THE CRAFT OF PROGRAMMING

Prentice-Hall International
Series in Computer Science

C. A. R. Hoare, Series Editor

Published

BACKHOUSE, R. C., *Syntax of Programming Languages: Theory and Practice*
de BAKKER, J. W., *Mathematical Theory of Program Correctness*
DUNCAN, F., *Microprocessor Programming and Software Development*
HENDERSON, P., *Functional Programming: Application and Implementation*
JONES, C. B., *Software Development: A Rigorous Approach*
REYNOLDS, J. C., *The Craft of Programming*
TENNENT, R. D., *Principles of Programming Languages*
WELSH, J. and ELDER, J., *Introduction to PASCAL*
WELSH, J. and MᶜKEAG, M., *Structured System Programming*

Future Titles

BJÖRNER, D. and JONES, C. B., *Formal Specification and Software Development*
DROMEY, G., *How to Solve it by Computer*
JACKSON, M. A., *System Design*
JOHNSTON, H., *Learning to Program with PASCAL*
LISTER, A. and GOLDSCHLAGER, L., *Computer Science: A Modern Introduction*
NAUR, P., *Studies in Program Analysis and Construction*
WELSH, J., ELDER, J. and BUSTARD, D., *Sequential and Concurrent Program Structures*

THE CRAFT OF PROGRAMMING

JOHN C. REYNOLDS

Syracuse University
Syracuse, New York

Prentice/Hall PHI International

ENGLEWOOD CLIFFS, NEW JERSEY   LONDON   NEW DELHI
SINGAPORE   SYDNEY   TOKYO   TORONTO   WELLINGTON

Library of Congress Cataloging in Publication Data

REYNOLDS, John C   1935–
    The craft of programming.

    Bibliography: p.
    Includes index
    1. Electronic digital computers—Programming
I. Title.
QA76.6.R47   001.64'2   80-24279
ISBN 0-13-188862-5

British Library Cataloguing in Publication Data

REYNOLDS, JOHN C
    The craft of programming.

        1. Electronic digital computers—Programming
        I. Title
        001.64'2   QA76.6
        ISBN 0-13-188862-5

ISBN 0-13-188862-5

PRENTICE-HALL INTERNATIONAL, INC., *London*
PRENTICE-HALL OF AUSTRALIA PTY., LTD., *Sydney*
PRENTICE-HALL CANADA, INC., *Toronto*
PRENTICE-HALL OF INDIA PRIVATE LIMITED, *New Delhi*
PRENTICE-HALL OF JAPAN, INC., *Tokyo*
PRENTICE-HALL OF SOUTHEAST ASIA PTE., LTD., *Singapore*
PRENTICE-HALL, INC., *Englewood Cliffs, New Jersey*
WHITEHALL BOOKS LIMITED, *Wellington, New Zealand*

Printed in the United States of America

10 9 8 7 6 5 4 3 2 1

CONTENTS

GLOSSARY OF NOTATION   ix

PREFACE   xi

1   **SIMPLE ITERATIVE PROGRAMS**   1

1.1   Computer Programs as Patterns of Behavior   1
   1.1.1   Patterns of Human Behavior: An Analogy   1
   1.1.2   Flowcharts   7
   1.1.3   Syntax   10

1.2   Variables, Expressions, and Assignment   12
   1.2.1   The State of the Computation   12
   1.2.2   Variables and Expressions   14

1.3   Top-Down Program Construction   17
   1.3.1   Computing Factorials   17
   1.3.2   Specification by Assertions   19
   1.3.3   Assertions as Comments   23
   1.3.4   Integer Division   27
   1.3.5   Fast Exponentiation   30
   1.3.6   Fibonacci Numbers   36

1.4   Assertions and Program Proving   38
   1.4.1   Assertions with Flowcharts   38
   1.4.2   Inference Rules for Specifications   42
   1.4.3   More Inference Rules   48

1.5   Declarations and Binding   52
   1.5.1   Local Variables and Simple Variable Declarations   52
   1.5.2   Binding and Alpha Conversion   55

1.6   Number Representations   58
   1.6.1   Integers   58
   1.6.2   Programming for an Idealized Computer   60
   *1.6.3   Fixed-Point Representation of Real Numbers   61
   *1.6.4   Floating-Point Representation of Real Numbers   62
   *1.6.5   The Propagation of Errors   65
   1.6.6   Real Variables and Expressions   69

v

2 ARRAYS 73

2.1 One-Dimensional Arrays 73
2.2 Programs that Use Arrays 76

    2.2.1 *Summation of an Array* 76
    2.2.2 *Interval Diagrams* 78
    2.2.3 *Partition Diagrams* 80
    2.2.4 *Summation Revisited* 85
    2.2.5 *Quantifiers* 89
    2.2.6 *Substitution and Identifier Collisions* 91
    2.2.7 *Maximum Finding* 93
    2.2.8 *Functions as Array Values* 95
    2.2.9 *Linear Search* 100
    2.2.10 *Binary Search* 102

2.3 Programs that Set Arrays 109

    2.3.1 *Two Simple Examples* 109
    2.3.2 *Inference for Array Assignments* 111
    2.3.3 *Sorting by Maximum Finding* 115
    2.3.4 *Rearrangement and Realignment* 119
    2.3.5 *Partitioning* 125
    2.3.6 *Merging* 127
    2.3.7 *Concatenation and Disjoint Union* 130
    2.3.8 *Preimages and Related Concepts* 137
    *2.3.9 *Ordering by Keys and Stability* 144

2.4 Multidimensional Arrays 148

    2.4.1 *Multidimensional Arrays in Algol W* 148
    2.4.2 *Assertions for Multidimensional Arrays* 149
    *2.4.3 *The Minimax of an Array* 150

3 PROCEDURES 157

3.1 Procedures in Algol W 158

    3.1.1 *Proper Procedures and the Copy Rule* 158
    3.1.2 *Specifiers and Phrase Types* 160
    3.1.3 *Identifier Collisions* 163
    3.1.4 *Interference and Parameter Assumptions* 166
    3.1.5 *Call by Value and Result* 168
    3.1.6 *Array Parameters* 172
    3.1.7 *Procedure Parameters* 177
    3.1.8 *Function Procedures* 180
    3.1.9 *A Summary* 181

3.2 Recursion 184

    3.2.1 *Simple Examples* 184
    3.2.2 *Sorting by Merging* 187
    3.2.3 *Quicksort* 195
    3.2.4 *Sorting by Range Partitioning* 200
    3.2.5 *Recursive Function Procedures* 201

3.3 Specification Logic 203

    3.3.1 Environments and Meanings 204
    3.3.2 Universal Specifications 210
    3.3.3 Additional Phrase and Data Types 211
    3.3.4 The Syntax and Semantics of Specifications 213
    3.3.5 Rules of Inference for Universal Specifications 217
    3.3.6 An Example of Inferences in Specification Logic 224
    3.3.7 Inference for Simple Variable Declarations 226
    3.3.8 Inference for Proper Procedure Declarations 228
    3.3.9 Examples of Inference about Procedures 232
    3.3.10 Further Examples 240
    3.3.11 Lambda Expressions 243
    *3.3.12 Abstract Specification Logic 247
    *3.3.13 Inference for Arrays 251
    *3.3.14 Inference for Function Procedures 257

4 ADDITIONAL CONTROL MECHANISMS 259

4.1 **for** Statements 259

    *4.1.1 **for** Statements in Algol W 259*
    *4.1.2 Inference for **for** Statements 262*
    *4.1.3 A Stronger Rule of Inference 266
    *4.1.4 Deriving the Inference Rules 267
    4.1.5 The Descending **for Statement 270*
    4.1.6 A Caution 271

4.2 **goto** Statements and Labels 272

    *4.2.1 **goto**'s and Labels in Algol W 272*
    *4.2.2 Using Assertions with **goto**'s and Labels 273*
    4.2.3 Inference for **goto's and Labels 275*
    *4.2.4 An Example of a Formal Proof 278
    4.2.5 Fast Exponentiation Revisited 281
    4.2.6 Transition Diagrams and Indeterminacy 286
    *4.2.7 Merging Revisited 291
    4.2.8 Another Caution 294

5 DATA REPRESENTATION STRUCTURING 297

5.1 Finding Paths in Directed Graphs 299

    5.1.1 Directed Graphs 299
    5.1.2 An Abstract Program for Reachability 301
    5.1.3 The Representation of Finite Sets 308
    5.1.4 Representation of the Set Variables T and U 310
    5.1.5 Representation of the Function Γ 316
    5.1.6 Representing Nodes 319
    5.1.7 The Computation of Paths 321

5.2   Finding Shortest Paths   324
>   *5.2.1   Directed Graphs with Edge Lengths   324*
>   *5.2.2   An Abstract Program for Minimum Distances   325*
>   *5.2.3   Representing U by a Heap   334*
>   *5.2.4   Representing Trees by Intervals   347*

*5.3   Using a Heap to Sort   351
>   **5.3.1   An Abstract Program   352*
>   **5.3.2   A Concrete Program   354*
>   **5.3.3   Further Transformations to Improve Efficiency   356*

5.4   Finding Strongly Connected Components   363
>   *5.4.1   Recursive Depth-First Search   363*
>   *5.4.2   An Abstract Program for Strongly Connected
>   Components   369*
>   *5.4.3   Transformation to a Concrete Program   374*

**APPENDIX A   NOTATION FOR SYNTACTIC
DEFINITION   383**

A.1   Backus-Naur Form   383
A.2   Extensions of Backus-Naur Form   391

APPENDIX B   THE SYNTAX OF A SUBSET OF ALGOL W   395

B.1   Syntax for Chapter 1   397
>   *B.1.1   Basic Symbols   397*
>   *B.1.2   Simple Variable Declarations   398*
>   *B.1.3   Variables and Expressions   399*
>   *B.1.4   Statements   401*
>   *B.1.5   Implicitly Declared Procedures   402*

B.2   Syntax for Chapter 2   404
>   *B.2.1   Array Declarations   404*
>   *B.2.2   Variables and Expressions Involving Arrays   404*

B.3   Syntax for Chapter 3   405
>   *B.3.1   Phrase Types   406*
>   *B.3.2   Formal Parameter Lists   407*
>   *B.3.3   Procedure Declarations   408*
>   *B.3.4   Binders and Identifiers   408*
>   *B.3.5   Procedure Statements and Function Designators   410*

B.4   Syntax for Chapter 4   412
>   *B.4.1   The **for** Statement   412*
>   *B.4.2   Labels and **goto** Statements   412*

APPENDIX C   INPUT AND OUTPUT IN ALGOL W   413

C.1   Input   414
C.2   Output   415
C.3   An Example of a Complete Program   416

REFERENCES   421

INDEX   428

GLOSSARY OF NOTATION

$\neg$	Negation, logical
$\{P\}\ S\ \{Q\}$	Specification of statement
$\{\ \dots\ \}$	Formal comment in program (e.g., assertion, invariant, extended specifier, or parameter assumption); also Specification of static assertion
I_0	Ghost identifier or parameter denoting initial value
$P\big\|_{F\to A}$	Substitution of A for F in P
ε_x	Absolute error
ρ_x	Relative error
$\displaystyle\sum_{i=a}^{b}$	Summation from a to b
$\displaystyle\sum_{i\in S}$	Summation over finite set
$a\boxed{\ b\ }$	Interval diagram
$a_0\boxed{\ a_1\ }\ \dots\ a_n$	Partition diagram
$\in$	Is a member of
$\notin$	Is not a member of
$\subseteq$	Subset
$\cup$	Union of sets
U	Union of set of sets
$\cap$	Intersection of sets
$\dot{\cap}$	Intersection of function with set
$-$	Subtraction of sets
$\dot{-}$	Subtraction of set from function
$\# S$	Size of set
$S\# E$	Specification of noninterference
$\{\}$	Empty set
$\{X\}$	Image of function; also Singleton set
$\{x_1,\ \dots\ ,\ x_n\}$	Set containing $x_1,\ \dots\ ,\ x_n$
$\langle\ \rangle$	Empty function
$\langle x,\ y\rangle$	Pair
$\langle x_1,\ \dots\ ,\ x_n\rangle$	Sequence
$\forall$	Quantifier, universal
$\exists$	Quantifier, existential
A	Quantifier of specification

$\restriction$	Restriction of function
ρ^*	Pointwise extension of relation
ord$_\rho$	Ordered function
$[X \mid i{:}\ y]$	Single-argument function variation
$F \cdot G$	Composition of functions
I_S	Identity function
F^{-1}	Inverse of function
$\sim$	Rearrangement
$\simeq$	Realignment
$\oplus$	Concatenation
$\oplus_{\text{seq}}$	Sequence concatenation
$\times$	Cartesian product of sets
$+$	Disjoint union of sets
$\mathscr{P}$	Preimage
M_θ	Set of meanings for phrase type
$[\![\ \dots\ ]\!]_\eta$	Meaning in an environment
$\&$	Conjunction of assumptions
$\Rightarrow$	Implication between specifications
gv	Specification of good variable
$\mathscr{F}$	Set of identifiers with free (statement-like, expression-like) occurrences
Σ_{proc}	Procedure assumptions
Σ_{pa}	Parameter assumptions
$\lambda(\ \dots\ ).\ B$	Lambda expression
Γ	Immediate successor function
Γ^*	Reachability (also T-free reachability) function
for $z \in S$ **do**	Iteration over set
δ	Length of edge
δ^*	Minimum distance
$\sqsubseteq$	Reachability in binary tree
∞	Infinity
$\langle\ \dots\ \rangle$	Nonterminal symbol (in productions)
$::=$	Production operator (in productions)
$\mid$	Alternative sign (in productions)
$[\![\ \dots\ ]\!]^k$	Repetition (in productions)
$[\![\ \dots\ ]\!]^k_\odot$	Repetition with commas (in productions)

PREFACE

In 1972 I started teaching programming to graduate students in Computer and Information Science at Syracuse University. I began with the conviction that programs should work correctly and that programmers should be able to explain clearly why they work correctly. This led to considerable emphasis on structured programming and the use of assertions. Gradually my own attitudes and ideas crystalized, programming methodology and proof methods became a major concern of my research, and the present book began to evolve.

The modern computer is so powerful that a casual knowledge of programming suffices for most of its users. However, a variety of circumstances can abruptly require a much deeper understanding: the need to structure a program carefully to avoid being overwhelmed by its complexity, the need to insure reliability beyond what can be achieved by debugging, or the need to utilize computing resources efficiently. Beyond such practical considerations, there is an inherent intellectual satisfaction in mastering the fundamental concepts of programming.

The aim of this book is to provide such mastery concept by concept. For example, the reader is expected to understand proofs of correctness and order-of-magnitude time requirements for simple integer algorithms—such as $\log n$ exponentiation—before the concept of arrays is introduced. A similarly thorough understanding of array-manipulating algorithms is expected before the introduction of procedures.

The programming language used in this book is Algol W or, more precisely, the subset of Algol W that represents a refinement of Algol 60. Originally the main factor determining this choice was the level of the language. It is sufficiently high-level to provide block structure, including dynamic arrays, and a powerful procedure mechanism, including recursion, call by name, and higher-order procedures. On the other hand, it is sufficiently close to the machine to facilitate the estimation of time and storage requirements. In addition, it has an unusually elegant syntactic structure which permits clean subsetting, and an efficient and unusually error-free implementation.

In retrospect, the advantages of Algol W seem even more compelling. It distinguishes clearly between the types of variables and the types of procedure parameters, and, with a straightforward extension of its parameter specification facility, it can be made completely type-safe. Its procedure mechanism is based upon the copy rule, so that call by name is more fundamental than call by value. My own work, both in program proving and denotational semantics, has convinced me that these characteristics form a sounder conceptual basis for programming than those that underlie such languages as Pascal or Algol 68. In any event, much of what is said in this book, particularly in Chapter 3, would be difficult or impossible to say in such languages.

This book reflects a conviction about the importance of program proving. Ideally at least, I believe that a programmer should be able to specify the behavior of his program precisely, and to give a rigorous argument that the program meets its specifications. Of course, such an argument might not be a formal proof in the sense of logic, but it must be an adequate guideline for a formal proof. In other words, an adequately commented program should enable a competent reader to fill in the details of a formal proof in a straightforward manner.

This implies that the programmer should master formal proof methods, not in order to give a formal proof of every program that he writes, but as a firm foundation for rigorous though informal reasoning about programs.

In this connection, something needs to be said about the special problems of teaching experienced programmers to program. Such students are unlikely to be attracted by either polemics or formalism, but they can be motivated by a sequence of programming problems of the right level of difficulty, given in an environment that precludes using the computer as a crutch. Most programmers believe that they should be able to write a correct program for, say, binary search without using the computer. Once they have failed to do so and their errors have been pointed out, they are likely to become receptive to formalisms and methodologies that can help.

An even greater benefit of having students program without using the computer is that it requires the instructor to read their programs, which is just as important in teaching programming as in teaching English composition. Moreover this is a reciprocal benefit; in my own case reading student programs has taught me profound lessons about programming style and the nature of useful comments.

In the main text of this book, syntax is treated informally to provide a reading knowledge of Algol W; the additional syntactic formalities needed to write programs, as well as a brief description of input and output facilities, are given in the appendices. Within the main text, sections marked with asterisks can be skipped without endangering the understanding of later material.

Although this is primarily a textbook, I have not hesitated to include the results of my own research. [Reynolds 79, 81 and 78b] provide the source of much of Chapter 2, Section 3.3, and Sections 4.2.5 to 4.2.8, respectively. This research was partly supported by National Science Foundation Grant MCS 75-22002, Rome Air Force Development Center Contract F30602-77-C-0235, and the Science Research Council of Great Britain.

I am thankful to the members of IFIP Working Group 2.3 for many specific ideas and, more importantly, for the basic outlook that underlies this book. In addition, Tony Hoare has provided much-needed encouragement for several years, and Edsger W. Dijkstra and David Gries have each made numerous helpful suggestions after careful reading of a preliminary draft. I am also indebted to Lockwood Morris, Ernie Sibert, Nancy McCracken, and Otway Pardee, each of whom has used parts of the book in teaching at Syracuse University, to Rod Burstall and Robin Milner, who were my gracious hosts during a sabbatical at Edinburgh University, and to numerous students, who have taught me much about how to program, how to write, and even how to spell. Finally, I am deeply grateful for the encouragement and endless patience of my wife Mary and our children Edward and Matthew.

J.C.R.

1 SIMPLE ITERATIVE PROGRAMS

1.1 COMPUTER PROGRAMS AS PATTERNS OF BEHAVIOR

1.1.1 Patterns of Human Behavior: An Analogy

A computer program is a pattern of behavior for a machine that manipulates numbers or symbols. This implies that a clear understanding of even elementary programming requires the mastery of two quite distinct concepts: behavior patterns and the manipulation of numbers or symbols. To separate these concepts, we will use a perspicuous idea taken from [Dijkstra 71]: We will begin by considering behavior patterns for humans performing everyday acts, and momentarily ignore the actual domain of computer activity. This will permit us to concentrate upon the aspect of programming that is usually called "control structure".

Consider my behavior on a particular morning. At a rather gross level of detail, I did the following:

> Eat breakfast;
>
> Put on clothes;
>
> Leave in car .

However, each of these acts can be expanded into a sequence of acts at a more detailed level, and this expansion can be repeated. For example:

1

Gross	*Detailed*	*More Detailed*
	Eat orange;	
Eat breakfast;	Eat cereal;	Put milk on cereal; Put sugar on cereal; Eat bite of cereal; Eat bite of cereal; Eat bite of cereal; Eat bite of cereal;
	Eat toast;	
Put on clothes;	Put on heavy coat; Put on galoshes; Put on gloves;	
Leave in car	Open garage door; Start car; Get car out of garage; Drive car down driveway .	

On a different day, I might have exhibited a behavior that was similar on a gross level, but different in its details, e.g.

Gross	*Detailed*
Eat breakfast;	Eat orange; Eat pancakes;
Put on clothes;	Put on light coat;
Leave in car	Start car; Get car out of garage; Drive car down driveway .

So far, we have two specific behaviors; we now want to abstract a common pattern that describes both of them, and possibly many others. There is no magic recipe for doing this, but two observations are obviously pertinent. First, my behavior differs from day to day because I perceive differences in my environment, e.g. what is on the breakfast table. (Note that we are ignoring anything like free will—this may not be appropriate for discussing human behavior, but hopefully it will be appropriate for machine behavior.)

Secondly, patterns of behavior are intimately connected with the hierarchical structure of "levels of detail". In particular, specific behaviors that are similar on a gross level become more and more different as we examine finer levels of detail.

At the most gross level, our pattern of behavior looks just like a particular behavior:

> **begin**
> Eat breakfast;
> Put on clothes;
> Leave in car
> **end** .

But at the next level of detail, something new happens: What I do when I eat breakfast depends upon how hungry I am and what is on the table, what I do when I put on clothes depends upon the weather, and what I do when I leave in the car depends upon whether the garage door is closed.

To describe this kind of "conditional behavior", we must extend the language we have been using. First we need some terminology: A *statement* is a phrase that describes an action. (In English we would call it an imperative statement.) A *logical expression* is a phrase that describes a test of the environment. (The reason for using the name "logical expression" will become apparent later.)

If L is a logical expression and S is a statement, then

> **if** L **then** S

is a statement, called a *conditional statement*, that describes the following action:

> (1) Test whether L is true or false.
> (2) If L is true then do S, otherwise do nothing.

We will also need a second kind of *conditional statement*: If L is a logical expression and both S_1 and S_2 are statements, then

> **if** L **then** S_1 **else** S_2

is a statement that describes the following action:

(1) Test whether L is true or false.

(2) If L is true then do S_1, otherwise do S_2.

These conditional statements allow us to describe a pattern of behavior that depends upon the environment:

> **begin**
>> **begin comment** Eat breakfast;
>> **if** hungry **and** orange on table **then** Eat orange;
>> **if** hungry **and** cereal on table **then** Eat cereal;
>> **if** hungry **and** toast on table **then** Eat toast;
>> **if** hungry **and** pancakes on table **then** Eat pancakes
>> **end**;
>> **begin comment** Put on clothes;
>> **if** cold **then** Put on heavy coat **else** Put on light coat;
>> **if** snow **then begin** Put on galoshes; Put on gloves **end**
>> **end**;
>> **begin comment** Leave in car;
>> **if** garage door closed **then** Open garage door;
>> Start car;
>> Get car out of garage;
>> Drive car down driveway
>> **end**
> **end**   .

Here, in addition to the two forms of conditional statement, we are also using another kind of statement. If $S_1, S_2, \ldots, S_n$ are all statements, then

> **begin** S_1; S_2; $\ldots$; S_n **end**

is a statement, called a *block*, that describes the following action:

(1) Do S_1.

(2) Do S_2.

$\vdots$

(n) Do S_n.

The symbols **begin** and **end** can be used to group statements together, just as parentheses are used in elementary algebra to group expressions together. In the above example, this grouping is used to relate different levels of detail; each elementary statement at the gross level becomes a block of statements at the more detailed level. (Note that the entire pattern is grouped into a block of blocks—revealing a still grosser level of detail.)

Blocks are also used to group statements within conditional statements. For example, we wrote

> **if** snow **then begin** Put on galoshes; Put on gloves **end**

instead of

> **if** snow **then** Put on galoshes; Put on gloves

to show that neither galoshes nor gloves will be put on when there is no snow.

Two other linguistic constructs have also been used. If C is any sequence of symbols that does not include a semicolon, then

> **comment** C;

is a *comment*. Comments, which can occur anywhere in a program (except in the middle of "words"), have no effect on the machine (or human) that obeys the program, but are intended to help a reader to understand the program. For example, in the behavior pattern above, comments are used at the beginning of blocks to identify the gross structure from which the current level of detail is descended.

Secondly, if L_1 and L_2 are logical expressions, then

> L_1 **and** L_2

is a logical expression that is true if (and only if) both L_1 and L_2 are true. This is one of a number of constructions which will be used to build logical expressions out of simpler expressions, in the same way that the conditional and block constructions can be used to build statements out of simpler statements.

At the next level of detail something new happens. The pattern for "Eat cereal" might look like this:

> **begin comment** Eat cereal;
> Put milk on cereal;
> Put sugar on cereal;
> **if** cereal in bowl **then** Eat bite of cereal;
> **if** cereal in bowl **then** Eat bite of cereal;
> **if** cereal in bowl **then** Eat bite of cereal;
> $\vdots$
> **end**   .

Presumably, we must have at least as many copies of "Eat bite of cereal" in our pattern as the maximum number of bites in any cereal bowl.

To avoid this foolishness, we introduce another kind of statement. If L is a logical expression and S is a statement, then

> **while** L **do** S

is a statement, called a **while** *statement*, that describes the following action:

> (1) Test whether L is true or false.
> (2) If L is true then do S and go back to step (1), otherwise do nothing.

(Note that if the first test of L gives false, then S will not be performed at all.)

Now we can write "Eat cereal" as

> **begin comment** Eat cereal;
> Put milk on cereal;
> Put sugar on cereal;
> **while** cereal in bowl **do** Eat bite of cereal
> **end** .

The **while** statement is our first example of an *iterative statement*, i.e. a statement that can cause an action to be performed repeatedly. Such statements are essential in computer programming in order to exploit the tremendous disparity in speed between human program writing and mechanical program execution.

However, the power of repetition brings a concomitant danger: It is all too easy to write a **while** statement that never terminates, i.e. to write **while** L **do** S where doing S never makes L false. Perhaps

> **while** cereal in bowl **do** Eat bite of cereal

is innocent, but

> **while** car stopped **do** Press ignition

is a disastrous prescription for dealing with a dead battery.

The language we are using to describe behavior patterns is a kind of pidgin Algol W whose similarity to natural English can be misleading. One particular warning must be sounded: Here and throughout this book, only sequential behavior is considered—two activities never occur simultaneously or overlap in time. Because of this, the **while** statement differs subtly from the use of "while" in English. In executing **while** L **do** S, the logical expression L is not tested *during* execution of the statement S. Thus, according to

> **while** hungry **and** pancakes on plate **do**
>   **begin**
>   Slice one pancake;
>   **while** slice on plate **do** Eat slice
>   **end** ,

I will always finish a sliced pancake, even though my appetite fails in the midst of eating it. A more rational (though perhaps less realistic) behavior would be specified by repeating the test of *hungry* in the inner **while** statement:

```
while hungry and pancakes on plate do
   begin
   Slice one pancake;
   while hungry and slice on plate do Eat slice
   end  .
```

This is as far as we will go in exploiting the analogy between human behavior and computation; we have managed to illustrate all the control mechanisms that will be used in this chapter. But one fundamental point deserves further emphasis: The structure of levels of detail (or looking the other way round, levels of abstraction) is vital for imposing a pattern on a diversity of specific behaviors. To an observer from Mars, unfamiliar with human motivation, specific instances of the behavior we have described might appear to be unstructured sequences of very simple actions. But by virtue of this fact, such an observer would find it difficult or impossible to perceive any common pattern behind the diversity of instances.

This naturally suggests that programs should be developed by beginning at a high level of abstraction and repeatedly refining the level of detail. This approach, often called structured programming, top-down programming, or programming by stepwise refinement, has received considerable emphasis in recent years [Dijkstra 71, 72, Wirth 71b]. Although it is not a panacea, it is an immensely powerful tool for attacking complexity, and its employment in various guises will be a recurring theme throughout this book.

More precisely, we will say that a program is *structured* when it reveals a variety of levels of detail to the reader, and we will reserve the term *top-down* for the process of creating such a program by proceeding from the abstract to the concrete. Occasionally the opposite order of attack, which might be called *bottom-up* programming, is called for, particularly when the ultimate goal of the program is ill-defined or changeable.

We are left with the question of when the repeated expansion of patterns into more detailed patterns should stop. Since the patterns are intended to be instructions, the pragmatic answer is to stop at a level of detail that can be understood by the recipient of the instructions. In particular, if the recipient is a computer then one stops when all instructions belong to the fixed repertoire of the programming language being used.

1.1.2 Flowcharts

Flowcharts are one of the oldest methods for describing the control structure of computer programs. Although their serious limitations have curtailed their popularity in recent years, they are still useful for illuminating the concepts introduced in the previous section.

A flowchart is a collection of boxes containing statements and logical expressions which are connected by arrows showing the order in which the boxes are to be executed. A statement is contained in a rectangular box with a single outgoing arrow, which points to the box to be executed next:

A logical expression is contained in a diamond-shaped or hexagonal box with two outgoing arrows, one pointing to the box to be executed next if the logical expression is true, and the other pointing to the box to be executed next if the logical expression is false. The outgoing arrows are labeled **true** and **false** to distinguish them:

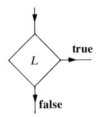

Special boxes marked **enter** and **exit** are used to indicate the beginning and end of execution:

As an example, the flowchart in Figure 1.1 describes the pattern of behavior for "Eat breakfast". It is evident that flowcharts are much less compact than the linguistic representation of behavior patterns, and that they obscure the basic hierarchical structure of the patterns (although one could use boxes containing smaller boxes as a kind of pictorial block). For these reasons, we will largely avoid their use (although the closely related concept of transition diagrams will be used in Sections 4.2.6 and 4.2.7).

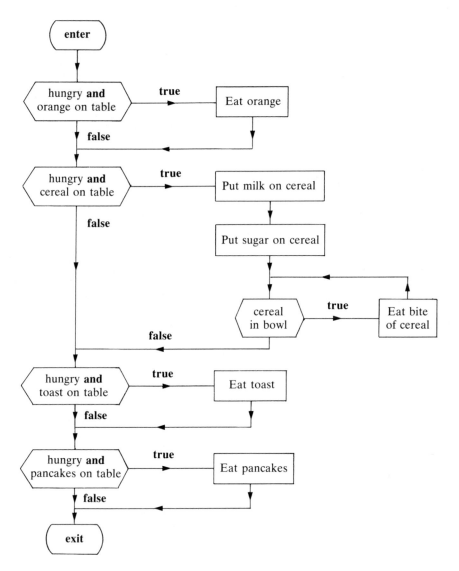

Figure 1.1   A Flowchart for the Behavior Pattern "Eat Breakfast".

However, it is helpful to use flowcharts to describe each of the linguistic constructions introduced in the previous section. In Figure 1.2, each of these constructions is defined by a simple flowchart. Indeed, one could almost say that these constructions have been chosen to correspond to the simplest possible ways of constructing flowcharts from individual statements and logical expressions.

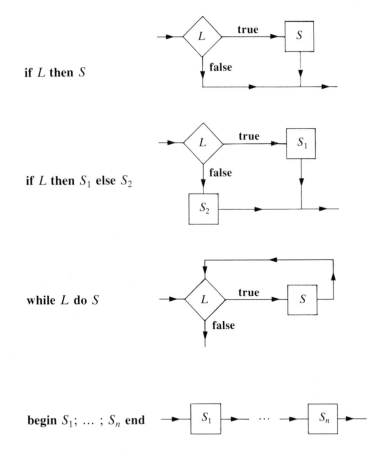

if L then S

if L then S_1 else S_2

while L do S

begin S_1; ... ; S_n end

Figure 1.2   The Basic Control Constructions Defined by Flowcharts.

Exercise

1. Write some behavior patterns. Try to include several levels of detail and to use
    each of the linguistic constructs discussed in this section. Translate the patterns
    into flowcharts.

1.1.3 Syntax

The analogy between human and computer behavior breaks down in one
respect. In reading a program, a computer lacks the human ability to correct
certain kinds of minor errors and ambiguities. (More precisely, this ability is
lacked by the compiler—the system program that translates a programming
language into the more elementary language used by the machine. Indeed,
most compilers, including the Algol W system, fall considerably short of

the present state-of-the-art of mechanical error correction [Morgan 70, Graham 75].)

As a consequence, programs to be executed by a computer must adhere to a rigid set of rules defining the *syntax* of the programming language being used. The behavior patterns we have presented adhere to these rules (except for the use of natural English for elementary statements and logical expressions), but it is all too easy to write statements that violate these rules yet remain intelligible to the human reader. For example, each of the following statements is syntactically erroneous:

> **if** hungry **and** orange on table **do** Eat orange
> **if** snow **then** Put on galoshes; Put on gloves **else**
>   Put on light overcoat
> **begin** Put on galoshes; Put on gloves; **comment** It is cold **end**

A further problem is *ambiguity*. Some statements, like puns in natural language, can be interpreted in more than one way. For example,

> **if** warm **then if** rain **then** Put on raincoat **else** Put on heavy coat

could reasonably mean either

> **if** warm **then**
> **begin if** rain **then** Put on raincoat **else** Put on heavy coat **end**

or

> **if** warm **then**
>   **begin if** rain **then** Put on raincoat **end**
> **else** Put on heavy coat   .

A human reader will use his entire understanding of context and meaning to resolve such ambiguities, often without becoming conscious of their existence. But the computer simply follows the syntax rules, even when the resulting interpretation would be unnatural for a human. For instance, in the above example, the Algol W compiler would choose the first interpretation.

Because of these problems, there is a great difference between the ability to read a programming language and the ability to write it for computer consumption. (The first encounter with this difference is often a traumatic experience for novice programmers.) In organizing this book, we have tried to separate material that is directed towards these two abilities. In the main text, syntax is treated informally to provide a reading knowledge of Algol W. The additional information needed to write programs is provided in the appendices: Appendix A presents a general notation for describing the syntax of programming languages, which is used in Appendix B to describe the portion of Algol W used in this book. Further information can be obtained from the Algol W Reference Manual [Sites 72].

The disparity between human and mechanical reading has other effects. In contrast to printing or handwriting, computer input is usually restricted to a small, fixed vocabulary of symbols that can be unnatural for the human reader. To alleviate this constraint, we will follow the practice, almost universal for Algol-like languages, of using a larger vocabulary for printed programs than for computer input. In particular, we will use lower-case letters freely, and will use boldface type for reserved words, i.e. words such as **if**, **then**, **begin**, and **end** that have fixed meanings and special syntactic roles. We will also use a few mathematical symbols, such as $\leq$, that are not available for computer input (with the IBM 360 implementation of Algol W), and we will use a variety of formats for various kinds of comments.

1.2   VARIABLES, EXPRESSIONS, AND ASSIGNMENT

1.2.1   The State of the Computation

We now turn from human behavior patterns to real computer programs. Just as a human acts upon and is affected by his environment, so the computer (actually the central processing unit of the computer) acts upon and is affected by the *state of the computation*. (See Figure 1.3.) As before, programs contain two fundamental kinds of phases: statements, describing actions that change the state, and expressions (logical and other types) describing information about the state that will influence the computation.

The main novelty is the nature of the state. The state is a collection of *variables*, each of which possesses a *current value*. For example,

x	0
$t2$	-7
cost	84

depicts a state containing variables named x, $t2$, and *cost*, in which x has the current value 0, $t2$ has the current value -7, and *cost* has the current value 84.

The basic statement for describing elementary changes in the state is the *assignment statement*, which affects the state by changing the current value of a single variable. It has the form

$$V := E$$

where V is a variable and E is an expression. The effect of an assignment statement is first to evaluate the expression on its right to obtain an integer (or other type of value), and then to make this integer the new current value of the variable named on the left. The current values of all other variables remain unchanged.

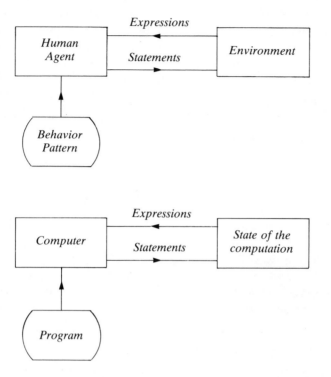

Figure 1.3   The Analogy between Human and Computer Behavior.

For example, after executing the three statements

$$x := 1; y := x+1; x := x+2 \quad ,$$

the current value of x is 3 and the current value of y is 2.

As a less trivial example, the following statement finds the quotient and remainder of two positive integers:

```
begin
r := x; q := 0;
while r≥y do
    begin r := r−y; q := q+1 end
end   .
```

Specifically, if before this statement is executed the current values of x and y are integers such that $x \geq 0$ and $y > 0$, then after execution the values of x and y will be unchanged, and the values of q and r will be integers such that $x = q \times y + r$ and $0 \leq r$ and $r < y$.

Consider performing this statement, starting with an initial state in which x has the value 7 and y has the value 3. The following table depicts the state of the computation after each execution of an assignment statement:

x	7	7	7	7	7	7	7
y	3	3	3	3	3	3	3
r	—	7	7	4	4	1	1
q	—	—	0	0	1	1	2

1.2.2   Variables and Expressions

Within a program, variables are denoted by *identifiers*, which are strings of letters and possibly digits that must begin with a letter, e.g. x, $t2$, or *cost*. (Notice the distinction between variables, which are part of the state of the computation, and identifiers, which are phrases of a program that denote variables. Eventually, we will introduce other ways of denoting variables, and other uses for identifiers.) A variable that always possesses integer values is called an *integer variable*.

An *integer expression* is a phrase that describes the computation of an integer whose value depends upon the state of the computation. It may have any of the following forms:

(1) An integer constant, i.e. a nonempty string of digits,

(2) An identifier denoting an integer variable,

(3) One or two integer subexpressions combined with an *arithmetic operator*, i.e. $+$, $-$, $\times$, **div**, **rem**, or **abs**.

(Other possible forms for integer expressions will be introduced later.) For example:

$$73$$
$$x$$
$$-x \times y$$
$$(x+y) \textbf{ div } 2$$
$$(x \times 3) \textbf{ rem } (y+1)$$
$$- \textbf{ abs } x$$

Most of the operators have the familiar meanings of elementary arithmetic, but some mention should be given to the operators **div** and **rem**, which indicate the quotient and remainder under integer division. Specifically, if x and y are integers, then x **div** y and x **rem** y are integers such that

$$x = (x \textbf{ div } y) \times y + (x \textbf{ rem } y) \quad ,$$
$$\text{When } x \geq 0, \; 0 \leq (x \textbf{ rem } y) < \textbf{ abs } y \quad ,$$
$$\text{When } x \leq 0, \; - \textbf{ abs } y < (x \textbf{ rem } y) \leq 0 \quad ,$$

where **abs** y denotes the absolute value of y.

Some expressions with more than one operator are potentially ambiguous. For example, $x-y-z$ might conceivably mean either $(x-y)-z$ or $x-(y-z)$. Such ambiguities are resolved by the syntax rules given in Appendix B. By and large, these rules follow customary mathematical usage (for example, $x-y-z$ means $(x-y)-z$), but in unfamiliar cases it is a kindness to human readers to put in extra parentheses.

We can now see the relationship between integer and logical expressions. In general an *expression* is a phrase that describes the computation of a value that depends upon the state of the computation; for an integer expression this value will be an integer, while for a logical expression, it will be a *logical value*, i.e. either **true** or **false**. Terms such as "integer" and "logical", which denote certain sets of values, are called *data types*.

A logical expression may have any of the following forms:

(1) The logical constant **true** or the logical constant **false**,

(2) An identifier denoting a *logical variable*, i.e. a variable that always possesses logical values,

(3) Two integer subexpressions combined by a *relational operator*, i.e. $=, \neq, <, \leq, >$, or $\geq$ (or two logical expressions combined by $=$ or $\neq$). A logical expression of this form is called a *relation*,

(4) One or two logical subexpressions combined with a *logical operator*, i.e. **and**, **or**, or $\neg$ (denoting logical negation),

(5) $odd(E)$, where E is an integer expression.

(Other possible forms will be introduced later.) For example,

> **true**
> p
> $x = y+1$
> $(0 \leq x)$ **and** $(x \leq y)$
> $(p$ **and** $\neg q)$ **or** $(q$ **and** $\neg p)$
> $\neg odd(x)$,

where p and q are logical variables and x and y are integer variables.

The relational operators have the familiar meanings of elementary arithmetic. The meanings of the logical operators are given by the following table:

p	q	p and q	p or q	$\neg p$
false	false	false	false	true
false	true	false	true	true
true	false	false	true	false
true	true	true	true	false

The expression $odd(x)$ has the value **true** if x is an odd integer and has the value **false** if x is an even integer.

Again, the potential ambiguities of expressions containing several operators are resolved by the syntax rules given in Appendix B.

The parallel treatment of the types **integer** and **logical** extends to assignment statements. An assignment statement can have the form $V := E$, where V and E are a variable and an expression of the same data type, i.e. where either

    (1) V is an integer variable and E is an integer expression,

or (2) V is a logical variable and E is a logical expression.

It is important to understand the distinction between an assignment statement such as $x := y+1$ and an equality relation such as $x = y+1$. The former denotes an action that changes the value possessed by x, while the latter denotes a computation that produces the value **true** or **false** without changing the state of the computation. It is not even true that an assignment statement will always "make" the corresponding equality relation true, for example, $x := x+1$ will not produce a state in which $x = x+1$ has the value **true.** (This distinction holds for almost all programming languages, although it is unfortunately obscured in languages such as PL/I where the same symbol = is used both as the assignment operator and the relational operator for equality.)

We have already seen the conditional statement **if** L **then** S_1 **else** S_2, which performs a "branch" on the value of the logical expression L. Algol W also provides a *conditional expression*, which performs a similar branch within the evaluation of an expression. If L is a logical expression and E_1 and E_2 are both integer expressions (or both logical expressions), then

    if L **then** E_1 **else** E_2

is an integer (or logical) conditional expression that is evaluated as follows:

    (1) Evaluate L to obtain **true** or **false**.
    (2) If L is **true** then evaluate E_1 to obtain the value of the conditional expression, otherwise evaluate E_2 to obtain the value of the conditional expression.

(There is no "one-way" conditional expression analogous to the conditional statement **if** L **then** S.) For example, the expression

    $2 \times ($**if** $x \leq y$ **then** x **else** $y)$

produces twice the minimum of x and y. (Notice the mixture of types—this is an integer expression containing the logical expression $x \leq y$, which in turn contains the two integer expressions x and y.)

Exercises

1. Execute the statement for finding quotients and remainders by hand for a few cases. What happens when
    (a) x is negative?
    (b) y is zero or negative?

2. Execute the following statement by hand for a few values of x:

    > **while** $x>1$ **do**
    > $\qquad x :=$ **if** $odd(x)$ **then** $3 \times x + 1$ **else** x **div** 2 .

    As far as is known, this statement will eventually terminate for any initial value of x, but no one has been able to prove this fifty-year-old conjecture [Terras 76, Crandall 78].

1.3   TOP-DOWN PROGRAM CONSTRUCTION

1.3.1   Computing Factorials

We have now introduced enough of our programming language to consider the construction of a simple program. Given an integer n, we want to write a statement whose execution will cause the computation of $n!$, i.e. the factorial of n. Specifically, the statement should, while leaving the value of n unchanged, set the variable f to the factorial of n.

We first note the following "facts" about the factorial function which may be useful in writing the program:

(I) $0! = 1$.

(II) $n! = n \times (n-1)!$ when $n > 0$.

(I) tells us the factorial of a particular number, zero, while (II) shows how to find the factorial of a new number if we already know some factorial. This suggests the following line of attack:

(1) Use (I) to compute the factorial of 0.

(2) Repeatedly use (II) to compute factorials of larger numbers until we find the factorial of the number we are interested in, i.e. n.

Suppose we use the variable f to save the last factorial we have computed, and an additional variable k to keep track of the number such that $f = k!$. Then the above plan becomes:

(1) Achieve $f = k!$ by setting k to 0 and f to 1.

(2) As long as k is different from n, increase k and change f in a way that will maintain the relation $f = k!$.

or in Algol W:

> **begin**
> $k := 0; f := 1;$
> **while** $k \neq n$ **do** "Increase k while maintaining $f = k!$"
> **end** .

This "program skeleton" is typical of the use of a **while** statement. Obviously, the body of a useful **while** statement (i.e. the substatement following **do**) should cause some change in the state of the computation—otherwise the **while** statement could never terminate. But, paradoxically, the key to understanding a **while** statement is not what its body changes but what it leaves unchanged—in this case, the relation $f = k!$. Such a relation is called an *invariant* of the **while** statement.

Our remaining task is to replace the specification "Increase k while maintaining $f = k!$" by an actual statement that will satisfy this specification. It is evident that if $f = k!$, then we can use (II) to find the factorial of the integer that is one larger than k. If we decide to change k first, we get

> **begin** $k := k+1;$ "Set f to reestablish $f = k!$" **end** .

Now consider the state of the computation just after the assignment statement $k := k+1$. Since we have increased k by one, the relation $f = k!$ will no longer be true; instead we will have $f = (k-1)!$. But by (II), $k! = k \times (k-1)! = k \times f$. Thus to reestablish $f = k!$ we write $f := k \times f$.

The complete statement for computing the factorial of n is thus

> **begin**
> $k := 0; f := 1;$
> **while** $k \neq n$ **do**
>   **begin** $k := k+1; f := k \times f$ **end**
> **end** .

However, the argument we have made to justify the construction of this statement is still seriously incomplete. In essence, the argument shows that f will be the factorial of n when *and if* execution of the statement is finished. However, since the statement contains a **while** construction, we must consider the possibility that its execution might never terminate. In particular, the fact that the body of the **while** statement increases the value of k does not automatically insure that k will eventually become equal to n.

To see that the program terminates, we note that k is initially set to zero, and is then incremented by one during each execution of the body of the **while** statement. Thus the test $k \neq n$ will be applied successively to the integers $k = 0, 1, 2, \ldots$. Eventually, $k \neq n$ will be false, the **while** statement will terminate, and therefore the entire program will terminate—*providing* $n \geq 0$. In the case of the factorial function, $n \geq 0$ is a reasonable restriction, since the factorials of negative integers are not defined.

However, termination considerations do not always work out so happily. By substituting (II) into itself, we can obtain the fact

(III) $n! = n \times (n-1) \times (n-2)!$ when $n > 1$,

which provides an alternative method of finding new factorials from old ones. Using (III) instead of (II) we can develop a factorial-computing program which increases k in steps of two:

begin
$k := 0; f := 1;$
while $k \neq n$ **do**
　　begin $k := k+2; f := k \times (k-1) \times f$ **end**
end .

Except for termination, this program is just as valid as the previous one, but it only terminates when n is an even nonnegative integer.

Overall, our construction of the factorial program is a microscopic example of top-down programming or programming by stepwise refinement. The basic idea is to progress in small, easily understood stages from an abstract specification of the program to a concrete realization. A more explicit description is the following rubric:

(1) Take an unwritten portion of the program whose purpose is precisely and completely specified.

(2) Replace this portion by a statement which may in turn contain portions that are unwritten but precisely and completely specified.

(3) Prove (or at least convince yourself) that the new statement will meet its specifications if its unwritten portions meet their specifications.

(4) Repeat the above process until the entire program is written.

This methodology dominates the whole area of modern, systematic programming, and it has proven invaluable for the development of large programs. But its success depends critically on the use of "precise and complete specifications". Most errors in complex programs can be traced to ambiguous or inadequate specifications.

So far our specifications have been informal and a bit vague. A remedy is provided in the next section.

1.3.2 Specification by Assertions

To provide "precise and complete specifications" for programs, we introduce the concept of assertions. An *assertion* is simply a description of possible states of the computation. For example, the assertion $x < y$ describes the states in which the variable x has a smaller current value than the variable y.

To specify the behavior of a statement S, we give an assertion P describing possible states before the execution of S, and a second assertion Q describing possible states after the execution of S. More precisely, we write the *specification*

$$\{P\}\; S\; \{Q\}$$

to specify that, if one executes S beginning with any state described by P, and if S terminates, then S will produce a state described by Q. For example,

$$\{x<y\}\; x := x+1\; \{x \le y\}$$

specifies that if $x<y$, then executing $x := x+1$ will produce a state in which $x \le y$. In the specification $\{P\}\; S\; \{Q\}$, the assertions P and Q are called the *precedent* and the *consequent* of S.

The idea of using assertions for specification in this manner is due to C. A. R. Hoare [Hoare 69, 71a]. (In Hoare's original notation statements, rather than assertions, are bracketed, so that one writes $P\{S\}\,Q$ rather than $\{P\}\, S\,\{Q\}$. However, we prefer the latter notation since it gives assertions the appearance of parenthetical remarks.)

It should be emphasized that, although they must be precise, assertions may be written in a variety of languages. Initially our assertions will be logical expressions (which take on the value **true** for the states they describe), but later we will use a variety of mathematical and logical symbolism, and occasionally we will fall back on ordinary English.

Specification by assertions can be used to make top-down programming rigorous. To illustrate, we will recapitulate our development of the factorial program.

We want to construct a statement "Compute Factorial" that meets the specification

$$\{n \ge 0\}\; \text{"Compute factorial"}\; \{f=n!\}\quad,$$

without changing the value of n. As before, we are going to achieve the invariant $f=k!$ and then use a **while** statement to repeatedly increase k while maintaining this invariant, until $k=n$. With a little foresight, however, we know that we are going to need *range information* about k to insure termination, and also to insure that k never takes on negative values, for which the factorial is undefined. Since k will start at zero and increase until it is equal to n, we expect that $0 \le k \le n$. By adding this range information, we get the invariant

$$f=k!\;\textbf{ and }\;0 \le k \le n\quad.$$

Thus we replace "Compute factorial" by

begin
"Achieve invariant";
while $k \neq n$ **do** "Increase k while maintaining invariant"
end   ,

which will meet its specification if the unwritten substatements meet the specifications

$$\{n \geq 0\} \text{ "Achieve invariant" } \{f = k! \text{ and } 0 \leq k \leq n\}$$

and

$$\{f = k! \text{ and } 0 \leq k \leq n \text{ and } k \neq n\}$$
"Increase k while maintaining invariant"
$$\{f = k! \text{ and } 0 \leq k \leq n\}   .$$

Notice that the invariant itself does not contain the test $k \neq n$; indeed when the **while** statement terminates the invariant will still be true but the test $k \neq n$ will be false, which permits us to infer $f = n!$. On the other hand, just before each execution of the body of the **while** statement, both the invariant and the test will be true, so that we can include $k \neq n$ in the precedent of the body "Increase k while maintaining invariant". The situation is clearly illustrated by the flowchart for the **while** statement:

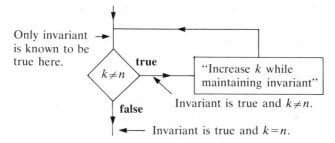

Only invariant is known to be true here.

$k \neq n$ **true**   "Increase k while maintaining invariant"

Invariant is true and $k \neq n$.

false

Invariant is true and $k = n$.

Since $0! = 1$, we can meet the specification of "Achieve invariant" by

$$k := 0; f := 1   .$$

(Strictly speaking, we should enclose this statement sequence in **begin** ... **end** to make it a statement, but this kind of parenthesization is a purely syntactic concern which we can ignore in writing specifications.)

For "Increase k while maintaining invariant", we write

begin $k := k+1$; "Set f to reestablish $f = k!$" **end**   .

Since $f = k!$ **and** $0 \leq k \leq n$ **and** $k \neq n$ will be true before executing $k := k+1$, the assertion $f = (k-1)!$ **and** $0 < k \leq n$ will be true afterwards. Thus our remaining unwritten subprogram must meet the specification

$\{f=(k-1)! \text{ and } 0<k\leq n\}$
"Set f to reestablish $f=k!$"
$\{f=k! \text{ and } 0\leq k\leq n\}$.

Since $k!=k\times(k-1)!$ when $k>0$, we can complete our program by replacing "Set f to reestablish $f=k!$" by

$f := k\times f$.

In summary, by using assertions to specify each part of our program during its development, we have demonstrated the specification

$\{n\geq 0\}$
begin
$k := 0; f := 1;$
while $k\neq n$ **do**
    begin $k := k+1; f := k\times f$ **end**
end
$\{f=n!\}$,

i.e. if $n\geq 0$ then executing the above program will, if the program terminates, produce a state in which $f=n!$.

As before, however, we must still make sure that the program terminates. Each execution of the body of the **while** statement increases k without changing n, yet produces a state in which the invariant, and therefore $k\leq n$, is still true. Since k cannot be increased forever without eventually growing larger than the unchanging value of n, the **while** statement must terminate.

In general, a specification of the form $\{P\}\,S\,\{Q\}$ does not specify that S terminates. In technical terms, such a specification shows the *conditional correctness*, as opposed to the *total correctness*, of a program. (For a specification method which shows total correctness, see [Dijkstra 75, 76].) This reflects the fact that, although the need for termination must be kept in mind when constructing a program, the actual argument that the program will terminate is separate from the argument that it will behave correctly if it does terminate.

However, the termination argument will usually be straightforward if the assertions are adequate. (Exercise 2 after Section 1.2.2 is an exception.) Typically, a termination argument is said to be *based* on some quantity that is always increased (or decreased) by the body of **while** statement, yet cannot be increased (or decreased) indefinitely. For example, the termination of the factorial program is based on k.

Another important property that cannot be specified in the form $\{P\}\,S\,\{Q\}$ is that a program leaves certain variables unchanged. For example, in our original specificat on of the factorial program we had to stipulate "without changing the value of n" informally. We will continue to treat such stipulations informally until Section 3.3.

The factorial example is typical of the use of the **while** statement. The key point is that one should decide on an invariant before writing the **while** statement, not afterwards. Indeed, one can give a general recipe for using the **while** statement to meet the specification $\{P\}\ S\ \{Q\}$:

(1) Choose an invariant I and a logical expression L.

(2) Replace S by:

> "Initialize";
> **while** L **do** "Change";
> "Finalize"   .

(3) Write substatements to meet the specifications

> $\{P\}$ "Initialize" $\{I\}$,
> $\{I$ **and** $L\}$ "Change" $\{I\}$,
> $\{I$ **and** $\neg L\}$ "Finalize" $\{Q\}$.

Here "Initialize" may be omitted if P implies I. Similarly, "Finalize" may be omitted if I **and** $\neg L$ implies Q—as in our factorial example. "Change" may never be omitted—it must have some effect on the state or termination cannot occur.

(4) Show termination—usually by showing that "Change" increases or decreases some quantity in a way that cannot be repeated forever without making I false (or making L false).

Exercise

1. Replace "Increase k while maintaining invariant" by

> **begin** $k := k+2;\ f := k \times (k-1) \times f$ **end**   ,

and find out where the program construction argument breaks down. See if you can save the situation by adding $even(n)$ to the precedent of the program and $even(k)$ **and** $even(n)$ to the invariant.

1.3.3   Assertions as Comments

In this section we turn our attention from program writing to program reading. There is a vast difference between a program being executable and being understandable—information sufficient to determine the behavior of a computer will seldom be sufficient to reveal the general nature of that behavior. For example, it is clear that the program developed in the previous section will set f to 6 if n is 3. But in the absence of comments it is hardly clear that this program will set f to the factorial of n whenever n is nonnegative.

Fortunately, the assertions used to specify parts of a program can also be used as comments. The essential idea is to add the assertions to the program, as though they were extra statements, in such a way that each specification $\{P\} \, S \, \{Q\}$ appears as part of the program. For example, assertions would be added to our factorial example as follows:

$\{n\geq0\}$
begin
$k := 0; f := 1;$
$\{f=k! \text{ and } 0\leq k\leq n\}$
while $k\neq n$ **do**
　　begin
　　$\{f=k! \text{ and } 0\leq k\leq n \text{ and } k\neq n\}$
　　$k := k+1;$
　　$\{f=(k-1)! \text{ and } 0<k\leq n\}$
　　$f := k\times f$
　　$\{f=k! \text{ and } 0\leq k\leq n\}$
　　end
end
$\{f=n!\}$　.

Unfortunately, the curly bracket convention is not part of Algol W—instead of $\{P\}$ one must write the more cumbersome form **comment** $P;$. Throughout this book, however, we will use curly brackets for comments that are assertions, and eventually for other kinds of comments that provide a formal specification of program behavior. It should also be mentioned that we are not following the syntax of Algol W logical expressions within our assertions. It is not necessary to do so within comments but, for example, if it were an executable part of the program, we would have to rewrite $0\leq k\leq n$ as $(0\leq k)$ **and** $(k\leq n)$.

Now something slightly mysterious appears. The assertions in a program like the one above can be interpreted in either of two ways:

(1) Whenever a statement S is surrounded by assertions, i.e. $\{P\} \, S \, \{Q\}$, it meets the specification implied by these assertions. For example, $k := k+1$ meets the specification

$$\{f=k! \text{ and } 0\leq k\leq n \text{ and } k\neq n\}$$
$$k := k+1 \; \{f=(k-1)! \text{ and } 0<k\leq n\} \quad .$$

At the opposite extreme, the entire program meets the specification

$$\{n\geq0\} \text{ begin } ... \text{ end } \{f=n!\} \quad .$$

(2) If the program is executed, beginning with any initial state which satisfies (i.e. is described by) the initial assertion, then whenever any assertion is "passed through", it will be a true description of the

current state of the computation. For example, if one begins with a state in which $n \geq 0$, then each time execution of $k := k+1$ is completed, the current state will satisfy $f = (k-1)!$ **and** $0 < k \leq n$.

This is not an accidental coincidence; we will see in Section 1.4.1 that a correct usage of assertions can always be interpreted in both of these ways.

Now consider the use of the **while** statement in a program with assertions as comments. It will always have the form

$\{I\}$
while L **do**
    begin $\{Q_1\}$ S $\{I\}$ **end**
$\{Q_2\}$

or, in terms of a flowchart,

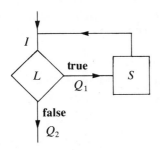

Here I is the invariant of the **while** statement, Q_1 is an assertion that is implied by I and L (i.e. it must be true for any state in which I and L are both true), and Q_2 is an assertion that is implied by I and $\neg L$. Notice that the invariant occurs (and must be true) at two points in the program: before the entire **while** statement and after each execution of the body S. These points correspond to the two arrows leading into the test in the flowchart.

This situation is such a commonly occurring cliché that it is worth adopting an abbreviation for it. We write

$\{$**whileinv**: $I\}$
while L **do** S .

Specifically, we label the invariant of the **while** statement with the symbol **whileinv** and only write it once, immediately before the **while** statement. We also omit Q_1 and Q_2 unless they are *nontrivial* consequences of I **and** L or of I **and** $\neg L$.

With this convention, the factorial program reduces to:

$\{n \geq 0\}$
begin
$k := 0; f := 1;$
$\{\textbf{whileinv: } f = k! \textbf{ and } 0 \leq k \leq n\}$
while $k \neq n$ **do**
    begin
    $k := k + 1;$
    $\{f = (k-1)! \textbf{ and } 0 < k \leq n\}$
    $f := k \times f$
    end
end
$\{f = n!\}$.

We will eventually see that even this is an excessive level of detail. For a simple program like this, it is sufficient to give just the initial and final assertions and the invariant of the **while** statement. However, it is vital that the given assertions should provide enough information. For instance, omission of the range information $0 \leq k \leq n$ would make the above program much harder to understand.

In general, the use of assertions as comments is important because it reveals the *statics* of the program. The statements of the program themselves reveal the dynamics, i.e. the changes that occur, so that a comment like

    comment increase x; $x := x + 1$

is simply redundant. But assertions reveal what the statements often hide— the unchanging aspects of the computation.

Exercises

1. Complete the following partially written programs for performing exponentiation. The programs should not change n or x. (Assume that $x^0 = 1$, even when $x = 0$.)

    (a) $\{n \geq 0\}$
        begin
        "Achieve invariant";
        $\{\textbf{whileinv: } y = x^k \textbf{ and } 0 \leq k \leq n\}$
        while $k \neq n$ **do**
            "Increase k while maintaining invariant"
        end
        $\{y = x^n\}$.

(b) $\{n \geq 0\}$
    begin
    "Achieve invariant";
    $\{$**whileinv:** $y \times x^k = x^n$ **and** $k \geq 0\}$
    while $k \neq 0$ **do**
        "Decrease k while maintaining invariant"
    end
    $\{y = x^n\}$.

2. Complete the following partially written programs for performing multiplication. The programs should not change x or y. (Do not use the "built-in" multiplication operator $\times$.)

(a) $\{y \geq 0\}$
    begin
    "Achieve invariant";
    $\{$**whileinv:** $z = x \times k$ **and** $k \leq y\}$
    while $k \neq y$ **do**
        "Increase k while maintaining invariant"
    end
    $\{z = x \times y\}$.

(b) $\{y \leq 0\}$
    begin
    "Achieve invariant";
    $\{$**whileinv:** $z = x \times k$ **and** $k \geq y\}$
    while $k \neq y$ **do**
        "Decrease k while maintaining invariant"
    end
    $\{z = x \times y\}$.

3. Combine the two programs in Exercise 2 to obtain a program satisfying

    $\{$**true**$\}$
    "Compute product"
    $\{z = x \times y\}$.

Note that the assertion **true** describes the set of all possible states of a computation.

1.3.4 Integer Division

As a second example of program construction, we consider a statement that, given two positive integers x and y, will set q and r to the quotient and remainder of x divided by y. Specifically, the statement should satisfy the specification

    $\{x \geq 0$ **and** $y > 0\}$
    "Compute quotient and remainder"
    $\{x = q \times y + r$ **and** $0 \leq r < y\}$

without changing x or y.

One way to find possible invariants is to ask how much of the final assertion can be achieved directly. In this case, we can get $x = q \times y + r$ simply by setting r to x and q to zero. This also gives $0 \leq r$ for free. Thus we will try

$$x = q \times y + r \text{ and } 0 \leq r$$

as the invariant of a **while** statement that tries to achieve $r < y$.

This gives us the partially written program

```
{x≥0 and y>0}
begin
r := x; q := 0;
{whileinv: x=q×y+r and 0≤r}
while r≥y do
      "Decrease r while maintaining invariant"
end
{x=q×y+r and 0≤r<y}   ,
```

where the body of the **while** statement must satisfy the specification

```
{x=q×y+r and y≤r}
"Decrease r while maintaining invariant"
{x=q×y+r and 0≤r}   .
```

(In the precedent of this specification, we do not need to include $0 \leq r$, since it is implied by $y \leq r$ when $y > 0$.)

With a little algebraic juggling, we can see that before the body of the **while** statement is executed

$$x = q \times y + r = (q + 1) \times y + (r - y)$$

will hold, so that decreasing r by y and increasing q by one will maintain the relation $x = q \times y + r$. Moreover, since beforehand $y \leq r$, decreasing r by y will give $0 \leq r$. Thus the statements

$$r := r - y; \ q := q + 1$$

meet the specification for "Decrease r while maintaining invariant".

The finished program is

```
{x≥0 and y>0}
begin
r := x; q := 0;
{whileinv: x=q×y+r and 0≤r}
while r≥y do
      begin r := r-y; q := q+1 end
end
{x=q×y+r and 0≤r<y}   .
```

Termination is based on r. Since $y>0$, each execution of the body of the **while** statement decreases r. (Notice that this argument would fail if $y=0$ were permitted.) Yet at the completion of each execution of the body, the invariant shows that $0 \leq r$. Since one cannot indefinitely decrease r without falsifying $0 \leq r$, the **while** statement must terminate.

So far all the programs we have constructed have set one or more *output* variables to values that depend upon one or more *input* variables, without changing the values of any input variables. For example, the above program sets q and r to values that depend upon x and y, without changing x or y. Such programs are said to be *input-preserving*.

However, consider the effect of deleting the initial assignment $r := x$. The resulting program is not input-preserving; it sets q and r to the quotient and remainder of the initial value of r divided by y, while destroying the initial value of r in the process.

A significant difficulty arises when we try to state this specification with assertions. It is a relationship between values in different states of the computation, but assertions can only relate values in the same state of the computation.

Fortunately, there is a standard method for overcoming this difficulty. One introduces an identifier, say r_0, that does not occur in the program being specified, and adds the equality $r=r_0$ to the precedent of the specification. Then since the program clearly does not change the value of r_0, this identifier can be used in assertions throughout the program to denote the initial value of r:

$$\{r \geq 0 \text{ and } y>0 \text{ and } r=r_0\}$$
begin
$q := 0;$
$\{\text{whileinv: } r_0=q \times y+r \text{ and } 0 \leq r\}$
while $r \geq y$ **do**
      begin $r := r-y; \ q := q+1$ **end**
end
$$\{r_0=q \times y+r \text{ and } 0 \leq r<y\} \quad .$$

An identifier, such as r_0, that occurs in the specification of a program (or in intermediate assertions) but does not occur in the program itself is called a *ghost identifier* of the specification. (Some authors, e.g. [Gries 80], call ghost identifiers "logical variables", which is a completely different usage of the latter term than in this book.) In specifying programs that do not preserve certain inputs, we will usually denote such inputs by ghost identifiers with the subscript zero.

Actually, almost all of the programs in Chapter 1 will be input-preserving. Such programs are obviously more flexible for their users, who may need to reference input values after the program has been executed. Moreover, the cost of preserving simple inputs such as integers or logical values is minor. This cost will escalate, however, when we consider array inputs in Chapter 2.

Exercises

1. In the program constructed in the above section, the relationship $x=q\times y+r$ would be preserved by a **while**-statement body of the form $r := r-(\alpha\times y); q := q+\alpha$, where α might be any integer. Show that $\alpha=1$ is the only choice of α that gives a correct program.

2. Complete the following partially written program for computing square roots. You may use multiplication by two but not by other numbers. (This is a reasonable restriction, since multiplication by two can be implemented by shifting on a computer with binary arithmetic.) The program should preserve the value of x.

    $\{x\geq0\}$
    begin
    "Achieve invariant";
    $\{$**whileinv:** $x=y^2+r$ **and** $r\geq0$ **and** $y\geq0\}$
    while $r\geq2\times y+1$ **do**
    　　"Decrease r while maintaining invariant"
    end
    $\{y^2\leq x<(y+1)^2\}$.

    (The algebraic juggling will involve the identity $(y+1)^2=y^2+2\times y+1$.)

3. From the program developed in the previous exercise, delete the initial assignment which preserves the input. Use a ghost identifier to specify the resulting program.

1.3.5   Fast Exponentiation

So far the heart of all the programs we have constructed has been a **while** statement whose body increases or decreases some variable by a constant amount. We now want to explore some more sophisticated computational behavior.

Consider the problem of computing x^n for $n\geq0$. In Exercise 1 after Section 1.3.3, we have already seen two solutions to this problem, but now we will construct a much faster program to meet the same specification. We begin with the solution to the second part of Exercise 1:

$\{n\geq0\}$
begin
$k := n; y := 1;$
$\{$**whileinv:** $y\times x^k=x^n$ **and** $k\geq0\}$
while $k\neq0$ **do**
　　begin $k := k-1; y := y\times x$ **end**
end
$\{y=x^n\}$.

In contrast to our factorial program, or to the first part of Exercise 1, the variable k in this program is repeatedly decreased rather than increased, and serves to keep track of the number of multiplications remaining to be done, rather than the number of multiplications already done.

To try to improve this program, we look for a more general invariant that will still imply the goal $y = x^n$ when $k = 0$. One possibility is to introduce an additional variable z, and use $y \times z^k = x^n$ instead of $y \times x^k = x^n$. The new invariant is almost as easy to achieve as the old one (if we also set z to x), but it gives us the extra freedom of changing z in the body of the **while** statement. We will see that this extra freedom allows us to write a much faster program.

At this stage our program is

$$\{n \geq 0\}$$
begin
$k := n; \ y := 1; \ z := x;$
$\{\textbf{whileinv}; \ y \times z^k = x^n \textbf{ and } k \geq 0\}$
while $k \neq 0$ **do**
     "Decrease k while maintaining invariant"
end
$\{y = x^n\}$,

where the body of the **while** statement must satisfy the specification

$$\{y \times z^k = x^n \textbf{ and } k > 0\}$$
"Decrease k while maintaining invariant"
$$\{y \times z^k = x^n \textbf{ and } k \geq 0\}   .$$

Since $z^k = z \times z^{k-1}$ when $k > 0$, the precedent here implies

$$x^n = y \times z^k = (y \times z) \times z^{k-1}   .$$

Thus decreasing k by one and multiplying y by z preserves the relation $y \times z^k = x^n$. Also, if $k > 0$ beforehand, then decreasing k by one will give $k \geq 0$. Thus we can replace "Decrease k while maintaining invariant" by

$$k := k - 1; \ y := y \times z   . \tag{S_-}$$

But this replacement takes no advantage of our more general invariant, and gives a program that is essentially the same as the second part of Exercise 1. We can do better by taking advantage of the freedom to change z, and using the exponential law

$$x^{2 \times m} = (x \times x)^m \text{ when } m \geq 0   .$$

Thus *if k is even* before executing "Decrease k while maintaining invariant", we will have

$$x^n = y \times z^k = y \times (z \times z)^{k \textbf{ div } 2}   ,$$

so that dividing k by two and squaring z will maintain $y \times z^k = x^n$. Also, if $k > 0$ (or even just $k \geq 0$) beforehand, then dividing k by two will give $k \geq 0$ afterwards.

This suggests a version of "Decrease k while maintaining invariant",

$$k := k \text{ div } 2; z := z \times z \quad , \qquad\qquad (S_{\text{div}})$$

that is potentially much faster than S_- (since repeated division by two will obviously make k decrease much more rapidly than repeated subtraction of one). But unfortunately the version S_{div} only works when k is even.

There are at least two ways around this dilemma. The obvious solution is to branch on whether k is odd or even, doing S_{div} when it is even and falling back on the slower S_- when it is odd:

> **if** $odd(k)$ **then**
>   **begin** $k := k-1; y := y \times z$ **end**
> **else**
>   **begin** $k := k \text{ div } 2; z := z \times z$ **end**   .
>
> $\qquad\qquad (S_{\text{branch}})$

A more subtle approach [Dijkstra 72] is to always do S_{div}, but to precede it by a statement that will *make k even*:

> "Make k even while maintaining invariant";
> $\{y \times z^k = x^n \text{ and } k \geq 0 \text{ and } even(k)\}$
> $k := k \text{ div } 2; z := z \times z$.

Then S_- provides an obvious method for fulfilling "Make k even while maintaining invariant": If k is odd do S_-, otherwise do nothing. This leads to the following version of "Decrease k while maintaining invariant":

> **if** $odd(k)$ **then begin** $k := k-1; y := y \times z$ **end**;
> $\{y \times z^k = x^n \text{ and } k \geq 0 \text{ and } even(k)\}$
> $k := k \text{ div } 2; z := z \times z$.
>
> $\qquad\qquad (S_{\text{makeeven}})$

Thus we have three possible versions, S_-, S_{branch}, and S_{makeeven}, of "Decrease k while maintaining invariant". For each version, termination is based on k. (The reader should check that S_{branch} and S_{makeeven} actually satisfy their specification and decrease k. Note that these statements would not always decrease k if their precedent permitted $k = 0$.)

Next, we consider the execution speed of the three ways of computing x^n. In all three cases, the program consists of a sequence of initialization statements followed by a single **while** statement. Thus the execution time will be smaller or equal to $\alpha + \beta \cdot l$, where α is the maximum time required for the initialization statements, β is the maximum time required for the body of the **while** statement, and l is the number of times the **while** statement body is executed. Notice that the bounds α and β only exist because:

(1) Neither the initialization statements nor the **while**-statement body contain **while** statements (or other iterative constructs).

(2) All the assignment statements and tests require a constant amount of time, or at least an amount of time that is bounded by some constant. (With slight exceptions which are irrelevant here, all the basic operations of the portion of Algol W used in this book have this property. In effect, the language is sufficiently "low-level" that there are no hidden iterations.)

When S_- is used, k begins with the value n and is decreased by one each time the **while**-statement body is executed, until it is equal to zero. Thus $l=n$.

When S_{makeeven} is used, each execution of the **while**-statement body will reduce k to no more than half its previous value. Since initially $k=n=2^{\log_2 n}$, the successive values of k will be bounded by

$$n=2^{\log_2 n}, \quad \frac{n}{2}=2^{\log_2 n-1}, \quad \frac{n}{4}=2^{\log_2 n-2}, \quad \cdots \quad.$$

Let $\lfloor \log_2 n \rfloor$ denote the largest integer that is smaller or equal to $\log_2 n$. Then it will take at most $\lfloor \log_2 n \rfloor$ iterations to reduce k to no more than

$$2^{\log_2 n - \lfloor \log_2 n \rfloor} \quad,$$

which is less than two. Then since k is an integer, it must be zero or one, so that at most one more iteration will complete the algorithm. Thus

$$l \leq \lfloor \log_2 n \rfloor + 1 \leq \log_2 n + 1.$$

The situation is slightly more complicated for S_{branch}. By considering even and odd k separately, it is easy to see that at most two iterations will be enough to reduce k to no more than half its previous value. Then the above argument shows that $l \leq 2 \cdot \log_2 n + 1$.

In summary, the time required by each of our programs to compute x^n is bounded by

$$\alpha + \beta \cdot n \qquad\qquad\qquad (S_-)$$
$$\alpha + \beta \cdot (\log_2 n + 1) \qquad\quad (S_{\text{makeeven}})$$
$$\alpha + \beta \cdot (2 \cdot \log_2 n + 1) \quad . \qquad (S_{\text{branch}})$$

Of course, the constants α and β are different in each case. Nevertheless, since the function $\log_2 n$ grows more slowly than n, it is clear that for sufficiently large n using either S_{makeeven} or S_{branch} will be faster than using S_-. Indeed, for any multiplier m, there will be sufficiently large n such that using S_{makeeven} or S_{branch} will be m times as fast as using S_-.

This kind of asymptotic behavior can be clarified by introducing the concept of *order of magnitude*. In general, a numerical function $f(n)$ is said to be *of order* $g(n)$ if there is a constant c such that, for all sufficiently large n, $f(n) \le c \cdot g(n)$. In particular,

$$\left. \begin{array}{l} \alpha + \beta \cdot n \\ \alpha + \beta \cdot (\log_2 n + 1) \\ \alpha + \beta \cdot (2 \cdot \log_2 n + 1) \end{array} \right\} \text{ is of order } \left\{ \begin{array}{l} n \\ \log n \\ \log n \end{array} \right. .$$

Note that we need not state the base of the logarithm explicitly, since choosing another base would only lead to a different value of the constant c. In other words, for any bases b and b' a function of order $\log_b n$ is also of order $\log_{b'} n$.

(Strictly speaking, any function, such as $\alpha + \beta \cdot (\log_2 n + 1)$, that is of order $\log n$ is also of order n, but the latter fact provides less information than the former. The real point is that the program using S_{makeeven} or S_{branch} requires time of order $\log n$, while the program using S_{-} requires time that is not of the order of any function which grows less rapidly than n.)

In many computing applications, the size of the computation is so large that order-of-magnitude considerations completely dominate the question of efficiency. Exponentiation is a marginal case, since one usually computes x^n for only moderate sized values of n, but more vivid examples will appear in later chapters.

Finally, we must compare S_{branch} and S_{makeeven}. Here, since the execution times are the same order of magnitude, the choice is less clearcut. The use of S_{branch} has the disadvantage of redundant testing: When k is odd, it will be decreased by one and then tested again to see whether it is odd, despite the fact that it must be even. On the other hand, S_{makeeven} has the disadvantage that the last execution of $k := k$ **div** $2; z := z \times z$ is always unnecessary, since k will already be zero. The time lost is not significant, but the final value of z can be much larger than x^n, and this can cause overflow problems. (See Section 1.6.1.)

It is natural to ask whether one can construct an exponentiation program which avoids the disadvantages of either S_{branch} or S_{makeeven}. We will return to this question in Section 4.2.5.

Exercises

1.   What is wrong with the following expansion of "Decrease k while maintaining invariant"?

   if *odd*(k) then begin $k := k-1; y := y \times z$ end;
   while $\lnot$ *odd*(k) do
      begin $k := k$ div $2; z := z \times z$ end   .

2.   For any positive integer n, let ξ be the number of bits in the binary representation of n, and let η be the number of such bits that are 1. For example, when

$n = 13 = 1101_{binary}$, $\xi = 4$ and $\eta = 3$. Show that the number of multiplications used to compute x^n is $\xi + \eta - 1$ when the program with S_{branch} is used, and $\xi + \eta$ when the program with $S_{makeeven}$ is used.

3. Complete the following partially written program for multiplication in such a way that it will require a time of order log y. Within the program, you may use multiplication and division by two, but not by other numbers. (As noted earlier, this is a natural restriction, since multiplication and division by two can be implemented by shifting on a computer with binary arithmetic.) The program should preserve x and y.

> $\{y \geq 0\}$
> **begin**
> "Achieve invariant";
> $\{$**whileinv**: $z + w \times k = x \times y$ **and** $k \geq 0\}$
> **while** $k \neq 0$ **do**
>   "Decrease k while maintaining invariant"
> **end**
> $\{z = x \times y\}$.

4. Complete the following partially written program for division in such a way that it will require a time of order log $(x$ **div** $y)$. Again, you may use multiplication and division by two, but not by other numbers. The program should preserve x and y.

> $\{x \geq 0$ **and** $y > 0\}$
> **begin**
> "Achieve first invariant";
> $\{$**whileinv**: $z = y \times 2^n$ **and** $n \geq 0$ **and** $x \geq 0\}$
> **while** $z \leq x$ **do**
>   "Increase z while maintaining invariant";
> "Achieve second invariant";
> $\{$**whileinv**: $x = q \times z + r$ **and** $0 \leq r < z$ **and** $z = y \times 2^n$ **and** $n \geq 0\}$
> **while** $n \neq 0$ **do**
>   "Decrease n while maintaining invariant"
> **end**
> $\{x = q \times y + r$ **and** $0 \leq r < y\}$.

5. Complete the following partially written program for computing square roots in such a way that it will require a time of order log x. The program should preserve x.

> $\{x \geq 0\}$
> **begin**
> "Achieve first invariant";
> $\{$**whileinv**: $z = 2^n$ **and** $n \geq 0$ **and** $x \geq 0\}$
> **while** $z \times z \leq x$ **do**
>   "Increase z while maintaining invariant";
> "Achieve second invariant";
> $\{$**whileinv**: $y^2 \leq x < (y + z)^2$ **and** $z = 2^n$ **and** $n \geq 0\}$
> **while** $n \neq 0$ **do**
>   "Decrease n while maintaining invariant"
> **end**
> $\{y^2 \leq x < (y + 1)^2\}$.

1.3.6 Fibonacci Numbers

So far our programs have all had the form

"Initialize"; **while** L **do** "Change"   .

The following example suggests that the situation does not always work out so simply.

We want to write a statement that, when given a nonnegative integer n, will set f to the nth Fibonacci number. Specifically, we want a statement that will satisfy the specification

$\{n \geq 0\}$ "Compute Fibonacci" $\{f = fib(n)\}$,

where fib is the function that satisfies

$$fib(0) = 0$$
$$fib(1) = 1$$
$$fib(n) = fib(n-1) + fib(n-2) .$$

We will use the same basic plan of attack as with the factorial function, but now we must keep track of two "adjacent" Fibonacci numbers. To do so, we will use three variables f, g, and k satisfying the relationship

$f = fib(k)$ **and** $g = fib(k-1)$.

Since we intend to increase k until it is equal to n, we add the appropriate range information $k \leq n$ to the invariant.

At this stage our program has the form

$\{n \geq 0\}$
begin
"Achieve invariant";
$\{$**whileinv**: $f = fib(k)$ **and** $g = fib(k-1)$ **and** $k \leq n\}$
while $k \neq n$ **do**
     "Increase k while maintaining invariant"
end
$\{f = fib(n)\}$.

Now consider the expansion of the **while** statement body. If we change k first, we have

$\{f = fib(k)$ **and** $g = fib(k-1)$ **and** $k < n\}$
$k := k+1;$
$\{f = fib(k-1)$ **and** $g = fib(k-2)$ **and** $k \leq n\}$
"Change f and g to reestablish invariant"
$\{f = fib(k)$ **and** $g = fib(k-1)$ **and** $k \leq n\}$.

To complete this program, it is evident that we must make the new value of f

be the sum of the old values of f and g, and make the new value of g be the old value of f.

But now we encounter a small dilemma: If we set f first, we will lose the old value of f and will be unable to set g, but if we set g first, we will lose the old value of g and be unable to set f. The simplest way out is to use an additional "temporary" variable t to save the information that will be needed. Then "Change f and g to reestablish invariant" can be replaced by

$$t := f+g; \; g := f; \; f := t \quad ,$$

or equally well by

$$t := f; \; f := f+g; \; g := t \quad .$$

Another problem occurs when we consider "Achieve invariant". The obvious replacement is

$$k := 1; \; g := 0; \; f := 1 \quad ,$$

which will achieve $f=fib(k)$ and $g=fib(k-1)$. But this initialization will not achieve $k \leq n$ when $n=0$—reflecting the fact that the **while** statement will run on forever when $n=0$.

This is slightly surprising. Usually, when a function is well-defined for zero, a reasonable program which works for all larger values will also work for zero. But there are exceptions, and the Fibonacci numbers are one of them. The most obvious solution is to use the program we have designed when $n \geq 1$, and to handle $n=0$ separately:

$$\{n \geq 0\}$$
if $n=0$ **then** $f := 0$ **else**
      begin
      $\{n \geq 1\}$
      $k := 1; \; g := 0; \; f := 1;$
      $\{$**whileinv**: $f=fib(k)$ **and** $g=fib(k-1)$ **and** $k \leq n\}$
      while $k \neq n$ **do**
         begin $k := k+1; \; t := f+g; \; g := f; \; f := t$ **end**
      end
$$\{f=fib(n)\} \quad .$$

Exercises

1.   A more elegant solution to the problem discussed above arises from the fact that the function fib can be consistently extended to -1. In particular, we can define $fib(-1)=1$, and still have $fib(n)=fib(n-1)+fib(n-2)$. Show that this extension permits one to write a program satisfying

$$\{n \geq 0\} \; \text{"Compute Fibonacci"} \; \{f=fib(n)\}$$

without including a special branch for $n=0$.

2.   The greatest common divisor $gcd(a, b)$ of two integers is the largest integer that divides both a and b. (This definition is meaningless when a and b are both zero, but by convention $gcd(0, 0) = 0$.) It is easily shown that

$$gcd(a, b) = gcd(b, a \textbf{ rem } b) \quad,$$
$$gcd(a, 0) = a \text{ when } a \geq 0 \quad.$$

Use these properties to construct a program (Euclid's algorithm) that will compute the greatest common divisor of any two nonnegative integers.

1.4   ASSERTIONS AND PROGRAM PROVING

In this section we will investigate the underlying nature of assertions, and show that they can be used to construct formal proofs that programs meet their specifications.

1.4.1   Assertions with Flowcharts

The nature of assertions is easily seen in the context of flowcharts, where they were originally introduced by R. W. Floyd [Floyd 67a], and independently by P. Naur [Naur 66]. In a flowchart, each assertion is attached to an arrow, and is meant to be a true description of the state of the computation whenever the arrow is traversed in moving from one box to another. (When several arrows join to lead to the same box or all lead to exit boxes, they must have the same assertion attached.) This is illustrated in Figure 1.4, where assertions are attached to a flowchart for the factorial-computing program.

Floyd's discovery was that, if adequate assertions are attached to a flowchart, then the correctness of the entire flowchart can be inferred from the correctness of its individual parts. By the correctness of the individual parts we mean that, for each box in the flowchart, the following *verification conditions* must hold:

(1)   If the box contains a statement S and has assertions P and Q attached to its incoming and outgoing arrows,

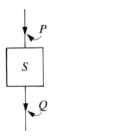

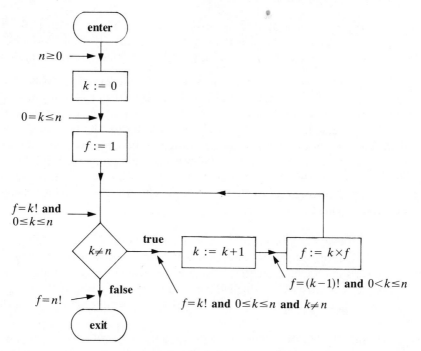

Figure 1.4   Flowchart with Assertions for Factorial-Computing Program.

then, for any state in which P is true, executing S must change that state into a state in which Q is true. In other words, S must meet the specification $\{P\}\ S\ \{Q\}$.

(2) If the box contains a logical expression L, has an assertion P attached to its incoming arrow, and has assertions Q_1 and Q_2 attached to its outgoing arrows marked **true** and **false**,

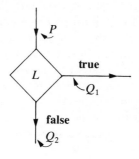

then Q_1 must be true for any state in which both P and L are true and Q_2 must be true for any state in which P is true and L is false. In other words, P **and** L must imply Q_1, and P **and** $\urcorner L$ must imply Q_2.

Now consider executing a flowchart in which every box satisfies these verification conditions (as is the case in Figure 1.4). If, at any time during this execution, the current state satisfies the assertion attached to the arrow that is being traversed, then the verification condition for the next box insures that, after execution of the statement or test in that box, the new state will satisfy the assertion attached to the new arrow being traversed. It is evident (by induction on the number of boxes that are executed) that this situation will continue throughout further execution. Thus the flowchart is "correct" in the following sense:

If every box of a flowchart satisfies the verification conditions, and if execution of the flowchart begins with an initial state that satisfies the assertion attached to **enter**, then as each arrow is traversed, the current state will satisfy the attached assertion, and when and if the program terminates, the final state will satisfy the assertion attached to **exit**.

In effect, the assertions attached to **enter** and **exit** are the precedent ($n \geq 0$ in Figure 1.4) and consequent ($f = n!$ in Figure 1.4) of the entire program, and the intermediate assertions provide enough information so that a reader can check (by using the verification conditions) that the program meets its specification.

Essentially, Floyd's discovery explains the "mysterious coincidence" of Section 1.3.3, since the use of assertions as comments is tantamount to attaching them to arrows in a flowchart.

Again, the qualification "when *and if* the program terminates" should be noticed. As with our earlier informal arguments, the use of assertions does not insure termination, but only shows conditional correctness. Nevertheless, it is usually easy to show termination separately if the assertions include enough range information about the relevant variables.

One other point deserves emphasis. Each arrow in a flowchart is both an outgoing arrow from one box and an incoming arrow to another box, so that the attached assertion must satisfy two verification conditions. The verification condition for the preceding box prevents the assertion from being too *strong*, i.e. from being an incorrect description of the current state. On the other hand, the verification condition for the succeeding box prevents the assertion from being too *weak*, i.e. from being an inadequate description of the current state.

For example, consider the circled assertion in the following portion of Figure 1.4:

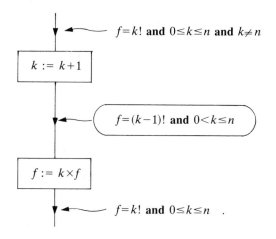

The verification condition for $k := k+1$ prevents us from strengthening this assertion to the point of incorrectness—for instance, we could not add the condition $k \neq n$. On the other hand, the verification condition for $f := k \times f$ prevents us from weakening this assertion to the point of inadequacy—for instance, we could not remove the condition $k \leq n$.

Here the notions of strengthening and weakening assertions involve implication. The following four statements are different ways of expressing the same relationship between two assertions P and Q:

(1) P is stronger than Q.

(2) Q is weaker than P.

(3) P implies Q.

(4) Every state described by P is also described by Q.

If P implies Q and also Q implies P, then P and Q are said to be *equivalent*. The assertion **true** is weaker than any assertion, since it describes every state. At the opposite extreme, the assertion **false** is stronger than any assertion, since it describes no state.

The adequacy of assertions can be described in another way. Let P be an assertion attached to some arrow in a flowchart, and imagine the following process:

(1) Execution of the flowchart begins with an initial state satisfying the assertion attached to **enter**.

(2) Execution is halted temporarily at some instant when the computation is traversing the arrow to which P is attached.

(3) A "demon" is permitted to make an arbitrary alteration in the current state of the computation, provided the altered state still satisfies the assertion P.

(4) Execution is resumed and permitted to continue to completion.

If there is nothing the demon can do that will lead to an incorrect final result, then the assertion P is adequate. If, in addition, there is nothing the demon can do that will lead to nontermination (although his actions might increase the number of steps to be executed), then P is also adequate for showing termination.

1.4.2 Inference Rules for Specifications

So far, we have relied upon our intuition to make sure that our programs actually satisfied their specifications. This is often sufficient, but it is hardly foolproof. Intuition can easily go wrong when one is dealing with a complex or subtle programming situation, and it can also go wrong if the exact meaning of the programming language is misunderstood. In these cases one needs a more rigorous method of proving that a program meets its specification.

The development of such methods has been a significant area of research in the last decade. It is a major (and controversial) thesis of this book that this development has progressed to the point where the serious programmer should be expected to prove his programs in the same sense that a mathematician is expected to prove his theorems.

However, one should carefully distinguish between the mathematician's concept of proof and the logician's concept of *formal* proof. A formal proof is a sequence of statements each of which is inferred from a subset of its predecessors according to a fixed and explicit set of *rules of inference*. In contrast, a mathematician's proof can be regarded as an adequate collection of hints for producing a formal proof. Specifically, a clear mathematical proof is one which provides just enough information to permit a well-trained reader to construct a formal proof without any trial-and-error. For example, the mathematician might write $q \times y + r = (q+1) \times y + (r-y)$ without further detail, confident that his reader understands the rules of arithmetic well enough to see how they could be used to infer this equation.

In a similar sense, an adequately commented program should provide just enough information to permit a well-trained reader, without trial-and-error, to construct a formal proof that the program meets its specification. This is the fundamental reason for studying formal methods for proving programs. One does not need to give a formal proof of an obviously correct program, but one needs a thorough understanding of formal proof methods to know when correctness is obvious.

In the first two chapters of this book, we will construct formal proofs using rules for inferring conditional-correctness specifications which were originally devised by C. A. R. Hoare [Hoare 69]. (A more elaborate formal system, capable of dealing with procedures, will be introduced in Section 3.3.) These inference rules represent a translation of Floyd's discovery about flowcharts into a form that is applicable to programs in an Algol-like language. Roughly speaking, for each way in which a statement can be constructed from simpler statements, there is a rule for inferring a specification of the constructed statement from specifications of its component statements.

Each inference rule consists of a sequence of zero or more specifications, called *premisses*, which are separated by a long bar from a single specification called the *conclusion*:

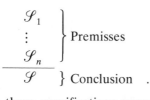

Within these specifications upper case letters, called *metavariables*, will occur in place of various types of phrases such as assertions, statements, variables, or expressions. An *instance* of an inference rule is obtained by replacing each metavariable by a phrase of the appropriate type, with the restriction that all occurrences of the same metavariable must be replaced by the same phrase. (A few rules will be prefaced by further restrictions on the permissible replacements.)

The meaning of an inference rule is that, for any instance, if the premisses are true specifications then the conclusion is a true specification. Thus in writing proofs, once the premisses of an instance have been proved, one may *infer* the conclusion of the instance.

We begin by developing a rule for the assignment statement. Suppose we have an assignment statement $X := E$, and that we wish an assertion P to be true after the assignment statement is finished. (Here X, E, and P are metavariables denoting an arbitrary variable identifier, expression, and assertion respectively.) What has to be true before the assignment statement begins? If we regard P as asserting that X has some property, then beforehand E must have the same property. To assert this, we can simply write down P and then replace each occurrence of X in P by E. More precisely, we must *substitute E for X in P*. (Eventually, when we encounter the phenomenon of *identifier collisions* in Section 2.2.6, we will adopt a more complex definition of substitution.)

Let us write $P\big|_{X \to E}$ to stand for the result of substituting E for X in P. Then the following inference rule describes assignment:

Simple Assignment:

$$\overline{\{P\,|\,_{X\to E}\}\ X := E\ \{P\}}\quad .$$

Although this rule is "justified" by the previous paragraph, the justification is only informal. Strictly speaking, one should regard the rule as a definition of the meaning of the assignment statement.

To obtain an instance of the assignment rule, we must replace the metavariables P, X, and E by a particular assertion, variable, and expression, and then carry out the indicated substitution. For example, suppose we replace P by $y<4$, X by y, and E by $y\times y$. Then the substitution $y<4\,|\,_{y\to y\times y}$ gives $y\times y<4$, so that we get the instance

$$\overline{\{y\times y<4\}\ y := y\times y\ \{y<4\}}\quad .$$

Similarly, if we replace P by $y\times y<4$, X by y, and E by $y-z$, we get the instance

$$\overline{\{(y-z)\times(y-z)<4\}\ y := y-z\ \{y\times y<4\}}\quad .$$

Like the assignment rule itself, these instances contain no premises. Thus, without proving anything beforehand, we may infer their conclusions.

Next, consider a compound statement of the form $S_1; S_2$. Suppose that whenever P is true executing S_1 will make Q true, and whenever Q is true executing S_2 will make R true. Then whenever P is true executing $S_1; S_2$ will make R true. Thus we have the rule

Statement Compounding:

$$\frac{\{P\}\ S_1\ \{Q\}}{\{Q\}\ S_2\ \{R\}}$$
$$\overline{\{P\}\ S_1;\ S_2\ \{R\}}\quad .$$

For example, if we make the replacements

$$P: (y-z)\times(y-z)<4 \qquad S_1: y := y-z$$
$$Q: y\times y<4 \qquad\qquad\quad S_2: y := y\times y \quad ,$$
$$R: y<4$$

we obtain the instance

$$\frac{\{(y-z)\times(y-z)<4\}\ y := y-z\ \{y\times y<4\}}{\{y\times y<4\}\ y := y\times y\ \{y<4\}}$$
$$\overline{\{(y-z)\times(y-z)<4\}\ y := y-z;\ y := y\times y\ \{y<4\}}\quad .$$

Here the two premises are the specifications that we proved by using the rule for simple assignment. Thus we may infer the conclusion.

Next suppose that P implies Q (i.e. that Q is true in any computational state for which P is true), and that whenever Q is true executing S will make R true. Obviously, whenever P is true executing S will make R true. Thus we have

Strengthening Precedent:

If P implies Q then

$$\frac{\{Q\}\ S\ \{R\}}{\{P\}\ S\ \{R\}}\ .$$

For example, since $-2 < y - z < 2$ implies $(y-z) \times (y-z) < 4$,

$P: -2 < y - z < 2 \qquad S: y := y - z;\ y := y \times y$
$Q: (y-z) \times (y-z) < 4 \qquad R: y < 4$

is a permissible replacement. Since the premiss of the resulting instance was inferred by the rule for statement compounding, we may infer the conclusion

$$\{-2 < y - z < 2\}\ y := y - z;\ y := y \times y\ \{y < 4\}\ .$$

On the other hand, suppose that whenever P is true executing S will make Q true, and that Q implies R. Obviously, whenever P is true executing S will make R true. Thus:

Weakening Consequent:

If Q implies R then

$$\frac{\{P\}\ S\ \{Q\}}{\{P\}\ S\ \{R\}}\ .$$

For example, $y < 4$ implies $y \leq 3$. This permits an obvious replacement that produces an instance whose premiss was proven in the previous paragraph. Thus we may infer the conclusion

$$\{-2 < y - z < 2\}\ y := y - z;\ y := y \times y\ \{y \leq 3\}\ .$$

At first sight, the last two rules seem too obvious to be worth mentioning. But although they are obvious, they are vital, since they are the essential mechanism that allows static mathematical facts to be used in proving program correctness. Notice that the specification

$$\{(y-z) \times (y-z) < 4\}\ y := y - z;\ y := y \times y\ \{y < 4\}$$

is purely concerned with programming; it depends upon the nature of the assignment statement and the operator ";", but has nothing to do with the fact that the values involved are a particular kind of mathematical entity called integers. On the other hand,

$$-2 < y - z < 2 \text{ implies } (y-z) \times (y-z) < 4 \quad,$$
$$y < 4 \text{ implies } y \leq 3$$

are purely mathematical facts which have nothing to do with programming, but which describe the nature of integers. (For example, the second fact holds for integers but not for real numbers.) In order to combine these two kinds of knowledge we must use the rules for strengthening precedents or weakening consequents.

It is evident that the explicit application of the rules for statement compounding, strengthening precedents, and weakening consequents involves a good deal of mechanical detail. Fortunately, there is a simple way of "automating" this detail.

Consider the following sequence of assertions and statements:

$$\{-2 < y - z < 2\}$$
$$\{(y-z) \times (y-z) < 4\}$$
$$y := y - z;$$
$$\{y \times y < 4\}$$
$$y := y \times y$$
$$\{y < 4\}$$
$$\{y \leq 3\} \quad .$$

Such a sequence is called a *tableau*. In general, a *tableau* is a sequence of intermixed assertions and statements that begins and ends with assertions.

A tableau is *valid* if:

(1) Whenever a triple of the form $\{P\}\, S\, \{Q\}$, where S is a statement or sequence of statements, occurs in the tableau, the triple is a true specification, and

(2) Whenever a pair of the form $\{P\}\, \{Q\}$ occurs in the tableau, the assertion P implies the assertion Q.

Thus, for example, the tableau given above is valid.

Now suppose a subsequence of the form $\{P\}\, S_1\, \{Q\}\, S_2\, \{R\}$ occurs in a valid tableau. Then $\{P\}\, S_1\, \{Q\}$ and $\{Q\}\, S_2\, \{R\}$ are true specifications, so that the rule for statement compounding can be used to infer $\{P\}\, S_1; S_2\, \{R\}$. Thus the tableau will remain valid if the intermediate assertion Q is deleted. Similarly, a subsequence of the form $\{P\}\, \{Q\}\, S\, \{R\}$ can be reduced to $\{P\}\, S\, \{R\}$ by the rule for strengthening precedents, and a subsequence of the form $\{P\}\, S\, \{Q\}\, \{R\}$ can be reduced to $\{P\}\, S\, \{R\}$ by the rule for weakening consequents. Finally, a subsequence of the form $\{P\}\, \{Q\}\, \{R\}$ can be reduced to $\{P\}\, \{R\}$ since, if P implies Q and Q implies R, then P implies R.

The repetition of this argument shows that a tableau will remain valid if all its intermediate assertions are deleted. But a valid tableau without intermediate assertions is simply a true specification. Thus any valid tableau constitutes a proof of the specification obtained by deleting its intermediate assertions. For example, since the tableau given above is valid, it is a proof of the specification

$$\{-2<y-z<2\}\ y := y-z;\ y := y\times y\ \{y\leq3\}\quad.$$

As a second example, we give a tableau which describes part of a real program: the body of the **while** statement in the Fibonacci number example of Section 1.3.6:

1. $\{f=fib(k)$ **and** $g=fib(k-1)$ **and** $k\leq n$ **and** $k\neq n\}$
    $\{f+g=fib(k+1)$ **and** $f=fib(k+1-1)$ **and** $k+1\leq n\}$
    $k := k+1;$
    $\{f+g=fib(k)$ **and** $f=fib(k-1)$ **and** $k\leq n\}$
    $t := f+g;$
    $\{t=fib(k)$ **and** $f=fib(k-1)$ **and** $k\leq n\}$
    $g := f;$
    $\{t=fib(k)$ **and** $g=fib(k-1)$ **and** $k\leq n\}$
    $f := t$
    $\{f=fib(k)$ **and** $g=fib(k-1)$ **and** $k\leq n\}\quad.$

Each specification in this tableau may be inferred from the assignment rule, and the implication that validates the pair of adjacent assertions is a consequence of elementary properties of the integers and the Fibonacci equation $fib(n)=fib(n-1)+fib(n-2)$. Thus the tableau is valid, so that we may infer that the body of the **while** statement satisfies the specification

$$\{f=fib(k)\ \textbf{and}\ g=fib(k-1)\ \textbf{and}\ k\leq n\ \textbf{and}\ k\neq n\}$$
$$k := k+1;\ t := f+g;\ g := f;\ f := t$$
$$\{f=fib(k)\ \textbf{and}\ g=fib(k-1)\ \textbf{and}\ k\leq n\}\quad.$$

At this point it is natural to ask how, given a specification to be proved about a sequence of statements, one can determine the intermediate assertions needed for a valid tableau. In general there is no answer (which is why adequately commented programs must contain certain intermediate assertions). However, an answer can be given for the simple case where the statements in the tableau are all assignment statements.

The rule for simple assignment has no premises, and the consequent of its conclusion is a single metavariable. Thus, when inferring a specification about an assignment statement, one is free to choose an arbitrary consequent. Hence, a tableau for a sequence of assignment statements can be constructed by working backwards, i.e. by generating the intermediate assertions in reverse order.

Suppose we wish to prove

$$\{P\}\ X_1 := E_1;\ X_2 := E_2;\ \dots\ ;\ X_n := E_n\ \{Q\}\quad.$$

Let Q_n be Q, Q_{n-1} be $Q_n|_{X_n \to E_n}$, Q_{n-2} be $Q_{n-1}|_{X_{n-1} \to E_{n-1}}$, and so forth. Then each specification in the tableau

$$\{P\} \{Q_0\} \, X_1 := E_1; \{Q_1\} \, X_2 := E_2; \dots ; \{Q_{n-1}\} \, X_n := E_n \{Q\}$$

will be inferable from the assignment rule, so that the tableau will be valid if P implies Q_0.

Of course it is possible that P may not imply Q_0, but it can be shown that in that case the specification one is trying to prove is false.

The reader may verify that the tableau for the Fibonacci **while**-statement body can be constructed by this method of working backwards.

Exercises

1. Use the method of working backwards to construct a valid tableau, different from that given in the above section, for the specification

   $$\{-2 < y - z < 2\} \, y := y - z; \, y := y \times y \, \{y \le 3\} \quad .$$

2. For the **while**-statement body in the Fibonacci program one can use

   $$k := k + 1; f := f + g; g := f - g \quad .$$

   Show that this alternative meets the same specification as was proved in the above section for the original **while**-statement body.

3. In the solution of Exercise 2 after Section 1.3.4, the **while** statement body can be either

   $$\textbf{begin } y := y + 1; \, r := r - 2 \times y + 1 \textbf{ end}$$

   or

   $$\textbf{begin } r := r - 2 \times y - 1; \, y := y + 1 \textbf{ end} \quad .$$

   Show that both of these statements meet the appropriate specification. More generally, show that these two statements are equivalent by showing that for any consequent P, repeated application of the assignment rule will produce equivalent precedents for the two statements.

1.4.3   More Inference Rules

We now introduce some more rules of inference, which will permit us to prove the correctness of the rest of the Fibonacci example.

Consider a **while** statement of the form **while** L **do** S, and suppose that S satisfies the specification $\{I \text{ and } L\} \, S \, \{I\}$. ($I$ obviously stands for "invariant".) If I is true before execution of the **while** statement begins, then (by induction on the number of executions of S) I will be true every time an execution of S is completed, so that I and $\neg L$ will be true if the **while** statement ever finishes its execution. Thus we have the inference rule

while Statement:

$$\{I \textbf{ and } L\}\ S\ \{I\}$$

$$\{I\} \textbf{ while } L \textbf{ do } S\ \{I \textbf{ and } \daleth L\}\quad.$$

This rule illustrates that knowledge of the invariant is the key to reasoning about the **while** statement. Once I is known to be the invariant of **while** L **do** S, it is evident that one must prove $\{I \textbf{ and } L\}\ S\ \{I\}$ about the body, and then infer $\{I\} \textbf{ while } L \textbf{ do } S\ \{I \textbf{ and } \daleth L\}$.

Next consider a conditional statement of the form **if** L **then** S_1 **else** S_2, and suppose that S_1 and S_2 satisfy the specifications $\{P \textbf{ and } L\}\ S_1\ \{Q\}$ and $\{P \textbf{ and } \daleth L\}\ S_2\ \{Q\}$. If P is true before the conditional statement begins, then either P **and** L will be true before S_1 is executed, or P **and** $\daleth L$ will be true before S_2 is executed. Either way, when the conditional statement is finished Q will be true, so that we have

Two-way Conditional Statement:

$$\{P \textbf{ and } L\}\ S_1\ \{Q\}$$
$$\{P \textbf{ and } \daleth L\}\ S_2\ \{Q\}$$

$$\{P\} \textbf{ if } L \textbf{ then } S_1 \textbf{ else } S_2\ \{Q\}\quad.$$

A similar line of reasoning justifies

One-way Conditional Statement:

If $(P \textbf{ and } \daleth L)$ implies Q then

$$\{P \textbf{ and } L\}\ S\ \{Q\}$$

$$\{P\} \textbf{ if } L \textbf{ then } S\ \{Q\}\quad.$$

These additional rules are sufficient to complete the proof of the Fibonacci program. We begin with the specification of the **while**-statement body that was established by Tableau 1 in the previous section:

$$\{f=fib(k) \textbf{ and } g=fib(k-1) \textbf{ and } k\leq n \textbf{ and } k\neq n\}$$
$$k := k+1;\ t := f+g;\ g := f;\ f := t$$
$$\{f=fib(k) \textbf{ and } g=fib(k-1) \textbf{ and } k\leq n\}\quad.$$

Then, if we take I to be "$f=fib(k)$ **and** $g=fib(k-1)$ **and** $k\leq n$" (the invariant) and use the rule for the **while** statement, we get

$$\{f=fib(k) \textbf{ and } g=fib(k-1) \textbf{ and } k\leq n\}$$
$$\textbf{while } k\neq n \textbf{ do}$$
$$\quad\textbf{begin } k := k+1;\ t := f+g;\ g := f;\ f := t \textbf{ end}$$
$$\{f=fib(k) \textbf{ and } g=fib(k-1) \textbf{ and } k\leq n \textbf{ and } \daleth k\neq n\}\quad.$$

From this specification, one can develop a tableau for the entire second part of the main conditional statement by working backwards through the initial assignment statements:

2. $\{n \geq 0$ **and** $\neg\, n=0\}$
$\{n \geq 1\}$
$\{1=fib(1)$ **and** $0=fib(1-1)$ **and** $1 \leq n\}$
$k := 1;$
$\{1=fib(k)$ **and** $0=fib(k-1)$ **and** $k \leq n\}$
$g := 0;$
$\{1=fib(k)$ **and** $g=fib(k-1)$ **and** $k \leq n\}$
$f := 1;$
$\{f=fib(k)$ **and** $g=fib(k-1)$ **and** $k \leq n\}$ ⎫
while $k \neq n$ **do** ⎪ from Tableau 1
begin $k := k+1;\ t := f+g;\ g := f;\ f := t$ **end** ⎬ by **while**-statement
$\{f=fib(k)$ **and** $g=fib(k-1)$ **and** $k \leq n$ **and** $\neg\, k \neq n\}$ ⎭ rule
$\{f=fib(n)\}$.

A more trivial tableau handles the first part of the main conditional statement:

3. $\{n \geq 0$ **and** $n=0\}$
$\{n=0\}$
$\{0=fib(n)\}$
$f := 0$
$\{f=fib(n)\}$.

Finally, from the specifications for the two parts of the main conditional statement, an application of the rule for the two-way conditional proves that the entire program meets its specification:

4. $\{n \geq 0\}$ ⎫
if $n=0$ **then** $f := 0$ **else** ⎪ from
begin ⎪ Tableaus
$k := 1;\ g := 0;\ f := 1;$ ⎪ 2 and 3
while $k \neq n$ **do** ⎬ by two-way
begin $k := k+1;\ t := f+g;\ g := f;\ f := t$ **end** ⎪ conditional
end ⎪ statement
$\{f=fib(n)\}$. ⎭ rule

The formal proof is completely conveyed by the tableaus numbered 1 to 4, along with marginal comments showing how steps in one tableau are inferred from the results of other tableaus. Each step in the proof is either an instance of some inference rule or an implication that is a consequence of the static mathematical nature of the data used by the program. At present, we have not formalized the proofs of these implications since only the familiar mathematics of integer arithmetic is involved. This situation will change, however, when arrays are introduced in Chapter 2.

The final inference of the proof is a conditional-correctness specification of the Fibonacci program. Thus the proof does not, by itself, insure that the program terminates, nor does it show the obvious but essential property that the program preserves the value of n.

Although our presentation has demonstrated that our proof is correct, i.e. that it is built out of instances of the rules of inference, it has not said much about how such proofs can be found. In fact, when a program is constructed from the top down, it is simplest to construct its proof in a similar manner, so that the tableaus are generated in the reverse of the order in which they are to be read.

In the present example, the overall specification to be proved completely determines tableau (4), whose body is a single two-way conditional statement. The need to apply the rule for the two-way conditional statement in turn determines tableaus (2) and (3), except for their intermediate assertions. Since (3) contains only assignment statements, it can be completed by working backwards, as discussed in the previous section.

On the other hand, (2) is less trivial to complete since it contains a **while** statement. However, knowledge of the invariant of this statement determines the instance of the rule for the **while** statement that must be used, which in turn determines the precedent and consequent of the **while** statement in (2) and the specification to be proved in (1). Then the rest of (2) and all of (1) can be filled in by working backwards through assignment statements.

Beyond the program itself and its overall specification, the one item of information needed to construct the formal proof is the invariant of the **while** statement. This pinpoints the invariant as the one intermediate assertion that should appear as a comment in the program.

In conclusion, we give three more inference rules which will be occasionally useful. The first describes a feature of Algol W which has not been discussed previously, the *empty* statement. In any context that permits a statement one can place an empty sequence of characters (i.e. a sequence of blanks or even nothing at all). The effect of executing such a statement is to leave the state of the computation unchanged. For example,

$$\left.\begin{array}{l}\textbf{if } L \textbf{ then } S \textbf{ else}\\ \textbf{if } L \textbf{ then else } S\\ \textbf{begin } S_1; \ ; \ S_2; \textbf{ end}\end{array}\right\} \begin{array}{c}\text{has the same}\\ \text{meaning as}\end{array} \left\{\begin{array}{l}\textbf{if } L \textbf{ then } S\\ \textbf{if } \lnot L \textbf{ then } S\\ \textbf{begin } S_1; \ S_2 \textbf{ end}\end{array}\right. .$$

The empty statement is succinctly characterized by the following rule of inference:

Empty Statement:

$$\underline{}$$
$$\{P\} \ \{P\} \quad .$$

Finally, two rules give methods for combining different specifications about the same statement:

Specification Conjunction:

$$\frac{\{P_1\} \; S \; \{Q_1\}}{\{P_1 \text{ and } P_2\} \; S \; \{Q_1 \text{ and } Q_2\}} \quad .$$

Specification Disjunction:

$$\frac{\{P_1\} \; S \; \{Q_1\}}{\{P_1 \text{ or } P_2\} \; S \; \{Q_1 \text{ or } Q_2\}} \quad .$$

Additional inference rules for new language features will be given in Sections 1.5.1, 2.3.2, and 2.4.2. With these additions, the rules are sufficient to deal with the programs in Chapters 1 and 2. However, the rules cannot encompass certain aspects of the procedure mechanism introduced in Chapter 3. In Section 3.3 we will resolve these difficulties by developing a system of inference based upon a more complex notion of specification.

Exercise

1. Give formal proofs that some of the programs in this chapter meet their specification. The fast exponentiation program in Section 1.3.5 and the programs in Exercises 3 to 5 after that section are excellent candidates.

   Be careful not to let the mathematics of the data creep into applications of the inference rules. In applying the **while**-statement rule, for example, if L is to be replaced by $r \geq y$, then $\neg L$ becomes $\neg r \geq y$ rather than $r < y$. Strictly speaking, "$\neg r \geq y$ implies $r < y$" is a mathematical fact about the integers.

   Also be careful not to get implications backwards. This is a surprisingly common error in first attempts at formal proof, perhaps because many (though hardly all) of the implications used in such proofs are actually equivalences.

1.5   DECLARATIONS AND BINDING

1.5.1   Local Variables and Simple Variable Declarations

In the program for computing Fibonacci numbers, the body of the **while** statement meets the following specification:

$$\{f = fib(k) \text{ and } g = fib(k-1) \text{ and } k \leq n \text{ and } k \neq n\}$$
$$k := k+1; \; t := f+g; \; g := f; f := t$$
$$\{f = fib(k) \text{ and } g = fib(k-1) \text{ and } k \leq n\} \quad .$$

Moreover this specification, along with the requirements that k be increased and n not be changed, is a complete description of the properties of the **while**-statement body needed to make the overall program correct.

Neither the precedent nor the consequent of this specification contain any occurrence of the integer variable t. This indicates that t has two important properties:

(1) The value possessed by t when the statement begins execution has no significant effect on its execution.

(2) The value possessed by t when the statement completes execution has no significant effect on the rest of the program.

When a variable possesses both of these properties with respect to a statement, it is said to be a *local variable* of the statement.

The importance of this concept is twofold. If the statement to which a variable is local is indicated explicitly in a program, then the identifier denoting the variable can be used for other purposes outside of that statement, and the storage used to hold the value of the variable can be used for other purposes when the statement is not being executed.

In Algol W, the fact that a variable is local to a statement can be indicated by *declaring* the variable, i.e. by mentioning the identifier denoting the variable in a *simple variable declaration* at the beginning of the statement. For example, the fact that t is a local integer variable of the above statement can be indicated by using the declaration **integer** t as follows:

> **begin integer** t;
> $k := k+1; t := f+g; g := f; f := t$
> **end** .

In general, a declaration describes the meaning that will be attached to one or more identifiers in a particular block that is called the *scope* of the declaration. (The definition of the scope of a declaration will be modified slightly in Section 2.1.) The declarations whose scope is a given block appear as a sequence at the beginning of that block. Thus the general form of a block is

> **begin** D_1; ... ; D_m; S_1; ... ; S_n **end**

where D_1 to D_m are zero or more declarations and S_1 to S_n are one or more statements. (Notice that all declarations in the block precede the first statement. Also notice that any statement can be made into the scope of a declaration by enclosing it in "statement brackets", e.g. **begin** D; S **end**.)

Eventually we will introduce a variety of declarations for giving different kinds of meaning to identifiers. Our present concern, however, is only with simple variable declarations, which indicate that identifiers denote variables. Specifically, if I_1, ... , I_n are distinct identifiers then

integer $I_1, \dots, I_n$

or

logical $I_1, \dots, I_n$

is a *simple variable declaration* indicating that $I_1, \dots, I_n$ denote distinct integer or logical variables. These variables will belong to the state of the computation during execution of the scope of the declaration.

Notice that the scope of a simple variable declaration such as **integer** t plays two roles. One role, which is common to all kinds of declarations (as well as other kinds of binding mechanisms) is that of a *static* scope, which is the program region in which the identifier t denotes a certain variable; outside this region t can be used for other purposes. The second role, which is specific to variable and array declarations, is that of a *dynamic* scope, which is the statement during whose execution the variable denoted by t belongs to the state of the computation.

The importance of the second role is that almost all implementations of Algol-like languages allocate storage for the value of a variable only during execution of the scope of its declaration, and use the same storage for other purposes at other times. As a consequence, when execution of the scope of **integer** t begins the value of t will be unpredictable, and when execution is completed the value of t will be lost. However, if t is local to the scope of its declaration then properties (1) and (2) given above insure that this behavior will not affect program correctness.

If we look at the outer block of the Fibonacci program (the second substatement of the conditional statement) we see that the variables k and g occur in neither the precedent $\{n \geq 1\}$ nor the consequent $\{f = fib(n)\}$. Thus these variables are local and can be declared in the outer block. When all local variables are declared, the program has the form

$$\{n \geq 0\}$$
if $n = 0$ **then** $f := 0$ **else**
　　begin integer k, g;
　　$\{n \geq 1\}$
　　$k := 1; g := 0; f := 1;$
　　$\{\text{whileinv: } f = fib(k) \text{ and } g = fib(k-1) \text{ and } k \leq n\}$
　　while $k \neq n$ **do**
　　　　begin integer t;
　　　　$k := k+1; t := f+g; g := f; f := t$
　　　　end
　　end
$\{f = fib(n)\}$　.

As is evident from the surrounding assertions, the variables n and f are not local to the program and therefore cannot be declared in it. This is due to the fact that the program is not complete—to actually run it on the computer one must precede it by statements that will produce a value of n and follow it by statements that will use the value of f.

A *complete program* is a statement that is sufficiently self-contained to describe an entire computation to be performed by the computer. In Algol W, as in most Algol-like languages, every identifier used in a complete program must be declared—the only exception is a small set of *implicitly declared* identifiers (such as *odd*) whose meanings are "built into" the language. Although this requirement can occasionally be tedious for the program writer, it is a considerable convenience for the reader, and also provides a helpful safeguard against accidental misspellings of identifiers.

Although it would be permissible to declare every identifier in the outermost block of a complete program, it is good programming style to place each declaration as "far in" as possible, i.e. to indicate explicitly for each variable the statement to which it is local. While this practice is slightly pedantic for small programs, it is vital for large programs, which may contain hundreds of declarations, since it minimizes the number of identifiers the reader (or writer) must consider at any particular point in the program. A secondary benefit is the minimization of storage requirements; this consideration is usually unimportant for the simple variables considered in this chapter, but it can be vital for the efficient treatment of large arrays, as will be illustrated in Section 3.2.2.

As with previous language features, there is a rule of inference for proving specifications of statements containing declarations:

Declarations:

If D is a simple variable (or array) declaration of identifiers $I_1, \ldots, I_n$, and if $I_1, \ldots, I_n$ do not occur (free) in P or Q then

$$\frac{\{P\}\ S\ \{Q\}}{\{P\}\ \textbf{begin}\ D;\ S\ \textbf{end}\ \{Q\}}\quad.$$

Note that the requirement that $I_1, \ldots, I_n$ do not occur in P or Q is tantamount to saying that these identifiers denote local variables of S.

Exercise

1. Examine the illustrative programs and exercises given so far. Determine which variables are local, and where and how they should be declared.

1.5.2   Binding and Alpha Conversion

Declarations are our first encounter with the phenomenon of binding, which will reoccur with several other constructions in Algol W and also in the language we use for assertions and specifications. In the statement

> **begin integer** t;
> $k := k+1; t := f+g; g := f; f := t$
> **end**   ,

for example, the occurrences of t are all bound by the occurrence in the declaration **integer** t. As a consequence, the meaning of this statement does not depend upon the particular choice of the identifier t. Indeed, we could replace the occurrences of t by any identifier other than k, f, or g without changing the meaning of the statement.

This kind of invariance under changes of bound identifiers, which is called *alpha convertibilty*, insures that the user of any phrase of a program can safely ignore the particular identifiers that are bound in the phrase. Although it is hardly important for the tiny programs in this book, it is vital for large programs which can contain hundreds of bound identifiers.

Indeed, alpha convertibility is the fundamental property of identifier binding in a well-designed language. This is an intentionally controversial assertion; although alpha convertibility holds for Algol 60 and most of its descendents, including PL/I and (fortunately) Algol W, it does not hold for such popular languages as LISP, SNOBOL, or APL. However, its failure in these languages, which only occurs in rather complex situations involving procedures, is a rich source of programming error.

(The term "alpha convertibility" comes from the study of a simple logical language called the *lambda calculus*, in which binding and substitution play major roles.)

In general, binding is caused by certain identifier occurrences called *binding occurrences*, or more briefly, *binders*. For each binder, there is an enclosing phrase called its *scope*, which is the extent of the program over which the binder has an effect.

In declarations, the binders are the occurrences of the identifiers being declared, e.g. $I_1, \dots, I_n$ in **integer** $I_1, \dots, I_n$, and their scope is the scope of the declaration itself, which is the immediately enclosing block (subject to a minor exception which will be discussed in Section 2.1).

Binders and their scopes can be used to define the concepts of free and bound identifier occurrences. Consider an occurrence of an identifier I in a phrase S. If S does not contain any binder of I whose scope contains this occurrence of I, then this occurrence is said to be *free in S*.

On the other hand, suppose S contains one or more binders of I whose scope contains the occurrence of I. Then one of these binders—call it B—will be innermost, i.e. its scope will not include the scope of any of the others. (It is a syntactic error to have two binders of the same identifier with the same scope.) In this case the occurrence of I is said to be *bound by B in S*. More loosely, we will sometimes say that the occurrence is bound by the declaration (or other phrase such as specifier, formal parameter list, or quantifier) that contains the binder B.

For example, in the statement

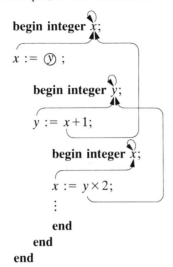

the single free identifier occurrence is circled, and bound occurrences are connected by arrows to the binders that bind them. It is evident that the same identifier, e.g. y, can have both free and bound occurrences in the same phrase. Moreover, the same occurrence can be bound in a phrase and free in a subphrase, e.g. the last occurrence of y is bound in the statement above, but free in the innermost block.

Now suppose S is a phrase containing the scope of a binder B of an identifier I, and let I' be some other identifier that does not occur at all in the scope of B. Let S' be obtained from S by replacing every occurrence of I bound by B in S (including B itself) by I'. Then S' is called an *alpha variant* of S, and the process of converting S to S' is called *alpha conversion*, or sometimes *renaming*. The principle of alpha convertibility is that alpha conversion always preserves meaning.

For example, S might be the **while** statement in the Fibonacci program,

> **while** $k \neq n$ **do**
> **begin integer** t;
> $k := k+1; t := f+g; g := f; f := t$
> **end**   ,

whose body is the scope of a binder of t. Since n does not occur in this scope, we can alpha convert S into

> **while** $k \neq n$ **do**
> **begin integer** n;
> $k := k+1; n := f+g; g := f; f := n$
> **end**   .

On the other hand, since f occurs in the scope of the binder of t, the result of replacing t by f,

> **while** $k \neq n$ **do**
>   **begin integer** f;
> $k := k+1; f := f+g; g := f; f := f$
> **end** ,

is *not* an alpha variant of S; the change of the bound identifier from t to f causes the original occurrences of f in S to change from free to bound occurrences and thereby changes the meaning.

Since alpha conversion preserves meaning, it can be used in proving program specifications, i.e. from a specification one can infer an alpha variant of that specification. This is sometimes necessary in applications of the rule for declarations given in the previous section. For example, one cannot use that rule directly to infer

$$\{x=0\} \textbf{ begin integer } x; x := 1 \textbf{ end } \{x=0\} \quad ,$$

since the declared variable occurs in the precedent and consequent. But one can use the rule to infer

$$\{x=0\} \textbf{ begin integer } y; y := 1 \textbf{ end } \{x=0\} \quad ,$$

and then alpha-convert this specification to replace y by x.

1.6 NUMBER REPRESENTATIONS

1.6.1 Integers

So far, we have assumed that the range of possible values of an integer variable is the entire set of integers. In fact, in a real computer this range must be limited to some finite subset of the integers. In this section we will explore the consequences of this limitation and then go on to consider the representation of numbers that are not restricted to be integers. We will consider general methods of number representation as well as the specific representations provided by the implementation of Algol W.

The *memory* (or *storage*) of a computer is composed of a large number of elementary *memory elements*, each of which can be in any of several states. The number r of possible states of a single memory element is called the *radix* of the computer; in practice, it is always either two (for a *binary* computer) or ten (for a *decimal* computer).

A variable is implemented by a group of memory elements called a *word*. The number w of elements in the word is called its *word length*, and is the same for all variables of the same type. (The term "word" is actually used in a variety of ways in the computer literature. The concept used here is sometimes called a *logical word*, in contrast to a *physical word*, which is a group of memory elements that can be read or changed simultaneously.)

Now suppose a variable is to range over a set S of possible values. Then each member of S must be represented by one or more configurations of the states of the memory elements in a word, so that the size of S cannot exceed r^w, the number of state configurations. Clearly S must be finite.

Thus the range of a so-called integer variable can only be some finite subset of the integers. Normally it is a set of consecutive integers, i.e. the set of integers i such that $minint \leq i \leq maxint$, where $minint$ and $maxint$ are the smallest and largest representable integers, and $maxint - minint + 1$ is the total number of representable integers, which must be no larger than r^w. When only non-negative integers are needed, the obvious choice is $minint = 0$ and $maxint = r^w - 1$.

When negative integers must be included, the choice of representation is less clearcut. For simplicity, one would like to have $minint = -maxint$, so that the set of representable integers is symmetric about zero. But then the number of representable integers will be $2 \times maxint + 1$, which is odd, while the number of possible representations r^w is even, at least when the radix is two or ten. Thus one must either waste a possible representation (usually by providing two representations for zero) or choose an asymmetric representation in which $minint$ is slightly different than $-maxint$.

In the implementation of Algol W for the IBM 360 or 370, an asymmetric representation is used for integer variables. Specifically,

$$r = 2$$
$$w = 32$$
$$maxint = 2^{31} - 1 = 2147483647$$
$$minint = -2^{31} = -2147483648 \quad .$$

Roughly speaking, an integer is representable if its magnitude is less than about two billion. This choice of representation is actually a property of the computer, rather than the programming language, since the representation is used by the computer circuitry which performs the elementary operations of integer arithmetic.

Obviously, it is possible for an integer operation to yield a non-representable result when applied to representable arguments. Such an occurrence is called an *overflow*. In Algol W, the occurrence of any overflow, or a division by zero, will terminate computation and produce an error message. (Actually, the language provides an *exceptional condition* facility, not discussed in this book, which permits one to alter this response to overflows.)

1.6.2 Programming for an Idealized Computer

The finite range of number representations is one of several limitations that distinguish real computers from idealized machines which would be far easier to program. Another obvious limitation is the finite total size of the computer memory. In dealing with such limitations, it is best to begin by programming for an idealized computer, taking the limitations into account in only a qualitative way.

For example, one deals with the limitations of finite-range integer arithmetic by pretending that all integers are representable, yet taking care to avoid numbers with unnecessarily large magnitudes. (This is the advantage of S_{branch} over S_{makeeven} discussed in Section 1.3.5.) The resulting program will be satisfactory if the integer range of the computer is normally adequate for the problem at hand, and if one can tolerate an occasional failure of the computer to produce an answer (which is usually much less serious than producing a wrong answer).

Sometimes, however, the integer range of the computer will be intrinsically inadequate to carry out the desired computation. In this situation, one must translate the *abstract* program for the idealized computer into a *concrete* program for the real machine, in which large integers are represented by arrays (or lists) of machine-representable integers. This is basically an instance of data representation structuring, discussed in Chapter 5, but the specific problem of programming basic arithmetic operations for multiple-word integer representations is a specialized topic.

A similar situation arises from the limited amount of memory available in a real computer. One begins by programming for an idealized machine with infinite memory, while taking care to avoid unnecessary storage usage. Occasionally, the amount of memory available will be intrinsically inadequate for the problem, and it will be necessary to translate the program into one for the real computer by using techniques such as overlays or virtual memory management, which permit the substitution of secondary memory (e.g. disks or tapes) for primary memory.

However, the limitations of the real computer require special attention in certain kinds of real-time programming (for example, process control), where failure to calculate an answer—usually within a specified time limit—can be as disastrous as a wrong answer. Even here, one should begin by programming for an idealized computer, but then one must deduce safe bounds on the time, storage, and arithmetic range required by the program, and show that these bounds do not exceed the capacity of the machine to be used.

The deduction of such bounds is quite different from proving that a program is correct. (An extension of correctness proofs that takes overflow into account has been provided by [Hoare 69], but it leads to extraordinary complex proofs.) Some of the flavor of such deductions is given by the discussion of the speed of fast exponentiation in Section 1.3.5, and by similar discussions of searching and sorting algorithms in Sections 2.2.10 and 3.2. A more thorough introduction to this methodology, which is part of the research area called "Analysis of Algorithms", is given in [Aho 74].

In summary, the main point is the value of the idealized machine as a tool for subdividing the programming task. The most severe limitation in real computing is the finiteness of the programmer's mind, which can only encompass simple problems without some kind of subdivision or structuring. A second point is the importance of an environment (the combination of language implementation and machine) in which overflows, storage exhaustion, and other actions where the real computer deviates from the ideal are always detected as errors—this point will reoccur with subscript errors in Chapter 2.

*1.6.3 Fixed-Point Representation of Real Numbers

Unfortunately, not all numbers are integers. When we need a variable to range over the real numbers, we must face the problem of approximation as well as the problem of limited range. Suppose that we wish a variable to range over the real interval from *minreal* to *maxreal*. Since we can only represent a finite subset of the uncountably many numbers in this interval, it is hopeless to try to represent every number that might occur in an exact calculation, and the best we can hope for is that every number in the interval will be *near* to some representable number.

A *fixed-point representation* for an interval of real numbers is one in which the representable numbers are equally spaced. If the spacing is σ, then the representable numbers will be

$$minreal, \; minreal + \sigma, \; \ldots \; , \; maxreal - \sigma, \; maxreal \quad .$$

(For simplicity, we assume that $maxreal - minreal$ is an exact multiple of σ.) Then the number of representable numbers is $(maxreal - minreal)/\sigma + 1$, which must be no greater than r^w, where r is the radix of the computer and w is the word length of the real variable. In essence, fixing the word length imposes an upper bound on the ratio between the interval size and the spacing.

Any nontrivial calculation involving real numbers will obviously be approximate. In general, when x is *approximated* by x', the *absolute error* of the approximation is the quantity $\varepsilon_x = |x - x'|$, i.e. the absolute value of the difference between x and x'.

Now let rnd(x) denote the representable number nearest to x (or one of the nearest representable numbers, if x is halfway between two representable numbers). Then, even when x is precisely known, its best representable approximation is rnd(x), which has an absolute *roundoff* error ε_x^{rnd} satisfying

$\varepsilon_x^{\text{rnd}} = \left| x - \text{rnd}(x) \right| \leq \sigma/2$ whenever *minreal*$\leq x \leq$*maxreal*. (The superscript rnd is meant to distinguish roundoff from other sources of error, such as will be considered in Section 1.6.5.)

In other words, there is a constant bound on the absolute roundoff error over the entire range of x. This fact is characteristic of a fixed-point representation.

Real variables with a fixed-point representation are not provided in Algol W; indeed, in most areas of computation, the use of fixed-point representation has been supplanted by floating-point representation, which is described in the next section. When necessary, a fixed-point real variable x with spacing σ can be represented by an integer variable xn such that $x = xn \cdot \sigma$. (For example, dollars with a spacing of .01 can be represented by an integer variable giving cents.) The use of this kind of representation, and the problem of choosing appropriate spacings for each variable, is called *scaling*.

*1.6.4 Floating-Point Representation of Real Numbers

Suppose an approximate real number denoting a distance is known to have an absolute error of no more than a hundred feet. If the distance is several million miles, this is an extraordinary accuracy which should be sufficient for any reasonable purpose, but if the distance is a few inches, the approximation is unusably crude. In certain kinds of calculations, where the gross magnitude of a quantity x is unknown or variable, the absolute error ε_x is an inadequate measure of accuracy. A better measure is the *relative error*:

$$\rho_x = \left| \frac{x - x'}{x} \right| = \frac{\varepsilon_x}{|x|} \ ,$$

which is the ratio between the absolute error and the magnitude of the quantity being approximated.

In this situation, a fixed-point representation will be inappropriate, since its relative roundoff error will grow in inverse proportion to the magnitude of x. What is needed is a representation in which the spacing decreases as x decreases, in such a way as to provide a constant bound on the relative roundoff error.

This requirement is met by *floating-point representation*, in which a real number is represented as the product of another real number with a very limited range times an integral power of a fixed integer $R > 1$ called the *base*. Specifically, let f be a fixed-point real variable with range $-1 < f < 1$ and spacing σ (note the exclusion of the extreme values $f = \pm 1$), and let e be an integer variable with range *minexp*$\leq e \leq$*maxexp*. Then the pair of values $\langle e, f \rangle$ is a *floating-point representation* of the number $x = f \cdot R^e$.

The pairs $\langle e, f \rangle$, $\langle e+1, f/R \rangle$, $\langle e+2, f/R^2 \rangle$, ... all represent the same number. To remove this multiplicity, we impose the *normalization* requirement that $|f| \geq 1/R$. However, since this requirement excludes any representation for zero, a special representation is introduced for zero.

An illustration (for an unrealistically large σ and small range of e) is given in Figure 1.5. The general situation is that, for each value of e between *minexp* and *maxexp*, the pairs

$$\langle e, R^{-1} \rangle, \langle e, R^{-1}+\sigma \rangle, \dots , \langle e, 1-\sigma \rangle, \langle e+1, R^{-1} \rangle$$

represent a sequence of equally spaced numbers from R^{e-1} to R^e inclusive, with a spacing of $\sigma \cdot R^e$. (We will neglect the fact that the last number will be missing when $e = maxexp$.) There is a similar sequence from $-R^e$ to $-R^{e-1}$.

Now suppose x is a real number such that $R^{minexp-1} \leq |x| < R^{maxexp}$. Then there will be an e such that $R^{e-1} \leq |x| < R^e$, and thus there will be a representable number $\mathrm{rnd}(x)$ no further than $\sigma \cdot R^e/2$ from x. In other words, the absolute roundoff error will satisfy $\varepsilon_x^{\mathrm{rnd}} \leq \sigma \cdot R^e/2$. But $|x| \geq R^{e-1}$. Thus the relative roundoff error will satisfy

$$\rho_x^{\mathrm{rnd}} = \frac{\varepsilon_x^{\mathrm{rnd}}}{|x|} \leq \frac{\varepsilon_x^{\mathrm{rnd}}}{R^{e-1}} \leq \frac{\sigma \cdot R^e/2}{R^{e-1}} = \sigma \cdot R/2 \quad ,$$

which provides a constant bound on the relative roundoff error over the range $R^{minexp-1} \leq |x| < R^{maxexp}$.

However, this bound does not hold in the center interval $-R^{minexp-1} < x < R^{minexp-1}$. In the worst case, when $\mathrm{rnd}(x) = 0$, we have $\rho_x^{\mathrm{rnd}} = |(x - \mathrm{rnd}(x))/x| = 1$.

This analysis suggests that one should use a floating-point representation when trying to control the relative error, but a fixed-point representation when trying to control the absolute error. But in fact, a floating-point representation is a "reasonable" substitute for a fixed-point representation. Suppose x ranges over the interval $-R^e \leq x \leq R^e$, where $minexp + \log_R(1/\sigma) - 1 \leq e \leq maxexp$. Then the largest spacing anywhere in the interval is $\sigma \cdot R^e$, and the absolute error must satisfy $\varepsilon_x^{\mathrm{rnd}} \leq \sigma \cdot R^e/2$. (The lower limit on e insures that the spaces surrounding zero do not exceed $\sigma \cdot R^e$; one could reduce this limit to *minexp* by permitting f to be unnormalized when $e = minexp$.) But this is as good as one could achieve for the interval $-R^e \leq x \leq R^e$ with a fixed-point representation with the same word length as f. In effect, the price of using a floating-point representation to replace a fixed-point representation is simply the memory space for the variable e.

The IBM 360 and 370 provide two forms of floating-point representation, called *single* and *double precision*, which differ in word length and spacing:

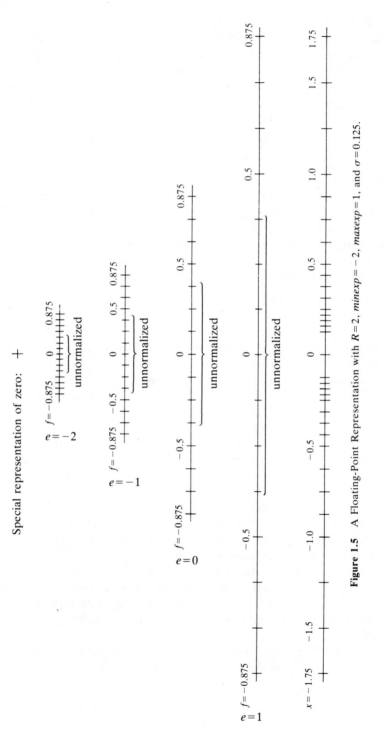

Figure 1.5   A Floating-Point Representation with $R=2$, $minexp=-2$, $maxexp=1$, and $\sigma=0.125$.

	single precision	double precision
w	32	64
R	16	16
$minexp$	-64	-64
$maxexp$	$+63$	$+63$
σ	2^{-24}	2^{-56}
$\sigma \cdot R/2$	$2^{-21} < 5 \times 10^{-7}$	$2^{-53} < 1.2 \times 10^{-16}$

With $R^{maxexp} > 7 \times 10^{75}$, the range $-R^{maxexp} < x < R^{maxexp}$ seems enormous, but it can be exceeded easily in moderately complicated calculations. The occurrence of an operation whose result is outside this range is an *overflow* and, as with integer overflow, causes termination with an error stop in Algol W.

The occurrence of an operation whose result has a magnitude less than $R^{minexp-1} < 5.4 \times 10^{-79}$ is called an *underflow*. In the Algol W implementation the result of an underflow is set to zero and the computation continues.

Regardless of whether fixed or floating point is used, computation with real numbers is dominated by the fact that these representations are only approximate. One obvious point is the danger implicit in testing two approximate values for equality. Instead of testing $x = y$, which is likely to be spuriously false because of approximation, one should usually test either

$$\mathbf{abs}(x - y) \le \varepsilon$$

or

$$\mathbf{abs}(x - y) \le \rho \times \mathbf{abs}(x) \quad ,$$

where ε or ρ is an appropriate positive constant. In other words, one should test whether x and y approximate one another with a sufficiently small absolute or relative error.

(Notice, however, that the above tests both differ from true equality in failing to satisfy the law of transitivity, e.g. $\mathbf{abs}(x - y) \le \varepsilon$ and $\mathbf{abs}(y - z) \le \varepsilon$ does not imply $\mathbf{abs}(x - z) \le \varepsilon$.)

One other small point deserves mention. In decimal notation, certain rational numbers have an exact finite representation which can be used to advantage in hand computation. In a binary computer—more precisely, when σ is a power of two—many of these numbers will no longer have exact representations. Thus for example, $1/5$ and $1/10$ are not exactly representable.

*1.6.5 The Propagation of Errors

Even for simple calculations with real numbers, careful attention must be paid to the effects of roundoff and other sources of numerical error. If one could begin with exact input data, carry out an exact calculation, and then round the result x to the nearest representable number, the error in this result would simply be the roundoff error $\varepsilon_x^{\mathrm{rnd}}$ or ρ_x^{rnd}, which could easily be controlled by the choice of representation of the result. But in actuality, the inputs themselves will usually be approximate, and a roundoff error will occur at each step of the computation. Each of these errors will induce a corresponding error in the final result.

The effects of input errors can be illustrated by a simple geometric example. Suppose the input data are coordinates of points p, q, r, and s in the plane, and that we wish to compute the coordinates of the intersection of the line passing through p and q with the line passing through r and s. As shown in Figure 1.6, if the two lines are nearly parallel or the points on one line are close to one another, then a small uncertainty in the input (indicated by drawing p, q, r, and s as small circles) will induce a large uncertainty in the output (indicated by the shaded regions).

This kind of error magnification is intrinsic in the problem being posed and cannot be avoided by programming. The general case can be described with a little calculus. Suppose we wish to compute a continuous and differentiable function $f(x_1, \ldots, x_n)$ for approximate values of the inputs $x_1', \ldots, x_n'$. To a first order approximation, the absolute error due to input errors is

$$
\begin{aligned}
\varepsilon_{f(x_1, \ldots, x_n)} &\\
&= \left| f(x_1, \ldots, x_n) - f(x_1', \ldots, x_n') \right| \\
&\simeq \left| \sum_{i=1}^{n} \frac{\partial}{\partial x_i} f(x_1, \ldots, x_n) \cdot (x_i - x_i') \right| \\
&\leq \sum_{i=1}^{n} \left| \frac{\partial}{\partial x_i} f(x_1, \ldots, x_n) \cdot (x_i - x_i') \right| \\
&= \sum_{i=1}^{n} \left| \frac{\partial}{\partial x_i} f(x_1, \ldots, x_n) \right| \cdot \varepsilon_{x_i} \quad ,
\end{aligned}
$$

and the relative error is

$$
\begin{aligned}
\rho_{f(x_1, \ldots, x_n)} &\\
&= \frac{\varepsilon_{f(x_1, \ldots, x_n)}}{\left| f(x_1, \ldots, x_n) \right|} \\
&\leq \sum_{i=1}^{n} \left| \frac{1}{f(x_1, \ldots, x_n)} \cdot \frac{\partial}{\partial x_i} f(x_1, \ldots, x_n) \right| \cdot \varepsilon_{x_i} \\
&= \sum_{i=1}^{n} \left| \frac{x_i}{f(x_1, \ldots, x_n)} \cdot \frac{\partial}{\partial x_i} f(x_1, \ldots, x_n) \right| \cdot \rho_{x_i} \quad .
\end{aligned}
$$

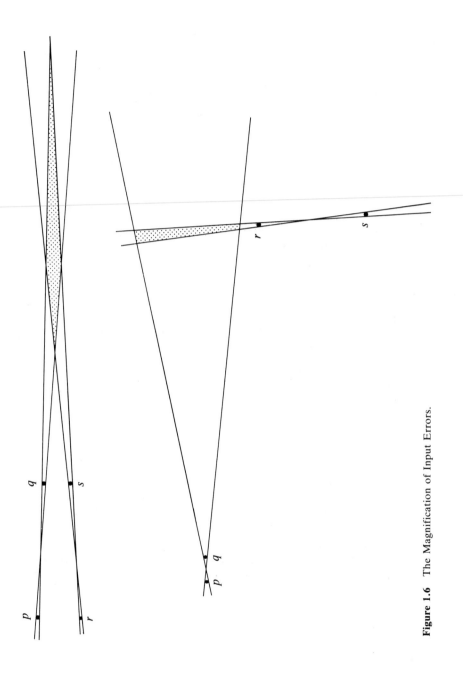

Figure 1.6   The Magnification of Input Errors.

In these formulas, the underlined coefficients of the input errors are called the (absolute and relative) *error propagation coefficients*.

For input errors, these coefficients are determined by the function f one is trying to compute and the inputs $x_1, \ldots, x_n$. When some of the coefficients are large, one is close to an "ill-defined" problem, and cannot avoid magnification of the error.

Further insight into the phenomenon of error propagation can be gained by considering the computation of the sum or product of two numbers. When $f(x_1, x_2) = x_1 + x_2$, the above formulas give

$$\varepsilon_{x_1+x_2} \leqslant 1 \cdot \varepsilon_{x_1} + 1 \cdot \varepsilon_{x_2} \quad ,$$

$$\rho_{x_1+x_2} \leqslant \left| \frac{x_1}{x_1+x_2} \right| \cdot \rho_{x_1} + \left| \frac{x_2}{x_1+x_2} \right| \cdot \rho_{x_2} \quad .$$

Thus for addition, absolute errors will not be magnified, but relative errors will be magnified when x_1 is near to $-x_2$.

For multiplication, taking $f(x_1, x_2) = x_1 \cdot x_2$ gives

$$\varepsilon_{x_1 \cdot x_2} \leqslant |x_2| \cdot \varepsilon_{x_1} + |x_1| \cdot \varepsilon_{x_2} \quad ,$$

$$\rho_{x_1 \cdot x_2} \leqslant 1 \cdot \rho_{x_1} + 1 \cdot \rho_{x_2} \quad .$$

Here the situation is reversed. Relative errors will not be magnified, but absolute errors will be magnified when $|x_1|$ or $|x_2|$ is large.

Although the propagation of input errors is essentially determined by the function one is trying to compute, the propagation of errors occuring in intermediate calculations can be profoundly influenced by the choice of computation method. Suppose $g(x_1, \ldots, x_n)$ is an intermediate result in the computation of $f(x_1, \ldots, x_n)$. Then the effect of $g(x_1, \ldots, x_n)$ on the final result will be given by some function h such that

$$f(x_1, \ldots, x_n) = h\big(g(x_1, \ldots, x_n), x_1, \ldots, x_n\big) \quad .$$

The problem is that a roundoff or other error in the calculation of $g(x_1, \ldots, x_n)$ will be magnified if the propagation coefficient for h with respect to its first argument is large, and that this can happen even when all of the propagation coefficients for f itself are small. In essence, a well-defined problem can be structured to give an ill-defined subproblem.

A vivid illustration is provided by the computation of derivatives. Suppose we wish to compute the first derivative of a function θ at the point x. Since this derivative is the limit of $[\theta(x+\delta) - \theta(x)]/\delta$ as δ goes to zero, an obvious method is to compute

$$f(x) = \frac{\theta(x+\delta) - \theta(x)}{\delta}$$

for some very small value of δ.

NUMBER REPRESENTATIONS   69

But consider the effect of a roundoff error in the computation of the intermediate result $\theta(x+\delta)$. In fact, we would be computing

$$f'(x) = \frac{\text{rnd}\big(\theta(x+\delta)\big) - \theta(x)}{\delta} \quad,$$

which would induce the absolute error

$$\varepsilon_{f(x)} = \big|\, f(x) - f'(x) \,\big| = \left| \frac{\theta(x+\delta) - \text{rnd}\big(\theta(x+\delta)\big)}{\delta} \right|$$

$$= \varepsilon_{\theta(x+\delta)}^{\text{rnd}} / \delta \quad,$$

which is inversely proportional to δ. Thus choosing too small a value of δ would catastrophically magnify the effect of an error in an intermediate result.

This kind of analysis is a trivial example of *numerical analysis*, a highly developed field which is intellectually quite distinct from the rest of computer science, but which is crucially important in many areas of application. At least when the results are going to be relied upon, a solid knowledge of the fundamentals of numerical analysis is needed to program any nontrivial calculation with real numbers.

Even an introduction to the field is beyond the scope of this book; we have only said enough to warn the reader that many pitfalls await the unwary. Good introductory texts are [Dorn 72] and [Hamming 71].

1.6.6   Real Variables and Expressions

Real numbers, with single- and double-precision floating-point representations, are provided in Algol W by the data types **real** and **long real**. Simple variables of these types are introduced by simple variable declarations of the form

> **real** $I_1, \ldots , I_n$

or

> **long real** $I_1, \ldots , I_n$

in which $I_1, \ldots , I_n$ are binders of identifiers that denote real or long real variables.

Constants are a bit complicated. In general, a numerical constant consists of the following items, in order from left to right:

(1) A nonempty string of digits, possibly containing a decimal point.

(2) A *scale factor* of the form $'N$, where N is an integer, possibly beginning with $+$ or $-$. The scale factor indicates that the number being represented is to be multiplied by 10^N.

(3) An optional letter L, which indicates that a double precision representation is to be used.

Either item (1) or (2), but not both, may be omitted. The data type of the constant is **long real** if L is present, otherwise it is **real** if a decimal point or a scale factor is present, otherwise it is **integer**.

For example, the following are constants of different numerical types which all represent the number ten:

integer	real	long real
10	10.	$10L$
	10.00	$10.L$
	$.1'2$	$10.00L$
	$100'-1$	$.1'2L$
	$'1$	$100'-1L$
		$'1L$

Note that the distinction between **real** and **long real** has nothing to do with the number of digits occurring in the constant.

Expressions of type **real** or **long real**, as well as **integer**, are built up from constants and variables by using the familiar operators of arithmetic. Moreover, such expressions may have mixed type, i.e. an expression of one numerical type may have subexpressions of different numerical types. In general, E **op** E' has type **integer** if E and E' are both **integer**, type **real** if either E or E' has type **real,** or type **long real** in any other case. However, there are the following exceptions:

(1) $E \times E'$ is **long real** unless E and E' are both **integer**.

(2) $E \ / \ E'$, denoting real division, is never **integer**; it will be **long real** when both E and E' are **integer**. In contrast E **div** E' and E **rem** E' are always **integer**, and are permitted only when E and E' are both **integer**. These are quite different operations. For example, $7 \ / \ 2 = 3.5L$, but 7 **div** $2 = 3$ and 7 **rem** $2 = 1$.

(3) E ** E', denoting E^E, is always **long real**, and is permitted only when E' is **integer**.

In a numerical assignment statement of the form $X := E$, X and E can have different numerical types, except that if X is **integer** then E must be **integer**.

A more complete and precise description of this syntax, including several additional operations, is given in Appendix B. Despite a few idiosyncrasies, the general effect is to give the programmer complete control over the precision of his calculations, while providing adequate precision in cases where the intention is not obvious from the program. For example, if all the variables are **real**, then

$$z := x1 \times y1 - x2 \times y2$$

will cause the intermediate results of the two multiplications to be represented in double precision. If the programmer wants these intermediate results to be represented in single precision (which is probably unwise, since the subtraction can cause a growth in the relative error), he must write

> **begin real** $t1$, $t2$;
> $t1 := x1 \times y1$; $t2 := x2 \times y2$; $z := t1 - t2$
> **end** .

Exercise

1. Write a statement that will set y to e^x, where x and y are **long real** variables. Use the Taylor series

$$e^x = \sum_{k=0}^{\infty} \frac{x^k}{k!} \quad .$$

More precisely, since one cannot sum all the terms of this infinite series, stop when

$$\sum_{k=0}^{n-1} \frac{x^k}{k!}$$

approximates

$$\sum_{k=0}^{n} \frac{x^k}{k!}$$

with a relative error of no more than 10^{-10}. Try executing this program for a variety of values of x. Explain why the program produces erroneous answers for large negative values of x, e.g. -20. Suggest a way of overcoming this deficiency.

2 ARRAYS

2.1 ONE-DIMENSIONAL ARRAYS

The programming language we have used so far has the fundamental limitation that all variables are denoted by identifiers occurring in the text of the program. As a consequence, every evaluation of the same expression will depend upon the values of the same set of variables, i.e. the variables denoted by the identifiers occurring in the expression. Similarly, every execution of the same assignment statement will affect the value of the same variable, i.e. the variable denoted by the identifier on the left side of the assignment statement.

Although an interesting variety of programs can be written within this limitation, it is frequently necessary to write a statement with the property that different executions can involve different members of some collection of variables, where the choice of the particular variables affected by a particular execution depends upon previously computed results.

For example, in a program that dealt with the variation of temperature throughout the day, one might need a collection of twenty-four real variables, each giving the temperature at a particular hour. Within this program, some statement might evaluate or assign to the particular variable giving the temperature at time t. Moreover, such a statement might occur within a loop that iterated over different values of t.

73

The basic facility that provides this kind of capability is called the *array*. A *one-dimensional array* is a finite collection of variables which is in one-to-one correspondence with some finite consecutive set of integers, called the *domain* of the array. If X is such an array, then the member of X corresponding to the integer i is called the *ith element of* X and is written $X(i)$. Conversely, the integer i is called the *subscript of* $X(i)$.

For example, if X is a real array with the domain $\{5, 6, 7\}$, then the elements of X are three distinct real variables denoted by $X(5)$, $X(6)$, and $X(7)$.

It is important to distinguish between $i=j$, which implies that $X(i)$ and $X(j)$ are the same variable, and $X(i)=X(j)$, which means that $X(i)$ and $X(j)$ are possibly distinct variables with the same value. If $i=j$, then $X(i)=X(j)$ will always be true, and an assignment to $X(i)$ will change the values of both $X(i)$ and $X(j)$. But if $i\neq j$, even though we may still have $X(i)=X(j)$, an assignment to $X(i)$ will leave $X(j)$ unchanged.

Just as with simple variables, each array used in a program must be declared in some block. A one-dimensional array declaration has the form

τ **array** $I_1, \ldots , I_m \ (L::U)$

where τ is **integer**, **real**, **long real**, or **logical**, $I_1, \ldots , I_m$ are binders of distinct identifiers, and L and U are integer expressions, called the *lower bound* and *upper bound* respectively. Such a declaration creates m distinct arrays, denoted by $I_1, \ldots , I_m$. Each of these arrays is a collection of variables of type τ, whose domain is the set of integers i such that $L \leq i \leq U$. These collections of variables will be part of the state of the computation during execution of the block which immediately encloses the array declaration.

If I has been declared to be an array identifier, and E is an integer expression, then

$I(E)$

is a phrase called an *array designator*, which denotes the Eth element of the array denoted by I. Since array designators denote variables, they can be used in the same contexts as other kinds of variable-denoting phrases such as variable identifiers.

For example, the declaration **real array** $X(0::99)$ will create an array containing one hundred real variables, whose domain is the set of integers between 0 and 99 inclusive. Within the block containing this declaration, the individual elements of the array can be referred to by real array designators such as $X(7)$, $X(i)$, or $X(i+j+1)$.

The possibility for different executions of the same statement to affect different array elements arises from the fact that an array designator such as $X(i+j+1)$ can have a subscript containing variables whose values are determined by the computation. The price one pays for this flexibility is the possibility that an evaluation of $X(E)$ can refer to a nonexistent element of X, which will happen when the value of E does not belong to the domain of X. Such an event is called a *subscript error*. During execution of an Algol W program, every subscript evaluation is checked for such errors, and the detection of an error causes program termination. Although this checking has a significant cost in computer time, it is well worth paying, since unchecked subscript errors can have unusually unpredictable and untraceable effects.

In contrast to many programming languages, Algol W provides a useful capability called *dynamic array allocation*, which permits the domain of an array, at the time the array is created, to depend upon previously computed quantities. This arises from the possibility that the lower and upper bounds in an array declaration can be integer expressions containing variables. These bounds are evaluated each time the block immediately enclosing the array declaration begins execution, so that different executions of this block can create different sized arrays. But once an array has been created, its domain remains fixed throughout the current execution of the enclosing block.

For example, in

```
begin integer n; n := 0;
while n < 100 do
    begin n := n+1;
        begin integer array X(1::n−1); S end
    end
end
```

the nth execution of the statement S will use an array whose domain runs from 1 to $n-1$. (Notice that this array will be empty for the first execution of S. It is permissible to declare an empty array, although any assignment to such an array will cause a subscript error.)

Dynamic arrays cause a rather subtle problem concerning the scope of declarations. A block such as

begin integer n; **integer array** $X(n :: X(1))$; ... **end**

appears to be nonsensical, since the variable n will have an unpredictable value, and the variable $X(1)$ will not even exist, when the bounds n and $X(1)$ are evaluated. In Algol W this nonsense is avoided by excluding array bounds from the scope of declarations in the same block. Specifically, the scope of any declaration, and of its binders, is the immediately enclosing block excluding lower and upper bounds of array declarations that are immediately enclosed by that block.

Thus the above block makes sense in a context where n and X are declared at a higher block level, e.g.

begin integer n; **integer array** $X(1::3)$;
$n := 7$; $X(1) := 9$;
  begin integer n; **integer array** $X(n::X(1))$; ... **end**
end   .

Here the occurrences of n and X in $n::X(1)$ are bound by the declarations in the outer block, so that the inner declaration of X will create an array with domain $\{7, 8, 9\}$. (However, this is not recommended as an example of clear programming style.)

2.2 PROGRAMS THAT USE ARRAYS

2.2.1 Summation of an Array

As a first example, consider a program for summing the elements of a real array. More precisely, we want a program that will set the real variable s to the sum of the values of those elements of an array X whose subscripts lie between the integers a and b inclusive.

It is not necessary for a and b to be the declared lower and upper bounds of the array X; we want our program to be applicable to an arbitrary *segment* of X rather than just the entire array. Any array-manipulation program can be generalized to handle segments rather than just entire arrays, and it is invariably good programming practice to do so.

At the completion of our program, we want the assertion

$$s = \sum_{i=a}^{b} X(i)$$

to hold, where the summation notation can be defined as follows:

(I) $\displaystyle\sum_{i=a}^{b} X(i) = 0$ when $b < a$,

(II) $\displaystyle\sum_{i=a}^{b} X(i) = \left(\sum_{i=a}^{b-1} X(i) \right) + X(b)$ when $b \geq a$.

An obvious approach is to achieve $s = \sum_{i=a}^{k} X(i)$ by setting k to $a-1$ and s to 0, and then to repeatedly increase k while maintaining $s = \sum_{i=a}^{k} X(i)$ until $k = b$. Thus we use the invariant

$$s = \sum_{i=a}^{k} X(i) \text{ and } a-1 \leq k \leq b   ,$$

which includes a specification of the range of k. The resulting program is

$\{a-1 \le b\}$
begin integer k;
$k := a-1; s := 0$;
$\{$**whileinv**: $s = \sum\limits_{i=a}^{k} X(i)$ **and** $a-1 \le k \le b\}$

while $\begin{bmatrix} k < b \\ k \ne b \end{bmatrix}$ **do**

   begin
   $k := k+1$;
   $\{s = \sum\limits_{i=a}^{k-1} X(i)$ **and** $a \le k \le b\}$
   $s := s + X(k)$
   end

end
$\{s = \sum\limits_{i=a}^{b} X(i)\}$.

The scheme of iteration is essentially the same as in the factorial program of Section 1.3.1, except that k ranges from $a-1$ to b instead of 0 to n. The reader may check that the assertions are correct, and should notice two salient points: First, the initial assertion $a-1 \le b$ is needed to insure $a-1 \le k \le b$ after the assignment $k := a-1$. Secondly, either the test $k < b$ or $k \ne b$ can be used in the **while** statement, since the presence of $k \le b$ in the invariant insures that either test will give the same outcome.

The program must terminate since one cannot increase k indefinitely without falsifying $k \le b$. However, now that we are using arrays, program correctness involves more than assertion correctness and termination; we must also consider the possibility of subscript errors.

Specifically, we must make sure that, for every execution of an array designator, the value of the subscript expression belongs to the declared domain of the indicated array. The only array designator in the above program is the occurrence of $X(k)$ in the statement $s := s + X(k)$, which is preceded by an assertion containing $a \le k \le b$. Thus the program will be correct with regard to subscript errors if every integer k, such that $a \le k \le b$, lies in the domain of X. As we will see in the next section, this condition can be written as $\boxed{a \quad b} \subseteq$ **dom** X, which should be added to the initial assertion of the program.

One final curious point remains. The initial assertion of the program contains $a-1 \le b$, yet our original problem, to set s to $\sum\limits_{i=a}^{b} X(i)$, is well-defined even when $a-1 > b$. Consider executing the program when $a-1 > b$. In contrast to the case covered by the assertions, the behavior of the program will depend upon the choice of the test in the **while** statement. If the test is $k \neq b$, then the initial condition $a - 1 > b$ will cause the program to run on forever. But if the test is $k < b$, then the initial condition $a - 1 > b$ will cause the **while** statement to terminate without ever executing its body, so that the final result will be $s = 0$, which is the correct result when $a - 1 > b$. Thus one can choose the **while**-statement test so that the program will still behave correctly when part of its initial assertion is violated. The reason for this rather surprising state of affairs will become apparent in the following sections.

Exercises

1. Investigate the effects of changing **while**-statement tests (e.g. from $\neq$ to $<$ or $>$) on the illustrative programs and exercises of Chapter 1.

2. Write a program that will examine an arbitrary array segment and count the number of elements whose value is zero.

2.2.2 Interval Diagrams

The introduction of arrays complicates the problem of specifying program behavior. The notation for assertions used in the previous chapter (with the addition of quantifiers, which will be discussed in Section 2.2.5) is theoretically adequate to specify array manipulations, but in practice it soon leads to unreadably long and complex assertions. To alleviate this complexity, we will introduce a variety of concepts, laws, and notations specifically oriented towards making assertions about arrays.

Many readers will find this material more difficult than the use of assertions in Chapter 1. This is largely due to unfamiliarity. In Chapter 1 we made extensive use of arithmetic concepts such as the distributive law, often without explicit mention. We were able to do so—without making things "difficult"—because these concepts have been understood for centuries and are now part of our common cultural heritage. But the analogous concepts about arrays, which are just as vital to the understanding of programming, are not centuries old. Indeed, their formulation is still a topic of current research [Reynolds 79].

To begin with, we consider relationships among different segments of the same array. Programmers have traditionally expressed such relationships by box-like diagrams. In this section and the next, we will provide a precise meaning for such diagrams which will permit their use in assertions.

Each segment of an array is in one-to-one correspondence with some finite consecutive set of integers; such a set is called an *interval*. In fact, the relationships we are interested in are really set-theoretic relationships among intervals.

In this section we will develop simple diagrams, called *interval diagrams*, which denote intervals themselves. For example:

$\boxed{a \quad |k}$ denotes the set of integers i such that $a \le i < k$,

$\boxed{k}$ denotes the set $\{k\}$ whose single member is k ,

$\boxed{k \quad b}$ denotes the set of integers i such that $k < i \le b$,

$\boxed{a \quad b}$ denotes the set of integers i such that $a \le i \le b$.

In the next section, we will use interval diagrams to compose more elaborate entities called *partition diagrams*, which assert relationships among intervals. For example, $\boxed{a \quad |k \quad b}$ asserts that the three intervals $\boxed{a \quad |k}$, $\boxed{k}$, and $\boxed{k \quad b}$ are disjoint (i.e. no integer belongs to more than one of these intervals), and that the union of these intervals is the interval $\boxed{a \quad b}$. It will turn out that this assertion is true if and only if $a \le k \le b$.

We now proceed to make these ideas precise. For any integer expressions a and b, a diagram of the form $\boxed{a \quad b}$ is called an *interval diagram*. We will use such a diagram in assertions as an expression denoting the set of integers i such that $a < i \le b$. On either side of the box, we may write $|a$ instead of $a-1|$ to improve readability. We may also write $\boxed{a}$ as an abbreviation for $\boxed{a \quad a}$, which denotes the *singleton* set whose only member is a. Thus

$$\left.\begin{array}{l} \boxed{a\quad b} \\[4pt] \boxed{a \quad b} \\[4pt] \boxed{a \quad |b} \\[4pt] \boxed{a \quad |b} \\[4pt] \boxed{a} \end{array}\right]\quad \text{denotes the set of integers } i \text{ such that} \quad \left[\begin{array}{l} a < i \le b \\[4pt] a \le i \le b \\[4pt] a < i < b \\[4pt] a \le i < b \\[4pt] i = a \quad . \end{array}\right.$$

When formulating general properties of interval (or partition) diagrams we will always use the standard form $\boxed{a \quad b}$, but when using the diagrams to make assertions we will freely employ all of the forms shown above.

For an array X we write **dom** X to denote the domain of X. Thus the assertion $\boxed{a \quad b} \subseteq$ **dom** X used in the previous section states that every integer i satisfying $a \le i \le b$ belongs to the domain of X. (The relation $S \subseteq S'$ means that S is a subset of S'. It should be emphasized that diagrams, the operator **dom**, and set-theoretic operators such as $\subseteq$ are not part of Algol W and can only be used in assertions.)

For any finite set S, we will write $\# S$ to denote the *size*, or number of members of S. At first sight, one might expect that $\# \boxed{a \quad b} = b - a$, but $b - a$ can be a negative number, while the size of a set is never less than zero. Actually,

$$\# \; a\boxed{b} = \textbf{if}\; b - a \ge 0 \;\textbf{then}\; b - a \;\textbf{else}\; 0 \quad .$$

The fact that we need a conditional expression to describe a fundamental property of intervals is a clear portent of a potential source of programming errors, i.e. the possibility that a program might be correct for one case of the conditional but not the other. To emphasize this situation we say that $a\boxed{b}$ is a *regular representation* of an interval when $a \le b$, and an *irregular representation* when $a > b$.

There are three possibilities:

If $b-a$	Then $a\boxed{b}$ is a
>0	regular representation of a nonempty set
$=0$	regular representation of the empty set
<0	irregular representation of the empty set.

Thus, only the empty set has irregular representations, but it also has regular representations.

Of course, the notions of size and irregularity can also be applied to interval diagrams in which one or both expressions appear to the right of a dividing line. For example,

$$\# \; \boxed{a\quad b} = \textbf{if}\; b - a + 1 \ge 0 \;\textbf{then}\; b - a + 1 \;\textbf{else}\; 0 \quad ,$$

and $\boxed{a\quad b}$ is an irregular representation of the empty set when $b - a + 1 < 0$.

The segment of an array X consisting of the array elements whose subscripts belong to an interval (or other set) S will be called the *segment of X over S*. For example, the program given in the previous section sums the values of the segment of X over $\boxed{a\quad b}$.

The one-to-one correspondence between array elements and their subscripts insures that the number of elements in a segment over S is the same as the size of S. (However, the number of elements in an array segment may be greater than the size of its set of values, since several array elements may have the same value.) When S has an irregular representation we will say that a segment over S is irregular. For example, the "final curious point" made in the previous section is that the summation program works correctly for irregular segments when the test $k < b$ is used in the **while** statement.

2.2.3 Partition Diagrams

For any integer expressions $a_0, a_1, a_2, \dots, a_n$, where $n \ge 1$, a diagram of the form

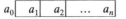

is called a *partition diagram*. The intervals denoted by $a_0 \boxed{\quad a_1}$, $a_1 \boxed{\quad a_2}$, ... , $a_{n-1} \boxed{\quad a_n}$ are called the *component intervals* of the partition diagram, and the interval denoted by $a_0 \boxed{\quad a_n}$ is called the *total interval* of the partition diagram.

We will use partition diagrams in assertions as logical expressions with the following meaning:

A partition diagram is true if and only if its component intervals are disjoint (i.e. no integer belongs to more than one of them), and the union of the component intervals is the total interval.

(In set-theoretic terminology, this is equivalent to saying that the component intervals form a *partition* of the total interval.)

Just as with interval diagrams, we may write $\ldots\ \boxed{\;|a}\ \ldots$ instead of $\ldots\ \boxed{a-1|\quad}\ \ldots$, and $\ldots\ \boxed{|a|}\ \ldots$ instead of $\ldots\ \boxed{|a\quad a|}\ \ldots$. For example,

$$a \ \boxed{\;|k|\;} \ b$$

is a partition diagram with the same meaning as

$$a \ \boxed{\;|k \quad k|\;} \ b \quad ,$$

which in turn has the same meaning as the standard-form diagram

$$a-1 \ \boxed{\;|k-1 \quad k|\;} \ b \quad .$$

Notice that, since these conventions work the same way for interval and partition diagrams, we can decompose a partition diagram into component and total interval diagrams without converting it into standard form. For example, $a \ \boxed{\;|k|\;} \ b$ decomposes into

Component Intervals	Total Interval
$a \ \boxed{\;|k}$	$\boxed{a \quad b}$,
$\boxed{|k|}$	
$\boxed{k| \quad }b$	

whose standard forms,

Component Intervals	Total Interval
$a-1 \boxed{\quad k-1}$	$a-1 \boxed{\quad b}$,
$k-1 \boxed{\quad k}$	
$k \boxed{\quad b}$	

are the same as the decomposition of $a-1 \ \boxed{\;|k-1 \quad k|\;} \ b$.

It is important to understand the distinction between interval diagrams, which will be used in assertions as expressions denoting intervals, and partition diagrams, which will be used in assertions as expressions denoting

true or **false**. A diagram with intermediate dividing lines can only be used as a partition diagram, but a diagram with only end lines can be used in either role.

Since a partition diagram asserts a relationship among intervals that are determined by integer expressions, the truth or falsity of the partition diagram depends only upon the values of these integer expressions. The following theorem shows that this dependency can also be expressed by ordering relations:

Theorem 1   The partition diagram

$$a_0 \boxed{\quad a_1 \mid a_2 \mid \ \ldots\ \ a_n \quad}$$

is true if and only if either

$$(i)\quad a_0 \leq a_1 \leq a_2 \leq\ \ldots\ \leq a_n$$

or

$$(ii)\quad a_0 \geq a_1 \geq a_2 \geq\ \ldots\ \geq a_n \quad.$$

Notice that (i) asserts that every component interval diagram is regular, while (ii) asserts that every component interval is empty.

Proof: (1) Suppose $a_0 \leq a_1 \leq a_2 \leq\ \ldots\ \leq a_n$. To show disjointness, suppose k belongs to some component interval $a_{i-1} \boxed{\quad a_i}$, and let $a_{j-1} \boxed{\quad a_j}$ be any other component. Then either $j < i$, so that $a_j \leq a_{i-1} < k$, or $i < j$, so that $k \leq a_i \leq a_{j-1}$. Either way, $a_{j-1} < k \leq a_j$ is false, so that k does not belong to $a_{j-1} \boxed{\quad a_j}$.

To show that the total interval is the union of the component intervals, suppose that k belongs to some component $a_{i-1} \boxed{\quad a_i}$. Then since $a_0 \leq a_{i-1} < k \leq a_i \leq a_n$, k belongs to the total interval $a_0 \boxed{\quad a_n}$. On the other hand, suppose that k belongs to $a_0 \boxed{\quad a_n}$. Since $a_0 < k$ but $k \leq a_n$, there is a smallest i such that $1 \leq i \leq n$ and $k \leq a_i$. Then $a_{i-1} < k \leq a_i$, so that k belongs to the component $a_{i-1} \boxed{\quad a_i}$.

(2) Suppose $a_0 \geq a_1 \geq a_2 \geq\ \ldots\ \geq a_n$. Then each component interval is empty, which establishes disjointness, and the total interval is also empty, and is therefore the union of the component intervals.

(3) Finally we come to the interesting case: We must show that, if the partition diagram is true, then either (i) or (ii) holds. The following proof is due to F. L. Morris.

Suppose $a_0 \boxed{\quad a_1 \mid \ \ldots\ \ a_n}$. A fundamental fact about partitions is that the size of the total interval must be the sum of the sizes of the component intervals, i.e.

$$\# \, a_0 \boxed{\;\;a_n} = \sum_{i=1}^{n} \# \, a_{i-1}\boxed{\;\;a_i} \quad, \tag{a}$$

where the size function $\# \, a\boxed{\;\;b} = $ **if** $b-a \geq 0$ **then** $b-a$ **else** 0 is always nonnegative and is zero if and only if $a\boxed{\;\;b}$ is empty.

However, for arbitrary a_i's simple cancellation gives

$$a_n - a_0 = \sum_{i=1}^{n} a_i - a_{i-1} \quad. \tag{b}$$

Now suppose we define the function

$$f(a, b) = b - a - \# a\boxed{\;\;b} = \text{ if } b-a\geq 0 \text{ then } 0 \text{ else } b-a \quad,$$

which is always nonpositive and is zero if and only if $a\boxed{\;\;b}$ is regular. Then subtraction of (a) from (b) gives

$$f(a_0, a_n) = \sum_{i=1}^{n} f(a_{i-1}, a_i) \quad. \tag{c}$$

The total interval diagram $a_0\boxed{\;\;a_n}$ must be either empty or regular (or both). Suppose it is empty. Then (a) asserts that a sum of nonnegative terms is zero, which implies that each term is zero. Thus, for each i, $a_{i-1}\boxed{\;\;a_i}$ is empty and $a_{i-1} \geq a_i$.

On the other hand, suppose $a_0\boxed{\;\;a_n}$ is regular. Then (c) asserts that a sum of nonpositive terms is zero, which implies that each term is zero. Thus, for each i, $a_{i-1}\boxed{\;\;a_i}$ is regular and $a_{i-1} \leq a_i$. []

From this theorem, we can derive some general rules for inferring one partition diagram from another. Note that all the vertical lines in a partition diagram are called *dividing lines*, which may be either *end lines* or *intermediate lines*.

Theorem 2 (1) (Erasure) A partition diagram implies any diagram that can be obtained from it by removing dividing lines (and their associated expressions).

(2) (Dividing line replication) Let

$$D_1 = a_0\boxed{\;\ldots\;a_m\;\;|\;\;\ldots\;a_n}$$

be any partition diagram, and let

$$D_2 = a_0\boxed{\;\ldots\;a_m\;\;|\;\;a_m\;\;|\;\;\ldots\;a_n}$$

be obtained from D_1 by adding a dividing line with the same associated expression as an·adjacent dividing line. Then D_1 implies D_2.

(3)   (Direct Substitution) Let

$$D_1 = a_0 \boxed{\ \ldots\ a_{m-1}\ |\ a_m\ |\ \ldots\ a_n\ }$$
$$D_2 = a_{m-1} \boxed{\ c_1\ |\ \ldots\ c_l\ |\ a_m\ }$$

be partition diagrams such that the end lines of D_2 have associated expressions which are the same as the associated expressions of two adjacent dividing lines in D_1. Then D_1 **and** D_2 implies D_3, where

$$D_3 = a_0 \boxed{\ \ldots\ a_{m-1}\ |\ c_1\ |\ \ldots\ c_l\ |\ a_m\ |\ \ldots\ a_n\ }$$

is obtained from D_1 by inserting the intermediate lines of D_2 between the adjacent lines of D_1.

Proof: (1) If $a_0 \le a_1 \le \ldots \le a_n$ is true, then it will remain so if we delete some of the a_i's. The $\ge$ case behaves similarly.

(2) If $a_0 \le \ldots \le a_m \le \ldots \le a_n$ then $a_0 \le \ldots \le a_m \le a_m \le \ldots \le a_n$. The $\ge$ case behaves similarly.

(3) If D_1 and D_2 are true then there are four possibilities:

(a) $a_0 \le \ldots \le a_{m-1} \le a_m \le \ldots \le a_n$
     and $a_{m-1} \le c_1 \le \ldots \le c_l \le a_m$,

(b) $a_0 \le \ldots \le a_{m-1} \le a_m \le \ldots \le a_n$
     and $a_{m-1} \ge c_1 \ge \ldots \ge c_l \ge a_m$,

(c) $a_0 \ge \ldots \ge a_{m-1} \ge a_m \ge \ldots \ge a_n$
     and $a_{m-1} \ge c_1 \ge \ldots \ge c_l \ge a_m$,

(d) $a_0 \ge \ldots \ge a_{m-1} \ge a_m \ge \ldots \ge a_n$
     and $a_{m-1} \le c_1 \le \ldots \le c_l \le a_m$.

In case (a) we have $a_0 \le \ldots \le a_{m-1} \le c_1 \le \ldots \le c_l \le a_m \le \ldots \le a_n$ directly. In case (b), $a_{m-1} \le a_m$ and $a_{m-1} \ge c_1 \ge \ldots \ge c_l \ge a_m$ give $a_{m-1} = c_1 = \ldots = c_l = a_m$, and again we have $a_0 \le \ldots \le a_{m-1} \le c_1 \le \ldots \le c_l \le a_m \le \ldots \le a_n$. The remaining cases are similar.   ▯

A final theorem gives more specific results:

Theorem 3   (1)   Any partition diagram without intermediate lines, e.g. $a \boxed{\ \ b\ }$, is always true.

(2)   The following are equivalent: $\boxed{a\ |\ b}$, $\boxed{a\ \ |b}$, $a \le b$, $\#\boxed{a\ \ b} \ge 1$, $a \in \boxed{a\ \ b}$, and $b \in \boxed{a\ \ b}$.

(3)   The following are equivalent: $\boxed{a\ |\ b\ |\ c}$, $a \le b \le c$, and $b \in \boxed{a\ \ c}$.

The proof is left to the reader.

Exercises

1. For each of the following assertions, give an equivalent partition diagram:

(a) $k \in \boxed{a \quad b}$ and $m \in \boxed{a \quad b}$ and $k < m$,

(b) $k \in \boxed{a \quad b}$ and $m \in \boxed{a \quad b}$ and $k \le m$,

(c) $k \in \boxed{a \quad m}$ and $\boxed{a \quad m} \subseteq \boxed{a \quad b}$.

2. Prove

(a) $\boxed{a_0 \; a_1 \; a_2 \; \dots \; a_n}$ is equivalent to

$\boxed{a_0 + c \quad a_1 + c \quad a_2 + c \; \dots \; a_n + c}$.

(b) $\boxed{a \quad \quad b}$ is equivalent to $\boxed{a \quad \quad b}$.

2.2.4 Summation Revisited

To illustrate the use of interval and partition diagrams, we shall reconstruct the program given in Section 2.2.1 for summing an array segment. We first introduce a more general notation for summation. Let $\sum_{i \in S} X(i)$ denote the sum of the values of $X(i)$ over all i in the set S. Then

(I) $\sum_{i \in S} X(i) = 0$ when S is empty   ,

(II) $\sum_{i \in \boxed{k}} X(i) = X(k)$,

(III) $\sum_{i \in S \cup S'} X(i) = \left(\sum_{i \in S} X(i) \right) + \left(\sum_{i \in S'} X(i) \right)$
when S and S' are disjoint sets.

In this notation, we want our program to achieve

$$s = \sum_{i \in \boxed{a \quad b}} X(i) .$$

If our program is to iterate over the integers in the interval $\boxed{a \quad b}$, then its invariant should assert that this interval is partitioned into subsets of "processed" and "unprocessed" integers, and that s is the sum of X over the processed subset. Moreover, if the iteration is to be in increasing order then both of these subsets will be intervals and the processed integers will all be smaller than the unprocessed integers. Using the integer variable k to keep track of the division between the two subintervals, we get the invariant

$$\boxed{a \quad k \quad b} \text{ and } s = \sum_{i \in \boxed{a \quad k}} X(i) ,$$

where the processed and unprocessed subintervals are the components $\boxed{a \quad k}$ and $\boxed{k \quad b}$ of the partition diagram.

(We could equally well have chosen to write $\boxed{\quad k}$ instead of $\boxed{k \quad}$. Roughly speaking, we have decided that k will denote the last processed integer rather than the first unprocessed integer.)

Initially, we can achieve the invariant by setting k to $a-1$ and s to zero, so that the processed interval is the empty interval $\boxed{a \quad a-1}$, the unprocessed interval is the total interval $a-1\boxed{\quad b} = \boxed{a \quad b}$, and s is the sum of X over the empty processed interval. On the other hand, when $k \geq b$ the unprocessed interval will be empty, and the partition diagram will imply

$$\boxed{a \quad k} = \boxed{a \quad k} \cup k\boxed{\quad b} = \boxed{a \quad b} \quad ,$$

so that the invariant will imply the consequent of our program. Thus we have

$$\{\boxed{a \quad b} \subseteq \mathbf{dom}\ X\}$$
$$\mathbf{begin\ integer}\ k;$$
$$k := a-1;\ s := 0;$$
$$\{\mathbf{whileinv:}\ \boxed{a \quad k}\boxed{\quad b}\ \mathbf{and}\ s = \sum_{i \in \boxed{a\ k}} X(i)\}$$
$$\mathbf{while}\ k < b\ \mathbf{do}$$
$$\qquad \text{``Process one integer''}$$
$$\mathbf{end}$$
$$\{s = \sum_{i \in \boxed{a\ b}} X(i)\} \quad .$$

The invariant can be rewritten as

$$\boxed{a \quad k+1 \quad b}\ \mathbf{and}\ s = \sum_{i \in \boxed{a}k+1} X(i) \quad ,$$

and the test $k < b$ implies $\boxed{k+1 \quad b}$ by Theorem 3(2). Thus Theorem 2(3) shows that, when "Process one integer" begins execution,

$$\boxed{a \quad k+1 \quad b}\ \mathbf{and}\ s = \sum_{i \in \boxed{a}k+1} X(i) \quad ,$$

so that increasing k by one will give

$$\boxed{a \quad k \quad b}\ \mathbf{and}\ s = \sum_{i \in \boxed{a}k} X(i) \quad .$$

Less formally, $k < b$ insures that $k+1$ belongs to the unprocessed interval, and $k := k+1$ transfers this integer into the processed interval, which is then the union of two disjoint subintervals: its former value $\boxed{a \quad k}$ and the singleton $\boxed{k}$. Then (II) and (III) imply

$$\sum_{i \in \boxed{a\ k}} X(i) = \sum_{i \in \boxed{a}k} X(i) + X(k)$$

so that the invariant can be regained by $s := s + X(k)$. Thus the summation program is

$\{\boxed{a \quad b} \subseteq \text{dom } X\}$

begin integer k;

$k := a - 1;\ s := 0;$

$\{$**whileinv**: $\boxed{a \quad k \quad b}$ **and** $s = \sum_{i \in \boxed{a\ k}} X(i)\}$

while $k < b$ **do**

   begin

   $k := k + 1;$

   $\{\boxed{a \quad k \quad b}$ **and** $s = \sum_{i \in \boxed{a\ }k} X(i)\}$

   $s := s + X(k)$

   end

end

$\{s = \sum_{i \in \boxed{a\ b}} X(i)\}$.

To show the role of interval and partition diagrams more explicitly, we give a complete formal proof of the correctness of this program. The proof consists of the two tableaus shown in Tables 2.1 and 2.2. The first tableau shows that the **while**-statement body S satisfies the specification $\{I$ **and** $L\}$ S $\{I\}$, where I is the invariant and L is the **while**-statement test. From this specification, the inference rule for **while** statements gives $\{I\}$ **while** L **do** S $\{I$ **and** $\neg L\}$. Then the second tableau uses this result to show that the entire program meets its specification. Justifications of the various inferences are given to the right of the tableaus. The terms "disjointness property" and "union property" refer to the two properties that define partition diagrams.

Termination is based on the size of the unprocessed interval $\boxed{k \quad b}$, which is decreased by the **while**-statement body and cannot be less than zero. The impossibility of subscript errors is shown by the initial assertion $\boxed{a \quad b} \subseteq$ **dom** X (which must hold throughout the program since a and b are not changed and **dom** X cannot be changed within the scope of the declaration of X), plus the partition diagram $\boxed{a \quad k \quad b}$, which is equivalent to $k \in \boxed{a \quad b}$ by Theorem 3(3) and which occurs in the precedent of the statement $s := s + X(k)$ containing the only array designator.

In contrast to Section 2.2.1, the correctness proof using interval and partition diagrams includes—without any extra analysis—the case where $\boxed{a \quad b}$ is irregular. Of course, the **while**-statement test that $\boxed{k \quad b}$ is nonempty must be $k < b$ rather than $k \neq b$.

Notice that both nontermination and the impossibility of subscript errors are shown by informal arguments which go beyond our formal logic for inferring specifications. Formally, subscript errors are a special kind of nontermination, so that $\{P\}$ S $\{Q\}$ means that if P holds beforehand then

$\{\boxed{a \quad k \quad b} \text{ and } s = \sum_{i \in \boxed{a\ k}} X(i) \text{ and } k < b\}$

$\{\boxed{a \quad k+1 \quad b} \text{ and } s = \sum_{i \in \boxed{a\ }k+1} X(i) \text{ and } \boxed{k+1 \quad b}\}$ Theorem 3(2)

$\{\boxed{a \quad k+1 \quad b} \text{ and } s = \sum_{i \in \boxed{a\ }k+1} X(i)\}$ Direct substitution

$k := k+1;$

$\{\boxed{a \quad k \quad b} \text{ and } s = \sum_{i \in \boxed{a\ }k} X(i)\}$ Assignment

$\{\boxed{a \quad k \quad b} \text{ and } s + X(k) = (\sum_{i \in \boxed{a\ }k} X(i)) + (\sum_{i \in \boxed{k}} X(i))\}$ (II)

$\{\boxed{a \quad k \quad b} \text{ and } s + X(k) = \sum_{i \in \boxed{a\ }k \cup \boxed{k}} X(i)\}$ (III) and disjointness property

$\{\boxed{a \quad k \quad b} \text{ and } \boxed{a \quad k} \text{ and } s + X(k) = \sum_{i \in \boxed{a\ }k \cup \boxed{k}} X(i)\}$ Erasure

$\{\boxed{a \quad k \quad b} \text{ and } s + X(k) = \sum_{i \in \boxed{a\ k}} X(i)\}$ Union property

$s := s + X(k)$

$\{\boxed{a \quad k \quad b} \text{ and } s = \sum_{i \in \boxed{a\ k}} X(i)\}$ Assignment

$\{\boxed{a \quad k \quad b} \text{ and } s = \sum_{i \in \boxed{a\ k}} X(i)\}$ Erasure

Table 2.1 Proof of the Summation Program, Part I.

$\{\boxed{a \quad b} \subseteq \textbf{dom } X\}$

$\{\boxed{a \quad b}\}$ Theorem 3(1)

$\{\boxed{a \quad a-1 \quad b}\}$ Dividing line replication

$\{\boxed{a \quad a-1 \quad b} \text{ and } 0 = \sum_{i \in \boxed{a\ a-1}} X(i)\}$ (I) and definition of interval diagram

$k := a-1;$

$\{\boxed{a \quad k \quad b} \text{ and } 0 = \sum_{i \in \boxed{a\ k}} X(i)\}$ Assignment

$s := 0;$

$\{\boxed{a \quad k \quad b} \text{ and } s = \sum_{i \in \boxed{a\ k}} X(i)\}$ Assignment

while $k < b$ **do begin** $k := k+1;\ s := s + X(k)$ **end**

$\{\boxed{a \quad k \quad b} \text{ and } s = \sum_{i \in \boxed{a\ k}} X(i) \text{ and } \neg\, k < b\}$ **while** statement

$\{\boxed{a \quad k \quad b} \text{ and } s = \sum_{i \in \boxed{a\ k}} X(i) \text{ and } k\boxed{\quad b} \text{ empty}\}$ Definition of interval diagram

$\{\boxed{a \quad k} = \boxed{a \quad b} \text{ and } s = \sum_{i \in \boxed{a\ k}} X(i)\}$ Union property

$\{s = \sum_{i \in \boxed{a\ b}} X(i)\}$ Substitution of equals

Table 2.2 Proof of the Summation Program, Part II.

executing S will, if S terminates *without an error message*, give a state in which Q holds. This view presupposes that all subscript errors will cause error messages; fortunately this is the case in Algol W.

Exercise

1. The following generalization of the factorial-computing problem shows that the kind of reasoning about intervals facilitated by interval and partition diagrams can be needed even in the absence of arrays. Write a program that will accept two arbitrary integers a and b, and will set the real variable s to $\Pi_{i \in \boxed{a \quad b}}\, i$, where

    (I) $\Pi_{i \in \{\}}\, i = 1$,
    (II) $\Pi_{i \in \boxed{k}}\, i = k$,
    (III) $\Pi_{i \in S \cup S'}\, i = (\Pi_{i \in S}\, i) \times (\Pi_{i \in S'}\, i)$
          when S and S' are disjoint .

2.2.5 Quantifiers

Our next example will be a program to find the subscript of a maximum element in an array segment: Given the segment of X over $\boxed{a \quad b}$, we want to find an integer j such that $\boxed{a \quad |j| \quad b}$ and $X(j)$ is at least as large as every element in the segment. However, before beginning to develop a program for this task, we must translate the previous sentence into a precise logical expression, and here we encounter a problem: How do we express "$X(j)$ is at least as large as *every* element in the segment"?

Given a particular integer i in $\boxed{a \quad b}$, it is easy enough to say that $X(i) \le X(j)$. The problem is that we want to assert this logical expression for *all i* in $\boxed{a \quad b}$, not just for a particular i. The solution is simply to introduce a new notation $(\forall\, I \in S)$ which is defined to mean "For all I in the set S." We then write

$$(\forall\, i \in \boxed{a \quad b})\; X(i) \le X(j) .$$

The phrase $(\forall\, I \in S)$ is called a *universal quantifier of I*. There is a second kind of quantifier, called an *existential quantifier of I*, which is written $(\exists\, I \in S)$ and means "For some I in the set S" or "There exists an I in the set S such that". The extension of logical expressions in assertions to include these two kinds of quantifiers produces a fundamental increase in their expressive power. (In the jargon of symbolic logic, we are moving from the propositional calculus to the first-order predicate calculus.)

Quantifiers, like declarations, are binding mechanisms. Specifically, the occurrence of the identifier I in $(\forall\, I \in S)\, P$ or $(\exists\, I \in S)\, P$ is a binder whose scope consists of itself plus the following expression P, i.e. the entire quantified expression excluding the set S.

For example, in $(\forall\, i \in \boxed{a \quad b})\, X(i) \le X(j)$ the scope of the binder of i is the binder itself plus $X(i) \le X(j)$, and the only identifiers occurring in this scope are i, X, and j. Thus the meaning of this assertion will remain unchanged if we alpha-convert it, as discussed in Section 1.5.2, by replacing the binder of i and the occurrence of i in $X(i) \le X(j)$ by any other identifier except X or j, e.g.

$$(\forall\ k \in \boxed{a\ \ b})\ X(k) \le X(j)\ \ ,$$

or even

$$(\forall\ a \in \boxed{a\ \ b})\ X(a) \le X(j)\ \ ,$$

but *not*

$$(\forall\ j \in \boxed{a\ \ b})\ X(j) \le X(j)\ \ .$$

The nature of the universal quantifier is explicated by the following laws:

$$\text{If } S \subseteq S' \text{ and } (\forall\ i \in S')\ P \text{ then } (\forall\ i \in S)\ P\ \ , \tag{1}$$

$$(\forall\ i \in \{\})\ P\ \ , \tag{2}$$

$$(\forall\ i \in S \cup S')\ P \text{ if and only if both } (\forall\ i \in S)\ P \text{ and } (\forall\ i \in S')\ P\ \ , \tag{3}$$

$$\text{If } (\forall\ i \in S)\ P \text{ and } E \in S \text{ then } P|_{i \to E}\ \ , \tag{4}$$

where $\{\}$ denotes the empty set and $S \cup S'$ denotes the union of the sets S and S'. Law (2) asserts that anything is true when universally quantified over the empty set; in this case the quantified expression is often said to be *vacuously* true. Law (4) asserts that, from a universally quantified expression one can infer anything obtained by substituting for the bound identifier an expression denoting a member of S.

The universal and existential quantifiers are related by the operation of negation: Something is true for all members of S if and only if it is not false for some member of S. In other words,

$$(\forall\ i \in S)\ P \text{ if and only if } \neg\ (\exists\ i \in S)\ \neg\ P\ \ , \tag{5}$$

and similarly

$$(\exists\ i \in S)\ P \text{ if and only if } \neg\ (\forall\ i \in S)\ \neg\ P\ \ . \tag{6}$$

Although quantifiers can be used in assertions, they cannot occur in logical expressions in Algol W programs themselves. This is not an accidental omission—it can be shown that it is theoretically impossible to write a computer program that will correctly evaluate an arbitrary logical expression containing quantifiers. (Actually, it would be possible to evaluate quantifiers over finite sets. But even permitting such limited quantifiers in programs would drastically change the nature of the programming language, since it would introduce expressions with unbounded evaluation times.)

Exercises

1. Explain the difference between

    $$(\forall\ i \in \boxed{a\ \ b})\ (\exists\ j \in \boxed{a\ \ b})\ i \neq j$$
    and
    $$(\exists\ j \in \boxed{a\ \ b})\ (\forall\ i \in \boxed{a\ \ b})\ i \neq j \quad .$$

2. Use quantifiers to formalize the following mathematical facts and definitions. You may use Int to denote the set of integers and Real to denote the set of real numbers. In (c) and (d) you may need the operator **implies** discussed in Section 2.2.10.

    (a)   For every integer, there is a larger integer.

    (b)   There is no maximum integer.

    (c)   There is a real number between every pair of distinct real numbers.

    (d)   For every real x, $\lfloor x \rfloor$ is the largest integer that is no more than x.

3. Prove that the formalizations of (a) and (b) in the previous exercise are equivalent.

4. Binding occurs in the summation notations used in Sections 2.2.1 and 2.2.4, and in the conventional notation for definite integrals. For each of these notations, describe the binders and their scopes.

2.2.6   Substitution and Identifier Collisions

Both law (4) in the previous section and the rule for assignment in Section 1.4.2 involve the application of substitution to assertions that, with the introduction of quantifiers, can contain bound identifier occurrences. Because of this, we must consider an interaction between substitution and binding which is often called *identifier collision*.

As an example, if Int denotes the set of integers then

$$(\forall\ i \in \text{Int})\ (\exists\ j \in \text{Int})\ i = j - 1$$

is an obviously true fact about the integers. Thus, since $j + 1$ is an integer expression, law (4) implies

$$(\exists\ j \in \text{Int})\ i = j - 1 \big|_{i \to j+1} \quad .$$

However, if we interpret the indicated substitution naively, then the above expression seems to be

$$(\exists\ j \in \text{Int})\ j + 1 = j - 1 \quad ,$$

which is patently false. The difficulty is that the free occurrence of j in $j + 1$ has been moved by the substitution into the scope of a binder of j, and has therefore been "captured" by the binder. More briefly, the two usages of j have *collided*.

In essence, this means that the naive interpretation of substitution is incorrect, and that a correct definition of substitution must preserve binding structure by avoiding collisions. The basic method for accomplishing this is to use alpha conversion to eliminate binders that could cause collisions.

In formulating such a definition of substitution, we include the case of simultaneous substitution for several identifiers, and we permit the substitution to involve phrases, such as statements, that occur in programs but not assertions. Although these generalizations are presently unnecessary, they will be needed in Section 3.1.1, where we will use substitution to describe the copy rule for procedures.

Suppose S is a phrase, $I_1, \ldots, I_n$ are distinct identifiers, and $A_1, \ldots, A_n$ are phrases. Let S' be an alpha variant of S (or possibly S itself) that contains no binder of any identifier that occurs free in any of the A_i's. Then

$$S\big|_{I_1, \ldots, I_n \to A_1, \ldots, A_n} \quad ,$$

called the result of *substituting* the A_i's for the I_i's in S, is the phrase obtained from S' by replacing every free occurrence of each I_i by the corresponding A_i.

For example, to obtain

$$(\exists\, j \in \text{Int})\ i = j - 1\big|_{i \to j+1} \quad ,$$

we cannot take S' to be $(\exists\, j \in \text{Int})\ i = j - 1$, since this phrase contains a binder of j, which occurs free in $j + 1$. Instead, we must take S' to be an alpha variant such as $(\exists\, k \in \text{Int})\ i = k - 1$, to obtain $(\exists\, k \in \text{Int})\ j + 1 = k - 1$ as the result of the substitution. (Which alpha variant we choose as S' doesn't matter—since they all have the same meaning—as long as it does not contain any binder of j.)

(Actually, the requirement that S' contain no binder of any identifier that occurs free in any of the A_i's is stronger than necessary. The following weaker but more complicated requirement is sufficient to avoid identifier collisions: For each I_i, S' must contain no free occurrence of I_i within the scope of a binder of any identifier occurring free in A_i.)

Two other aspects of substitution require comment. The replacement of occurrences of I_i by A_i must be carried out in terms of phrases rather than strings of characters. For example, $x \times y = 0\big|_{x \to a+b}$ is $(a + b) \times y = 0$, not $a + b \times y = 0$. In general, each A_i must be enclosed in parentheses (or **begin ... end**) whenever this is necessary to preserve its identity as a subphrase of the result of the replacement.

Finally, it should be noted that simultaneous substitution can produce a different result than repeated substitution. For example, $x \le y\big|_{x,y \to y,x}$ is $y \le x$, but $(x \le y\big|_{x \to y})\big|_{y \to x}$ is $x \le x$.

Exercise

1. Suppose the consequent $(\forall\ i \in \boxed{a \quad b})\ X(i) \le X(j)$ is to hold after executing the assignment $j := i+1$. What is the precedent that must hold before execution of this assignment?

2.2.7 Maximum Finding

Now that we have introduced quantifiers and dealt with the interaction of binding and substitution, we can attack the problem of maximum finding. We want a program that, given the segment of X over $\boxed{a \quad b}$, will set the variable j to satisfy the consequent

$$\boxed{a \ |j| \quad b} \ \text{and} \ (\forall\ i \in \boxed{a \quad b})\ X(i) \le X(j) \quad .$$

An obvious plan of attack is to sequence through the elements in order of increasing subscripts while always keeping j set to the subscript of the largest element encountered so far. If we use a variable k to keep track of the subscript of the last-examined element, then our invariant will be:

$$\boxed{a \ |j| \ k \quad b} \ \text{and} \ (\forall\ i \in \boxed{a \quad k})\ X(i) \le X(j) \quad ,$$

which asserts that $\boxed{a \quad b}$ is partitioned into a processed interval $\boxed{a \quad k}$ and an unprocessed interval $\boxed{k \quad b}$, and that j is the subscript of a maximum element of the subsegment of X over the processed interval.

When $k \ge b$, the unprocessed interval will be empty, the processed interval will equal $\boxed{a \quad b}$, and the invariant will imply the final assertion. However, unlike the summation program, we cannot start with the initialization $k := a-1$, for then there could be no value of j satisfying $\boxed{a \ |j| \ k}$. The smallest $\boxed{a \quad k}$ we can start with is a one-element interval. Moreover, since this one-element interval must be a subset of $\boxed{a \quad b}$, we must impose the initial condition that $\boxed{a \quad b}$ be nonempty, or equivalently $\boxed{a| \quad b}$. In fact, this initial condition is inherent in the problem we are trying to solve—if $\boxed{a \quad b}$ were empty it would be meaningless to ask for the subscript of its maximum element.

If $\boxed{a| \quad b}$, then the initialization $j := a;\ k := a$ will give $\boxed{a \ |j| \ k \quad b}$, and also $\boxed{a \quad k} = \boxed{|j|}$, which implies $(\forall\ i \in \boxed{a \quad k})\ X(i) \le X(j)$. Thus this initialization will achieve the invariant.

If we increase k at the beginning of the **while**-statement body, we get the program skeleton

$\{\boxed{a\ \ \ b}\}$
begin integer k;
$j := a$; $k := a$;
$\{$**whileinv:** $\boxed{a\ \ |j\ \ |\ k|\ \ b}$ **and** $(\forall\ i \in \boxed{a\ \ k})\ X(i) \leq X(j)\}$
while $k < b$ **do**
    begin $k := k+1$; "Inspect one element" **end**
end
$\{\boxed{a\ \ |j\ \ |\ b}$ **and** $(\forall\ i \in \boxed{a\ \ b})\ X(i) \leq X(j)\}$.

At the beginning of the **while**-statement body, the invariant will be true and $\boxed{k\ \ \ b}$ will be nonempty, so that $\boxed{a\ \ |j\ \ \ |k+1|\ \ b}$ will hold. Then increasing k by one will give

$$\boxed{a\ \ |j\ \ |k|\ \ b}\ \textbf{and}\ (\forall\ i \in \boxed{a\ \ }k)\ X(i) \leq X(j)\quad .$$

With this assertion as precedent, "Inspect one element" must reestablish the invariant.

At this stage, since $\boxed{a\ \ k}$ will be the union of $\boxed{a\ \ }k$ and $\boxed{k}$, the maximum element of X over $\boxed{a\ \ k}$ will be the larger of the maximum over $\boxed{a\ \ }k$, which will be $X(j)$, and the maximum over $\boxed{k}$, which will be $X(k)$. Thus j can be left unchanged if $X(k) \leq X(j)$, and j can be reset to k if $X(k) \geq X(j)$. (Notice that $\boxed{a\ \ |j\ \ |\ k|\ \ b}$ will not be falsified by $j := k$ since $k \in \boxed{a\ \ k}$, and that either alternative can be taken when $X(k) = X(j)$.)

As with the summation program, termination is assured by the decreasing size of the unprocessed interval $\boxed{k\ \ \ b}$. The only array designators are $X(k)$ and $X(j)$ in "Inspect one element", whose precedent contains $\boxed{a\ \ |j\ \ |k|\ \ b}$. Thus subscript errors will be precluded by adding $\boxed{a\ \ b} \subseteq$ **dom** X to the initial assertion.

The final program is

$\{\boxed{a\ \ b} \subseteq$ **dom** X **and** $\boxed{a\ \ \ b}\}$
begin integer k;
$j := a$; $k := a$;
$\{$**whileinv:** $\boxed{a\ \ |j\ \ |\ k|\ \ b}$ **and** $(\forall\ i \in \boxed{a\ \ k})\ X(i) \leq X(j)\}$
while $k < b$ **do**
    begin $k := k+1$; **if** $\begin{bmatrix} X(k) > X(j) \\ X(k) \geq X(j) \end{bmatrix}$ **then** $j := k$ **end**
end
$\{\boxed{a\ \ |j\ \ |\ b}$ **and** $(\forall\ i \in \boxed{a\ \ b})\ X(i) \leq X(j)\}$.

Either choice of the relation which compares $X(k)$ with $X(j)$ gives a program that meets the specification. However, this choice can make a difference in the result of the computation. (Consider the extreme case where all elements of X have the same value.) In fact, we have intentionally provided a indeterminate specification; when the segment of X over $\boxed{a \quad b}$ has more than one maximum element, the specification leaves the program free to produce the subscript of any maximum element.

Exercises

1. For each of the two versions of the maximum-finding program, give a correct specification and invariant that are determinate, i.e. that cannot be met by a program with different behavior.

2. (Suggested by F. L. Morris) Write program that will produce the subscripts of both a maximum and a minimum element of an array segment. Use a single **while** statement, so that the array segment is only scanned once. With a bit of cleverness, this program can be written so that the number of executed comparisons of array elements is no more than $3/2$ times the size of the segment.

    (*Hint*: Process the array elements two at a time.)

2.2.8 Functions as Array Values

So far we have taken the view that an array is a collection of variables which, like the simple variables used in Chapter 1, possess numerical or logical values. For many purposes, however, it is more convenient to view an array as a single "giant" variable, whose value is a function.

A function F consists of three sets:

> (1) A set **dom** F, called the *domain* of F,
>
> (2) A set **cod** F, called the *codomain* of F,
>
> (3) A set, called the *graph* of F, consisting of pairs $\langle i, r \rangle$ such that i belongs to **dom** F and r belongs to **cod** F,

which satisfy the following relationship:

> For each i in **dom** F there is *exactly one* r in **cod** F such that $\langle i, r \rangle$ belongs to the graph of F.

A function F is often said to be a function *from* **dom** F *to* **cod** F. For any i in **dom** F, we write $F(i)$ to denote the unique value such that $\langle i, F(i) \rangle$ belongs to the graph of F; this unique value is called the *result of applying F to i*, and F is said to *map i* into $F(i)$. Two functions F and G are equal if and only if they have the same domain, codomain, and graph, i.e. **dom** $F =$ **dom** G, **cod** F = **cod** G, and $F(i) = G(i)$ for all i in **dom** F.

Consider an array X in a particular state of some computation. Let F be the function such that

(1)   **dom** $F=$ **dom** X.

(2)   **cod** F is the set of values (e.g. the set of integers, the set of reals, or the set {**true, false**}) that are associated with the data type of the elements of X.

(3)   For all $i \in$ **dom** F, $F(i)$ is the current value of the array element $X(i)$.

Then the function F is said to be the *current value* of the array X.

Now suppose $X(i)$ is an array designator in an expression, e.g. on the right side of an assignment statement or in an assertion. Instead of saying that $X(i)$ denotes the value of the ith element of X, we can equally well say that $X(i)$ is the result of applying the value of X to i.

Suppose, for example, that sq is an integer array with domain $\boxed{-5 \quad 5}$ such that, in the older view, each $sq(i)$ is a variable whose current value is the square of the number i. In the functional view, sq itself has a current value, which is the "squaring function" from $\boxed{-5 \quad 5}$ to the set of integers, and an expression such as $sq(3)$ denotes the result of applying this function to 3. The contrast between these views is pictured in Figure 2.3.

Henceforth, in discussing expressions or assertions we will often ignore the distinction between an array and its value, e.g. we will say "the function X" rather than "the function that is the value of the array X". Actually, this is no worse than saying "the integer x" instead of "the integer that is the value of the variable x".

At present, the main reason for emphasizing the functional view is to introduce several mathematical concepts about functions and their sets of results which will allow assertions to be expressed more succinctly.

The first of these concepts is restriction. If X is a function and S is a subset of its domain, then the *restriction of X to S*, written $X \uparrow S$, is the function from S to the codomain of X that gives the same result as X when applied to any member of S. In other words, if $S \subseteq$ **dom** X then

$$\mathbf{dom}\ X \uparrow S = S\ , \tag{1}$$

$$\mathbf{cod}\ X \uparrow S = \mathbf{cod}\ X\ , \tag{2}$$

$$(\forall i \in S)\ (X \uparrow S)\ (i) = X(i)\ . \tag{3}$$

This concept can be used to describe the value of a segment of an array: The value of the segment of X over S is just the restriction $X \uparrow S$ of the value of X to S. For example, the value of the segment of sq over $\boxed{2 \quad 4}$ is $sq \uparrow \boxed{2 \quad 4}$, which is the squaring function from $\boxed{2 \quad 4}$ to the set of integers.

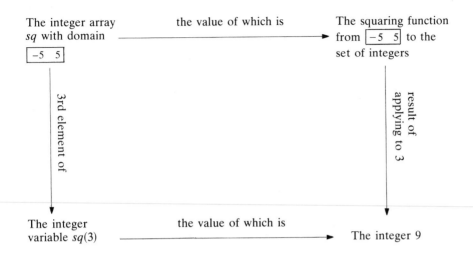

Figure 2.3 Two Views of an Array.

It is easy to see that restriction obeys the following laws:

$$X \upharpoonright \textbf{dom } X = X \quad , \tag{4}$$

$$\text{If } S' \subseteq S \subseteq \textbf{dom } X \text{ then } (X \upharpoonright S) \upharpoonright S' = X \upharpoonright S' \quad , \tag{5}$$

$$X \upharpoonright \{\} = \langle \rangle \quad . \tag{6}$$

In the last line, $\langle \rangle$ denotes the unique function from the empty set to the codomain of X, whose graph must necessarily be empty. In general, we will write $\langle \rangle$ for such a function without explicitly stating its codomain, which will usually be evident from context. Notice that $\langle \rangle$ is the only possible value of an empty array.

A second useful concept is the *image* of a function, which is the set of results that can be obtained by applying the function to all members of its domain. We write $\{X\}$ to denote the image of X. Thus r belongs to $\{X\}$ if and only if there is an i in the domain of X such that $X(i) = r$. For example,

$$\{sq\} = \{0, 1, 4, 9, 16, 25\} \quad ,$$
$$\{sq \upharpoonright \boxed{2 \quad 4}\} = \{4, 9, 16\} \quad .$$

Notice that, if a function maps several arguments into the same result, then its image will be smaller than its domain.

It is easily seen that images obey the following laws:

$$\{X\} \subseteq \textbf{cod } X \quad , \tag{7}$$

$$\text{If } S \subseteq \textbf{dom } X \text{ then } \{X \uparrow S\} \subseteq \{X\} \quad , \tag{8}$$

$$\{X\} = \{\} \text{ if and only if } X = \langle \rangle \quad , \tag{9}$$

$$\text{If } \textbf{dom } X = S \cup S' \text{ then } \{X\} = \{X \uparrow S\} \cup \{X \uparrow S'\} \quad , \tag{10}$$

$$\{X \uparrow \boxed{i}\} = \{X(i)\} \quad , \tag{11}$$

$$\# \{X\} \le \# \textbf{dom } X \text{ when } \textbf{dom } X \text{ is a finite set} \quad . \tag{12}$$

In (11), $\{X(i)\}$ denotes the *singleton* set whose only member is $X(i)$. This standard mathematical usage of curly brackets should not be confused with our notation for an image—since $X(i)$ is not a function.

Finally, to describe relations between sets such as images, we will use the concept of the pointwise extension of a relation. Suppose ρ is a binary relation between values of some type. If S and T are sets of such values, then $S \rho^* T$ is a logical expression that is true if and only if $x \rho y$ is true for all x in S and y in T. The entity ρ^*, which is a binary relation between sets, is called the *pointwise extension* of ρ.

Strictly speaking, we should say that if ρ relates values in some set U to values in some set U', then ρ^* relates subsets of U to subsets of U'. However, we can gloss over the specification of U when ρ is $=$ or $\ne$, which are defined for all kinds of values, or $<$, $\le$, $>$, or $\ge$, which are defined for all kinds of numeric values, and which will be extended to certain other kinds of values in Section 2.3.7. When the latter relations are defined between all members of a set, we will say that the *standard ordering* is defined for that set.

As an example,

$$\{2, 3\} \le^* \{3, 4\} \ , \quad \{2, 3\} \ne^* \{4, 5\}$$

are both true, but

$$\{2, 3\} <^* \{3, 4\} \ , \quad \{2, 3\} =^* \{2, 3\} ., \quad \{2, 3\} \ne^* \{2, 3\}$$

are all false. (The last two examples show that $\ne^*$ is not the negation of $=^*$. Moreover $=^*$ and $\ne^*$ are different from the relations $=$ and $\ne$ between sets. This is why the asterisk is needed to indicate pointwise extension explicitly.)

It is easily seen that for any relation ρ, the pointwise extension of ρ satisfies the following laws:

$$\text{If } S' \subseteq S \text{ and } S \rho^* T \text{ then } S' \rho^* T \quad ,$$
$$\text{If } T' \subseteq T \text{ and } S \rho^* T \text{ then } S \rho^* T' \quad , \tag{13}$$

$$\{\} \rho^* T \quad ,$$
$$S \rho^* \{\} \quad , \tag{14}$$

$$\{x\} \rho^* \{y\} \text{ if and only if } x \rho y \quad , \tag{15}$$

$$(S \cup S') \rho^* T \text{ if and only if both } S \rho^* T \text{ and } S' \rho^* T \quad ,$$
$$S \rho^* (T \cup T') \text{ if and only if both } S \rho^* T \text{ and } S \rho^* T' \quad , \tag{16}$$

Here (14) is justified since any logical expression quantified by "for all x in S" is vacuously true when S is empty.

Very frequently, the set on one side or the other of a pointwise-extended relation will have a single member. We write $x \, \rho^* \, T$ as an abbreviation for $\{x\} \, \rho^* \, T$ and $S \, \rho^* \, y$ as an abbreviation for $S \, \rho^* \, \{y\}$. For example, for any integers a and b, $a <^* a\boxed{\quad b}$ and $a\boxed{\quad b} \leq^* b$.

Some additional laws relate the pointwise extension of different relations:

> If $x \, \rho \, y$ implies $x \, \rho' \, y$ for all x and y,
> then $S \, \rho^* \, T$ implies $S \, \rho'^* \, T$ for all S and T. $\qquad$ (17)

> If $x \, \rho \, y$ and $y \, \rho' \, z$ implies $x \, \rho'' \, z$ for all x, y, and z,
> then $S \, \rho^* \, T$ and $T \, \rho'^* \, U$ implies $S \, \rho''^* \, U$ for all S and U $\quad$ (18)
> and nonempty T.

Notice that (18) does not hold when T is empty, since then $S \, \rho^* \, T$ and $T \, \rho'^* \, U$ are vacuously true, even though $S \, \rho''^* \, U$ may be false. Taking T to be the singleton set $\{y\}$ gives the special case:

> If $x \, \rho \, y$ and $y \, \rho' \, z$ implies $x \, \rho'' \, z$ for all x, y, and z,
> then $S \, \rho^* \, y$ and $y \, \rho'^* \, U$ implies $S \, \rho''^* \, U$ for all S, y, and U. $\quad$ (19)

Both (18) and (19) are particularly useful in the case where ρ, ρ', and ρ'' are the same relation. If $x \, \rho \, y$ and $y \, \rho \, z$ implies $x \, \rho \, z$ for all x, y, and z, then ρ is said to be a *transitive* relation.

The reason for introducing the concepts of restriction, image, and pointwise extension is that they permit many (though hardly all) assertions about arrays to be expressed without explicit quantifiers. For example, in the invariant used in the previous section we wrote

$$(\forall i \in \boxed{a\ \ k}) \; X(i) \leq X(j)$$

to indicate that $X(j)$ is a maximum element of the segment of X over $\boxed{a\ \ k}$. We can now express this assertion more succinctly as

$$\{X \uparrow \boxed{a\ \ k}\} \leq^* X(j) \quad .$$

The reasoning used to justify the assignment $j := k$ when $X(k) \geq X(j)$ can now be given more formally by using the laws developed in this section. Suppose

$$\boxed{a\ \ k} \text{ and } \{X \uparrow \boxed{a\ \ k}\} \leq^* X(j) \text{ and } X(j) \leq X(k) \quad .$$

Since $\leq$ is a transitive relation, (19) implies $\{X \uparrow \boxed{a\ \ k}\} \leq^* X(k)$. On the other hand, (11) and (15) give $\{X \uparrow \boxed{k}\} = \{X(k)\} \leq^* X(k)$. Then, since $\boxed{a\ \ k}$ implies $\boxed{a\ \ k} = \boxed{a\ \ k} \cup \boxed{k}$, laws (10), (5), and (16) give

$$\{X \uparrow \boxed{a\ \ k}\} = \{X \uparrow \boxed{a\ \ k}\} \cup \{X \uparrow \boxed{k}\} \leq^* X(k) \quad .$$

The notations defined in this section are not part of Algol W and can only be used in assertions. (Notice that this prevents any confusion between the use of curly brackets to enclose assertions and the use of such brackets inside assertions to indicate images or other sets.)

Exercises

1. Determine which of the relations $=, \neq, <, \leq, >, \geq$ satisfy which of the following laws:

    (a) (Transitivity) $x \rho y$ and $y \rho z$ implies $x \rho z$

    (b) (Reflexivity) $x \rho x$

    (c) (Antisymmetry) $x \rho y$ and $y \rho x$ implies $x = y$

    (d) (Totality) $x \rho y$ or $y \rho x$

    (e) (Symmetry) $x \rho y$ implies $y \rho x$.

    A relation is said to be *preorder* if it satisfies (a) and (b), a *partial order* if it satisfies (a) through (c), a *total order* if it satisfies (a) through (d), and an *equivalence* if it satisfies (a), (b), and (e).

2. Determine when the law $x \rho y$ implies $x \rho' y$ holds for the various relations listed in Exercise 1. When this law holds ρ' is said to *include* ρ, since the set of pairs related by ρ' includes the set of pairs related by ρ.

2.2.9 Linear Search

We next consider the problem of searching an array segment to find an occurrence of a specified value. More precisely, we want a program that will accept the segment of an array X over $\boxed{a \quad b}$ and a single value y, and will set a variable j to an integer in $\boxed{a \quad b}$ such that $X(j) = y$. However, we must also deal with the possibility that the value of y may not occur in the array segment being searched. For this reason, we introduce a logical variable *present*, and require our program to set *present* to **true** if it is able to achieve the above criterion or to **false** if it is impossible to do so. Thus our program must set *present* and j to satisfy the final assertion

$$\textbf{if } present \textbf{ then } \boxed{a \;\; \boxed{j} \;\; b} \textbf{ and } X(j) = y \textbf{ else } \{X \uparrow \boxed{a \quad b}\} \neq^* y \quad .$$

Notice the use of a logical conditional expression within an assertion. An equivalent but less readable assertion would be *present* **and** $\boxed{a \;\; \boxed{j} \;\; b}$ **and** $X(j) = y$ **or** $\neg$ *present* **and** $\{X \uparrow \boxed{a \quad b}\} \neq^* y$.

The basic idea is to test each $X(j)$, in order of increasing subscript, until either the search criterion is satisfied or the array segment is exhausted. The invariant asserts that if *present* is **true** then the search criterion has been satisfied, while if *present* is **false,** then $\boxed{a \quad j}$ is a subinterval of $\boxed{a \quad b}$ for which the search criterion cannot be satisfied:

$$\textbf{if } present \textbf{ then } \boxed{a \;\; |j| \;\; b} \textbf{ and } X(j)=y$$
$$\textbf{else } \boxed{a \;\; j \;\; b} \textbf{ and } \{X \uparrow \boxed{a \;\; j}\} \neq^* y \quad .$$

This invariant will imply the final assertion if either *present* is **true** or $\boxed{j \quad b}$ is empty. On the other hand, it can be achieved initially by setting j to $a-1$ and *present* to **false.** Thus we obtain a program of the form

$$\{\boxed{a \quad b} \subseteq \textbf{dom } X\}$$
begin
$$j := a-1; \; present := \textbf{false};$$
$$\{\textbf{whileinv: if } present \textbf{ then } \boxed{a \;\; |j| \;\; b} \textbf{ and } X(j)=y$$
$$\textbf{else } \boxed{a \;\; j \;\; b} \textbf{ and } \{X \uparrow \boxed{a \;\; j}\} \neq^* y \}$$
while $\neg$ *present* **and** $(j<b)$ **do**
    begin $j := j+1;$ "Test next element" **end**
end
$$\{\textbf{if } present \textbf{ then } \boxed{a \;\; |j| \;\; b} \textbf{ and } X(j)=y \textbf{ else } \{X \uparrow \boxed{a \;\; b}\} \neq^* y\} \quad .$$

At the beginning of the **while**-statement body the invariant will be true, *present* will be false, and $\boxed{j \quad b}$ will be nonempty, which implies

$$\neg \, present \textbf{ and } \boxed{a \;\; |j+1| \;\; b} \textbf{ and } \{X \uparrow \boxed{a \;\; j}\} \neq^* y \quad .$$

Taking into account the action of $j := j+1$, we see that "Test next element" must meet the specification

$$\{ \neg \, present \textbf{ and } \boxed{a \;\; |j| \;\; b} \textbf{ and } \{X \uparrow \boxed{a \;\; j}\} \neq^* y\}$$
"Test next element"
$$\{\textbf{if } present \textbf{ then } \boxed{a \;\; |j| \;\; b} \textbf{ and } X(j)=y$$
$$\textbf{else } \boxed{a \;\; j \;\; b} \textbf{ and } \{X \uparrow \boxed{a \;\; j}\} \neq^* y \} \quad .$$

If $X(j)=y$ then *present* should obviously be set to **true** by "Test next element", while if $X(j) \neq y$ then *present* can be left **false,** since

$$\{X \uparrow \boxed{a \;\; j}\} = \{X \uparrow \boxed{a \;\; j} \cup \boxed{j}\} = \{X \uparrow \boxed{a \;\; j}\} \cup \{X \uparrow \boxed{j}\} \neq^* y \quad .$$

Thus "Test next element" can be replaced by

$$\textbf{if } X(j)=y \textbf{ then } present := \textbf{true} \quad .$$

The finished program is

$\{\boxed{a \quad b} \subseteq \textbf{dom } X\}$

begin

$j := a - 1;\ present := \textbf{false};$

$\{\textbf{whileinv: if } present \textbf{ then } \boxed{a \quad |j| \quad b} \textbf{ and } X(j) = y$

  $\textbf{else } \boxed{a \quad j \quad b} \textbf{ and } \{X \upharpoonright \boxed{a \quad j}\} \neq^* y\ \}$

while $\lnot\ present$ **and** $(j < b)$ **do**

  begin $j := j + 1;$ **if** $X(j) = y$ **then** $present := $ **true end**

end

$\{\textbf{if } present \textbf{ then } \boxed{a \quad |j| \quad b} \textbf{ and } X(j) = y \textbf{ else } \{X \upharpoonright \boxed{a \quad b}\} \neq^* y\}$.

Termination is assured since the **while**-statement body either sets *present* to **true** or eventually reduces $\boxed{j \quad b}$ to the empty interval. Subscript errors are precluded by $\boxed{a \quad b} \subseteq \textbf{dom } X$ and the presence of $\boxed{a \quad |j| \quad b}$ in the precedent of "Test next element".

The contrast between this program and that of Section 2.2.7 reveals an intrinsic difference between finding a maximum and finding an element with a given value. The property "being a maximum" depends upon the entire array segment in such a way that every element must always be examined. But "being an element with a given value" is a property of the element by itself, so that a successful search can sometimes terminate without examining every element.

It is natural to ask if the above program is the best we can do. Intuitively at least, the answer is yes; in the absence of any information about the values of X, we must continue to test the elements of X over $\boxed{a \quad b}$ until either our search is successful or all elements have been tested, and there is no reason to prefer one order of search over another. However, as we will see in the next section, the situation can be dramatically different if the programmer possesses a priori information about the values of the array being searched.

2.2.10 Binary Search

A much more efficient method for searching an array segment can be used in the special but practically important case where the array segment is known to be *ordered*.

The concept of ordering will be used in many programs. Let X be a function with numerical arguments and results, such as the value of an integer or real array. Then X is *ordered in increasing order* if and only if

$$(\forall\ i \in \textbf{dom } X)\ (\forall\ j \in \textbf{dom } X)\ i < j \textbf{ implies } X(i) \le X(j) \quad .$$

However, increasing order is only one way in which a function can be ordered. To deal with a variety of such possibilities we generalize the relation between $X(i)$ and $X(j)$ to an arbitrary binary relation ρ. Suppose X is a function such that the standard ordering is defined for its domain and ρ is defined for its codomain. Then we write $\mathbf{ord}_\rho\ X$, and say that X is *ordered with respect to* ρ, if and only if

$$(\forall\ i \in \mathbf{dom}\ X)\ (\forall\ j \in \mathbf{dom}\ X)\ i<j\ \mathbf{implies}\ X(i)\ \rho\ X(j)\quad.$$

In this definition we have used **implies** as a logical operator with the following meaning:

p	q	p **implies** q
false	false	true
false	true	true
true	false	false
true	true	true

We have previously used implication as a relationship between assertions: "P implies Q" is an English sentence meaning that every computational state described by P is also described by Q. Now we will also use **implies** (in boldface) as a logical operator (akin to **and** and **or** except that it is not part of Algol W) within assertions. The connection between these usages is that the sentence "P implies Q" is true if and only if the assertion P **implies** Q describes all computational states.

A worthwhile generalization should have several useful special cases and satisfy nontrivial general laws. Useful special cases of $\mathbf{ord}_\rho$ include:

> $\mathbf{ord}_\leq X$: increasing order
> $\mathbf{ord}_< X$: strict increasing order
> $\mathbf{ord}_\geq X$: decreasing order
> $\mathbf{ord}_> X$: strict decreasing order
> $\mathbf{ord}_= X$: all elements have equal values
> $\mathbf{ord}_{\neq} X$: all elements have distinct values   ,

and general laws include:

> If $S \subseteq \mathbf{dom}\ X$ and $\mathbf{ord}_\rho\ X$ then $\mathbf{ord}_\rho\ X \upharpoonright S$,   (1)

> If $\#\ \mathbf{dom}\ X \leq 1$ then $\mathbf{ord}_\rho\ X$,   (2)

> Suppose $\mathbf{dom}\ X = S \cup T$ and $S <^* T$. Then $\mathbf{ord}_\rho\ X$ holds if and only if:
> > (a) $\mathbf{ord}_\rho\ X \upharpoonright S$,
> > and (b) $\mathbf{ord}_\rho\ X \upharpoonright T$,   (3)
> > and (c) $\{X \upharpoonright S\}\ \rho^*\ \{X \upharpoonright T\}$.

Also, since $a\boxed{\quad b\quad c}$ implies $a\boxed{\quad b} <^* b\boxed{\quad c}$, one can obtain the following special case of (3) for intervals:

Suppose $\mathbf{dom}\ X = a\boxed{\quad}c$ and $a\boxed{\quad b\quad}c$. Then $\mathbf{ord}_\rho\ X$ holds if and only if

(a) $\mathbf{ord}_\rho\ X \uparrow a\boxed{\ b\ }$,

and (b) $\mathbf{ord}_\rho\ X \uparrow b\boxed{\ c\ }$, (4)

and (c) $\{X \uparrow a\boxed{\ b\ }\}\ \rho^*\ \{X \uparrow b\boxed{\ c\ }\}$.

Further laws hold for certain relations. If $x\ \rho\ x$ holds for all x, then ρ is said to be *reflexive*; for example $\le$ is reflexive. It is easily seen that

If ρ is reflexive and $\mathbf{dom}\ X = \boxed{a\quad b}$ is nonempty, then $\mathbf{ord}_\rho\ X$ implies $X(a)\ \rho^*\ \{X\}$ and $\{X\}\ \rho^*\ X(b)$. (5)

Another obvious law is:

If $x\ \rho\ y$ implies $x\ \rho'\ y$ for all x and y, then $\mathbf{ord}_\rho\ X$ implies $\mathbf{ord}_{\rho'}\ X$ for all X . (6)

For example, $\mathbf{ord}_<\ X$ implies both $\mathbf{ord}_\le\ X$ and $\mathbf{ord}_{\ne}\ X$.

Returning to the problem at hand, we want a program that will satisfy

$\{\boxed{a\quad b} \subseteq \mathbf{dom}\ X \text{ and } \mathbf{ord}_\le\ X \uparrow \boxed{a\quad b}\}$
"Search"
$\{\textbf{if}\ present\ \textbf{then}\ \boxed{a\quad j\quad b}\ \text{and}\ X(j) = y\ \textbf{else}\ \{X \uparrow \boxed{a\quad b}\} \ne^* y\}$.

The essential idea is that if inspection of an array element gives $X(j) \ne y$, then one can test whether $X(j) < y$ or $X(j) > y$; in the first case the ordering of the segment implies that all elements to the left of $X(j)$ must be less than y, while in the second case the ordering implies that all elements to the right must be greater than y. Either way, one is able to exclude from further search an entire segment of elements rather than a single element.

As with linear search, the heart of our program will be a **while** statement whose invariant asserts that if *present* is **true** then the search criterion has been met, while if *present* is **false** then there is a portion of the interval $\boxed{a\quad b}$ for which the criterion cannot be met. But now this portion can consist of both a left and a right subinterval of $\boxed{a\quad b}$, which enclose the subinterval remaining to be searched. If we use the variables c and d to delimit these subintervals then the invariant is

if *present* **then** $\boxed{a\quad j\quad b}$ **and** $X(j) = y$ **else**
$\boxed{a\quad c\quad d\quad b}$ **and** $\{X \uparrow \boxed{a\quad c}\} \ne^* y$ **and** $\{X \uparrow d\boxed{\quad b}\} \ne^* y$.

This invariant can be achieved with a trivial initialization. On the other hand, it will imply the final assertion if either *present* is **true** or $\boxed{c\quad d}$ is empty. The latter case holds since the partition diagram $\boxed{a\quad c\quad d\quad b}$ implies that

$\boxed{a \quad b} = \boxed{a \quad}c \cup d\boxed{\quad b}$ when $\boxed{c \quad d}$ is empty. Thus we obtain the program skeleton:

> $\{\boxed{a \quad b} \subseteq \textbf{dom } X \text{ and } \textbf{ord}_{\le} X \uparrow \boxed{a \quad b}\}$
> **begin integer** c, d;
> $c := a; d := b; present := \textbf{false};$
> $\{\textbf{whileinv: if } present \textbf{ then } \boxed{a \quad \boxed{j} \quad b} \text{ and } X(j)=y \textbf{ else}$
> $\boxed{a \quad \boxed{c \quad d} \quad b} \text{ and } \{X \uparrow \boxed{a \quad \boxed{c}}\} \ne^* y \text{ and } \{X \uparrow \boxed{d \boxed{\quad} b}\} \ne^* y \}$
> **while** $\urcorner present$ **and** $(c \le d)$ **do**
>   "Reduce $\boxed{c \quad d}$ while maintaining invariant"
> **end**
> $\{\textbf{if } present \textbf{ then } \boxed{a \quad \boxed{j} \quad b} \text{ and } X(j)=y \textbf{ else } \{X \uparrow \boxed{a \quad b}\} \ne^* y\}$.

At the beginning of "Reduce $\boxed{c \quad d}$ while maintaining invariant" we will have

$$\boxed{a \quad \boxed{c \quad d} \quad b} \text{ and } \{X \uparrow \boxed{a \quad \boxed{c}}\} \ne^* y \text{ and } \{X \uparrow \boxed{d \boxed{\quad} b}\} \ne^* y$$
$$\textbf{and } \urcorner present \textbf{ and } c \le d \quad .$$

At this point we want to set j to some subscript in the interval $\boxed{c \quad d}$, which is known to be nonempty, and then do a three-way branch upon whether the jth element is equal to, less than, or greater than y. If we assume that "Pick j" is a statement that sets j to satisfy

$$\{c \le d\} \text{ "Pick } j\text{" } \{c \le j \le d\} \quad ,$$

then we get the following expansion of "Reduce $\boxed{c \quad d}$ while maintaining invariant":

> **begin**
> "Pick j";
> $\{\boxed{a \quad \boxed{c} \quad \boxed{j} \quad d \quad b} \text{ and } \{X \uparrow \boxed{a \quad \boxed{c}}\} \ne^* y$
> $\text{and } \{X \uparrow \boxed{d \boxed{\quad} b}\} \ne^* y \text{ and } \urcorner present \}$
> **if** $X(j)=y$ **then** "Maintain invariant when $X(j)=y$"
>   **else if** $X(j)<y$ **then** "Maintain invariant when $X(j)<y$"
>   **else** "Maintain invariant when $X(j)>y$"
> **end**   .

When $X(j)=y$, since $\boxed{a \quad \boxed{j} \quad b}$ will also hold, we can set $present$ to **true**. When $X(j)<y$, since the subsegment of X over $\boxed{a \quad j} \subseteq \boxed{a \quad b}$ is ordered, we will have $\{X \uparrow \boxed{a \quad j}\} \le^* X(j)$ by (5), which gives $\{X \uparrow \boxed{a \quad j}\} \ne^* y$ by (19) in Section 2.2.8. Thus the invariant will be maintained if we set c to $j+1$.

Similarly, when $X(j)>y$, which implies $\{X \upharpoonright \boxed{j\ \ b}\} \neq^* y$ because of the ordering, we may set d to $j-1$.

At this stage the overall program is:

$\{\boxed{a\ \ b} \subseteq \textbf{dom } X \textbf{ and ord}_\le X \upharpoonright \boxed{a\ \ b}\}$
begin integer c, d;
$c := a;\ d := b;\ present := \textbf{false}$;
$\{$**whileinv:** **if** $present$ **then** $\boxed{a\ \ |j|\ \ b}$ **and** $X(j)=y$ **else**
$\qquad \boxed{a\ |c\ \ d|\ b}$ **and** $\{X \upharpoonright \boxed{a\ \ |c}\} \neq^* y$ **and** $\{X \upharpoonright \boxed{d\ \ |\ \ b}\} \neq^* y \ \}$
while $\neg\, present$ **and** $(c \le d)$ **do**
$\qquad$**begin**
$\qquad$ "Pick j";
$\qquad$ **if** $X(j)=y$ **then** $present := \textbf{true}$
$\qquad\qquad$ **else if** $X(j)<y$ **then** $c := j+1$
$\qquad\qquad$ **else** $d := j-1$
$\qquad$**end**
end
$\{$**if** $present$ **then** $\boxed{a\ \ |j|\ \ b}$ **and** $X(j)=y$ **else** $\{X \upharpoonright \boxed{a\ \ b}\} \neq^* y\}$.

Termination is assured by the fact that each execution of the body of the **while** statement either sets $present$ to **true** or decreases the size of $\boxed{c\ \ d}$, and these operations cannot be repeated indefinitely without falsifying $\neg\, present$ **and** $(c \le d)$. (Note that termination would not be assured if the assignment to c or d was $c := j$ or $d := j$.) The impossibility of subscript errors follows from the fact that "Pick j" will insure $\boxed{a\ |c\ \ |j|\ \ d|\ b}$ before execution of the conditional statement which tests $X(j)$.

Our final task is to fill in the statement "Pick j", which must satisfy

$$\{c \le d\} \text{ "Pick } j \text{"} \{c \le j \le d\}   .$$

But here the problem is not just to produce a correct statement—for example, $j := c$ or $j := d$ would be correct—but to make the program as fast as possible.

Ideally, we would like to minimize the number of array elements that will remain to be searched, which will be $\#\,\boxed{j\ \ |\ d}$ if $X(j)<y$, or $\#\,\boxed{c\ \ |j}$ if $X(j)>y$. But at this stage we don't know whether $X(j)$ is smaller or larger than y. The best we can do is to pick j to minimize the maximum of $\#\,\boxed{j\ \ |\ d}$ and $\#\,\boxed{c\ \ |j}$, which will occur if j is as close as possible to the middle of the interval $\boxed{c\ \ d}$. Since the "middle" is just the mean $(c+d)\,/\,2$, we replace "Pick j" by

$$j := (c+d) \textbf{ div } 2   .$$

But here there is a subtle complication. When $c+d$ is even, this statement will produce $(c+d)/2$, and will obviously meet its specification. But when $c+d$ is odd, the mean will not be an integer, the operation **div** will round the mean downward or upward, and it is not obvious that the necessary condition

$$c \leq d \text{ implies } c \leq (c+d) \text{ div } 2 \leq d$$

will be satisfied.

At first sight, this seems to mean that we are going to have to look at the exact definition of the operation **div**, which would lead to a complicated analysis. (Remember that $c+d$ might be negative.) But in fact our necessary condition is a consequence of a simple property which holds for any reasonable definition of integer division (including the one used in Algol W). All we need to know about integer division rounding is that division by two is *monotone*, i.e.

For all integers i and j, if $i \leq j$ then
$(i \text{ div } 2) \leq (j \text{ div } 2)$.

Because if $c \leq d$ then $(c+c) \leq (c+d) \leq (d+d)$, and by monotonicity, $(c+c)$ **div** $2 \leq (c+d)$ **div** $2 \leq (d+d)$ **div** 2. But in the first and third cases, the divisor is even, so that **div** gives an exact result of c or d respectively. Thus $c \leq (c+d)$ **div** $2 \leq d$.

It is important to realize that the algorithm we have just described, which is called *binary search*, is an order of magnitude faster than the linear search algorithm given in the previous section. The previous search algorithm required a time of the order of $\# \boxed{a \quad b}$—the size of the array segment being searched—at least in the worst case where the element being sought is not present. But binary search requires a time of the order of the logarithm of $\# \boxed{a \quad b}$. Fundamentally, this is because each execution of the **while**-statement body reduces the size of the interval $\boxed{c \quad d}$ to at most half of its previous value. By an argument similar to that in Section 1.3.5, the execution time of the program is bounded by $\alpha + \beta \cdot (\log_2 \# \boxed{a \quad b} + 1)$, where α and β are bounds on the time required for initialization and for the **while**-statement body.

This is our first encounter with a pervasive phenomenon: The efficiency of many algorithms for manipulating arrays (or other representations of sequences of data) can often be improved by an order of magnitude if the arrays are known to be ordered according to some easily tested ordering relation. Curiously, this phenomenon has nothing to do with the "meaning" of the ordering relation. Indeed, it is a common practice to obtain these efficiencies by ordering data in accordance with a completely arbitrary ordering convention. (Of course, this idea is much older than machine computation; it is the rationale behind alphabetic ordering.)

Exercises

1. In general, a function X is said to be *monotone* when

    $$(\forall\ i \in \mathbf{dom}\ X)\ (\forall\ j \in \mathbf{dom}\ X)\ i \leq j \ \textbf{implies}\ X(i) \leq X(j)\ \ ,$$

    to be *injective* when

    $$(\forall\ i \in \mathbf{dom}\ X)\ (\forall\ j \in \mathbf{dom}\ X)\ i \neq j\ \textbf{implies}\ X(i) \neq X(j)\ \ ,$$

    and to be *strictly monotone* when it is both monotone and injective. Prove that X is monotone if and only if $\mathbf{ord}_{\leq}\ X$, injective if and only if $\mathbf{ord}_{\neq}\ X$, and strictly monotone if and only if $\mathbf{ord}_{<}\ X$. In your proof, indicate the roles of the following laws about the standard ordering:

    (a) (Transitivity) $x \leq y$ and $y \leq z$ implies $x \leq z$
    (b) (Reflexivity) $x \leq x$
    (c) (Antisymmetry) $x \leq y$ and $y \leq x$ implies $x = y$
    (d) (Totality) $x \leq y$ or $y \leq x$
    (e) (Definition of $<$) $x < y$ if and only if both
         $x \leq y$ and $\neg\ y \leq x$.

2. Prove law (3) given in the above section. As in the previous exercise, indicate the roles of the laws about the standard ordering.

3. (Suggested by S. Winograd)   On a computer with short word length, unnecessary overflow can be caused by using $j := (c + d)\ \mathbf{div}\ 2$ for "Pick j", since $c + d$ can be out of range even when c, d, and $(c + d)\ \mathbf{div}\ 2$ are all in range. In this situation, a better alternative is $j := c + (d - c)\ \mathbf{div}\ 2$. Use a monotonicity argument to show the correctness of this version of "Pick j".

4. (Suggested by C. J. Rimkus)   The version of binary search developed in this section may perform as many as two tests of $X(j)$ per iteration. Write an alternative version that meets the same specification but only performs a single test in the body of its **while** statement, at the minor expense of always continuing the iteration until $\boxed{c\ \ d}$ is reduced to at most one element. The basic idea is to use an invariant which asserts that if the search criterion is met by some integer in $\boxed{a\ \ b}$ then it is met by some integer in $\boxed{c\ \ d}$, or equivalently if the criterion fails throughout $\boxed{c\ \ d}$ then it fails throughout $\boxed{a\ \ b}$:

    $$\boxed{a\ |c\ \ d|\ b}\ \textbf{and}\ (\{X \uparrow \boxed{c\ \ d}\} \neq^* y\ \textbf{implies}\ \{X \uparrow \boxed{a\ \ b}\} \neq^* y)\ \ .$$

5. Suppose an *increasing zero* of an array X is an integer i such that $X(i) \leq 0$ and $X(i+1) > 0$. Write a program that will accept a segment of the array X over $\boxed{a\ \ b}$ such that $a < b$ and $X(a) \leq 0$ and $X(b) > 0$, and will set i to an increasing zero of X

such that $a \le i < b$. As with binary search, each iteration should roughly halve the size of the segment being searched. Notice that a proof of correctness and termination for this program constitutes a proof of the existence of an increasing zero under the specified precedent.

6. Suppose a *run* in an array segment is a subsegment whose elements all have the same value. Write a program that will accept a nonempty segment of the array X over $\boxed{a \quad b}$ and set i and j to integers such that the segment over $\boxed{i \quad j}$ is (one of) the longest runs in the given segment. The program should require a time of the order of the size of $\boxed{a \quad b}$.

2.3 PROGRAMS THAT SET ARRAYS

In the previous section, we have described programs that use arrays without creating or altering them, i.e. that evaluate array elements but do not assign to them. We now turn to programs that also assign to array elements.

2.3.1 Two Simple Examples

As a first example, consider a program for creating a table of the values of some function such as the factorial. Given a segment of an array F over $\boxed{0 \quad n}$, we want to set each element $F(k)$ of the segment to $k!$, i.e. we want a program satisfying

$$\{\boxed{0 \quad n} \subseteq \textbf{dom } F\}$$
"Tabulate Factorial"
$$\{(\forall\, i \in \boxed{0 \quad n})\; F(i)=i!\} \quad .$$

Trivially, we could iterate over $\boxed{0 \quad n}$ in any order, computing each factorial by means of the algorithm we have already developed in Section 1.3.1:

$$\{\boxed{0 \quad n} \subseteq \textbf{dom } F\}$$
begin integer k;
$k := -1$;
$\{\textbf{whileinv:}\ \boxed{0 \quad k \quad n}\ \textbf{and}\ (\forall\, i \in \boxed{0 \quad k})\; F(i)=i!\}$
while $k < n$ **do**
      begin $k := k+1$; "Compute $k!$ and assign it to $F(k)$" **end**
end
$\{(\forall\, i \in \boxed{0 \quad n})\; F(i)=i!\} \quad .$

But this is ludicrously inefficient, since it does not take advantage of the fact that our method of computing $k!$ will compute all smaller factorials "on the way". Actually, once we have set $F(0)$ to $0!$, if we iterate over increasing k, then we can always obtain $k!$ directly from the stored value of $F(k-1)=(k-1)!$.

In this approach the iterative structure is somewhat different. Each execution of the **while**-statement body still computes a single factorial, but now this computation presupposes the presence of a previously computed factorial. This presupposition is reflected in the invariant by the assertion that $\boxed{0 \quad k}$ must be nonempty. In turn, this causes the initial assertion to contain the requirement that $\boxed{0 \quad n}$ be nonempty:

$$\{\boxed{0 \quad n} \text{ and } \boxed{0 \quad n} \subseteq \text{dom } F\}$$
begin integer k;
$k := 0; \ F(0) := 1;$
$\{\textbf{whileinv: } \boxed{0 \quad k \quad n} \text{ and } (\forall \ i \in \boxed{0 \quad k}) \ F(i)=i!\}$
while $k<n$ **do**
    begin $k := k+1; \ F(k) := k \times F(k-1)$ **end**
end
$\{(\forall \ i \in \boxed{0 \quad n}) \ F(i)=i!\}$.

One can view this program as a modification of the program given in Section 1.3.1, in which the successive values of $k!$ are stored in distinct array elements rather than in a single simple variable. It is common to make this kind of modification when the intermediate results of a computation can be used effectively later in the program.

As a second example, we consider a program for shifting each element of an array segment one place to the left. We want a program satisfying

$$\{\boxed{a \quad b} \text{ and } \boxed{a \quad b} \subseteq \text{dom } X \text{ and } X=X_0\}$$
"Shift left"
$$\{(\forall \ i \in \boxed{a \quad b}) \ X(i)=X_0(i+1)\}$$.

Notice that, since this program is non input-preserving, we must use a ghost identifier X_0 to denote the initial value of the array X.

The program scans from left to right, copying each array element into the element on its left. The invariant asserts that the segment of X over $\boxed{a \quad b}$ is partitioned into a lefthand segment which has already been shifted and a righthand segment which retains its initial value, with a hole in the middle which has been copied but not yet copied into:

$\{\boxed{a \quad b}$ and $\boxed{a \quad b} \subseteq \text{dom } X$ and $X = X_0\}$
begin integer k;
$k := a$;
$\{$**whileinv:** $\boxed{a \quad k \quad b}$ and $(\forall\ i \in \boxed{a \quad}k)\ X(i) = X_0(i+1)$
   and $(\forall\ i \in k\boxed{\quad b})\ X(i) = X_0(i)\ \}$
while $k < b$ **do**
   begin $k := k+1$; $X(k-1) := X(k)$ **end**
end
$\{(\forall\ i \in \boxed{a \quad}b)\ X(i) = X_0(i+1)\}$.

Exercises

1. Write a program that will set $F(k)$ to the kth Fibonacci number $fib(k)$, for each element of the segment of F over $\boxed{0 \quad n}$, where $\boxed{0 \quad n}$ contains at least two elements.

2. As above, but for each element of an arbitrary segment over $\boxed{a \quad b}$. Use $fib(n-2) = fib(n) - fib(n-1)$ to define fib for negative n.

3. By comparing it with the left-shifting program given above, one might expect the following to be a right-shifting program:

   begin integer k; $k := a$;
    while $k < b$ **do begin** $k := k+1$; $X(k) := X(k-1)$ **end**
   end   .

In fact its behavior is quite different since, after the first iteration, the expression $X(k-1)$ yields a value that has been stored during the previous iteration. Describe the behavior of this program by giving an invariant and initial and final assertions.

2.3.2 Inference for Array Assignments

So far we have relied upon the reader's intuition to see that assignment statements which assign to array elements satisfy their specifications. Before proceeding further, we will develop an inference rule which can be used to verify such assignments rigorously.

In the first place, it is easily seen that the inference rule for simple assignment given in Section 1.4.2,

$$\overline{\{P\mid_{X \to E}\}\ X := E\ \{P\}}\quad ,$$

is inadequate to deal with assignments to array elements. If we try to apply this rule to an array assignment such as $X(i) := y$, we get

$$\{P\mid_{X(i) \to y}\}\ X(i) := y\ \{P\}\quad .$$

But it is not clear what $P|_{X(i) \to y}$ means. We might reasonably infer

$$\{y=z\}\ X(i) := y\ \{X(i)=z\}$$

or

$$\{w=z\}\ X(i) := y\ \{w=z\}\quad,$$

but the rule falls apart in a situation such as

$$\{?\}\ X(i) := y\ \{X(j)=z\}\quad.$$

In fact, if $j=i$ we must have $y=z$ before executing $X(i) := y$, while if $j \neq i$ we must have $X(j)=z$. Thus

$$\{(\textbf{if } j=i \textbf{ then } y \textbf{ else } X(j))=z\}\ X(i) := y\ \{X(j)=z\}\quad.$$

But this is hardly a consequence of the inference rule for simple assignment.

As first pointed out in [Hoare 72a, 73], the simplest and cleanest way to reason about array assignments is to regard them as operations which change the value of an entire array rather than a single element. (This idea draws upon earlier work in [McCarthy 67].) Specifically, $X(i) := y$ can be regarded as an operation that assigns to X the function that is just like the old value of X except that it maps i into y.

To formalize this idea we need a notation for describing the variation of a function at a single argument. Suppose X is a function such that i belongs to its domain and y belongs to its codomain. Then we write $[X \mid i\colon y]$ to denote the function such that

$$\textbf{dom } [X \mid i\colon y] = \textbf{dom } X\quad,\tag{1}$$
$$\textbf{cod } [X \mid i\colon y] = \textbf{cod } X\quad,\tag{2}$$
$$[X \mid i\colon y](i) = y\quad,\tag{3}$$
$$\text{If } j \neq i \text{ then } [X \mid i\colon y](j) = X(j)\quad.\tag{4}$$

Using this notation we can regard an assignment statement of the form $X(S) := E$, which assigns to an array element, as an abbreviation for $X := [X \mid S\colon E]$, which assigns to an entire array. The latter form is acceptable to the inference rule for simple assignment, which gives $\{P|_{X \to [X \mid S\colon E]}\}\ X := [X \mid S\colon E]\ \{P\}$. Thus we have the following inference rule [Hoare 72a, 73]:

Array Assignment:

$$\overline{\{P|_{X \to [X \mid S\colon E]}\}\ X(S) := E\ \{P\}}\quad.$$

Notice that the precedent of this inference rule does not contain a condition such as $S \in \textbf{dom } X$ which would preclude subscript errors. The absence of such a condition is consistent with our view that subscript errors are a special kind of nontermination, so that their absence must be shown by informal arguments.

As an example of the use of the array assignment rule, consider the statement $F(k) := k \times F(k-1)$ in the factorial tabulation program given in the previous section. To show the correctness of this program, one must show that

$$\{\boxed{0 \quad k-1 \, k \quad n} \text{ and } (\forall\, i \in \boxed{0 \quad k})\ F(i)=i!\}$$
$$F(k) := k \times F(k-1)$$
$$\{\boxed{0 \quad k \quad n} \text{ and } (\forall\, i \in \boxed{0 \quad k})\ F(i)=i!\} \quad .$$

Let P be the consequent. Then we must show that the precedent implies $P\big|_{F\to[F \mid k:\, k \times F(k-1)]}$, which is

$$\boxed{0 \quad k \quad n} \text{ and } (\forall\, i \in \boxed{0 \quad k})\ [F \mid k:\, k \times F(k-1)]\,(i)=i! \quad .$$

The partition diagram $\boxed{0 \quad k-1 \, k \quad n}$ gives $\boxed{0 \quad k \quad n}$ by erasure, and also implies $k-1 \in \boxed{0 \quad k}$ and $\boxed{0 \quad k} = \boxed{0 \quad k} \cup \boxed{k}$.

According to the last result (along with (3) in Section 2.2.5), in order to show

$$(\forall\, i \in \boxed{0 \quad k})\ [F \mid k:\, k \times F(k-1)]\,(i)=i!$$

it is sufficient to show

$$(\forall\, i \in \boxed{0 \quad k})\ [F \mid k:\, k \times F(k-1)]\,(i)=i!$$

and

$$(\forall\, i \in \boxed{k})\ [F \mid k:\, k \times F(k-1)]\,(i)=i! \quad .$$

But $i \in \boxed{0 \quad k}$ implies $i \neq k$, and $i \in \boxed{k}$ is equivalent to $i=k$. Thus by the definition of $[F \mid k:\, k \times F(k-1)]$, the two conditions above are equivalent to

$$(\forall\, i \in \boxed{0 \quad k})\ F(i)=i!$$

and

$$k \times F(k-1)=k! \quad .$$

The first of these conditions is given directly by the precedent, while the second is a straightforward consequence of the precedent and the definition of the factorial function.

It is evident that repeated application of the array assignment rule can create expressions of the form

$$[\ ... \ [X \mid i_1:\, y_1]\ ...\ \mid i_n:\, y_n] \quad .$$

This kind of nesting is common enough that it is useful to abbreviate it: To stand for the above expression we will write

$$[X \mid i_1:\, y_1\ ...\ \mid i_n:\, y_n] \quad .$$

As with the other concepts we have introduced, there are useful laws about the variation of a function at a single argument. Suppose i and j belong to **dom** X, y and z belong to **cod** X, and $S \subseteq$ **dom** X. Then

$$[X \mid i\colon X(i)] = X \quad , \tag{5}$$
$$[X \mid i\colon y \mid i\colon z] = [X \mid i\colon z] \quad , \tag{6}$$
$$\text{If } i \neq j \text{ then } [X \mid i\colon y \mid j\colon z] = [X \mid j\colon z \mid i\colon y] \quad , \tag{7}$$
$$\text{If } i \in S \text{ then } [X \mid i\colon y] \uparrow S = [X \uparrow S \mid i\colon y] \quad , \tag{8}$$
$$\text{If } i \notin S \text{ then } [X \mid i\colon y] \uparrow S = X \uparrow S \quad , \tag{9}$$
$$\{[X \mid i\colon y]\} = \{X \uparrow (\textbf{dom } X - \{i\})\} \cup \{y\} \quad , \tag{10}$$
$$\{[X \mid i\colon X(j) \mid j\colon X(i)]\} = \{X\} \quad . \tag{11}$$

The last of these laws says that the image of an array value is preserved by an exchange operation. In (10), the operator $-$ denotes the subtraction of sets, i.e. $S - T$ is the set of those values which belong to S but not to T.

Since expressions denoting array values and other functions are useful in assertions, the reader may wonder why such expressions, or even assignment statements that assign values to entire arrays, are not permitted in the programming language itself. Although such features are provided in some programming languages, notably APL and PL/I, their use makes it difficult to control or even estimate the time and space requirements of programs. So we have chosen to use a "lower level" language that forces the user to express his programs at a level of detail much closer to the actual operation of the computer. (An additional pedagogical benefit is that even fairly simple programming tasks lead to programs with significant structure.)

Exercises

1. For the left-shifting program given in Section 2.3.1, and the program given in Exercise 3 following that section, determine the appropriate specification for the array assignment statement, and prove that this specification is met.

2. Prove law (11).
   (*Hint:* Treat the cases $i = j$ and $i \neq j$ separately.)

3. An additional subtlety of array assignment arises when an array occurs in its own subscript. For example, one might expect that, for any variable-denoting phrase L, the two statements $L := 7$ and $L := 7; L := 7$ should have the same effect. But in fact, the two statements $X(X(1)) := 7$ and $X(X(1)) := 7; X(X(1)) := 7$ have different effects if $X(1) = 1$ before execution. Show that the inference rule for array assignment describes this situation correctly.

2.3.3 Sorting by Maximum Finding

Next we consider a program for sorting an array segment, i.e. for rearranging the values of the elements so that the segment becomes ordered in increasing order. One approach is to build upon the program given in Section 2.2.7 for finding the maximum element of a segment; the idea is to find the maximum of the entire segment and move it to the right, then find the maximum of the remaining elements and move it to the right, etc. We begin by writing an invariant that describes the typical situation in the midst of program execution. The array will be divided into two subsegments such that the right subsegment is already ordered, and each element in the left subsegment is smaller or equal to each element in the right subsegment. If we use the variable m to keep track of the right end of the left subsegment, then the invariant is

$$\boxed{a\ \ m\ \ \ \ b}\ \text{and}\ \text{ord}_\leq X \upharpoonright m\boxed{\ \ \ b}\ \text{and}\ \{X \upharpoonright \boxed{a\ \ m}\} \leq^* \{X \upharpoonright m\boxed{\ \ \ b}\}\ \ .$$

The invariant can be achieved by setting m to b, so that $m\boxed{\ \ \ b}$ is empty and $\boxed{a\ \ m} = \boxed{a\ \ b}$, and it implies the final assertion when $\boxed{a\ \ m}$ is empty. Thus we get the program skeleton:

$$\{\boxed{a\ \ b} \subseteq \textbf{dom}\ X\}$$
begin integer m;
$m := b$;
$\{$**whileinv**: $\boxed{a\ \ m\ \ \ \ b}$ and $\text{ord}_\leq X \upharpoonright m\boxed{\ \ \ b}$
     and $\{X \upharpoonright \boxed{a\ \ m}\} \leq^* \{X \upharpoonright m\boxed{\ \ \ b}\}$ $\}$
while $a \leq m$ **do**
    "Maintain invariant while decreasing m"
end
$\{\text{ord}_\leq X \upharpoonright \boxed{a\ \ b}\}$.

Within "Maintain invariant while decreasing m", we want to find a maximum element of the left subsegment and move it to the right of that subsegment. When execution begins, we know that the left subsegment is not empty, so that we can use our previously written program to set a variable j to the subscript of a maximum element in this subsegment. At this point the invariant will still be true, and we will also know that

$$\boxed{a\ \ j\ \ \ m\ \ \ \ b}\ \text{and}\ \{X \upharpoonright \boxed{a\ \ m}\} \leq^* X(j)\ \ .$$

Next we will exchange the elements $X(j)$ and $X(m)$. Since these elements fall outside the subsegment over $m\boxed{}b$, $X \uparrow m\boxed{}b$ will still be ordered. Also $\{X \uparrow \boxed{a\quad m}\} \le^* \{X \uparrow m\boxed{}b\}$ will remain true, since the image $\{X \uparrow \boxed{a\quad m}\}$ will be unaffected by an exchange of elements within the segment over $\boxed{a\quad m}$. But now $X(m)$ will be a maximum of the subsegment over $\boxed{a\quad m}$.

So far "Maintain invariant while decreasing m" has the form:

> **begin integer** j;
> "Set j to the subscript of a maximum of X over $\boxed{a\quad m}$";
> $\{\boxed{a\quad j\quad m\quad b}$ **and ord**$_\le X \uparrow m\boxed{}b$ **and**
> $\qquad \{X \uparrow \boxed{a\quad m}\} \le^* \{X \uparrow m\boxed{}b\}$ **and** $\{X \uparrow \boxed{a\quad m}\} \le^* X(j)\ \}$
> "Exchange $X(j)$ and $X(m)$";
> $\{\boxed{a\quad j\quad m\quad b}$ **and ord**$_\le X \uparrow m\boxed{}b$ **and**
> $\qquad \{X \uparrow \boxed{a\quad m}\} \le^* \{X \uparrow m\boxed{}b\}$ **and** $\{X \uparrow \boxed{a\quad m}\} \le^* X(m)\ \}$
> $\vdots$
>
> **end**   .

At this stage, the fact that all elements in the left subsegment are smaller or equal to those in the right subsegment implies that the right subsegment will remain ordered if we decrease m by one, and the fact that the rightmost element of the left subsegment is a maximum implies that the elements in the left subsegment will still be less than all the elements in the right subsegment if we decrease m by one.

To make this argument more formal, we first note that the partition diagram $\boxed{a\quad j\quad m\quad b}$ implies that $\boxed{a\quad m}$ is not empty, and therefore $\boxed{a\quad m\quad b}$. Then $\{X \uparrow \boxed{a\quad m}\} \le^* \{X \uparrow m\boxed{}b\}$ implies $X(m) \le^* \{X \uparrow m\boxed{}b\}$ which, in conjunction with **ord**$_\le X \uparrow m\boxed{}b$, implies **ord**$_\le X \uparrow \boxed{m\quad b}$. Also, $\{X \uparrow \boxed{a\quad m}\} \le^* X(m)$ and $\{X \uparrow \boxed{a\quad m}\} \le^* \{X \uparrow m\boxed{}b\}$ implies $\{X \uparrow \boxed{a\quad m}\} \le^* \{X \uparrow \boxed{m\quad b}\}$ and therefore $\{X \uparrow \boxed{a\quad m}\} \le^* \{X \uparrow \boxed{m\quad b}\}$. Thus the last assertion in the above program implies

$$\boxed{a\quad m\quad b}\ \textbf{and ord}_\le X \uparrow \boxed{m\quad b}\ \textbf{and}\ \{X \uparrow \boxed{a\quad m}\} \le^* \{X \uparrow \boxed{m\quad b}\}\quad ,$$

which shows that the invariant will still be true if we complete "Maintain invariant while decreasing m" with the statement $m := m-1$.

To finish the program, we replace "Set j to the subscript of a maximum of X over $\boxed{a\quad m}$" by our program for maximum finding, with m substituted for b, and replace "Exchange $X(j)$ and $X(m)$" by an obvious program for exchanging the values of two variables (which will have no effect when the variables are the same). This gives:

$\{\boxed{a \quad b} \subseteq \mathbf{dom}\ X\}$

begin integer m;

$m := b$;

$\{$**whileinv:** $\boxed{a \quad m \quad b}$ **and ord**$_\le X \uparrow m \boxed{\quad b}$

    and $\{X \uparrow \boxed{a \quad m}\} \le^* \{X \uparrow m \boxed{\quad b}\}\ \}$

while $a \le m$ **do**

    begin integer j;

    $\{\boxed{a \quad m} \subseteq \mathbf{dom}\ X$ **and** $\boxed{a \quad m}\}$

        begin integer k;

        $j := a;\ k := a$;

        $\{$**whileinv:** $\boxed{a \quad j \quad k \quad m}$ **and** $\{X \uparrow \boxed{a \quad k}\} \le^* X(j)\}$

        while $k < m$ **do**

            begin $k := k+1$; **if** $X(k) > X(j)$ **then** $j := k$ **end**

        end ;

    $\{\boxed{a \quad j \quad m \quad b}$ **and ord**$_\le X \uparrow m \boxed{\quad b}$ **and**

        $\{X \uparrow \boxed{a \quad m}\} \le^* \{X \uparrow m \boxed{\quad b}\}$ **and** $\{X \uparrow \boxed{a \quad m}\} \le^* X(j)\ \}$

    begin integer t; $t := X(j)$; $X(j) := X(m)$; $X(m) := t$ **end**;

    $\{\boxed{a \quad j \quad m \quad b}$ **and ord**$_\le X \uparrow m \boxed{\quad b}$ **and**

        $\{X \uparrow \boxed{a \quad m}\} \le^* \{X \uparrow m \boxed{\quad b}\}$ **and** $\{X \uparrow \boxed{a \quad m}\} \le^* X(m)\ \}$

    $m := m-1$

    end

end

$\{\mathbf{ord}_\le X \uparrow \boxed{a \quad b}\}$.

Termination is based on the size of $\boxed{a \quad m}$. We have already seen that the precedent $\boxed{a \quad m} \subseteq \mathbf{dom}\ X$ will preclude subscript errors in the maximum-finding subprogram. Subscript errors in the exchange statement are precluded by the precedent $\boxed{a \quad j \quad m \quad b}$ and the initial assertion $\boxed{a \quad b} \subseteq \mathbf{dom}\ X$.

The maximum-finding subprogram will, on the average, take time proportional to half the size of $\boxed{a \quad b}$. The outer **while** statement will repeat this subprogram, along with some statements which require a constant amount of time, once for each member of $\boxed{a \quad b}$. Thus the execution time for the whole program will be of the order of the square of the size of the segment being sorted. This is an order of magnitude worse than what can be achieved by more sophisticated methods. In Section 3.2 we will develop programs that can sort a segment of size n in time of order $n \cdot \log n$.

Exercises

1. Show that the sorting program given above remains correct (and becomes slightly faster) if the test $a \leq m$ in the outer **while** statement is replaced by $a < m$.

2. Give a formal proof that the exchange statement within the sorting program meets the specification given by its surrounding assertions.

3. Complete the following partially written program for removing duplicate values from an ordered array segment. The program should set only X and c (and local variables), should require a time of order $\#\ \boxed{a\ \ b}$, and should not use any local arrays.

$\{\boxed{a\ \ b} \subseteq \text{dom } X \text{ and ord}_\leq X \uparrow \boxed{a\ \ b} \text{ and } X = X_0\}$
begin integer d;
"Achieve invariant";
$\{$**whileinv:** $\boxed{a\ \ c\ \ d\ \ b}$ **and ord**$_< X \uparrow \boxed{a\ \ c}$
$\quad$ **and** $\{X \uparrow \boxed{a\ \ c}\} = \{X_0 \uparrow \boxed{a\ \ d}\}$ **and** $X \uparrow \boxed{d\ \ b} = X_0 \uparrow \boxed{d\ \ b}\ \}$
while $d \leq b$ **do**
$\quad$ "Reduce $\boxed{d\ \ b}$ while maintaining invariant"
end
$\{\boxed{a\ \ c\ \ b} \text{ and ord}_< X \uparrow \boxed{a\ \ c} \text{ and } \{X \uparrow \boxed{a\ \ c}\} = \{X_0 \uparrow \boxed{a\ \ b}\}\}$.

4. Another method for sorting an array segment is to build up an ordered subsegment by repeated insertion of new elements. The simplest way to perform the insertion while maintaining the ordering is to "slide" the new element from one end of the subsegment to its proper destination by repeated exchanges of adjacent elements.

   Complete the following partially written program for sorting by insertion. The program should set only X (and local variables), should require a time of order $(\#\ \boxed{a\ \ b})^2$, and should not use any local arrays.

$\{\boxed{a\ \ b} \subseteq \text{dom } X\}$
begin integer d;
"Achieve invariant";
$\{$**whileinv:** $\boxed{a\ \ d\ \ b}$ **and ord**$_\leq X \uparrow \boxed{a\ \ d}\}$
while $d < b$ **do**
$\quad$ **begin**
$\quad\quad$ $d := d+1$;
$\quad\quad$ "Reestablish invariant by sliding $X(d)$ leftward"
$\quad$ **end**
end
$\{\text{ord}_\leq X \uparrow \boxed{a\ \ b}\}$.

5. Write a program that will set the segment of an integer array D over $\boxed{2\ \ n}$ so that $D(k)$ is the smallest factor of k that is larger than one, i.e. the least integer i such that $i > 1$ and k **rem** $i = 0$. An obvious approach is to test k **rem** i for each k and each i such that $1 < i \leq k$, but you should be able to find a more efficient method.

2.3.4   Rearrangement and Realignment

The sorting program given in the previous section was shown to satisfy the specification

$$\{\boxed{a \quad b} \subseteq \mathbf{dom}\ X\}\ \text{``Sort''}\ \{\mathbf{ord}_{\leq}\ X \restriction \boxed{a \quad b}\}\quad .$$

In fact, this specification is seriously incomplete, since it does not specify that the final value of the segment will be some rearrangement of the initial value. (For example, the specification could be trivially met by a program that sets every element to zero.) Intuitively, it is obvious that the sorting program satisfies this "rearrangement condition" since all the program ever does to change the segment is to repeatedly exchange pairs of elements. But a surprising amount of mathematics is needed to give a rigorous proof of the rearrangement condition, or even a rigorous definition of the concept of rearrangement.

One approach is to formalize the idea that X is a rearrangement of Y when every value occurs the same number of times as a result of X and of Y. Another approach is to formalize the idea that X is a rearrangement of Y when there is a one-to-one correspondence or *bijection* between the domains of these functions such that X and Y give the same result when applied to corresponding values. We will pursue the second approach since, by imposing restrictions on the one-to-one correspondence, we will also be able to define the concept of an order-preserving rearrangement, or *realignment*. Eventually, in Section 2.3.8, we will show that these two approaches are equivalent.

First we will introduce the concepts of function composition and identity functions. Then we will use these concepts to define bijections, and finally we will use bijections to define rearrangement and realignment.

If F is a function from S to T and G is a function from T to U, then $F \cdot G$, called the *composition* of F with G, is the function from S to U such that $(F \cdot G)(i) = G(F(i))$ for all i in S. (Note that the order of composition is the reverse of the order of application.) If S is a set, then I_S, called the *identity function on S*, is the function from S to S such that $I_S(i) = i$ for all i in S.

Composition is associative, and identity functions behave like identity elements with regard to composition, i.e. if F is a function from S to T, G is a function from T to U, and H is a function from U to V, then

$$(F \cdot G) \cdot H = F \cdot (G \cdot H)\quad , \tag{1}$$
$$I_S \cdot F = F\quad , \tag{2}$$
$$F \cdot I_T = F\quad . \tag{3}$$

Further laws relate composition and identity functions to the various concepts about functions which we have introduced previously. Suppose F is a function from S to T, G is a function from T to U, $S' \subseteq S$, $i \in S$, and $j \in T$. Then

$$(F \cdot G) \uparrow S' = (F \uparrow S') \cdot G \quad , \tag{4}$$
$$\{F \cdot G\} = \{G \uparrow \{F\}\} \quad , \tag{5}$$
$$\{I_S \uparrow S'\} = S' \quad , \tag{6}$$
$$[F \mid i\colon j] \cdot G = [F \cdot G \mid i\colon G(j)] \quad , \tag{7}$$
If $\mathbf{ord}_< F$ and $\mathbf{ord}_\rho G$ then $\mathbf{ord}_\rho F \cdot G \quad , \tag{8}$
$$\mathbf{ord}_< I_S \quad . \tag{9}$$

A function F is said to be *injective* when

$$(\forall\, i \in \mathbf{dom}\ F)\ (\forall\, j \in \mathbf{dom}\ F)\ i \neq j \text{ implies } F(i) \neq F(j) \quad ,$$

i.e. when for every k in its codomain there is at most one i in its domain such that $F(i) = k$. When the standard ordering is defined for its domain, F is injective if and only if $\mathbf{ord}_{\neq} F$. (See Exercise 1 after Section 2.2.10.) However, the concept of an injective function is meaningful for any domain.

On the other hand, F is said to be *surjective* when $\{F\} = \mathbf{cod}\ F$, i.e. when for every k in its codomain there is at least one i in its domain such that $F(i) = k$. When F is both injective and surjective, i.e. when for every k in its codomain there is exactly one i in its domain, it is called a *bijection*, or sometimes a *one-to-one correspondence*.

Now suppose F is a function from S to T and F^{-1} is a function from T to S such that

$$F \cdot F^{-1} = I_S \text{ and } F^{-1} \cdot F = I_T \quad .$$

Then F^{-1} is called an *inverse* of F. In fact, a function cannot have more than one inverse, since if F^{-1} and $F^{-1'}$ are both inverses of F then

$$F^{-1'} = F^{-1'} \cdot I_S = F^{-1'} \cdot F \cdot F^{-1} = I_T \cdot F^{-1} = F^{-1} \quad .$$

(Strictly, we should write

$$\ldots = F^{-1'} \cdot I_S = F^{-1'} \cdot (F \cdot F^{-1}) = (F^{-1'} \cdot F) \cdot F^{-1} = \ldots \quad .$$

However, we will often elide the application of an associativity law by omitting parentheses in multiple compositions.) Thus we are justified in calling F^{-1} *the* inverse of F.

However, not every function possesses an inverse. Indeed:

A function possesses an inverse if and only if it is a bijection. (10)

To see this, suppose F possesses an inverse F^{-1}. If i and j are distinct members of $\mathbf{dom}\ F$, we cannot have $F(i) = F(j)$ since this would imply $i = F^{-1}(F(i)) = F^{-1}(F(j)) = j$; thus F is injective. Moreover, if k is a member of $\mathbf{cod}\ F$, then $F^{-1}(k)$ is a member of $\mathbf{dom}\ F$ such that $F(F^{-1}(k)) = k$, so that $k \in \{F\}$; thus F is surjective. On the other hand, if F is a bijection then F^{-1} can be taken to be the function which maps each k in $\mathbf{cod}\ F$ into the unique i in $\mathbf{dom}\ F$ such that $F(i) = k$.

If the standard ordering is defined for its domain and codomain, a function F is said to be *monotone* when

$$(\forall\ i \in \textbf{dom}\ F)\ (\forall\ j \in \textbf{dom}\ F)\ i \leq j \ \textbf{implies}\ F(i) \leq F(j)\ \ .$$

It is easy to see that $\textbf{ord}_{\leq}\ F$ holds if and only if F is monotone, and that $\textbf{ord}_{<}\ F$ holds if and only if F is both monotone and injective. (See Exercise 1 after Section 2.2.10.)

Suppose B is a bijection from S to T and C is a bijection from T to U. Then

$$B \cdot C \cdot C^{-1} \cdot B^{-1} = B \cdot I_T \cdot B^{-1} = B \cdot B^{-1} = I_S\ \ ,$$

and

$$C^{-1} \cdot B^{-1} \cdot B \cdot C = C^{-1} \cdot I_T \cdot C = C^{-1} \cdot C = I_U\ \ .$$

Moreover, if $\textbf{ord}_{<}\ B$ and $\textbf{ord}_{<}\ C$ then, by (8), $\textbf{ord}_{<}\ B \cdot C$. Thus

> If B and C are (monotone) bijections then $B \cdot C$ is a (monotone) bijection with $(B \cdot C)^{-1} = C^{-1} \cdot B^{-1}$.   (11)

Here we are using a common mathematical convention for combining two similar propositions: the above statement is true if either all the parenthesized phrases are included or if they are all omitted.

Since $I_S \cdot I_S = I_S$ and, by (9), $\textbf{ord}_{<}\ I_S$,

> I_S is a (monotone) bijection with $I_S^{-1} = I_S$.   (12)

If B is a bijection from S to T then $B \cdot B^{-1} = I_S$ and $B^{-1} \cdot B = I_T$, and interchanging the order of these equations shows that B^{-1} is a bijection from T to S whose inverse is B. Moreover, if $\textbf{ord}_{<}\ B$ then $\textbf{ord}_{<}\ B^{-1}$. To see this, suppose i and j are members of $\textbf{cod}\ B = \textbf{dom}\ B^{-1}$ such that $i < j$. We cannot have $B^{-1}(i) > B^{-1}(j)$, since $\textbf{ord}_{<}\ B$ would imply $i = B(B^{-1}(i)) > B(B^{-1}(j)) = j$. We cannot have $B^{-1}(i) = B^{-1}(j)$ since $i \neq j$ and B^{-1} is injective. Therefore we must have $B^{-1}(i) < B^{-1}(j)$. Thus

> If B is a (monotone) bijection, then B^{-1} is a (monotone) bijection with $(B^{-1})^{-1} = B$.   (13)

This development should seem familiar to readers who know abstract algebra. For a given set S, functions from S to S form a monoid with composition as multiplication and I_S as the identity element, and bijections from S to S (often called permutations) form a group that is a subalgebra of this monoid. Moreover, monotone bijections also form a group that is a subalgebra of the monoid. (However, we are interested in functions between arbitrary sets, which have a richer structure than an ordinary algebra: sets and the functions between them form a category in which bijections are the isomorphisms.)

Additional laws establish that "interchange" functions and functions between singleton sets are bijections. We leave it to the reader to verify that:

If $i \in S$ and $j \in S$ then $[I_S \mid i{:}\, j \mid j{:}\, i]$ is a
bijection which is its own inverse. $\quad\quad$ (14)

The function B from $\{i\}$ to $\{j\}$ such that $B(i) = j$ is a
monotone bijection with an inverse such that $B^{-1}(j) = i$. $\quad$ (15)

At last we can define rearrangement and realignment. Suppose X and Y are functions with the same codomain. We write $X \sim Y$, and say X is a *rearrangement* of Y, when there is a bijection B from **dom** X to **dom** Y such that $X = B \cdot Y$. We write $X \simeq Y$, and say X is a *realignment* of Y, when there is a monotone bijection B from **dom** X to **dom** Y such that $X = B \cdot Y$. Obviously,

If $X \simeq Y$ then $X \sim Y$. $\quad\quad$ (16)

If there are (monotone) bijections B and C such that $X = B \cdot Y$ and $Y = C \cdot Z$, then $X = B \cdot C \cdot Z$ where, by (11), $B \cdot C$ is a (monotone) bijection. Therefore

(Transitivity)
If $X \sim Y$ and $Y \sim Z$ then $X \sim Z$, $\quad\quad$ (17)
If $X \simeq Y$ and $Y \simeq Z$ then $X \simeq Z$.

By similar reasoning, (12) leads to

(Reflexivity)
$X \sim X$, $\quad\quad$ (18)
$X \simeq X$,

and (13) leads to

(Symmetry)
If $X \sim Y$ then $Y \sim X$, $\quad\quad$ (19)
If $X \simeq Y$ then $Y \simeq X$.

Thus $\sim$ and $\simeq$ are equivalence relations.

Two more laws establish that exchanging array elements creates a rearrangement and that functions with singleton domains and equal results are realignments of each other. From (14) and (7) we have

If $i \in$ **dom** X and $j \in$ **dom** X then
$[X \mid i{:}\, X(j) \mid j{:}\, X(i)] \sim X$, $\quad\quad$ (20)

and from (15) we have

If **dom** $X = \{i\}$ and **dom** $Y = \{j\}$ and $X(i) = Y(j)$
then $X \simeq Y$. $\quad\quad$ (21)

Further laws show that rearrangement preserves images and realignment preserves ordering. If there is a bijection B such that $X = B \cdot Y$ then (5) gives $\{X\} = \{B \cdot Y\} = \{Y \mathbin{\lceil} \{B\}\} = \{Y \mathbin{\lceil} \mathbf{cod}\ B\} = \{Y \mathbin{\lceil} \mathbf{dom}\ Y\} = \{Y\}$. Moreover, if $\mathbf{ord}_< B$ and $\mathbf{ord}_\rho\ Y$ then (8) gives $\mathbf{ord}_\rho\ X$. Thus

$$\text{If } X \sim Y \text{ then } \{X\} = \{Y\} \quad , \tag{22}$$

and

$$\text{If } X \simeq Y \text{ and } \mathbf{ord}_\rho\ Y \text{ then } \mathbf{ord}_\rho\ X \quad . \tag{23}$$

Finally, we note that if $X = B \cdot Y$ then $X \cdot Z = B \cdot Y \cdot Z$. Thus rearrangement and realignment are both preserved by composition on the right:

$$\begin{aligned}
&\text{If } X \sim Y \text{ then } X \cdot Z \sim Y \cdot Z \quad , \\
&\text{If } X \simeq Y \text{ then } X \cdot Z \simeq Y \cdot Z \quad .
\end{aligned} \tag{24}$$

With these mathematical preliminaries, we can return to the sorting problem. To specify the rearrangement condition, i.e. that the final value of $X \mathbin{\lceil} \boxed{a\ \ b}$ is a rearrangement of the initial value, we use a ghost identifier:

$$\{\boxed{a\ \ b} \subseteq \mathbf{dom}\ X \text{ and } X = X_0\} \text{ ``Sort'' } \{X \mathbin{\lceil} \boxed{a\ \ b} \sim X_0 \mathbin{\lceil} \boxed{a\ \ b}\} \quad .$$

By reflexivity, the initial assertion implies $X \mathbin{\lceil} \boxed{a\ \ b} \sim X_0 \mathbin{\lceil} \boxed{a\ \ b}$, so that this specification can be proved by showing that every part of the program preserves $X \mathbin{\lceil} \boxed{a\ \ b} \sim X_0 \mathbin{\lceil} \boxed{a\ \ b}$. In other words, we must show that each program part will continue to meet its specification if we add this condition to all assertions. This is trivial for the parts that do not assign to the array X. The only interesting part is "Exchange $X(j)$ and $X(m)$", which can be proved as follows:

$$\{\boxed{a\ \ |j|\ \ m|\ \ b} \text{ and } X \mathbin{\lceil} \boxed{a\ \ b} \sim X_0 \mathbin{\lceil} \boxed{a\ \ b}\}$$
$$\{\boxed{a\ \ |j|\ \ m|\ \ b} \text{ and } [X \mathbin{\lceil} \boxed{a\ \ b} \mid j{:}\ X(m) \mid m{:}\ X(j)] \sim X_0 \mathbin{\lceil} \boxed{a\ \ b}\}$$
$$\{[X \mid j{:}\ X(m) \mid m{:}\ X(j)] \mathbin{\lceil} \boxed{a\ \ b} \sim X_0 \mathbin{\lceil} \boxed{a\ \ b}\}$$
$$t := X(j);$$
$$\{[X \mid j{:}\ X(m) \mid m{:}\ t] \mathbin{\lceil} \boxed{a\ \ b} \sim X_0 \mathbin{\lceil} \boxed{a\ \ b}\}$$
$$X(j) := X(m);$$
$$\{[X \mid m{:}\ t] \mathbin{\lceil} \boxed{a\ \ b} \sim X_0 \mathbin{\lceil} \boxed{a\ \ b}\}$$
$$X(m) := t$$
$$\{X \mathbin{\lceil} \boxed{a\ \ b} \sim X_0 \mathbin{\lceil} \boxed{a\ \ b}\} \quad .$$

The first step is a consequence of transitivity and (20), and the second step is a consequence of (8) in Section 2.3.2. (A similar argument applies to the insertion sorting program of Exercise 4 after Section 2.3.3.)

The concept of realignment plays no role in the specification of the sorting program since the ordering of the final value of X is not affected by the ordering of the initial value. A simple example of the use of realignment is the following annotation of the left-shifting program, with assertions that avoid the quantifiers used in Section 2.3.1:

$$\{ \boxed{a \quad b} \text{ and } \boxed{a \quad b} \subseteq \text{dom } X \text{ and } X = X_0 \}$$
begin integer k;

$k := a$;

$\{ \textbf{whileinv: } \boxed{a \quad k \quad b} \text{ and } X \restriction (\boxed{a \quad k} \cup k\boxed{\quad b}) \simeq X_0 \restriction a\boxed{\quad b} \}$
while $k < b$ **do**

      begin $k := k+1; \ X(k-1) := X(k)$ **end**

end

$$\{ X \restriction \boxed{a \quad b} \simeq X_0 \restriction a\boxed{\quad b} \} \ .$$

Notice that the invariant expresses the idea of an array with a hole in the middle by using a function whose domain $\boxed{a \quad k} \cup k\boxed{\quad b}$ is not an interval.

Exercises

1. Prove law (5) in the above section.

2. Show the following generalization of (8): If $\textbf{ord}_\rho \ F$ and $\textbf{ord}_{\rho'} \ G$ then $\textbf{ord}_{\rho''} \ F \cdot G$, where ρ'' is expressed in terms of ρ and ρ' by

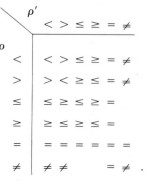

3. Show that if B is a monotone bijection from an interval to an interval, then there must be a constant s such that, for all $i \in \textbf{dom } B$, $B(i) = i+s$. This implies that if $X \simeq Y$ and the domains of X and Y are both intervals, then there is an s such that $X(i) = Y(i+s)$, i.e. X is a "shift" of Y.

4. Actually, our specification of "Sort" is still too weak, since we should also show that the elements of X outside of the segment over $\boxed{a \quad b}$ are left unchanged. Show that the assertion $X \restriction (\textbf{dom } X - \boxed{a \quad b}) = X_0 \restriction (\textbf{dom } X - \boxed{a \quad b})$ can be added to the consequent of the program.

2.3.5 Partitioning

We next consider a program to rearrange an array segment so that it is partitioned into a subsegment whose values are smaller or equal to a given number r, and a second subsegment whose values are larger than r. Specifically, we want a program that, when given the segment of X over $\boxed{a \quad b}$ and a number r, will rearrange the segment and set an integer variable c so that

$$\boxed{a \;\; c \;\; b} \text{ and } \{X \uparrow \boxed{a \;\; c}\} \leq^* r \text{ and } r <^* \{X \uparrow \boxed{c \;\; b}\} \quad .$$

In the midst of program execution, there will be three subsegments, with values known to be at most r on the left, values known to be larger than r on the right, and values that remain to be processed in the middle. Thus the invariant will be

$$\boxed{a \;\; c \;\; d \;\; b} \text{ and } \{X \uparrow \boxed{a \;\; c}\} \leq^* r \text{ and } r <^* \{X \uparrow \boxed{d \;\; b}\} \quad .$$

This invariant can be achieved initially by making $\boxed{a \;\; c}$ and $\boxed{d \;\; b}$ empty and $\boxed{c \;\; d}$ equal to $\boxed{a \;\; b}$, and it will imply the final result when $\boxed{c \;\; d}$ is empty. Thus we get:

$$\{\boxed{a \;\; b} \subseteq \textbf{dom } X\}$$
begin integer d;
$c := a;\ d := b$;
$\{$**whileinv:** $\boxed{a \;\; c \;\; d \;\; b}$
$\quad$ and $\{X \uparrow \boxed{a \;\; c}\} \leq^* r$ and $r <^* \{X \uparrow \boxed{d \;\; b}\} \}$
while $c \leq d$ **do**
$\quad$ "Reduce $\boxed{c \;\; d}$ while maintaining invariant"
end
$$\{\boxed{a \;\; c \;\; b} \text{ and } \{X \uparrow \boxed{a \;\; c}\} \leq^* r \text{ and } r <^* \{X \uparrow \boxed{c \;\; b}\}\} \quad .$$

For the body of the **while** statement, a straightforward approach is to compare some element in the middle subsegment with r, move it to the left or right of the middle subsegment by exchange, and then increase c or decrease d to incorporate the tested element into the left or right subsegment. A portion of the exchanges can be avoided if the tested element is already at the left (or equally well at the right) of the middle segment. Thus "Reduce $\boxed{c \;\; d}$ while maintaining invariant" can be filled in with

$$\textbf{if } X(c) \le r \textbf{ then } c := c+1 \textbf{ else}$$
$$\textbf{begin } \text{``Exchange } X(c) \text{ and } X(d)\text{''}; \; d := d-1 \textbf{ end} \quad .$$

But this still does an unnecessary amount of exchanging. A better approach is to notice that $\boxed{c \quad d}$ can be reduced without any rearrangement if either $X(c) \le r$ or $X(d) > r$:

$$\textbf{if } X(c) \le r \textbf{ then } c := c+1 \textbf{ else}$$
$$\textbf{if } X(d) > r \textbf{ then } d := d-1 \textbf{ else} \ldots \quad .$$

In the remaining case we can exchange $X(c)$ and $X(d)$ to achieve $X(c) \le r$ and $X(d) > r$, which suggests that we can then both increase c and decrease d. But this operation will violate the partition diagram $\boxed{a \mid c \quad d \mid b}$ by making $\boxed{c \quad d}$ irregular unless $\# \boxed{c \quad d} \ge 2$ beforehand. Fortunately, $X(c) \le r$ and $X(d) > r$ implies $X(c) \ne X(d)$, and therefore $c \ne d$, so that $\# \boxed{c \quad d} \ge 2$.

The final program is:

$$\{\boxed{a \quad b} \subseteq \textbf{dom } X\}$$
$$\textbf{begin integer } d;$$
$$c := a; \; d := b;$$
$$\{\textbf{whileinv: } \boxed{a \mid c \quad d \mid b}$$
$$\text{and } \{X \uparrow \boxed{a \quad c}\} \le^* r \text{ and } r <^* \{X \uparrow \boxed{d \quad b}\} \; \}$$
$$\textbf{while } c \le d \textbf{ do}$$
$$\qquad \textbf{if } X(c) \le r \textbf{ then } c := c+1 \textbf{ else}$$
$$\qquad \textbf{if } X(d) > r \textbf{ then } d := d-1 \textbf{ else}$$
$$\qquad\qquad \textbf{begin}$$
$$\qquad\qquad \{\boxed{c \quad\quad d}\}$$
$$\qquad\qquad \textbf{begin integer } t; \; t := X(c); \; X(c) := X(d); \; X(d) := t \textbf{ end};$$
$$\qquad\qquad c := c+1; \; d := d-1$$
$$\qquad\qquad \textbf{end}$$
$$\textbf{end}$$
$$\{\boxed{a \mid c \quad b} \text{ and } \{X \uparrow \boxed{a \quad c}\} \le^* r \text{ and } r <^* \{X \uparrow \boxed{c \quad b}\}\} \quad .$$

Termination and the impossibility of subscript errors are obvious. Since the exchange operation is the only part of the program that alters the array, the argument given in the previous section shows that the final value of X over $\boxed{a \quad b}$ is a rearrangement of the initial value.

It is easily seen that the maximum time taken to partition an array segment of size n is of order n.

2.3.6 Merging

Next we consider *merging*. The basic problem is to copy the combined values of two ordered array segments into a single segment, while performing a rearrangement so that the final segment is ordered. Trivially, we could copy one segment after the other and then sort the result, but a much faster program is possible if we take advantage of the ordering of the input segments.

Let the input segments be X over $\boxed{ax \quad bx}$ and Y over $\boxed{ay \quad by}$, and let the output segment be Z over $\boxed{az \quad bz}$. For simplicity, we assume that the output segment is exactly the right size to hold the result. Then the program specification is:

$$\{ \boxed{ax \quad bx} \subseteq \textbf{dom } X \textbf{ and } \boxed{ay \quad by} \subseteq \textbf{dom } Y \textbf{ and } \boxed{az \quad bz} \subseteq \textbf{dom } Z$$

$$\textbf{and ord}_{\leq} X \uparrow \boxed{ax \quad bx} \textbf{ and ord}_{\leq} Y \uparrow \boxed{ay \quad by}$$

$$\textbf{and } \# \boxed{ax \quad bx} + \# \boxed{ay \quad by} = \# \boxed{az \quad bz} \}$$

"Merge"

$$\{ \textbf{ord}_{\leq} Z \uparrow \boxed{az \quad bz} \} \quad .$$

Just as with the sorting and partitioning programs, we will postpone the problem of showing that the output segment is a rearrangement of the combined input segments.

The basic idea is to scan all three segments from left to right, while copying individual elements from X or Y into Z. Thus each array segment will be divided into a left subsegment containing copied values and a right subsegment containing uncopied values (or unused space in the case of Z). We expect that the Z segment will be ordered as it is built up, and that every copied value will be smaller or equal to every uncopied value. The latter condition insures that the uncopied values can eventually be moved into Z without disturbing the values that are already present. Thus if we use the variables kx, ky, and kz to keep track of the scanning positions in the three segments, we will have the invariant

$$\boxed{ax \quad kx \quad bx} \textbf{ and } \boxed{ay \quad ky \quad by} \textbf{ and } \boxed{az \quad kz \quad bz}$$

$$\textbf{and ord}_{\leq} Z \uparrow \boxed{az \quad kz}$$

$$\textbf{and } \{ Z \uparrow \boxed{az \quad kz} \} \leq^* \{ X \uparrow \boxed{kx \quad bx} \} \cup \{ Y \uparrow \boxed{ky \quad by} \}$$

$$\textbf{and } \# \boxed{kx \quad bx} + \# \boxed{ky \quad by} = \# \boxed{kz \quad bz} \quad .$$

The last line asserts that there is exactly enough space left in Z to accommodate the uncopied values.

The obvious initialization is to make the three lefthand segments empty, and we can terminate when $\boxed{kz \quad bz}$ is empty, or equivalently when both $\boxed{kx \quad bx}$ and $\boxed{ky \quad by}$ are empty. This gives the program form:

$$\{ \boxed{ax \quad bx} \subseteq \textbf{dom } X \textbf{ and } \boxed{ay \quad by} \subseteq \textbf{dom } Y \textbf{ and } \boxed{az \quad bz} \subseteq \textbf{dom } Z$$
$$\textbf{and ord}_{\leq} X \uparrow \boxed{ax \quad bx} \textbf{ and ord}_{\leq} Y \uparrow \boxed{ay \quad by}$$
$$\textbf{and } \# \boxed{ax \quad bx} + \# \boxed{ay \quad by} = \# \boxed{az \quad bz} \}$$

begin integer kx, ky, kz;

$kx := ax$; $ky := ay$; $kz := az$;

{**whileinv**: as above}

while $kz \leq bz$ **do**

  "Copy one element"

end

$\{\textbf{ord}_{\leq} Z \uparrow \boxed{az \quad bz}\}$.

To preserve the condition that copied values must be smaller or equal to uncopied values, "Copy one element" must move the smallest member of $\{X \uparrow \boxed{kx \quad bx}\} \cup \{Y \uparrow \boxed{ky \quad by}\}$ into $Z \uparrow \boxed{az \quad kz}$. Since X and Y are ordered, this smallest member will be either $X(kx)$ or $Y(ky)$. At first sight, it might appear sufficient to compare these two components, but this overlooks the possibility that one of them may not exist. We do not know that *both* of the segments over $\boxed{kx \quad bx}$ and $\boxed{ky \quad by}$ are nonempty. If only one of them is nonempty, then its leftmost component should be copied without being compared with a nonexistent component of the other segment.

Thus "Copy one element" has the form:

if $\left(\textbf{if } ky > by \textbf{ then true else if } kx > bx \textbf{ then false else } X(kx) \leq Y(ky)\right)$
  then $\{ \boxed{kx \quad bx} \textbf{ and } \boxed{kz \quad bz}$
    and $X(kx) \leq^{*} \{X \uparrow \boxed{kx \quad bx}\} \cup \{Y \uparrow \boxed{ky \quad by}\} \}$
    "Copy X"
  else $\{ \boxed{ky \quad by} \textbf{ and } \boxed{kz \quad bz}$
    and $Y(ky) \leq^{*} \{X \uparrow \boxed{kx \quad bx}\} \cup \{Y \uparrow \boxed{ky \quad by}\} \}$
    "Copy Y" .

Notice the use of a logical conditional expression to avoid evaluating $X(kx) \leq Y(ky)$ in a context that could cause a subscript error.

In "Copy X" we will perform $Z(kz) := X(kx)$ to copy the least uncopied value, $kx := kx+1$ to exclude this component from the uncopied segment of X, and $kz := kz+1$ to include it in the copied segment of Z.

The fact that the previously copied values are all smaller or equal to the uncopied values, including $X(kx)$, insures that $Z \uparrow \boxed{az \quad kz}$ will remain ordered. Moreover, the fact that $X(kx)$ is a least uncopied value insures that the copied values will continue to be smaller or equal to the uncopied values.

The development of "Copy Y" is similar. The final program is:

$$\{\;\fbox{$ax \quad bx$} \subseteq \textbf{dom } X \textbf{ and } \fbox{$ay \quad by$} \subseteq \textbf{dom } Y \textbf{ and } \fbox{$az \quad bz$} \subseteq \textbf{dom } Z$$

$$\textbf{and ord}_\le X \uparrow \fbox{$ax \quad bx$} \textbf{ and ord}_\le Y \uparrow \fbox{$ay \quad by$}$$

$$\textbf{and } \# \fbox{$ax \quad bx$} + \# \fbox{$ay \quad by$} = \# \fbox{$az \quad bz$} \;\}$$

begin integer kx, ky, kz;

$kx := ax; \; ky := ay; \; kz := az;$

$\{\textbf{whileinv: } \fbox{$ax \quad kx \quad bx$} \textbf{ and } \fbox{$ay \quad ky \quad by$} \textbf{ and } \fbox{$az \quad kz \quad bz$}$

$\quad \textbf{and ord}_\le Z \uparrow \fbox{$az \quad kz$}$

$\quad \textbf{and } \{Z \uparrow \fbox{$az \quad kz$}\} \le^* \{X \uparrow \fbox{$kx \quad bx$}\} \cup \{Y \uparrow \fbox{$ky \quad by$}\}$

$\quad \textbf{and } \# \fbox{$kx \quad bx$} + \# \fbox{$ky \quad by$} = \# \fbox{$kz \quad bz$} \;\}$

while $kz \le bz$ **do**

$\quad$ **if** $\big($**if** $ky > by$ **then true else if** $kx > bx$ **then false else**

$\qquad X(kx) \le Y(ky)\big)$

$\quad$ **then** $\{\fbox{$kx \quad bx$} \textbf{ and } \fbox{$kz \quad bz$}$

$\qquad \textbf{and } X(kx) \le^* \{X \uparrow \fbox{$kx \quad bx$}\} \cup \{Y \uparrow \fbox{$ky \quad by$}\}\}$

$\qquad$ **begin** $Z(kz) := X(kx); \; kx := kx + 1; \; kz := kz + 1$ **end**

$\quad$ **else** $\{\fbox{$ky \quad by$} \textbf{ and } \fbox{$kz \quad bz$}$

$\qquad \textbf{and } Y(ky) \le^* \{X \uparrow \fbox{$kx \quad bx$}\} \cup \{Y \uparrow \fbox{$ky \quad by$}\}\}$

$\qquad$ **begin** $Z(kz) := Y(ky); \; ky := ky + 1; \; kz := kz + 1$ **end**

end

$\{\textbf{ord}_\le Z \uparrow \fbox{$az \quad bz$}\}$.

Termination is based on the size of $\fbox{$kz \quad bz$}$. The impossibility of subscript errors is left to the reader. The time required by the program is obviously of order $\# \fbox{$az \quad bz$}$.

It is tempting to replace the logical expression

$\quad$ **if** $ky > by$ **then true else**

$\qquad$ **if** $kx > bx$ **then false else** $X(kx) \le Y(ky)$

by the more compact expression

$$(ky > by) \textbf{ or } (kx \le bx) \textbf{ and } \big(X(kx) \le Y(ky)\big)\quad,$$

but the latter expression does not make it obvious that the array designators $X(kx)$ and $Y(ky)$ will only be evaluated when the appropriate segments are nonempty. In fact, this situation hinges upon a rather subtle point of language design. The expressions E_1 **or** E_2 and E_1 **and** E_2 have the property that, if their first operand is true or false respectively, then the result is independent of the second operand. In some programming languages, including

Algol W and LISP, the second operand will not be evaluated under these circumstances, so that the more compact expression given above is correct. However, in many other languages, there is no guarantee that the second operand will not be evaluated, so that the more cumbersome conditional expression must be used.

It may be noted that the merge program involves some redundant testing. For example, before copying an element from X to Z, the program will have tested whether the right subsegment of Y is empty. Yet the next time around the **while**-loop this test will be repeated, despite the fact that its outcome cannot be different. In Section 4.2.7 we will develop a version of the program that avoids this inefficiency.

2.3.7 Concatenation and Disjoint Union

Just as with the sorting program in Section 2.3.3, the treatment of merging in the previous section avoided specifying a rearrangement condition. In this case, we want to show that the result of "Merge" is a rearrangement of the combined input segments, but to do this we must formalize the notation of combining or *concatenating* functions.

Ordinarily, concatenation is only defined for sequences. For $n \geq 0$, a *sequence* of length n is a function whose domain is $\boxed{1 \quad n}$. If X and Y are sequences of length m and n with the same codomain, then $X \oplus_{\text{seq}} Y$, called the *sequence concatenation* of X and Y, is the sequence of length $m+n$, with the same codomain as X and Y, such that

$$(X \oplus_{\text{seq}} Y)\,(i) = \textbf{if } i \leq m \textbf{ then } X(i) \textbf{ else } Y(i-m)$$

for all i in $\boxed{1 \quad m+n}$. It is easily seen that

    a. **dom** $(X \oplus_{\text{seq}} Y)$ is the union of the disjoint sets
        $\boxed{1 \quad m}$ and $\boxed{m \quad m+n}$,

    b. $(X \oplus_{\text{seq}} Y) \upharpoonright \boxed{1 \quad m} \simeq X$,

    c. $(X \oplus_{\text{seq}} Y) \upharpoonright \boxed{m \quad m+n} \simeq Y$,

    d. $\boxed{1 \quad m} <^* \boxed{m \quad m+n}$.

However, we are going to need to consider the concatenation of functions which are not sequences: The rearrangement condition for "Merge" involves concatenating functions whose domains are intervals which might not begin with one, later in this chapter we will need to concatenate functions whose domains are not intervals, and in Section 5.3.1 we will concatenate functions whose domains are not even sets of integers. Unfortunately, the above definition does not generalize cleanly to such cases.

The way out of this difficulty is to realize that, for most purposes, the specific domain of the concatenation of X and Y does not matter; all that matters is that this domain should partition into sets, akin to $\boxed{1 \quad m}$ and $\boxed{m \quad m+n}$, that possess the properties stated above. The simplest general way to produce such a domain is to pair or "tag" the members of **dom** X with some value, say one, and to tag the members of **dom** Y with some distinct value, say two.

For sets S_1 and S_2, we write $S_1 \times S_2$, called the *Cartesian product* of S_1 and S_2, to denote the set of pairs $\langle i_1, i_2 \rangle$ such that $i_1 \in S_1$ and $i_2 \in S_2$. Then, for any sets S and T, $\{1\} \times S$ and $\{2\} \times T$ are disjoint sets in one-to-one correspondence with S and T respectively, so that we can define $S+T$, called the *disjoint union* of S and T, to be the set

$$S+T = \{1\} \times S \cup \{2\} \times T \quad .$$

It is easily seen that

$$\text{If } S' \subseteq S \text{ and } T' \subseteq T \text{ then } S'+T' \subseteq S+T \quad , \tag{1}$$

$$(S+T) \cup (S'+T') = (S \cup S') + (T \cup T') \quad ,$$
$$(S+T) \cap (S'+T') = (S \cap S') + (T \cap T') \quad , \tag{2}$$
$$(S+T) - (S'+T') = (S-S') + (T-T') \quad ,$$

$$\# (S+T) = (\# S) + (\# T) \text{ when } S \text{ and } T \text{ are finite sets.} \tag{3}$$

In (3), notice that $+$ stands for the disjoint union of sets on the left, but for the ordinary addition of integers on the right.

Now suppose X is a function from S to U and Y is a function from T to U. Then we define $X \oplus Y$, called the *concatenation* of X and Y, to be the function from $S+T$ to U such that

$$(X \oplus Y) (\langle 1, i \rangle) = X(i) \text{ for all } i \in S \quad ,$$
$$(X \oplus Y) (\langle 2, j \rangle) = Y(j) \text{ for all } j \in T \quad .$$

The relationship between this definition of $\oplus$ and the earlier definition of $\oplus_{\text{seq}}$ is illustrated by Figure 2.4.

Let B be the function from $\{1\} \times S$ to S such that $B(\langle 1, i \rangle) = i$ for all i in S, and C be the function from $\{2\} \times T$ to T such that $C(\langle 2, j \rangle) = j$ for all j in T. Then B and C are bijections such that $(X \oplus Y) \uparrow (\{1\} \times S) = B \cdot X$ and $(X \oplus Y) \uparrow (\{2\} \times T) = C \cdot Y$. Thus

    a. **dom**$(X \oplus Y)$ is the union of the disjoint sets
        $\{1\} \times$ **dom** X and $\{2\} \times$ **dom** Y ,
    b. $(X \oplus Y) \uparrow (\{1\} \times$ **dom** $X) \sim X$,   (4)
    c. $(X \oplus Y) \uparrow (\{2\} \times$ **dom** $Y) \sim Y$.

However, we want realignments, not merely rearrangements, and we also want the property $\{1\} \times$ **dom** $X <^* \{2\} \times$ **dom** Y. For these notions to be

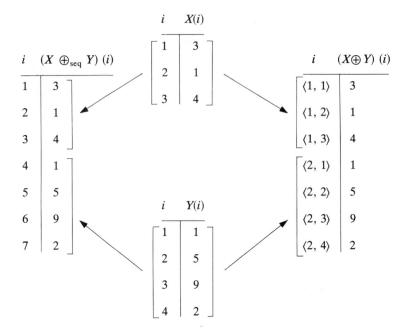

Figure 2.4   Two Kinds of Concatenation.

meaningful, we must extend the standard ordering to encompass the pairs in $S+T$.

If the standard ordering is defined for S and T, then we extend it to $S+T$ as follows:

$$\langle x, y\rangle \leq \langle x', y'\rangle \text{ if and only if } x<x' \text{ or } (x=x' \text{ and } y \leq y') \quad ,$$
$$\langle x, y\rangle < \langle x', y'\rangle \text{ if and only if } x<x' \text{ or } (x=x' \text{ and } y<y') \quad .$$

This kind of ordering is often called *lexicographic ordering*, since it is a special case of the word ordering used in dictionaries. (Think of two-letter words as pairs of letters.) Notice that repeated use of this definition extends the standard ordering to sets constructed by repeated use of +.

When $S+T$ is ordered lexicographically, $\langle 1, i\rangle \leq \langle 1, i'\rangle$ implies $i \leq i'$, so that the bijection B is monotone, $\langle 2, j\rangle \leq \langle 2, j'\rangle$ implies $j \leq j'$, so that bijection C is monotone, and $\langle 1, i\rangle < \langle 2, j\rangle$ always holds, so that $\{1\} \times S <^* \{2\} \times T$. Thus (4) can be strengthened to:

If the standard ordering is defined for **dom** X and **dom** Y, then:

    a. **dom**$(X \oplus Y)$ is the union of the disjoint sets
        $\{1\} \times$ **dom** X and $\{2\} \times$ **dom** Y ,

    b. $(X \oplus Y) \uparrow (\{1\} \times$ **dom** $X) \simeq X$,   (5)

    c. $(X \oplus Y) \uparrow (\{2\} \times$ **dom** $Y) \simeq Y$,

    d. $\{1\} \times$ **dom** $X <^* \{2\} \times$ **dom** Y .

This is similar to the basic properties of $\oplus_{\text{seq}}$, except that the sets $\{1\} \times \textbf{dom } X$ and $\{2\} \times \textbf{dom } Y$ of pairs have replaced the intervals $\boxed{1 \quad m}$ and $m\boxed{\quad m+n}$.

Concatenation is related to the restriction and composition of functions by simple laws. If X and Y are functions with the same codomain then

$$\text{If } S \subseteq \textbf{dom } X \text{ and } T \subseteq \textbf{dom } Y \text{ then}$$
$$(X \oplus Y) \upharpoonright (S+T) = (X \upharpoonright S) \oplus (Y \upharpoonright T) \quad . \tag{6}$$

Moreover, if Z is a function whose domain is the common codomain of X and Y then

$$(X \oplus Y) \cdot Z = X \cdot Z \oplus Y \cdot Z \quad . \tag{7}$$

For each of these equations, the reader may verify that the functions denoted by the two sides of the equation have the same domain and the same codomain, and that these functions give the same result when applied to any member of their common domain.

From (4) we can obtain an equation for the image of a concatenation. By (10) in Section 2.2.8, we have

$$\{X \oplus Y\} = \{X \oplus Y \upharpoonright \{1\} \times \textbf{dom } X\} \cup \{X \oplus Y \upharpoonright \{2\} \times \textbf{dom } Y\} \quad ,$$

so that by (22) in Section 2.3.4,

$$\{X \oplus Y\} = \{X\} \cup \{Y\} \quad . \tag{8}$$

Similarly, from (5) we can obtain a relationship between concatenation and ordering. From (3) in Section 2.2.10,

$$\textbf{ord}_\rho (X \oplus Y) \text{ if and only if}$$
$$\text{(a)} \quad \textbf{ord}_\rho (X \oplus Y) \upharpoonright \{1\} \times \textbf{dom } X$$
$$\text{and (b)} \quad \textbf{ord}_\rho (X \oplus Y) \upharpoonright \{2\} \times \textbf{dom } Y$$
$$\text{and (c)} \quad \{(X \oplus Y) \upharpoonright \{1\} \times \textbf{dom } X\} \, \rho^* \, \{(X \oplus Y) \upharpoonright \{2\} \times \textbf{dom } Y\} \quad ,$$

so that by (23) and (22) in Section 2.3.4,

$$\textbf{ord}_\rho (X \oplus Y) \text{ if and only if}$$
$$\text{(a)} \quad \textbf{ord}_\rho X$$
$$\text{and (b)} \quad \textbf{ord}_\rho Y \tag{9}$$
$$\text{and (c)} \quad \{X\} \, \rho^* \, \{Y\} \quad .$$

A number of further laws relate concatenation to rearrangement and realignment. Each of these laws arises from the existence of a bijection between sets that are constructed by disjoint unions. We assume that X, Y, Z, X', and Y' are functions with the same codomain, and that the standard ordering is defined for their domains. (If the standard ordering is not so defined then the laws we derive still hold with $\simeq$ replaced by $\sim$.)

The function B from $(\textbf{dom } X + \textbf{dom } Y) + \textbf{dom } Z$ to $\textbf{dom } X + (\textbf{dom } Y + \textbf{dom } Z)$ such that $B(\langle 1, \langle 1, i \rangle \rangle) = \langle 1, i \rangle$, $B(\langle 1, \langle 2, j \rangle \rangle) = \langle 2, \langle 1, j \rangle \rangle$, and $B(\langle 2, k \rangle) = \langle 2, \langle 2, k \rangle \rangle$ is a monotone bijection satisfying $(X \oplus Y) \oplus Z = B \cdot (X \oplus (Y \oplus Z))$. Thus

$$(X \oplus Y) \oplus Z \simeq X \oplus (Y \oplus Z) \quad . \tag{10}$$

The function B from **dom** $X + \{\}$ to **dom** X such that $B(\langle 1, i \rangle) = i$ is a monotone bijection satisfying $X \oplus \langle \rangle = B \cdot X$. Thus

$$X \oplus \langle \rangle \simeq X \quad . \tag{11}$$

Similarly, the function B from $\{\} + $ **dom** X to **dom** X such that $B(\langle 2, j \rangle) = j$ is a monotone bijection satisfying $\langle \rangle \oplus X = B \cdot X$, so that

$$\langle \rangle \oplus X \simeq X \quad . \tag{12}$$

The function B from **dom** $X + $ **dom** Y to **dom** $Y + $ **dom** X such that $B(\langle 1, i \rangle) = \langle 2, i \rangle$ and $B(\langle 2, j \rangle) = \langle 1, j \rangle$ is a bijection—but not a monotone bijection—satisfying $X \oplus Y = B \cdot (Y \oplus X)$. Thus

$$X \oplus Y \sim Y \oplus X \quad . \tag{13}$$

Next, suppose that there are (monotone) bijections B and C such that $X = B \cdot X'$ and $Y = C \cdot Y'$. Let D be the function from **dom** $X + $ **dom** Y to **dom** $X' + $ **dom** Y' such that $D(\langle 1, i \rangle) = \langle 1, B(i) \rangle$ and $D(\langle 2, j \rangle) = \langle 2, C(j) \rangle$. Then D is a (monotone) bijection such that $X \oplus Y = D \cdot (X' \oplus Y')$. Thus

$$\begin{aligned} &\text{If } X \sim X' \text{ and } Y \sim Y' \text{ then } X \oplus Y \sim X' \oplus Y' \quad . \\ &\text{If } X \simeq X' \text{.and } Y \simeq Y' \text{ then } X \oplus Y \simeq X' \oplus Y' \quad . \end{aligned} \tag{14}$$

The reader who is familiar with abstract algebra will recognize the import of laws (10) to (14). Functions with a common codomain form an algebra in which $\oplus$ is a binary operation and $\langle \rangle$ is a constant. By (14) the equivalence relations $\sim$ and $\simeq$ are congruences on this algebra, by (10) to (12) the quotient of this algebra by $\simeq$ is a monoid, and by (10) to (13) the quotient of this algebra by $\sim$ is a commutative monoid. While we will not use these algebraic concepts explicitly, they suggest that (10) to (14) are likely to be pervasive laws about concatenation.

Finally, suppose that **dom** $X = S \cup T$ where S and T are disjoint sets. Let B be the function from $S \cup T$ to $S + T$ such that $B(i) = \textbf{if } i \in S \textbf{ then } \langle 1, i \rangle \textbf{ else } \langle 2, i \rangle$. Then B is a bijection such that $X = B \cdot ((X \uparrow S) \oplus (X \uparrow T))$. Moreover, if $S <^* T$ then B is monotone. Thus

$$\begin{aligned} &\text{If } \textbf{dom } X = S \cup T \text{ and } S \text{ and } T \text{ are disjoint} \\ &\quad \text{then } X \sim (X \uparrow S) \oplus (X \uparrow T) \quad . \\ &\text{If } \textbf{dom } X = S \cup T \text{ and } S <^* T \\ &\quad \text{then } X \simeq (X \uparrow S) \oplus (X \uparrow T) \quad . \end{aligned} \tag{15}$$

As a special case where S and T are intervals:

$$\begin{aligned} &\text{If } \textbf{dom } X = a \boxed{} c \text{ and } a \boxed{ b } c \\ &\quad \text{then } X \simeq (X \uparrow a \boxed{} b) \oplus (X \uparrow b \boxed{} c) \quad . \end{aligned} \tag{16}$$

We can now formulate and prove the rearrangement condition for the merging program. To show that the result of "Merge" is a rearrangement of the concatenation of its input segments, we must show that

$$(Z \uparrow \boxed{az \quad bz}) \sim (X \uparrow \boxed{ax \quad bx}) \oplus (Y \uparrow \boxed{ay \quad by})$$

can be added to the consequent of the program. (Since the program does not alter X or Y, we do not need to use ghost identifiers.) The obvious addition to the invariant is

$$(Z \uparrow \boxed{az \quad | kz}) \sim (X \uparrow \boxed{ax \quad | kx}) \oplus (Y \uparrow \boxed{ay \quad | ky}) \quad ,$$

which will imply the final result when $\boxed{kx \quad bx}$, $\boxed{ky \quad by}$, and $\boxed{kz \quad bz}$ are empty. To show that the invariant is still preserved it is sufficient to show that "Copy X" satisfies the specification

$$\{ \boxed{ax \quad |kx| \quad bx} \text{ and } \boxed{az \quad |kz| \quad bz}$$
$$\text{and } (Z \uparrow \boxed{az \quad | kz}) \sim (X \uparrow \boxed{ax \quad | kx}) \oplus (Y \uparrow \boxed{ay \quad | ky}) \}$$
$$\textbf{begin } Z(kz) := X(kx); \ kx := kx+1; \ kz := kz+1 \textbf{ end}$$
$$\{ (Z \uparrow \boxed{az \quad | kz}) \sim (X \uparrow \boxed{ax \quad | kx}) \oplus (Y \uparrow \boxed{ay \quad | ky}) \} \quad ,$$

and that "Copy Y" satisfies an analogous specification.

To prove this specification, we will show that its precedent implies the precedent of the following specification, which is a direct consequence of the inference rules for array assignment and simple assignment:

$$\{ ([Z \mid kz: X(kx)] \uparrow \boxed{az \quad kz}) \sim (X \uparrow \boxed{ax \quad kx}) \oplus (Y \uparrow \boxed{ay \quad | ky}) \}$$
$$\textbf{begin } Z(kz) := X(kx); \ kx := kx+1; \ kz := kz+1 \textbf{ end}$$
$$\{ (Z \uparrow \boxed{az \quad | kz}) \sim (X \uparrow \boxed{ax \quad | kx}) \oplus (Y \uparrow \boxed{ay \quad | ky}) \} \quad .$$

Thus, assume the first precedent. Then:

$$[Z \mid kz: X(kx)] \uparrow \boxed{az \quad kz}$$
$$\simeq ([Z \mid kz: X(kx)] \uparrow \boxed{az \quad |}kz) \oplus ([Z \mid kz: X(kx)] \uparrow \boxed{kz}) \quad (16)$$
$$= (Z \uparrow \boxed{az \quad |}kz) \oplus ([Z \mid kz: X(kx)] \uparrow \boxed{kz}) \quad (9 \text{ in } 2.3.2)$$
$$\simeq (Z \uparrow \boxed{az \quad |}kz) \oplus (X \uparrow \boxed{kx}) \quad (21 \text{ in } 2.3.4, 14)$$
$$\sim (X \uparrow \boxed{ax \quad |}kx) \oplus (Y \uparrow \boxed{ay \quad |}ky) \oplus (X \uparrow \boxed{kx}) \quad (\text{hypothesis}, 14)$$
$$\sim (X \uparrow \boxed{ax \quad |}kx) \oplus (X \uparrow \boxed{kx}) \oplus (Y \uparrow \boxed{ay \quad |}ky) \quad (13, 14)$$
$$\simeq (X \uparrow \boxed{ax \quad kx}) \oplus (Y \uparrow \boxed{ay \quad |}ky) \quad . \quad (16, 14)$$

Here we have hidden applications of the associativity law (10) by writing the fifth and sixth lines without parentheses; even though the functions denoted by the two ways of parenthesizing one of these lines are not equal, they are realignments of one another, and that is enough for our purposes. By (16), and (18) in Section 2.3.4, each adjacent pair of lines is related by $\sim$. Thus the desired conclusion follows from the fact that $\sim$ is transitive. The proof for "Copy Y" is similar.

Sometimes concatenation can be used to good effect in proving specifications where it does not appear explicitly. An example is provided by the version of the left-shifting program given at the end of Section 2.3.4. To show that the **while**-statement body meets its specification, we must show that

$$\boxed{a \mid k{-}1 \mid k \mid \ b}\ \text{and}\ X \uparrow (\boxed{a \mid k{-}1} \cup k{-}1\boxed{\ \ b}) \simeq X_0 \uparrow a\boxed{\ \ b}$$

implies

$$[X \mid k{-}1: X(k)] \uparrow (\boxed{a \mid k} \cup k\boxed{\ \ b}) \simeq X_0 \uparrow a\boxed{\ \ b}\quad .$$

This can be proved by a sequence of realignments involving concatenations:

$$[X \mid k{-}1: X(k)] \uparrow (\boxed{a \mid k} \cup k\boxed{\ \ b})$$

$$\simeq ([X \mid k{-}1: X(k)] \uparrow \boxed{a \mid} k) \oplus ([X \mid k{-}1: X(k)] \uparrow k\boxed{\ \ b})\quad (15)$$

$$\simeq ([X \mid k{-}1: X(k)] \uparrow \boxed{a \mid} k{-}1) \oplus ([X \mid k{-}1: X(k)] \uparrow \boxed{k{-}1})$$

$$\oplus ([X \mid k{-}1: X(k)] \uparrow k\boxed{\ \ b})\qquad\qquad (16, 14)$$

$$\simeq (X \uparrow \boxed{a \mid} k{-}1) \oplus (X \uparrow \boxed{k}) \oplus (X \uparrow k\boxed{\ \ b})$$

$$(9\ \text{in}\ 2.3.2,\ 21\ \text{in}\ 2.3.4,\ 14)$$

$$\simeq (X \uparrow \boxed{a \mid} k{-}1) \oplus (X \uparrow k{-}1\boxed{\ \ b})\qquad\qquad (16, 14)$$

$$\simeq X \uparrow (\boxed{a \mid} k{-}1 \cup k{-}1\boxed{\ \ b})\qquad\qquad (15)$$

$$\simeq X_0 \uparrow a\boxed{\ \ b}\quad .\qquad\qquad (\text{hypothesis})$$

Exercises

1. Show that the lexicographic extension of the standard ordering is consistent with the laws given in Exercise 1 after Section 2.2.10, i.e. prove that if these laws are satisfied by members of S and T then they are satisfied by members of $S+T$.

2. Prove that if X and Y are sequences with the same codomain then $X \oplus_{\text{seq}} Y$ is the unique sequence which is a realignment of $X \oplus Y$. Then use this fact to show that laws (7) to (14) and (16) hold for sequences when $\oplus$ is replaced by $\oplus_{\text{seq}}$ and $\simeq$ by $=$.

    (*Hint*: The result of Exercise 3 after Section 2.3.4 implies that if X and Y are sequences such that $X \simeq Y$ then $X = Y$.)

3. Suppose S and T are sets, J is the function from S to $S+T$ such that $J(i) = \langle 1, i \rangle$ for all i in S, and K is the function from T to $S+T$ such that $K(j) = \langle 2, j \rangle$ for all j in T. Prove that:

    If U is a set, X is a function from S to U, and Y is a function from T to U, then there is exactly one function from $S+T$ to U, namely $X \oplus Y$, such that $J \cdot (X \oplus Y) = X$ and $K \cdot (X \oplus Y) = Y$.

    (This property characterizes disjoint union in terms of category theory by asserting that $S+T$ is a "coproduct" in the category of sets.)

4. Write a program to merge two strictly ordered array segments into a strictly ordered array segment, eliminating duplicate values. The program should set only Z and kz, should require time of order $\#\ \boxed{ax\quad bx} + \#\ \boxed{ay\quad by}$, and should not use any local arrays. It should satisfy

$$\{\boxed{ax\quad bx} \subseteq \textbf{dom}\ X \text{ and } \boxed{ay\quad by} \subseteq \textbf{dom}\ Y \text{ and } \boxed{az\quad bz} \subseteq \textbf{dom}\ Z$$
$$\textbf{and ord}_< X \uparrow \boxed{ax\quad bx} \text{ and } \textbf{ord}_< Y \uparrow \boxed{ay\quad by}$$
$$\textbf{and } \#\ \boxed{ax\quad bx} + \#\ \boxed{ay\quad by} \le \#\ \boxed{az\quad bz}\ \}$$
"Strict Merge"
$$\{\boxed{az\quad kz\quad bz} \text{ and } \textbf{ord}_< Z \uparrow \boxed{az\quad kz}$$
$$\textbf{and } \{Z \uparrow \boxed{az\quad kz}\} = \{X \uparrow \boxed{ax\quad bx}\} \cup \{Y \uparrow \boxed{ay\quad by}\}\ \}\quad .$$

5. (Suggested by W. J. Gadbow) Write a program to merge two ordered array segments that takes one of its inputs from an upper subsegment of its output segment. This is possible since the processed part of the output segment will never overlap the unprocessed part of the input segment. The program should set only X, should require a time of order $\#\ \boxed{ax\quad bx}$, and should not use any local arrays. It should satisfy

$$\{\boxed{ax\quad bx} \subseteq \textbf{dom}\ X \text{ and } \boxed{ay\quad by} \subseteq \textbf{dom}\ Y \text{ and } \boxed{ax\quad cx\quad bx}$$
$$\textbf{and ord}_\le X \uparrow \boxed{cx\quad bx} \text{ and } \textbf{ord}_\le Y \uparrow \boxed{ay\quad by}$$
$$\textbf{and } \#\ \boxed{ax\quad cx} = \#\ \boxed{ay\quad by} \text{ and } X = X_0\ \}$$
"Overwriting Merge"
$$\{\textbf{ord}_\le X \uparrow \boxed{ax\quad bx} \text{ and }$$
$$(X \uparrow \boxed{ax\quad bx}) \sim (X_0 \uparrow \boxed{cx\quad bx}) \oplus (Y \uparrow \boxed{ay\quad by})\ \}\quad .$$

6. Write a program to eliminate all values in an ordered array segment that do *not* occur in another ordered array segment. At the same time the program should eliminate duplicate values. It should set only X and cx, should require time of order $\#\ \boxed{ax\quad bx} + \#\ \boxed{ay\quad by}$, and should not use any local arrays. It should satisfy

$$\{\boxed{ax\quad bx} \subseteq \textbf{dom}\ X \text{ and } \boxed{ay\quad by} \subseteq \textbf{dom}\ Y$$
$$\textbf{and ord}_\le X \uparrow \boxed{ax\quad bx} \text{ and } \textbf{ord}_\le Y \uparrow \boxed{ay\quad by} \text{ and } X = X_0\}$$
"Intersect and remove duplicates"
$$\{\boxed{ax\quad cx\quad bx} \text{ and } \textbf{ord}_< X \uparrow \boxed{ax\quad cx}$$
$$\textbf{and } \{X \uparrow \boxed{ax\quad cx}\} = \{X_0 \uparrow \boxed{ax\quad bx}\} \cap \{Y \uparrow \boxed{ay\quad by}\}\ \}\quad .$$

2.3.8   Preimages and Related Concepts

In this section we introduce some additional concepts about functions that are useful in specifying array manipulations. Most important is the notion of a preimage. If U is a subset of the codomain of a function X then $\mathcal{P}(U, X)$, called the *preimage of U under X*, is the subset of the domain of X whose members are mapped by X into members of U. In other words, $i \in \mathcal{P}(U, X)$ if and only if $i \in \textbf{dom}\ X$ and $X(i) \in U$.

Let U and U' be subsets of **cod** X. Then it is easily seen that $\mathcal{P}$ preserves set inclusion:

$$\text{If } U' \subseteq U \text{ then } \mathcal{P}(U', X) \subseteq \mathcal{P}(U, X) \quad , \tag{1}$$

distributes with $\cup$, $\cap$, and $-$:

$$\begin{aligned}
\mathcal{P}(U \cup U', X) &= \mathcal{P}(U, X) \cup \mathcal{P}(U', X) \quad , \\
\mathcal{P}(U \cap U', X) &= \mathcal{P}(U, X) \cap \mathcal{P}(U', X) \quad , \\
\mathcal{P}(U - U', X) &= \mathcal{P}(U, X) - \mathcal{P}(U', X) \quad ,
\end{aligned} \tag{2}$$

and takes on its maximum or minimum values when U includes or excludes the entire image of X:

$$\mathcal{P}(U, X) = \mathbf{dom}\ X \text{ if and only if } \{X\} \subseteq U \quad , \tag{3}$$

$$\mathcal{P}(U, X) = \{\} \text{ if and only if } U \text{ and } \{X\} \text{ are disjoint} \quad . \tag{4}$$

There are also some obvious relationships with composition and identity functions. If $X \cdot Y$ is defined and U is a subset of the codomain of Y then

$$\mathcal{P}(U, X \cdot Y) = \mathcal{P}(\mathcal{P}(U, Y), X) \quad , \tag{5}$$

and if U' is a subset of U then

$$\mathcal{P}(U', I_U) = U' \quad . \tag{6}$$

Somewhat more subtle are the relationships among preimages, restriction, and images. Suppose $S \subseteq \mathbf{dom}\ X$ and $U \subseteq \mathbf{cod}\ X$. Then $\mathcal{P}(U, X \upharpoonright S)$ consists of the members of $\mathbf{dom}(X \upharpoonright S) = S$ that are mapped by X into members of U, which are just the members of $\mathcal{P}(U, X)$ that are also members of S. Thus

$$\mathcal{P}(U, X \upharpoonright S) = \mathcal{P}(U, X) \cap S \quad . \tag{7}$$

If we start with a set $S \subseteq \mathbf{dom}\ X$ of arguments, form the set $\{X \upharpoonright S\}$ of results obtained by applying X to these arguments, and then form the set $\mathcal{P}(\{X \upharpoonright S\}, X)$ of all arguments that give these results, we must end with at least the arguments we began with, i.e.

$$S \subseteq \mathcal{P}(\{X \upharpoonright S\}, X) \quad . \tag{8}$$

Going in the other direction we can give even more information. If we start with a set $U \subseteq \mathbf{cod}\ X$ of results, form the set $\mathcal{P}(U, X)$ of arguments that give these results, and then form the set $\{X \upharpoonright \mathcal{P}(U, X)\}$ of results obtained from these arguments, we must get exactly the members of U that can be obtained by applying X to any argument, i.e.

$$\{X \upharpoonright \mathcal{P}(U, X)\} = U \cap \{X\} \quad . \tag{9}$$

Next, we connect preimages with concatenation. Suppose U is a subset of the common codomain of X and Y. Since $\mathbf{dom}(X \oplus Y) = \mathbf{dom}\ X + \mathbf{dom}\ Y = \{1\} \times \mathbf{dom}\ X \cup \{2\} \times \mathbf{dom}\ Y$, we can use (7) and (5) to obtain

$$
\begin{aligned}
&\mathscr{P}(U,\ X \oplus Y) \\
&= (\mathscr{P}(U,\ X \oplus Y) \cap (\{1\} \times \mathbf{dom}\ X)) \\
&\quad \cup (\mathscr{P}(U,\ X \oplus Y) \cap (\{2\} \times \mathbf{dom}\ Y)) \\
&= \mathscr{P}(U,\ (X \oplus Y) \upharpoonright (\{1\} \times \mathbf{dom}\ X)) \\
&\quad \cup \mathscr{P}(U,\ (X \oplus Y) \upharpoonright (\{2\} \times \mathbf{dom}\ Y)) \\
&= \mathscr{P}(U,\ B \cdot X) \cup \mathscr{P}(U,\ C \cdot Y) \\
&= \mathscr{P}(\mathscr{P}(U,\ X),\ B) \cup \mathscr{P}(\mathscr{P}(U,\ Y),\ C) \quad,
\end{aligned}
$$

where B is the bijection from $\{1\} \times \mathbf{dom}\ X$ to $\mathbf{dom}\ X$ such that $B(\langle 1, i \rangle) = i$ and C is the bijection from $\{2\} \times \mathbf{dom}\ Y$ to $\mathbf{dom}\ Y$ such that $C(\langle 2, j \rangle) = j$. Then the preimage of $\mathscr{P}(U,\ X)$ under B is $\{1\} \times \mathscr{P}(U,\ X)$, the preimage of $\mathscr{P}(U,\ Y)$ under C is $\{2\} \times \mathscr{P}(U,\ Y)$, and the union of these preimages is $\mathscr{P}(U,\ X) + \mathscr{P}(U,\ Y)$. Thus

$$\mathscr{P}(U,\ X \oplus Y) = \mathscr{P}(U,\ X) + \mathscr{P}(U,\ Y) \quad. \tag{10}$$

Finally, we relate preimages to rearrangement and realignment. Suppose B is a (monotone) bijection from $\mathbf{dom}\ X$ to $\mathbf{dom}\ Y$, and S is a subset of $\mathbf{dom}\ X$. Since $B(i) \in \{B \upharpoonright S\}$ for all i in S, we can define a function B_S by first restricting B to S and then reducing its codomain to $\{B \upharpoonright S\}$. In other words, B_S is the function from S to $\{B \upharpoonright S\}$ such that $B_S(i) = B(i)$ for all i in S. This function is obviously surjective, and it inherits the injectivity (and monotonicity) of B. Thus B_S is a (monotone) bijection from S to $\{B \upharpoonright S\}$.

Now suppose $X = B \cdot Y$, where X and Y are functions with the same codomain, and suppose U is a subset of that codomain. Then $B_{\mathscr{P}(U,\ X)}$ will be a (monotone) bijection from $\mathscr{P}(U,\ X)$ to $\{B \upharpoonright \mathscr{P}(U,\ X)\}$. But from (5) and (9) and the fact that B is surjective, we have

$$
\begin{aligned}
\{B \upharpoonright \mathscr{P}(U,\ X)\} &= \{B \upharpoonright \mathscr{P}(U,\ B \cdot Y)\} \\
&= \{B \upharpoonright \mathscr{P}(\mathscr{P}(U,\ Y),\ B)\} = \{B\} \cap \mathscr{P}(U,\ Y) \\
&= \mathbf{cod}\ B \cap \mathscr{P}(U,\ Y) = \mathscr{P}(U,\ Y) \quad.
\end{aligned}
$$

Thus the composition $B_{\mathscr{P}(U,\ X)} \cdot (Y \upharpoonright \mathscr{P}(U,\ Y))$ is well-defined. Moreover, for all i in $\mathscr{P}(U,\ X)$,

$$(Y \upharpoonright \mathscr{P}(U,\ Y))\ (B_{\mathscr{P}(U,\ X)}\ (i)) = Y(B(i)) = X(i) \quad,$$

so that $(X \upharpoonright \mathscr{P}(U,\ X)) = B_{\mathscr{P}(U,\ X)} \cdot (Y \upharpoonright \mathscr{P}(U,\ Y))$. Thus when U is a subset of the common codomain of X and Y, we have

$$
\begin{aligned}
&\text{If } X \sim Y \text{ then } X \upharpoonright \mathscr{P}(U,\ X) \sim Y \upharpoonright \mathscr{P}(U,\ Y) \quad, \\
&\text{If } X \simeq Y \text{ then } X \upharpoonright \mathscr{P}(U,\ X) \simeq Y \upharpoonright \mathscr{P}(U,\ Y) \quad.
\end{aligned}
\tag{11}
$$

The first part of this law is one step in proving a fundamental theorem about the nature of rearrangement:

Theorem   If X and Y are functions with the same codomain, then the following statements are equivalent:

(a) $X \sim Y$,

(b) For all $U \subseteq \text{cod } X$, $X \upharpoonright \mathscr{P}(U, X) \sim Y \upharpoonright \mathscr{P}(U, Y)$,

(c) For all $U \subseteq \text{cod } X$, $\# \, \mathscr{P}(U, X) = \# \, \mathscr{P}(U, Y)$,

(d) For all $r \in \text{cod } X$, $X \upharpoonright \mathscr{P}(\{r\}, X) \sim Y \upharpoonright \mathscr{P}(\{r\}, Y)$,

(e) For all $r \in \text{cod } X$, $\# \, \mathscr{P}(\{r\}, X) = \# \, \mathscr{P}(\{r\}, Y)$.

Notice that the equivalence of (a) and (e) captures the idea that X is a rearrangement of Y when every value occurs the same number of times as a result of X and of Y.

Proof: From the first part of (11), we see that (a) implies (b). To see that (b) implies (c), suppose $X \upharpoonright \mathscr{P}(U, X) \sim Y \upharpoonright \mathscr{P}(U, Y)$. Then there is a bijection from $\mathscr{P}(U, X)$ to $\mathscr{P}(U, Y)$, so that $\# \, \mathscr{P}(U, X) = \# \, \mathscr{P}(U, Y)$ follows from the well-known proposition of set theory that two sets have the same size if and only if there is a bijection between them. (For finite sets, this can be proved by induction on the size of the sets; for infinite sets it is the definition of "have the same size".)

Since (d) is a special case of (b) and (e) is a special case of (c), (b) implies (d) and (c) implies (e). Moreover, (d) implies (e) for the same reason that (b) implies (c).

Finally, we must show that (e) implies (a). If (e) holds then the above-mentioned proposition of set theory insures that, for each r in **cod** X, there will be a bijection C_r from $\mathscr{P}(\{r\}, X)$ to $\mathscr{P}(\{r\}, Y)$. Since each i in **dom** X belongs to $\mathscr{P}(\{X(i)\}, X)$, we can define C to be the function from **dom** X to **dom** Y such that $C(i) = C_{X(i)}(i)$. Similarly, we can define D to be the function from **dom** Y to **dom** X such that $D(j) = C_{Y(j)}{}^{-1}(j)$.

For each $i \in$ **dom** X, $C(i) = C_{X(i)}(i)$ will belong to $\mathscr{P}(\{X(i)\}, Y)$, so that $Y(C(i)) = X(i)$, and $D(C(i)) = C_{Y(C(i))}{}^{-1}(C(i)) = C_{X(i)}{}^{-1}(C_{X(i)}(i)) = i$. Thus $X = C \cdot Y$ and $C \cdot D = I_{\textbf{dom } X}$.

Similarly, for each $j \in$ **dom** Y, $D(j) = C_{Y(j)}{}^{-1}(j)$ will belong to $\mathscr{P}(\{Y(j)\}, X)$, so that $X(D(j)) = Y(j)$, and $C(D(j)) = C_{X(D(j))}(D(j)) = C_{Y(j)}(C_{Y(j)}{}^{-1}(j)) = j$. Thus $D \cdot C = I_{\textbf{dom } Y}$.

Combining these results, we see that D is the inverse of C, so that C is a bijection, and $X = C \cdot Y$, so that $X \sim Y$.

In summary, (a) implies (b), (b) implies (c) and (d), either (c) or (d) implies (e), and (e) implies (a). Thus if any of these statements are true, they must all be true. $\square$

For a function X and a set U, the restriction $X \upharpoonright \mathscr{P}(\textbf{cod } X \cap U, X)$ retains just those domain elements which are mapped into members of U. This is a sufficiently useful notion that it is worth defining $X \mathbin{\hat{\cap}} U$, called the *intersection* of the function X with the set U, to be $X \upharpoonright \mathscr{P}(\textbf{cod } X \cap U, X)$.

Since $\{X\} \subseteq \mathbf{cod}\ X, \{X\} \subseteq U$ holds if and only if $\{X\} \subseteq \mathbf{cod}\ X \cap U$ which, by (3), holds if and only if $\mathscr{P}(\mathbf{cod}\ X \cap U, X) = \mathbf{dom}\ X$. In turn, this holds if and only if $X \uparrow \mathscr{P}(\mathbf{cod}\ X \cap U, X) = X$. Thus

$$X \mathbin{\hat\cap} U = X \text{ if and only if } \{X\} \subseteq U \quad . \tag{12}$$

On the other hand, U and $\{X\}$ are disjoint if and only if $\mathbf{cod}\ X \cap U$ and $\{X\}$ are disjoint, if and only if, by (4), $\mathscr{P}(\mathbf{cod}\ X \cap U, X) = \{\}$, if and only if $X \uparrow \mathscr{P}(\mathbf{cod}\ X \cap U, X) = \langle\rangle$. Thus

$$X \mathbin{\hat\cap} U = \langle\rangle \text{ if and only if } U \text{ and } \{X\} \text{ are disjoint} \quad . \tag{13}$$

Since restriction doesn't alter codomains, we have $\mathbf{cod}(X \mathbin{\hat\cap} U) = \mathbf{cod}\ X$. Thus

$$
\begin{aligned}
\mathscr{P}(\mathbf{cod}(X \mathbin{\hat\cap} U) \cap U', X \mathbin{\hat\cap} U) \\
= \mathscr{P}(\mathbf{cod}\ X \cap U', X \uparrow \mathscr{P}(\mathbf{cod}\ X \cap U, X)) \\
= \mathscr{P}(\mathbf{cod}\ X \cap U', X) \cap \mathscr{P}(\mathbf{cod}\ X \cap U, X) \\
= \mathscr{P}(\mathbf{cod}\ X \cap U \cap U', X) \quad ,
\end{aligned}
$$

where the last two lines are consequences of (7) and (2). Then

$$
\begin{aligned}
(X \mathbin{\hat\cap} U) \mathbin{\hat\cap} U' &= (X \mathbin{\hat\cap} U) \uparrow \mathscr{P}(\mathbf{cod}\ (X \mathbin{\hat\cap} U) \cap U', X \mathbin{\hat\cap} U) \\
&= (X \mathbin{\hat\cap} U) \uparrow \mathscr{P}(\mathbf{cod}\ X \cap U \cap U', X) \\
&= (X \uparrow \mathscr{P}(\mathbf{cod}\ X \cap U, X)) \uparrow \mathscr{P}(\mathbf{cod}\ X \cap U \cap U', X) \\
&= X \uparrow \mathscr{P}(\mathbf{cod}\ X \cap U \cap U', X) \quad ,
\end{aligned}
$$

i.e.

$$(X \mathbin{\hat\cap} U) \mathbin{\hat\cap} U' = X \mathbin{\hat\cap} (U \cap U') \quad . \tag{14}$$

If X and Y, and therefore $X \oplus Y$, have the same codomain, then (10), along with (6) in Section 2.3.7, gives

$$
\begin{aligned}
(X \oplus Y) \mathbin{\hat\cap} U &= (X \oplus Y) \uparrow \mathscr{P}(\mathbf{cod}\ (X \oplus Y) \cap U, X \oplus Y) \\
&= (X \oplus Y) \uparrow (\mathscr{P}(\mathbf{cod}\ X \cap U, X) + \mathscr{P}(\mathbf{cod}\ Y \cap U, Y)) \\
&= (X \uparrow \mathscr{P}(\mathbf{cod}\ X \cap U, X)) \oplus (Y \uparrow \mathscr{P}(\mathbf{cod}\ Y \cap U, Y)) \quad ,
\end{aligned}
$$

i.e.

$$(X \oplus Y) \mathbin{\hat\cap} U = (X \mathbin{\hat\cap} U) \oplus (Y \mathbin{\hat\cap} U) \quad . \tag{15}$$

Further laws relate $\hat\cap$ to images, rearrangement, and realignment. From (9) we get

$$\{X \mathbin{\hat\cap} U\} = \{X\} \cap U \quad , \tag{16}$$

which shows why $\hat\cap$ is called intersection. From (11) we get

$$
\begin{aligned}
&\text{If } X \sim Y \text{ then } X \mathbin{\hat\cap} U \sim Y \mathbin{\hat\cap} U \quad , \\
&\text{If } X \simeq Y \text{ then } X \mathbin{\hat\cap} U \simeq Y \mathbin{\hat\cap} U \quad .
\end{aligned}
\tag{17}
$$

Sometimes one needs to consider the restriction of a function X that eliminates, rather than retains, just those domain elements that are mapped into members of a set U. In this case it is useful to define $X \doteq U$, called the *subtraction* of U from X, to be $X \upharpoonright \mathscr{P}(\mathbf{cod}\ X - U,\ X) = X \mathbin{\dot\cap} (\mathbf{cod}\ X - U)$. Each of the laws (12) to (17) for intersection has an analogue for subtraction, which can be derived in a similar manner:

$$X \doteq U = X \text{ if and only if } U \text{ and } \{X\} \text{ are disjoint} \quad, \qquad (12-)$$
$$X \doteq U = \langle\rangle \text{ if and only if } \{X\} \subseteq U \quad, \qquad (13-)$$
$$(X \doteq U) \doteq U' = X \doteq (U \cup U') \quad, \qquad (14-)$$
$$(X \oplus Y) \doteq U = (X \doteq U) \oplus (Y \doteq U) \quad, \qquad (15-)$$
$$\{X \doteq U\} = \{X\} - U \quad, \qquad (16-)$$
$$\begin{aligned} &\text{If } X \sim Y \text{ then } X \doteq U \sim Y \doteq U \quad,\\ &\text{If } X \simeq Y \text{ then } X \doteq U \simeq Y \doteq U \quad. \end{aligned} \qquad (17-)$$

A simple illustration of these concepts is provided by the following program, which restricts the array segment $X \upharpoonright \boxed{a\ \ b}$ to eliminate all values outside of the interval $\boxed{r\ \ s}$, and realigns the result so that its domain is a left subinterval of $\boxed{a\ \ b}$:

$$\{\boxed{a\ \ b} \subseteq \mathbf{dom}\ X \text{ and } X = X_0\}$$
begin integer d; $c := a$; $d := a$;
$\{$**whileinv:** $\boxed{a\ \ |c\ \ |d\ \ b}$ and $X \upharpoonright \boxed{a\ \ |c} \simeq (X_0 \upharpoonright \boxed{a\ \ |d}) \mathbin{\dot\cap} \boxed{r\ \ s}$
    and $X \upharpoonright \boxed{d\ \ b} = X_0 \upharpoonright \boxed{d\ \ b}\}$
while $d \le b$ **do**
    if $(X(d) < r)$ **or** $(s < X(d))$ **then** $d := d+1$
    else begin $X(c) := X(d)$; $c := c+1$; $d := d+1$ **end**
end
$\{\boxed{a\ \ |c\ \ b} \text{ and } X \upharpoonright \boxed{a\ \ |c} \simeq (X_0 \upharpoonright \boxed{a\ \ b}) \mathbin{\dot\cap} \boxed{r\ \ s}\}$.

The heart of the correctness proof for this program is to show that the invariant and $d \le b$ and $X(d) \notin \boxed{r\ \ s}$ imply

$$X \upharpoonright \boxed{a\ \ |c} \simeq (X_0 \upharpoonright \boxed{a\ \ d}) \mathbin{\dot\cap} \boxed{r\ \ s} \quad,$$

and that the invariant and $d \le b$ and $X(d) \in \boxed{r\ \ s}$ imply

$$[X \mid c: X(d)] \upharpoonright \boxed{a\ \ |c} \simeq (X_0 \upharpoonright \boxed{a\ \ d}) \mathbin{\dot\cap} \boxed{r\ \ s} \quad.$$

To see this, assume the invariant and $d \le b$. Then $\boxed{a\ \ |d}$ and $\boxed{a\ \ |c}$ and $X \upharpoonright \boxed{d} = X_0 \upharpoonright \boxed{d}$, so that

$$(X_0 \uparrow \boxed{a \quad d}) \mathbin{\dot\cap} \boxed{r \quad s}$$
$$\simeq ((X_0 \uparrow \boxed{a \quad d}) \oplus (X_0 \uparrow \boxed{\ d\ })) \mathbin{\dot\cap} \boxed{r \quad s} \qquad \text{(16 in 2.3.7, 17)}$$
$$= ((X_0 \uparrow \boxed{a \quad d}) \mathbin{\dot\cap} \boxed{r \quad s}) \oplus ((X_0 \uparrow \boxed{\ d\ }) \mathbin{\dot\cap} \boxed{r \quad s}) \qquad (15)$$
$$\simeq (X \uparrow \boxed{a \quad c}) \oplus ((X_0 \uparrow \boxed{\ d\ }) \mathbin{\dot\cap} \boxed{r \quad s}) \qquad \text{(hypothesis, 14 in 2.3.7)}$$
$$= (X \uparrow \boxed{a \quad c}) \oplus ((X \uparrow \boxed{\ d\ }) \mathbin{\dot\cap} \boxed{r \quad s}) \quad .$$

If $X(d) \notin \boxed{r \quad s}$, then $\boxed{r \quad s}$ and $\{X \uparrow \boxed{\ d\ }\} = \{X(d)\}$ are disjoint sets, so that (13) gives $(X \uparrow \boxed{\ d\ }) \mathbin{\dot\cap} \boxed{r \quad s} = \langle\rangle$, and the above concatenation equals

$$(X \uparrow \boxed{a \quad c}) \oplus \langle\rangle$$
$$\simeq X \uparrow \boxed{a \quad c} \quad . \qquad \text{(11 in 2.3.7)}$$

On the other hand, if $X(d) \in \boxed{r \quad s}$ then $\{X \uparrow \boxed{\ d\ }\} \subseteq \boxed{r \quad s}$, so that (12) gives $(X \uparrow \boxed{\ d\ }) \mathbin{\dot\cap} \boxed{r \quad s} = X \uparrow \boxed{\ d\ }$, and the above concatenation equals

$$(X \uparrow \boxed{a \quad c}) \oplus (X \uparrow \boxed{\ d\ })$$
$$\simeq ([X \mid c: X(d)] \uparrow \boxed{a \quad c}) \oplus ([X \mid c: X(d)] \uparrow \boxed{\ c\ })$$
$$\text{(9 in 2.3.2, 21 in 2.3.4, 14 in 2.3.7)}$$
$$\simeq [X \mid c: X(d)] \uparrow \boxed{a \quad c} \quad . \qquad \text{(16 in 2.3.7)}$$

Exercises

1. Prove

   If $U \subseteq \mathbf{cod}\ X$ then $\mathscr{P}(U, X) = \mathscr{P}(U \cap \{X\}, X)$,
   $X \mathbin{\dot\cap} U = X \mathbin{\dot\cap} (U \cap \{X\})$,
   $X \mathbin{\dot-} U = X \mathbin{\dot-} (U \cap \{X\})$.

2. Write a program to eliminate all values in an ordered array segment that do *not* occur in another ordered array segment, without eliminating duplicates of the values that are retained. The program should set only X and cx, should require time of order $\#\boxed{ax \quad bx} + \#\boxed{ay \quad by}$, and should not use any local arrays. It should satisfy

   $\{\boxed{ax \quad bx} \subseteq \mathbf{dom}\ X \text{ and } \boxed{ay \quad by} \subseteq \mathbf{dom}\ Y$
        and $\mathbf{ord}_{\le} X \uparrow \boxed{ax \quad bx}$ and $\mathbf{ord}_{\le} Y \uparrow \boxed{ay \quad by}$ and $X = X_0 \}$
   "Intersect segments"
   $\{\boxed{ax \quad cx \quad bx}$
        and $X \uparrow \boxed{ax \quad cx} \simeq (X_0 \uparrow \boxed{ax \quad bx}) \mathbin{\dot\cap} \{Y \uparrow \boxed{ay \quad by}\} \}$.

   (Compare the consequent of this specification with that in Exercise 6 after Section 2.3.7.)

3. As in the previous exercise, except that the X-values to be eliminated are those that *do* occur in the segment of Y. The program specification is the same as in the previous exercise, except that $\dot-$ replaces the occurrence of $\dot\cap$.

4. (Suggested by O. O'M. Pardee) Write a program to remove, from an array segment with nonnegative values in decreasing order, all elements whose values are squares of values in the original array segment. The program should set only X and c, should require time of order $\#\,\boxed{a\ \ b}$, and should not use any local arrays. It should satisfy

$$\{\boxed{a\ \ b} \subseteq \textbf{dom } X \textbf{ and ord}_\geq X \uparrow \boxed{a\ \ b} \textbf{ and } \{X \uparrow \boxed{a\ \ b}\} \geq^* 0$$
$$\textbf{and } X = X_0 \,\}$$

"Remove squares"

$$\{\boxed{a\quad c\quad b}$$
$$\textbf{and } X \uparrow \boxed{a\quad c} \simeq (X_0 \uparrow \boxed{a\ \ b}) \div \{X_0 \cdot Sq \uparrow \boxed{a\ \ b}\}\,\}\quad,$$

where Sq is the function from integers to integers such that $Sq(i) = i \times i$.

*2.3.9 Ordering by Keys and Stability

In our programs for sorting, partitioning, and merging, the order of occurrence of values in the output array is specified in terms of an ordering relation which is applied to the values themselves. In the merging program of Section 2.3.6, for example, the order of occurrence in the output array is specified by $\textbf{ord}_\leq Z \uparrow \boxed{az\ \ bz}$, which is

$$(\forall\, i \in \boxed{az\ \ bz})\, (\forall\, j \in \boxed{az\ \ bz})\, i < j \textbf{ implies } Z(i) \leq Z(j)\quad.$$

In many applications, however, the values in an array such as Z are complex records, and the order of their occurrence depends upon the application of an ordering relation to values called *keys* which appear in certain fields of these records.

Abstractly, we can formalize this situation by assuming that there is a function K, from the codomain of the array being ordered to the set of keys, that maps each record into the value of its key field. (We are assuming here that a set of records can be described by a data type. In fact, we are anticipating problem-oriented, or user-defined types, which will be discussed in Chapter 5.) Then the order of occurrence of values in an array can be specified in terms of the composition of that array with K. In specifying a merging program, for example, one would assert $\textbf{ord}_\leq Z \cdot K \uparrow \boxed{az\ \ bz}$, which is

$$(\forall\, i \in \boxed{az\ \ bz})\, (\forall\, j \in \boxed{az\ \ bz})\, i < j \textbf{ implies } K(Z(i)) \leq K(Z(j))\quad.$$

In fact, the generalization of a program such as "Merge" to handle ordering by keys is usually straightforward. In tests of the values of array elements and assertions about such values, the arrays are replaced by their composition with K. However, this replacement is not applied to statements which move values of array elements, or to assertions about rearrangement or realignment—it is the records themselves, not their keys, that are to be rearranged.

For instance, the generalization of "Merge" to ordering by keys is:

$\{\,\boxed{ax \quad bx} \subseteq \mathbf{dom}\ X$ and $\boxed{ay \quad by} \subseteq \mathbf{dom}\ Y$ and $\boxed{az \quad bz} \subseteq \mathbf{dom}\ Z$

$\qquad$ and $\mathrm{ord}_{\le}\ X \cdot K \uparrow \boxed{ax \quad bx}$ and $\mathrm{ord}_{\le}\ Y \cdot K \uparrow \boxed{ay \quad by}$

$\qquad$ and $\#\boxed{ax \quad bx} + \#\boxed{ay \quad by} = \#\boxed{az \quad bz}\,\}$

begin integer $kx,\ ky,\ kz;$

$kx := ax;\ ky := ay;\ kz := az;$

$\{\mathbf{whileinv}\!:\ \boxed{ax \quad kx \quad bx}$ and $\boxed{ay \quad ky \quad by}$ and $\boxed{az \quad kz \quad bz}$

$\qquad$ and $\mathrm{ord}_{\le}\ Z \cdot K \uparrow \boxed{az \quad kz}$

$\qquad$ and $\{Z \cdot K \uparrow \boxed{az \quad kz}\} \le^* \{X \cdot K \uparrow \boxed{kx \quad bx}\}$

$\qquad \cup \{Y \cdot K \uparrow \boxed{ky \quad by}\}$

$\qquad$ and $\#\boxed{kx \quad bx} + \#\boxed{ky \quad by} = \#\boxed{kz \quad bz}$

$\qquad$ and $(Z \uparrow \boxed{az \quad kz}) \sim (X \uparrow \boxed{ax \quad kx}) \oplus (Y \uparrow \boxed{ay \quad ky})\,\}$

while $kz \le bz$ **do**

$\qquad$ **if** $(\mathbf{if}\ ky > by\ \mathbf{then}\ \mathrm{true}\ \mathbf{else\ if}\ kx > bx\ \mathbf{then}\ \mathrm{false}\ \mathbf{else}$

$\qquad\qquad K(X(kx)) \le K(Y(ky)))$

$\qquad$ **then** $\{\,\boxed{kx \quad bx}$ and $\boxed{kz \quad bz}$

$\qquad\qquad$ and $K(X(kx)) \le^* \{X \cdot K \uparrow \boxed{kx \quad bx}\} \cup \{Y \cdot K \uparrow \boxed{ky \quad by}\}\,\}$

$\qquad\qquad$ **begin** $Z(kz) := X(kx);\ kx := kx+1;\ kz := kz+1$ **end**

$\qquad\qquad\qquad\qquad\qquad$ "Copy X"

$\qquad$ **else** $\{\,\boxed{ky \quad by}$ and $\boxed{kz \quad bz}$

$\qquad\qquad$ and $K(Y(ky)) \le^* \{X \cdot K \uparrow \boxed{kx \quad bx}\} \cup \{Y \cdot K \uparrow \boxed{ky \quad by}\}\,\}$

$\qquad\qquad$ **begin** $Z(kz) := Y(ky);\ ky := ky+1;\ kz := kz+1$ **end**

$\qquad\qquad\qquad\qquad\qquad$ "Copy Y"

end

$\{\mathrm{ord}_{\le}\ Z \cdot K \uparrow \boxed{az \quad bz}$

$\qquad$ and $(Z \uparrow \boxed{az \quad bz}) \sim (X \uparrow \boxed{ax \quad bx}) \oplus (Y \uparrow \boxed{ay \quad by})\,\}$.

The specification of this program illustrates a curious characteristic of ordering by keys. If distinct records can have the same key, i.e. if the function K is not injective, then the specification is indeterminate: its consequent would remain true if one were to rearrange output records with the same key.

Although this indeterminacy is often acceptable, in some applications it is necessary to strengthen the program specification by adding a condition called *stability*. Roughly speaking, a program which rearranges records to meet some ordering criterion is said to be stable if records with the same keys occur in the same order in the output as in the input.

This idea can be described rigorously by using the concepts of realignment, preimages, and array intersection. Suppose X, Y, and K are functions such that $\mathbf{cod}\ X = \mathbf{cod}\ Y = \mathbf{dom}\ K$. Then X is said to be a *stable rearrangement of Y with respect to K* when

$$(\forall\ k \in \mathbf{cod}\ K)\ X \dot{\cap} \mathscr{P}(\{k\}, K) \simeq Y \dot{\cap} \mathscr{P}(\{k\}, K)\ \ .$$

The following theorem shows that stability is preserved by exchanging array segments which have no keys in common:

Theorem   If X, Y, and K are functions such that
$\mathbf{cod}X = \mathbf{cod}\ Y = \mathbf{dom}\ K$ and $\{X \cdot K\} \neq^* \{Y \cdot K\}$ then
$(\forall\ k \in \mathbf{cod}\ K)\ (X \oplus Y) \dot{\cap} \mathscr{P}(\{k\}, K) \simeq (Y \oplus X) \dot{\cap} \mathscr{P}(\{k\}, K).$

Proof: Let k be a member of $\mathbf{cod}\ K$. Since $\{X \cdot K\}$ and $\{Y \cdot K\}$ are disjoint sets, either $k \notin \{X \cdot K\}$ or $k \notin \{Y \cdot K\}$.

Suppose $k \notin \{X \cdot K\}$. Then $\{k\}$ and $\{X \cdot K\}$ are disjoint, so that by (4) in Section 2.3.8, $\mathscr{P}(\{k\}, X \cdot K) = \{\}$, and therefore $X \restriction \mathscr{P}(\{k\}, X \cdot K) = \langle\rangle$, Thus, using (5) in Section 2.3.8 and the definition of $\dot{\cap}$, we have $X \restriction \mathscr{P}(\{k\}, X \cdot K) = X \restriction \mathscr{P}(\mathscr{P}(\{k\}, K), X) = X \dot{\cap} \mathscr{P}(\{k\}, K) = \langle\rangle$. Similarly, if $k \notin \{Y \cdot K\}$ then $Y \dot{\cap} \mathscr{P}(\{k\}, K) = \langle\rangle$.

From (15) in Section 2.3.8, we have

$$(X \oplus Y) \dot{\cap} \mathscr{P}(\{k\}, K) = (X \dot{\cap} \mathscr{P}(\{k\}, K)) \oplus (Y \dot{\cap} \mathscr{P}(\{k\}, K))\ \ ,$$
$$(Y \oplus X) \dot{\cap} \mathscr{P}(\{k\}, K) = (Y \dot{\cap} \mathscr{P}(\{k\}, K)) \oplus (X \dot{\cap} \mathscr{P}(\{k\}, K))\ \ .$$

Then, since either $X \dot{\cap} \mathscr{P}(\{k\}, K)$ or $Y \dot{\cap} \mathscr{P}(\{k\}, K)$ is $\langle\rangle$, the identity laws for $\langle\rangle$ with regard to $\oplus$ (i.e. (11) and (12) in Section 2.3.7) establish that the right sides of these equations are realignments of one another. $\Box$

To illustrate the application of this theorem, we show part of a proof that the generalization of "Merge" to ordering by keys is stable. At the outset, it should be stressed that this stability hinges upon the use of the test $K(X(kx)) \leq K(Y(ky))$ to compare array elements; had we chosen to use $K(X(kx)) < K(Y(ky))$ the program would still have met its previous specification but would not have been stable.

We replace the rearrangement condition in the consequent by an assertion that $Z \restriction \boxed{az \quad bz}$ is a stable rearrangement of the concatenation of $X \restriction \boxed{ax \quad bx}$ and $Y \restriction \boxed{ay \quad by}$ with respect to K:

$$(\forall \ k \in \mathbf{cod} \ K) \ (Z \uparrow \boxed{az \quad bz}) \ \hat{\cap} \ \mathscr{P}(\{k\}, K)$$
$$\simeq ((X \uparrow \boxed{ax \quad bx}) \oplus (Y \uparrow \boxed{ay \quad by})) \ \hat{\cap} \ \mathscr{P}(\{k\}, K) \quad .$$

Similarly, we replace the rearrangement condition in the invariant by an assertion that the concatenation of the processed subsegment of Z, the unprocessed subsegment of X, and the unprocessed subsegment of Y is a stable rearrangement of the concatenation of $X \uparrow \boxed{ax \quad bx}$ and $Y \uparrow \boxed{ay \quad by}$ with respect to K:

$$(\forall \ k \in \mathbf{cod} \ K)$$
$$((Z \uparrow \boxed{az \quad kz}) \oplus (X \uparrow \boxed{kx \quad bx}) \oplus (Y \uparrow \boxed{ky \quad by})) \ \hat{\cap} \ \mathscr{P}(\{k\}, K)$$
$$\simeq ((X \uparrow \boxed{ax \quad bx}) \oplus (Y \uparrow \boxed{ay \quad by})) \ \hat{\cap} \ \mathscr{P}(\{k\}, K) \quad .$$

Also, as a consequence of $\mathbf{ord}_{\leq} \ X \cdot K \uparrow \boxed{ax \quad bx}$ and the falsity of the test which branches between "Copy X" and "Copy Y", we add $\{Y \cdot K \uparrow \boxed{ky}\} \neq^*$ $\{X \cdot K \uparrow \boxed{kx \quad bx}\}$ to the precedent of "Copy Y".

The heart of the correctness proof is the demonstration that "Copy Y" preserves the stability assertion which we have added to the invariant. After propagating the invariant backwards through the assignments in "Copy Y", we are left with the task of showing that the invariant and the precedent of "Copy Y" imply

$$(\forall \ k \in \mathbf{cod} \ K)$$
$$(([Z \mid kz: Y(ky)] \uparrow \boxed{az \quad kz}) \oplus (X \uparrow \boxed{kx \quad bx}) \oplus (Y \uparrow ky \boxed{\quad by}))$$
$$\hat{\cap} \ \mathscr{P}(\{k\}, K)$$
$$\simeq ((X \uparrow \boxed{ax \quad bx}) \oplus (Y \uparrow \boxed{ay \quad by})) \ \hat{\cap} \ \mathscr{P}(\{k\}, K) \quad .$$

We assume the invariant and the precedent of "Copy Y", and write $\mathscr{P}$ as an abbreviation for $\mathscr{P}(\{k\}, K)$. Then, for any k in $\mathbf{cod} \ K$,

$$(([Z \mid kz: Y(ky)] \uparrow \boxed{az \quad kz}) \oplus (X \uparrow \boxed{kx \quad bx}) \oplus (Y \uparrow ky \boxed{\quad by}))$$
$$\hat{\cap} \ \mathscr{P}$$
$$\simeq ((Z \uparrow \boxed{az \quad kz}) \oplus (Y \uparrow \boxed{ky}) \oplus (X \uparrow \boxed{kx \quad bx}) \oplus (Y \uparrow ky \boxed{\quad by}))$$
$$\hat{\cap} \ \mathscr{P} \quad .$$

At this point, we need to interchange $Y \uparrow \boxed{ky}$ and $X \uparrow \boxed{kx \quad bx}$. (Such an interchange is not needed in proving the analogous implication for "Copy X".) Using (15) in Section 2.3.8, the theorem we have just proved, and the assumption that $\{Y \cdot K \uparrow \boxed{ky}\}$ and $\{X \cdot K \uparrow \boxed{kx \quad bx}\}$ are disjoint, we see that the above expression is a realignment of

$$((Z \uparrow \boxed{az \quad} kz) \cap \mathscr{P})$$
$$\oplus (((Y \uparrow \boxed{ky}) \oplus (X \uparrow \boxed{kx \quad bx})) \cap \mathscr{P})$$
$$\oplus ((Y \uparrow ky \boxed{\quad by}) \cap \mathscr{P})$$
$$\simeq ((Z \uparrow \boxed{az \quad} kz) \cap \mathscr{P})$$
$$\oplus (((X \uparrow \boxed{kx \quad bx}) \oplus (Y \uparrow \boxed{ky})) \cap \mathscr{P})$$
$$\oplus ((Y \uparrow ky \boxed{\quad by}) \cap \mathscr{P})$$
$$\simeq ((Z \uparrow \boxed{az \quad} kz) \oplus (X \uparrow \boxed{kx \quad bx}) \oplus (Y \uparrow \boxed{ky}) \oplus (Y \uparrow ky \boxed{\quad by}))$$
$$\cap \mathscr{P}$$
$$\simeq ((Z \uparrow \boxed{az \quad} kz) \oplus (X \uparrow \boxed{kx \quad bx}) \oplus (Y \uparrow \boxed{ky \quad by})) \cap \mathscr{P}$$
$$\simeq ((X \uparrow \boxed{ax \quad bx}) \oplus (Y \uparrow \boxed{ay \quad by})) \cap \mathscr{P} \quad ,$$

where the last step follows from the stability condition in the invariant.

Exercises

1. Prove that a stable rearrangement is a rearrangement, i.e. that

    $$(\forall \ k \in \mathbf{cod} \ K) \ X \cap \mathscr{P}(\{k\}, K) \simeq Y \cap \mathscr{P}(\{k\}, K)$$

    implies $X \sim Y$.

    (*Hint*: Use the equivalence of (a) and (d) of the Theorem in Section 2.3.8.)

2. Generalize the insertion-sorting program of Exercise 4 after Section 2.3.3 to ordering by keys, and prove that it is stable.

3. Give examples to show that the generalizations to ordering by keys of the programs for sorting by maximum finding (Section 2.3.3) and for partitioning (Section 2.3.5) are *not* stable.

2.4 MULTIDIMENSIONAL ARRAYS

2.4.1 Multidimensional Arrays in Algol W

So far we have only considered arrays whose domains are intervals, i.e. finite consecutive sets of integers, but conceptually an array domain could be any set. A case of particular practical importance is *multidimensional* arrays, whose domains are finite sets of finite sequences (or "tuples") of integers. Ever since FORTRAN, most programming languages have provided facilities for multidimensional arrays, which are especially useful in numerical calculations, e.g. for the representation of matrices or tables of multi-argument functions. (More recent languages, such as Pascal [Wirth 71a], provide an even richer variety of arrays.)

In Algol W, an n-dimensional array declaration has the form

$$\tau \; \textbf{array} \; I_1 , \; \ldots \; , I_m \; (L_1 :: U_1, \; \ldots \; , L_n :: U_n)$$

where τ is **integer**, **real**, **long real**, or **logical**, $I_1, \; \ldots \; , I_m$ are binders of distinct identifiers, and $L_1, \; \ldots \; , L_n$ and $U_1, \; \ldots \; , U_n$ are integer expressions, called the *lower bounds* and *upper bounds* respectively. Such a declaration creates m distinct arrays, denoted by $I_1, \; \ldots \; , I_m$. Each of these arrays is a collection of variables of type τ whose domain is the set of integer sequences $\langle i_1, \; \ldots \; , i_n \rangle$ such that $L_1 \leq i_1 \leq U_1, \; \ldots \; , L_n \leq i_n \leq U_n$.

If I has been declared to be an n-dimensional array identifier, and $E_1, \; \ldots \; , E_n$ are integer expressions, then

$$I(E_1, \; \ldots \; , E_n)$$

is an array designator denoting the array element corresponding to the domain member $\langle E_1, \; \ldots \; , E_n \rangle$. E_i is called the ith subscript of $I(E_1, \; \ldots \; , E_n)$.

For example, the declaration **real array** $X(1::4, \; -2::2)$ will create a two-dimensional array containing twenty real variables, whose domain is the set of integer pairs $\langle i, j \rangle$ such that $1 \leq i \leq 4$ and $-2 \leq j \leq 2$.

In the case of a two-dimensional array, the elements can be visualized in a rectangular arrangement, e.g.

$$
\begin{array}{ccccc}
X(1,-2) & X(1,-1) & X(1,0) & X(1,1) & X(1,2) \\
X(2,-2) & X(2,-1) & X(2,0) & X(2,1) & X(2,2) \\
X(3,-2) & X(3,-1) & X(3,0) & X(3,1) & X(3,2) \\
X(4,-2) & X(4,-1) & X(4,0) & X(4,1) & X(4,2) \quad .
\end{array}
$$

As suggested by this arrangement, the *ith row* of a two-dimensional array is the set of elements whose first subscript is i, and the *ith column* is the set of elements whose second subscript is i.

As with one-dimensional arrays, the *value* of an n-dimensional array X is the function with the same domain as X which maps $\langle i_1, \; \ldots \; , i_n \rangle$ into the value of the element $X(i_1, \; \ldots \; , i_n)$.

2.4.2 Assertions for Multidimensional Arrays

Most of the concepts and notations we have introduced for assertions about one-dimensional arrays carry over to multidimensional arrays. The main novelty is the use of the Cartesian product to describe domains. In Section 2.3.7 we introduced the binary Cartesian product, but now we must generalize to a product of n sets: If $S_1, \; \ldots \; , S_n$ are sets, then the *Cartesian product* $S_1 \times \; \ldots \; \times S_n$ is the set of sequences $\langle i_1, \; \ldots \; , i_n \rangle$ such that $i_1 \in S_1, \; \ldots \; , i_n \in S_n$. It is easily seen that

$$S_1 \times \ldots \times S_n \text{ is empty if any } S_i \text{ is empty} \quad , \tag{1}$$

$$\text{If } S_1 \subseteq T_1 \text{ and } \ldots \text{ and } S_n \subseteq T_n \text{ then} \\ S_1 \times \ldots \times S_n \subseteq T_1 \times \ldots \times T_n \quad , \tag{2}$$

$$S_1 \times \ldots \times (S_i \cup T_i) \times \ldots \times S_n \\ = (S_1 \times \ldots \times S_i \times \ldots \times S_n) \cup (S_1 \times \ldots \times T_i \times \ldots \times S_n) \quad , \tag{3}$$

$$\# (S_1 \times \ldots \times S_n) = (\# S_1) \times \ldots \times (\# S_n) \\ \text{when } S_1, \ldots , S_n \text{ are finite sets} \quad . \tag{4}$$

(Note that $\times$ denotes a Cartesian product on the left of (4), but an ordinary numerical product on the right of the same line.) If all of the S_i's are intervals, then $S_1 \times \ldots \times S_n$ is called a *block*. Thus for example, the declaration **real array** $X(l_1 :: u_1, \ldots , l_n :: u_n)$ creates an array whose domain is the block $\boxed{l_1 \quad u_1} \times \ldots \times \boxed{l_n \quad u_n}$.

Suppose S is a block that is a subset of the domain of X. Then the portion of X consisting of the elements $X(\sigma)$ such that $\sigma \in S$, is called the *segment of X over S*. For example, if **dom** $X = S \times T$, then the ith row of X is the segment of X over $\boxed{i} \times T$ and the jth column of X is the segment of X over $S \times \boxed{j}$.

If $\langle i_1, \ldots , i_n \rangle$ belongs to the domain of a function X, then $[X \mid \langle i_1, \ldots , i_n \rangle : y]$ denotes the function with the same domain such that

$$[X \mid \langle i_1, \ldots , i_n \rangle : y] (j_1, \ldots , j_n) \\ = \textbf{if } i_1 = j_1 \text{ and } \ldots \text{ and } i_n = j_n \textbf{ then } y \\ \textbf{else } X(j_1, \ldots , j_n) \quad .$$

The obvious extension of the inference rule for array assignments is:

Multidimensional Array Assignment:

$$\{P|_{X \to [X \mid \langle S_1, \ldots , S_n \rangle : E]}\} \; X(S_1, \ldots , S_n) := E \; \{P\} \quad .$$

*2.4.3   The Minimax of an Array

As an example of the use of a multidimensional array, we consider a problem arising in game theory: finding the minimax of a two-dimensional array segment. Consider a nonempty segment of a two-dimensional array X over $\boxed{1 \quad m} \times \boxed{1 \quad n}$. $X(i0, j0)$ is a *minimax* of this segment if and only if

(1) $X(i0,j0)$ is a maximum of the $i0$th row,
(2)   The maximum of each row is at least $X(i0,j0)$.

Thus our program should set the integer variables $i0$ and $j0$ to meet the specification

$$\{\boxed{1 \quad m} \times \boxed{1 \quad n} \subseteq \textbf{dom } X \text{ and } \boxed{1 \quad m} \text{ and } \boxed{1 \quad n}\}$$
"Find Minimax"
$$\{\boxed{1 \quad i0 \quad m} \text{ and } \boxed{1 \quad j0 \quad n}$$
$$\text{and } \{X \uparrow \boxed{i0} \times \boxed{1 \quad n}\} \leq^* X(i0,j0)$$
$$\text{and } (\forall\, i \in \boxed{1 \quad m})\,(\forall\, j \in \boxed{1 \quad n})$$
$$\{X \uparrow \boxed{i} \times \boxed{1 \quad n}\} \leq^* X(i,j) \text{ implies } X(i0,j0) \leq X(i,j)\,\}\quad.$$

On the main level, our program will iterate over successive rows, using a variable k to keep track of the last row processed. The invariant asserts that $X(i0,j0)$ is the minimax of the part of X processed so far, i.e. the segment over $\boxed{1 \quad k} \times \boxed{1 \quad n}$:

$$\boxed{1 \quad i0 \quad k \quad m} \text{ and } \boxed{1 \quad j0 \quad n}$$
$$\text{and } \{X \uparrow \boxed{i0} \times \boxed{1 \quad n}\} \leq^* X(i0,j0)$$
$$\text{and } (\forall\, i \in \boxed{1 \quad k})\,(\forall\, j \in \boxed{1 \quad n})$$
$$\{X \uparrow \boxed{i} \times \boxed{1 \quad n}\} \leq^* X(i,j) \text{ implies } X(i0,j0) \leq X(i,j)\quad.$$

This will imply the final consequent when $\boxed{k \quad m}$ is empty. On the other hand it can be achieved initially by setting k to one and $i0$ and $j0$ to the subscripts of a maximum of the first row. Thus the program has the form:

```
begin integer k;
"Set j0 to second subscript of maximum of first row";
i0 := 1; k := 1;
```
$$\{\textbf{whileinv: } \boxed{1 \quad i0 \quad k \quad m} \text{ and } \boxed{1 \quad j0 \quad n}$$
$$\text{and } \{X \uparrow \boxed{i0} \times \boxed{1 \quad n}\} \leq^* X(i0,j0)$$
$$\text{and } (\forall\, i \in \boxed{1 \quad k})\,(\forall\, j \in \boxed{1 \quad n})$$
$$\{X \uparrow \boxed{i} \times \boxed{1 \quad n}\} \leq^* X(i,j) \text{ implies } X(i0,j0) \leq X(i,j)\,\}$$
```
while k < m do
    begin k := k+1;
    "Process kth row"
    end
end .
```

At the beginning of "Process kth row" we will have

$$\boxed{1 \; |i0| \; k| \; m} \text{ and } \boxed{1 \; |j0| \; n}$$

$$\text{and } \{X \uparrow \boxed{i0} \times \boxed{1 \; n}\} \leq^* X(i0,j0)$$

$$\text{and } (\forall \; i \in \boxed{1 \; k}) \; (\forall \; j \in \boxed{1 \; n})$$

$$\{X \uparrow \boxed{i} \times \boxed{1 \; n}\} \leq^* X(i,j) \text{ implies } X(i0,j0) \leq X(i,j) \quad .$$

To regain the invariant, the obvious thing to do is to scan the kth row to find its maximum and, if the new maximum is smaller than $X(i0,j0)$, to reset $i0$ and $j0$ to the subscripts of the new maximum.

But one can do better than this. While scanning the kth row, we can compare each element with $X(i0,j0)$. If we find any element which is at least $X(i0,j0)$ then, without completing the scan, we can infer that the maximum must also be at least $X(i0,j0)$, so that $i0$ and $j0$ will not be reset.

Thus, suppose we begin "Process kth row" with

> **begin logical** *new*; **integer** $j1$;
> "Scan kth row";
>
> $\vdots$
>
> **end** ,

where "Scan kth row" either sets *new* to **true** and $j1$ to the second subscript of a row maximum which is smaller than $X(i0,j0)$, or sets *new* to **false** if there is some row element which is at least $X(i0,j0)$:

> $\{\boxed{1 \; k| \; m} \text{ and } \boxed{1 \; n}\}$
> "Scan kth row"
> $\{\textbf{if } new \textbf{ then } \boxed{1 \; |j1| \; n} \text{ and } \{X \uparrow \boxed{k} \times \boxed{1 \; n}\} \leq^* X(k,j1)$
> $\qquad \text{and } X(k,j1) < X(i0,j0)$
> $\quad \textbf{else } (\exists \; j \in \boxed{1 \; n}) \; X(i0,j0) \leq X(k,j) \} \quad .$

By the reasoning of the previous paragraph, this consequent implies that if *new* is **false** then the maximum of the kth row is at least $X(i0,j0)$. Thus "Process kth row" can be completed with

> **if** *new* **then begin** $i0 := k$; $j0 := j1$ **end**   .

The invariant of "Scan kth row" is similar to the consequent except that, if *new* is **true**, it only asserts that $X(k,j1)$ is a maximum of a subsegment of the kth row over $\boxed{1 \; j}$. This invariant will imply the consequent when either *new* is **false** or $\boxed{j \; n}$ is empty, and can be achieved initially by setting j and $j1$ to one and *new* to $X(k,1) < X(i0,j0)$. Thus "Scan kth row" has the form

begin integer j;

$j := 1; j1 := 1; new := X(k,1) < X(i0,j0)$;

{**whileinv: if** *new* **then** $\boxed{1 \quad \boxed{j1} \quad j \quad n}$

and $\{X \uparrow \boxed{k} \times \boxed{1 \quad j}\} \leq^* X(k,j1)$

and $X(k,j1) < X(i0,j0)$

else $(\exists\, j \in \boxed{1 \quad n})\ X(i0,j0) \leq X(k,j)$ }

while *new* **and** $(j<n)$ **do**

$\quad$ **begin** $j := j+1$; "Inspect $X(k,j)$" **end**

end   .

At the beginning of "Inspect $X(k,j)$" we will have

$\boxed{1 \quad \boxed{j1} \quad j \quad n}$ **and** $\{X \uparrow \boxed{k} \times \boxed{1 \quad j}\} \leq^* X(k,j1)$

and $X(k,j1) < X(i0,j0)$.

If $X(i0,j0) \leq X(k,j)$ then we can set *new* to **false**; otherwise we can proceed as in a conventional maximum-finding program. Thus "Inspect $X(k,j)$" can be replaced by

$\quad$ **if** $X(i0,j0) \leq X(k,j)$ **then** *new* := **false else**

$\quad$ **if** $X(k,j1) < X(k,j)$ **then** $j1 := j$.

Filling in "Set $j0$ to second subscript of maximum of first row" with the obvious subprogram, we obtain the following final program:

$\{ \boxed{1\quad m} \times \boxed{1\quad n} \subseteq \textbf{dom } X \textbf{ and } \boxed{1\quad m} \textbf{ and } \boxed{1\quad n} \}$

begin integer k;
   begin integer j;
   $j := 1; j0 := 1$;
   while $j < n$ **do**
      begin $j := j+1$; **if** $X(1,j0) < X(1,j)$ **then** $j0 := j$ **end**
   end;
$i0 := 1; k := 1$;
$\{$**whileinv:** $\boxed{1\quad i0\quad k\quad m}$ **and** $\boxed{1\quad j0\quad n}$
   and $\{X \uparrow \boxed{i0} \times \boxed{1\quad n}\} \leq^* X(i0, j0)$
   and $(\forall\, i \in \boxed{1\quad k})\, (\forall\, j \in \boxed{1\quad n})$
      $\{X \uparrow \boxed{i} \times \boxed{1\quad n}\} \leq^* X(i,j)$ **implies** $X(i0,j0) \leq X(i,j)\,\}$
while $k < m$ **do**
   begin $k := k+1$;
      begin logical *new*; **integer** $j1$;
         begin integer j;
         $j := 1; j1 := 1; new := X(k,1) < X(i0,j0)$;
         $\{$**whileinv: if** *new* **then** $\boxed{1\quad j1\quad j\quad n}$
            and $\{X \uparrow \boxed{k} \times \boxed{1\quad j}\} \leq^* X(k,j1)$
            and $X(k,j1) < X(i0,j0)$
            else $(\exists\, j \in \boxed{1\quad n})\, X(i0,j0) \leq X(k,j)\,\}$
         while *new* **and** $(j < n)$ **do**
            begin $j := j+1$;
            if $X(i0,j0) \leq X(k,j)$ **then** *new* := **false else**
               if $X(k,j1) < X(k,j)$ **then** $j1 := j$
            end
         end;
         if *new* **then begin** $i0 := k; j0 := j1$ **end**
      end
   end
end
$\{\boxed{1\quad i0\quad m}$ **and** $\boxed{1\quad j0\quad n}$
   and $\{X \uparrow \boxed{i0} \times \boxed{1\quad n}\} \leq^* X(i0,j0)$
   and $(\forall\, i \in \boxed{1\quad m})\, (\forall\, j \in \boxed{1\quad n})$
      $\{X \uparrow \boxed{i} \times \boxed{1\quad n}\} \leq^* X(i,j)$ **implies** $X(i0,j0) \leq X(i,j)\,\}$

Termination and the impossibility of subscript errors are left to the reader.

The idea of aborting the row scan when encountering an element larger or equal to $X(i0,j0)$ is a special case of J. McCarthy's "alpha-beta heuristic", which is an algorithm for the more general problem of finding the minimax of a tree with numerical node values [Slagle 69].

Exercises

1. For many array-manipulation problems, reasonable efficiency requires substantially different approaches to the input-preserving case and the non-input-preserving or "inplace" case. A simple illustration is provided by the problem of transposing a two-dimensional array.

    Write two programs, one for placing the transpose of $X \uparrow \boxed{1~~m} \times \boxed{1~~n}$ in $Y \uparrow \boxed{1~~n} \times \boxed{1~~m}$ and the other for placing the transpose of $X \uparrow \boxed{1~~n} \times \boxed{1~~n}$ in X itself. The programs should require time of order $\# \boxed{1~~m} \times \boxed{1~~n}$ and $\# \boxed{1~~n} \times \boxed{1~~n}$ respectively, and should not use any local arrays. They should satisfy

$$\{\boxed{1~~m} \times \boxed{1~~n} \subseteq \textbf{dom } X \text{ and } \boxed{1~~n} \times \boxed{1~~m} \subseteq \textbf{dom } Y\}$$
    "Input-preserving transposition"
$$\{(\forall\, i \in \boxed{1~~m})\,(\forall\, j \in \boxed{1~~n})\ Y(j, i) = X(i, j)\}$$

    and

$$\{\boxed{1~~n} \times \boxed{1~~n} \subseteq \textbf{dom } X \text{ and } X = X_0\}$$
    "Inplace transposition"
$$\{(\forall\, i \in \boxed{1~~n})\,(\forall\, j \in \boxed{1~~n})\ X(j, i) = X_0(i, j)\}\quad.$$

2. (Suggested by R. W. Floyd) Write a program that will examine the segment of a logical array T over $\boxed{1~~m} \times \boxed{1~~n}$ to determine the largest square subblock within which the values of T are all true.

    Let

$$squ(i, j, d) \equiv$$
$$i - d\boxed{~~i} \times j - d\boxed{~~j} \subseteq \boxed{1~~m} \times \boxed{1~~n}$$
$$\textbf{and } \{T \uparrow i - d\boxed{~~i} \times j - d\boxed{~~j}\} =^* \textbf{true}$$

    Then the program should set integer variables i, j, and d, and satisfy

$$\{\boxed{1~~m} \times \boxed{1~~n} \subseteq \textbf{dom } T\}$$
    "Find largest square"
$$\{squ(i, j, d) \textbf{ and } (\forall\, i' \in \boxed{1~~m})\,(\forall\, j' \in \boxed{1~~n})\,(\forall\, d' \geq 0)$$
$$(squ(i', j', d') \textbf{ implies } d' \leq d)\}\quad.$$

    With some ingenuity, it is possible to construct such a program that requires time of order $m \cdot n$.

3 PROCEDURES

Most programming languages provide facilities that, to at least a limited extent, permit the programmer to define and then use new kinds of statements and expressions. In Algol-like languages, this capability is provided by *procedures*: new statements called *procedure statements* are defined by *proper procedure declarations*, and new expressions called *function designators* are defined by *function procedure declarations*. (Most of our attention will focus on proper procedures; function procedures will be introduced in Section 3.1.8.)

The use of procedures can sometimes save considerable writing and also reduce the space needed to store a program in the computer. But the real importance of procedures is their usefulness for displaying program structure. One can encapsulate as a procedure a conceptually subordinate program for performing some task, and then treat the performance of this task as an elementary operation on the same level as the basic statements and expressions of the programming language.

Of necessity, our discussion of procedures will be more language-dependent than that of previous topics, since facilities for procedures (often called "subroutines" or "macros") vary substantially among different programming languages. Fortunately, the procedure facility of Algol W, based upon that of Algol 60 [Naur 60, 63], is exceptionally powerful, elegant, and amenable to formal reasoning. Indeed, this is one of the main reasons that Algol W, as opposed to Pascal for example, is used in this book.

3.1   PROCEDURES IN ALGOL W

3.1.1   Proper Procedures and the Copy Rule

Suppose a statement S occurs several times in some block of a program:

begin ... ; S; ... ; S; ... ; S; ... **end**   .

Rather than writing out each occurrence of S, we may declare some identifier P to stand for S, and then write P instead of S:

begin procedure P; S;
  ... ; P; ... ; P; ... ; P; ... **end**   .

Here **procedure** P; S is a *procedure declaration* whose *body* is S, and the other occurrences of P are *procedure statements*. The procedure statements are said to *call* the procedure defined by the procedure declaration.

Under the scope of the declaration **procedure** P; S, the procedure statement P will have the same meaning as S. For example, under the scope of

procedure *stepx*; $x := x + 1$,

the statement *stepx* will have the same meaning as $x := x + 1$.

In this form, the procedure facility has limited usefulness; it is unusual to need exactly the same statement in several places. More often, one needs statements that are similar in form but different in the occurrences of certain subphrases. To accomplish this kind of variation, we introduce *parameters*.

The basic idea is to add a parenthesized list of distinct identifiers F_1; ... ; F_n, called *formal parameters*, to the procedure declaration:

procedure $P(F_1; \ldots ; F_n)$; S

and to add a corresponding list of phrases $A_1, \ldots , A_n$, called *actual* parameters to each procedure statement:

$P(A_1, \ldots , A_n)$.

Then, under the scope of the above declaration, $P(A_1, \ldots , A_n)$ will have the same meaning as the statement obtained by substituting $A_1, \ldots , A_n$ for $F_1, \ldots , F_n$ in S.

For example, if we declare

procedure *incx*(**integer** $\{$**exp**$\}$ y); $x := x + y$

(the occurrence of **integer** $\{$**exp**$\}$ here will be explained in the next section), then the procedure statement *incx*(3) will have the same meaning as $x := x + 3$, and the procedure statement *incx*($a \times b$) will have the same meaning as $x := x + a \times b$.

Actually, the exact definition of the meaning of procedures, called the *copy rule*, is somewhat more complicated than is indicated by the above discussion. Before stating the copy rule, however, we must describe the binding properties of procedure declarations, which are more complex than those of other declarations.

Like all declarations, a procedure declaration binds the identifier which it declares, i.e. in

$$\textbf{procedure } P(F_1; \ldots ; F_n); \; S$$

the occurrence of P is a binder whose scope is the scope of the declaration, which is the immediately enclosing block, excluding lower and upper bounds of array declarations that are immediately enclosed by that block. However, the occurrences of $F_1, \ldots, F_n$ in the formal parameter list are also binders, whose scope is different than that of the declaration: the scope of $F_1, \ldots, F_n$ is the formal parameter list itself plus the body S of the procedure declaration.

This binding structure is illustrated by

$$\textbf{begin procedure } incx(\textbf{integer } \{exp\} \; y); \; \textcircled{x} := \textcircled{x} + y;$$

$$\vdots$$

$$incx(\textcircled{y} + 1)$$

$$\textbf{end} \quad ,$$

where we have circled free identifier occurrences and drawn arrows from bound occurrences to the binders that bind them. Notice that the procedure statement $incx(\textcircled{y} + 1)$ falls within the scope of the binder of $incx$, but not within the scope of the binder of y. Also notice that a procedure body can contain free occurrences of identifiers, such as x, that are not formal parameters. In general, the free identifier occurrences in the body of a procedure declaration that are not bound by the formal parameter list of that declaration are said to be *global* occurrences.

We can now state the *copy rule*: Let $P(A_1, \ldots, A_n)$ be a procedure statement in which the occurrence of P is bound by the declaration

$$\textbf{procedure } P(F_1; \ldots ; F_n); \; S \quad .$$

Suppose that, for every identifier G occurring globally in S, there is no binder of G whose scope includes the procedure statement but not the procedure declaration. Then $P(A_1, \ldots, A_n)$ has the same meaning as

$$S \big|_{F_1, \ldots, F_n \to A_1, \ldots, A_n} \quad .$$

The restriction on binders of global identifiers is needed to avoid identifier collisions. As will be illustrated in Section 3.1.3, this restriction can always be satisfied by alpha-converting the scope of the offending binders.

It should be emphasized that the copy rule describes the meaning of procedures rather than their implementation. One could implement procedures (excepting recursive procedures, which will be introduced in Section 3.2) by using the copy rule to eliminate procedure statements prior to translation into machine code; such an approach is often called an "open subroutine" or "macro-expansion" implementation. In the implementation of Algol W, however, "closed subroutines" are used: procedure declarations and statements are compiled into separate segments of code, and during the execution of a procedure statement control passes back and forth between these segments in a complex manner that simulates the copy rule.

We will not discuss the details of this implementation method, which is described in [Dijkstra 60] and [Randell 64]. Its overall effect, however, is to reduce the storage needed for machine code at the expense of increasing execution time and the storage needed for data. However, these increases do not affect order of magnitude bounds on time or storage space.

3.1.2 Specifiers and Phrase Types

In the previous discussion, we glossed over the possibility that the formal and actual parameters of a procedure may not match, so that the substitution prescribed by the copy rule gives a syntactically invalid statement.

Consider a procedure declaration with n formal parameters:

procedure $P(F_1; \ldots ; F_n); S$

Under the scope of this declaration, each procedure statement $P(A_1, \ldots, A_n)$ must obviously have n actual parameters. Beyond this, however, each A_i must be a phrase that can meaningfully replace F_i at all of its free occurrences in the procedure body S. For example, under the declaration of *incx* given in the previous section, the statement *incx*(**true**) would be erroneous, since substituting **true** for y in the body $x := x + y$ would give the syntactically invalid $x := x + \textbf{true}$.

It is important to be able to detect this kind of error during compilation rather than execution. ("During execution" can be long after the program has been written, tested, and falsely presumed correct.) For this purpose, Algol W requires the programmer to specify the types of all formal parameters. A procedure declaration with n formal parameters actually has the form

procedure $P(\sigma_1; \ldots ; \sigma_n); S$

where each σ_i is a *specifier*, which not only names the formal parameter F_i but also describes its type. Using the type information in σ_i, the compiler checks both the occurrences of F_i in S and the corresponding actual parameter A_i in each procedure statement that calls P. The type information is also used to improve the efficiency of the closed-subroutine implementation.

For example, the specifier **integer** y in

   procedure *incx*(**integer** y); $x := x + y$

permits the compiler to detect an incorrect usage, such as $x := x$ **and** y, of the formal parameter y in the body of the procedure declaration, and to detect a procedure statement, such as *incx*(**true**), with an incorrect actual parameter.

   Ideally, these checks by the compiler should insure that no parameter mismatches can occur during execution of a program, i.e. that the substitution prescribed by the copy rule never gives a syntactically invalid statement. Unfortunately, however, the specifiers used in Algol W are inadequate to achieve this goal. For example, one can declare

   procedure *setzero*(**integer** y); $y := 0$.

In contrast to the situation with *incx*, a procedure statement such as *setzero*(7) is erroneous, since the substitution of 7 for y would give the invalid statement $7 := 0$. Similarly, *setzero*$(a + 1)$ is erroneous, since it would lead to $a + 1 := 0$. In general, however, this kind of error cannot be detected in Algol W programs before execution.

   This inadequacy is the most serious design mistake in the language. It postpones the detection of a significant class of errors from compilation to execution. Moreover, the need to detect such errors during execution degrades the efficiency of the procedure mechanism.

   At the time Algol W was developed, the design of adequate specifiers was not understood. Since then, however, largely through the development of Algol 68 [van Wijngaarden 69], the problem has been solved. In this book, we will apply the solution retroactively to Algol W.

   Essentially, we will change Algol W by extending the form of specifiers to eliminate their inadequacies. Of course, we will not actually change the compiler to accept a different form of specifier or to detect more errors. The extra information in our extended specifiers will really be comments—indicated by the perennial curly brackets—but these comments will be used in a formally prescribed manner that will insure the correctness of parameter matching.

   For example, we will write

   procedure *incx*(**integer** {**exp**} y); $x := x + y$

to indicate that the formal parameter y is used in the procedure body as an integer expression, but not in a context, such as the left side of an assignment statement, that requires a variable. This permits procedure statements such as *incx*(7) or *incx*$(a + 1)$, though it prohibits statements such as *incx*(**true**) or *incx*(3.5) where the actual parameter is not an *integer* expression.

   On the other hand, we will write

   procedure *setzero*(**integer** {**var**} y); $y := 0$

to indicate that the formal parameter y may be assigned to (as well as evaluated) in the procedure body. This permits statements such as *setzero*(a) or *setzero*$(X(1))$, but prohibits statements such as *setzero*(7) or *setzero*($a + 1$) where the actual parameter is not a variable.

In general, what an (extended) specifier specifies is the *phrase type* of the formal parameter that it binds. At the outset, it must be emphasized that phrase types are quite different than data types. A data type, such as **integer**, describes a set of values that can be taken on by a particular kind of variable. On the other hand, a phrase type, such as **integer variable**, **integer expression**, or **procedure(integer expression)**, describes a set of phrases that have a particular kind of meaning. When a formal parameter is specified to have the phrase type θ, it must only occur in contexts that would permit any phrase of type θ (perhaps after parenthesization), and each corresponding actual parameter must be a phrase of type θ.

For instance, for any data type τ, the specifier τ {**var**} F specifies that F has phrase type τ **variable**. Phrases of this type include not only appropriately declared identifiers, but also array designators such as $X(1)$, where X denotes a one–dimensional τ array. On the other hand, the specifier τ {**exp**} F specifies that F has phrase type τ **expression**. Phrases of this type include not only phrases of type τ **variable**, but also various constants and compound expressions. Since the variety of phrases is greater for τ **expression** than for τ **variable**, the variety of contexts that permit formal parameters is more limited, e.g. it excludes the left sides of assignment statements.

Formal parameters of phrase type τ **variable** or τ **expression** are often called *simple* parameters. In Section 3.1.5 we will introduce other specifiers for simple parameters, and in Sections 3.1.6 to 3.1.8 we will introduce specifiers for parameters of other phrase types.

Frequently, several formal parameters of the same procedure will have similar specifiers. When such specifiers appear consecutively in the formal parameter list they may be combined into a single *compound* specifier. For example, the formal parameter list

$$\textbf{integer } \{\textbf{exp}\} \ i; \ \textbf{integer } \{\textbf{exp}\} \ j; \ \textbf{real } \{\textbf{var}\} \ x; \ \textbf{real } \{\textbf{var}\} \ y$$

can be abbreviated by

$$\textbf{integer } \{\textbf{exp}\} \ i, j; \ \textbf{real } \{\textbf{var}\} \ x, y$$

Note that, just as with declarations, specifiers are separated by semicolons, while formal parameters within compound specifiers are separated by commas.

Not only specifiers, but all binding mechanisms specify the phrase type of the identifiers that they bind. For example, the declaration $\tau \ I_1, \ldots, I_n$ specifies that $I_1, \ldots, I_n$ have phrase type τ **variable**. The quantifiers $(\forall I \in S)$ and $(\exists I \in S)$ each specify that I has phrase type τ **expression**, where τ is the data type of the members of S. (One needs τ **expression** here, rather than τ **variable**, so that constants or compound expressions can be substituted for I when applying law (4) of Section 2.2.5.)

The nature of specifiers and phrase types is formalized by the syntax in Appendix B, where phrases of type θ are the phrases that can be derived from the nonterminal $\langle\theta\rangle$, and the contexts that permit formal parameters and other identifiers of phrase type θ are the contexts that permit the nonterminal $\langle\theta$ identifier$\rangle$. In Section B.3 of Appendix B, it is shown that correctness with regard to this syntax is preserved by the copy rule.

3.1.3 Identifier Collisions

Most of the programs developed in previous chapters might reasonably occur within complete programs as the bodies of procedure declarations. An example is the following declaration of a procedure for computing the factorial:

> **procedure** *fact*(**integer** {**exp**} n; **integer** {**var**} f);
> $\{n \geq 0\}$
>   **begin integer** k;
> $k := 0; f := 1;$
>   **while** $k \neq n$ **do**
>   **begin** $k := k+1; f := k \times f$ **end**
>   **end**
> $\{f = n!\}$.

Suppose a, b, c are integer variables, and x is a real variable. It is easily seen from the copy rule that, under the scope of this declaration, the procedure statement *fact*(a, b) will set b to the factorial of a, *fact*$(3, a)$ will set a to 6, and *fact*$(a + b, c)$ will set c to the factorial of $a + b$. On the other hand, because of the rules for parameter matching, *fact*(a, b, c), *fact*(**true**, a), *fact*(x, a), *fact*$(3, x)$, *fact*$(3, 4)$, and *fact*$(3, a+b)$ are all erroneous.

A more interesting case is the procedure statement *fact*(k, a). At first sight, it might appear that the copy rule asserts that this is equivalent to

> **begin integer** k;
> $k := 0; a := 1;$
> **while** $k \neq k$ **do**
>   **begin** $k := k+1; a := k \times a$ **end**
> **end**   .

But this statement will not compute the factorial correctly, since the actual parameter k has been captured by the declaration of the local variable k.

This is another instance of the interaction between substitution and binding called identifier collision, which was first encountered in Section

2.2.6. The definition of substitution given there requires that, before substituting $A_1, \ldots, A_n$ for $F_1, \ldots, F_n$ in S, S must be alpha-converted to eliminate binders of identifiers that occur free in any A_i. In this case, since k occurs free in an actual parameter, the procedure body must be converted to eliminate the binder of k before substituting k,a for n,f. Thus the procedure statement $fact(k, a)$ is equivalent to

$$\begin{aligned}
&\textbf{begin integer } k'; \\
&k' := 0;\ a := 1; \\
&\textbf{while } k' \neq k \textbf{ do} \\
&\quad \textbf{begin } k' := k' + 1;\ a := k' \times a \textbf{ end} \\
&\textbf{end} \quad ,
\end{aligned}$$

where the bound occurrences of k have been renamed k'. As one would hope, this statement will set a to the factorial of k. (Strictly speaking, k' is not a legal Algol W identifier, but for expository purposes the use of primes to indicate renaming is irresistible.)

When a program is to be encapsulated as a procedure, one must decide which of the identifiers occurring free in the program are to be bound as formal parameters and which are to be left as globals. In general, it is clearest to parameterize only those identifiers whose meaning will vary among different calls of the procedure. Thus one would declare

$$\textbf{procedure } incx(\textbf{integer } \{\textbf{exp}\}\ y);\ x := x + y$$

to increase the particular variable x by a variety of values,

$$\textbf{procedure } incbyy(\textbf{integer } \{\textbf{var}\}\ x);\ x := x + y$$

to increase a variety of variables by the particular value y, and

$$\textbf{procedure } inc(\textbf{integer } \{\textbf{var}\}\ x;\ \textbf{integer } \{\textbf{exp}\}\ y);\ x := x + y$$

to increase a variety of variables by a variety of values.

Global identifier occurrences introduce further possibilities for identifier collisions. Consider, for example,

$$\begin{aligned}
&\textbf{begin integer } x; \\
&\textbf{procedure } incx(\textbf{integer } \{\textbf{exp}\}\ y);\ x := x + y; \\
&\quad \vdots \\
&\quad \textbf{begin integer } x;\ \ldots\ incx(3);\ \ldots\ \textbf{end} \\
&\textbf{end} \quad .
\end{aligned}$$

Here the global occurrences of x are bound by the first declaration of x, so that $incx$ is a procedure for increasing the particular variable denoted by that declaration. Thus this block should not be equivalent to

> **begin integer** x;
>
> $\vdots$
>
> > **begin integer** x; ... $x := x + 3$; ... **end**
> **end**   ,

in which $x := x + 3$ increases the variable denoted by the second declaration of x.

This is the rationale for the proviso in the copy rule that "for every identifier G occurring globally in S, there is no binder of G whose scope includes the procedure statement but not the procedure declaration." To meet this proviso, we must alpha-convert our example to eliminate the second declaration of x before applying the copy rule. This gives

> **begin integer** x;
>
> $\vdots$
>
> > **begin integer** x'; ... $x := x + 3$; ... **end**
> **end**   ,

in which $x := x + 3$ increases the variable declared by the first declaration.

Exercise

1. For each identifier occurrence in the following statements, indicate whether it is free or bound and, if it is bound, indicate the binder that binds it. Then use the copy rule, with alpha conversion when necessary, to produce equivalent statements that do not contain procedure statements.

    (a) **begin integer** x;
         procedure *powerx*(**integer** {**exp**} n; **integer** {**var**} y);
             begin integer k; $k := 0$; $y := 1$;
             while $k \neq n$ **do begin** $k := k+1$; $y := x \times y$ **end**
             end;
         $x := 3$;
             begin integer x; ... *powerx*($k+1$, x); ... **end**
         end   .

    (b) **begin**
         procedure p(**integer** {**var**} y);
             begin
             procedure p(**integer** {**var**} y, z);
                 begin integer x; $x := y$; $y := z$; $z := x$ **end**;
             $p(x, y)$
             end;
         begin integer x; ... $p(x)$; ... **end**
         end   .

3.1.4 Interference and Parameter Assumptions

Although the copy rule avoids identifier collisions by alpha conversion, it does not avoid another phenomenon called *interference*. A simple illustration is provided by the procedure statement *fact*(a, a), which is equivalent to

> **begin integer** k;
> $k := 0$; $a := 1$;
> **while** $k \neq a$ **do**
> > **begin** $k := k + 1$; $a := k \times a$ **end**
>
> **end**   .

This statement does not set the variable a to the factorial of its previous value. The difficulty is that the two formal parameters n and f, which we expected to denote distinct variables when we wrote the procedure body, have both been replaced by actual parameters denoting the same variable. This replacement causes f to *interfere* with n, i.e. an assignment to f will change the value of n. In fact, the assignment $f := 1$ will obliterate the value of n whose factorial we are trying to compute.

More generally, interference can occur whenever an actual parameter of phrase type τ **variable** occurs in some other actual parameter. For example, *fact*$(a + b, a)$ will not set a to the factorial of $a + b$. Again, the replacement of formal by actual parameters causes f to interfere with n.

Interference can also take place between formal parameters and global identifiers. For example,

> **procedure** *powerx*(**integer** {**exp**} n; **integer** {**var**} y);
> > {$n \geq 0$}
>
> **begin integer** k;
> $k := 0$; $y := 1$;
> **while** $k \neq n$ **do**
> > **begin** $k := k + 1$; $y := x \times y$ **end**
>
> **end**
> > {$y = x^n$}

will normally set y to the nth power of the global variable x. But this procedure will not behave correctly if y interferes with either the formal parameter n or the global identifier x. Thus both *powerx*(a, a) and *powerx*(a, x) would be erroneous calls.

These examples make it clear that the correctness of a procedure statement will often depend upon assumptions of noninterference that restrict the replacement of formal by actual parameters. A clearly documented procedure declaration must include a description of these *parameter assumptions*.

For this purpose we will write $X \mathbin{\#} E$, where X is a variable and E is an expression, to indicate that X must not interfere with E, i.e. that no assignment to X may affect the value of E. (Normally, X and E will be formal parameters or global identifiers.) When more than one such assumption is necessary, they will be joined together with the symbol & (meaning "and"). The parameter assumptions will then be labeled with the symbol **pa**, surrounded by curly brackets (since they are formal comments about program correctness), and placed between the formal parameter list and the procedure body (before the precedent of the body if it is present).

For example, a correctly annotated version of *fact* is

> **procedure** *fact*(**integer** {**exp**} n; **integer** {**var**} f);
> {**pa**: $f \# n$}
> {$n \geq 0$}
> **begin integer** k;
> $k := 0; f := 1$;
> **while** $k \neq n$ **do**
>   **begin** $k := k + 1; f := k \times f$ **end**
> **end**
> {$f = n!$} .

Similarly, for *powerx* we would write

> **procedure** *powerx*(**integer** {**exp**} n; **integer** {**var**} y);
> {**pa**: $y \# n$ & $y \# x$}
> {$n \geq 0$}
> **begin integer** k;
> $k := 0; y := 1$;
> **while** $k \neq n$ **do**
>   **begin** $k := k + 1; y := x \times y$ **end**
> **end**
> {$y = x^n$} .

It is important to understand the distinction between assertions, parameter assumptions, and specifiers. Assertions describe states of the computation. Parameter assumptions and specifiers describe restrictions on the replacement of formal by actual parameters. The distinction between the latter two entities is that specifiers describe *syntactic* restrictions, i.e. restrictions that can be expressed by a syntactic description of the programming language (as in Appendix B), and that can be enforced by a compiler (even though the existing Algol W compiler does not enforce our extended specifiers). In contrast, parameter assumptions describe restrictions that are, in general, too subtle to be treated syntactically or to be enforced by a compiler.

(Actually, the possibility of devising syntactic restrictions to control interference is a current research topic of considerable importance, especially for the design of programming languages for concurrent computation [Reynolds 78a]. However, such an approach to the problem of interference is beyond the scope of this book.)

3.1.5 Call by Value and Result

For simple parameters, there is a standard method for avoiding the problems of interference. The basic idea is to replace occurrences of formal parameters in the procedure body by local variables. Then the formal parameters that convey input information are used to initialize the corresponding local variables, while the formal parameters that convey output information are assigned the final values of the corresponding local variables.

For example, the result of applying this transformation to the procedure *fact* would give

> **procedure** *fact*(**integer** {**exp**} n; **integer** {**var**} f);
>   **begin integer** n', f';
> $n' := n$;
>   **begin integer** k;
> $k := 0; f' := 1$;
>   **while** $k \neq n'$ **do**
>   **begin** $k := k + 1; f' := k \times f'$ **end**
>   **end**;
> $f := f'$
>   **end** .

In this form, the procedure will still work correctly when f interferes with n, since this will not cause the local variables f' and n' to interfere, and since the procedure never examines the possibly altered value of n after assigning to f.

For example, *fact*($a+b$, a) has the same meaning as

> **begin integer** n', f';
> $n' := a + b$;
>   **begin integer** k;
> $k := 0; f' := 1$;
>   **while** $k \neq n'$ **do**
>   **begin** $k := k + 1; f' := k \times f'$ **end**
>   **end**;
> $a := f'$
> **end** .

Of course, this statement will change the value of $a + b$, so that $a = (a + b)$! will not hold after execution. But the final value of a will be the factorial of the initial value of $a + b$, i.e.

$$\{a+b\geq0 \text{ and } a+b=n_0\} \ fact(a+b,\ a) \ \{a=n_0!\} \quad .$$

This kind of transformation is so commonly useful that an equivalent mechanism is built into Algol W. To define the procedure given above, one need only write the declaration

> **procedure** *fact*(**integer value** n; **integer result** f);
>   **begin integer** k;
> $k := 0; f := 1;$
>   **while** $k \neq n$ **do**
>   **begin** $k := k+1; f := k \times f$ **end**
>   **end**   .

The general mechanism is the following: Instead of using the specifiers τ {**var**} F or τ {**exp**} F (where τ is some data type), one may use any of the following specifiers:

> τ **value** F
> τ **result** F
> τ **value result** F .

In these cases the formal parameter F is said to be *called by value*, *called by result*, or *called by value and result*, respectively. In contrast, a formal parameter with any other form of specifier is said to be *called by name*.

(Although these terms are firmly entrenched in the computing literature, they are slightly illogical. One normally speaks of a procedure statement "calling" a procedure, e.g. *fact*($a+b, c$) calls *fact*. But "call by name" or "by value" or "by result" describes the behavior of a parameter, not a procedure.)

The effect of these new specifiers is equivalent to transforming the body of the procedure declaration as follows:

(1)   All free occurrences of formal parameters called by value or by result (or both) are renamed. (We will indicate this renaming by adding primes to the parameter occurrences.)

(2)   The procedure body is enclosed in a block in which the renamed parameters are declared as local variables, with the data types indicated by their specifiers.

(3)   For each formal parameter F_i called by value, or by value and result, the assignment $F_i' := F_i$ is added to the beginning of the block enclosing the body.

(4)   For each formal parameter F_i called by result, or by value and result, the assignment $F_i := F_i'$ is added to the end of the block enclosing the body.

After the procedure body has been transformed in this manner, specifiers of the form τ **value** F should be replaced by τ {**exp**} F, and specifiers of the form τ **result** F and τ **value result** F should be replaced by τ {**var**} F.

This transformation preserves syntactic correctness if each formal parameter specified by τ **value**, τ **result**, or τ **value result** is used as a τ variable within the procedure body. For τ **result** and τ **value result**, the corresponding actual parameters must also be τ variables, but for τ **value**, the corresponding actual parameters may be τ expressions. (Thus τ **value** is anomalous in specifying one phrase type, τ **variable**, for the identifier that it binds but another phrase type, τ **expression**, for corresponding actual parameters.)

In addition to avoiding the problems of interference, call by value and call by result are usually more efficient than call by name. This is especially true when a formal parameter that is repeatedly evaluated in the procedure body is replaced by an actual parameter that is a complex expression. For example, consider $fact((a + b) \times c, d)$. When the formal parameter n (corresponding to $(a + b) \times c$) is called by name, this statement is equivalent to

> **begin integer** k;
> $k := 0; d := 1$;
> **while** $k \neq (a + b) \times c$ **do**
>   **begin** $k := k + 1; d := k \times d$ **end**
> **end**   ,

which will repeatedly evaluate $(a + b) \times c$. On the other hand, when n is called by value, the expression $(a + b) \times c$ will only be evaluated once, at the beginning of the procedure body.

In most cases, it is best to call simple parameters by value and/or result. One should specify **value** if the formal parameter conveys input information, and **result** if it conveys output information. Indeed, the Algol W compiler encourages the use of call by value and result by giving a warning message whenever a simple parameter is called by name. Conceptually, however, call by name is more fundamental, since it is defined directly by the copy rule, while call by value and result are defined in terms of call by name in the manner we have just described.

Nevertheless, there are situations where call by name is needed for simple parameters. One case occurs when it is necessary to avoid evaluation of some parameter for certain values of other parameters. Consider

> **procedure** *setimply*(**logical result** p; **logical value** q;
>   **logical** {**exp**} r);
> $p :=$ **if** q **then** r **else true**   .

If P is a logical variable and Q and R are logical expressions, then the procedure statement

> *setimply*(P, Q, R)

has the same effect as $P := $ **if** Q **then** R **else true**, or $P := Q$ **implies** R (which cannot be written in Algol W since the language does not provide the logical operator **implies**). Calling r by name rather than by value avoids the unnecessary evaluation of R when Q is **false**. This is vital if R is ill-defined for certain states in which Q is **false**. For example, suppose X is an array with domain $\boxed{a \quad b}$. Then the use of call by name for r is necessary to avoid subscript errors in a procedure statement such as

$$setimply(zerovalue, (a \leq i) \textbf{ and } (i \leq b), X(i) = 0) \quad .$$

A more profound application of call by name, known as Jensen's device, turns the phenomena of repeated evaluation and interference into advantages. Consider

```
procedure sum(integer {var} i; integer {exp} e);
    begin s := 0; i := a − 1;
    while i < b do
        begin i := i + 1; s := s + e end
    end   .
```

Suppose I is an integer variable and E is an integer expression. Then the procedure statement $sum(I, E)$ is equivalent to

```
begin s := 0; I := a − 1;
while I < b do
    begin I := I + 1; s := s + E end
end   .
```

At first sight this statement appears to sum the same value of E repeatedly, i.e. to be an unusually inefficient way of setting s to $(\#\boxed{a \quad b}) \times E$. But suppose that the variable I interferes with the expression E. Then each execution of the **while**-statement body will evaluate E for a different value of I, and the program will set s to the sum

$$\sum_{I=a}^{b} E \quad .$$

For example, if a is 1, b is 100, and X is an array with the domain $\boxed{1 \quad 100}$, then $sum(j, X(j) \times X(j))$ will set s to

$$\sum_{j=1}^{100} X(j) \times X(j) \quad ,$$

i.e. to the vector product of X with itself.

Call by name and call by value are peculiar to Algol-like languages, and call by result is an original feature of Algol W. Most programming languages, including FORTRAN and PL/I, treat parameters by a method known as *call by reference* or *by address*. In this approach, a formal parameter F_i denotes the same variable as the corresponding actual parameter A_i when A_i denotes a variable, but F_i denotes a local variable initialized to A_i when A_i is a constant or a compound expression. Roughly speaking, variables are called by name, while constants and compound expressions are called by value. Repeated (or avoided) parameter evaluation never occurs, but interference is still possible. Call by reference is less powerful than the combination of call by name and by value, but it can be given a more efficient implementation.

This brief description glosses over some subtle differences between call by reference and call by name which have profound repercussions upon the formal definition of programming languages and methods for proving program correctness. Although call by reference is more prevalent in present-day programming languages, the author believes that call by name is a more sound conceptual basis for the procedure mechanism.

Exercises

1. Show that, for the procedure *fact*, interference problems will be avoided if n is called by value and f by name, or if n is called by name and f by result.

2. When call by value is specified, one can assign to the formal parameter without affecting the corresponding actual parameter. Use this capability to write a version of *fact* whose only local variables are the "hidden" local variables implicit in the use of call by value or result.
    (*Hint*: Use the invariant $f \times (n!) = n_0!$ **and** $n \geq 0$, where n_0 is a ghost identifier referring to the value of the formal parameter n when execution of the procedure body begins.)

3. Consider how the examples and exercises in Chapter 1 might be encapsulated as procedures. In particular, determine which identifiers should be formal parameters, and what their specifiers should be. Are there any cases in which call by name might be useful?

3.1.6   Array Parameters

So far, we have only considered simple parameters, whose phrase type is τ **variable** or τ **expression**. In this section and the next we move on to parameters with other phrase types. The copy rule is sufficiently general to handle these extensions, but additional specifiers must be introduced.

An array specifier in Algol W has the form τ **array** $F(*, \ldots, *)$, where τ is a data type and the parenthesized list, called a *dimension list*, contains $n \geq 1$ asterisks. This specifies that F denotes an n-dimensional array whose elements have data type τ. A corresponding actual parameter must also denote an n-dimensional array whose elements have data type τ.

Just as with simple call-by-name parameters, we will extend array specifiers by adding {**exp**} or {**var**}. The specifier

$$\tau \text{ array } \{\text{exp}\} \ F(*, \ldots, *)$$

which establishes the phrase type τ **array expression**(*, ... , *), will be used if no element of F can be assigned to or changed by executing the procedure, while

$$\tau \text{ array } \{\text{var}\} \ F(*, \ldots, *)$$

which establishes the phrase type τ **array variable**(*, ... , *), will be used otherwise.

In this case, the use of {**exp**} or {**var**} is not needed to ensure that the copy rule preserves syntactic correctness, since there is no phrase in Algol W that denotes an array value but not an array whose elements can be assigned to. However, such array expressions are conceptually possible; indeed, much of Chapter 2 was devoted to defining such expressions, e.g. $[X \,|\, i: e]$ or $X \cdot Y$, for use in assertions. Moreover, the use of {**exp**} or {**var**} provides essential information about a procedure by indicating which parameters denote arrays whose values may be changed by the procedure.

Similar array specifiers that occur consecutively can be combined. For example,

integer array {**exp**} $X(*)$; **integer array** {**exp**} $Y(*)$

can be abbreviated by the compound array specifier

integer array {**exp**} $X, Y(*)$.

Array parameters are always called by name, so that interference between arrays can affect correctness. One should be wary whenever the same array identifier occurs more than once as an actual parameter in a procedure statement.

The omission of call by value or result for arrays is motivated by both consistency and efficiency. The provision of these facilities would introduce implicit array assignments into a language that does not permit explicit array assignments, and would obscure the space and time requirements of array-handling procedures. Although, as we will see below, there are situations where arrays must be copied to avoid interference, such copying can have a major impact on the time and space requirements of a program, so that it is better to program the copying explicitly rather than hide it in a parameter-passing mechanism.

As an example of the use of array parameters, the following procedure encapsulates the program constructed in Section 2.2.7 for finding the subscript of a maximum of an array segment:

procedure max(**integer value** a, b; **integer result** j;

    integer array {**exp**} $X(*)$);

$\{\boxed{a\quad b} \subseteq \text{\bf dom } X \text{ \bf and } \boxed{a\quad b}\}$

begin integer k;

$j := a; k := a;$

$\{$**whileinv**: $\boxed{a\quad\boxed{j}\quad\boxed{k}\quad b}$ **and** $\{X \uparrow \boxed{a\quad k}\} \leq^* X(j)\}$

while $k < b$ **do**

    begin $k := k+1$; **if** $X(k) > X(j)$ **then** $j := k$ **end**

end

$\{\boxed{a\quad\boxed{j}\quad b} \text{ \bf and } \{X \uparrow \boxed{a\quad b}\} \leq^* X(j)\}$.

Similarly, we can present the sorting program of Section 2.3.3 as a procedure. But now we can express the way in which this sorting program uses maximum-finding as a subsidiary operation by having the sorting procedure call the previously defined maximum-finding procedure, i.e. by using a procedure statement referring to max in the body of the declaration of $maxsort$:

procedure $maxsort$(**integer value** a, b; **integer array** {**var**} $X(*)$);

    $\{\boxed{a\quad b} \subseteq \text{\bf dom } X \text{ \bf and } X = X_0\}$

begin integer m;

$m := b$;

$\{$**whileinv**: $\boxed{a\quad m\quad b}$ **and** $\text{ord}_\leq X \uparrow \boxed{m\quad b}$

    and $\{X \uparrow \boxed{a\quad m}\} \leq^* \{X \uparrow \boxed{m\quad b}\}$

    and $X \uparrow \boxed{a\quad b} \sim X_0 \uparrow \boxed{a\quad b}$ $\}$

while $a \leq m$ **do**

    begin integer j;

    $max(a, m, j, X)$;

    begin integer t; $t := X(j)$; $X(j) := X(m)$; $X(m) := t$ **end**;

    $m := m - 1$

    end

end

$\{\text{ord}_\leq X \uparrow \boxed{a\quad b} \text{ \bf and } X \uparrow \boxed{a\quad b} \sim X_0 \uparrow \boxed{a\quad b}\}$.

We could also express the subsidiary operation of exchanging two array elements as a separate procedure, i.e. we could define

procedure $exchange$(**integer value** i, j; **integer array** {**var**} $X(*)$);

    begin integer t; $t := X(i)$; $X(i) := X(j)$; $X(j) := t$ **end** ,

and then write

procedure *maxsort*(**integer value** a, b; **integer array** {**var**} $X(*)$);
$\{\boxed{a \quad b} \subseteq \textbf{dom } X \text{ and } X = X_0\}$
begin integer m;
$m := b$;
{**whileinv**: ... }
while $a \leq m$ **do**
  begin integer j;
  $max(a, m, j, X)$;
  $exchange(j, m, X)$;
  $m := m - 1$
  end

end
$\{\text{ord}_\leq X \uparrow \boxed{a \quad b} \text{ and } X \uparrow \boxed{a \quad b} \sim X_0 \uparrow \boxed{a \quad b}\}$.

Notice that the specifier of X contains {**var**}, even though no assignment to an element of X appears in the body of *maxsort*. One must still use {**var**} to indicate that executing *maxsort* will change X, even though the change is caused by calling another procedure.

Two more examples of array-manipulating procedures are constructed from the partition program of Section 2.3.5:

procedure *partition*(**integer value** a, b, r;
    integer result c; **integer array** {**var**} $X(*)$);
    $\{\boxed{a \quad b} \subseteq \textbf{dom } X \text{ and } X = X_0\}$
    begin integer d;
    $c := a$; $d := b$;
    {**whileinv**: $\boxed{a \quad c \quad d \quad b}$ and $\{X \uparrow \boxed{a \quad c}\} \leq^* r$
        and $r <^* \{X \uparrow \boxed{d \quad b}\}$ and $X \uparrow \boxed{a \quad b} \sim X_0 \uparrow \boxed{a \quad b}$ }
    while $c \leq d$ **do**
        if $X(c) \leq r$ **then** $c := c + 1$ **else**
        if $X(d) > r$ **then** $d := d - 1$ **else**
            begin
            $\{\boxed{c \quad d}\}$
            begin integer t; $t := X(c)$; $X(c) := X(d)$; $X(d) := t$ **end**;
            $c := c + 1$; $d := d - 1$
            end

    end
    $\{\boxed{a \quad c \quad b} \text{ and } \{X \uparrow \boxed{a \quad c}\} \leq^* r \text{ and } r <^* \{X \uparrow \boxed{c \quad b}\}$
        and $X \uparrow \boxed{a \quad b} \sim X_0 \uparrow \boxed{a \quad b}\}$,

and from the merging program of Section 2.3.6:

> **procedure** *merge*(**integer value** ax, bx, ay, by, az, bz;
>   **integer array** {exp} X, $Y(*)$; **integer array** {var} $Z(*)$);
> {**pa**: $Z \# X$ & $Z \# Y$}
> {$\boxed{ax\;\;bx} \subseteq$ **dom** X **and** $\boxed{ay\;\;by} \subseteq$ **dom** Y **and** $\boxed{az\;\;bz} \subseteq$ **dom** Z
>   **and** $\mathrm{ord}_{\leq} X \uparrow \boxed{ax\;\;bx}$ **and** $\mathrm{ord}_{\leq} Y \uparrow \boxed{ay\;\;by}$
>   **and** $\# \boxed{ax\;\;bx} + \# \boxed{ay\;\;by} = \# \boxed{az\;\;bz}$ }
> **begin integer** kx, ky, kz;
> $kx := ax$; $ky := ay$; $kz := az$;
> {**whileinv**: $\boxed{ax\;\;kx\;\;bx}$ **and** $\boxed{ay\;\;ky\;\;by}$ **and** $\boxed{az\;\;kz\;\;bz}$
>   **and** $\mathrm{ord}_{\leq} Z \uparrow \boxed{az\;\;kz}$
>   **and** $\{Z \uparrow \boxed{az\;\;kz}\} \leq^{*} \{X \uparrow \boxed{kx\;\;bx}\} \cup \{Y \uparrow \boxed{ky\;\;by}\}$
>   **and** $\# \boxed{kx\;\;bx} + \# \boxed{ky\;\;by} = \# \boxed{kz\;\;bz}$
>   **and** $(Z \uparrow \boxed{az\;\;kz}) \sim (X \uparrow \boxed{ax\;\;kx}) \oplus (Y \uparrow \boxed{ay\;\;ky})$ }
> **while** $kz \leq bz$ **do**
>   **if** (**if** $ky > by$ **then true else if** $kx > bx$ **then false else**
> $X(kx) \leq Y(ky)$)
>   **then begin** $Z(kz) := X(kx)$; $kx := kx+1$; $kz := kz+1$ **end**
>   **else begin** $Z(kz) := Y(ky)$; $ky := ky+1$; $kz := kz+1$ **end**
> **end**
> {$\mathrm{ord}_{\leq} Z \uparrow \boxed{az\;\;bz}$
>   **and** $(Z \uparrow \boxed{az\;\;bz}) \sim (X \uparrow \boxed{ax\;\;bx}) \oplus (Y \uparrow \boxed{ay\;\;by})$ } .

Since the last procedure has several array parameters, one of which is changed by the procedure, it raises the possibility of interference between the array parameters. Consider a procedure statement *merge*(...) in which the same array identifier occurs twice as an actual parameter. There is no problem if the actual parameters corresponding to the formal parameters X and Y are the same, since neither of these arrays is changed by the procedure. But *merge* may not behave correctly if the actual parameters corresponding to X and Z, or to Y and Z, are the same. In this situation, the procedure may perform assignments to elements of Z that are yet-to-be-processed elements of X or Y. Thus, correct usage of *merge* requires that Z must not interfere with X or Y.

We have indicated this requirement as a parameter assumption. In general, if X and Y are arrays, we write $X \# Y$ to indicate that no assignment to an element of X should affect the value of an element of Y. Similarly, if X is an array and E is an expression, we write $X \# E$ to indicate that no assignment to an element of X should affect the value of E.

Of course, even though we cannot call arrays by value or result, we could overcome the interference problem by simulating call by result for Z (or call by value for X and Y). We could simply replace Z in the body of *merge* by a local array ZZ, and add a statement for copying ZZ into Z to the end of the body:

```
procedure merge(integer value ax, bx, ay, by, az, bz;
        integer array {exp} X, Y(*); integer array {var} Z(*));
    begin integer array ZZ(az::bz);
    begin ... end;
        begin integer k; k := az − 1;
        while k<bz do
            begin k := k + 1; Z(k) := ZZ(k) end
        end
    end
```

(where **begin ... end** is the previous procedure body with Z replaced by ZZ). But now we have increased the space and time requirements of *merge* substantially and, more crucially, we have imposed this penalty on all usages of *merge* to accommodate a particular kind of usage. A far more flexible approach, encouraged by the absence of call by value or result for arrays, is to retain the original version of *merge*, to state its limitations clearly, and to leave the problem of circumventing these limitations to its users.

Exercise

1. For Exercises 4 to 6 following Section 2.3.7, encapsulate the solution of each exercise as a procedure by constructing an appropriate heading. Include the necessary parameter assumptions.

3.1.7 Procedure Parameters

In Algol W, a parameter of a procedure can itself denote a procedure. Thus one procedure can be passed as a parameter to a second procedure, and then called from within the body of the second procedure. For example, if we declare

```
procedure p(procedure q {integer exp, integer var});
    begin ... q(a + b, c) ... end
```

then the statement *p(fact)* has the same meaning as the result of substituting *fact* for q in the body of p, so that $q(a + b, c)$ becomes $fact(a + b, c)$.

In Algol W, the specifier **procedure** F is used to indicate that the formal parameter F denotes a proper procedure. However, just as with other kinds of parameters, this form of specifier must be extended to provide enough information to check parameter matching. As illustrated above, we will include in the specifier of a procedure parameter a list of the phrase types of the parameters to which the procedure parameter can be applied. In general, we will use a specifier of the form

$$\textbf{procedure } F \{\theta_1, \dots, \theta_n\}$$

to indicate that the formal parameter F denotes a proper procedure that in turn accepts $n \geq 1$ parameters of types $\theta_1, \dots, \theta_n$. The phrase type established by this specification is $\textbf{procedure}(\theta_1, \dots, \theta_n)$.

When $n = 0$, i.e. when F denotes a "parameterless" procedure, an interesting possibility arises. Within the body of the procedure in which F is a formal parameter, any call of F will be a procedure statement consisting of F by itself, which will remain syntactically correct if F is replaced by any statement. Thus an actual parameter corresponding to F can be any statement, rather than just an identifier denoting a parameterless procedure.

In fact, this possibility is permitted in Algol W. Thus we say that the specifier **procedure** F (where the absence of curly brackets indicates $n = 0$) establishes the phrase type **statement**, indicating that an actual parameter corresponding to F can be any statement.

As an example, consider

       procedure *repeat*(**procedure** *s*; **logical** {**exp**} *l*);
          begin *s*; **while** ⌐*l* **do** *s* **end**   .

If S is a statement and L is a logical expression, then *repeat*(S, L) is equivalent to **begin** S; **while** ⌐L **do** S **end**, or to the flowchart

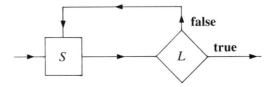

Thus *repeat*(S, L) is equivalent to the statement **repeat** S **until** L, which is not provided in Algol W, but occurs in several other languages and expositions of programming [Wirth 71a, Dijkstra 71].

As a second example, consider

        procedure *iterate*(**integer value** *a*, *b*; **procedure** *p* {**integer exp**});
          begin integer *k*; *k* := *a* − 1;
          while *k* < *b* **do**
              begin *k* := *k* + 1; *p*(*k*) **end**
          end   .

The effect of this procedure is to apply p to every integer in $\boxed{a \quad b}$, in increasing order. (Notice that {**integer exp**} in the specification indicates that $p(k)$ should not change the value of k.) Thus, for example, the following statement will set s to the sum of the segment of X over $\boxed{a \quad b}$:

> **begin**
> **procedure** *addoneelement*(**integer** {**exp**} i); $s := s + X(i)$;
> $s := 0$; *iterate*(a, b, *addoneelement*)
> **end** .

To see this, we first apply the copy rule (and the rule for call by value) to the call of *iterate*:

> **begin**
> **procedure** *addoneelement*(**integer** {**exp**} i); $s := s + X(i)$;
> $s := 0$;
>   **begin integer** a', b';
> $a' := a$; $b' := b$;
>   **begin integer** k; $k := a' - 1$;
>   **while** $k < b'$ **do**
>   **begin** $k := k + 1$; *addoneelement*(k) **end**
>   **end**
>   **end**
> **end** ,

and then apply the copy rule to the resulting call of *addoneelement*:

> **begin**
> **procedure** *addoneelement*(**integer** {**exp**} i); $s := s + X(i)$;
> $s := 0$;
>   **begin integer** a', b';
> $a' := a$; $b' := b$;
>   **begin integer** k; $k := a' - 1$;
>   **while** $k < b'$ **do**
>   **begin** $k := k + 1$; $s := s + X(k)$ **end**
>   **end**
>   **end**
> **end** .

Procedures that accept procedure parameters are often called *higher-order* procedures. As illustrated by *repeat* and *iterate*, such procedures can be used to describe control mechanisms. Indeed in Section 4.1.1 we will see that the Algol W **for** statement can be viewed as a call of *iterate*. Further examples of higher-order procedures will occur in Chapter 5.

3.1.8 Function Procedures

Just as proper procedure declarations can be used to define new statements called procedure statements, so *function procedure declarations* can be used to define new expressions called *function designators*.

Let τ denote **integer**, **real**, **long real**, or **logical**. Then a τ function declaration has the form

$$\tau \textbf{ procedure } P(\sigma_1; \ldots ; \sigma_n); \; E$$

where each σ_i is a specifier of a formal parameter F_i, and E is a τ expression. Within the scope of this declaration, one can write a τ expression of the form

$$P(A_1, \ldots, A_n)$$

which is called a *function designator*. The meaning of $P(A_1, \ldots, A_n)$ is again defined by the copy rule: it is the same as the meaning of

$$E \big|_{F_1, \ldots, F_n \rightarrow A_1, \ldots, A_n} \quad ,$$

with the proviso about global identifiers that is needed to avoid identifier collisions. The form of specifiers, the rules for matching formal and actual parameters, and the behavior of call by value and result are the same as for proper procedures.

The following examples should be obvious:

> **integer procedure** *maximum*(**integer value** m, n);
>   **if** $m > n$ **then** m **else** n;
> **logical procedure** *even*(**integer value** x); $\neg\, odd(x)$;
> **logical procedure** *implies*(**logical value** q; **logical** $\{$**exp**$\}$ r);
>   **if** q **then** r **else true**   .

Function procedures may also be used as parameters to either proper or function procedures. For $n \geq 1$, the extended specifier

$$\tau \textbf{ procedure } F \{\theta_1, \ldots, \theta_n\}$$

establishes the phrase type τ **procedure**$(\theta_1, \ldots, \theta_n)$. When $n = 0$, a corresponding actual parameter may be any τ expression, rather than just a τ function procedure, since any call of F will be a function designator consisting of F by itself, which will remain syntactically correct if F is replaced by any (parenthesized) τ expression. Although this possibility is not mentioned in [Sites 72], it is a natural analogue of the situation for proper procedures which appears (on the basis of several test cases) to be supported by the Algol W implementation. Thus the specifier τ **procedure** F (where the absence of curly brackets indicates $n = 0$) establishes the phrase type τ **expression**. In fact, τ **procedure** F has the same meaning as τ $\{$**exp**$\}$ F.

Algol W permits the bodies of function procedures to be a kind of phrase called a *block expression* which can contain assignments and other statements. Unfortunately, the introduction of block expressions permits the construction of expressions with *side effects*, i.e. expressions whose evaluation can change the state of the computation.

The use of side effects can make programs very difficult to understand. More fundamentally, side effects invalidate our whole approach to specifying programs and proving their correctness, which relies upon the assumption that any expression which can be written in the programming language can also appear in assertions. The occurrence of an expression with side effects in an assertion is meaningless, and thus the introduction of a language feature permitting side effects would undermine the rigor of our logic.

For this reason we will not use block expressions in this book, nor will we use call by result for the parameters of function procedures.

On the other hand, we will use call by value. The formal explanation of call by value given in Section 3.1.5 does not extend to function procedures (since we have proscribed block expressions), but the reader's intuitive understanding should be adequate. Call by value is usually preferable to call by name (for simple parameters) since it prevents repeated evaluation of an actual parameter. However, as indicated by the above declaration of *implies*, call by name may be needed to avoid unnecessary evaluation.

Exercise

1. Most of the programs in Section 2.2, which use arrays but do not alter them, can be recast as proper procedures that accept function procedures that in turn accept integers. Encapsulate the program for binary search in Section 2.2.10 as a proper procedure that accepts a function X and searches over an interval for an integer j such that $X(j) = y$.

3.1.9 A Summary

Since our exposition of the various aspects of procedures has been rather discursive, it is useful to summarize their characteristics. Throughout this summary, the symbol τ stands for any of the four data types **integer**, **real**, **long real**, or **logical**.

A *proper procedure declaration* has the form

$$\textbf{procedure } P(\sigma_1; \ldots ; \sigma_n); \ S$$

where the body S is a statement, and a τ *function procedure declaration* has the form

$$\tau \ \textbf{procedure } P(\sigma_1; \ldots ; \sigma_n); \ E$$

where the body E is a τ expression. In each case P is a binder of an identifier, and $\sigma_1; \ldots ; \sigma_n$ is a *formal parameter list* in which each σ_i is a specifier. When $n = 0$ the parentheses enclosing the formal parameter list are omitted.

In the sequel we will only describe specifiers that contain a single binder of an identifier, which is called a *formal parameter*. However, any specifier can be compounded by listing several formal parameters, separated by commas, in place of a single formal parameter.

The scope of the binder P in a procedure declaration is the immediately enclosing block, excluding lower and upper bounds in array declarations immediately enclosed by that block. The scope of the binders in the formal parameter list is the formal parameter list plus the following procedure body; the identifier occurrences which are free in the body and not bound by these binders are called *global* occurrences.

The meaning of a procedure declaration can be obtained by first using the transformation described in Section 3.1.5 to eliminate the specifiers τ **value** F, τ **result** F, and τ **value result** F, and then using the copy rule described in Section 3.1.1.

We have extended the form of specifiers in Algol W, by adding formally prescribed comments in curly brackets, to achieve a syntax that guarantees that the copy rule will preserve syntactic correctness. This syntax, precisely described in Appendix B, is based on the idea that every binder establishes the *phrase type* of the identifier occurrences that it binds, which in turn determines the contexts that can contain these occurrences. In particular, an identifier P of phrase type **procedure**$(\theta_1, \dots, \theta_n)$ can only occur in a procedure statement $P(A_1, \dots, A_n)$ if each actual parameter A_i is a phrase of type θ_i. A similar requirement is imposed upon an identifier occurrence of type τ **procedure**$(\theta_1, \dots, \theta_n)$ in a function designator. As a consequence, the substitution prescribed by the copy rule is always *type-correct*, i.e. it replaces identifier occurrences by phrases of the same phrase type. In Section B.3.5 of Appendix B, we will show that, with appropriate parenthesization, such substitutions preserve syntactic correctness.

The following is a list of the phrase types used in programs in this book, along with a description of the declarations, specifiers, and other binders that establish these phrase types:

(1) τ **variable**. This phrase type is established by the declaration τ I_1, $\dots$, I_n, or by the specifier τ {**var**} F, τ **value** F, τ **result** F, or τ **value result** F.

(2) τ **expression**. This phrase type is established by the declaration τ **procedure** P; E, or by the specifier τ {**exp**} F or τ **procedure** F. Moreover, as we will see in Section 4.1.1, the phrase type **integer expression** is established by the binder in a **for** statement.

(3) τ **array variable**(*, $\dots$, *). This phrase type is established by the declaration τ **array** I_1, $\dots$, $I_m(L_1::U_1, \dots, L_n::U_n)$, or by the specifier τ **array** {**var**} $F(*, \dots, *)$. The number $n \geq 1$ of asterisks indicates the number of dimensions of the array.

(4) τ **array expression**(*, ... , *). This phrase type is established by the specifier τ **array** {**exp**} F(*, ... , *). Again, the number of asterisks indicates the number of dimensions.

(5) **statement**. This phrase type is established by the declaration **procedure** P; S, or by the specifier **procedure** F.

(6) **procedure**$(\theta_1, ... , \theta_n)$, where $n \geq 1$ and each θ_i is a phrase type. This phrase type is established by the declaration **procedure** $P(\sigma_1; ... ; \sigma_n)$; S, where each σ_i is a specifier establishing the phrase type θ_i, except that if σ_i is τ **value**, θ_i is τ **expression**. It is also established by the specifier **procedure** F {$\theta_1, ... , \theta_n$}.

(7) τ **procedure**$(\theta_1, ... , \theta_n)$, where $n \geq 1$ and each θ_i is a phrase type. This phrase type is established by the declaration τ **procedure** $P(\sigma_1; ... ; \sigma_n)$; E, where each σ_i determines θ_i as described in (6) above. It is also established by the specifier τ **procedure** F {$\theta_1, ... , \theta_n$}.

Exercise

1. Consider the following procedure declaration.
    (a) For each identifier occurrence, show the binder that binds it.
    (b) For each binder, show the phrase type that it establishes.
    (c) Use the copy rule to obtain an equivalent procedure declaration that does not contain any calls of the procedures *iter* or *q*.

```
procedure doubleiter(procedure p {integer exp, integer exp});
    begin
    procedure iter(procedure p {integer exp});
        begin integer k; k := 0;
        while k < 100 do
            begin k := k + 1; p(k) end
        end;
    procedure q(integer {exp} i);
        begin
        procedure q(integer {exp} j); p(i, j);
        iter(q)
        end;
    iter(q)
    end   .
```

3.2 RECURSION

Since the scope of a procedure declaration is a block that includes the body of the declaration, a procedure can be called from its own body, or from the body of any other procedure declared in the same block. Thus a procedure can call itself, and a family of procedures declared in the same block can call one another. This capability is called *recursion*.

So far, we have used procedures to encapsulate parts of programs in order to clarify structure and to avoid replicating similar parts of programs. But the use of recursion goes far beyond this. It is a profound extension of our programming language, which provides an essentially new way of writing programs.

3.2.1 Simple Examples

Consider the procedure

> **procedure** *fact*(**integer value** n; **integer result** f);
> $\{n \geq 0\}$
> **if** $n = 0$ **then** $f := 1$ **else**
>   **begin** *fact*$(n-1, f)$; $f := n \times f$ **end**
> $\{f = n!\}$,

which calls itself via the procedure statement *fact*$(n-1, f)$. Obviously, *fact*$(0, f)$ sets f to the factorial of zero, since it only executes the assignment $f := 1$. But then *fact*$(1, f)$ must set f to the factorial of one, since in this case the recursive call *fact*$(n-1, f)$ is *fact*$(0, f)$. Similarly, *fact*$(2, f)$ will call *fact*$(1, f)$ and will set f to the factorial of two, etc.

In summary, *fact*$(0, f)$ works correctly, and for $n > 0$, the correctness of *fact*$(n-1, f)$ implies the correctness of *fact*(n, f). Thus by induction on n, *fact*(n, f) is correct for all $n \geq 0$. However, the procedure does not work for $n < 0$; in this case it will continue to call itself forever with increasingly negative values of n. Just as with the **while** statement, the use of recursion can produce nonterminating computations.

Recursion can be explained by means of the copy rule. Of course, applying the copy rule to a procedure statement that calls a recursive procedure will always give another statement that still contains one or more procedure statements as substatements—one can never eliminate such statements completely. However, for any particular terminating execution of a recursive procedure statement, there will be some finite number of copy-rule applications such that the remaining procedure statements will not be executed. For example, applying the copy rule twice to *fact*(n, f) (and using the rules for call by value and result) gives

```
begin integer n', f'; n' := n;
if n' = 0 then f' := 1 else
    begin
        begin integer n", f"; n" := n' - 1;
        if n" = 0 then f" := 1 else
            begin fact(n" - 1, f"); f" := n" × f" end;
        f' := f"
        end;
    f' := n' × f'
    end;
f := f'
end   ,
```

which will set f to the factorial of n, when $0 \leq n < 2$, without executing the recursive procedure statement $fact(n" - 1, f")$. More generally, N applications of the copy rule will be sufficient for $0 \leq n < N$.

In general, recursion can be used to solve a problem if:

(1) There is some integer characteristic of the problem, which we will call the *size* of the problem, that has a minimum value.
(2) Minimal-sized cases can be solved directly, i.e. without recursion.
(3) The solution of any nonminimal-sized case can be expressed in terms of the solution of (perhaps several) cases with smaller sizes.

A problem with these characteristics can be solved by a recursive procedure of the form:

```
procedure solve( ... );
    if "Size is minimal" then "Direct solution"
        else "General solution"   ,
```

where "General solution" will use recursive calls of *solve* to obtain solutions for smaller cases. A proof of correctness and termination will involve induction on the size of the problem.

For the problem of setting f to $n!$, the size is n, the minimum size is zero, the direct solution for $n = 0$ is $f := 1$, and the general solution for $n > 0$ is $fact(n - 1, f)$; $f := n × f$.

Computing factorials is a trivial application of recursion; a program using iteration by means of a **while** statement will be nearly as clear and somewhat faster. A more significant example is a puzzle called the "Towers of Hanoi" [Dijkstra 71].

This puzzle consists of three pegs and n disks of distinct sizes which can be piled on the pegs. In a legal configuration every disk will be on some peg, and no disk will be on top of a smaller disk. (See Figure 3.1.) A move consists of removing the topmost disk from one peg and placing it on top of another

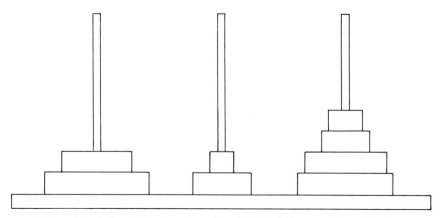

Figure 3.1 A Legal Configuration of an Eight-disk Tower of Hanoi Puzzle.

peg, without violating the constraint that no disk can be on top of a smaller disk. Starting with all disks on one peg, the problem is to find a sequence of moves that will place all disks on one other peg.

The key to solving the puzzle is to notice that the problem of moving the k smallest disks from one peg to another is unaffected by the presence of larger disks on any of the pegs—the larger disks simply remain unmoved beneath the moving ones, and they cannot violate the constraint that no disk can be on top of a smaller one.

To treat the problem of moving the k smallest disks recursively, we take k to be the size. Then the minimal case is $k = 0$, and the direct solution is to do nothing.

For $k > 0$, the general solution is to move $k - 1$ disks to the "intermediate" peg (the one that is neither the start nor the destination), to move a single disk from the start to the destination peg, and then to move $k - 1$ disks from the intermediate peg to the destination.

To express this solution as a recursive procedure, we represent the pegs by three distinct integers, and we assume the existence of a procedure *moveone*(**integer value** a, b) for moving the topmost disk from peg a to peg b. (In practice *moveone* might simply print a record of the move from a to b.) Then the following procedure will move k disks from peg a to peg b, using peg c as an intermediary:

```
procedure movemany(integer value k, a, b, c);
    if k>0 then
        begin
        movemany(k−1, a, c, b);
        moveone(a, b);
        movemany(k−1, c, b, a)
        end    .
```

In contrast to the factorial computation, this procedure expresses the general solution in terms of more than one smaller solution. In other words, a single execution of the body of *movemany* may cause two immediate calls of *movemany*. This situation is usually characteristic of a nontrivial use of recursion.

Exercises

1. Show that *movemany*(k, a, b, c) will execute $2^k - 1$ moves.

2. The following recursive procedure, which sets f to the nth Fibonacci number, is very similar to the factorial example:

    > **procedure** *fib*(**integer value** n; **integer result** f);
    > $\{n \geq 0\}$
    >   **if** $n = 0$ **then** $f := 0$ **else if** $n = 1$ **then** $f := 1$ **else**
    >   **begin integer** g;
    >   *fib*($n - 2$, g); *fib*($n - 1$, f); $f := f + g$
    >   **end**
    > $\{f = fib(n)\}$.

    However, this is an extremely inefficient way to compute Fibonacci numbers. Why?

3. The computational power of recursion subsumes that of the **while** statement. To show this, define a recursive procedure *whiledo*, whose body does not contain a **while** statement, such that *whiledo*(L, S) has the same meaning as **while** L **do** S.

3.2.2 Sorting by Merging

To provide further examples, we will explore several ways of applying recursion to the problem of sorting an array segment. An obvious measure of the size of this problem is the size of the segment to be sorted. The minimal case occurs when the segment contains zero or one elements—in this case the segment is already ordered and nothing needs to be done.

For larger segments, we can divide the segment into two smaller subsegments, recursively sort each of the subsegments, and then merge them, i.e. rearrange the ordered subsegments so that the entire segment is ordered. Thus our program has the form:

procedure *mergesort*(**integer value** a, b;
    integer array {**var**} $X(*)$);
   $\{\boxed{a\ \ b} \subseteq \textbf{dom } X \textbf{ and } X = X_0\}$
   if $a < b$ **then**
      begin integer m;
      "Pick m";
      $\{\boxed{a\ \ m\ \ \ b} \textbf{ and } \# \boxed{a\ \ m} < \# \boxed{a\ \ b} \textbf{ and } \# \boxed{m\ \ \ b} < \# \boxed{a\ \ b}\}$
      mergesort(a, m, X); *mergesort*($m + 1$, b, X);
      $\{\textbf{ord}_\leq X \uparrow \boxed{a\ \ m} \textbf{ and ord}_\leq X \uparrow \boxed{m\ \ \ b}$
         $\textbf{and } X \uparrow \boxed{a\ \ m} \sim X_0 \uparrow \boxed{a\ \ m}$
         $\textbf{and } X \uparrow \boxed{m\ \ \ b} \sim X_0 \uparrow \boxed{m\ \ \ b}\}$
      "Merge"
      end
   $\{\textbf{ord}_\leq X \uparrow \boxed{a\ \ b} \textbf{ and } X \uparrow \boxed{a\ \ b} \sim X_0 \uparrow \boxed{a\ \ b}\}$.

At first sight, one might expect to replace "Merge" by

$$merge(a, m, m + 1, b, a, b, X, X, X)\quad,$$

where *merge* is the procedure defined in Section 3.1.6. But, as discussed in that section, this would cause the formal parameter Z to interfere with the formal parameters X and Y, which would cause *merge* to malfunction. To overcome this difficulty, we will declare a separate local array to hold the result of *merge*, and then copy this array back into X. Thus "Merge" is replaced by

    begin integer array $Y(a::b)$; **integer** k;
    $merge(a, m, m + 1, b, a, b, X, X, Y)$;
    $\{\textbf{ord}_\leq Y \textbf{ and } Y \sim X_0 \uparrow \boxed{a\ \ b}\}$
    $k := a - 1$;
    while $k < b$ **do begin** $k := k + 1$; $X(k) := Y(k)$ **end**
    end .

To insure termination of our recursive procedure, we must program "Pick m" so that both $\boxed{a\ \ m}$ and $\boxed{m\ \ \ b}$ are smaller than $\boxed{a\ \ b}$, i.e. so that

$$\{a < b\} \text{ "Pick } m \text{" } \{a \leq m < b\}\quad.$$

Moreover, to maximize speed, we want to make $\# \boxed{a\ \ m}$ and $\# \boxed{m\ \ \ b}$ as nearly equal as possible. The solution is to replace "Pick m" by

$$m := (a + b - 1) \textbf{ div } 2\quad.$$

Correctness can be shown by a monotonicity argument similar to that given in Section 2.2.10.

The complete procedure is

> **procedure** *mergesort*(**integer value** a, b;
>   **integer array** {**var**} $X(*)$);
> $\{\boxed{a\ \ b} \subseteq \mathbf{dom}\ X\ \mathbf{and}\ X = X_0\}$
> **if** $a < b$ **then**
>   **begin integer** m;
> $m := (a + b - 1)\ \mathbf{div}\ 2$;
> $\{\boxed{a\ \ m\ \ b}\ \mathbf{and}\ \#\ \boxed{a\ \ m} < \#\ \boxed{a\ \ b}$
> $\mathbf{and}\ \#\ \boxed{m\ \ \ b} < \#\ \boxed{a\ \ b}\ \}$
>   *mergesort*(a, m, X); *mergesort*$(m + 1, b, X)$;
> $\{\mathbf{ord}_{\leq} X \upharpoonright \boxed{a\ \ m}\ \mathbf{and}\ \mathbf{ord}_{\leq} X \upharpoonright \boxed{m\ \ \ b}$
> $\mathbf{and}\ X \upharpoonright \boxed{a\ \ m} \sim X_0 \upharpoonright \boxed{a\ \ m}$
> $\mathbf{and}\ X \upharpoonright \boxed{m\ \ \ b} \sim X_0 \upharpoonright \boxed{m\ \ \ b}\ \}$
>   **begin integer array** $Y(a::b)$; **integer** k;
>   *merge*$(a, m, m+1, b, a, b, X, X, Y)$;
> $\{\mathbf{ord}_{\leq} Y\ \mathbf{and}\ Y \sim X_0 \upharpoonright \boxed{a\ \ b}\}$
> $k := a - 1$;
>   **while** $k < b$ **do begin** $k := k + 1$; $X(k) := Y(k)$ **end**
>   **end**
>   **end**
> $\{\mathbf{ord}_{\leq} X \upharpoonright \boxed{a\ \ b}\ \mathbf{and}\ X \upharpoonright \boxed{a\ \ b} \sim X_0 \upharpoonright \boxed{a\ \ b}\}$.

(For simplicity, we have used slightly incomplete assertions. As discussed in Exercise 4 after Section 2.3.4, we should also specify that *mergesort* has no effect on the elements of X outside of the segment over $\boxed{a\ \ b}$. For this purpose, $X \upharpoonright (\mathbf{dom}\ X - \boxed{a\ \ b}) = X_0 \upharpoonright (\mathbf{dom}\ X - \boxed{a\ \ b})$ could be added to all assertions.)

To determine the time required by this procedure, we must investigate the pattern of recursive calls that occur during execution. This pattern can be described by a *calling tree* in which each node represents a call of *mergesort*, and one node is a subnode of another if the call represented by the lower node occurs during execution of the call represented by the higher node. At each node of the tree we will place the size of the segment being sorted by the corresponding call. For example, Figure 3.2 shows a calling tree for sorting a segment of size 7.

A node without subnodes is called *terminal*. The *depth* of any node is its distance from the top node, and the *depth* of the tree is the depth of its

depth=

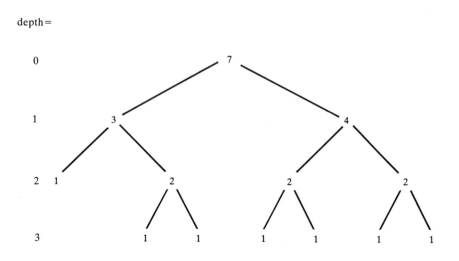

Figure 3.2   A Calling Tree for *mergesort* with $n=7$, $d=3$, $t=13$, and $s=27$.

deepest node. In Figure 3.2, one terminal node has a depth of 2 while the others have depths of 3; the depth of the tree is 3.

The nature of *mergesort* ensures that its calling tree will have the following properties:

(1) A node is terminal if and only if its attached size is one.
(2) A node is nonterminal if and only if its attached size is greater than one. In this case the node will have exactly two immediate subnodes (i.e. the calling tree will be a binary tree), and the size attached to the node will be the sum of the sizes attached to the immediate subnodes.

(We are ignoring the case where the attached size is zero, which will not occur in a calling tree except in the trivial special case where the entire array being sorted is empty.)

From these local properties of calling trees, we can establish certain global properties. Consider a calling tree with the following parameters:

n = size attached to top node,
d = depth of tree,
t = total number of nodes,
s = sum of sizes attached to nodes,

Then

$$(3)\ t = 2 \cdot n - 1,$$
$$(4)\ s \leq n \cdot (d + 1) \quad .$$

To show that (3) and (4) are consequences of (1) and (2), we use induction on tree depth, i.e. in proving (3) and (4) for an arbitrary tree, we assume that (3) and (4) hold for its subtrees. If the tree consists of a single terminal node, then $n = 1$, $d = 0$, $t = 1$, and $s = 1$, so that (3) and (4) are obviously true.

Otherwise, the calling tree has the form shown in Figure 3.3.

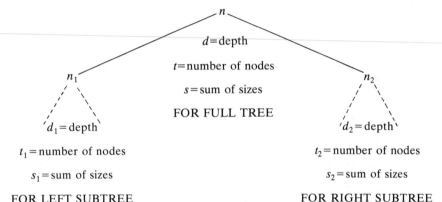

Figure 3.3   The General Case for Induction on the Depth of a Calling Tree.

The induction hypothesis for the two immediate subtrees gives

$$t_1 = 2 \cdot n_1 - 1 \qquad\qquad t_2 = 2 \cdot n_2 - 1$$
$$s_1 \leq n_1 \cdot (d_1 + 1) \qquad\qquad s_2 \leq n_2 \cdot (d_2 + 1) \quad .$$

Then

$$\begin{aligned}
t &= t_1 + t_2 + 1 \\
&= (2 \cdot n_1 - 1) + (2 \cdot n_2 - 1) + 1 \\
&= 2 \cdot (n_1 + n_2) - 1 \\
&= 2 \cdot n - 1 \quad ,
\end{aligned}$$

and

$$\begin{aligned}
s &= s_1 + s_2 + n \\
&\leq n_1 \cdot (d_1 + 1) + n_2 \cdot (d_2 + 1) + n \\
&\leq n_1 \cdot d + n_2 \cdot d + n \\
&= (n_1 + n_2) \cdot d + n \\
&= n \cdot (d + 1) \quad ,
\end{aligned}$$

where the second inequality holds because the depth of a tree is one larger than the maximum depth of its immediate subtrees.

Now consider the time required to execute a single call of *mergesort* for an array of size n, exclusive of the time required to execute any recursive subcalls. The only iterations are the **while** statement within *merge* and the **while** statement that copies from Y into X. Thus the time for a single call will be bounded by a linear function of n, say $\alpha + \beta \cdot n$.

It follows that the total time required by *mergesort*, including recursive calls, will be bounded by the sum of $\alpha + \beta \cdot n$ over the nodes of the calling tree, which is $\alpha \cdot t + \beta \cdot s$. Then (3) and (4) show that the time to sort an array segment of size n is bounded by

$$\alpha \cdot (2 \cdot n - 1) + \beta \cdot n \cdot (d + 1) \quad .$$

This formula shows the importance of minimizing the depth of the calling tree. For a given n, this depth will be minimized if the tree is *almost balanced*, i.e. if the depths of the highest and lowest terminal nodes in the tree differ by at most one. For example, the calling tree in Figure 3.2 is almost balanced, while the tree in Figure 3.4 is highly unbalanced, and has much larger values of d and s.

In fact, *mergesort* produces an almost balanced tree because, at each recursive level, the segment to be sorted is split as nearly as possible into equal parts. Specifically, the calling tree satisfies

  (5) For any nonterminal node with attached size $n \geq 2$, if n is even then both immediate subnodes have attached size $n/2$, while if n is odd then the immediate subnodes have attached sizes $(n-1)/2$ and $(n+1)/2$.

Let $\lfloor \log_2 n \rfloor$ be the largest integer that is at most $\log_2 n$, and let $\lceil \log_2 n \rceil$ be the smallest integer that is at least $\log_2 n$. Then (5) implies

  (6) Every terminal node has a depth d' such that $\lfloor \log_2 n \rfloor \leq d' \leq \lceil \log_2 n \rceil$.

Again the proof is by induction on tree depth. For a single-node tree, $n = 1$ and $d' = 0$, so that (6) is obvious. Otherwise, we have the situation shown in Figure 3.3, and the induction hypothesis implies that, for every terminal node in the left subtree, the depth in the full tree satisfies

$$\lfloor \log_2 n_1 \rfloor + 1 \leq d' \leq \lceil \log_2 n_1 \rceil + 1 \quad .$$

(Remember that the depth of a node in the full tree is one larger than its depth in an immediate subtree.) Then since $\lfloor \log_2 \ n_1 \rfloor + 1 = \lfloor (\log_2 n_1) + 1 \rfloor = \lfloor \log_2 (2 \cdot n_1) \rfloor$, and similarly for $\lceil \log_2 \cdot n_1 \rceil + 1$, we have

$$\lfloor \log_2 (2 \cdot n_1) \rfloor \leq d' \leq \lceil \log_2 (2 \cdot n_1) \rceil \quad .$$

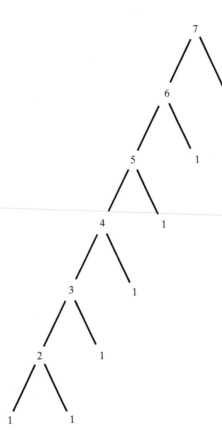

Figure 3.4 A Highly Unbalanced Calling Tree with $n = 7$, $d = 6$, $t = 13$, and $s = 34$.

By a similar argument, for every terminal node in the right subtree, the depth in the full tree satisfies

$$\lfloor \log_2 (2 \cdot n_2) \rfloor \le d' \le \lceil \log_2 (2 \cdot n_2) \rceil \quad .$$

When n is even, $2 \cdot n_1 = 2 \cdot n_2 = n$, so that every terminal node satisfies (6). On the other hand, when n is odd, either $2 \cdot n_1 = n - 1$ and $2 \cdot n_2 = n + 1$ or vice-versa. Thus every terminal node satisfies

$$\lfloor \log_2 (n - 1) \rfloor \le d' \le \lceil \log_2 (n + 1) \rceil \quad .$$

But here n is an odd integer and is not one (since it is attached to a nonterminal node), so it is not an exact power of two. This implies $\lfloor \log_2 n \rfloor = \lfloor \log_2 (n - 1) \rfloor$ and $\lceil \log_2 n \rceil = \lceil \log_2 (n + 1) \rceil$, which again establishes (6).

From (6), we see that the calling tree for *mergesort* is almost balanced, and that its depth is bounded by $\lceil \log_2 n \rceil < \log_2 n + 1$. Thus the time required by *mergesort* is bounded by

$$\alpha \cdot (2 \cdot n - 1) + \beta \cdot n \cdot (\log_2 n + 2)$$
$$= 2 \cdot (\alpha + \beta) \cdot n - \alpha + \beta \cdot n \cdot \log_2 n \quad ,$$

which is of order $n \cdot \log n$.

This result shows that sorting by merging is an order of magnitude faster than sorting by maximum finding, which requires a time of order n^2. It also shows that the time to sort large arrays is dominated by the coefficient β, so that attempts to improve the speed of *mergesort* for large arrays should focus on the bodies of the **while** statements within *merge* and the copying operation. Thus, for example, the speed for large arrays would not be significantly improved by treating $\# \boxed{a \quad b} = 2$ as a special case to be sorted by a simple exchange. (For an improvement that does reduce β, see Exercise 2 below.)

Finally, we must consider the space required by *mergesort*. For an order-of-magnitude estimate we can ignore individual variables and only consider the local array Y. Of course, each recursive call of *mergesort* will use its own local array, but no two of these arrays will exist at the same time. This is because the recursive calls of *mergesort* are outside the block in which Y is declared. As a result, all storage used by lower-level recursive calls will be released before the block using Y is entered. Another way of seeing this is to notice that, although repeated application of the copy rule will create many blocks with local arrays, these blocks will never overlap.

Thus the local storage used by *mergesort* is the size of the largest local array, which is obviously the one at the top level of recursion whose size is $\# \boxed{a \quad b}$.

The situation would be completely different if the declaration of Y were moved outward to the block containing the recursive calls. Then several local arrays would be used simultaneously, and their combined size would be the sum of the sizes along some path in the calling tree, which could be nearly twice the size of the largest single array. This is a vivid instance of the importance of declaring arrays as locally as possible.

On the other hand, as discussed in Exercise 3 at the end of this section, there is an ingenious method of reducing the storage requirements of *mergesort*—but not to the point where they are negligible. The need 'for substantial extra storage to avoid interference is inherent in the underlying method of sorting by merging, and is the most serious limitation of this method in comparison with others.

Exercises

1. Show that, for any tree in which every node has either zero or two immediate subnodes, the number of terminal nodes is one more than the number of nonterminal nodes.

2. Although the need for temporary storage is inherent in sorting by merging, it is possible to avoid performing the copying operation after each call of *merge*. This will significantly reduce the coefficient β of the term in the time bound that is dominant for large n.

    Define two procedures *insort* and *outsort* that satisfy the following specifications:

    > **procedure** *insort*(**integer value** a, b; **integer array** {**var**} $X,Y(*)$);
    > $\{$**pa**: $X \# Y$ & $Y \# X\}$
    > $\{\boxed{a \quad b} \subseteq \mathbf{dom}\ X$ **and** $\boxed{a \quad b} \subseteq \mathbf{dom}\ Y$ **and** $X = X_0\}$
    > $\vdots$
    > $\{\mathbf{ord}_{\leq} X \upharpoonright \boxed{a \quad b}$ **and** $X \upharpoonright \boxed{a \quad b} \sim X_0 \upharpoonright \boxed{a \quad b}\}$;

    > **procedure** *outsort*(**integer value** a, b; **integer array** {**var**} $X,Y(*)$);
    > $\{$**pa**: $X \# Y$ & $Y \# X\}$
    > $\{\boxed{a \quad b} \subseteq \mathbf{dom}\ X$ **and** $\boxed{a \quad b} \subseteq \mathbf{dom}\ Y$ **and** $X = X_0\}$
    > $\vdots$
    > $\{\mathbf{ord}_{\leq} Y \upharpoonright \boxed{a \quad b}$ **and** $Y \upharpoonright \boxed{a \quad b} \sim X_0 \upharpoonright \boxed{a \quad b}\}$.

    Insort should sort the segment of X over $\boxed{a \quad b}$ and leave its result in the same place; it should use the segment of Y over $\boxed{a \quad b}$ as its temporary storage. *Outsort* should sort the segment of X over $\boxed{a \quad b}$ and leave its result in the segment of Y over $\boxed{a \quad b}$. The two procedures will be mutually recursive, i.e. each will call the other (and both will call *merge*). The provision of a second array as a parameter obviates the need for declaring a local array.

3. (Suggested by W. J. Gadbow) Use the "Overwriting Merge" program of Exercise 5 after Section 2.3.7 to develop a variation of *mergesort* that uses less storage.

4. Show that, when *merge* is generalized to ordering by keys as discussed in Section 2.3.9, *mergesort* is stable.

3.2.3 Quicksort

We next consider a different recursive sorting method, called *quicksort*, which was invented by C. A. R. Hoare [Hoare 62, Foley 71]. As before, we will take the size of the problem to be the size of the segment to be sorted, so that the minimal case of zero or one elements can be treated by doing nothing, and we will treat the general case by dividing the segment into two smaller subsegments and sorting the subsegments recursively.

In *mergesort*, we followed the recursive calls by an operation that rearranged the ordered subsegments into a completely ordered segment. Now we will reverse the approach: we will precede the recursive calls by an operation such that sorting the subsegments will make the entire segment ordered without further computation. A sufficient condition is that, before the recursive calls, all values in the left subsegment should be smaller or equal to all values in the right subsegment.

Thus our procedure has the form:

> **procedure** *quicksort*(**integer value** a, b; **integer array** {**var**} $X(*)$);
> $\quad\{\boxed{a\ \ b}\subseteq \textbf{dom } X \text{ and } X=X_0\}$
> $\quad$**if** $a<b$ **then**
> $\quad\quad$**begin integer** c;
> $\quad\quad$"Prepare";
> $\quad\quad$*quicksort*$(a,\ c-1,\ X)$; *quicksort*$(c,\ b,\ X)$
> $\quad\quad$**end**
> $\quad\{\textbf{ord}_\le X\uparrow\boxed{a\ \ b} \text{ and } X\uparrow\boxed{a\ \ b}\sim X_0\uparrow\boxed{a\ \ b}\}$,

where "Prepare" must satisfy

> $\quad\{\boxed{a\ \ b}\subseteq \textbf{dom } X \text{ and } \boxed{a|\ \ |b} \text{ and } X=X_0\}$
> $\quad$"Prepare"
> $\quad\{\boxed{a|\ \ |c|\ \ |b} \text{ and } \{X\uparrow\boxed{a\ \ |c}\}\le^*\{X\uparrow\boxed{c\ \ b}\}$
> $\quad\quad \text{and } X\uparrow\boxed{a\ \ b}\sim X_0\uparrow\boxed{a\ \ b}\}$.

Notice that the consequent asserts that $\boxed{a\ \ |c}$ and $\boxed{c\ \ b}$ are both nonempty, and therefore both smaller than $\boxed{a\ \ b}$, which is necessary to insure termination of the recursion.

An obvious possibility for "Prepare" is to choose some integer r and then use the procedure *partition* given in Section 3.1.6 to obtain two subsegments whose values are smaller or equal to r and larger than r:

> **begin integer** r;
> "Choose r";
> *partition*$(a,\ b,\ r,\ c,\ X)$
> **end**   .

But *partition* gives no guarantee that both $\boxed{a\ \ |c}$ and $\boxed{c\ \ b}$ will be nonempty. Moreover, this situation cannot be remedied by a careful choice of r; in the extreme case where all segment values are equal, one of the subsegments will be empty, regardless of the choice of r.

A simple way around this problem is to treat the outermost elements of the segment separately, and to apply *partition* to the interior. The details of the argument are evident from the assertions in this version of "Prepare":

$\{ \fbox{$a \quad b$} \subseteq \textbf{dom } X \text{ and } \fbox{$a \quad b$} \}$
begin integer r;
if $X(a) > X(b)$ **then** "Exchange $X(a)$ and $X(b)$";
$\{ X(a) \le X(b) \}$
"Choose r";
$\{ X(a) \le r \le X(b) \}$
partition$(a+1, b-1, r, c, X)$
end
$\{ \fbox{$a \quad c \quad b$} \text{ and } X(a) \le r \text{ and } \{ X \uparrow \fbox{$a \quad c$} \} \le^* r$
    and $r <^* \{ X \uparrow \fbox{$c \quad b$} \}$ and $r \le X(b) \}$
$\{ \fbox{$a \quad c \quad b$} \text{ and } \{ X \uparrow \fbox{$a \quad c$} \} \le^* \{ X \uparrow \fbox{$c \quad b$} \} \}$.

(For clarity, the obvious rearrangement conditions have been omitted from the assertions.)

To maximize speed we want to choose r, within the constraint $X(a) \le r \le X(b)$, to make the segments $\fbox{$a \quad c$}$ and $\fbox{$c \quad b$}$ as nearly equal in size as is possible without doing a time-consuming operation. If we exclude the possibility of examining more than the outermost elements, the obvious choice is $r := (X(a) + X(b))$ **div** 2, which satisfies $X(a) \le r \le X(b)$ by a monotonicity argument similar to that in Section 2.2.10.

The final version of the procedure is:

procedure *quicksort*(**integer value** a, b; **integer array** $\{$**var**$\}$ $X(*)$);
    $\{ \fbox{$a \quad b$} \subseteq \textbf{dom } X \text{ and } X = X_0 \}$
    if $a < b$ **then**
        begin integer c;
            begin integer r;
            if $X(a) > X(b)$ **then**
                begin integer t;
                $t := X(a); X(a) := X(b); X(b) := t$
                end;
            $r := (X(a) + X(b))$ **div** 2;
            $\{ X(a) \le r \le X(b) \}$
            partition$(a+1, b-1, r, c, X)$
            end;
            $\{ \fbox{$a \quad c \quad b$} \text{ and } \{ X \uparrow \fbox{$a \quad c$} \} \le^* \{ X \uparrow \fbox{$c \quad b$} \}$
                and $X \uparrow \fbox{$a \quad b$} \sim X_0 \uparrow \fbox{$a \quad b$} \}$
            quicksort$(a, c-1, X)$; *quicksort*(c, b, X)
        end
    $\{ \textbf{ord}_\le X \uparrow \fbox{$a \quad b$} \text{ and } X \uparrow \fbox{$a \quad b$} \sim X_0 \uparrow \fbox{$a \quad b$} \}$.

(As with *mergesort*, we have omitted the specification that this procedure must not disturb X outside of the segment $\boxed{a\ \ b}$.)

In contrast to *mergesort*, this procedure does not use any local arrays, so that its storage requirements are negligible in comparison with the array being sorted (with the exception discussed in Exercise 2 below).

The time required by *quicksort* presents a phenomenon we have not encountered before: there is an order-of-magnitude difference between the worst-case behavior and the average behavior. In the worst case, at each recursive level $X(a)$ and $X(b)$ might be the largest two elements in the segment over $\boxed{a\ \ b}$. In this situation the calling tree will be extremely unbalanced, as in Figure 3.4, and the time required to sort a segment of size n will be of order n^2. But if the execution time is averaged over a reasonable distribution of segments of size n, then the probability of a nearly balanced tree is high enough that the average time is of order $n \cdot \log n$ (as is shown in [Aho 74]).

Some refinements of *quicksort* are discussed in the following exercises. A thorough discussion of improvements to the algorithm, with an extremely detailed analysis of time requirements is given in [Sedgewick 77, 78]. With such improvements, the algorithm is the best general-purpose method for sorting large arrays (unless the arrays are so large they must be kept in secondary storage devices such as disks or tapes). The only important qualifications are the anomalous worst-case behavior, which renders *quicksort* unsuitable for certain kinds of real-time applications, and a lack of stability.

Exercises

1. Hoare's version of *quicksort* [Hoare 62, Foley 71] uses the notion of "stoppers" to achieve a faster partitioning operation than the version given above. The basic idea is as follows: Suppose $\{X \uparrow \boxed{c\ \ b}\}$ contains a value, called a *stopper*, which is larger or equal to r. Since $\boxed{c\ \ b}$ must be nonempty, we can examine $X(c)$ without fear of a subscript error. If we find that $X(c)$ is smaller than r, then it cannot be a stopper, so that $\{X \uparrow \boxed{c\ \ b}\}$ must contain a stopper. Moreover, if we also know $\boxed{c\ \ d\ \ b}$ and $\{X \uparrow \boxed{d\ \ b}\} \geq^* r$, then $\boxed{c\ \ d\ \ b}$.

    Hoare's algorithm maintains the existence of a stopper in $\boxed{c\ \ b}$ that is at least r and a stopper in $\boxed{a\ \ d}$ that is at most r. In addition to justifying a reduction in the number of tests executed during the partitioning process, these stoppers insure that the recursively sorted subsegments will both be strictly smaller than the segment over $\boxed{a\ \ b}$.

    Check the correctness, including termination and lack of subscript errors, of the following slight variation of Hoare's algorithm. Within assertions, I stands for

$\boxed{a \quad c \quad d \quad b}$ and $\{X \uparrow \boxed{a \quad c}\} \leq^* r$ and $\{X \uparrow \boxed{d \quad b}\} \geq^* r$
and $(\exists i \in \boxed{c \quad b})\ X(i) \geq r$ and $(\exists i \in \boxed{a \quad d})\ X(i) \leq r$
and $X \uparrow \boxed{a \quad b} \sim X_0 \uparrow \boxed{a \quad b}$.

procedure $quickersort$(**integer value** a, b; **integer array** $\{$**var**$\}$ $X(*)$);
    $\{\boxed{a \quad b} \subseteq$ **dom** X and $X = X_0\}$
    if $a < b$ **then**
        begin integer c, d, r;
        "Choose r";
        $\{(\exists i \in \boxed{a \quad b})\ X(i) \geq r$ and $(\exists i \in \boxed{a \quad b})\ X(i) \leq r\}$
        $c := a;\ d := b$;
        $\{$whileinv: $I\}$ **while** $X(c) < r$ **do** $c := c + 1$;
        $\{$whileinv: I and $X(c) \geq r\}$ **while** $X(d) > r$ **do** $d := d - 1$;
        $\{$whileinv: I and $X(c) \geq r$ and $X(d) \leq r\}$
        while $c < d$ **do**
            begin
            begin integer t; $t := X(c)$; $X(c) := X(d)$; $X(d) := t$ **end**;
            $c := c + 1$; $d := d - 1$;
            $\{$whileinv: $I\}$ **while** $X(c) < r$ **do** $c := c + 1$;
            $\{$whileinv: I and $X(c) \geq r\}$ **while** $X(d) > r$ **do** $d := d - 1$
            end;
        $\{I$ and $\{X \uparrow \boxed{c \quad d}\} =^* r\}$
        $quickersort(a,\ c-1,\ X)$; $quickersort(d+1,\ b,\ X)$
        end
    $\{$**ord**$_{\leq} X \uparrow \boxed{a \quad b}$ and $X \uparrow \boxed{a \quad b} \sim X_0 \uparrow \boxed{a \quad b}\}$.

Notice that the specification of "Choose r" can be met by setting r to any value in the segment of X over $\boxed{a \quad b}$. To minimize the probability of worst-case behavior it might be better to set r to the median of a small sample of segment values, which would also meet the specification.

2.   Consider the worst case, in which the calling tree for $quicksort$ has the extremely unbalanced form shown in Figure 3.4. Even though there are no local arrays, the individual variable c, plus some storage space used by the procedure linkage mechanism, will be allocated at each level of recursion, so that the total storage needed will be proportional to the size of the array segment being sorted.

    To overcome this problem, one can combine recursion and iteration. The basic idea is that the body of $quicksort$ should contain a **while** statement with the invariant:

$\boxed{a_0 \quad a \quad b \quad b_0}$ and **ord**$_{\leq} X \uparrow \boxed{a_0 \quad a}$ and **ord**$_{\leq} X \uparrow \boxed{b \quad b_0}$
and $\{X \uparrow \boxed{a_0 \quad a}\} \leq^* \{X \uparrow \boxed{a \quad b_0}\}$
and $\{X \uparrow \boxed{a_0 \quad b}\} \leq^* \{X \uparrow \boxed{b \quad b_0}\}$
and $X \uparrow \boxed{a_0 \quad b_0} \sim X_0 \uparrow \boxed{a_0 \quad b_0}$,

where a_0 and b_0 are ghost identifiers recording the values of a and b upon entry to *quicksort*. Within the body of the **while** statement, one can partition X over $\boxed{a\ \ b}$ into two smaller subsegments, sort the smaller of these subsegments with a single recursive call of *quicksort*, and then reset a or b so that the remaining subsegment becomes the segment of X over $\boxed{a\ \ b}$.

This is an application of a general method for replacing recursion by iteration which is discussed in [Knuth 74].

3.2.4 Sorting by Range Partitioning

Finally, we consider a third recursive sorting method, which is applicable when the values occurring in the array segment to be sorted lie within a known finite range. This method is distinguished from *mergesort* and *quicksort* by the use of a different notion of size.

Suppose that X is an integer array, and that there is a finite interval $\boxed{r\ \ s}$ such that $\{X \uparrow \boxed{a\ \ b}\} \subseteq \boxed{r\ \ s}$. We can then regard the size of $\boxed{r\ \ s}$ to be the size of the problem of sorting X over $\boxed{a\ \ b}$. The minimal case occurs when $\boxed{r\ \ s}$ has zero or one members, which implies that X over $\boxed{a\ \ b}$ is already ordered. In the general case, we can use *partition* to obtain two subsegments with ranges which are each smaller than $\boxed{r\ \ s}$, and then sort each of these subsegments recursively. If we make the ranges of the subsegments as nearly equal as possible, we get

> **procedure** *rangesort*(**integer value** a, b, r, s;
>   **integer array** $\{$**var**$\}$ $X(*)$);
> $\{\boxed{a\ \ b} \subseteq$ **dom** X **and** $\{X \uparrow \boxed{a\ \ b}\} \subseteq \boxed{r\ \ s}$ **and** $X = X_0\}$
>   **if** $r < s$ **then**
>   **begin integer** c, t;
> $t := (r + s - 1)$ **div** 2;
> $\{\boxed{r\ \ t\ \ s}\}$
>   *partition*(a, b, t, c, X);
> $\{\{X \uparrow \boxed{a\ \ c}\} \subseteq \boxed{r\ \ t}$ **and** $\{X \uparrow \boxed{c\ \ b}\} \subseteq \boxed{t\ \ s}\}$
>   *rangesort*$(a, c-1, r, t, X)$; *rangesort*$(c, b, t+1, s, X)$
>   **end**
> $\{$**ord**$_\leq X \uparrow \boxed{a\ \ b}$ **and** $X \uparrow \boxed{a\ \ b} \sim X_0 \uparrow \boxed{a\ \ b}\}$.

This procedure bears a curious relation to *quicksort*: Their forms are similar yet the reasons for their termination, and also the times which they require, are completely different. A calling tree for *rangesort* will still satisfy $s \leq n \cdot (d + 1)$, but now the depth of the tree will be the least integer k such that $\# \boxed{r\ \ s} \leq 2^k$. Thus the time required for *rangesort* to sort an array segment of size n will be of order of magnitude $n \cdot \log(\# \boxed{r\ \ s})$.

In most cases this will be worse than $n \cdot \log n$. But sometimes one needs to sort an array whose range is smaller than its size. In practice this situation arises when one is sorting a large file of records, not on the entire value of the records, but only on the value of some key field whose number of possible values is less than the number of records. (In the extreme case the key might only have two possible values, so that *partition* itself could be used to do the sorting.)

In using *rangesort* in practice, one would probably replace the test in the conditional statement by $(r<s)$ **and** $(a<b)$, so that termination will occur when the segment being sorted has either minimal range or domain size.

3.2.5   Recursive Function Procedures

Algol W permits function procedures as well as proper procedures to be recursive. For example, one can define

> **integer procedure** *factorial*(**integer value** n);
>   **if** $n=0$ **then** 1 **else** $n \times factorial(n-1)$

or

> **real procedure** *power*(**real value** x; **integer value** n);
>   **if** $n=0$ **then** 1 **else if** $odd(n)$ **then** $x \times power(x, n-1)$
>   **else** $power(x \times x, n$ **div** $2)$.

It is evident that this kind of definition can possess a high degree of clarity and elegance. Indeed, one well-known programming language—LISP [McCarthy 60]—is built around the concept of recursively defined functions.

Nevertheless, with much regret, we will avoid the use of recursive function procedures in this book. The reason is similar to that for avoiding expressions with side effects. Our approach to specifying programs and proving their correctness relies upon the fact that any expression which can be written in the programming language can also appear in assertions. But if recursive functions are permitted, then expressions such as *factorial*(-1) can denote nonterminating computations. Unfortunately, the possibility that such expressions might occur in assertions cannot be accommodated by the logic we are using for program specification.

Exercises

1.   The purpose of this exercise is to show how recursion can be used to do simple parsing. A *parser* is the input-processing routine of a compiler which determines whether the input is syntactically legal and, if so, how it is divided into sub-phrases.

Suppose that an *S-expression* is a sequence of characters which is either the single letter A or a pair of S-expressions, enclosed in parentheses and separated by a period. In other words, in the notation of Appendix A, S-expressions are defined by the productions

$$\langle \text{S-expression} \rangle ::= A \mid (\langle \text{S-expression} \rangle . \langle \text{S-expression} \rangle)$$

Thus for example, the following character sequences are S-expressions:

A
$(A.A)$
$((A.A).((A.A).(A.A)))$

while the following character sequences are not S-expressions:

$($ (AA)
$()$ $(A.A.A)$
(A) $(A.A))$

To represent a sequence of characters, one can use a one-dimensional integer array in which the ith element has the value 1, 2, 3, or 4 depending upon whether the ith character of the sequence is A, a left parenthesis, a period, or a right parenthesis respectively. (Alternatively, one could use the string processing facilities of Algol W, which are not described in this book.)

Write a recursive procedure

> **procedure** *parse*(**integer value** a, b; **integer result** c;
> **logical result** *correct*; **integer array** $\{$**exp**$\}$ $X(*)$);
> ...

that will examine the segment of X over $\boxed{a \quad b}$ to determine whether the character sequence represented by this array segment *begins* with an S-expression. More precisely,

(1) If there is an integer c such that $\boxed{a \quad c \quad b}$ and $X \uparrow \boxed{a \quad c}$ represents an S-expression, then c should be set to this integer (which must be unique, since an S-expression cannot be an initial subsequence of any other S-expression) and *correct* should be set to **true**.

(2) Otherwise, *correct* should be set to **false**.

The reader should be warned that the problems which arise in parsing programming languages can be far more difficult than is indicated by this exercise. We have purposely chosen a language whose parsing can be accomplished by a straightforward use of recursion. Good general references for the construction of parsers are [Aho 72, Gries 71, Backhouse 79].

2. (Suggested by P. J. Landin) The function procedure in the following block does not use our extended specifiers, and violates the parameter-matching discipline described in Section 3.1. Nevertheless, it is legal Algol W, and its meaning can be explained by the copy rule.

```
begin
integer procedure strange(integer n; integer procedure h);
   if n=0 then 1 else n × h(n−1, h);
b := strange(a, strange)
end  .
```

(a) Show that there is no way of extending the specifiers in this program that will obey the parameter-matching discipline used in this book.

(b) Use the copy rule to explain the behavior of this program. (Assume that a and b are integer variables.)

(c) Explain why this program might be said to exemplify "hidden recursion".

3.3 SPECIFICATION LOGIC

The introduction of procedures has greatly enriched the variety of meanings that can be denoted by identifiers. Because of this, the logic for proving program correctness introduced earlier cannot encompass the procedure mechanism. In this section, we describe a more complex system, called specification logic, that provides the generality needed to cope with procedures.

Proof methods for procedures have been the goal of considerable research. Most of this work, beginning with [Hoare 71b] and including [Hoare 73], [London 78], and [Gries 80] (which is unusually clear and readable), has focused on call by reference and value, and has neglected the binding or "block" structure of Algol-like languages (though the use of subsidiary deduction in [Hoare 71b] is a first step in this direction). The result has been some exceedingly complicated inference rules, which fall considerably short of dealing with the full generality of the Algol procedure mechanism. In particular, these approaches cannot handle interference, call by name, statement parameters, or higher-order procedures.

In contrast, specification logic uses a more elaborate logical framework in which the meaning of specifications depends upon environments, which are mappings of identifiers into their meanings. New forms of specifications are introduced to deal with this dependency, and to permit the formulation and inference of universal specifications, which are true in all environments. Call by name is regarded as fundamental, with call by value and result treated as abbreviational mechanisms in the sense of Section 3.1.5.

It should be admitted at the outset that, at least in its present form, specification logic is still seriously incomplete. As discussed in [Reynolds 81], call by reference cannot be encompassed, and an interaction between interference and higher-order procedures prevents the proof of certain useful programs. Nevertheless, the author believes that specification logic is more general than alternative approaches and also conceptually simpler (especially in the abstract version discussed in Section 3.3.12).

To see the inadequacy of the logical framework used in previous chapters, consider the specification

$$\{a+b\geq 0\}\; p(a+b,\, c)\; \{c=(a+b)!\}\quad.$$

Without further information, we cannot say whether this specification is true or false; it is true if the "meaning" of p is a procedure that computes the factorial and false otherwise.

One might be tempted to say that the truth or falsity of the above specification depends upon the context of the statement $p(a+b, c)$, i.e. upon the declaration that binds the occurrence of p. But this view is inadequate since $p(a+b, c)$ may occur in the body of a higher-order procedure in which p is a formal parameter. In this case, the meaning of p can range over a variety of procedures during different executions of the same occurrence of $p(a+b, c)$.

Indeed, occurrences of formal parameters can falsify specifications that do not refer to procedures explicitly and that are inferable in the logic of Chapters 1 and 2. In that logic, for example, one can infer

$$\{y\leq z\}\ x:=3\ \{y\leq z\}\quad.$$

However, if x or y or z is a formal parameter, then x can interfere with $y\leq z$, and such interference will falsify this specification.

The solution to these difficulties is to recognize that the meaning of a specification, as well as the meaning of any kind of phrase that can occur in a specification, depends upon the meanings of the identifiers that occur free in the phrase. More precisely, the meaning of a phrase depends upon an *environment* which maps these identifiers into their meanings.

3.3.1   Environments and Meanings

To understand environments and meanings, we must introduce some of the basic concepts of the semantics of programming languages. First, it must be understood that environments and states of the computation are quite different entities:

An *environment* is a function that maps identifiers into their meanings. The kind of meaning appropriate for a particular identifier depends upon its phrase type.

A *state of the computation*, or more briefly, a *state*, is a function that maps variables into their values. The kind of value appropriate for a particular variable depends upon its data type.

The distinction between these entities, and the fact that both are needed to describe an Algol-like language, was first realized in the early work of Strachey and Landin [Barron 63, Landin 65, 66a, 66b]. These authors called variables "L-values", and they called states "stores", which is the British term for computer memories. This terminology was meant to suggest that states were an abstraction of the contents of a computer memory. (The meaning of "environment" introduced here is different from the informal meaning of the term used in Section 1.1.)

The meanings of identifiers or phrases of type τ **variable** are variables that can possess values of data type τ. When we speak of the value of a variable identifier x, we really mean the value, in a particular state, of the variable that is the meaning, in a particular environment, of x.

For example, if we say that, in an environment η and a state σ, the values of x and y are both seventeen, we might be describing either of two situations:

(a) The meanings of x and y in η are distinct variables, which are both mapped by σ into seventeen,

or (b) The meanings of x and y in η are the same variable, which is mapped by σ into seventeen.

The distinction between these situations shows how interference between variables is described: In (a) x and y do not interfere, while in (b) each interferes with the other.

In general, we write M_θ for the set of meanings appropriate to the phrase type θ, and $[\![X]\!]_\eta$ for the meaning of an identifier or phrase X in the environment η. Thus, if X has phrase type θ then $[\![X]\!]_\eta \in M_\theta$, and if X is an identifier then $[\![X]\!]_\eta = \eta(X)$.

For example, $M_{\tau \text{ variable}}$ is the set of variables that can possess values of data type τ. The two cases distinguished above can be described more succinctly as

(a) $[\![x]\!]_\eta \neq [\![y]\!]_\eta$ and $\sigma([\![x]\!]_\eta) = \sigma([\![y]\!]_\eta) = 17$,

or (b) $[\![x]\!]_\eta = [\![y]\!]_\eta$ and $\sigma([\![x]\!]_\eta) = 17$.

The meaning of an expression or assertion determines a value that depends upon the state of the computation, so that this meaning is a function from states to values. Thus $M_{\tau \text{ expression}}$ is the set of functions from the set of states to the set of values of data type τ, and $M_{\text{assertion}}$ is the set of functions from the set of states to {**true, false**}. For example, if x and y are integer variable identifiers, then $[\![x+y]\!]_\eta$ is the function that maps σ into $\sigma([\![x]\!]_\eta) + \sigma([\![y]\!]_\eta)$. Similarly, $[\![3]\!]_\eta$ is the constant function that maps σ into 3.

For an assertion P, we say that $[\![P]\!]_\eta$ *describes* a state σ, or that σ *satisfies* $[\![P]\!]_\eta$, when $[\![P]\!]_\eta(\sigma)$ is true.

For statements, $M_{\text{statement}}$ is the set of functions from the set of states to the set of sequences of states. In particular, the meaning of a statement maps a state σ into the sequence of states (excluding σ itself) that occur during execution of the statement beginning with σ. If this execution does not terminate then the sequence is infinite, otherwise it concludes with a *final* state.

Assignment statements give rise to statement sequences consisting of a final state by itself. If X and E are phrases of type τ **variable** and τ **expression**, then

$$[\![X := E]\!]_\eta(\sigma) = \langle [\sigma \mid [\![X]\!]_\eta : [\![E]\!]_\eta(\sigma)] \rangle \quad ,$$

where the final state is similar to σ except that it maps the variable that is the meaning of X into the value of E in σ.

For example, if x and y are integer variable identifiers then

$$[\![x := 3]\!]_\eta(\sigma) = \langle [\sigma \mid [\![x]\!]_\eta : [\![3]\!]_\eta(\sigma)] \rangle$$
$$= \langle [\sigma \mid [\![x]\!]_\eta : 3] \rangle \quad ,$$
$$[\![y := x+y]\!]_\eta(\sigma) = \langle [\sigma \mid [\![y]\!]_\eta : [\![x+y]\!]_\eta(\sigma)] \rangle$$
$$= \langle [\sigma \mid [\![y]\!]_\eta : \sigma([\![x]\!]_\eta) + \sigma([\![y]\!]_\eta)] \rangle \quad .$$

Longer sequences of states occur for compound statements. Suppose S_1 and S_2 are statements. If $[\![S_1]\!]_\eta(\sigma)$ is an infinite sequence then $[\![S_1; S_2]\!]_\eta(\sigma) = [\![S_1]\!]_\eta(\sigma)$. Otherwise, if $[\![S_1]\!]_\eta(\sigma)$ concludes with the final state σ_f, then $[\![S_1; S_2]\!]_\eta(\sigma) = [\![S_1]\!]_\eta(\sigma) \oplus_{\text{seq}} [\![S_2]\!]_\eta(\sigma_f)$.

For example,

$$[\![x := 3; y := x+y]\!]_\eta(\sigma)$$
$$= \langle [\sigma \mid [\![x]\!]_\eta : 3] \rangle \oplus_{\text{seq}} [\![y := x+y]\!]_\eta([\sigma \mid [\![x]\!]_\eta : 3])$$
$$= \langle [\sigma \mid [\![x]\!]_\eta : 3], [\sigma \mid [\![x]\!]_\eta : 3 \mid [\![y]\!]_\eta : [\![x+y]\!]_\eta([\sigma \mid [\![x]\!]_\eta : 3])] \rangle$$
$$= \langle [\sigma \mid [\![x]\!]_\eta : 3], [\sigma \mid [\![x]\!]_\eta : 3 \mid [\![y]\!]_\eta : $$
$$[\sigma \mid [\![x]\!]_\eta : 3]([\![x]\!]_\eta) + [\sigma \mid [\![x]\!]_\eta : 3]([\![y]\!]_\eta)] \rangle$$
$$= \langle [\sigma \mid [\![x]\!]_\eta : 3], [\sigma \mid [\![x]\!]_\eta : 3 \mid [\![y]\!]_\eta : $$
$$3 + [\sigma \mid [\![x]\!]_\eta : 3]([\![y]\!]_\eta)] \rangle \quad .$$

In the last line, notice that $[\sigma \mid [\![x]\!]_\eta : 3]([\![y]\!]_\eta)$ cannot be simplified to $\sigma([\![y]\!]_\eta)$ unless we know that $[\![x]\!]_\eta \neq [\![y]\!]_\eta$, i.e. that x does not interfere with y in the environment η.

Finally, as an example of nontermination,

$$[\![x := 0; \textbf{ while true do } x := x+1]\!]_\eta(\sigma)$$
$$= \langle [\sigma \mid [\![x]\!]_\eta : 0], [\sigma \mid [\![x]\!]_\eta : 1], [\sigma \mid [\![x]\!]_\eta : 2], \dots \rangle \quad .$$

We can now define the meaning of specifications of the form $\{P\} S \{Q\}$. The informal definition:

> $[\![\{P\} S \{Q\}]\!]_\eta$ is true if and only if, starting with any state described by $[\![P]\!]_\eta$, executing $[\![S]\!]_\eta$ will either never terminate or will terminate with a final state described by $[\![Q]\!]_\eta$.

is formalized by:

> $[\![\{P\} S \{Q\}]\!]_\eta$ is true if and only if, for any state σ such that $[\![P]\!]_\eta(\sigma)$ is true, the sequence $[\![S]\!]_\eta(\sigma)$ is either infinite or concludes with a final state σ_f such that $[\![Q]\!]_\eta(\sigma_f)$ is true.

Notice that there is an implicit quantification over states but not environments. This reflects the way in which specifications differ fundamentally from assertions: their truth or falsity depends upon only an environment rather than both an environment and a state.

For most purposes, including the above definition, the only relevant information about the sequence $[\![S]\!]_\eta(\sigma)$ is whether it is finite and, if so, what its final state is. However, to define noninterference specifications in Section

3.3.4, we will need to consider the intermediate states that occur during execution of a statement.

It is evident that a statement describes a change of state, but not a change of environment. In contrast, environments are "changed" by binding mechanisms. For example, the meaning of **begin integer** I; S **end** in an environment η is the meaning of S in the environment $[\eta \mid I: V]$ that is similar to η except that it maps I into a "new" variable V that is distinct from all variables relevant to the meanings prescribed by η.

In general, for any phrase P, $[\![P]\!]_\eta$ depends only upon the part of η that gives meanings to the identifiers occurring free in P. If P is the scope of binders of the identifiers $I_1, \dots, I_n$, then $[\![P]\!]_\eta$ is some function of the meanings of the immediate subphrases of P in environments that differ from η only for $I_1, \dots, I_n$. More generally, if P' is any subphrase of P, and $I_1, \dots, I_n$ are the identifiers occurring free in P' but bound in P, then $[\![P]\!]_\eta$ depends upon the meaning of P' in environments that differ from η only for $I_1, \dots, I_n$.

Operationally, one can think of the execution or evaluation of P as creating new environments for the execution or evaluation of subphrases, but these new environments do not "persist" in the sense that changes of state persist.

There is a fundamental relationship between environments and substitution called the *substitution law*: If P is any phrase, η is any environment, and $F_1, \dots, F_n \rightarrow A_1, \dots, A_n$ is any type-correct substitution, then

$$[\![P \mid F_1, \dots, F_n \rightarrow A_1, \dots, A_n]\!]_\eta = [\![P]\!]_{[\eta \mid F_1: \, [\![A_1]\!]_\eta \, \dots \mid F_n: \, [\![A_n]\!]_\eta]} \quad .$$

Essentially, the effect of the substitution $F_1, \dots, F_n \rightarrow A_1, \dots, A_n$ is the same as a change of environment that maps each F_i into the meaning of A_i.

We can now describe the meaning of proper procedures. The meaning $[\![H(A_1, \dots, A_n)]\!]_\eta$ of a procedure statement can only depend upon the meaning $[\![H]\!]_\eta$ of the procedure being called and the meanings $[\![A_1]\!]_\eta, \dots, [\![A_n]\!]_\eta$ of the actual parameters. Therefore, since the only role of procedures is to determine the effect of their calls, $[\![H]\!]_\eta$ can be taken to be the function that maps $[\![A_1]\!]_\eta, \dots, [\![A_n]\!]_\eta$ into $[\![H(A_1, \dots, A_n)]\!]_\eta$. Thus $M_{\text{procedure}(\theta_1, \dots, \theta_n)}$ is the set of functions from $M_{\theta_1} \times \dots \times M_{\theta_n}$ to $M_{\text{statement}}$, and

$$[\![H(A_1, \dots, A_n)]\!]_\eta = [\![H]\!]_\eta([\![A_1]\!]_\eta, \dots, [\![A_n]\!]_\eta) \quad .$$

Now consider the declaration **procedure** $H(\theta_1 \, F_1; \dots ; \theta_n \, F_n)$; B_{proc}. (Here and in the rest of this chapter we will use $\theta_1 \, F_1; \dots ; \theta_n \, F_n$ as the general form of a parameter list, ignoring call by value and result, compound specifiers, and such syntactic trivia as the fact that one writes **real array** $\{$**var**$\}$ F (∗) instead of **real array variable**(∗) F.) As with any declaration, the meaning of the enclosing block in an environment η is the meaning of the block body in an environment that is similar to η except for giving a new meaning to the identifier being declared:

$$[\![\textbf{begin procedure } H(\theta_1\ F_1;\ \dots\ ;\ \theta_n\ F_n);\ B_{\text{proc}};\ B\ \textbf{end}]\!]_\eta = [\![B]\!]_{\eta'}\ ,$$

where

$$\eta' = [\eta \mid H{:}\ h]\ .$$

In this case, the new meaning h is the function from $M_{\theta_1} \times \dots \times M_{\theta_n}$ to $M_{\text{statement}}$ such that

$$h(f_1,\ \dots\ ,f_n) = [\![B_{\text{proc}}]\!]_{[\eta' \mid F_1{:}\ f_1 \mid\ \dots\ \mid F_n{:}\ f_n]}\ .$$

For example,

$$
\begin{aligned}
&[\![\textbf{begin}\\
&\textbf{procedure } q(\textbf{integer } \{\textbf{var}\}\ v;\ \textbf{integer } \{\textbf{exp}\}\ e);\\
&\quad \textbf{begin } x := 3;\ v := e\ \textbf{end};\\
&q(y,\ x+y)\\
&\textbf{end}]\!]_\eta\\
&= [\![q(y,\ x+y)]\!]_{\eta'}\ ,
\end{aligned}
$$

where $\eta' = [\eta \mid q{:}\ h]$ and h is the function such that

$$h(f_1,\ f_2) = [\![x := 3;\ v := e]\!]_{[\eta' \mid v{:}\ f_1 \mid e{:}\ f_2]}\ .$$

Thus

$$
\begin{aligned}
[\![q(y,\ x+y)]\!]_{\eta'} &= [\![q]\!]_{\eta'}([\![y]\!]_{\eta'},\ [\![x+y]\!]_{\eta'})\\
&= h([\![y]\!]_{\eta'},\ [\![x+y]\!]_{\eta'})\\
&= [\![x := 3;\ v := e]\!]_{[\eta' \mid v{:}\ [\![y]\!]_{\eta'} \mid e{:}\ [\![x+y]\!]_{\eta'}]}\\
&= [\![x := 3;\ v := e \mid v,\ e \to y,\ x+y]\!]_{\eta'}\\
&= [\![x := 3;\ y := x+y]\!]_{\eta'}\ ,
\end{aligned}
$$

where the penultimate step is an application of the substitution law. Thus the meaning of the block enclosing the declaration of q, in an arbitrary environment η, will remain the same if $q(y, x+y)$ is replaced by $x := 3;\ y := x+y$. Notice that this coincides with the prescription of the copy rule.

In fact, the copy rule can be derived from the semantics of procedures and the general properties of environments given in this section. Consider the block

$$\textbf{begin procedure } H(\theta_1\ F_1;\ \dots\ ;\ \theta_n\ F_n);\ B_{\text{proc}};\ B\ \textbf{end}\ ,$$

and suppose that B contains a procedure statement $H(A_1, \dots, A_n)$ in which the occurrence of H is bound by the procedure declaration. Also suppose that, for every identifier G occurring globally in B_{proc}, there is no binder of G whose scope includes the procedure statement but not the procedure declaration. Then the meaning of the block enclosing the procedure declaration, in an environment η, will only depend upon the meaning of $H(A_1, \dots, A_n)$ in environments η'' that agree with $\eta' = [\eta \mid H{:}\ h]$ for H (since the occurrence of H is bound by the procedure declaration) and the identifiers occurring globally in B_{proc} (since there are no intervening binders of these identifiers). For such an environment η'',

$$\llbracket H(A_1, \ldots, A_n)\rrbracket_{\eta''}$$
$$= \llbracket H\rrbracket_{\eta''}(\llbracket A_1\rrbracket_{\eta''}, \ldots, \llbracket A_n\rrbracket_{\eta''})$$
$$= h(\llbracket A_1\rrbracket_{\eta''}, \ldots, \llbracket A_n\rrbracket_{\eta''})$$
$$= \llbracket B_{\text{proc}}\rrbracket_{[\eta' \mid F_1: \llbracket A_1\rrbracket_{\eta''} \mid \ldots \mid F_n: \llbracket A_n\rrbracket_{\eta''}]} \quad .$$

The environment here agrees with $[\eta'' \mid F_1: \llbracket A_1\rrbracket_{\eta''} \mid \ldots \mid F_n: \llbracket A_n\rrbracket_{\eta''}]$ for both the formal parameters and the identifiers occurring globally in B_{proc}, and therefore for all identifiers occurring free in B_{proc}. Thus the above meaning is the same as

$$= \llbracket B_{\text{proc}}\rrbracket_{[\eta'' \mid F_1: \llbracket A_1\rrbracket_{\eta''} \mid \ldots \mid F_n: \llbracket A_n\rrbracket_{\eta''}]}$$
$$= \llbracket B_{\text{proc}} \mid F_1, \ldots, F_n \to A_1, \ldots, A_n\rrbracket_{\eta''} \quad ,$$

where the last step is an application of the substitution law. Thus the meaning of the block enclosing the declaration of H, in an arbitrary environment η, will remain unchanged if $H(A_1, \ldots, A_n)$ is replaced by $B_{\text{proc}} \mid F_1, \ldots, F_n \to A_1, \ldots, A_n$.

This argument also leads to a conclusion which will be used in Section 3.3.8 when we justify an inference rule for procedures, and which is obtained by taking the actual parameters $A_1, \ldots, A_n$ to be the same as the formal parameters $F_1, \ldots, F_n$, so that the substitution of actuals for formals has no effect on B_{proc}: If η'' is an environment that agrees with $\eta' = [\eta \mid H: h]$ for H and the identifiers occurring globally in B_{proc}, then $\llbracket H(F_1, \ldots, F_n)\rrbracket_{\eta''} = \llbracket B_{\text{proc}}\rrbracket_{\eta''}$.

Although this discussion of semantics is enough to preface the presentation of specification logic, it is not a general exposition of the subject. Three omissions in particular should be noted:

(1) Saying that $M_{\tau\,\text{variable}}$ is a set of variables precludes phrases of type τ **variable**, such as array designators, that can denote different variables depending upon the state of the computation. To encompass such phrases, the members of $M_{\tau\,\text{variable}}$ must be functions from the set of states to the set of variables that can possess values of data type τ.

(2) In the definition of the meaning of procedure declarations, the equations

$$\eta' = [\eta \mid H: h]$$

and

$$h(f_1, \ldots, f_n) = \llbracket B_{\text{proc}}\rrbracket_{[\eta' \mid F_1: f_1 \mid \ldots \mid F_n: f_n]}$$

are mutually recursive; in effect a recursive semantic definition is needed to define the semantics of recursive procedures. Although it is nontrivial to show that these equations possess a solution, the real difficulty lies in the opposite direction: there are a variety of solutions, and the particular solution that describes procedures is the least solution in a certain partial ordering that can be imposed on the set of procedure meanings. This is the subject matter of *fixed-point theory*, which is a major topic in modern semantics.

(3) The semantics we have described, often called *direct semantics*, cannot easily accommodate labels and **goto** statements, which will be introduced in Section 4.2. To describe these entities, one must use a more complex approach called *continuation semantics*.

Two useful survey papers on semantics are [Reynolds 72], which deals with operational semantics, and [Tennent 76], which deals with denotational semantics. A good text is [Stoy 77]. A more elementary text is [Tennent 81], which uses the underlying concepts of semantics to describe a variety of programming languages.

3.3.2 Universal Specifications

It is now clear that the meaning of a specification such as

$$\{a+b\geq 0\}\ p(a+b,\ c)\ \{c=(a+b)!\}$$

or

$$\{y\leq z\}\ x:=3\ \{y\leq z\}$$

depends upon an environment. Thus the "truest" kind of specification is one that, unlike these examples, is true for all environments (that provide type-appropriate meanings to the identifiers occurring free in the specification). We will call such a specification *universal*. Unfortunately, because of the problem of interference, there are hardly any universal specifications of the form $\{P\}\,S\,\{Q\}$. To obtain universal specifications, we must enlarge the language of specifications radically.

For example, if X is a variable and E is an expression, we will write $X\#E$ to specify that X does not interfere with E. More precisely, the specification $X\#E$ is true in those environments in which assignments to the variable that is the meaning of X cannot affect the value of E.

We will also use a kind of implication to construct compound specifications. If $\mathscr{S}_1$ and $\mathscr{S}_2$ are specifications, then $\mathscr{S}_1\Rightarrow\mathscr{S}_2$ is a specification meaning "if $\mathscr{S}_1$ then $\mathscr{S}_2$" or "$\mathscr{S}_1$ implies $\mathscr{S}_2$". More precisely, $\mathscr{S}_1\Rightarrow\mathscr{S}_2$ is true in those environments in which either $\mathscr{S}_1$ is false or $\mathscr{S}_2$ is true.

Using notations such as these, we can write nontrivial specifications that are universal. For example,

$$x \# (y \le z) \Rightarrow \{y \le z\} \ x := 3 \ \{y \le z\}$$

is true in all environments.

A particularly desirable advantage of universality is that it is preserved by substitution. The result of performing any type-correct substitution upon a universal specification is another universal specification. This is a consequence of the substitution law stated in the previous section. If $[\![\mathscr{S}]\!]_\eta$ is true for all environments η, then

$$[\![\mathscr{S} \, | \, F_1, \ldots, F_n {\to} A_1, \ldots A_n]\!]_{\eta'} = [\![\mathscr{S}]\!]_{[\eta' \, | \, F_1: \, [\![A_1]\!]_{\eta'} \, | \, \ldots \, | \, F_n: \, [\![A_n]\!]_{\eta'}]}$$

is true for all η'.

For example, consider the substitution that replaces x and y by the same identifier w. When applied to the *non*universal specification

$$\{y \le z\} \ x := 3 \ \{y \le z\} \quad ,$$

this substitution gives

$$\{w \le z\} \ w := 3 \ \{w \le z\} \quad ,$$

which is patently false. But when applied to the universal specification

$$x \# (y \le z) \Rightarrow \{y \le z\} \ x := 3 \ \{y \le z\} \quad ,$$

the same substitution gives

$$w \# (w \le z) \Rightarrow \{w \le z\} \ w := 3 \ \{w \le z\} \quad ,$$

which is true—indeed universal—since $w \# (w \le z)$ is false.

3.3.3 Additional Phrase and Data Types

A vital property of both assertions and specifications is that the language in which they are written is as similar as possible to the language in which programs are written. In particular, identifiers have the same kinds of meaning, and binding and substitution behave in the same way. For example, the meaning of assertions and specifications, like that of programs, is preserved by alpha conversion.

However, to obtain the full expressive power of specifications, we must introduce additional phrase types. To see this, consider the following universal specification, which succinctly characterizes **while** statements:

$$\{i \textbf{ and } l\} \ s \ \{i\} \Rightarrow \{i\} \textbf{ while } l \textbf{ do } s \ \{i \textbf{ and } \neg \, l\} \quad .$$

Here l is a logical expression identifier, s is a statement identifier, and i is an *assertion* identifier. Since this specification is universal, it holds for all meanings of l, s, and i that are appropriate for logical expressions, statements, and assertions respectively. As a consequence, we may perform any type-correct substitution, such as

$$l \rightarrow k \neq n$$
$$s \rightarrow \textbf{begin } k := k+1; f := k \times f \textbf{ end}$$
$$i \rightarrow f = k! \textbf{ and } 0 \leq k \leq n \quad ,$$

which gives

$$\{f = k! \textbf{ and } 0 \leq k \leq n \textbf{ and } k \neq n\}$$
$$\quad \textbf{begin } k := k+1; f := k \times f \textbf{ end}$$
$$\quad \{f = k! \textbf{ and } 0 \leq k \leq n\}$$
$$\Rightarrow$$
$$\{f = k! \textbf{ and } 0 \leq k \leq n\}$$
$$\quad \textbf{while } k \neq n \textbf{ do begin } k := k+1; f := k \times f \textbf{ end}$$
$$\quad \{f = k! \textbf{ and } 0 \leq k \leq n \textbf{ and } \neg\, k \neq n\} \quad .$$

It is evident that this universal specification conveys the same information as the **while**-statement rule given in Section 1.4.3.

This example illustrates the usefulness of identifiers that stand for assertions. To permit such identifiers we will add **assertion** to the set of phrase types. An identifier of type **assertion** can be used in any context that permits an assertion, while a phrase of type **assertion** can be any assertion.

This generalization seems less startling if one remembers that assertions are similar to logical expressions—both are phrases whose meanings map states into truth values. (Indeed, when we defined $M_{\textbf{assertion}}$ in Section 3.3.1, we were treating **assertion** as a phrase type.) The difference is that assertions are not part of the programming language and may even be uncomputable in principle. Thus assertions, including assertion identifiers, cannot occur within executable phrases such as statements and expressions (except as comments).

In fact, we will go a step further and introduce procedures whose calls are assertions, by adding **assertion procedure** $(\theta_1, \ldots, \theta_n)$ to the set of phrase types. (Here $\theta_1, \ldots, \theta_n$ is a list of phrase types.) Of course, such procedures cannot be called from statements or expressions, but they still can be used to define concepts that are needed to make assertions intelligible.

For example, the concept of increasing order introduced in Section 2.2.10 can be defined by

> **assertion procedure** *incord*(**integer array** {**exp**} $X(*)$);
> $(\forall i \in \textbf{dom } X)(\forall j \in \textbf{dom } X)\ i < j \textbf{ implies } X(i) \leq X(j)$.

We can even define the concept of ordering with respect to an arbitrary binary relation on integers if we regard such a relation as an assertion procedure accepting two integers:

> **assertion procedure** *ord*{**assertion procedure** *rho* {**integer exp**,
> **integer exp**}; **integer array** {**exp**} $X(*)$);
> $(\forall i \in \textbf{dom } X)(\forall j \in \textbf{dom } X)\ i < j \textbf{ implies } rho\big(X(i), X(j)\big)$.

Another useful generalization will be to use data types that do not occur in executable programs. In Sections 3.3.13 and 4.1 we will treat **integer set** as a data type, so that interval diagrams are phrases of type **integer set expression**. Then in Chapter 5 we will introduce abstract data types that are specific to the problems our programs are intended to deal with.

One final point about specifications and phrase types requires emphasis. Specifications will usually contain free identifier occurrences. In this situation it is essential to state the phrase types of the free identifiers. For example, when we gave the universal specification for the **while** statement, we were careful to indicate that l had type **logical expression**, s had type **statement**, and i had type **assertion**. This point is crucial since some specifications are syntactically correct for several assignments of phrase types to their free identifiers, but universal only for some of these type assignments.

3.3.4 The Syntax and Semantics of Specifications

We now introduce the full variety of specifications used in the rest of this book. The reader who has difficulty with the formal definitions of the meaning of these specifications should return to them after reading the later sections describing inference rules and illustrating their usage.

First we have the form $\{P\}\, S\, \{Q\}$ that was introduced in Chapter 1. As described in Section 3.3.1:

(1) If P and Q are assertions and S is a statement then $[\![\{P\}\, S\, \{Q\}]\!]_\eta$ is true if and only if, for any state σ such that $[\![P]\!]_\eta(\sigma)$ is true, the sequence $[\![S]\!]_\eta(\sigma)$ is either infinite or concludes with a final state σ_f such that $[\![Q]\!]_\eta(\sigma_f)$ is true.

Secondly, we introduce a specification of the form $\{P\}$ to indicate that an assertion P is *static*, i.e. that P holds for all states of the computation and therefore cannot be falsified by executing any statement:

(2) If P is an assertion then $[\![\{P\}]\!]_\eta$ is true if and only if $[\![P]\!]_\eta(\sigma)$ is true for all states σ.

For example, if k is an integer expression identifier then $\{k > 4 \text{ implies } k \geq 5\}$ is universal, and $\{odd(2 \times k + 1)\}$ is true in any environment in which odd has its predeclared meaning. (Notice, however, that neither of these specifications is true if k is a real expression identifier; this illustrates the importance of stating the phrase types of free identifiers explicitly.)

Next, we have forms of specifications containing subspecifications. If $\mathscr{S}_1, \ldots, \mathscr{S}_n$ and $\mathscr{S}$ are specifications then $\mathscr{S}_1 \& \ldots \& \mathscr{S}_n \Rightarrow \mathscr{S}$ is a specification meaning "if $\mathscr{S}_1$ and ... and $\mathscr{S}_n$ then $\mathscr{S}$" or "$\mathscr{S}_1$ and ... and $\mathscr{S}_n$ implies $\mathscr{S}$". More precisely:

(3) For $n \geq 1$, if $\mathscr{S}_1, \ldots, \mathscr{S}_n$ and $\mathscr{S}$ are specifications then $[\![\mathscr{S}_1 \, \& \, \ldots \, \& \, \mathscr{S}_n \Rightarrow \mathscr{S}]\!]_\eta$ is true if and only if either $[\![\mathscr{S}]\!]_\eta$ is true or some $[\![\mathscr{S}_i]\!]_\eta$ is false.

Notice that $\&$ and $\Rightarrow$ play roles in the formation of specifications analogous to the roles of **and** and **implies** in the formation of assertions. We have intentionally chosen different symbols to emphasize that specifications are different from assertions. Also notice that this kind of compound specification has a more restricted form than the analogous forms for assertions: $\&$ can only appear on the left of $\Rightarrow$, and there are no operations corresponding to **or** or $\neg$. The use of this restricted form is based on Gentzen's notion of natural deduction [Gentzen 35].

In the form $\mathscr{S}_1 \, \& \, \ldots \, \& \, \mathscr{S}_n \Rightarrow \mathscr{S}$, the subspecifications $\mathscr{S}_1, \ldots, \mathscr{S}_n$ are called *assumptions*.

We will also use a universal quantifier $\forall$ that is analogous to $\forall$ for assertions. The specification $(\forall \theta \, I) \, \mathscr{S}$ means that $\mathscr{S}$ is true for every meaning of I that is appropriate to the phrase type θ. More precisely:

(4) If I is an identifier and $\mathscr{S}$ is a specification such that the free occurrences of I in $\mathscr{S}$ have phrase type θ, then $[\![(\forall \theta \, I) \, \mathscr{S}]\!]_\eta$ is true if and only if, for all meanings m appropriate to θ, $[\![\mathscr{S}]\!]_{[\eta \mid I: \, m]}$ is true.

Next we consider noninterference specifications. We have already mentioned the case $V \# E$, where V is a variable and E is an expression; then $V \# E$ means that assigning to V does not affect the value of E. The left side of $\#$ can also be a statement, in which case $S \# E$ means that executing S does not affect the value of E. More precisely, it means that, starting with any state, the value of E will not be affected at any time during the execution of S:

(5a) If S is a statement and E is a τ expression or assertion then $[\![S \# E]\!]_\eta$ is true if and only if, for all states σ and σ' such that σ' occurs in the sequence $[\![S]\!]_\eta(\sigma)$, $[\![E]\!]_\eta(\sigma') = [\![E]\!]_\eta(\sigma)$.

For example,

$$\textbf{begin } x := x + 1; \; x := x - 1 \textbf{ end } \# \; x$$

is *not* true. On the other hand,

$$\textbf{while true do } x := x + 1 \; \# \; y$$

is true if x and y denote distinct variables.

We can define the case where a variable occurs on the left of $\#$ in terms of (5a), by saying that $V \# E$ holds if no assignment to V interferes with E:

(5b) If V is a τ variable, E is a τ' expression or assertion, and I is an identifier not occurring free in V or E then, for all environments, $V \# E$ has the same meaning as

$$(\forall \tau \textbf{ exp } I) \, (V := I) \; \# \; E \quad .$$

In fact, we will generalize noninterference specifications further, to permit any *statement-like* phrase to appear on the left of #, and any *expression-like* phrase to appear on the right. The classification of various types of phrases as statement-like or expression-like is given in Table 3.5. Roughly speaking, statement-like phrases describe ways of changing states, while expression-like phrases describe ways of computing values from states. Notice, however, that simple and array variables are both statement-like, since assigning to a variable causes a change of state, and expression-like, since any variable is also an expression.

Phrase Type	Statement-like	Expression-like
τ **variable**	X	X
τ **expression**		X
τ **array variable**(*, ... , *)	X	X
τ **array expression**(*, ... , *)		X
statement	X	
assertion		X
procedure$(\theta_1, ... , \theta_n)$	X	
τ **procedure**$(\theta_1, ... , \theta_n)$		X
assertion procedure$(\theta_1, ... , \theta_n)$		X

Table 3.5   Statement-like and Expression-like Phrases.

An array variable does not interfere with an expression or assertion E if none of its elements interfere with E:

(5c) If X is an n-dimensional τ array variable, E is a τ' expression or assertion, and $I_1, ... , I_n$ are distinct identifiers not occurring free in X or E then, for all environments, $X \# E$ has the same meaning as

$$(\forall \text{ integer exp } I_1) ... (\forall \text{ integer exp } I_n) \, X(I_1, ... , I_n) \# E \quad .$$

A procedure does not interfere with E if the only calls of the procedure that interfere with E are ones in which statement-like actual parameters interfere with E.

(5d) If H is a procedure$(\theta_1, ... , \theta_n)$, E is a τ expression or assertion, $I_1, ... , I_n$ are distinct identifiers that do not occur free in H or E, and $\theta_{i_1}, ... , \theta_{i_k}$ are the statement-like members of $\{\theta_1, ... , \theta_n\}$ then, for all environments, $H \# E$ has the same meaning as

$$(\forall \theta_1 I_1) ... (\forall \theta_n I_n) \left(I_{i_1} \# E \, \& \, ... \, \& \, I_{i_k} \# E \Rightarrow H(I_1, ... , I_n) \# E \right) \quad .$$

Roughly speaking, H does not interfere with E if no call of H interferes with E by means of global identifiers. For example, in the environment created by the declaration

procedure $p(\text{integer } \{\textbf{var}\} \, z);$ **begin** $z := z + 1; \, x := z$ **end**   ,

$p(I) \# E$ holds whenever $x \# E$ and $I \# E$, so that $p \# E$ holds whenever $x \# E$.

Next we generalize the right side of $\#$. A statement-like phrase does not interfere with an array expression if it only interferes with applications of the expression to subscripts when it interferes with the subscripts:

> (5e) If S is a statement-like phrase, Y is an n-dimensional τ array expression, and $I_1, \dots, I_n$ are distinct identifiers not occurring free in S or Y then, for all environments, $S \# Y$ has the same meaning as
>
> $$(\forall \text{ integer exp } I_1) \dots (\forall \text{ integer exp } I_n)$$
> $$\left(S \# I_1 \ \& \ \dots \ \& \ S \# I_n \Rightarrow S \# Y(I_1, \dots, I_n)\right) \quad .$$

Finally, a statement-like phrase does not interfere with a function (or assertion) procedure if it only interferes with calls of the function procedure when it interferes with expression-like actual parameters:

> (5f) If S is a statement-like phrase, F is a τ procedure $(\theta_1, \dots, \theta_n)$ or an assertion procedure $(\theta_1, \dots, \theta_n)$, $I_1, \dots, I_n$ are distinct identifiers not occurring free in S or F, and $\theta_{i_1}, \dots, \theta_{i_k}$ are the expression-like members of $\{\theta_1, \dots, \theta_n\}$ then, for all environments, $S \# F$ has the same meaning as
>
> $$(\forall \theta_1 I_1) \dots (\forall \theta_n I_n)\left(S \# I_{i_1} \ \& \ \dots \ \& \ S \# I_{i_k} \Rightarrow S \# F(I_1, \dots, I_n)\right) \quad .$$

Again the effect is to specify an absence of interference through globals.

Sometimes it is necessary to quantify a specification about noninterference over an identifier of an arbitrary statement-like (or expression-like) type rather than a specific phrase type. For example,

$$(\forall \text{ sta-like } s) \ (s \# x \ \& \ s \# y \Rightarrow s \# z)$$

specifies that something interferes with z only when it interferes with x or y, where the "something" could be a simple variable, statement, array variable, or procedure. The generalization of (4) is straightforward:

> (4′) If I is an identifier and $\mathscr{S}$ is a specification such that all free occurrences of I in $\mathscr{S}$ have the form $I \# \dots$ (or $\dots \# I$), then $[\![(\forall \text{ sta-like } I) \mathscr{S}]\!]_\eta$ (or $[\![(\forall \text{ exp-like } I) \mathscr{S}]\!]_\eta$) is true if and only if, for all meanings m appropriate to any statement-like (or expression-like) type, $[\![\mathscr{S}]\!]_{[\eta \mid I: m]}$ is true.

The final form of specification that we will use is $\mathbf{gv}(V)$, where V is a τ variable. This specification holds if assigning any value to V will transform any state into a state in which V possesses that value; in this situation we say that V is a *good* variable.

At first sight, it might seem that $\mathbf{gv}(V)$ should be true for all variables and all environments. But the syntax of Algol W permits phrases of type τ **variable,** such as the array designator $X(X(1))$, that are not good variables.

(See Exercise 3 after Section 2.3.2.) For a state in which the array elements $X(1)$ and $X(7)$ have the values 1 and 2 respectively, execution of $X(X(1)):=7$ will produce a state in which $X(X(1))$ has the value 2. Thus $\mathbf{gv}(X(X(1)))$ is false. Moreover, the use of $X(X(1))$ as an actual parameter will create an environment in which the corresponding formal parameter is not a good variable.

The formal definition of $\mathbf{gv}(V)$ is based on the idea that this specification holds when, for any value E and any property Π of values, the assignment $V:=E$ will transform a state in which Π holds for E into a state in which Π holds for V. The formalization of Π is an assertion procedure (τ expression) that is not interfered with by V:

(6) If V is a τ variable, and E and Π are distinct identifiers that do not occur free in V then, for all environments, $\mathbf{gv}(V)$ has the same meaning as

$$(\forall\ \tau\ \mathbf{exp}\ E)\ (\forall\ \mathbf{assertion\ procedure}(\tau\ \mathbf{exp})\ \Pi)$$
$$(V \# \Pi \Rightarrow \{\Pi(E)\}\ V:=E\ \{\Pi(V)\})\ \ .$$

The relationship between this definition and an axiom for assignment will be explored in Section 3.3.12.

3.3.5 Rules of Inference for Universal Specifications

Specification logic is a system for inferring universal specifications. In this section we present most of the rules of inference dealing with arbitrary specifications, and with the parts of the programming language that do not involve binding mechanisms. These inference rules replace the ones given in Sections 1.4.2 and 1.4.3, which do not take into account the effects of interference and other phenomena that can occur when procedures are used.

The form of the rules is essentially the same as in Chapter 1. Each rule consists of a sequence of zero or more specifications called *premisses*, separated by a horizontal bar from a single specification called the *conclusion*. Again, an instance of a rule will be formed by replacing capital letters, called *metavariables*, by phrases, subject to restrictions that preface the rule. These restrictions will state the types of phrases that can replace metavariables, and will sometimes restrict these phrases to be identifiers. In the latter case, the phrase type stated for the identifier must be the phrase type of all free occurrences of that identifier in the premisses and conclusion of the instance of the rule.

The essential change from Chapter 1 is that the rules describe the inference of universal specifications, rather than specifications that are true in a particular environment. Thus the meaning of a rule is that, for any instance, if all the premisses of the instance are true in all environments, then the conclusion of the instance is true in all environments.

Some special conventions apply to specifications of the form $\mathscr{S}_1$ & ... & $\mathscr{S}_n \Rightarrow \mathscr{S}$. It is evident that the meaning of such a specification does not depend upon the order in which the assumptions $\mathscr{S}_1$ & ... & $\mathscr{S}_n$ are written, nor does the meaning change if duplicate occurrences of the assumptions are added. For these reasons, we can regard $\mathscr{S}_1$ & ... & $\mathscr{S}_n$ as a (finite) set of specifications.

Because of this, we will permit expressions denoting finite sets of specifications to appear on the left of $\Rightarrow$ in inference rules. In constructing such expressions we will use the metavariables Σ and $\mathscr{S}$ (with occasional subscripts and superscripts) to stand for finite sets of specifications and individual specifications respectively. We will write Σ & Σ' to denote the union of the sets Σ and Σ', and Σ & $\mathscr{S}$ to denote the union of Σ and $\{\mathscr{S}\}$. When such an expression is replaced by a specific set of assumptions, these assumptions can be written in any order and can be duplicated. For example, if Σ stands for $\{\mathscr{S}_1, \mathscr{S}_2\}$ and Σ' stands for $\{\mathscr{S}_2, \mathscr{S}_3\}$, then Σ & Σ' & $\mathscr{S}_4 \Rightarrow \mathscr{S}$ stands for any of the following equivalent specifications (among others):

$$\mathscr{S}_1 \ \& \ \mathscr{S}_2 \ \& \ \mathscr{S}_3 \ \& \ \mathscr{S}_4 \Rightarrow \mathscr{S}$$
$$\mathscr{S}_2 \ \& \ \mathscr{S}_4 \ \& \ \mathscr{S}_3 \ \& \ \mathscr{S}_1 \Rightarrow \mathscr{S}$$
$$\mathscr{S}_4 \ \& \ \mathscr{S}_2 \ \& \ \mathscr{S}_3 \ \& \ \mathscr{S}_4 \ \& \ \mathscr{S}_1 \ \& \ \mathscr{S}_3 \Rightarrow \mathscr{S} \ \ .$$

We can even include the case where the set of assumptions is empty. If Σ stands for the empty set, then $\Sigma \Rightarrow \mathscr{S}$ simply stands for $\mathscr{S}$.

Our first rules of inference describe the basic properties of $\Rightarrow$ and &:

(R1) Self-Implication
$$\overline{\mathscr{S} \Rightarrow \mathscr{S}} \ \ .$$

(R2) Adding Assumptions
$$\frac{\Sigma \Rightarrow \mathscr{S}}{\Sigma \ \& \ \Sigma' \Rightarrow \mathscr{S}} \ \ .$$

(R3) Separating Assumptions
$$\frac{\Sigma \ \& \ \Sigma' \Rightarrow \mathscr{S}}{\Sigma \Rightarrow (\Sigma' \Rightarrow \mathscr{S})} \ \ .$$

(R4) Combining Assumptions
$$\frac{\Sigma \Rightarrow (\Sigma' \Rightarrow \mathscr{S})}{\Sigma \ \& \ \Sigma' \Rightarrow \mathscr{S}} \ \ .$$

(R5) Modus Ponens
$$\Sigma_1 \Rightarrow \mathscr{S}_1$$
$$\vdots$$
$$\frac{\Sigma_n \Rightarrow \mathscr{S}_n \quad \Sigma \ \& \ \mathscr{S}_1 \ \& \ ... \ \& \ \mathscr{S}_n \Rightarrow \mathscr{S}}{\Sigma \ \& \ \Sigma_1 \ \& \ ... \ \& \ \Sigma_n \Rightarrow \mathscr{S}} \ \ .$$

The first rule says that any specification implies itself. The second rule says that assumptions can always be added to a specification. The third rule shows how multiple assumptions can be separated by introducing an extra $\Rightarrow$, and the fourth rule shows how such separation can be removed. The fifth rule says that assumptions can be replaced by other assumptions that imply them. It is called "Modus Ponens" by analogy with classical logic.

The next three rules deal with quantifiers of the form $(\forall \theta\ I)$:

(R6) Quantifier Introduction

   If I is an identifier of phrase type θ that does not occur free in Σ then

$$\frac{\Sigma \Rightarrow \mathscr{S}}{\Sigma \Rightarrow (\forall \theta\ I)\ \mathscr{S}}\ \ .$$

(R7) Quantifier Removal

   If $I_1, \ldots, I_n$ are distinct identifiers of phrase types $\theta_1, \ldots, \theta_n$, and $A_1, \ldots, A_n$ are phrases of types $\theta_1, \ldots, \theta_n$ then

$$\frac{}{(\forall \theta_1\ I_1) \ldots (\forall \theta_n\ I_n)\ \mathscr{S} \Rightarrow \mathscr{S}|_{I_1, \ldots, I_n \to A_1, \ldots, A_n}}\ \ .$$

(R8) Free Substitution

   If $\mathscr{S}|_{I_1, \ldots, I_n \to A_1, \ldots, A_n}$ is a type-correct substitution, then

$$\frac{\mathscr{S}}{\mathscr{S}|_{I_1, \ldots, I_n \to A_1, \ldots, A_n}}\ \ .$$

Rule (R8) says that substitution preserves the universality of specifications. In fact, this rule can be derived from the more general rules (R6) and (R7). To see this, suppose $\mathscr{S}$ is a universal specification and $I_1, \ldots, I_n \to A_1, \ldots, A_n$ is a type-correct substitution. Then there are phrase types $\theta_1, \ldots, \theta_n$ such that each free occurrence of I_i in $\mathscr{S}$ has type θ_i and each A_i has type θ_i. By applying rule (R6) n times to $\mathscr{S}$ (taking Σ to be the empty set), one can infer $(\forall\ \theta_1\ I_1) \ldots (\forall\ \theta_n\ I_n)\ \mathscr{S}$. Then from rule (R7) and modus ponens (R5), one can infer $\mathscr{S}|_{I_1, \ldots, I_n \to A_1, \ldots, A_n}$.

The next rules deal with specifications of the form $\{P\}$, which hold in a particular environment if P is a static assertion, i.e. if P is true for all states:

(R9)   Mathematical Fact Introduction

   If P is an assertion that is a mathematical fact then

$$\frac{}{\{P\}}\ \ .$$

(R10) Reductio ad Absurdum

$$\frac{}{\{\textbf{false}\} \Rightarrow \mathscr{S}}\ \ .$$

(R11) Static Implication

   If P and Q are assertions then

$$\frac{}{\{P\}\ \&\ \{P\ \textbf{implies}\ Q\} \Rightarrow \{Q\}}\ \ .$$

Rule (R9) says that mathematical facts (typically about various data types) are true in any environment and state. Rule (R10) says that the specification {**false**}, which is not true in any environment, implies anything. Rule (R11) says that static assertions can be combined according to the usual laws of mathematical reasoning.

In fact, rule (R11) can be expressed in a different way. By substituting the assertion identifiers p and q for the metavariables P and Q, we can infer the particular universal specification

(R11′) Static Implication (Axiom)

$$\{p\} \ \& \ \{p \ \textbf{implies} \ q\} \Rightarrow \{q\} \ \ .$$

On the other hand, from (R11′) we can use rule (R8) for free substitution to obtain $\{P\} \ \& \ \{P \ \textbf{implies} \ Q\} \Rightarrow \{Q\}$ for any assertions P and Q. Thus the single universal specification (R11′) has the same power in our logic as the rule of inference (R11).

Of course, a universal specification such as (R11′) can be viewed as a very simple kind of inference rule, with no premises and no metavariables. But it is simpler to view it as an *axiom*, i.e. a particular specification that, because it is known to be universal, can be written as part of a proof without being inferred from anything that precedes it.

In fact, most of the rules of inference given in Sections 1.4.2 and 1.4.3 can be reformulated as axioms in specification logic. In stating these axioms, we use p, q, r, i, p_1, p_2, q_1, and q_2 as assertion identifiers, s, s_1, and s_2 as statement identifiers, and l as a logical expression identifier:

(R12) Statement Compounding (Axiom)

$$\{p\} \ s_1 \ \{q\} \ \& \ \{q\} \ s_2 \ \{r\} \Rightarrow \{p\} \ s_1; \ s_2 \ \{r\} \ \ .$$

(R13) Strengthening Precedent (Axiom)

$$\{p \ \textbf{implies} \ q\} \ \& \ \{q\} \ s \ \{r\} \Rightarrow \{p\} \ s \ \{r\} \ \ .$$

(R14) Weakening Consequent (Axiom)

$$\{p\} \ s \ \{q\} \ \& \ \{q \ \textbf{implies} \ r\} \Rightarrow \{p\} \ s \ \{r\} \ \ .$$

(R15) **while** statement (Axiom)

$$\{i \ \textbf{and} \ l\} \ s \ \{i\} \Rightarrow \{i\} \ \textbf{while} \ l \ \textbf{do} \ s \ \{i \ \textbf{and} \ \neg \ l\} \ \ .$$

(R16) Two-way Conditional Statement (Axiom)

$$\{p \ \textbf{and} \ l\} \ s_1 \ \{q\} \ \& \ \{p \ \textbf{and} \ \neg \ l\} \ s_2 \ \{q\} \Rightarrow \{p\} \ \textbf{if} \ l \ \textbf{then} \ s_1 \ \textbf{else} \ s_2 \ \{q\} \ \ .$$

(R17) One-way Conditional Statement (Axiom)

$$\{p \ \textbf{and} \ l\} \ s \ \{q\} \ \& \ \{(p \ \textbf{and} \ \neg \ l) \ \textbf{implies} \ q\} \Rightarrow \{p\} \ \textbf{if} \ l \ \textbf{then} \ s \ \{q\} \ \ .$$

(R18) Empty Statement (Axiom)

$\{p\}\,\{p\}$.

(R19) Specification Conjunction (Axiom)

$\{p_1\}\,s\,\{q_1\}\,\&\,\{p_2\}\,s\,\{q_2\} \Rightarrow \{p_1 \text{ and } p_2\}\,s\,\{q_1 \text{ and } q_2\}$.

(R20) Specification Disjunction (Axiom)

$\{p_1\}\,s\,\{q_1\}\,\&\,\{p_2\}\,s\,\{q_2\} \Rightarrow \{p_1 \text{ or } p_2\}\,s\,\{q_1 \text{ or } q_2\}$.

To see the relationship between these axioms and the rules of Chapter 1, consider (R12). Let P, Q, and R be any assertions and S_1 and S_2 be any statements. Then by applying the rule of free substitution (R8) to axiom (R12), we may infer $\{P\}\,S_1\,\{Q\}\,\&\,\{Q\}\,S_2\,\{R\} \Rightarrow \{P\}\,S_1; S_2\,\{R\}$.

If $\{P\}\,S_1\,\{Q\}$ and $\{Q\}\,S_2\,\{R\}$ have been shown to be universal specifications then, by modus ponens (R5), we may infer $\{P\}\,S_1; S_2\,\{R\}$. In form, this is exactly the inference permitted by the rule for statement compounding given in Section 1.4.2. However, in specification logic it is no longer a very useful inference. The problem is that it is very rare for specifications of the form $\{P\}\,S_1\,\{Q\}$ or $\{Q\}\,S_2\,\{R\}$ to be universal.

The usual situation is that $\{P\}\,S_1\,\{Q\}$ will only be true in all environments satisfying some set Σ_1 of assumptions, and $\{Q\}\,S_2\,\{R\}$ will only be true in all environments satisfying some set Σ_2 of assumptions. In other words, $\Sigma_1 \Rightarrow \{P\}\,S_1\,\{Q\}$ and $\Sigma_2 \Rightarrow \{Q\}\,S_2\,\{R\}$ will be universal specifications. In this situation, we may use modus ponens and (R12) to infer $\Sigma_1\,\&\,\Sigma_2 \Rightarrow \{P\}\,S_1; S_2\,\{R\}$. Thus $\{P\}\,S_1; S_2\,\{R\}$ will be true in all environments satisfying both Σ_1 and Σ_2.

More generally, if

$$\Sigma_1 \Rightarrow \mathscr{S}_1$$
$$\vdots$$
$$\Sigma_n \Rightarrow \mathscr{S}_n$$

are universal specifications, and $\mathscr{S}_1\,\&\,\ldots\,\&\,\mathscr{S}_n \Rightarrow \mathscr{S}$ can be obtained from an axiom A by type-correct substitution, then free substitution and modus ponens can be used to infer

$$\Sigma_1\,\&\,\ldots\,\&\,\Sigma_n \Rightarrow \mathscr{S}$$.

Henceforth, we will simply say that such an inference is obtained "by applying A".

It is this ability to carry along and combine assumptions about environments that distinguishes specification logic from the logic of Chapter 1.

Next we consider specifications of the form $S\,\#\,E$, which specify that S does not interfere with E. The essential idea we want to capture is that everything that can cause interference is named by an identifier. Thus if I_1, $\dots$, I_n are the identifiers occurring free in S, we would expect $I_1 \# E$ & $\dots$ & $I_n \# E$ to imply $S \# E$.

However, this form of reasoning needs to be strengthened. For example, $x \# (y+z) \Rightarrow (x := y) \# (y+z)$ holds despite the fact that y interferes with $y+z$. The reason is that the only occurrence of y in $x := y$ is in a context—the expression on the right side of an assignment statement—that is not statement-like, and therefore cannot describe any action that might cause interference.

To make this precise, we must develop some notation for identifier occurrences. Let P be any phrase. We write $\mathscr{F}(P)$ for the set of identifiers that have free occurrences in P.

We say that an occurrence in P of an identifier (or more generally, an occurrence of a subphrase) is *statement-like* if the type of every subphrase of P enclosing the occurrence is statement-like. This concept can be defined more formally by using the terminology of Appendix A: A statement-like identifier or subphrase occurrence in P corresponds to a subtree in a derivation tree for P such that every node on the path from the root of the derivation tree to the root of the subtree has a statement-like phrase type. We write $\mathscr{F}_{\text{sta-like}}(P)$ for the subset of $\mathscr{F}(P)$ consisting of those identifiers that have statement-like free occurrences in P.

Then we have the following inference rule:

(R21) Left-Side Noninterference Decomposition

If S is a statement-like phrase, E is an expression-like phrase, and $\mathscr{F}_{\text{sta-like}}(S) = \{I_1, \dots, I_n\}$, then

$$\frac{}{I_1 \# E \ \& \ \dots \ \& \ I_n \# E \Rightarrow S \# E} \quad .$$

A similar rule deals with the identifiers occurring on the right side of $\#$. We say that an identifier or subphrase occurrence in a phrase P is *expression-like* if the type of every subphrase of P enclosing the occurrence is expression-like, and we write $\mathscr{F}_{\text{exp-like}}(P)$ for the set of identifiers that have free expression-like occurrences in P. Then:

(R22) Right-Side Noninterference Decomposition

If S is a statement-like phrase, E is an expression-like phrase, and $\mathscr{F}_{\text{exp-like}}(E) = \{I_1, \dots, I_n\}$, then

$$\frac{}{S \# I_1 \ \& \ \dots \ \& \ S \# I_n \Rightarrow S \# E} \quad .$$

For example, since $\mathscr{F}_{\text{exp-like}}(y+z) = \{y, z\}$, rule (R22) gives $x \# y$ & $x \# z \Rightarrow x \# (y+z)$. Then since $\mathscr{F}_{\text{sta-like}}(x := y) = \{x\}$, rule (R21) gives $x \# (y+z) \Rightarrow (x := y) \# (y+z)$. Using modus ponens to combine these two specifications gives $x \# y$ & $x \# z \Rightarrow (x := y) \# (y+z)$. In this way, these two rules can be used to express any noninterference specification in terms of its free identifiers.

Our next rule describes an important consequence of noninterference. Suppose a statement S does not interfere with an assertion P, and consider executing S with an initial state for which P is true. Then P will continue to be true during execution of S and will still be true when (and if) S terminates. Thus if S satisfies $\{Q\}\ S\ \{R\}$, it will also satisfy $\{Q$ and $P\}\ S\ \{R$ and $P\}$.

This reasoning is captured by the following axiom, in which s is a statement identifier, and p, q and r are assertion identifiers:

(R23) Constancy (Axiom)

$$s \# p\ \&\ \{q\}\ s\ \{r\} \Rightarrow \{q \text{ and } p\}\ s\ \{r \text{ and } p\} \quad .$$

Finally, we come to the inference rule for assignment. In Chapter 1 we gave the rule $\{P|_{X\to E}\}\ X := E\ \{P\}$, which can be falsified by various effects caused by the procedure mechanism. To avoid such falsification, we must preface this specification with the assumptions that X is a good variable and that X does not interfere with any other identifier that has a free expression-like occurrence in P. Thus we have

(R24) Simple Assignment

Let X be a τ variable identifier, E be a τ expression, and P be an assertion such that all free occurrences of X in P have type τ expression. Let $\{I_1, \dots, I_n\} = \mathscr{F}_{\text{exp-like}}(P) - \{X\}$. Then

$$\mathrm{gv}(X)\ \&\ X \# I_1\ \&\ \dots\ \&\ X \# I_n \Rightarrow \{P|_{X \to E}\}\ X := E\ \{P\} \quad .$$

Notice why this rule makes sense syntactically. The free occurrences of X in P are in contexts that permit τ expressions, and therefore τ variables, since a variable can always be used as an expression. Thus we can either substitute the expression E for X in P, or leave X unchanged while changing its type from τ **expression** to τ **variable**.

Exercise

1. Derive the following rules of inference from the rules given in the preceding section:

(a)
$$\frac{}{\Sigma\ \&\ (\Sigma \Rightarrow \mathscr{S}) \Rightarrow \mathscr{S}} \quad .$$

(b)
$$\frac{\Sigma \Rightarrow \mathscr{S}_1}{(\mathscr{S}_1 \Rightarrow \mathscr{S}_2) \Rightarrow (\Sigma \Rightarrow \mathscr{S}_2)} \quad .$$

(c) If I has phrase type θ then

$$\frac{\mathscr{S}_1\ \&\ \dots\ \&\ \mathscr{S}_n \Rightarrow \mathscr{S}}{(\forall \theta\ I)\ \mathscr{S}_1\ \&\ \dots\ \&\ (\forall \theta\ I)\ \mathscr{S}_n \Rightarrow (\forall \theta\ I)\ \mathscr{S}} \quad .$$

(d)   If I_1 and I_2 have phrase types θ_1 and θ_2 then

$$\overline{(\forall \theta_1\, I_1)\ (\forall \theta_2\, I_2)\ \mathscr{S} \Rightarrow (\forall \theta_2\, I_2)\ (\forall \theta_1\, I_1)\ \mathscr{S}}\quad .$$

(e)   If I and J have phrase type θ then

$$\overline{(\forall \theta\, I)\ (\forall \theta\, J)\ \mathscr{S} \Rightarrow (\forall \theta\, I)\ (\mathscr{S}|_{J \rightarrow I})}\quad .$$

(f)   Axiom

$$\{q\}\ s\ \{r\}\ \&\ \{p\} \Rightarrow \{q\}\ s\ \{p \text{ and } r\}\quad .$$

3.3.6   An Example of Inferences in Specification Logic

We have now accumulated enough rules to give an extended example. Let k, f, and n be integer variable identifiers. Then the following two universal specifications are instances of the assignment rule (R24):

$$\begin{aligned}
&\mathbf{gv}(k)\ \&\ k\#f\ \&\ k\#n \Rightarrow \\
&\quad \{(k+1) \times f = (k+1)! \text{ and } 0 \le k+1 \le n\} \\
&\quad k := k+1\ \{k \times f = k! \text{ and } 0 \le k \le n\} \\
&\mathbf{gv}(f)\ \&\ f\#k\ \&\ f\#n \Rightarrow \\
&\quad \{k \times f = k! \text{ and } 0 \le k \le n\} \\
&\quad f := k \times f\ \{f = k! \text{ and } 0 \le k \le n\}\quad .
\end{aligned}$$

By applying axiom (R12) for statement compounding, we get

$$\begin{aligned}
&\mathbf{gv}(k)\ \&\ k\#f\ \&\ k\#n\ \&\ \mathbf{gv}(f)\ \&\ f\#k\ \&\ f\#n \Rightarrow \\
&\quad \{(k+1) \times f = (k+1)! \text{ and } 0 \le k+1 \le n\} \\
&\quad k := k+1;\, f := k \times f\ \{f = k! \text{ and } 0 \le k \le n\}\quad .
\end{aligned}$$

Next, the rule for introducing mathematical facts gives

$$\begin{aligned}
&\{(f = k! \text{ and } 0 \le k \le n \text{ and } k \ne n) \\
&\quad \textbf{implies}\ ((k+1) \times f = (k+1)! \text{ and } 0 \le k+1 \le n)\ \}\quad ,
\end{aligned}$$

since the assertion within curly brackets is a mathematical fact about the integers. Then by applying axiom (R13) for strengthening precedents, we get

$$\begin{aligned}
&\mathbf{gv}(k)\ \&\ k\#f\ \&\ k\#n\ \&\ \mathbf{gv}(f)\ \&\ f\#k\ \&\ f\#n \Rightarrow \\
&\quad \{f = k! \text{ and } 0 \le k \le n \text{ and } k \ne n\} \\
&\quad k := k+1;\, f := k \times f\ \{f = k! \text{ and } 0 \le k \le n\}\quad .
\end{aligned}$$

Just as in Chapter 1, reasoning that involves the rules for statement compounding, strengthening precedents, and weakening consequents can be concisely communicated by using a tableau. The only change is that now the tableau must be prefaced with the union of the assumptions used in each step of the reasoning. For example, the chain of reasoning we have just given can be described by the following tableau:

$$\begin{matrix} \mathbf{gv}(k) \ \& \ k\#f \ \& \ k\#n \\ \& \ \mathbf{gv}(f) \ \& \ f\#k \ \& \ f\#n \end{matrix} \Bigg\} \ \Rightarrow \ \begin{cases} \{f=k! \ \mathbf{and} \ 0 \le k \le n \ \mathbf{and} \ k \ne n\} \\ \{(k+1) \times f = (k+1)! \ \mathbf{and} \ 0 \le k+1 \le n\} \\ k := k+1; \\ \{k \times f = k! \ \mathbf{and} \ 0 \le k \le n\} \\ f := k \times f \\ \{f=k! \ \mathbf{and} \ 0 \le k \le n\} \end{cases} .$$

The general situation is that a tableau has the form $\Sigma \Rightarrow L$, where L is a list of intermixed assertions and statements that begins and ends with assertions. Such a tableau is *valid* if:

(1) Whenever the triple $\{P\} \ S \ \{Q\}$ occurs in L, where S is a statement or sequence of statements, $\Sigma \Rightarrow \{P\} \ S \ \{Q\}$ is a universal specification,

and (2) Whenever the pair $\{P\}\{Q\}$ occurs in L, $\Sigma \Rightarrow \{P \ \mathbf{implies} \ Q\}$ is a universal specification.

If a tableau $\Sigma \Rightarrow L$ is valid, then $\Sigma \Rightarrow \{P\} \ S_1; \ \ldots \ ; \ S_n \ \{Q\}$ is a universal specification, where $\{P\} \ S_1; \ \ldots \ ; \ S_n \ \{Q\}$ is obtained from L by deleting intermediate assertions.

From the result of the above tableau, we can use the **while**-statement axiom (R15) to infer the universal specification:

$$\mathbf{gv}(k) \ \& \ k\#f \ \& \ k\#n \ \& \ \mathbf{gv}(f) \ \& \ f\#k \ \& \ f\#n \Rightarrow$$
$$\{f=k! \ \mathbf{and} \ 0 \le k \le n\}$$
$$\mathbf{while} \ k \ne n \ \mathbf{do}$$
$$\mathbf{begin} \ k := k+1; f := k \times f \ \mathbf{end}$$
$$\{f=k! \ \mathbf{and} \ 0 \le k \le n \ \mathbf{and} \ \lnot \ k \ne n\} \ ,$$

which is the main step in the following tableau:

$$\begin{matrix} \mathbf{gv}(k) \ \& \ k\#f \ \& \ k\#n \\ \& \ \mathbf{gv}(f) \ \& \ f\#k \ \& \ f\#n \end{matrix} \Bigg\} \ \Rightarrow \ \begin{cases} \{n \ge 0\} \\ \{1=0! \ \mathbf{and} \ 0 \le 0 \le n\} \\ k := 0; \\ \{1=k! \ \mathbf{and} \ 0 \le k \le n\} \\ f := 1; \\ \{f=k! \ \mathbf{and} \ 0 \le k \le n\} \\ \mathbf{while} \ k \ne n \ \mathbf{do} \\ \quad \mathbf{begin} \ k := k+1; f := k \times f \ \mathbf{end} \\ \{f=k! \ \mathbf{and} \ 0 \le k \le n \ \mathbf{and} \ \lnot \ k \ne n\} \\ \{f=n!\} \end{cases} .$$

The remaining steps are obvious applications of the rules for assignment statements and for introducing mathematical facts. Notice that these steps do not introduce any additional assumptions.

This example shows that specification logic treats assignment and control statements in much the same way as in Chapter 1. The difference is that each assignment statement introduces assumptions about the relevant identifiers. In the following sections we will see how these assumptions are eliminated or "discharged" by declarations and other binding mechanisms.

Exercise

1. Determine the necessary set of assumptions Σ, and prove

$$\Sigma \Rightarrow \{n \geq 0\}$$
$$k := 0; \ y := 1;$$
$$\textbf{while } k \neq n \textbf{ do}$$
$$\qquad \textbf{begin } k := k+1; \ y := x \times y \textbf{ end}$$
$$\{y = x^n\} \quad .$$

3.3.7   Inference for Simple Variable Declarations

The fundamental shortcoming of the kind of reasoning about programs used in Chapters 1 and 2 is that the specification of a statement is always inferred independently of the context in which the statement occurs. This is in sharp contrast to the way in which one reads a program in a language with block structure. As the reader descends into the program, each declaration provides information about the identifier being declared which can be used in understanding the statements within the scope of the declaration. Similarly, specifiers and parameter assumptions provide information about formal parameters. In specification logic this information is conveyed by assumptions.

Consider a block **begin integer** X; B **end**, which contains a single simple variable declaration, and suppose that we wish to show that this block satisfies $\{P\}$ **begin integer** X; B **end** $\{Q\}$. If the block is not a complete program, this will not be a universal specification, but it should be implied by some set Σ of relevant assumptions that have been established by declarations in enclosing blocks. In other words, we want to show that $\Sigma \Rightarrow \{P\}$ **begin integer** X; B **end** $\{Q\}$ is universal.

To do this, we must obviously show that the block body B satisfies $\{P\}$ B $\{Q\}$. But now, in addition to the assumptions Σ, we may use certain additional assumptions arising from the nature of the declaration **integer** X. Specifically, we may assume that X is a good variable, and that there is no interference between X and any phrase that does not contain a free occurrence of X.

This reasoning is captured by the following rule of inference:

(R25) Simple Variable Declarations

> If X is a τ variable identifier, B is a statement, P and Q are assertions, $E_1, \ldots , E_m$ are expression-like phrases, $S_1, \ldots , S_n$

are statement-like phrases, and X does not occur free in Σ, P, Q, E_1, $\dots$, E_m, S_1, $\dots$, S_n, then

$$\frac{\Sigma \ \& \ \mathbf{gv}(X) \ \& \ X\#E_1 \ \& \ \dots \ \& \ X\#E_m \ \& \ S_1\#X \ \& \ \dots \ \& \ S_n\#X \Rightarrow \{P\}\ B\ \{Q\}}{\Sigma \Rightarrow \{P\}\ \mathbf{begin}\ \tau\ X;\ B\ \mathbf{end}\ \{Q\}} \quad .$$

The reason that X must not occur free in Σ, P, or Q is that the meaning of this identifier outside the block is unrelated to its meaning inside the block.

As an example, we apply this rule to the specification proved at the end of the previous section. To match the premiss to this specification, we take X to be k and

$$\overbrace{\mathbf{gv}(f) \ \& \ f\#n \ \& \ \mathbf{gv}(k)}^{\Sigma} \ \& \ \overbrace{k\#f}^{E_1} \ \& \ \overbrace{k\#n}^{E_2} \ \& \ \overbrace{f\#k}^{S_1} \Rightarrow$$

$$\overbrace{\{n \geq 0\}}^{P}$$

$$B \left\{ \begin{array}{l} k:=0;\ f := 1; \\ \mathbf{while}\ k \neq n\ \mathbf{do} \\ \qquad \mathbf{begin}\ k := k+1;\ f := k \times f\ \mathbf{end} \end{array} \right.$$

$$\overbrace{\{f = n!\}}^{Q} \quad .$$

Then the rule for simple variable declarations gives

$$\begin{array}{l} \mathbf{gv}(f) \ \& \ f\#n \Rightarrow \\ \quad \{n \geq 0\} \\ \quad \mathbf{begin\ integer}\ k; \\ \quad k:=0;\ f := 1; \\ \quad \mathbf{while}\ k \neq n\ \mathbf{do} \\ \qquad \mathbf{begin}\ k := k+1:\ f := k \times f\ \mathbf{end} \\ \quad \mathbf{end} \\ \quad \{f = n!\} \quad . \end{array}$$

Informally, we say that the declaration **integer** k *discharges* the assumptions $\mathbf{gv}(k) \ \& \ k\#f \ \& \ k\#n \ \& \ f\#k$ which were used in reasoning about the body of the block.

Notice that there is no choice about which assumptions are discharged by a declaration $\tau\ X$. The undischarged assumptions Σ must be those not containing free occurrences of X, while each discharged assumption must have one of the forms $\mathbf{gv}(X)$ or $X\#E$ or $S\#X$, where S and E contain no free occurrences of X. In effect rule (R25) tells us everything we can assume about X and nothing else.

Of course, the rule for simple variable declarations only applies to a block that contains the declaration of a single variable. However, a block containing a multiple declaration or a sequence of declarations can be expanded into a nest of blocks in which each block contains the declaration of a single variable.

Exercise

1. Using the result of Exercise 1 after the previous section, determine the necessary set of assumptions Σ and prove

$$\Sigma \Rightarrow \{n \geq 0\}$$
$$\textbf{begin integer } k;$$
$$k := 0; \ y := 1;$$
$$\textbf{while } k \neq n \textbf{ do}$$
$$\qquad \textbf{begin } k := k + 1; \ y := x \times y \textbf{ end}$$
$$\textbf{end}$$
$$\{y = x^n\} \quad .$$

3.3.8 Inference for Proper Procedure Declarations

Now we come to the heart of our development: the formulation of an inference rule for proper procedure declarations. Because of its importance and complexity, we will give a more rigorous justification for this rule than for others: we will prove the correctness of a version of the rule that is adequate for nonrecursive procedures, and only rely upon the reader's intuition to justify the strengthening of this rule that is necessary to handle recursion.

Suppose we wish to infer a universal specification about a block containing the declaration of a proper procedure, i.e.

$$\Sigma \Rightarrow \{P\} \textbf{ begin procedure } H(\theta_1 \ F_1; \ \dots \ ; \ \theta_n \ F_n); \ B_{\text{proc}}; \ B \textbf{ end } \{Q\} \quad (1)$$

where $H, F_1, \dots, F_n$ are distinct identifiers. To do this we must show that the block body satisfies $\{P\} \ B \ \{Q\}$, using both the inherited assumptions Σ and additional assumptions Σ_{proc} that describe the nature of the procedure being declared. In other words, we must have a premiss of the form

$$\Sigma \ \& \ \Sigma_{\text{proc}} \Rightarrow \{P\} \ B \ \{Q\} \quad . \qquad (2)$$

Since the procedure identifier H has a different meaning in B than outside the block containing the procedure declaration, we assume that H does not occur free in Σ, P, or Q.

With a simple variable declaration, the analogue of Σ_{proc} is completely determined by the declaration. With a procedure declaration, however, the situation is more complex: to make an assumption about calls of a procedure, one must first prove something about the body of its declaration. Thus our rule will have a specification of B_{proc} as an additional premiss, and the form of Σ_{proc} will depend upon this premiss as well as upon the procedure declaration itself.

The premiss about B_{proc} has the form

$$\Sigma' \ \& \ \Sigma_{\text{pa}} \Rightarrow \{P_{\text{proc}}\} \ B_{\text{proc}} \ \{Q_{\text{proc}}\} \ . \tag{3}$$

Here the assumptions needed to insure $\{P_{\text{proc}}\} B_{\text{proc}} \{Q_{\text{proc}}\}$ are divided in Σ', which is a subset of the inherited assumptions Σ that describes global identifiers in B_{proc}, and Σ_{pa}, which is the set of parameter assumptions discussed in Section 3.1.4. We assume that Σ' contains no free occurrences of the formal parameters $F_1, \ldots, F_n$, since these identifiers have a different meaning in B_{proc} than outside the enclosing block. We also assume that H does not occur free in Σ_{pa}, P_{proc}, or Q_{proc}.

The complexity of the rule for proper procedure declarations lies in the form of Σ_{proc}. Rather than stating this form ad hoc, we will develop it while proving that the rule is correct, i.e. that if (2) and (3) are universal specifications then (1) is a universal specification.

Assume (2) and (3) are universal, and led η be any environment in which Σ is true. Then we must show that

$$\{P\} \ \textbf{begin procedure} \ H(\theta_1 \ F_1; \ \ldots \ ; \ \theta_n \ F_n); \ B_{\text{proc}}; \ B \ \textbf{end} \ \{Q\}$$

is true in η. But the block in the above specification has the same meaning in η as its body B has in $\eta' = [\eta \mid H{:}h]$, where h is the meaning of the procedure being declared, as described in Section 3.3.1. Moreover, P and Q have the same meaning in η and η' since H does not occur free in these assertions. Thus it is sufficient to show that $\{P\} \ B \ \{Q\}$ is true in η'.

Since H does not occur free in Σ, the truth of Σ in η implies the truth of Σ in η'. Thus the universality of (2) implies the desired result that $\{P\} B \{Q\}$ is true in η', providing Σ_{proc} is true in η'.

Now consider (3), and let η'' be any environment that gives meanings of the appropriate type to the identifiers occurring free in (3), and that gives the same meaning as η' to H and to the identifiers that occur free in Σ' or globally in B_{proc}. We know that Σ is true in η', Σ' is a subset of Σ, and η'' agrees with η' for the identifiers occurring free in Σ'; thus Σ' is true in η''. Then the universality of (3) implies that

$$\Sigma_{\text{pa}} \Rightarrow \{P_{\text{proc}}\} \ B_{\text{proc}} \ \{Q_{\text{proc}}\}$$

is true in η''. Moreover, as shown in Section 3.3.1, since η'' agrees with η' for H and the identifiers occurring globally in B_{proc}, $H(F_1, \ldots, F_n)$ has the same meaning in η'' as B_{proc}, so that

$$\Sigma_{\text{pa}} \Rightarrow \{P_{\text{proc}}\} \ H(F_1, \ldots, F_n) \ \{Q_{\text{proc}}\}$$

is true in η''. It follows from the definition of quantified specifications that the above specification, quantified over any of the identifiers for which η'' can differ from η', is true in the environment η', and can therefore be an assumption in Σ_{proc}.

These quantified identifiers can include the formal parameters $F_1, \ldots , F_n$, which are distinct from H and do not occur free in Σ' or globally in B_{proc}. Moreover, we can also quantify over other identifiers that are distinct from H and do not occur free in Σ' or B_{proc}. If such identifiers have any free occurrences in (3) (which is the only case of interest), then they are ghost identifiers of (3); we therefore call them *ghost parameters*.

Thus Σ_{proc} can contain the assumption

$$(\forall \ \theta_1 \ F_1) \ \ldots \ (\forall \ \theta_n \ F_n) \ (\forall \ \theta'_1 \ G_1) \ \ldots \ (\forall \ \theta'_k G_k)$$
$$(\Sigma_{\text{pa}} \Rightarrow \{P_{proc}\} \ H(F_1, \ \ldots \ , F_n) \ \{Q_{\text{proc}}\}) \quad ,$$

where the ghost parameters $G_1, \ldots , G_k$ can be any identifiers, of phrase types $\theta'_1, \ldots , \theta'_k$, that are distinct from each other and H, $F_1, \ldots , F_n$, and do not occur free in Σ' or B_{proc}.

However, we will also need a second assumption in Σ_{proc} that describes noninterference properties of the procedure being declared. To derive this assumption, let $I_1, \ldots , I_m$ be the identifiers with global statement-like occurrences in B_{proc}, i.e.

$$\{I_1, \ \ldots \ , I_m\} = \mathscr{F}_{\text{sta-like}}(B_{\text{proc}}) - \{F_1, \ \ldots \ , F_n\} \quad ,$$

and let E be some identifier distinct from $F_1, \ldots , F_n$, H, and the identifiers occurring globally in B_{proc}. Since every member of $\mathscr{F}_{\text{sta-like}}(B_{\text{proc}})$ must be either an I_i or a statement-like formal parameter, we can use rule (R21) for left-side noninterference decomposition to infer the universal specification

$$I_1 \# E \ \& \ \ldots \ \& \ I_m \# E \Rightarrow (F_{i_1} \# E \ \& \ \ldots \ \& \ F_{i_j} \# E \Rightarrow B_{\text{proc}} \# E) \quad ,$$

where $F_{i_1}, \ldots , F_{i_j}$ are the formal parameters with statement-like phrase type.

Let e be any meaning, appropriate to an expression-like phrase type, such that $I_1 \# E \ \& \ \ldots \ \& \ I_m \# E$ is true in $[\eta' \mid E: e]$, and let η'' be any environment that gives the same meaning as $[\eta' \mid E: e]$ to all identifiers except the formal parameters. Since the formal parameters do not occur in $I_1 \# E \ \& \ \ldots \ \& \ I_m \# E$, this specification is true in η'', so that the universal specification in the previous paragraph implies that

$$F_{i_1} \# E \ \& \ \ldots \ \& \ F_{i_j} \# E \Rightarrow B_{\text{proc}} \# E$$

is true in η''. But B_{proc} and $H(F_1, \ldots , F_n)$ have the same meaning in η'', since this environment agrees with η' for H and the identifiers occurring globally in B_{proc}. Thus the above specification, with B_{proc} replaced by $H(F_1, \ldots , F_n)$, is also true in η'', and since η'' gives arbitrary meaning to the formal parameters and agrees with $[\eta' \mid E: e]$ for other identifiers,

$$(\forall\theta_1\,F_1)\,...\,(\forall\theta_n\,F_n)\,\big(F_{i_1}\#\,E\;\&\;...\;\&\;F_{i_j}\#\,E\Rightarrow H(F_1,\,...\,,F_n)\#\,E\big)$$

is true in $[\eta'\mid E\colon e]$.

By (5d) in Section 3.3.4, this specification is the definition of $H\#\,E$, so that $H\#\,E$ is true in $[\eta'\mid E\colon e]$. Then since e is any expression-like meaning such that $I_1\#\,E\;\&\;...\;\&\;I_m\#\,E$ is true in $[\eta'\mid E\colon e]$, the specification

$$(\forall\ \text{exp-like}\ E)\,(I_1\#\,E\;\&\;...\;\&\;I_m\#\,E\Rightarrow H\#\,E)$$

is true in η' and can be taken as the second assumption in Σ_{proc}. (A minor generalization of the form of this assumption, obtained by alpha-conversion, is that E can be any identifier distinct from $I_1,\,...\,,I_m$, and H.)

This argument shows the correctness of a rule that is adequate for nonrecursive procedures. To handle recursion, the rule must be strengthened in two ways:

(a) The assumptions Σ_{proc} must be added to the premiss (3). Essentially, we must be able to make the same assumptions about calls of a procedure from within its body as from elsewhere in its scope.

(b) H must be excluded from the identifiers $I_1,\,...\,,I_m$ in the noninterference part of Σ_{proc}. Essentially, a procedure only interferes with something if some global identifier other than the procedure name interferes with it.

Thus we have:

(R26) Proper Procedure Declarations

Suppose

$F_1,\,...\,,F_n,\,G_1,\,...\,,G_k,\,H$ are distinct identifiers of phrase types $\theta_1,\,...\,,\theta_n,\,\theta'_1,\,...\,,\theta'_k$, $\mathbf{procedure}(\theta_1,\,...\,,\theta_n)$,

$B_{\text{proc}},\,B$ are statements,

$P_{\text{proc}},\,Q_{\text{proc}},\,P,\,Q$ are assertions,

$\Sigma,\,\Sigma',\,\Sigma_{\text{pa}}$ are finite sets of specifications,

such that

$\Sigma'\subseteq\Sigma$,

$F_1,\,...\,,F_n$ do not occur free in Σ',

$G_1,\,...\,,G_k$ do not occur free in B_{proc} or Σ',

H does not occur free in $P_{\text{proc}},\,Q_{\text{proc}},\,P,\,Q,\,\Sigma,\,\Sigma'$, or Σ_{pa}.

Let Σ_{proc} be

$$(\forall\theta_1 F_1)\,...\,(\forall\theta_n F_n)\,(\forall\theta'_1 G_1)\,...\,(\forall\theta'_k G_k)$$
$$\big(\Sigma_{\text{pa}}\Rightarrow\{P_{\text{proc}}\}\,H(F_1,\,...\,,F_n)\,\{Q_{\text{proc}}\}\big)$$
$$\&\;(\forall\ \text{exp-like}\ E)\,(I_1\#\,E\;\&\;...\;\&\;I_m\#\,E\Rightarrow H\#\,E)\quad,$$

where $\{I_1, \ldots, I_m\} = \mathcal{F}_{\text{sta-like}}(B_{\text{proc}}) - \{F_1, \ldots, F_n, H\}$ and E is some identifier that is distinct from $I_1, \ldots, I_m$ and H. Then

$$\frac{\Sigma' \;\&\; \Sigma_{\text{pa}} \;\&\; \Sigma_{\text{proc}} \Rightarrow \{P_{\text{proc}}\}\; B_{\text{proc}}\; \{Q_{\text{proc}}\} \qquad \Sigma \;\&\; \Sigma_{\text{proc}} \Rightarrow \{P\}\; B\; \{Q\}}{\Sigma \Rightarrow \{P\}\; \textbf{begin procedure } H(\theta_1 F_1; \ldots; \theta_n F_n);\; B_{\text{proc}};\; B\; \textbf{end}\; \{Q\}} \quad .$$

As with the rule for simple variable declarations, this rule only applies to blocks that contain a single declaration. Usually, blocks with multiple declarations can be expanded into nests of blocks with single declarations, but this approach will not handle groups of mutually recursive procedures. To handle mutual recursion, one must extend the above rule to multiple procedure declarations. Although such an extension is conceptually straightforward, the resulting rule is so complicated that we will not try to formulate it.

On the other hand, the full generality of the single-declaration rule given above is frequently unnecessary. In reasoning about nonrecursive procedures, the assumption Σ_{proc} may be omitted from the first premiss. When this premiss does not contain ghost identifiers, there will be no need for the ghost parameters $G_1, \ldots, G_k$. When B_{proc} contains no global identifiers, or when the only assumptions about global identifiers also involve formal parameters, Σ' will be empty.

3.3.9 Examples of Inference about Procedures

Our first example of the use of the rule for proper procedure declarations does not involve recursion, ghost parameters, or inherited assumptions. Consider the specification proved in Section 3.3.7:

$$\overbrace{\text{gv}(f) \;\&\; f \# n}^{\Sigma_{\text{pa}}} \Rightarrow$$

$$\overbrace{\{n \geq 0\}}^{P_{\text{proc}}}$$

$$B_{\text{proc}} \left\{ \begin{array}{l} \textbf{begin integer } k; \\ k := 0;\; f := 1; \\ \textbf{while } k \neq n \textbf{ do} \\ \qquad \textbf{begin } k := k+1;\; f := k \times f \textbf{ end} \\ \textbf{end} \end{array} \right.$$

$$\overbrace{\{f = n!\}}^{Q_{\text{proc}}} \quad .$$

We will encapsulate the statement in this specification as the body of a procedure declaration with the heading

$$
\overset{H}{\overbrace{\textbf{procedure } fact}}(\overset{\theta_1}{\overbrace{\textbf{integer } \{\textbf{exp}\}}} \overset{F_1}{\overbrace{n}} ; \overset{\theta_2}{\overbrace{\textbf{integer } \{\textbf{var}\}}} \overset{F_2}{\overbrace{f}}); \ldots \quad .
$$

The metavariables in the procedure rule must be replaced so that the procedure declaration in the conclusion matches the declaration of *fact*, and the first premiss matches the specification of the procedure body. Most of these replacements are indicated above. Since there are no global identifier occurrences in B_{proc}, Σ' is empty. Since there are no ghost identifiers in the specification of B_{proc}, there are no ghost parameters.

These replacements map the first premiss of the procedure rule (with Σ_{proc} omitted since there is no recursion) into the universal specification given above, and map Σ_{proc} into the procedure assumptions

$$
(\forall \textbf{ integer exp } n) \ (\forall \textbf{ integer var } f)
$$
$$
\big(\textbf{gv}(f) \ \& \ f \# n \Rightarrow \{n \geq 0\} \ fact(n, f) \ \{f = n!\}\big)
$$
$$
\& \ (\forall \textbf{ exp-like } e) \ fact \# e \quad .
$$

In the last line, there are no $I_1, \ldots, I_m$ since there are no global identifiers in B_{proc}.

Thus the rule for proper procedure declarations shows that, from an instance of the second premiss,

$$
\Sigma \ \& \ \Sigma_{\text{proc}} \Rightarrow \{P\} \ B \ \{Q\} \quad ,
$$

we can infer an instance of the conclusion,

$$
\Sigma \Rightarrow \{P\}
$$
$$
\textbf{begin procedure } fact(\textbf{integer } \{\textbf{exp}\} \ n; \textbf{ integer } \{\textbf{var}\} \ f);
$$
$$
\qquad \textbf{begin } \ldots \textbf{ end};
$$
$$
B
$$
$$
\textbf{end}
$$
$$
\{Q\} \quad .
$$

Notice that, in addition to $f \# n$, the parameter assumptions include the assumption $\textbf{gv}(f)$, which was omitted from the informal presentation of this procedure in Section 3.1.4. In fact, the use of $\textbf{gv}$ in parameter assumptions is so stereotyped that it would be pedantic to include it in program comments. Normally, $\textbf{gv}(F)$ will occur as a parameter assumption for each formal parameter F of type τ **variable**.

To illustrate how the assumption Σ_{proc} is used in reasoning about the block body, we consider the procedure statement $fact(a + b, c)$. From rule (R22) for right-side noninterference decomposition, we have

$$
c \# a \ \& \ c \# b \Rightarrow c \# (a + b) \quad ,
$$

and from rule (R7) for removing quantifiers, we have

$$((\forall \text{integer exp } n)\ (\forall\ \text{integer var } f)$$
$$(\mathbf{gv}(f)\ \&\ f \# n \Rightarrow \{n \ge 0\}\ fact(n, f)\ \{f = n!\}))$$
$$\Rightarrow (\mathbf{gv}(c)\ \&\ c \# (a+b) \Rightarrow \{a+b \ge 0\}\ fact(a+b, c)\ \{c = (a+b)!\})\quad .$$

Thus

$$\mathbf{gv}(c)\ \&\ c \# a\ \&\ c \# b\ \&\ \Sigma_{\text{proc}}$$
$$\Rightarrow \{a+b \ge 0\}\ fact(a+b, c)\ \{c = (a+b)!\}$$

is a universal specification about the procedure statement $fact(a+b, c)$.

However, Σ_{proc} also contains $(\forall\ \text{exp-like } e)\ fact \# e$. To see the role of this assumption, we will show that $fact(a+b, c)$ preserves the assertion $a+b \ge 0$. The rule for right-side noninterference decompositon gives

$$c \# a\ \&\ c \# b \Rightarrow c \# (a+b \ge 0)\quad ,$$

quantifier removal gives

$$((\forall\ \text{exp-like } e)\ fact \# e) \Rightarrow fact \# (a+b \ge 0)\quad ,$$

and left-side noninterference decomposition gives

$$fact \# (a+b \ge 0)\ \&\ c \# (a+b \ge 0) \Rightarrow fact(a+b, c) \# (a+b \ge 0)$$

since the occurrences of a and b in $fact(a+b, c)$ are not statement-like.

Next we employ the rule of constancy (R23). By substituting $fact(a+b, c)$ for s, $a+b \ge 0$ for both p and q, and $c = (a+b)!$ for r, we get

$$fact(a+b, c) \# (a+b \ge 0)$$
$$\&\ \{a+b \ge 0\}\ fact(a+b, c)\ \{c = (a+b)!\}$$
$$\Rightarrow \{a+b \ge 0\}\ fact(a+b, c)\ \{c = (a+b)!\ \textbf{and }\ a+b \ge 0\}\quad .$$

Then using modus ponens to combine the last five specifications gives

$$\overbrace{\mathbf{gv}(c)\ \&\ c \# a\ \&\ c \# b\ \&\ \Sigma_{\text{proc}}}^{\Sigma} \Rightarrow$$

$$\overbrace{\{a+b \ge 0\}}^{P}\ \overbrace{fact(a+b, c)}^{B}\ \overbrace{\{c = (a+b)!\ \textbf{and }\ a+b \ge 0\}}^{Q}\quad .$$

It is easy to see how this kind of reasoning could be extended to a block body containing several calls of $fact$. However, if we just take the metavariables as indicated, the above specification becomes an instance of the second premiss of the procedure rule, so that we may infer

$\mathbf{gv}(c)$ & $c\#a$ & $c\#b \Rightarrow$
$\quad \{a+b \geq 0\}$
$\quad$ **begin procedure** *fact*(**integer** $\{$**exp**$\}$ n; **integer** $\{$**var**$\}$ f);
$\quad\quad$ **begin** ... **end**;
$\quad$ *fact*$(a+b, c)$
$\quad$ **end**
$\quad \{c = (a+b)! \text{ and } a+b \geq 0\}$.

As a second example, we consider a recursive procedure for computing factorials:

$$\overbrace{H}\quad\overbrace{\theta_1}\quad\overbrace{F_1}\quad\overbrace{\theta_2}\quad\overbrace{F_2}$$
$$\textbf{procedure } \textit{fact}(\textbf{integer } \{\textbf{exp}\}\ n\ ;\ \textbf{integer } \{\textbf{var}\}\ f\ );$$

$$\overbrace{\Sigma_{\text{pa}}}$$
$$\{\textbf{pa: } \mathbf{gv}(f)\ \&\ f\#n\}$$

$$\overbrace{P_{\text{proc}}}$$
$$\{\overbrace{n \geq 0}\}$$

$$B_{\text{proc}} \begin{cases} \textbf{if } n=0 \textbf{ then } f := 1 \textbf{ else} \\ \quad \textbf{begin } \textit{fact}(n-1, f);\ f := n \times f \textbf{ end} \end{cases}$$

$$\overbrace{Q_{\text{proc}}}$$
$$\{\overbrace{f=n!}\}\quad.$$

With a recursive procedure, we cannot proceed by first proving a specification of the body and then matching this specification against the first premiss of the procedure rule to determine Σ_{proc}, since we need to know Σ_{proc} while proving the specification of the body. However, an adequately commented procedure declaration, such as the one above, will contain enough information to determine the metavariable replacements that give the first premiss and Σ_{proc}. (Notice that the stereotyped parameter assumption $\mathbf{gv}(f)$ has been included since f has type τ **variable**.)

If we replace the metavariables as indicated, take Σ' to be empty since there are no global identifiers, and use no ghost parameters since there are no ghost identifiers, then the first premiss of the procedure rule becomes

$\quad \mathbf{gv}(f)$ & $f\#n$ & $\Sigma_{\text{proc}} \Rightarrow$
$\quad\quad \{n \geq 0\}$
$\quad\quad$ **if** $n=0$ **then** $f := 1$ **else**
$\quad\quad\quad$ **begin** *fact*$(n-1, f)$; $f := n \times f$ **end**
$\quad\quad \{f=n!\}$,

where Σ_{proc} is

$$(\forall \text{ integer exp } n) \ (\forall \text{ integer var } f)$$
$$\big(\mathbf{gv}(f) \ \& \ f\#n \Rightarrow \{n \geq 0\} \ fact(n, f) \ \{f=n!\}\big)$$
$$\& \ (\forall \text{ exp-like } e) \ fact\#e \quad .$$

Actually, this is the same Σ_{proc} as in the previous example, which is hardly surprising since the two procedures are intended to have the same meaning.

However, we must now prove the above specification of B_{proc}, using Σ_{proc} as an assumption. This reflects the basic method of reasoning about recursion: In showing the correctness of the procedure body, one assumes that recursive calls behave correctly.

As a first step, an argument similar to that given for the previous example shows that the statement $fact(n-1, f)$ satisfies

$$\mathbf{gv}(f) \ \& \ f\#n \ \& \ \Sigma_{\text{proc}} \Rightarrow$$
$$\{n-1 \geq 0\} \ fact(n-1, f) \ \{f=(n-1)! \text{ and } n-1 \geq 0\} \quad .$$

Then the following tableau establishes a specification for the compound statement in the procedure body:

$$\mathbf{gv}(f) \ \& \ f\#n \ \& \ \Sigma_{\text{proc}} \Rightarrow \begin{cases} \{n \geq 0 \text{ and } \neg \, n=0\} \\ \{n-1 \geq 0\} \\ fact(n-1, f) \\ \{f=(n-1)! \text{ and } n-1 \geq 0\} \\ \{n \times f = n!\} \\ f := n \times f \\ \{f=n!\} \quad . \end{cases}$$

The other half of the conditional statement satisfies

$$\mathbf{gv}(f) \ \& \ f\#n \Rightarrow \begin{cases} \{n \geq 0 \text{ and } n=0\} \\ \{1=n!\} \\ f := 1 \\ \{f=n!\} \quad . \end{cases}$$

Finally, the desired premiss about the procedure body can be inferred by using rule (R16) for the two-way conditional statement:

$$\mathbf{gv}(f) \ \& \ f\#n \ \& \ \Sigma_{\text{proc}} \Rightarrow$$
$$\{n \geq 0\}$$
$$\text{if } n=0 \text{ then } f := 1 \text{ else}$$
$$\quad \text{begin } fact(n-1, f); f := n \times f \text{ end}$$
$$\{f=n!\} \quad .$$

Since Σ_{proc} is the same as in the previous example, its usage in reasoning about the body of the block containing the procedure declaration is similar.

For a third example, we consider a nonrecursive factorial-computing procedure that uses call by value and result:

procedure *fact*(**integer value** n; **integer result** f);

$$B_0 \begin{cases} \textbf{begin integer } k; \\ k:=0; f:=1; \\ \textbf{while } k \neq n \textbf{ do} \\ \qquad \textbf{begin } k:=k+1; f:=k\times f \textbf{ end} \\ \textbf{end} \quad . \end{cases}$$

This procedure declaration will lead to a Σ_{proc} which is stronger than in the previous examples, reflecting the fact that this procedure will still behave correctly when its parameters interfere. However, to express this extra strength we will need to use ghost identifiers and parameters.

Let B_0 be the body of the above procedure declaration, and let B_0' be $B_0|_{n,\ f\to n',\ f'}$. Then according to the transformation described in Section 3.1.5, the above declaration is equivalent to

$$\overbrace{\textbf{procedure } fact}^{H}(\overbrace{\textbf{integer } \{\textbf{exp}\}}^{\theta_1}\ \overbrace{n}^{F_1}\ ;\ \overbrace{\textbf{integer } \{\textbf{var}\}}^{\theta_2}\ \overbrace{f}^{F_2}\ );$$

$$B_{\text{proc}} \begin{cases} \textbf{begin integer } n', f'; \\ n':=n; B_0'; f:=f' \\ \textbf{end} \quad . \end{cases}$$

As in our first example, B_0 satisfies

$$\textbf{gv}(f)\ \&\ f\#n \Rightarrow \{n\geq 0\}\ B_0\ \{f=n!\} \quad .$$

Moreover, since f is the only identifier with a free statement-like occurrence in B_0, the rules for noninterference decomposition give

$$f\#n\ \&\ f\#n_0 \Rightarrow B_0\#(n=n_0) \quad .$$

Next, we use the rule of constancy (R23) to obtain

$$B_0\#(n=n_0)\ \&\ \{n\geq 0\}\ B_0\ \{f=n!\} \Rightarrow$$
$$\{n\geq 0 \textbf{ and } n=n_0\}\ B_0\ \{f=n! \textbf{ and } n=n_0\} \quad .$$

Then by combining these results and weakening the consequent, we obtain

$$\textbf{gv}(f)\ \&\ f\#n\ \&\ f\#n_0 \Rightarrow \{n\geq 0 \textbf{ and } n=n_0\}\ B_0\ \{f=n_0!\} \quad .$$

At first sight, it may seem surprising that we will need this kind of ghost-identifier description of the behavior of B_0. Intuitively the reason is that, since n is called by value, a caller of *fact* will have no access to the value of n after B_0 has completed execution, and therefore no interest in the fact that $f=n!$ will hold. What is important to the caller is that f will be the factorial of the value n_0 possessed by n before execution of B_0, since n_0 will also be the value of the corresponding actual parameter.

Next, we apply the substitution $n, f \rightarrow n', f'$ to the above specification, to obtain

$$\textbf{gv}(f') \;\&\; f' \,\#\, n' \;\&\; f' \,\#\, n_0 \Rightarrow \{n' \geq 0 \text{ and } n' = n_0\} \; B_0' \;\{f' = n_0!\} \quad ,$$

which is the main step in the following tableau:

$$\left.\begin{array}{l}\textbf{gv}(n') \;\&\; n' \,\#\, n_0 \\ \&\; \textbf{gv}(f') \;\&\; f' \,\#\, n' \;\&\; f' \,\#\, n_0 \\ \&\; \textbf{gv}(f) \;\&\; f \,\#\, n_0 \end{array}\right\} \Rightarrow \left\{\begin{array}{l} \{n \geq 0 \text{ and } n = n_0\} \\ n' := n; \\ \{n' \geq 0 \text{ and } n' = n_0\} \\ B_0'; \\ \{f' = n_0!\} \\ f := f' \\ \{f = n_0!\} \end{array}\right. .$$

Then two applications of rule (R25) for simple variable declarations give

$$\overbrace{\textbf{gv}(f) \;\&\; f \,\#\, n_0}^{\Sigma_{\text{pa}}} \Rightarrow$$

$$\overbrace{\{n \geq 0 \text{ and } n = n_0\}}^{P_{\text{proc}}}$$

$$B_{\text{proc}} \left\{\begin{array}{l} \{n \geq 0 \text{ and } n = n_0\} \\ \textbf{begin integer } n', f'; \\ n' := n; B_0'; f := f' \\ \textbf{end} \end{array}\right.$$

$$\overbrace{\{f = n_0!\}}^{Q_{\text{proc}}} .$$

The indicated metavariable replacements map this specification into the first premiss of the procedure rule. As in our previous examples, since there are no global identifiers, Σ' is empty. But now, since n_0 is a ghost identifier of the above specification, it becomes a ghost parameter in Σ_{proc}. Thus we take G_1 to be n_0 and θ_1' to be its phrase type **integer expression**. Thus Σ_{proc} is

$$(\forall \textbf{ integer exp } n) \; (\forall \textbf{ integer var } f) \; (\forall \textbf{ integer exp } n_0)$$
$$(\textbf{gv}(f) \;\&\; f \,\#\, n_0 \Rightarrow \{n \geq 0 \text{ and } n = n_0\} \; fact(n, f) \; \{f = n_0!\})$$
$$\&\; (\forall \textbf{ exp-like } e) \; fact \,\#\, e \quad .$$

The reader may verify that this Σ_{proc} implies the Σ_{proc} of the two previous factorial-computing procedures. (Hint: Substitute n for n_0, using parts (c), (d) and (e) of Exercise 1 following Section 3.3.5.) Thus the present procedure will behave correctly whenever the previous ones do so.

On the other hand, as an example of the additional capabilities provided by call by value and result, the present Σ_{proc} implies

$$(\forall \text{ integer exp } n_0)$$
$$(\mathbf{gv}(a) \ \& \ a \# n_0 \Rightarrow$$
$$\{a+b \geq 0 \text{ and } a+b = n_0\} \ fact(a+b, a) \ \{a = n_0!\}) \quad ,$$

which characterizes the kind of call that will not behave correctly when call by name is used.

Exercises

1. For each of the following procedures, determine Σ_{proc} and prove the appropriate instance of the first premiss of rule (R26) for proper procedure declarations.

   (a) **procedure** *powerx*(**integer** {**exp**} n; **integer** {**var**} y);
       begin integer k;
       $k := 0$; $y := 1$;
       while $k \neq n$ **do**
           begin $k := k+1$; $y := x \times y$ **end**
       end   .

   Here the specification of the procedure body is the result of Exercise 1 after Section 3.3.7. Despite the presence of the global identifier x, Σ' is empty, since the only assumption about x is $y \# x$, which also involves a formal parameter and must therefore be part of Σ_{pa}.

   (b) **procedure** *powerxy*(**integer** {**exp**} n);
       begin integer k;
       $k := 0$; $y := 1$;
       while $k \neq n$ **do**
           begin $k := k+1$; $y := x \times y$ **end**
       end   .

   Again, the specification of the procedure body is the result of Exercise 1 after Section 3.3.7. Now, however, Σ' is $\mathbf{gv}(y) \ \& \ y \# x$.

   (c) **procedure** *powerxy*(**integer** {**exp**} n);
       {**pa**: $y \# n$}
       $\{n \geq 0\}$
       if $n = 0$ **then** $y := 1$ **else**
           begin *powerxy*$(n-1)$; $y := x \times y$ **end**
       $\{y = x^n\}$.

   As in the previous case, Σ' is $\mathbf{gv}(y) \ \& \ y \# x$.

   (d) The procedure described in Exercise 2 following Section 3.1.5.

2. Show that the procedure declaration

> **procedure** *swap*(**integer** {**var**} *x*, *y*);
>   **begin integer** *t*; *t*:=*x*; *x*:=*y*; *y*:=*t* **end**

gives rise to the procedure assumption $\Sigma_{\text{proc}} \equiv$

> ($\forall$ **integer var** *x*) ($\forall$ **integer var** *y*) ($\forall$ **integer exp** x_0) ($\forall$ **integer exp** y_0)
>   (gv(*x*) & gv(*y*) & $x \# x_0$ & $x \# y_0$ & $y \# x_0$ & $y \# y_0$ & $y \# x \Rightarrow$
> $\{x = x_0 \text{ and } y = y_0\}$ *swap*(*x*, *y*) $\{y = x_0 \text{ and } x = y_0\}$)
> & ($\forall$ **exp-like** *e*) *swap* $\# e$.

Notice the asymmetry between *x* and *y*.

3.3.10 Further Examples

The examples in the previous section show the application of specification logic to procedures that can be proved by more conventional methods, e.g. [Hoare 71b]. The only significant novelty is the treatment of call by value and result as abbreviational constructs in the sense of Section 3.1.5, which avoids the complications of the procedure rule that would be necessary to include these parameter-passing mechanisms explicitly.

We now consider two examples, involving statement parameters and the use of call by name to repeatedly evaluate expressions with changing values, that cannot be treated by other approaches. In both of these examples, we will use parameter assumptions that go beyond the simple noninterference and good-variable specifications used previously.

The first example is the higher-order procedure

$$\overbrace{\text{procedure } \textit{repeat}(}^{H} \quad \overbrace{\textbf{procedure}}^{\theta_1 = \textbf{statement } F_1} \; s \; \overbrace{; \textbf{logical } \{\textbf{exp}\}}^{\theta_2} \; \overbrace{l}^{F_2} \;);$$

$$\overbrace{\textbf{begin } s; \textbf{ while } \neg l \textbf{ do } s \textbf{ end}}^{B_{\text{proc}}} \quad ,$$

which was introduced in Section 3.1.7. Suppose the identifier *p* denotes an assertion that will be true when the body of this procedure begins execution, and the identifier *i* denotes the invariant of the **while** statement. Then the statement *s* should satisfy the specifications $\{p\}$ *s* $\{i\}$ and $\{i \text{ and } \neg l\}$ *s* $\{i\}$, or equivalently the single specification $\{p \text{ or } (i \text{ and } \neg l)\}$ *s* $\{i\}$. The key to reasoning about the procedure is to take this specification as the parameter assumption.

We begin with the obvious tableau

$$\{p \text{ or } (i \text{ and } \neg l)\} \; s \; \{i\} \Rightarrow \begin{cases} \{i \text{ and } \neg l\} \\ \{p \text{ or } (i \text{ and } \neg l)\} \\ s \\ \{i\} \end{cases} .$$

Then an application of the **while**-statement axiom (R15) gives the main step in the following tableau:

$$\{p \text{ or } (i \text{ and } \neg l)\} \ s \ \{i\} \Rightarrow \left\{ \begin{array}{l} \{p\} \\ \{p \text{ or } (i \text{ and } \neg l)\} \\ s; \\ \{i\} \\ \textbf{while } \neg l \textbf{ do } s \\ \{i \text{ and } \neg (\neg l)\} \\ \{i \text{ and } l\} \end{array} \right. .$$

To match the result of this tableau with the first premiss of rule (R26), we use the metavariable replacements

$$\overbrace{\{p \text{ or } (i \text{ and } \neg l)\} \ s \ \{i\}}^{\Sigma_{\text{pa}}} \Rightarrow \overbrace{\{p\}}^{P_{\text{proc}}} \ \overbrace{s; \textbf{while } \neg l \textbf{ do } s}^{B_{\text{proc}}} \ \overbrace{\{i \text{ and } l\}}^{Q_{\text{proc}}} \ .$$

Since there are no global identifiers, Σ' is empty. Since p and i are ghost identifiers, they become ghost parameters, of phrase type **assertion**. Thus Σ_{proc} is

      ($\forall$ **statement** s) ($\forall$ **logical exp** l) ($\forall$ **assertion** p) ($\forall$ **assertion** i)
        ($\{p \text{ or } (i \text{ and } \neg l)\} \ s \ \{i\} \Rightarrow \{p\} \ repeat(s, l) \ \{i \text{ and } l\}$)
      & ($\forall$ **exp-like** e) $repeat \# e$.

The second line of Σ_{proc} is similar to the kind of axiom one would give about a **repeat** statement if it were available in Algol W. However, Σ_{proc} is not a universal specification; it only holds in environments in which the identifier *repeat* has an appropriate meaning.

Our second example is the procedure given in Section 3.1.5 that uses Jensen's device to compute an iterated sum:

      procedure *sum*(**integer** {**var**} i; **integer** {**exp**} e);
        begin $s := 0$; $i := a - 1$;
        while $i < b$ **do**
           begin $i := i + 1$; $s := s + e$ **end**
      end .

To describe the body of this procedure, we introduce a ghost identifier θ, of phrase type **integer procedure(integer expression)**, that expresses the value of e as a function of i. The relationship between these three identifiers is expressed by the static assertion $\{e = \theta(i)\}$, which will appear as a parameter assumption.

The invariant of the **while** statement asserts that $\boxed{a \quad b}$ is partitioned into a processed interval $\boxed{a \quad i}$ and an unprocessed interval $i\boxed{\quad b}$, and that s is the sum of θ over the processed interval:

$$\boxed{a \quad i \quad b} \text{ and } s = \sum_{j \in \boxed{a \quad i}} \theta(j) \quad .$$

The following tableau shows that this invariant is preserved by the **while**-statement body:

$$
\begin{array}{l}
\mathbf{gv}(i) \ \& \ i \# a \ \& \ i \# b \\
\& \ i \# s \ \& \ i \# \theta \\
\& \{e = \theta(i)\} \\
\& \ \mathbf{gv}(s) \ \& \ s \# a \ \& \ s \# b \\
\& \ s \# i \ \& \ s \# \theta
\end{array}
\Rightarrow
\left\{
\begin{array}{l}
\{\boxed{a \quad i \quad b} \text{ and } s = \sum_{j \in \boxed{a \quad i}} \theta(j) \text{ and } i < b\} \\
\{\boxed{a \quad i+1 \quad b} \text{ and } s = \sum_{j \in \boxed{a \quad i+1}} \theta(j)\} \\
i := i+1; \\
\{\boxed{a \quad i \quad b} \text{ and } s = \sum_{j \in \boxed{a \quad i}} \theta(j)\} \\
\{\boxed{a \quad i \quad b} \text{ and } s + \theta(i) = \sum_{j \in \boxed{a \quad i}} \theta(j)\} \\
\{\boxed{a \quad i \quad b} \text{ and } s + e = \sum_{j \in \boxed{a \quad i}} \theta(j)\} \\
s := s + e \\
\{\boxed{a \quad i \quad b} \text{ and } s = \sum_{j \in \boxed{a \quad i}} \theta(j)\} \quad .
\end{array}
\right.
$$

Then the **while**-statement axiom gives the main step in

$$
\begin{array}{l}
\mathbf{gv}(i) \ \& \ i \# a \ \& \ i \# b \\
\& \ i \# s \ \& \ i \# \theta \\
\& \{e = \theta(i)\} \\
\& \ \mathbf{gv}(s) \ \& \ s \# a \ \& \ s \# b \\
\& \ s \# i \ \& \ s \# \theta
\end{array}
\Rightarrow
\left\{
\begin{array}{l}
\{\mathbf{true}\} \\
\{0 = 0\} \\
s := 0; \\
\{s = 0\} \\
\{\boxed{a \quad a-1 \quad b} \text{ and } s = \sum_{j \in \boxed{a \quad a-1}} \theta(j)\} \\
i := a - 1; \\
\{\boxed{a \quad i \quad b} \text{ and } s = \sum_{j \in \boxed{a \quad i}} \theta(j)\} \\
\mathbf{while} \ i < b \ \mathbf{do} \\
\quad \mathbf{begin} \ i := i+1; \ s := s+e \ \mathbf{end} \\
\{\boxed{a \quad i \quad b} \text{ and } s = \sum_{j \in \boxed{a \quad i}} \theta(j) \text{ and } \neg \ i < b\} \\
\{s = \sum_{j \in \boxed{a \quad b}} \theta(j)\} \quad .
\end{array}
\right.
$$

The following metavariable replacements map the first premiss of the procedure rule into the result of this tableau:

$$\overbrace{\mathbf{gv}(s) \ \& \ s \# a \ \& \ s \# b}^{\Sigma'}$$

$$\overbrace{\& \ \mathbf{gv}(i) \ \& \ i \# a \ \& \ i \# b \ \& \ i \# s \ \& \ i \# \theta \ \& \ s \# i \ \& \ s \# \theta \ \& \ \{e = \theta(i)\}}^{\Sigma_{\mathrm{pa}}} \Rightarrow$$

$$\overbrace{P_{\text{proc}}}$$
$$\{\textbf{true}\}$$

$$B_{\text{proc}} \begin{cases} s:=0;\ i:=a-1; \\ \textbf{while } i<b \textbf{ do} \\ \qquad \textbf{begin } i:=i+1;\ s:=s+e \textbf{ end} \end{cases}$$

$$\overbrace{Q_{\text{proc}}}$$
$$\{s=\textstyle\sum_{j\,\in\,\boxed{a\ \ b}}\ \theta(j)\} \quad .$$

The formal parameters are i and e, and the ghost parameter is θ. Thus Σ_{proc} is

($\forall$ **integer var** i) ($\forall$ **integer exp** e)
    ($\forall$ **integer procedure(integer exp)** θ)
    $(\textbf{gv}(i)\ \&\ i\#a\ \&\ i\#b\ \&\ i\#s\ \&\ i\#\theta\ \&\ s\#i\ \&\ s\#\theta\ \&\ \{e=\theta(i)\}$
        $\Rightarrow\{\textbf{true}\}\ sum(i,\,e)\ \{s=\textstyle\sum_{j\,\in\,\boxed{a\ \ b}}\ \theta(j)\}\ )$
& ($\forall$ **exp-like** e) $(s\#e\Rightarrow sum\#e)$.

   In the next section, we will show how these assumptions can be used to reason about calls of *sum*.

Exercise

1.   The procedure *whiledo* described in Exercise 3 following Section 3.2.1 uses recursion to obtain the effect of a **while** statement. Show that the declaration of *whiledo* leads to a Σ_{proc} bearing a close relation to axiom (R15) for the **while** statement.

3.3.11 Lambda Expressions

A significant shortcoming of Algol W is that it does not provide any way to denote a procedure without using an identifier to name the procedure. This deficiency is particularly painful for procedures that are actual parameters in calls of other procedures. For example, in Section 3.1.7 we used the following statement to sum an array segment:

```
begin
procedure addoneelement(integer {exp} i); s := s + X(i);
s := 0; iterate(a, b, addoneelement)
end   .
```

Here the only usage of the procedure named by *addoneelement* is in the call of *iterate*, but we are forced to name this procedure by an identifier and to define the meaning of this identifier at a point remote from the only point where it is used. The program would be simpler and clearer if we could write an expression denoting this procedure directly as an actual parameter of the call of *iterate*.

This kind of facility is provided by a procedure-denoting expression called a *lambda expression*, which consists of the symbol λ, followed by a parenthesized formal parameter list, a period, and a procedure body, e.g.

$$\lambda(\textbf{integer } \{\textbf{exp}\} \ i). \ s := s + X(i) \quad .$$

A lambda expression defines the same procedure as would be defined by a procedure declaration with the same formal parameter list and body, but leaves the procedure unnamed. Instead, the lambda expression is written directly at the point where the procedure is used. For example, the array-summing program given above could be written as

> **begin**
> $s := 0; \ iterate(a, \ b, \ \lambda(\textbf{integer } \{\textbf{exp}\} \ i). \ s := s + X(i))$
> **end** .

Syntactically, a lambda expression of the form

$$\lambda(\theta_1 \ F_1; \ \dots \ ; \ \theta_n \ F_n). \ B$$

is a phrase of type **procedure**$(\theta_1, \dots, \theta_n)$, τ **procedure**$(\theta_1, \dots, \theta_n)$, or **assertion procedure**$(\theta_1, \dots, \theta_n)$, depending upon whether the body B is a statement, a τ expression, or an assertion. As with procedure declarations, the occurrences of $F_1, \dots, F_n$ in the formal parameter list are binders whose scope is the formal parameter list plus the following procedure body, i.e. the entire lambda expression.

Just as the meaning of procedure declarations can be explained by the copy rule, so the meaning of lambda expressions can be explained by a process called *beta reduction*. Consider a procedure statement or function designator that begins with a lambda expression:

$$\left(\lambda(\theta_1 \ F_1; \ \dots \ ; \ \theta_n \ F_n). \ B\right) (A_1, \ \dots \ , A_n) \quad .$$

Such a phrase is called a *beta redex*. Its meaning is always the same as the meaning of the phrase obtained from the procedure body B by substituting each A_i for F_i:

$$B\big|_{F_1, \ \dots \ , F_n \to A_1, \ \dots \ , A_n} \quad .$$

The replacement of a beta redex by the result of this substitution is called *beta reduction*. (The terms beta redex and beta reduction, like the term alpha conversion, are taken from the study of the lambda calculus, which is a logical language based upon the use of lambda expressions.)

In this description of beta reduction, we have assumed that call by value or result is not used in the lambda expression. When such usage occurs, it must be eliminated by means of the transformation described in Section 3.1.5, before the process of beta reduction is performed.

As an example, suppose *iterate* is defined by the declaration

> **procedure** *iterate*(**integer** {**exp**} a, b; **procedure** p {**integer exp**});
>   **begin integer** k; $k := a - 1$;
>   **while** $k < b$ **do**
>   **begin** $k := k + 1$; $p(k)$ **end**
>   **end**   .

(To keep the example simple, we use call by name, rather than call by value as in Section 3.1.7.) Then an application of the copy rule shows that

$$iterate\big(a,\ b,\ \lambda(\textbf{integer } \{\textbf{exp}\}\ i).\ s := s + X(i)\big)$$

is equivalent to

> **begin integer** k; $k := a - 1$;
> **while** $k < b$ **do**
>   **begin** $k := k + 1$;
> $(\lambda(\textbf{integer } \{\textbf{exp}\}\ i).\ s := s + X(i))\ (k)$
>   **end**
> **end**   .

Next, the beta redex in the fourth line can be reduced to $s := s + X(k)$, so that the call of *iterate* is equivalent to

> **begin integer** k; $k := a - 1$;
> **while** $k < b$ **do**
>   **begin** $k := k + 1$; $s := s + X(k)$ **end**
> **end**   .

Although lambda expressions are not available in Algol W, they are provided in several programming languages, including LISP and (with slightly different notation) Algol 68. In the rest of this book, we will occasionally use them in programs to improve clarity. In such cases they can be eliminated by declaring a procedure with a dummy name. Specifically, one can replace a lambda expression of the form $\lambda(\theta_1\ F_1; \ldots ; \theta_n\ F_n).\ B$ by an identifier D that does not occur elsewhere in the program, and then insert the declaration

> **procedure** $D(\theta_1\ F_1; \ldots ; \theta_n\ F_n)$; B

in a block enclosing the occurrence of D. One should be careful that the enclosing block is small enough to fall within the scope of all binders of the identifiers occurring globally in B. As an example, this transformation would convert our array-summing program back into the form containing a declaration of *addoneelement* that was given at the beginning of this section.

However, our main reason for introducing lambda expressions is to use them in specification logic. Since lambda expressions denote procedures, they are among the phrases that can be substituted for identifiers of procedural types. Moreover, since beta reduction preserves meaning, it can be used as a rule of inference, i.e. the reduction of a beta redex occurring in a universal specification gives another universal specification. Indeed, one can even use beta reduction backwards to create a redex in a specification.

To illustrate the use of lambda expressions in specification logic, consider the procedure *sum* discussed in the previous section. By applying rule (R7) for quantifier removal to the Σ_{proc} obtained for this procedure, with the substitution

$$i, e, \theta \rightarrow j, X(j) \times X(j), \lambda(\textbf{integer } \{\textbf{exp}\} \ k). \ X(k) \times X(k) \quad ,$$

one can infer

$$
\begin{aligned}
\Sigma_{\text{proc}} \ \& \ \textbf{gv}(j) \ \& \ j\#a \ \& \ j\#b \ \& \ j\#s \\
\& \ j\# \left(\lambda(\textbf{integer } \{\textbf{exp}\} \ k). \ X(k) \times X(k)\right) \\
\& \ s\#j \ \& \ s\# \left(\lambda(\textbf{integer } \{\textbf{exp}\} \ k). \ X(k) \times X(k)\right) \\
\& \ \{X(j) \times X(j) = \left(\lambda(\textbf{integer } \{\textbf{exp}\} \ k). \ X(k) \times X(k))(j)\right\} \\
\Rightarrow \{\textbf{true}\} \ sum(j, X(j) \times X(j)) \\
\{s = \textstyle\sum_{j \in \boxed{a \ \ b}} \left(\lambda(\textbf{integer } \{\textbf{exp}\} \ k). \ X(k) \times X(k))(j)\right\} \quad .
\end{aligned}
$$

By beta-reducing the two redexes, we infer

$$
\begin{aligned}
\Sigma_{\text{proc}} \ \& \ \textbf{gv}(j) \ \& \ j\#a \ \& \ j\#b \ \& \ j\#s \\
\& \ j\# \left(\lambda(\textbf{integer } \{\textbf{exp}\} \ k). \ X(k) \times X(k)\right) \\
\& \ s\#j \ \& \ s\# \left(\lambda(\textbf{integer } \{\textbf{exp}\} \ k). \ X(k) \times X(k)\right) \\
\& \ \{X(j) \times X(j) = X(j) \times X(j)\} \\
\Rightarrow \{\textbf{true}\} \ sum(j, X(j) \times X(j)) \ \{s = \textstyle\sum_{j \in \boxed{a \ \ b}} X(j) \times X(j)\} \quad .
\end{aligned}
$$

Then, since $X(j) \times X(j) = X(j) \times X(j)$ is a mathematical fact, and right-side noninterference decomposition gives

$$j\#X \Rightarrow j\# \left(\lambda(\textbf{integer } \{\textbf{exp}\} \ k). \ X(k) \times X(k)\right)$$

and

$$s\#X \Rightarrow s\# \left(\lambda(\textbf{integer } \{\textbf{exp}\} \ k). \ X(k) \times X(k)\right)$$

(since only X occurs free in the lambda expression), we have

$$
\begin{aligned}
\Sigma_{\text{proc}} \ \& \ \textbf{gv}(j) \ \& \ j\#a \ \& \ j\#b \ \& \ j\#s \ \& \ j\#X \ \& \ s\#j \ \& \ s\#X \\
\Rightarrow \{\textbf{true}\} \ sum(j, X(j) \times X(j)) \ \{s = \textstyle\sum_{j \in \boxed{a \ \ b}} X(j) \times X(j)\} \quad .
\end{aligned}
$$

Next, rule (R25) for simple variable declarations gives

$$
\begin{aligned}
\Sigma_{\text{proc}} \ \& \ s\#X \Rightarrow \\
\{\textbf{true}\} \\
\textbf{begin integer } j; \ sum(j, X(j) \times X(j)) \ \textbf{end} \\
\{s = \textstyle\sum_{j \in \boxed{a \ \ b}} X(j) \times X(j)\} \quad .
\end{aligned}
$$

Thus, if we take this specification as the second premiss of the procedure rule, remembering that $\Sigma' = \mathbf{gv}(s)$ & $s \# a$ & $s \# b$ must be a subset of Σ, we obtain the conclusion

$$\mathbf{gv}(s) \ \& \ s \# a \ \& \ s \# b \ \& \ s \# X \Rightarrow$$
$$\{\mathbf{true}\}$$
$$\mathbf{begin}$$
$$\mathbf{procedure} \ sum(\mathbf{integer} \ \{\mathbf{var}\} \ i; \ \mathbf{integer} \ \{\mathbf{exp}\} \ e);$$
$$\mathbf{begin} \ s := 0; \ i := a - 1;$$
$$\mathbf{while} \ i < b \ \mathbf{do}$$
$$\mathbf{begin} \ i := i + 1; \ s := s + e \ \mathbf{end}$$
$$\mathbf{end};$$
$$\mathbf{begin \ integer} \ j; \ sum\big(j, \ X(j) \times X(j)\big) \ \mathbf{end}$$
$$\mathbf{end}$$
$$\{s = \textstyle\sum_{j \in \boxed{a \ \ b}} X(j) \times X(j)\} \quad .$$

Exercise

1. Use the copy rule and beta reduction to eliminate the procedure statements from the following program, which computes the sum of a segment of a two-dimensional array:

    $$\mathbf{begin} \ s := 0;$$
    $$iterate(a1, \ b1, \ \lambda(\mathbf{integer} \ \{\mathbf{exp}\} \ i).$$
    $$iterate(a2, \ b2, \ \lambda(\mathbf{integer} \ \{\mathbf{exp}\} \ j). \ s := s + X(i, j)) \ )$$
    $$\mathbf{end}$$

    (Assume the formal parameters a and b of *iterate* are called by name.) Also, use the method of introducing declared procedures with dummy names to convert this program to conventional Algol W.

*3.3.12   Abstract Specification Logic

Once lambda expressions have been introduced into specification logic, with beta reduction as an inference mechanism, the logic can be simplified significantly. In particular one can give axioms, which we will call *abstract axioms*, from which several of the more complicated inference rules can be derived by substituting lambda expressions and then using beta reduction. In effect, much of the complexity of the logic can be encapsulated in the mechanism of beta reduction.

For example, the following is an abstract axiom for assignment, in which x is a τ variable identifier, e is a τ expression identifier, and π is an assertion procedure(τ expression) identifier:

248 PROCEDURES

(R27) Simple Assignment (Axiom)

$$\mathbf{gv}(x) \ \& \ x \# \pi \Rightarrow \{\pi(e)\} \ x := e \ \{\pi(x)\} \quad .$$

From this axiom, we can derive our previous rule (R24) for assignment as follows: Suppose X is a τ variable identifier, E is a τ expression, and P is an assertion such that the free occurrences of X in P have phrase type τ **expression**. By substituting X for x, E for e, and $\lambda(\tau \ \mathbf{exp} \ X). \ P$ for π in rule (R27), we can infer

$$\mathbf{gv}(X) \ \& \ X \# \left(\lambda(\tau \ \mathbf{exp} \ X). \ P\right) \Rightarrow$$
$$\left\{\left(\lambda(\tau \ \mathbf{exp} \ X). \ P\right)(E)\right\} \ X := E \ \left\{\left(\lambda(\tau \ \mathbf{exp} \ X). \ P\right)(X)\right\} \quad .$$

Then by beta-reducing the precedent and consequent, we get

$$\mathbf{gv}(X) \ \& \ X \# \left(\lambda(\tau \ \mathbf{exp} \ X). \ P\right) \Rightarrow \{P|_{X \to E}\} \ X := E \ \{P\} \quad ,$$

since beta-reducing the consequent leads to the substitution $X \to X$, which leaves P unaffected.

However, by right-side noninterference decomposition, we have

$$X \# I_1 \ \& \ \dots \ \& \ X \# I_n \Rightarrow X \# \left(\lambda(\tau \ \mathbf{exp} \ X). \ P\right) \quad ,$$

where $\{I_1, \dots, I_n\} = \mathcal{F}_{\text{exp-like}}\left(\lambda(\tau \ \mathbf{exp} \ X). \ P\right) = \mathcal{F}_{\text{exp-like}}(P) - \{X\}$. Then modus ponens can be used to infer the conclusion of rule (R24).

From rules (R6) and (R7) for the introduction and removal of quantifiers, it can be seen that axiom (R27) is equivalent to

$$\mathbf{gv}(x) \Rightarrow (\forall \tau \ \mathbf{exp} \ e) \ (\forall \ \mathbf{assertion} \ \mathbf{procedure}(\tau \ \mathbf{exp}) \ \pi)$$
$$\left(x \# \pi \Rightarrow \{\pi(e)\} \ x := e \cdot \{\pi(x)\}\right) \quad .$$

In this form, the axiom is an obvious consequence of the definition (6) of **gv** given in Section 3.3.4, as is the converse implication

(R28) Good Variables (Axiom)

$$(\forall \ \tau \ \mathbf{exp} \ e) \ (\forall \ \mathbf{assertion} \ \mathbf{procedure}(\tau \ \mathbf{exp}) \ \pi)$$
$$\left(x \# \pi \Rightarrow \{\pi(e)\} \ x := e \ \{\pi(x)\}\right)$$
$$\Rightarrow \mathbf{gv}(x) \quad .$$

In the next section, we will use (R28) to obtain conditions for insuring that array designators are good variables.

Another abstract axiom describes nonrecursive proper procedures. Let m be a procedure$(\theta_1, \dots, \theta_n)$ identifier and σ be a procedure$\big(\text{procedure } (\theta_1, \dots, \theta_n)\big)$ identifier, and consider the block

$$\mathbf{begin} \ \mathbf{procedure} \ h(\theta_1 \ f_1; \ \dots \ ; \ \theta_n \ f_n); \ m(f_1, \dots, f_n); \ \sigma(h) \ \mathbf{end} \quad .$$

Obviously the effect of the procedure declaration is to give h the same meaning as m, so that $\sigma(h)$ inside the block has the same meaning as $\sigma(m)$ outside the block. This justifies the following abstract axiom, where p and q are assertion identifiers:

(R29) Nonrecursive Proper Procedure Declarations (Axiom)

$$\{p\}\,\sigma(m)\,\{q\}\Rightarrow$$
$$\{p\}$$
begin procedure $h(\theta_1\,f_1;\,\dots\,;\,\theta_n\,f_n);\,m(f_1,\,\dots\,,f_n);$
$$\sigma(h)$$
end
$$\{q\}\quad.$$

(Strictly speaking, this is a family of axioms, one for each choice of $n \geq 1$ and $\theta_1, \dots, \theta_n$.)

Despite the seeming triviality of this axiom, it can be used to derive the nonrecursive case of rule (R26) for proper procedure declarations. Suppose that $F_1, \dots, F_n, G_1, \dots, G_k, H, E$ are distinct identifiers, B_{proc}, B are statements, $P_{\mathrm{proc}}, Q_{\mathrm{proc}}, P, Q$ are assertions, and $\Sigma, \Sigma', \Sigma_{\mathrm{pa}}$ are finite sets of specifications, that satisfy the restrictions given in rule (R26) and also the restriction that H does not occur free in B_{proc} (since we are not considering recursion).

Suppose that the first premiss of rule (R26), with Σ_{proc} omitted since we are avoiding recursion,

$$\Sigma'\ \&\ \Sigma_{\mathrm{pa}}\Rightarrow\{P_{\mathrm{proc}}\}\,B_{\mathrm{proc}}\,\{Q_{\mathrm{proc}}\}$$

is a universal specification. Since the F's and G's do not occur free in Σ', we can introduce quantifiers to infer

$$\Sigma'\Rightarrow(\forall F,\,G)\,(\Sigma_{\mathrm{pa}}\Rightarrow\{P_{\mathrm{proc}}\}\,B_{\mathrm{proc}}\,\{Q_{\mathrm{proc}}\})\quad,$$

where we have written $(\forall F,\,G)$ to abbreviate the list of quantifiers $(\forall\,\theta_1 F_1)\,\dots\,(\forall\,\theta_n F_n)\,(\forall\,\theta_1' G_1)\,\dots\,(\forall\,\theta_k'\,G_k)$.

By using left-side noninterference decomposition and introducing a quantifier, we can infer

$$(\forall\ \textbf{exp-like}\ E)\,(I_1 \# E\ \&\ \dots\ \&\ I_m \# E\Rightarrow$$
$$(\lambda(\theta_1 F_1;\,\dots\,;\,\theta_n F_n).\,B_{\mathrm{proc}})\# E)\quad,$$

where $\{I_1, \dots, I_m\}=\mathscr{F}_{\textbf{sta-like}}(\lambda(\theta_1 F_1;\,\dots\,;\,\theta_n F_n).\,B_{\mathrm{proc}})=\mathscr{F}_{\textbf{sta-like}}(B_{\mathrm{proc}})-\{F_1, \dots, F_n, H\}$.

Next, suppose that the second premiss of rule (R26),

$$\Sigma\ \&\ (\forall F,\,G)\,(\Sigma_{\mathrm{pa}}\Rightarrow\{P_{\mathrm{proc}}\}\,H(F_1, \dots, F_n)\,\{Q_{\mathrm{proc}}\})$$
$$\&\ (\forall\ \textbf{exp-like}\ E)\,(I_1 \# E\ \&\ \dots\ \&\ I_m \# E\Rightarrow H\# E)$$
$$\Rightarrow\{P\}\,B\,\{Q\}\quad,$$

is a universal specification. Since beta reduction preserves meaning, we can replace B by the redex $(\lambda(\textbf{procedure}(\theta_1, \dots, \theta_n)\,H).\,B)(H)$ which reduces to B, i.e. we can do beta-reduction backwards. Then we can substitute $\lambda(\theta_1 F_1;\,\dots\,;\,\theta_n F_n).\,B_{\mathrm{proc}}$ for H. Since the F's, G's, and E do not occur free in

$\lambda(\theta_1 F_1; \ldots; \theta_n F_n).\ B_{\text{proc}}$, there is no alpha conversion. Since H does not occur free in Σ, Σ_{pa}, P_{proc}, Q_{proc}, P, Q, or $\lambda(\textbf{procedure}(\theta_1, \ldots, \theta_n)\ H).\ B$, these phrases are not changed by the substitution. On the other hand, the statement $H(F_1, \ldots, F_n)$ changes to $(\lambda(\theta_1 F_1; \ldots; \theta_n F_n).\ B_{\text{proc}})\ (F_1, \ldots, F_n)$, which beta-reduces to B_{proc}. Thus we have

$$\Sigma\ \&\ (\forall F,\, G)\ (\Sigma_{\text{pa}} \Rightarrow \{P_{\text{proc}}\}\ B_{\text{proc}}\ \{Q_{\text{proc}}\})$$
$$\&\ (\forall\ \textbf{exp-like}\ E)\ (I_1 \# E\ \&\ \ldots\ \&\ I_m \# E \Rightarrow$$
$$(\lambda(\theta_1 F_1; \ldots; \theta_n F_n).\ B_{\text{proc}}) \# E)$$
$$\Rightarrow \{P\}\ (\lambda(\textbf{procedure}(\theta_1, \ldots, \theta_n)\ H).\ B)$$
$$(\lambda(\theta_1 F_1; \ldots; \theta_n F_n).\ B_{\text{proc}})\ \{Q\}\quad.$$

Next we use axiom (R29). First we use alpha conversion to replace $f_1, \ldots, f_n$, and h by $F_1, \ldots, F_n$, and H. (Without loss of generality, we can assume that these identifiers are distinct from p, q, m, and σ.) Then we substitute P for p, Q for q, $\lambda(\theta_1 F_1; \ldots; \theta_n F_n).\ B_{\text{proc}}$ for m, and $\lambda(\textbf{procedure}(\theta_1, \ldots, \theta_n)\ H).\ B$ for σ. Since $F_1, \ldots, F_n$, and H do not occur free in the first of these lambda expressions and H does not occur free in the second, the substitution does not cause any alpha conversion. However, the substitution does convert the statements $m(F_1, \ldots, F_n)$ and $\sigma(H)$ into redexes. After beta-reducing these redexes, we have

$$\{P\}\ (\lambda(\textbf{procedure}(\theta_1, \ldots, \theta_n)\ H).\ B)$$
$$(\lambda(\theta_1 F_1; \ldots; \theta_n F_n).\ B_{\text{proc}})\ \{Q\}$$
$$\Rightarrow \{P\}\ \textbf{begin procedure}\ H(\theta_1 F_1; \ldots; \theta_n F_n);\ B_{\text{proc}};\ B\ \textbf{end}\ \{Q\}\quad.$$

Finally, from the results of the last four paragraphs and the restriction $\Sigma' \subseteq \Sigma$, we can use modus ponens to infer the conclusion of rule (R26):

$$\Sigma \Rightarrow \{P\}\ \textbf{begin procedure}\ H(\theta_1 F_1; \ldots; \theta_n F_n);\ B_{\text{proc}};\ B\ \textbf{end}\ \{Q\}\quad.$$

Thus in the nonrecursive case, lambda expressions and beta reduction can be used to derive the complex rule (R26) from the almost trivial abstract axiom (R29).

Unfortunately, this approach cannot be extended to encompass recursion. To give an abstract axiom for recursion, one must introduce *specification*-valued procedures. Moreover, to insure the soundness of the axiom one must restrict the bound occurrences of identifiers in lambda expressions denoting these procedures so that, in the language of fixed-point theory, the meanings of these lambda expressions are *continuous* functions. These considerations, which are beyond the scope of this book, are discussed in [Reynolds 81].

Exercise

1. Simple variable declarations can be described by a family of abstract axioms indexed by the integers $m \geq 0$ and $n \geq 0$. Let $e_1, \ldots , e_m$ be identifiers of expression-like types, $s_1, \ldots , s_n$ be identifiers of statement-like types, p and q be assertion identifiers, and σ be a procedure(τ variable) identifier. Then:

    $$(\forall \; \tau \; \mathbf{var} \; x) \; \big(\mathbf{gv}(x) \; \& \; x \# e_1 \; \& \; \ldots \; \& \; x \# e_m$$
    $$\& \; s_1 \# x \; \& \; \ldots \; \& \; s_n \# x \Rightarrow \{p\} \; \sigma(x) \; \{q\}\big)$$
    $$\Rightarrow \{p\} \; \mathbf{begin} \; \tau \; x; \; \sigma(x) \; \mathbf{end} \; \{q\} \quad .$$

    Derive rule (R25) from this family of axioms, and vice-versa.

*3.3.13   Inference for Arrays

In this section we give a brief account of the inference rules that describe assignment to array elements and the declaration of arrays. For simplicity, this account is limited to the one-dimensional case.

In Section 2.3.2, we gave the rule $\{P|_{X \to [X \, | \, S: \; E]}\} \; X(S) := E \; \{P\}$ for assignment to array elements. Just as with simple assignment, the generalization to specification logic requires us to preface this specification with assumptions about noninterference, namely that assigning to $X(S)$ will not affect the meaning of any identifier other than X that has a free occurrence in P. However, we do not need to assume that X is a "good" array variable since, in the subset of Algol W used in this book, all array variables have good behavior. (It is array *designators*, not array variables, that can behave badly.) Thus there will be no analogue of the specification $\mathbf{gv}(V)$ for arrays.

As in Section 2.3.2, our rule will not take subscript errors into account, i.e. we will assume that such errors are akin to nontermination and must be treated by informal arguments outside of our conditional logic.

These considerations lead to the following rule, which plays the same role for assignments to array elements that rule (R24) plays for simple assignments:

(R30)   Array Assignment

> Let X be an identifier of type τ **array variable**($*$), S be an integer expression, E be a τ expression, and P be an assertion such that all free occurrences of X in P have type τ **array expression**($*$). Let $\{I_1, \ldots , I_n\} = \mathscr{F}_{\mathbf{exp\text{-}like}}(P) - \{X\}$. Then

$$X(S) \# I_1 \; \& \; \ldots \; \& \; X(S) \# I_n \Rightarrow \{P|_{X \to [X \, | \, S: \; E]}\} \; X(S) := E \; \{P\} \quad .$$

The same rule can be stated more abstractly as an axiom, analogous to rule (R27) for simple assignment, in which x is a τ array variable ($*$) identifier, s is an integer expression identifier, e is a τ expression identifier, and ρ is an assertion procedure(τ array expression ($*$)) identifier:

(R30′) Array Assignment (Axiom)

$$x(s) \# \rho \Rightarrow \{\rho([x \mid s: e])\}\ x(s) := e\ \{\rho(x)\}\quad .$$

We leave it to the reader to verify that (R30) and (R30′) can each be derived from the other.

In a sense, either rule (R30) or (R30′) tells us everything that we need to know about assignment to array elements. In practice, however, we need additional rules to deal with the use of array designators as actual parameters. For example, let Σ_{proc} be the procedure assumptions obtained in Section 3.3.9 that describe a factorial-computing procedure using call by name. It is easy to infer the following specification about the call $fact(X(i), X(j))$, where X is an integer array:

$$\Sigma_{\text{proc}}\ \&\ \mathbf{gv}(X(j))\ \&\ X(j) \# X(i) \Rightarrow$$
$$\{X(i) \geq 0\}\ fact(X(i),\ X(j))\ \{X(j) = X(i)!\}\quad .$$

But to make use of such a specification we need rules to show when we can assume that an array designator is good, e.g. $\mathbf{gv}(X(j))$, or that two array designators referring to the same array do not interfere with one another, e.g. $X(j) \# X(i)$.

The following rule serves the first of these purposes. Here x is a τ array variable (∗) identifier and s is an integer expression identifier:

(R31) Good Array Designators (Axiom)

$$x(s) \# s \Rightarrow \mathbf{gv}(x(s))\quad .$$

This rule can be derived from (R30′) and (R28). To see this, let π be an assertion procedure (τ exp) identifier. By substituting $\lambda(\tau\ \mathbf{array\ exp}\ (\ast)\ x).$ $\pi(x(s))$ for ρ in (R30′) and using right-side noninterference decomposition and beta reduction, we have

$$x(s) \# s\ \&\ x(s) \# \pi \Rightarrow \{\pi([x \mid s: e](s))\}\ x(s) := e\ \{\pi(x(s))\}\quad ,$$

or since $[x \mid s: e](s) = e$,

$$x(s) \# s\ \&\ x(s) \# \pi \Rightarrow \{\pi(e)\}\ x(s) := e\ \{\pi(x(s))\}\quad .$$

Next, we separate assumptions and introduce quantifiers to obtain

$$x(s) \# s \Rightarrow$$
$$(\forall\ \tau\ \mathbf{exp}\ e)\ (\forall\ \mathbf{assertion\ procedure}\ (\tau\ \mathbf{exp})\ \pi)$$
$$(x(s) \# \pi \Rightarrow \{\pi(e)\}\ x(s) := e\ \{\pi(x(s))\})\quad .$$

Then modus ponens can be used to derive rule (R31) from this result and rule (R28) for good variables.

Notice that the assumption $x(s) \# s$ normally precludes $x(s)$ from being an array designator such as $X(X(1))$.

The next two axioms describe noninterference. They show circumstances in which assigning to an array element will not affect another element of the same array, or even a segment of the same array. Here s and t are integer expression identifiers, x is a τ array variable (*) identifier, and ν is an integer set expression identifier:

(R32) Array Element Noninterference (Axiom)

$$\{s \neq t\} \ \& \ x(s) \# t \Rightarrow x(s) \# x(t) \quad .$$

(R33) Array Segment Noninterference (Axiom)

$$\{s \notin \nu\} \ \& \ x(s) \# \nu \Rightarrow x(s) \# x \restriction \nu \quad .$$

These axioms go significantly beyond the previously given rules for noninterference, since they specify noninterference between parts of an entity named by a single identifier. Notice the use of static assertions to insure that noninterference will hold for any state.

Also notice that in defining the phrase type of ν we have introduced **integer set** as a new data type. As described in Section 3.3.3, this is a straightforward extension of specification logic, despite the fact that **integer set** is not one of the data types provided in Algol W. In making inferences from rule (R33), one is free to substitute for ν any expression, such as an interval diagram, which denotes a set of integers.

We have remarked that the last three axioms are needed to deal with the use of array designators as actual parameters. As a simple example, consider the following program, which uses the procedure *fact* to create a table of the factorial function:

$$\{\boxed{0 \quad n} \subseteq \mathbf{dom} \ X\}$$
begin integer k;
$k := -1$;
$\{\mathbf{whileinv}: \boxed{0 \quad k| \quad n} \ \text{and} \ (\forall \ i \in \boxed{0 \quad k}) \ X(i) = i!\}$
while $k < n$ **do**
    begin $k := k + 1; \ fact(k, X(k))$ **end**
end
$\{(\forall \ i \in \boxed{0 \quad n}) \ X(i) = i!\} \quad .$

(As pointed out in Section 2.3.1, this is a ludicrously inefficient way of computing a table of factorials. However, it serves nicely to illustrate the points we are trying to make.)

We assume that *fact* has been declared to be either of the procedures in Section 3.3.9 that use call by name, so that the appropriate procedure assumptions Σ_{proc} are

$$(\forall \ \mathbf{integer} \ \mathbf{exp} \ n) \ (\forall \ \mathbf{integer} \ \mathbf{var} \ f)$$
$$(\mathbf{gv}(f) \ \& \ f \# n \Rightarrow \{n \geq 0\} \ fact(n, f) \ \{f = n!\})$$
$$\& \ (\forall \ \mathbf{exp\text{-}like} \ e) \ fact \# e \quad .$$

Then we may infer by quantifier elimination

$$\Sigma_{\text{proc}} \ \& \ \mathbf{gv}(X(k)) \ \& \ X(k)\#k \Rightarrow \{k \geq 0\} \ fact(k, X(k)) \ \{X(k)=k!\} \quad,$$

and by rule (R31)

$$\Sigma_{\text{proc}} \ \& \ X(k)\#k \Rightarrow \{k \geq 0\} \ fact(k, X(k)) \ \{X(k)=k!\} \quad.$$

Next we develop some relevant noninterference specifications. The rather complicated reasoning used here is typical of programs in which array designators are used as actual parameters. Let z be an integer variable identifier and Y be an integer array expression (∗) identifier. By noninterference decomposition we have

$$fact\#k \ \& \ fact\#Y \ \& \ z\#k \ \& \ z\#Y \Rightarrow$$
$$fact(k, z)\#(\forall \ i \in \boxed{0 \quad}k) \ Y(i)=i! \quad,$$

since the occurrence of k in $fact(k, z)$ is not statement-like. Thus since Σ_{proc} contains $(\forall \ \mathbf{exp\text{-}like} \ e) \ fact\#e$, we have

$$\Sigma_{\text{proc}} \ \& \ z\#k \ \& \ z\#Y \Rightarrow fact(k, z)\#(\forall \ i \in \boxed{0 \quad}k) \ Y(i)=i! \quad.$$

Then by substituting $X(k)$ for z and $X \uparrow \boxed{0 \quad}k$ for Y we get

$$\Sigma_{\text{proc}} \ \& \ X(k)\#k \ \& \ X(k)\#X \uparrow \boxed{0 \quad}k \Rightarrow$$
$$fact(k, X(k))\#(\forall \ i \in \boxed{0 \quad}k) \ (X \uparrow \boxed{0 \quad}k)(i)=i! \quad.$$

To deal with the third assumption, we use rule (R33) to obtain

$$\{k \notin \boxed{0 \quad}k\} \ \& \ X(k)\#\boxed{0 \quad}k \Rightarrow X(k)\#X \uparrow \boxed{0 \quad}k \quad.$$

Here the first assumption is a mathematical fact and the second assumption is implied by $X(k)\#k$. Thus we have

$$\Sigma_{\text{proc}} \ \& \ X(k)\#k \Rightarrow$$
$$fact(k, X(k)) \ \# \ (\forall \ i \in \boxed{0 \quad}k) \ (X \uparrow \boxed{0 \quad}k)(i)=i! \quad.$$

The results of the last two paragraphs may be combined by using the rule of constancy:

$$\Sigma_{\text{proc}} \ \& \ X(k)\#k \Rightarrow$$
$$\{(\forall \ i \in \boxed{0 \quad}k) \ (X \uparrow \boxed{0 \quad}k)(i)=i! \ \textbf{and} \ k \geq 0\}$$
$$fact(k, X(k))$$
$$\{(\forall \ i \in \boxed{0 \quad}k) \ (X \uparrow \boxed{0 \quad}k)(i)=i! \ \textbf{and} \ X(k)=k!\} \quad.$$

Then another application of the rule of constancy gives

$$\Sigma_{\text{proc}} \ \& \ X(k)\#k \ \& \ fact(k, X(k))\#\boxed{0 \quad k \quad n} \Rightarrow$$
$$\{\boxed{0 \quad k \quad n} \ \textbf{and} \ (\forall \ i \in \boxed{0 \quad}k) \ (X \uparrow \boxed{0 \quad}k)(i)=i! \ \textbf{and}$$
$$k \geq 0 \}$$
$$fact(k, X(k))$$
$$\{\boxed{0 \quad k \quad n} \ \textbf{and} \ (\forall \ i \in \boxed{0 \quad}k) \ (X \uparrow \boxed{0 \quad}k)(i)=i! \ \textbf{and}$$
$$X(k)=k! \} \quad.$$

In conjunction with

$$\Sigma_{\text{proc}} \Rightarrow fact\#k \ \& \ fact\#n$$

and the noninterference decompositions

$$fact\#k \ \& \ fact\#n \ \& \ X\#k \ \& \ X\#n \Rightarrow fact(k, X(k))\#\boxed{0 \ \ k \ \ n}$$

and

$$X\#k \Rightarrow X(k)\#k \quad ,$$

the result of the previous paragraph gives the main step in the following tableau:

$$
\left.
\begin{array}{l}
\mathbf{gv}(k) \\
\& \ k\#n \ \& \ k\#X \\
\& \ \Sigma_{\text{proc}} \\
\& \ X\#k \ \& \ X\#n
\end{array}
\right\}
\Rightarrow
\left\{
\begin{array}{l}
\{\boxed{0 \ k \ \ n} \text{ and } (\forall \ i \in \boxed{0 \ \ k}) \ X(i)=i! \text{ and } k<n\} \\
\{\boxed{0 \ \ k{+}1 \ \ n} \text{ and } (\forall \ i \in \boxed{0 \ \ k}{+}1) \ X(i)=i!\} \\
k := k+1; \\
\{\boxed{0 \ k \ \ n} \text{ and } (\forall \ i \in \boxed{0 \ \ k}) \ X(i)=i!\} \\
\{\boxed{0 \ k \ \ n} \text{ and} \\
\quad (\forall \ i \in \boxed{0 \ \ k})(X \uparrow \boxed{0 \ \ k})(i)=i! \text{ and } k\geq 0\} \\
fact(k, X(k)) \\
\{\boxed{0 \ k \ \ n} \text{ and} \\
\quad (\forall \ i \in \boxed{0 \ \ k})(X \uparrow \boxed{0 \ \ k})(i)=i! \text{ and } X(k)=k!\} \\
\{\boxed{0 \ k \ \ n} \text{ and } (\forall \ i \in \boxed{0 \ \ k}) \ X(i)=i!\} \quad .
\end{array}
\right.
$$

Then the application of the **while**-statement rule to the result of this tableau gives the main step in

$$
\left.
\begin{array}{l}
\mathbf{gv}(k) \\
\& \ k\#n \ \& \ k\#X \\
\& \ \Sigma_{\text{proc}} \\
\& \ X\#k \ \& \ X\#n
\end{array}
\right\}
\Rightarrow
\left\{
\begin{array}{l}
\{\mathbf{true}\} \\
\{\boxed{0 \ {-}1 \ \ n} \text{ and } (\forall \ i \in \boxed{0 \ \ {-}1}) \ X(i)=i!\} \\
k := -1; \\
\{\boxed{0 \ k \ \ n} \text{ and } (\forall \ i \in \boxed{0 \ \ k}) \ X(i)=i!\} \\
\mathbf{while} \ k<n \ \mathbf{do} \\
\quad \mathbf{begin} \ k := k+1; \ fact(k, X(k)) \ \mathbf{end} \\
\{\boxed{0 \ k \ \ n} \text{ and } (\forall \ i \in \boxed{0 \ \ k}) \ X(i)=i! \text{ and} \\
\quad \neg \ k<n\} \\
\{(\forall \ i \in \boxed{0 \ \ n}) \ X(i)=i!\} \quad ,
\end{array}
\right.
$$

and the application of the rule for simple variable declarations gives

$$\Sigma_{\text{proc}} \ \& \ X \# n \Rightarrow$$
$$\{\textbf{true}\}$$
$$\textbf{begin integer } k;$$
$$k := -1;$$
$$\textbf{while } k < n \textbf{ do}$$
$$\quad \textbf{begin } k := k+1; \ fact(k, \ X(k)) \textbf{ end}$$
$$\textbf{end}$$
$$\{(\forall \ i \in \boxed{0 \quad n}) \ X(i) = i!\} \quad .$$

This matches the informal description of the program except for the absence of the initial assumption $\boxed{0 \quad n} \subseteq \textbf{dom } X$, which is only needed to insure against subscript errors.

To complete the treatment of arrays we must deal with their declarations. The following rule is a straightforward generalization of rule (R25) for simple variable declarations; the only novelty is the treatment of array bounds:

(R34) Array Declarations

> If X is a τ array variable(*) identifier, B is a statement, P and Q are assertions, L and U are integer expressions, $E_1, \ldots, E_m$ are expression-like phrases, $S_1, \ldots, S_n$ are statement-like phrases, and X does not occur free in $\Sigma, P, Q, L, U, E_1, \ldots, E_m, S_1, \ldots, S_n$, then

$$\dfrac{\Sigma \ \& \ X \# E_1 \ \& \ \ldots \ \& \ X \# E_m \ \& \ S_1 \# X \ \& \ \ldots \ \& \ S_n \# X}{\Rightarrow \{P \textbf{ and dom } X = \boxed{L \quad U}\} \ B \ \{Q\}}$$
$$\overline{\Sigma \Rightarrow \{P\} \textbf{ begin } \tau \textbf{ array } X \ (L::U); \ B \textbf{ end } \{Q\}} \quad .$$

Finally, the following axiom expresses the fact that, once an array has been declared, its domain cannot be changed by executing any statement. If s is an identifier of any statement-like type and x is a τ array variable (*) identifier, then

(R35) Domain Constancy (Axiom)

$$s \# \textbf{dom } x \quad .$$

Exercises

1. Derive rule (R30) from (R30′).

2. Let Σ_{proc} be the procedure assumption obtained in Exercise 2 after Section 3.3.9. Infer the following universal specification:

$$\Sigma_{\text{proc}} \ \& \ \textbf{gv}(i) \ \& \ i \ \# x_0 \ \& \ i \ \# y_0 \ \& \ X \# i \ \& \ X \# x_0 \ \& \ X \# y_0 \Rightarrow$$
$$\{i = x_0 \textbf{ and } X(i) = y_0\} \ swap(i, \ X(i)) \ \{X(i) = x_0 \textbf{ and } i = y_0\} \quad .$$

What goes wrong when one tries to infer a similar specification about $swap(X(i), \ i)$?

*3.3.14 Inference for Function Procedures

To complete our discussion of specification logic, we consider function procedures. At the abstract level, the appropriate axiom is identical to axiom (R29) for nonrecursive proper procedures, except for a change of types. Let p and q be assertion identifiers, m be a τ procedure $(\theta_1, \ldots, \theta_n)$ identifier, and σ be a procedure $\big(\tau$ procedure $(\theta_1, \ldots, \theta_n)\big)$ identifier. Then:

(R36)   Function Procedure Declarations (Axiom)

$$\{p\}\, \sigma(m)\, \{q\} \Rightarrow$$
$$\{p\}$$
$$\textbf{begin } \tau \textbf{ procedure } h(\theta_1 f_1; \ldots; \theta_n f_n);\ m(f_1, \ldots, f_n);$$
$$\sigma(h)$$
$$\textbf{end}$$
$$\{q\} \quad .$$

At a more concrete level we need a rule that is similar in nature to (R26) for proper procedures. However, the concrete rule for function procedures is simpler than that for proper procedures. For a proper procedure, the main part of the procedure assumptions embodies some property that must be proved about the procedure body. But for a function procedure the corresponding property is self-evident; it is just that the value of any procedure call will be equal to the value of the procedure body (after appropriate substitutions). Since this property is independent of the state, it can be expressed by a static assertion of equality.

This idea is captured by the following rule:

(R36$'$)   Function Procedure Declarations

    Suppose

        $F_1, \ldots, F_n, H$ are distinct identifiers of phrase
            types $\theta_1, \ldots, \theta_n, \tau \textbf{ procedure}(\theta_1, \ldots, \theta_n)$,
        B_{fproc} is a τ expression,
        B is a statement,
        P, Q are assertions,
        Σ is a finite set of specifications,

    such that H does not occur free in $\Sigma, P, Q,$ or B_{fproc}.
    Let Σ_{fproc} be

        $(\forall\ \theta_1 F_1) \ldots (\forall\ \theta_n F_n)\, \{H(F_1, \ldots, F_n) = B_{\text{fproc}}\}$
            & $(\forall\ \textbf{sta-like } S)\, (S \# I_1\ \&\ \ldots\ \&\ S \# I_m \Rightarrow S \# H)$,

    where $\{I_1, \ldots, I_m\} = \mathscr{F}_{\textbf{exp-like}}(B_{\text{fproc}}) - \{F_1, \ldots, F_n\}$ and S is some
    identifier that is distinct from $I_1, \ldots, I_m$ and H. Then

$$\frac{\Sigma\ \&\ \Sigma_{\text{fproc}} \Rightarrow \{P\}\, B\, \{Q\}}{\Sigma \Rightarrow \{P\}\ \textbf{begin } \tau \textbf{ procedure } H(\theta_1 F_1; \ldots; \theta_n F_n);\ B_{\text{fproc}};\ B\ \textbf{end}\ \{Q\}} \quad .$$

Notice that neither rule (R36) nor (R36′) permits recursion. For the reasons discussed in Section 3.2.5, recursive function procedures cannot be treated by specification logic.

Exercise

1. Derive rule (R36′) from (R36). The following is an outline of the derivation:

   (a) Assume that the premiss of (R36′) is universal. Use beta reduction backwards to replace B by $\left(\lambda(\tau\ \textbf{procedure}(\theta_1, \ldots, \theta_n)\ H).\ B\right)(H)$. Then substitute $\lambda(\theta_1 F_1;\ \ldots;\ \theta_n F_n).\ B_{\text{fproc}}$ for H.

   (b) In the result of (a), use rule (R9) for introducing mathematical facts to eliminate the assumption containing a static assertion, and use rule (R22) for right-side noninterference decomposition to eliminate the assumption about noninterference.

   (c) In axiom (R36), use alpha conversion to replace $f_1, \ldots, f_n$ and h by $F_1, \ldots, F_n$, and H, and then substitute

   $$p \to P$$
   $$q \to Q$$
   $$m \to \lambda(\theta_1 F_1;\ \ldots;\ \theta_n F_n).\ B_{\text{fproc}}$$
   $$\sigma \to \lambda(\tau\ \textbf{procedure}(\theta_1, \ldots, \theta_n)\ H).\ B \quad .$$

   After appropriate beta reduction, use modus ponens to combine this result with the result of (b) to infer the conclusion of (R36′).

4 ADDITIONAL CONTROL MECHANISMS

In this chapter, we will consider additional language facilities for describing control structures. On the one hand, we will introduce an iterative statement, called the **for** statement, that is more specialized than the **while** statement. On the other hand, we will consider labels and **goto** statements, which can be used to describe a wider variety of control structures than the language used in previous chapters.

4.1 for STATEMENTS

4.1.1 for Statements in Algol W

In the programs we have seen so far, some (but not all) of the **while** statements have served a particularly simple purpose: to cause some statement within their bodies to be repeatedly executed while some integer variable takes on successive values in a predetermined interval. This is such a common situation in programming that Algol W (like most higher-level programming languages) provides a special kind of iterative statement for describing it.

Let K be an identifier, L and U be integer expressions, and S be a statement. Then the **for** statement

$$\textbf{for } K := L \textbf{ until } U \textbf{ do } S$$

causes the following actions: First L and U are evaluated, and then the integers in the interval $\boxed{L \quad U}$ are sequenced through in ascending order. For each such integer, the integer is made the value of K, and the statement S is executed.

For example, the program in Section 2.2.4 for summing an array segment can be rewritten as follows using a **for** statement:

$$\{\boxed{a \quad b} \subseteq \textbf{dom } X\}$$
$$\textbf{begin } s := 0;$$
$$\textbf{for } k := a \textbf{ until } b \textbf{ do } s := s + X(k)$$
$$\textbf{end}$$
$$\{s = \Sigma_{i \in \boxed{a \quad b}} X(i)\} \quad .$$

Although nearly every higher-order programming language provides an iterative construct that is roughly similar to the **for** statement, the precise meaning of these constructs varies significantly from one language to another. (As an extreme example, the DO statement in FORTRAN always executes its body at least once.) Fortunately, the **for** statement in Algol W is unusually clean and elegant.

The simplest way to specify the precise meaning of the Algol W **for** statement is to define it to be an abbreviation for some statement built out of previously understood language constructs. However, since a correct definition of this kind is surprisingly subtle, we will approach it through several stages of plausible though inaccurate definitions. This approach will also suggest why the analogous constructs in other languages exhibit such diversity.

At first sight, one might expect that **for** $K := L$ **until** U **do** S should have the same meaning as

$$\textbf{begin } K := L - 1;$$
$$\textbf{while } K < U \textbf{ do}$$
$$\quad \textbf{begin } K := K + 1; \ S \textbf{ end} \tag{1}$$
$$\textbf{end} \quad .$$

However, this definition is inaccurate in several respects. In the first place, it does not have the correct binding structure. In the **for** statement, the initial occurrence of K is a binder whose scope is the entire **for** statement, excluding L and U. Thus if K is declared in some block enclosing the **for** statement, then the variable defined by this declaration will be unaffected by execution of the **for** statement.

This binding structure is captured by the following definition: If K does not occur free in L or U, then **for** $K := L$ **until** U **do** S has the same meaning as

$$\textbf{begin integer } K; \; K := L - 1;$$
$$\textbf{while } K < U \textbf{ do}$$
$$\qquad \textbf{begin } K := K + 1; \; S \textbf{ end} \qquad\qquad (2)$$
$$\textbf{end} \quad .$$

(If K does occur free in L or U, one must alpha-convert the **for** statement before applying this definition.)

In the second place, Algol W syntactically prohibits S from performing any action that could affect the value of K. This insures that successive executions of S will be performed for successive integers. To express this prohibition we add to our definition the requirement that all free occurrences of K in S must have the phrase type **integer expression** (as opposed to **integer variable**).

It is slightly surprising that Algol W enforces this requirement for **for** statements, even though it does not make a syntactic distinction between expressions and variables as procedure parameters. (In [Sites 72] the occurrences of K in S are described by the nonterminal symbol ⟨control identifier⟩, which is equivalent to our ⟨integer expression identifier⟩.)

Finally, Algol W evaluates the upper bound U once before any execution of S, but not repeatedly after each execution of S. Not only does this improve the efficiency of the **for** statement, but it insures that S cannot alter the interval being iterated over by interfering with U.

To capture this characteristic, we introduce a local variable U' to save the initial value of U. For the sake of symmetry, we also introduce L' to save the initial value of L. Thus we define **for** $K := L$ **until** U **do** S to have the same meaning as

$$\textbf{begin integer } L', U'; \; L' := L; \; U' := U;$$
$$\qquad \textbf{begin integer } K; \; K := L' - 1;$$
$$\qquad \textbf{while } K < U' \textbf{ do}$$
$$\qquad\qquad \textbf{begin } K := K + 1; \; S \textbf{ end} \qquad\qquad (3)$$
$$\qquad \textbf{end}$$
$$\textbf{end} \quad ,$$

where L' and U' are distinct identifiers that do not occur in the original **for** statement.

Except for overflow considerations, (3) is a precise definition of the Algol W **for** statement. It implies that (in contrast to many programming languages) there is a firm guarantee on the number of times a **for** statement will execute its body. Let N be the size of $\boxed{L \quad U}$ before the execution of **for** $K := L$ **until** U **do** S. Then S will be executed at most N times, and if S terminates without an error stop or a **goto** to an external label, then it will be executed exactly N times. As a consequence, a **for** statement will always terminate if its body always terminates. This is the most important distinction between the **for** statement and the more general iterative mechanism provided by the **while** statement.

The **for** statement is closely related to the procedure *iterate* which was defined in Section 3.1.7 and used as an example in Section 3.3.11. In fact, **for** $K := L$ **until** U **do** S is equivalent to the statement

$$iterate\big(L,\ U,\ \lambda(\textbf{integer } \{\textbf{exp}\}\ K).\ S\big)\quad,$$

where *iterate* is defined by

> **procedure** *iterate*(**integer value** a, b; **procedure** p $\{$**integer exp**$\}$);
>   **begin integer** k; $k := a-1$;
>   **while** $k<b$ **do**
>   **begin** $k := k+1$; $p(k)$ **end**
>   **end**   .

By using the call-by-value transformation of Section 3.1.5, the copy rule, and beta reduction, it can be seen that this definition is equivalent to (3). Moreover, if the parameters a and b of *iterate* are called by name, rather than by value, then this definition becomes equivalent to (2). For this reason, we will say that (2) and (3) define the call-by-name and call-by-value *variants* of the **for** statement, respectively.

4.1.2 Inference for **for** Statements

As with the **while** statement, the key to reasoning about the **for** statement **for** $K := L$ **until** U **do** S is an invariant that holds both initially and after each execution of the body S. The most obvious approach is to take this invariant to be a function of K that holds for $K = L-1$ before execution, and for the succession of integers in $\boxed{L\ \ U}$ after each iteration. But this approach leads to a complication: One must pursue separate lines of reasoning for the two cases where the interval $\boxed{L\ \ U}$ is regular and irregular.

A more elegant approach, given in [Hoare 72b], is to regard the invariant as a function of the interval $\boxed{L\ \ K}$ of integers that have been "processed so far". We will follow Hoare's approach since it unifies the regular and irregular cases, and meshes nicely with the use of interval and partition diagrams.

As an example, the invariant of the array summation program given in the previous section is $s = \sum_{i \in \boxed{a\ \ k}} X(i)$, which asserts that s is the sum of the elements of X over the processed interval. The **for**-statement body $s := s + X(k)$ maintains this invariant in the following sense: If the invariant holds for $\boxed{a \quad}k$ (and if $k \in \boxed{a \quad b}$) before execution, then the invariant holds for $\boxed{a \quad k}$ after execution, i.e.

$$\{s = \sum_{i \in \boxed{a \,}k} X(i) \text{ and } \boxed{a \quad k \quad b}\}$$
$$s := s + X(k) \,\{s = \sum_{i \in \boxed{a \; k}} X(i)\} \quad .$$

As a consequence, if the invariant holds for the empty interval before execution of the entire **for** statement, then it will hold for $\boxed{a}$, $\boxed{a \quad a+1}$, $\boxed{a \quad a+2}$, ... after successive executions of the body, and for the complete interval $\boxed{a \quad b}$ after the entire **for** statement has finished. Thus we may infer

$$\{s = \sum_{i \in \{\}} X(i)\} \text{ for } k := a \text{ until } b \text{ do } s := s + X(k)$$
$$\{s = \sum_{i \in \boxed{a \; b}} X(i)\} \quad .$$

In specification logic, the general case of this reasoning is given by the following rule of inference:

(R37) **for** Statements

Suppose

K and N are distinct identifiers of phrase types
     integer expression and **integer set expression,**
L and U are integer expressions,
S is a statement,
I is an assertion,
Σ is a finite set of specifications,

such that K does not occur free in L, U, I, or Σ.
Let $\{S_1, \ldots, S_m\} = \mathscr{F}_{\text{sta-like}}(S)$ and $S_{m+1}, \ldots, S_n$ be any other identifiers distinct from K. Then

$$\Sigma \ \& \ S_1 \ \# \ K \ \& \ \ldots \ \& \ S_n \ \# \ K \Rightarrow$$
$$\{I|_{N \to \boxed{L \quad}K}} \text{ and } \boxed{L \quad K \quad U}\} \, S \, \{I|_{N \to \boxed{L \; K}}\}$$

$$\overline{\Sigma \ \& \ S_1 \ \# \ L \ \& \ \ldots \ \& \ S_m \ \# \ L \ \& \ S_1 \ \# \ U \ \& \ \ldots \ \& \ S_m \ \# \ U \Rightarrow}$$
$$\{I|_{N \to \{\}}\} \text{ for } K := L \text{ until } U \text{ do } S \, \{I|_{N \to \boxed{L \; U}}\} \quad .$$

Notice that in defining the type of N we are using **integer set** as a data type. The identifier N, which serves to indicate the dependence of I upon the interval of processed integers, never actually occurs in the premiss or conclusion of the inference rule, since it is always replaced by either $\{\}$ or some interval diagram. (In most applications, n will be equal to m.)

As an example of the formal use of this rule, let

K be k U be b

N be v S be $s := s + X(k)$

S_1 be s I be $s = \sum_{i \in v} X(i)$

L be a Σ be $\mathbf{gv}(s)$ & $s \# a$ & $s \# X$.

Then the premiss of rule (R37) matches the result of the tableau

$$\left. \begin{array}{l} \mathbf{gv}(s) \ \& \ s \# a \\ \& \ s \# X \ \& \ s \# k \end{array} \right\} \Rightarrow \left\{ \begin{array}{l} \{s = \sum_{i \in \boxed{a \quad}_k} X(i) \ \textbf{and} \ \boxed{a \ | \ k | \ b}\} \\ \{s + X(k) = \sum_{i \in \boxed{a \ k}} X(i)\} \\ s := s + X(k) \\ \{s = \sum_{i \in \boxed{a \ k}} X(i)\} \quad , \end{array} \right.$$

so that we may infer the conclusion

$$\mathbf{gv}(s) \ \& \ s \# a \ \& \ s \# X \ \& \ s \# b \Rightarrow$$
$$\{s = \sum_{i \in \{\}} X(i)\}$$
$$\textbf{for } k := a \textbf{ until } b \textbf{ do } s := s + X(k)$$
$$\{s = \sum_{i \in \boxed{a \ b}} X(i)\} \quad .$$

The remainder of a correctness proof for the summation program is obvious.

Less formally, a clearly annotated program should include the invariants of nontrivial **for** statements. For this purpose, we will adopt the convention of writing the invariant of a **for** statement in the form $I|_{N \to \boxed{L \ K}}$, labeling it with the symbol **forinv**, and placing it immediately before the **for** statement. For example, the array summation program would be annotated:

$$\{\boxed{a \ b} \subseteq \textbf{dom } X\}$$
$$\textbf{begin } s := 0;$$
$$\{\textbf{forinv: } s = \sum_{i \in \boxed{a \ k}} X(i)\}$$
$$\textbf{for } k := a \textbf{ until } b \textbf{ do } s := s + X(k)$$
$$\textbf{end}$$
$$\{s = \sum_{i \in \boxed{a \ b}} X(i)\} \quad .$$

Notice that, in contrast with the **while** case, the invariant of a **for** statement does not contain range information such as $a \leq k \leq b$. Essentially, this information is built into the structure of the **for** statement itself.

Also notice that, since K must not occur free in I, it can only occur free in $I|_{N \to \boxed{L \ K}}$ in the context of the interval expression $\boxed{L \ K}$. This restriction insures that the invariant is actually a function of the interval of processed integers rather than of K itself. Although it is occasionally nontrivial to express the invariant in this way, the advantage of doing so is that the inferred specification of the **for** statement will include the case where $\boxed{L \ U}$ is irregular. For example, an appropriate invariant of the following factorial-computing program is that f is the product $\prod_{i \in \boxed{1 \ k}} i$ of the members of the processed interval (which is 1 when the processed interval is empty):

$\{\textbf{true}\}$
$\textbf{begin } f := 1;$
$\{\textbf{forinv: } f = \Pi_{i \in \boxed{1\ k}}\ i\}$
$\textbf{for } k := 1 \textbf{ until } n \textbf{ do } f := k \times f$
$\textbf{end}$
$\{f = \Pi_{i \in \boxed{1\ n}}\ i = \textbf{if } n \geq 0 \textbf{ then } n! \textbf{ else } 1\}$.

Similarly, the invariant of a (slow) exponentiation program can be expressed in terms of the size of the processed interval:

$\{\textbf{true}\}$
$\textbf{begin } y := 1;$
$\{\textbf{forinv: } y = x^{\#\ \boxed{1\ k}}\}$
$\textbf{for } k := 1 \textbf{ until } n \textbf{ do } y := x \times y$
$\textbf{end}$
$\{y = x^{\#\ \boxed{1\ n}} = \textbf{if } n \geq 0 \textbf{ then } x^n \textbf{ else } 1\}$.

Note that for both examples, in contrast with the program specifications given for similar programs in Chapter 1, the case $n < 0$ is included without any extra analysis.

A more complicated example is a **for**-statement version of the program for finding the subscript of a maximum element of an array, which was developed in Section 2.2.7 and encapsulated as a procedure in Section 3.1.6. In this case, one might expect the invariant of

$$\textbf{for } k := a+1 \textbf{ until } b \textbf{ do if } X(k) > X(j) \textbf{ then } j := k$$

to be

$$j \in \boxed{a\ k} \text{ and } \{X \uparrow \boxed{a\ k}\} \leq^* X(j) .$$

But this invariant must not depend upon k except through the interval of processed elements, which is $\boxed{a+1\ k} = a\boxed{\ k}$. Thus we must replace $\boxed{a\ k}$ by $\boxed{a} \cup a\boxed{\ k}$, which gives

$$\textbf{procedure } max(\textbf{integer value } a, b; \textbf{ integer result } j;$$
$$\qquad \textbf{integer array } \{\textbf{exp}\}\ X(*));$$
$$\{\boxed{a} \cup a\boxed{\ b} \subseteq \textbf{dom } X\}$$
$$\textbf{begin}$$
$$j := a;$$
$$\{\textbf{forinv: } j \in \boxed{a} \cup a\boxed{\ k} \text{ and } \{X \uparrow \boxed{a} \cup a\boxed{\ k}\} \leq^* X(j)\}$$
$$\textbf{for } k := a+1 \textbf{ until } b \textbf{ do if } X(k) > X(j) \textbf{ then } j := k$$
$$\textbf{end}$$
$$\{j \in \boxed{a} \cup a\boxed{\ b} \text{ and } \{X \uparrow \boxed{a} \cup a\boxed{\ b}\} \leq^* X(j)\} .$$

In this case the reasoning seems rather unnatural, but it correctly reflects the "unnatural" behavior of the procedure when $a > b$.

Exercise

1. Review the examples and exercises of previous chapters to determine which instances of iteration can be clarified by use of the **for** statement. In these instances, formulate an appropriate invariant. In one or two cases, give a formal proof using specification logic.

*4.1.3 **A Stronger Rule of Inference**

Consider the statement

> **for** $k := 1$ **until** n **do** $n := n+k$.

Unlike the examples given previously, the body of this **for** statement changes its upper bound. Thus its behavior distinguishes between the call-by-value and call-by-name variants of the **for** statement defined in Section 4.1.1. With the call-by-value variant, the upper bound of the iteration is fixed by the initial value of n, so that the **for** statement increases n by the sum of the numbers between one and its initial value. With the call-by-name variant, if the initial value of n is greater than zero, then the upper bound keeps increasing and never drops below the current value of k, so that the statement never terminates.

With the call-by-value variant, which is actually used in Algol W, the specification

$$\mathbf{gv}(n) \ \& \ n \ \# \ n_0 \Rightarrow$$
$$\{n=n_0\}$$
$$\textbf{for } k := 1 \textbf{ until } n \textbf{ do } n := n+k$$
$$\{n=n_0 + \textstyle\sum_{i \in \boxed{1 \ \ n_0}} i\}$$

is universal. However, this specification cannot be proved by using inference rule (R37) given in the previous section. The difficulty is that, if we take U to be n and S to be $n := n+k$, then the unsatisfiable assumption $n \# n$ appears in the conclusion of the rule.

In fact, (R37) is a valid rule of inference for both the call-by-name and call-by-value variants of the **for** statement, and therefore it cannot be used to reason about programs whose behavior is different in these two cases. However, it is possible to give a stronger rule that is specific to the call-by-value variant:

(R38) Strong **for** Statement Rule

Suppose

K and N are distinct identifiers of phrase types
integer expression and **integer set expression**,
L, U, L_0, and U_0 are integer expressions,
S is a statement,
I is an assertion,
Σ is a finite set of specifications,

such that K does not occur free in L_0, U_0, I, or Σ.
Let $\{S_1, \ldots, S_m\} = \mathcal{F}_{\text{sta-like}}(S)$ and $S_{m+1}, \ldots, S_n$ be any other
identifiers distinct from K. Then

$$\Sigma \ \& \ S_1 \ \# \ K \ \& \ \ldots \ \& \ S_n \ \# \ K \Rightarrow$$
$$\{I|_{N \to \boxed{L_0}K} \text{ and } \boxed{L_0 \mid K \mid U_0}\} \ S \ \{I|_{N \to \boxed{L_0 \ K}}\}$$

$$\Sigma \ \& \ S_1 \ \# \ L_0 \ \& \ \ldots \ \& \ S_m \ \# \ L_0 \ \& \ S_1 \ \# \ U_0 \ \& \ \ldots \ \& \ S_m \ \# \ U_0 \Rightarrow$$
$$\{I|_{N \to \{\}} \text{ and } L = L_0 \text{ and } U = U_0\}$$
$$\textbf{for } K := L \textbf{ until } U \textbf{ do } S \ \{I|_{N \to \boxed{L_0 \ U_0}}\} \quad .$$

By taking L_0 to be the same as L and U_0 to be the same as U, and
strengthening the precedent of the conclusion to eliminate $L = L$ and $U = U$,
it is easy to derive rule (R37) from rule (R38). However, although (R38) is
stronger than (R37), it is also more complicated, so that it is usually simpler
to use (R37) in the cases where it suffices, i.e. where S does not interfere with
L or U. (Indeed, the greater complexity of (R38) directly mirrors the fact
that **for** statements that alter their bounds are unnecessarily difficult to
understand.)

Exercise

1. Use rule (R38) to prove the universal specification given in the beginning of the
   above section.

*4.1.4 Deriving the Inference Rules

Since the **for** statement can be defined in terms of previously introduced
features of Algol W, we can "check" its inference rules by deriving them
from the definition. In this section we will show that (R37) holds for the
call-by-name variant of the **for** statement. An analogous but somewhat more
complicated demonstration that (R38) holds for the call-by-value variant is
left to the reader (as Exercise 2 below).

Suppose that the premiss of rule (R37),

$$\Sigma \ \& \ S_1 \ \# \ K \ \& \ \ldots \ \& \ S_n \ \# \ K \Rightarrow$$
$$\{I|_{N \to \boxed{L}K} \text{ and } \boxed{L \mid K \mid U}\} \ S \ \{I|_{N \to \boxed{L \ K}}\} \quad ,$$

is a universal specification in which the metavariables stand for phrases that satisfy the restrictions in the rule. By noninterference decomposition, we have

$$S_1 \# L \ \& \ \dots \ \& \ S_m \# L \ \& \ S_1 \# K \ \& \ \dots \ \& \ S_m \# K$$
$$\& \ S_1 \# U \ \& \ \dots \ \& \ S_m \# U$$
$$\Rightarrow S \# \boxed{L \ \ \boxed{K} \ \ U} \ .$$

From this specification and the premiss of rule (R37), we may use the rule of constancy (R23) to infer the main step in the following tableau:

$$
\left.
\begin{aligned}
&\mathbf{gv}(K) \ \& \ K \# L \ \& \ K \# U \\
&\& \ K \# E_1 \ \& \ \dots \ \& \ K \# E_l \\
&\& \ \Sigma \\
&\& \ S_1 \# L \ \& \ \dots \ \& \ S_m \# L \\
&\& \ S_1 \# K \ \& \ \dots \ \& \ S_n \# K \\
&\& \ S_1 \# U \ \& \ \dots \ \& \ S_m \# U
\end{aligned}
\right\}
\Rightarrow
\left\{
\begin{aligned}
&\{I|_{N \to \boxed{L \ \ K}} \text{ and } \boxed{L \ \boxed{K} \ U} \text{ and } K < U\} \\
&\{I|_{N \to \boxed{L}\,K+1} \text{ and } \boxed{L \ \boxed{K+1} \ U}\} \\
&K := K+1; \\
&\{I|_{N \to \boxed{L}\,K} \text{ and } \boxed{L \ \boxed{K} \ U}\} \\
&S \\
&\{I|_{N \to \boxed{L \ \ K}} \text{ and } \boxed{L \ \boxed{K} \ U}\} \\
&\{I|_{N \to \boxed{L \ \ K}} \text{ and } \boxed{L \ K \ U}\} \ ,
\end{aligned}
\right.
$$

where $\{E_1, \dots, E_l\} = \mathscr{F}_{\mathbf{exp\text{-}like}}(I) - \{N\}$.

Next, the **while** statement rule gives the main step in

$$
\left.
\begin{aligned}
&\mathbf{gv}(K) \ \& \ K \# L \ \& \ K \# U \\
&\& \ K \# E_1 \ \& \ \dots \ \& \ K \# E_l \\
&\& \ \Sigma \\
&\& \ S_1 \# L \ \& \ \dots \ \& \ S_m \# L \\
&\& \ S_1 \# K \ \& \ \dots \ \& \ S_n \# K \\
&\& \ S_1 \# U \ \& \ \dots \ \& \ S_m \# U
\end{aligned}
\right\}
\Rightarrow
\left\{
\begin{aligned}
&\{I|_{N \to \{\}}\} \\
&\{I|_{N \to \boxed{L \ \ L-1}} \text{ and } \boxed{L \ \boxed{L-1} \ U}\} \\
&K := L-1; \\
&\{I|_{N \to \boxed{L \ \ K}} \text{ and } \boxed{L \ \boxed{K} \ U}\} \\
&\text{\textbf{while} } K < U \text{ \textbf{do}} \\
&\quad \text{\textbf{begin} } K := K+1; \ S \text{ \textbf{end}} \\
&\{I|_{N \to \boxed{L \ \ K}} \text{ and } \boxed{L \ \boxed{K} \ U} \text{ and } \neg \ K < U\} \\
&\{I|_{N \to \boxed{L \ \ U}}\} \ .
\end{aligned}
\right.
$$

Here K is distinct from $E_1, \dots, E_l, S_1, \dots, S_n$, and does not occur free in Σ, L, U, or the initial or final assertion. Thus we may use the rule for simple variable declarations to infer

$$\Sigma \ \& \ S_1 \# L \ \& \ \dots \ \& \ S_m \# L \ \& \ S_1 \# U \ \& \ \dots \ \& \ S_m \# U \Rightarrow$$
$$\{I|_{N \to \{\}}\}$$
$$\text{\textbf{begin integer} } K; \ K := L-1;$$
$$\text{\textbf{while} } K < U \text{ \textbf{do begin} } K := K+1; \ S \text{ \textbf{end}}$$
$$\text{\textbf{end}}$$
$$\{I|_{N \to \boxed{L \ \ U}}\} \ .$$

The statement in this specification is the definition (2) of the call-by-name variant of the **for** statement given in Section 4.1.1. Thus we may replace this statement by **for** $K := L$ **until** U **do** S, which converts the specification into the conclusion of rule (R37).

Exercises

1. The following statement can be used in place of (2) in Section 4.1.1 as an alternative definition of the call-by-name variant of the **for** statement:

> **begin integer** K; $K := L$;
> **while** $K \le U$ **do**
>   **begin** S; $K := K+1$ **end**
> **end** .

(Except for overflow considerations, the two definitions are equivalent.) Show that this alternative definition can be used in place of (2) to derive rule (R37).

2. Derive rule (R38) for the definition of the call-by-value variant of the **for** statement. Notice that, since (R37) can be derived from (R38), this implies that (R37) describes the call-by-value, as well as the call-by-name variant.

    (*Hint*: The derivation follows the same lines as that given in the preceding section. The invariant of the **while** statement should be $I|_{N \to \boxed{L_0 \ \ K}}$ and $\boxed{L_0 \ \ K \ \ U_0}$ and $L' = L_0$ and $U' = U_0$, where L' and U' are distinct identifiers that do not occur in (the instance of) rule (R38).)

3. At the beginning of Section 4.1.2, we said that the most obvious approach to reasoning about **for** $K := L$ **until** U **do** S was to take the invariant to be a function of K. However, since this approach requires separate lines of reasoning for the two cases where $\boxed{L \ \ U}$ is regular and irregular, we chose instead to regard the invariant as a function of the processed interval.

    Nevertheless, the "most obvious approach" is more natural when only the regular case is relevant, as for example in the maximum-finding program. This approach is embodied in the following rule of inference:

    Suppose
    > K is an identifier of type **integer expression,**
    > L and U are integer expressions,
    > S is a statement,
    > J is an assertion,
    > Σ is a finite set of specifications,

    such that K does not occur free in L, U, or Σ.
    Let $\{S_1, \dots, S_m\} = \mathscr{F}_{\text{sta-like}}(S)$ and $S_{m+1}, \dots, S_n$ be any other identifiers distinct from K. Then

$$\frac{\Sigma \ \& \ S_1 \ \# \ K \ \& \ \dots \ \& \ S_n \ \# \ K \Rightarrow \{J|_{K \to K-1} \text{ and } L \le K \le U\} \ S \ \{J\}}{\begin{array}{c} \Sigma \ \& \ S_1 \ \# \ L \ \& \ \dots \ \& \ S_m \ \# \ L \ \& \ S_1 \ \# \ U \ \& \ \dots \ \& \ S_m \ \# \ U \Rightarrow \\ \{J|_{K \to L-1} \text{ and } L-1 \le U\} \\ \textbf{for} \ K := L \ \textbf{until} \ U \ \textbf{do} \ S \ \{J|_{K \to U}\} \end{array}} \quad .$$

Derive this rule from rule (R37).
(*Hint*: Replace I in rule (R37) by $J|_{K \to L-1+\#N}$.)

*4.1.5 The Descending for Statement

Occasionally it is useful to iterate through an interval in descending rather than ascending order. For this purpose, one can use a **for** statement with the form

$$\textbf{for } K := U \textbf{ step } -1 \textbf{ until } L \textbf{ do } S$$

which is equivalent to

$$\begin{aligned}
&\textbf{begin integer } U',\, L';\ U' := U;\ L' := L;\\
&\quad \textbf{begin integer } K;\ K := U'+1;\\
&\quad \textbf{while } K > L' \textbf{ do}\\
&\qquad \textbf{begin } K := K-1;\ S \textbf{ end}\\
&\quad \textbf{end}\\
&\textbf{end}\quad,
\end{aligned}$$

where L' and U' are distinct identifiers that do not occur in the original **for** statement. As in the ascending case, occurrences of K in S must have the type **integer expression**, so that S cannot change the value of K. (Actually, Algol W provides a more general **for** statement with an arbitrary integer step size, but in this book we will only use the simple cases that correspond to the step sizes $+1$ and -1.)

The following rule of inference describes the descending **for** statement:

(R39) Descending **for** Statements

Suppose

K and N are distinct identifiers of phrase types
integer expression and **integer set expression**,
L and U are integer expressions,
S is a statement,
I is an assertion,
Σ is a finite set of specifications,

such that K does not occur free in L, U, I, or Σ.
Let $\{S_1, \ldots, S_m\} = \mathscr{F}_{\text{sta-like}}(S)$ and $S_{m+1}, \ldots, S_n$ be any other identifiers distinct from K. Then

$$\Sigma\ \&\ S_1 \# K\ \&\ \ldots\ \&\ S_n \# K \Rightarrow$$
$$\{I|_{N \to K\boxed{\ \ U}}\ \text{and}\ \boxed{L\ \ \boxed{K}\ \ U}\}\ S\ \{I|_{N \to \boxed{K\ \ U}}\}$$

$$\overline{}$$

$$\Sigma\ \&\ S_1 \# L\ \&\ \ldots\ \&\ S_m \# L\ \&\ S_1 \# U\ \&\ \ldots\ \&\ S_m \# U \Rightarrow$$
$$\{I|_{N \to \{\}}\}\ \textbf{for } K := U\, \textbf{step } -1\, \textbf{until } L\, \textbf{do } S\ \{I|_{N \to \boxed{L\ \ U}}\}\quad.$$

An example of the use of the descending **for** statement is provided by the following version of the program for sorting by maximum finding, which was originally developed in Section 2.3.3 and encapsulated as a procedure in Section 3.1.6:

procedure *maxsort*(**integer value** a, b; **integer array** {**var**} $X(*)$);
    $\{\boxed{a \;\; b} \subseteq \textbf{dom } X \textbf{ and } X = X_0\}$
    $\{\textbf{forinv: } \text{ord}_\le \; X \uparrow \boxed{m \;\; b} \textbf{ and } X \uparrow \boxed{a \;\; b} \sim X_0 \uparrow \boxed{a \;\; b}$
       $\textbf{and } \{X \uparrow \boxed{a \;\; b} - \boxed{m \;\; b}\} \le^* \{X \uparrow \boxed{m \;\; b}\}\,\}$
    for $m := b$ **step** -1 **until** a **do**
       begin integer j;
       $max(a, m, j, X)$;
       begin integer t; $t := X(j)$; $X(j) := X(m)$; $X(m) := t$ **end**
    end
    $\{\text{ord}_\le \; X \uparrow \boxed{a \;\; b} \textbf{ and } X \uparrow \boxed{a \;\; b} \sim X_0 \uparrow \boxed{a \;\; b}\}$.

Notice the convention of writing the invariant in the form $I\big|_{N \to \boxed{K \;\; U}}$.

The developments of the preceding sections can be recapitulated for the descending case: call-by-name and call-by-value variants of the descending **for** statement can be defined, rule (R39) can be derived from the call-by-name definition, and a stronger rule can be derived from the call-by-value definition. The details are left to the reader.

4.1.6   A Caution

When it is necessary to iterate an action over a predetermined interval, the **for** statement provides a notation that is clearer and more concise than the **while** statement. However, a significant number of the iterations in well-written programs do not fit this pattern. The danger of the **for** statement is that it can narrow the programmer's viewpoint to a particular kind of iteration that, though often useful, is also often inappropriate.

It is all too easy to approach a programming task with the unspoken assumption that the main loop will be a **for** statement. In many cases—*partition* in Section 2.3.5 is a good example—this assumption seems perfectly reasonable, yet it precludes any simple or efficient solution. In all but the most cut-and-dried situations, the programmer must constantly remind himself that there is more to iteration than the **for** statement.

For this reason, some authors, notably [Dijkstra 71, 72, 76], avoid the **for** statement completely. We are unwilling to go so far, but have postponed its introduction until after the reader has been exposed to a substantial number of programs that cannot be fit into the mold of the **for** statement.

4.2   goto STATEMENTS AND LABELS

In contrast with the **for** statement, **goto** statements and labels can be used to construct a wider variety of control structures than the language described in previous chapters. Although their use has been the subject of considerable controversy [Dijkstra 68]—precisely because of their generality—we believe there are programming situations where their judicious employment can be beneficial. Certainly their use is compatible with the basic nature of structured programming.

4.2.1   goto's and Labels in Algol W

As discussed in Section 1.5, a block has the form

$$\textbf{begin } D_1; \ldots ; D_m; S_1; S_2; \ldots ; S_n \textbf{ end}$$
$$\uparrow \quad \uparrow \qquad\quad \uparrow$$

where $D_1; \ldots ; D_m$ is a sequence of zero or more declarations and $S_1; \ldots ; S_n$ is a sequence of one or more statements. In front of each statement in this sequence, i.e. at the positions indicated by the arrows, one can place any number of *label definitions* of the form

$$L:$$

where L is an identifier which is said to *label* the following statement. Strictly speaking, one cannot place a label definition between S_n and **end**, but the same effect (and appearance) can be achieved by making S_n a labeled empty statement.

A label definition $L:$ is a binder of L whose scope is the immediately enclosing block. Within this scope the **goto** statement

$$\textbf{goto } L$$

can be used to interrupt the normal control sequence and cause the computation to "jump" to the statement following the label definition that binds the occurrence of L in **goto** L.

For example, the array summation programs given in Sections 2.2.4 and 4.1.1 could be rewritten as

```
      begin integer k;
      k := a − 1; s := 0;
loop: if k ≥ b then goto done;
      k := k + 1; s := s + X(k);
      goto loop;
done: end   .
```

(Note that *done* labels an empty statement.) However this program, which is harder to understand than either previous version, is an obvious misuse of the **goto**. It is typical of the kind of poor programming style that has been fostered by obsolete languages with inadequate control mechanisms.

On the other hand, the following program for linear search is rather clearer than that given in Section 2.2.9:

```
        begin
        for k := a until b do
            if X(k) = y then
                begin present := true; j := k; goto out end;
            present := false;
   out:   end    .
```

Here the use of a **goto** clearly conveys the basic idea of aborting a sequential examination of array elements when the search criterion is met.

In the latter example, the **goto** statement causes a jump out of the scope of a binder of the identifier k. In general, such a jump causes the meaning of the identifier to become inaccessible just as when control leaves a scope in the normal manner. In this particular case, the value of k is saved by assigning it to the variable j before leaving the scope of the binder of k.

The syntax of Algol W prohibits any jump from entering a scope.

4.2.2 Using Assertions with **goto**'s and Labels

In the next section, we will extend specification logic to encompass programs containing **goto** statements and labels. Before doing so, however, it is useful to examine the use of assertions in such programs from a more intuitive viewpoint. In particular, we will consider the use of assertions as formal comments, as originally discussed in Section 1.3.3.

From this viewpoint one thinks of the flow of control as passing through assertions, and the fundamental property of a correctly annotated program is that, once control has passed through some assertion P with a current state of the computation which satisfies P, then at any later time when control passes through an assertion P' the current state of the computation will satisfy P'.

Now consider a **goto** statement with its surrounding assertions:

$$\ldots \{P\} \text{ goto } L \{Q\} \ldots ,$$

and suppose that L is bound by a label definition attached to a statement S with precedent P':

$$L: \{P'\} \ S \ldots \quad .$$

Suppose that control passes through P with a current state of the computation which satisfies P. Then the **goto** statement will send control through P' without changing the state of the computation. Thus, to insure that the state satisfies P', it must be the case that P implies P'.

On the other hand, consider Q. Since it immediately follows a **goto** statement, control will never pass through Q, and Q can be any assertion. In particular, Q can be the strongest possible assertion, **false**, which is not satisfied by any state of the computation, and therefore can only appear at a program point through which control will never pass.

In summary, the precedent of **goto** L must imply the precedent of the statement following the label definition that binds L, and the consequent of **goto** L can be any assertion, even **false**.

For example, the following is a thoroughly annotated version of the linear search program:

$$\{\boxed{a \quad b} \subseteq \textbf{dom } X\}$$

begin

$\{\textbf{forinv}\colon \{X \uparrow \boxed{a \quad k}\} \neq^* y\}$

for $k := a$ **until** b **do**

    if $X(k)=y$ **then**

        begin

        present := **true**; $j := k$;

        $\{\textit{present} \textbf{ and } \boxed{a \quad \boxed{j} \quad b} \textbf{ and } X(j)=y\}$

        goto *out*

        $\{\textbf{false}\}$

        end;

$\{\{X \uparrow \boxed{a \quad b}\} \neq^* y\}$

present := **false**;

$\{\neg \textit{present} \textbf{ and } \{X \uparrow \boxed{a \quad b}\} \neq^* y\}$

  out: $\{\textbf{if } \textit{present} \textbf{ then } \boxed{a \quad \boxed{j} \quad b} \textbf{ and } X(j)=y \textbf{ else } \{X \uparrow \boxed{a \quad b}\} \neq^* y$

end

$\{\textbf{if } \textit{present} \textbf{ then } \boxed{a \quad \boxed{j} \quad b} \textbf{ and } X(j)=y \textbf{ else } \{X \uparrow \boxed{a \quad b}\} \neq^* y$.

Here the assertion preceding **goto** *out* implies the assertion preceding the empty statement labeled by *out*. In addition, the latter assertion is also implied by the assertion following the statement *present* := **false**; this reflects the fact that control can pass to the labeled statement from the preceding statement, as well as from the **goto** statement. The assertion immediately following **goto** *out* is **false**, indicating that control will never pass through this point in the program.

These assertions suggest that, in reasoning about the **for** statement, its body

$$\textbf{if } X(k)=y \textbf{ then begin } \ldots \textbf{ ; goto } out \textbf{ end}$$

can be thought of as a statement that "achieves" $X(k) \neq y$ by jumping to a free label if this condition is false. Then the **for** statement itself can be thought of as a statement which achieves $X(k) \neq y$ for all k in $\boxed{a \quad b}$.

From the use of assertions as comments, we turn to the use of assertions to specify statements. Here the basic question is when the specification $\{P\}$ **goto** $L \{Q\}$ is true. At first sight, since regardless of the state of the computation control will never reach the end of the **goto** statement, one might expect that this specification would be true for any P and Q, even in the extreme case $\{\textbf{true}\}$ **goto** L $\{\textbf{false}\}$. However, as suggested by the preceding discussion, P must insure that the computation will behave correctly after control reaches the statement labeled by L, so that P must imply the precedent of the labeled statement.

The problem is that this is a condition on P that is not a property of **goto** L by itself, but rather of the context in which **goto** L occurs. This kind of context dependency cannot be described by the logic used in Chapters 1 and 2. However, it can be described in specification logic, where the truth of $\{P\}$ **goto** L $\{Q\}$ depends upon an environment that can reflect the context in which **goto** L occurs.

*4.2.3   Inference for goto's and Labels

We now describe the extension of specification logic to encompass **goto** statements and labels. The basic idea behind this extension was first presented in [Clint 72]. To avoid a full-fledged exposition of continuation semantics, which is beyond the scope of this book, our description will be somewhat informal.

Since labels are identifiers, an environment must specify some kind of meaning for labels. We define the meaning of a label to be a set of states, and say that a state belonging to the meaning of a label is *permissible* for that label. In other words, an environment specifies whether a state is permissible for a label. Intuitively, when $[\![\textbf{goto } L]\!]_\eta$ is executed, the current state will cause the rest of the computation to behave correctly if it is permissible for L in η.

Next we enlarge the variety of circumstances in which a specification of the form $\{P\}$ S $\{Q\}$ is true. Specifically, we define $[\![\{P\}$ S $\{Q\}]\!]_\eta$ to be true if and only if, starting with any state described by $[\![P]\!]_\eta$, executing $[\![S]\!]_\eta$ will either:

      (1)   Never terminate,

or   (2)   Terminate with a final state described by $[\![Q]\!]_\eta$, or   (3)   Execute a jump to a label L occurring free in S with a current state that is permissible for L in η, i.e. that belongs to the set $[\![L]\!]_\eta$.

From this definition, it is evident that $[\![\{P\} \textbf{ goto } L \{Q\}]\!]_\eta$ will be true if every state described by $[\![P]\!]_\eta$ belongs to $[\![L]\!]_\eta$. Notice that there is no dependency upon Q.

We must now develop a rule of inference that will enable us to infer a universal specification about a block of the form

$$\textbf{begin } S_0; \ L_1: S_1; \ \ldots \ ; \ L_n: S_n \textbf{ end}$$

from universal specifications about the statements $S_0, \ldots, S_n$. The essential idea is that in reasoning about the component statements we will assume that a state is permissible for L_i if it satisfies the precedent of S_i.

To carry out this argument in detail, suppose that the following specifications are universal:

$$\Sigma \ \& \ \Sigma_{\text{label}} \Rightarrow \{P_0\} \ S_0 \ \{P_1\}$$
$$\vdots$$
$$\Sigma \ \& \ \Sigma_{\text{label}} \Rightarrow \{P_n\} \ S_n \ \{P_{n+1}\} \quad ,$$

where Σ_{label} is the set of assumptions

$$\{P_1\} \textbf{ goto } L_1 \textbf{ \{false\}} \ \& \ \ldots \ \& \ \{P_n\} \textbf{ goto } L_n \textbf{ \{false\}} \quad .$$

Here $P_0, \ldots, P_{n+1}$ are assertions and Σ is a finite set of assumptions such that neither the P_i's nor Σ contain free occurrences of $L_1, \ldots, L_n$.

Let η be any environment in which the assumptions Σ are true. For each assertion P_i, let Δ_i be the set of states described by $[\![P_i]\!]_\eta$. Then let

$$\eta' = [\eta \mid L_1: \Delta_1 \mid \ldots \mid L_n: \Delta_n]$$

be the environment that is similar to η except that it maps each L_i into Δ_i.

Since the assumptions Σ contain no free occurrences of the L_i, they will be true in η'. Similarly, since each assertion P_i contains no free occurrence of the L_i, $[\![P_i]\!]_{\eta'} = [\![P_i]\!]_\eta$ will describe the set of states $\Delta_i = [\![L_i]\!]_{\eta'}$. As a consequence, the assumptions Σ_{label} will be true in η'.

Thus by our universal specifications about the S_i, for $0 \le i \le n$, $\{P_i\} \ S_i \ \{P_{i+1}\}$ will be true in η'. It follows from axiom (R12) for statement compounding that, for $0 \le i \le n$, the specification

$$\{P_i\} \ S_i; \ \ldots \ ; \ S_n \ \{P_{n+1}\}$$

will be true in η'.

Thus, starting with any state described by $[\![P_i]\!]_{\eta'}$, executing $[\![S_i; \ldots ; S_n]\!]_{\eta'}$ will either:

(1)   Never terminate,

or   (2)   Terminate with a final state described by $[\![P_{n+1}]\!]_{\eta'}$, or   (3)   Execute a jump to a label other than L_1, ... , L_n, with a current state that is permissible for that label in η',

or   (4)   Execute a jump to some L_i, with a current state that belongs to $[\![L_i]\!]_{\eta'}$, and is therefore described by $[\![P_i]\!]_{\eta'}$.

Now consider the execution of

$$[\![\textbf{begin } S_0;\ L_1\colon S_1;\ \dots\ ;\ L_n\colon S_n \textbf{ end}]\!]_{\eta'}\ ,$$

starting with a state described by $[\![P_0]\!]_{\eta'}$. This execution will be the same as that of $S_0; S_1; \dots ; S_n$ until when and if a jump to some L_i occurs, at which point the current state will be described by $[\![P_i]\!]_{\eta'}$. Thereafter the continued execution will be the same as that of $S_i; \dots ; S_n$ until when and if another jump to some L_i occurs, again with a current state described by the corresponding $[\![P_i]\!]_{\eta'}$.

Repeating this argument, it is evident that every time a jump to an L_i occurs, the state will satisfy $[\![P_i]\!]_{\eta'}$ and the continued execution will be the same as that of $S_i; \dots ; S_n$ until the next jump. Ultimately, there will either be an endless sequence of jumps, in which case the execution will never terminate, or there will be a last jump, after which the continued execution will be the same as that of some $S_i; \dots ; S_n$ and will lead to one of the conditions (1) to (3) given above.

Either way, starting with a state described by $[\![P_0]\!]_{\eta'}$, executing $[\![\textbf{begin } S_0;\ L_1\colon S_1;\ \dots\ ;\ L_n\colon S_n \textbf{ end}]\!]_{\eta'}$ will lead to one of the conditions (1) to (3). It follows that the specification

$$\{P_0\}\ \textbf{begin } S_0;\ L_1\colon S_1;\ \dots\ ;\ L_n\colon S_n \textbf{ end}\ \{P_{n+1}\}$$

will be true in η'. Moreover, since this specification contains no free occurrences of L_1, ... , L_n, it will also be true in η.

Thus, since η can be any environment in which Σ is true,

$$\Sigma \Rightarrow \{P_0\}\ \textbf{begin } S_0;\ L_1\colon S_1;\ \dots\ ;\ L_n\colon S_n \textbf{ end}\ \{P_{n+1}\}$$

is a universal specification.

This argument leads to the following rule of inference:

(R40) **goto** Statements and Labels

Suppose

L_1, ... , L_n are distinct identifiers of phrase type **label**,
S_0, ... , S_n are statements,
P_0, ... , P_{n+1} are assertions,
Σ is a finite set of specifications,

such that L_1, ... , L_n do not occur free in P_0, ... , P_{n+1}, or Σ.
Let Σ_{label} be

$$\{P_1\}\ \textbf{goto } L_1\ \{\textbf{false}\}\ \&\ \dots\ \&\ \{P_n\}\ \textbf{goto } L_n\ \{\textbf{false}\}\ .$$

Then

$$\Sigma \ \& \ \Sigma_{label} \Rightarrow \{P_0\} \ S_0 \ \{P_1\}$$

$$\vdots$$

$$\Sigma \ \& \ \Sigma_{label} \Rightarrow \{P_n\} \ S_n \ \{P_{n+1}\}$$

$$\overline{\Sigma \Rightarrow \{P_0\} \ \textbf{begin} \ S_0; \ L_1\colon S_1; \ \dots \ ; \ L_n\colon S_n \ \textbf{end} \ \{P_{n+1}\}} \quad .$$

Notice that we have introduced **label** as an additional phrase type in specification logic. Phrases of type **label**, which will always be identifiers, are neither statement-like nor expression-like.

Unfortunately, **label** is not a full-fledged phrase type in Algol W, since labels cannot be used as parameters to procedures. This is a minor anomaly in the design of the language. It causes no harm in practice, since in place of a label parameter one can always use a **goto** statement that refers to the label. However, it complicates the description of the language by introducing a usage of identifiers with unnecessarily different behavior than all other usages.

*4.2.4 An Example of a Formal Proof

To illustrate the use of the inference rule derived in the previous section, we will prove that the linear search program of Section 4.2.1 satisfies an appropriate specification. We begin by defining the appropriate assumption for the label *out*:

$$\Sigma_{label} \equiv$$
$$\{\textbf{if } present \textbf{ then } \boxed{a \ | \ j \ | \ b} \textbf{ and } X(j)=y \textbf{ else } \{X \uparrow \boxed{a \ \ b}\} \neq^* y\}$$
$$\textbf{goto } out$$
$$\{\textbf{false}\} \quad .$$

Then the inmost block of the program satisfies the tableau

$$
\begin{aligned}
&\begin{rcases}
\textbf{gv}(present) \ \& \ present \ \# \ a \\
\& \ present \ \# \ k \ \& \ present \ \# \ b \\
\& \ present \ \# \ X \ \& \ present \ \# \ y \\
\& \ \textbf{gv}(j) \ \& \ j \ \# \ present \\
\& \ j \ \# \ a \ \& \ j \ \# \ b \\
\& \ j \ \# \ X \ \& \ j \ \# \ y \\
\& \ \Sigma_{label}
\end{rcases}
\Rightarrow
\begin{cases}
\{\{X \uparrow \boxed{a \ | \ k} \} \neq^* y \textbf{ and } \boxed{a \ | \ k \ | \ b} \\
\quad \textbf{and } X(k)=y \} \\
\{\textbf{true and } \boxed{a \ | \ k \ | \ b} \textbf{ and } X(k)=y\} \\
present := \textbf{true}; \\
\{present \textbf{ and } \boxed{a \ | \ k \ | \ b} \textbf{ and } X(k)=y\} \\
j := k; \\
\{present \textbf{ and } \boxed{a \ | \ j \ | \ b} \textbf{ and } X(j)=y\} \\
\{\textbf{if } present \\
\quad \textbf{then } \boxed{a \ | \ j \ | \ b} \textbf{ and } X(j)=y \\
\quad \textbf{else } \{X \uparrow \boxed{a \ \ b}\} \neq^* y \} \\
\textbf{goto } out \\
\{\textbf{false}\} \\
\{\{X \uparrow \boxed{a \ \ k}\} \neq^* y\} \quad .
\end{cases}
\end{aligned}
$$

From the result of this tableau and the mathematical fact

$$(\{X \uparrow \boxed{a \quad k}\} \neq^* y \text{ and } \boxed{a \quad k \quad b} \text{ and } \neg X(k) = y)$$
$$\text{implies } \{X \uparrow \boxed{a \quad k}\} \neq^* y \quad,$$

we may use rule (R17) for the one-way conditional statement to infer

$$\mathbf{gv}(present) \ \& \ present \ \# \ a \ \& \ present \ \# \ k \ \& \ present \ \# \ b$$
$$\& \ present \ \# \ X \ \& \ present \ \# \ y \ \& \ \mathbf{gv}(j) \ \& \ j \ \# \ present$$
$$\& \ j \ \# \ a \ \& \ j \ \# \ b \ \& \ j \ \# \ X \ \& \ j \ \# \ y \ \& \ \Sigma_{\text{label}} \Rightarrow$$
$$\{\{X \uparrow \boxed{a \quad k}\} \neq^* y \text{ and } \boxed{a \quad k \quad b}\}$$
$$\text{if } X(k) = y \text{ then}$$
$$\qquad \mathbf{begin} \ present := \mathbf{true}; \ j := k; \ \mathbf{goto} \ out \ \mathbf{end}$$
$$\{\{X \uparrow \boxed{a \quad k}\} \neq^* y\} \quad .$$

Next we use rule (R37) for the **for** statement, taking the invariant I to be $X \uparrow N \neq^* y$. This discharges the assumption *present # k* and gives the main step in the following tableau:

$$
\left.
\begin{array}{l}
\mathbf{gv}(present) \ \& \ present \ \# \ a \\
\& \ present \ \# \ b \\
\& \ present \ \# \ X \ \& \ present \ \# \ y \\
\& \ \mathbf{gv}(j) \ \& \ j \ \# \ present \\
\& \ j \ \# \ a \ \& \ j \ \# \ b \\
\& \ j \ \# \ X \ \& \ j \ \# \ y \\
\& \ \Sigma_{\text{label}}
\end{array}
\right\}
\Rightarrow
\left\{
\begin{array}{l}
\{\boxed{a \quad b} \subseteq \mathbf{dom} \ X\} \\
\{\mathbf{true}\} \\
\{\{X \uparrow \{\}\} \neq^* y\} \\
\mathbf{for} \ k := a \ \mathbf{until} \ b \ \mathbf{do} \\
\quad \mathbf{if} \ X(k) = y \ \mathbf{then} \\
\qquad \mathbf{begin} \\
\qquad\quad present := \mathbf{true}; \\
\qquad\quad j := k; \ \mathbf{goto} \ out \\
\qquad \mathbf{end}; \\
\{\{X \uparrow \boxed{a \quad b}\} \neq^* y\} \\
\{\neg \ \mathbf{false} \ \text{and} \ \{X \uparrow \boxed{a \quad b}\} \neq^* y\} \\
present := \mathbf{false} \\
\{\neg \ present \ \text{and} \ \{X \uparrow \boxed{a \quad b}\} \neq^* y\} \\
\{\mathbf{if} \ present \\
\quad \mathbf{then} \ \boxed{a \quad j \quad b} \ \text{and} \ X(j) = y \\
\quad \mathbf{else} \ \{X \uparrow \boxed{a \quad b}\} \neq^* y \ \} \quad .
\end{array}
\right.
$$

Notice that the initial assertion $\boxed{a \quad b} \subseteq \mathbf{dom} \ X$ is irrelevant here. Its only purpose is to insure against subscript errors in the evaluation of the logical expression $X(k) = y$, and such errors are not treated formally in our logic.

Now we apply rule (R40) for **goto**'s and labels, taking L_1 to be *out*, S_0 to be the statement sequence in the above tableau, S_1 to be the empty statement, P_0 to be $\boxed{a \quad b} \subseteq \mathbf{dom} \ X$, P_1 and P_2 to both be

if *present* **then** $\boxed{a \quad \boxed{j} \quad b}$ **and** $X(j) = y$ **else** $\{X \uparrow \boxed{a \quad b}\} \neq^* y$,

and Σ to be all of the assumptions in the above tableau except Σ_{label}. Then the first premiss of rule (R40) is the result of the above tableau and the second premiss is an obvious consequence of rule (R18) for the empty statement. We may therefore infer the conclusion

$\textbf{gv}(present)$ & $present \,\#\, a$ & $present \,\#\, b$ & $present \,\#\, X$ & $present \,\#\, y$
& $\textbf{gv}(j)$ & $j \,\#\, present$ & $j \,\#\, a$ & $j \,\#\, b$ & $j \,\#\, X$ & $j \,\#\, y \Rightarrow$
    $\{\boxed{a \quad b} \subseteq \textbf{dom}\ X\}$
    begin
    for $k := a$ **until** b **do**
        if $X(k) = y$ **then**
            begin *present* := **true**; $j := k$; **goto** *out* **end**;
        present := **false**;
    out: **end**
    $\{$**if** *present* **then** $\boxed{a \quad \boxed{j} \quad b}$ **and** $X(j) = y$ **else** $\{X \uparrow \boxed{a \quad b}\} \neq^* y\}$.

Specification logic, and rule (R40) in particular, can be used to prove program correctness even in situations where **goto**'s and labels interact with the full generality of the procedure mechanism (as in Exercise 2 below). By itself, however, a logic for proving program correctness says little about how to create programs in the first place. In the rest of this chapter we will deal with this prior question with regard to **goto**'s and labels. Since we will not be using procedures, we will leave specification logic in abeyance, and return to the use of assertions as comments in the style of Section 4.2.2.

Exercises

1. Definition (2) of the call-by-name variant of the **for** statement, given in Section 4.1.1, will overflow unnecessarily if L is the smallest representable integer. Similarly, the definition given in Exercise 1 after Section 4.1.4 will overflow unnecessarily if U is the largest representable integer.

    Write two definitions of the call-by-name variant of the **for** statement that avoid these problems. One version should use **goto**'s and labels, and should only contain a single occurrence of the **for**-statement body S. The other version should not use **goto**'s or labels, but will contain more than one occurrence of S.

2. The following program performs linear search by using a subsidiary recursive procedure containing a jump to a global label. It is a complicated and inefficient way to search an array segment, but it illustrates a basic method that is useful for searching recursively defined data structures such as trees or list structures.

    Prove that this program satisfies the same specification as the linear search program considered in the preceding section.

$\{\boxed{a \quad b} \subseteq \textbf{dom } X\}$
begin
   begin
   procedure *search*(**integer** $\{\textbf{exp}\}$ c, d);
      $\{\textbf{pa}: present \# c \ \& \ present \# d \ \& \ j \# c \ \& \ j \# d\}$
      $\{\boxed{a \quad c \quad d \quad b}\}$
      if $c \le d$ **then**
         begin integer k;
         $k := (c+d)$ **div** 2;
         if $X(k) = y$ **then**
            begin *present* := **true**; $j := k$; **goto** *out* **end**
         else
            begin *search*($c, k-1$); *search*($k+1, d$) **end**
         end;
      $\{\{X \uparrow \boxed{c \quad d}\} \ne^* y\}$
   search(a, b)
   end;
  $\{\{X \uparrow \boxed{a \quad b}\} \ne^* y\}$
  present := **false**;
out: **end**
  $\{\textbf{if } present \textbf{ then } \boxed{a \quad j \quad b} \textbf{ and } X(j) = y \textbf{ else } \{X \uparrow \boxed{a \quad b}\} \ne^* y\}$.

4.2.5 Fast Exponentiation Revisited

For most programming, an adequate variety of control structures can be
formed by using conditional and **while** statements, as illustrated in the earlier
chapters of this book. Occasionally, however, one needs a control structure
that is difficult or even impossible to express with these constructs, and it is
necessary to use the more general mechanism of **goto** statements and labels.
Nevertheless, one can still construct programs systematically. In particular,
the concept of an invariant is still relevant [van Emden 79, Reynolds 78b].

    As an example, consider the fast exponentiation program introduced in
Section 1.3.5. It can be written in the overall form

      $\{n \ge 0\}$
      begin integer k, z;
      $k := n$; $y := 1$; $z := x$;
      $\{I\}$
      "Achieve $k = 0$ while preserving I"
      end
      $\{y = x^n\}$,

where I is the invariant

$$y \times z^k = x^n \text{ and } k \geq 0 \quad .$$

Moreover, there are two invariant-preserving operations which can be used to construct "Achieve $k=0$ while preserving I":

$$k := k-1; \, y := y \times z \qquad\qquad\qquad (S_-)$$

and

$$k := k \text{ div } 2; \, z := z \times z \quad , \qquad\qquad\qquad (S_{\text{div}})$$

which satisfy the specifications

$$\{I \text{ and } k \neq 0\} \, S_- \, \{I\}$$

and

$$\{I \text{ and } even(k)\} \, S_{\text{div}} \, \{I\} \quad .$$

In Section 1.3.5, we constructed two versions of "Achieve $k=0$ while preserving I":

> **while** $k \neq 0$ **do**
>   **if** $odd(k)$ **then** S_- **else** S_{div}

and

> **while** $k \neq 0$ **do**
>   **begin if** $odd(k)$ **then** S_- ; S_{div} **end** .

However, each of these versions has a deficiency: In the first, there are unnecessary executions of the test $odd(k)$, while in the second, the last execution of S_{div} is unnecessary (and can cause unnecessary overflow). We now want to devise a version of "Achieve $k=0$ while preserving I" that overcomes both of these deficiencies.

The first step is to determine the exact precedent under which each invariant-preserving operation will be performed. If k is zero, then an exit should occur, since the desired goal has been achieved. If k is nonzero and even, then S_{div} should be performed. Finally, if k is odd (and therefore nonzero) S_- should be performed. (Of course, it would also be correct to do S_- when k was nonzero and even, but S_{div} is faster.)

Having established their precedents, we can reexamine S_{div} and S_- to see if we can strengthen their consequents. In fact, it is easily seen that S_{div} will never give $k=0$, and that S_- will always give an even k, i.e.

$$\{I \text{ and } k \neq 0 \text{ and } even(k)\} \, S_{\text{div}} \, \{I \text{ and } k \neq 0\}$$
$$\{I \text{ and } odd(k)\} \, S_- \, \{I \text{ and } even(k)\} \quad .$$

These specifications encapsulate all we need to know about the invariant I in order to write "Achieve $k=0$ while preserving I". As long as we use S_{div} and S_- in accordance with these specifications and do not use any other statements which interfere with I, we can be sure that I will be preserved. Indeed, at the level of abstraction where S_{div} and S_- are considered as indivisible actions, the invariant I will hold continuously. In this situation we say that I is a *general invariant*.

At this level of abstraction, we can forget the invariant and concentrate on the remaining conditions $k=0$ and $odd(k)$ that occur in the above specifications. We intend to realize "Achieve $k=0$ while preserving I" by a sequence of labeled statements in which the assertion at each label is a conjunction built out of $k=0$ and $odd(k)$ or their negations. The key point is that the variety of such conjunctions that might be relevant to our program is so small that we can reason about it exhaustively.

First we must enumerate all possibly relevant assertions. Suppose for a moment that we were only interested in the conditions $k=0$. Then there would be three possibly relevant assertions:

> **true**
> $k \neq 0$
> $k = 0$.

Informally, these describe the "states of information" in which it is unknown whether k is zero, k is known to be nonzero, and k is known to be zero.

If the conditions $k=0$ and $odd(k)$ were independent of each other, then the three assertions about each condition would combine to give $3 \times 3 = 9$ composite assertions:

> **true** $even(k)$ $odd(k)$
> $k \neq 0$ $k \neq 0$ **and** $even(k)$ $k \neq 0$ **and** $odd(k)$
> $k = 0$ $k = 0$ **and** $even(k)$ $k = 0$ **and** $odd(k)$.

However, since zero is an even number, the conditions are not independent, and the number of relevant assertions is less than nine. In general, we need not consider an assertion that is impossible, i.e. that is not satisfied by any state of the computation (that satisfies the invariant). Moreover, we need not distinguish between two assertions that are equivalent, i.e. that are satisfied by the same set of (invariant-satisfying) states. In this particular case, $k=0$ **and** $odd(k)$ is impossible, $k \neq 0$ **and** $odd(k)$ is equivalent to $odd(k)$, and $k=0$ **and** $even(k)$ is equivalent to $k=0$. Thus there are only six relevant assertions:

> **true**
> $k \neq 0$
> $even(k)$
> $odd(k)$
> $k \neq 0$ **and** $even(k)$
> $k = 0$.

As a consequence, "Achieve $k=0$ while preserving I" will contain six labels, so that our program has the form:

$\{n \geq 0\}$
begin integer k, z;
$k := n; y := 1; z := x$;
$\{\textbf{geninv: } y \times z^k = x^n \textbf{ and } k \geq 0\}$
... ;
tr: $\{\textbf{true}\}$ ... ;
nz: $\{k \neq 0\}$ ... ;
ev: $\{even(k)\}$ ... ;
od: $\{odd(k)\}$ ... ;
$nzev$: $\{k \neq 0 \textbf{ and } even(k)\}$ ... ;
zr: $\{k = 0\}$ ...
end
$\{y = x^n\}$.

Here we have used the symbol **geninv** to indicate that I is a general invariant. We adopt the convention that an assertion prefixed by **geninv** must hold continuously from the occurrence of the assertion to the end of the immediately enclosing block.

The specification

$$\{I \textbf{ and } k \neq 0 \textbf{ and } even(k)\} \ S_{\text{div}} \ \{I \textbf{ and } k \neq 0\}$$

shows that S_{div} can be performed at the label $nzev$, and followed by a jump to nz. Similarly,

$$\{I \textbf{ and } odd(k)\} \ S_- \ \{I \textbf{ and } even(k)\}$$

shows that S_- can be performed at od, and followed by a jump to ev.

Since the initialization $k := n; y := 1; z := x$ achieves the invariant without providing any knowledge about $k = 0$ or $odd(k)$, it must be followed by a jump to tr. On the other hand, since an exit should occur when $k = 0$, the label zr should be attached to an empty statement at the end of the block. (In fact, we have had the foresight to place zr in this position.)

At this stage our program has the form

$\{n \geq 0\}$
begin integer k, z;
$k := n; y := 1; z := x$;
$\{\textbf{geninv: } y \times z^k = x^n \textbf{ and } k \geq 0\}$
goto tr;
tr: $\{\textbf{true}\}$ ... ;
nz: $\{k \neq 0\}$ ... ;
ev: $\{even(k)\}$ ... ;
od: $\{odd(k)\}$ S_-; **goto** ev;
$nzev$: $\{k \neq 0 \textbf{ and } even(k)\}$ S_{div}; **goto** nz;
zr: $\{k = 0\}$
end
$\{y = x^n\}$.

At the remaining labels, the assertions are insufficient to imply the precedent of any operation, so that testing must be performed. At *nz* one can obviously test $odd(k)$ and go to either *od* or *nzev*. Similarly, at *ev* one can test $k=0$ and go to either *zr* or *nzev*. At *tr*, either test will provide useful information; if we choose the test $k=0$, then our final program is:

$$\{n \geq 0\}$$
begin integer k, z;
$k := n; y := 1; z := x;$
$\{\textbf{geninv } I: y \times z^k = x^n \textbf{ and } k \geq 0\}$
goto *tr*;
tr: $\{\textbf{true}\}$ **if** $k=0$ **then goto** *zr* **else goto** *nz*;
nz: $\{k \neq 0\}$ **if** $odd(k)$ **then goto** *od* **else goto** *nzev*;
ev: $\{even(k)\}$ **if** $k=0$ **then goto** *zr* **else goto** *nzev*;
od: $\{odd(k)\}$ **begin**$_I$ $k := k-1; y := y \times z$ **end**;
    goto *ev*;
nzev: $\{k \neq 0 \textbf{ and } even(k)\}$ **begin**$_I$ $k := k$ **div** $2; z := z \times z$ **end**;
    goto *nz*;
zr: $\{k=0\}$
end
$$\{y = x^n\} \quad .$$

Here we have expanded S_- and S_{div} into blocks. In doing so, we have dropped below the level of abstraction at which the general invariant is continuously true, i.e. there will be points in the interior of these blocks at which the general invariant does not hold.

To indicate this situation we adopt the following notational convention: When an assertion is used as a general invariant, it is given a name (e.g. I in this example). Then this name is placed as a subscript at the beginning of each block within whose interior the general invariant may be momentarily falsified. Such blocks must be regarded as indivisible actions when we say that the general invariant holds continuously from its point of occurrence to the end of the immediately enclosing block.

For clarity, we have used **goto** statements whenever control passes to a labeled statement, so that control never passes through a label from the previous statement. As a consequence, except for the attachment of *zr* to the end of the block, the meaning of the program is independent of the order of the labels.

In fact, this order has been chosen to clarify the proof that the program terminates. Since the only backward jumps (from a **goto** statement to a lexically preceding label definition) follow the occurrences of S_- and S_{div}, it follows that every loop must contain an occurrence of S_- or S_{div}. Thus termination is based on k, which will be decreased by S_- and by S_{div} whenever their precedents are satisfied.

This program avoids both the redundant testing and unnecessary execution of S_{div} that occurred in the versions of Section 1.3.5. On the other hand, it is longer and more difficult to write than the earlier versions, and it would only be justified in a programming situation where execution speed was extremely important.

Nevertheless it is still a structured program. There is a clear separation between two levels of abstraction: a detailed level at which the invariant-preserving operations S_- and S_{div} are formulated, and a gross level at which the invariant can be ignored since it is preserved by the primitive operations. Indeed, this kind of invariant suppression is essential to the program development, since it permits the programmer to limit his attention to the conditions beyond the invariant—$k=0$ and $odd(k)$—which are so simple that one can treat them exhaustively by enumerating all relevant assertions.

4.2.6   Transition Diagrams and Indeterminacy

When control structure becomes as complex as in the previous example, it is helpful to use a graphical representation such as a flowchart. For many purposes, however, a clearer graphical representation is provided by a *transition diagram*.

In a transition diagram, labels and other program points where assertions can occur are represented by nodes, whilst statements and tests are represented by arrows or *arcs* from one node to another. As shown in Figure 4.1, a statement S is represented by a solid arc, marked with S, from the program point where its precedent occurs to the program point where its consequent occurs. As shown in Figure 4.2, a test L is represented by a pair of dashed arcs: an arc marked with L from the point before testing to the point to be reached if L is **true**, and an arc marked with the negation of L from the point before testing to the point to be reached if L is **false**.

One can think of a computer executing a transition diagram by moving from node to node along arcs. When a test arc marked with L is encountered, it is only traversed if L is **true**. When a statement arc marked with S is encountered, the statement S is executed.

Transition diagrams are given in Figure 4.3 for the basic control constructs used in Chapter 1. These diagrams may be compared with the equivalent flowcharts given in Figure 1.2.

Figure 4.1 $\{P\}$ S $\{Q\}$ as a Transition Diagram.

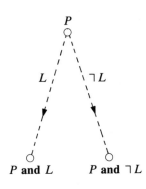

Figure 4.2   A Test L Performed in a State Satisfying P.

if L then S

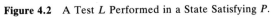

if L then S_1 else S_2

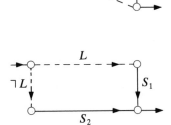

while L do S

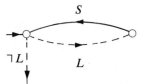

begin S_1; ... ; S_n end

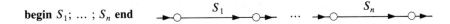

Figure 4.3   The Basic Control Constructions Defined by Transition Diagrams.

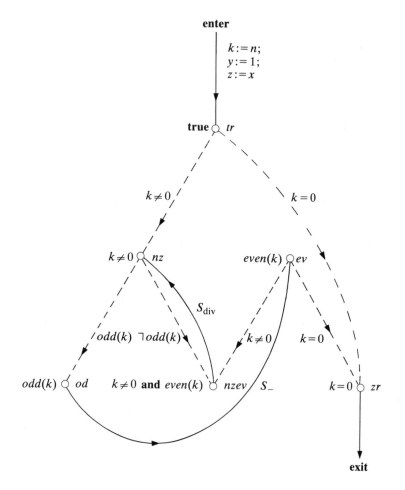

Figure 4.4 A Transition Diagram for Fast Exponentiation.

Figure 4.4 gives a transition diagram for the fast exponentiation program developed in the previous section. The diagram reveals the logic behind the program more directly that the Algol W program itself. The nodes correspond to the relevant assertions, and the arcs for S_- and S_{div} are directly attached to the appropriate precedents and consequents.

In order for a transition diagram to determine the behavior of a computer completely, there must be exactly one way out of each node—either a single statement arc or a pair of complementary test arcs. Suppose we say that a test arc marked with L is *permissible* for those states of the computation in which L is **true**, and that a statement arc (or exit arc) is *permissible* for all states of the computation. Then a transition diagram will completely determine computational behavior if, for each node and each possible state of the computation, there is exactly one permissible arc emanating from the node.

However, transition diagrams that violate this condition are still meaningful—and sometimes useful. For a given node, if there are any states of the computation for which no outgoing arc is permissible, then the node is a *dead end*, whose effect is a kind of nontermination. More interestingly, if there are any states of the computation for which more than one outgoing arc is permissible, then the node (and the transition diagram containing it) is said to be *indeterminate*.

In executing an indeterminate transition diagram, the computer is "allowed" to traverse any permissible arc, so that its behavior is only partly determined. Nevertheless, such a diagram is correct if every possible behavior that it allows meets the program specification.

For example, when developing the fast exponentiation program in the previous section, we made an arbitrary choice between the tests $k = 0$ and $odd(k)$ at the label *tr*. Avoiding this choice leads to the indeterminate transition diagram shown in Figure 4.5. At the node *tr* in this diagram, the computer is free to traverse either of two test arcs, both of which lead to correct behavior.

Further indeterminacy would be introduced by adding an arc marked S_- from *nz* to *tr*, as indicated by the dotted line in Figure 4.5. This change still leaves the program correct, but it introduces serious inefficiencies—essentially it allows the computer to choose between fast and slow exponentiation.

In recent years, the importance of indeterminacy in programming has increased, and at least one author has advocated a programming language with indeterminate control mechanisms [Dijkstra 75, 76]. There are at least three reasons for this development:

(1) As shown in the next section, the intelligibility of a program can be enhanced by avoiding unnecessary choices that do not affect correctness.

(2) As discussed in Chapter 5, it is often profitable to attack complex problems by first writing an abstract program using problem-oriented types of data, and then translating this program into a concrete program using a particular data representation. In this approach, it is often vital to leave the abstract program indeterminate in order to postpone choices that require knowledge of the data representation.

(3) In some kinds of parallel processing, the actual program executed by the computer may be indeterminate. Consider, for example, searching a large data file, stored on several magnetic tapes or disks, for any of several records giving the age of a particular

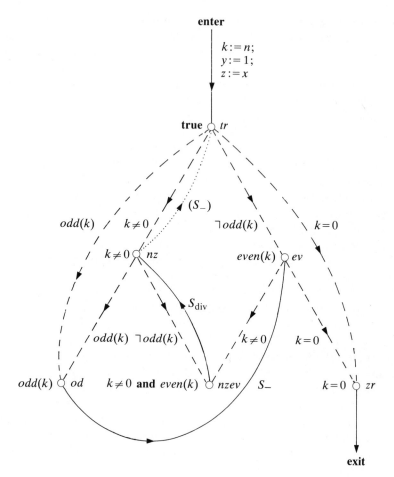

enter

$$k := n;$$
$$y := 1;$$
$$z := x$$

true tr

(S_-)

$odd(k)$ / $k \neq 0$ $\neg odd(k)$ $k = 0$

$k \neq 0$ nz $even(k)$ ev

S_{div}

/ $odd(k)$ $\neg odd(k)$ $k \neq 0$ $k = 0$

$odd(k)$ od $k \neq 0$ **and** $even(k)$ $nzev$ / S_- $k = 0$ zr

exit

Figure 4.5 An Indeterminate Transition Diagram for Fast Exponentiation.

person. The particular record examined might not be determined by the program, and could depend upon factors such as the relative speeds of motors in different storage devices.

In all of these situations, the key point is that an indeterminate program is only correct if *all* of its possible executions are correct. (This point requires special emphasis since there is another notion of indeterminacy used in automata theory and artificial intelligence in which—roughly speaking—a program is correct if *some* possible execution is correct [Floyd 67b].)

*4.2.7 Merging Revisited

In Section 2.3.6, we developed a program for merging two ordered array segments. Just as with fast exponentiation, a more efficient version of this program can be obtained by considering transitions among all relevant assertions built out of certain simple conditions.

The overall program can be written in the form:

$$\{\boxed{ax \quad bx} \subseteq \textbf{dom } X \textbf{ and } \boxed{ay \quad by} \subseteq \textbf{dom } Y \textbf{ and } \boxed{az \quad bz} \subseteq \textbf{dom } Z$$
$$\textbf{and ord}_\leq X \uparrow \boxed{ax \quad bx} \textbf{ and ord}_\leq Y \uparrow \boxed{ay \quad by}$$
$$\textbf{and } \# \boxed{ax \quad bx} + \# \boxed{ay \quad by} = \# \boxed{az \quad bz} \}$$
begin integer kx, ky, kz;
$kx := ax$; $ky := ay$; $kz := az$;
$\{I\}$
"Achieve $kx > bx$ and $ky > by$ while preserving I"
end
$\{\textbf{ord}_\leq Z \uparrow \boxed{az \quad bz}\}$,

where I is the invariant

$$\boxed{ax \quad kx \quad bx} \textbf{ and } \boxed{ay \quad ky \quad by} \textbf{ and } \boxed{az \quad kz \quad bz}$$
$$\textbf{and ord}_\leq Z \uparrow \boxed{az \quad kz}$$
$$\textbf{and } \{Z \uparrow \boxed{az \quad kz}\} \leq^* \{X \uparrow \boxed{kx \quad bx}\} \cup \{Y \uparrow \boxed{ky \quad by}\}$$
$$\textbf{and } \# \boxed{kx \quad bx} + \# \boxed{ky \quad by} = \# \boxed{kz \quad bz}   .$$

(As in Section 2.3.6, we are ignoring the rearrangement condition.)

The real work of "Achieve $kx > bx$ and $ky > by$ while preserving I" will be done by two invariant-preserving operations that copy the leftmost element of either $X \uparrow \boxed{kx \quad bx}$ or $Y \uparrow \boxed{ky \quad by}$ into the rightmost position of $Z \uparrow \boxed{az \quad kz}$:

$$Z(kz) := X(kx); \; kx := kx+1; \; kz := kz+1 \qquad \text{(Copy } X)$$
$$Z(kz) := Y(ky); \; ky := ky+1; \; kz := kz+1 . \qquad \text{(Copy } Y)$$

These operations satisfy the specifications

$$\{I \textbf{ and } kx \leq bx \textbf{ and } (ky > by \textbf{ or } (ky \leq by \textbf{ and } X(kx) \leq Y(ky)))\}$$
$$\text{"Copy } X\text{" } \{I\}$$
$$\{I \textbf{ and } ky \leq by \textbf{ and } (kx > bx \textbf{ or } (kx \leq bx \textbf{ and } Y(ky) \leq X(kx)))\}$$
$$\text{"Copy } Y\text{" } \{I\} .$$

In effect, if either $\boxed{kx \quad bx}$ or $\boxed{ky \quad by}$ is empty one must copy the leftmost element of the other nonempty segment, while if both segments are nonempty, then one must copy the lesser of their leftmost elements.

In Section 2.3.6, "Achieve $kx > bx$ and $ky > by$ while preserving I" was realized by

> **while** $kz \le bz$ **do**
>   **if** $\big($**if** $ky > by$ **then true else if** $kx > bx$ **then false else**
> $X(kx) \le Y(ky)\big)$
>   **then** "Copy X" **else** "Copy Y" .

This clearly involves redundant testing. For example, after executing "Copy X", the program will test $ky > by$, although the outcome of this test cannot differ from its previous outcome before executing "Copy X".

Saying that "Copy X" preserves the outcome of $ky > by$ is tantamount to saying that it satisfies the following pair of specifications:

$$\{I \textbf{ and } kx \le bx \textbf{ and } ky > by\} \text{ "Copy } X\text{" } \{I \textbf{ and } ky > by\}$$
$$\{I \textbf{ and } kx \le bx \textbf{ and } ky \le by \textbf{ and } X(kx) \le Y(ky)\}$$
$$\text{"Copy } X\text{" } \{I \textbf{ and } ky \le by\} \quad .$$

Similarly "Copy Y" satisfies

$$\{I \textbf{ and } kx > bx \textbf{ and } ky \le by\} \text{ "Copy } Y\text{" } \{I \textbf{ and } kx > bx\}$$
$$\{I \textbf{ and } kx \le bx \textbf{ and } ky \le by \textbf{ and } X(kx) \ge Y(ky)\}$$
$$\text{"Copy } Y\text{" } \{I \textbf{ and } kx \le bx\} \quad .$$

The significant conditions are obviously $kx \le bx$, $ky \le by$, and $X(kx) \le Y(ky)$. The first two are obviously independent, and give rise to nine relevant assertions. However, the condition $X(kx) \le Y(ky)$ is only well-defined when both $\boxed{kx \quad bx}$ and $\boxed{ky \quad by}$ are nonempty, i.e. when $kx \le bx$ **and** $ky \le by$. In general, an assertion of the form C_1 **and** ... **and** C_n is not relevant if there is any (invariant-satisfying) state for which no C_i is false and some C_i is undefined. Thus in this particular case, $X(kx) \le Y(ky)$ gives rise to only two more relevant assertions: $kx \le bx$ **and** $ky \le by$ **and** $X(kx) \le Y(ky)$, and $kx \le bx$ **and** $ky \le by$ **and** $X(kx) \ge Y(ky)$. $\big($Strictly speaking, $X(kx) \ge Y(ky)$ is not the negation of $X(kx) \le Y(ky)$, but the "overlap" between the two conditions will not cause any difficulties.$\big)$

Thus we have the eleven assertions shown in the transition diagram in Figure 4.6. The operations "Copy X" and "Copy Y" each occur twice, in accordance with their specifications. The placement of tests is obvious. Entrance after initialization occurs at the node marked **true**, since none of the significant conditions is known. Exit occurs when the goal $kx > bx$ **and** $ky > by$ has been achieved.

The transition diagram is indeterminate at two points: at **true**, where it is immaterial whether one tests the emptyness of $\boxed{kx \quad bx}$ or of $\boxed{ky \quad by}$, and at

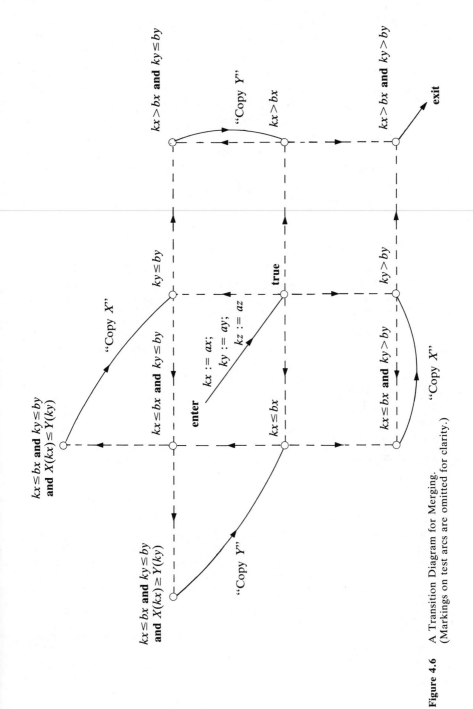

Figure 4.6   A Transition Diagram for Merging. (Markings on test arcs are omitted for clarity.)

$kx \leq bx$ and $ky \leq by$, where one can perform either "Copy X" or "Copy Y" when $X(kx) = Y(ky)$. (Here we are ignoring the question of stability, discussed in Section 2.3.9.) In this form the transition diagram reveals the symmetry between X and Y which is characteristic of the merging problem: Interchanging X and Y, ax and ay, bx and by, and kx and ky has the same effect as reflecting the transition diagram along a diagonal.

The diagram has been drawn so that every test arc moves further from the central node marked **true**. This makes it evident that every loop contains either "Copy X" or "Copy Y". Thus termination is insured since both of these operations decrease the sum of the sizes of $\boxed{kx \quad bx}$ and $\boxed{ky \quad by}$.

After resolving the indeterminacies arbitrarily, it is staightforward to translate the transition diagram into an Algol W program.

4.2.8 Another Caution

In Sections 4.2.5 to 4.2.7, we have presented a method of programming based upon the enumeration of relevant assertions which eventually become labels in the program. The method is systematic, and there are occasions when its employment gives a worthwhile improvement in execution speed.

Nevertheless, experience shows that this method should be used with great discretion. It usually yields a modest gain in execution speed at considerable cost in program length, complexity, and opportunity for error. Execution speed is rarely that important. Even when the speed of a complete program is vital, it is usually dominated by the speed of a small number of key parts of the program. On the other hand, complexity always has its price, which is usually underestimated.

One should never try to write the fastest program until one has written the simplest program, and then examined it to find where speed is worth its price in complexity.

Exercises

1. Without using **goto** statements or labels, write a program that is equivalent to the fast exponentiation program given in Section 4.2.5, in the sense that for any given input both programs execute the same sequence of tests and assignment statements. You may need to use more than one occurrence of S_- or S_{div}. (The author is indebted to D. Gries for showing him that this can be done.)

2. Show that the fast exponentiation program in Section 4.2.5 is free of redundant testing. More precisely, show that for every path through the transition diagram in Figure 4.4, there is an input value of n which will cause the program to execute that path.

3. Apply the methodology of Sections 4.2.5 to 4.2.7 to eliminate redundant testing in the array partitioning program devised in Section 2.3.5. The relevant assertions are built out of the conditions $c \le d$, $X(c) \le r$, and $X(d) \le r$. You should be able to take advantage of the fact that the statement $d := d - 1$ cannot change the outcome of the test $X(c) \le r$.

4. The speed of the partitioning program discussed in the previous problem can be further improved by using "stoppers". Once $c := c + 1$ has been executed, $\{X \uparrow$ $\boxed{a \quad c}\}$ will be nonempty and will contain a "stopper" whose value is less than or equal to r. Thus $X(d)$ will be well-defined, and if $X(d) > r$, $\boxed{c \quad d}$ will be nonempty. Similarly, once $d := d - 1$ has been executed $X(c)$ will be well-defined, and if $X(c) \le r$ then $\boxed{c \quad d}$ will again be nonempty. As a consequence, one can frequently avoid any explicit test of the emptiness of $\boxed{c \quad d}$.

    To take advantage of this situation, one must consider the conditions $a < c$, $c \le d$, $d < b$, $X(c) \le r$, and $X(d) \le r$. The total number of possibly relevant assertions is unworkably large, but the problem becomes tractable if one only considers assertions for labels that can be reached from the initial state, and if potential indeterminacy is resolved as soon as it is encountered. Even so, this problem represents an extreme case of complexity for the sake of speed, in which "exhaustive reasoning" becomes a double-entendre. (It should be compared with the much simpler use of stoppers in Exercise 1 after Section 3.2.3, where the initialization insures the existence of stoppers.)

5 DATA REPRESENTATION STRUCTURING

The programs developed in previous chapters have all been expressed directly in terms of concepts that are provided by Algol W and most other programming languages. In more complex and realistic programs, however, this kind of direct expression is often unworkable, and one must consider concepts that are germane to the problem being solved but are not provided by the language in which the program must ultimately be written. For example, in writing a program to perform geometric calculations, one would expect to consider entities such as points and lines.

Such entities are data types, in exactly the same sense as **integer**, **real**, and **logical**. Although they are not provided by our programming language, it is conceptually straightforward to extend that language to include them. In particular, everything we have learned about constructing and verifying programs remains applicable to such an extended language.

At the outset, it should be emphasized that there are two complementary aspects to data types. On the one hand, for any data type there must be a mathematically well-defined set that serves as the range of values of variables and expressions of that type. On the other hand, for any data type or family of related data types, there must be a collection of primitive operations. For instance, for the data types **integer** and **logical**, Algol W provides primitive arithmetic operations such as $+$, relational operations such as $\leq$, and logical operations such as **and**. Similarly, for the data types **point** and **line**, an extended language might provide primitive operations for finding the line connecting two points or the point that is the intersection of two lines.

Our main thesis is that the introduction of "problem-oriented" or "user-defined" data types separates the development of a program into two phases. In the first phase one writes—and shows the correctness of—an *abstract program* in which the new types appear on the same footing as the built-in types. For example, there might be point and line variables, whose values are computed by connecting points and finding intersections. In the second phase, one designs representations for the new data types, and then uses these representations to transform the abstract program into a *concrete program* in which the new types have been eliminated. For example, a point might be represented by its x- and y-coordinates, so that each point variable in the abstract program would be transformed into a pair of real variables in the concrete program.

Over the last decade, data representation structuring has been the subject of considerable research. The earliest roots of this work lie in the design of specific programming languages, notably SIMULA 67 [Dahl 68] and even Algol W (in the record and reference facilities, which are not discussed in this book). However, as typified by [Dahl 72], [Hoare 72a], and [Hoare 72c], the subject was soon viewed as a fundamental aspect of programming methodology, independent of specific languages. More recent work has included both language design to support this methodology, e.g. [Liskov 75] and [Wulf 76], and language-independent developments, e.g. [Guttag 77] and [Jones 80].

In this book, by using Algol W (indeed a subset of Algol W that excludes the record and reference facilities) we perforce view data representation structuring as a methodology, i.e. as a way of constructing programs. This choice of language will not inhibit our development of programs, since we are free in our thinking about programs to extend or modify a programming language in any consistent way. But our final concrete programs will be less clear in Algol W than they would be in a more modern language. In effect, we will still develop programs in a structured manner, but the structure will be less apparent in the final programs.

In compensation, we will be free to transform abstract programs into concrete programs in ways that go beyond the work mentioned above. For example, we will occasionally use distinct representations for different abstract variables of the same type, compound representations that simultaneously represent more than one abstract variable, incomplete representations that leave some abstract values unrepresented, and even ambiguous representations that give the same representation to distinct abstract values. We will also make considerable use of indeterminate abstract programs.

One small warning is needed to avoid getting off on the wrong foot. Just because an abstract program is *abstract* does not imply that it is more profound or difficult to write than a concrete program. In many cases the intellectual heart of a program lies in an ingenious choice of data representation rather than in the abstract algorithm.

5.1 FINDING PATHS IN DIRECTED GRAPHS

5.1.1 Directed Graphs

To illustrate data representation structuring, it is useful to explore a variety of programs in the same problem area. Thus most of this chapter will be devoted to several programs for finding properties of directed graphs. However, it should be emphasized that our primary purpose is to demonstrate a methodology for constructing programs, and that we will only skim the surface of the subject of direct-graph algorithms. A much more comprehensive discussion of this subject is given in [Aho 74].

A *directed graph* consists of a set **node** whose members are called *nodes*, and a set **edge** whose members are called *edges* (or sometimes *arcs*). Each edge is an ordered pair $\langle x, y \rangle$ of nodes which is said to *go from x to y*. We will only consider finite directed graphs. More specifically, we will assume that the sizes of **node** and **edge** are bounded by integers N and E respectively.

Conventionally, a directed graph is pictured by using points to represent nodes and arrows to represent edges. For example, Figure 5.1 illustrates the directed graph such that

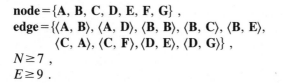

$$\begin{aligned}
&\textbf{node} = \{A, B, C, D, E, F, G\}\,, \\
&\textbf{edge} = \{\langle A, B \rangle,\ \langle A, D \rangle,\ \langle B, B \rangle,\ \langle B, C \rangle,\ \langle B, E \rangle, \\
&\qquad\quad\ \langle C, A \rangle,\ \langle C, F \rangle,\ \langle D, E \rangle,\ \langle D, G \rangle\}\,, \\
&N \geq 7\,, \\
&E \geq 9\,.
\end{aligned}$$

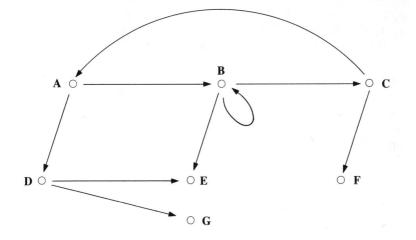

Figure 5.1 A Picture of a Directed Graph.

A node y is said to be an *immediate successor of* x if and only if there is an edge from x to y. We write Γ for the function from nodes to sets of nodes such that $\Gamma(x)$ is the set of immediate successors of x. Thus $y \in \Gamma(x)$ if and only if $\langle x, y \rangle \in$ **edge**.

For our purposes it will be convenient to regard the function Γ, rather than the set **edge**, as the fundamental description of the edge structure of a directed graph. It will also be convenient to extend this function to accept sets of nodes. When S is a set of nodes we write $\Gamma(S)$ for the set of nodes that are immediate successors of some member of S. Thus, $y \in \Gamma(S)$ if and only if $y \in \Gamma(x)$ for some $x \in S$. For example, for the graph in Figure 5.1, $\Gamma(\{\mathbf{A}, \mathbf{B}, \mathbf{F}\}) = \{\mathbf{B}, \mathbf{C}, \mathbf{D}, \mathbf{E}\}$.

A nonempty sequence $\langle x_0, x_1, \ldots, x_n \rangle$ of nodes is said to be a *path* of n steps from x_0 to x_n if and only if each adjacent pair of nodes is an edge, i.e. if $x_i \in \Gamma(x_{i-1})$ for each i in $\boxed{1 \quad n}$. For example, in Figure 5.1:

> $\langle \mathbf{A}, \mathbf{B}, \mathbf{C}, \mathbf{F} \rangle$, is a path of three steps from $\mathbf{A}$ to $\mathbf{F}$,
> $\langle \mathbf{B}, \mathbf{C}, \mathbf{A}, \mathbf{B}, \mathbf{B} \rangle$ is a path of four steps from $\mathbf{B}$ to $\mathbf{B}$,
> $\langle \mathbf{B}, \mathbf{E} \rangle$ is a path of one step from $\mathbf{B}$ to $\mathbf{E}$,
> $\langle \mathbf{G} \rangle$ is a path of zero steps from $\mathbf{G}$ to $\mathbf{G}$.

Notice that the step number is the number of edges in a path, which is one less than the number of nodes, that the minimum step number is zero, and that a path of one step is just an edge.

A node y is said to be *reachable* from a node x if and only if there is a path (of any number of steps) from x to y, Just as the edge structure can be represented by the function Γ, so reachability can be represented by the function Γ^*, from nodes to sets of nodes, such that $\Gamma^*(x)$ is the set of nodes that are reachable from x. Thus $y \in \Gamma^*(x)$ if and only if there is a path from x to y. (This use of the asterisk is unrelated to its use, in Section 2.2.8, for indicating the pointwise extension of relations.) For example, Γ^* for the graph in Figure 5.1 is given by

x	$\Gamma^*(x)$
A	$\{\mathbf{A}, \mathbf{B}, \mathbf{C}, \mathbf{D}, \mathbf{E}, \mathbf{F}, \mathbf{G}\}$
B	$\{\mathbf{A}, \mathbf{B}, \mathbf{C}, \mathbf{D}, \mathbf{E}, \mathbf{F}, \mathbf{G}\}$
C	$\{\mathbf{A}, \mathbf{B}, \mathbf{C}, \mathbf{D}, \mathbf{E}, \mathbf{F}, \mathbf{G}\}$
D	$\{\mathbf{D}, \mathbf{E}, \mathbf{G}\}$
E	$\{\mathbf{E}\}$
F	$\{\mathbf{F}\}$
G	$\{\mathbf{G}\}$.

As with Γ, we will extend Γ^* to act on sets of nodes by defining $\Gamma^*(S)$ to be the set of nodes that are reachable from some member of S.

Exercise

1. The transition diagrams introduced in Section 4.2.6 are directed graphs, and
    programs for finding their properties play an important role in compilers which
    attempt to optimize machine code. Tabulate Γ and Γ^* for the transition diagram
    in Figure 4.4.

5.1.2 An Abstract Program for Reachability

As a first example of a program dealing with a directed graph, we consider
computing, for a given node x, the set $\Gamma^*(x)$ of nodes that can be reached
from x. Such a computation is called *single-source* to emphasize that $\Gamma^*(x)$ is
to be computed for a particular x rather than for all nodes in the graph. (Of
course, a multiple-source computation could be obtained by iterating a
single-source computation over different nodes, but this approach would be
inefficient. In fact, the best multiple-source algorithms [Warshall 62, Aho
74] are quite different from the single-source algorithms considered in this
chapter.)

In the abstract version of our program, we will use two new data types:
node, whose values are nodes of the graph, and **set**, whose values are sets of
nodes. The relevant primitive operations will be conventional mathematical
operations on sets and their members. The input will be the node x and the
function Γ that describes the edge structure of the graph. The output will be a
set variable T whose final value will be $\Gamma^*(x)$.

The basic idea of the algorithm is to "grow" the set T by starting with the
set $\{x\}$ and repeatedly adding nodes that can be reached from x. Thus T will
always satisfy the invariant

$$I\colon T \subseteq \Gamma^*(x) \text{ and } x \in T \ .$$

The growth will be carried out by repeatedly adding to T nodes that can be
reached in a single step from some node that is already in T, and the
algorithm will stop when such growth is no longer possible. This will occur
when $\Gamma(T) \subseteq T$, i.e. when every node that can be reached in one step from a
member of T is already a member of T.

Thus an initial version of the abstract algorithm is

node {exp} x; **set procedure** Γ **{node exp}; set {var}** T;

$\vdots$

{true}
begin
$T := \{x\}$;
{geninv I: $T \subseteq \Gamma^*(x)$ **and** $x \in T$**}**
while $\neg\, \Gamma(T) \subseteq T$ **do**
    begin node y;
    $y :=$ a member of T;
    {geninv II: $y \in \Gamma^*(x)$**}**
    $T := T \cup \Gamma(y)$
    end
end
{$T = \Gamma^*(x)$**}**   .

Since they describe input and output, the identifiers x, Γ, and T are not bound in this program. We adopt the convention of specifying the phrase types of such identifiers in a preface to the program.

As discussed in Section 4.2.5, the symbol **geninv** indicates that I and II are *general invariants*. This means that each of these assertions holds continuously (at the present level of abstraction) from its point of occurrence to the end of the immediately enclosing block.

The outer invariant I insures that the statement $y :=$ a member of T will achieve the inner invariant II. In turn, II insures that $T := T \cup \Gamma(y)$ will preserve I, since $y \in \Gamma^*(x)$ implies $\Gamma(y) \subseteq \Gamma^*(x)$.

Notice that $y :=$ a member of T is an indeterminate operation, since it does not specify which member of T is to become the value of y. This indeterminacy will turn out to be useful when we transform our program into concrete form, since it will provide a degree of freedom that will permit us to construct a faster program.

When the program terminates, the invariant I will insure $x \in T$ and the falsity of the **while**-statement test will insure $\Gamma(T) \subseteq T$. It follows that $\Gamma^*(x) \subseteq T$, i.e. that T contains every node that can be reached from x. The proof is by induction on the number of steps. The only node that can be reached in zero steps is x itself, whose presence in T is insured by $x \in T$. If a node w can be reached in $n+1$ steps, then it can be reached in one step from some node z that can be reached in n steps. By the induction hypothesis z belongs to T, so that w belongs to $\Gamma(T)$, and the halting condition $\Gamma(T) \subseteq T$ implies that w belongs to T.

On the other hand, the invariant I insures $T \subseteq \Gamma^*(x)$, i.e. that every node in T can be reached from x. In conjunction with $\Gamma^*(x) \subseteq T$, this implies the desired consequent of the program.

The next step in developing an abstract algorithm is to express the statement $T := T \cup \Gamma(y)$ in terms of more elementary operations. For this purpose, we introduce an extension of the **for** statement that describes iteration over the members of a finite set. In general, we write **for** $K \in S$ **do** B to indicate that B is to be performed once for each member of the set S, with K denoting each member in turn. The order in which the members of S are iterated over is left indeterminate.

This construct can be used to express the addition of $\Gamma(y)$ to T as an iteration over $\Gamma(y)$ of a statement that adds individual nodes to T. Thus we replace $T := T \cup \Gamma(y)$ by

$$\textbf{for } z \in \Gamma(y) \textbf{ do } T := T \cup \{z\} \quad .$$

The virtue of this replacement is that it decouples the representations of T and Γ. If we left $T := T \cup \Gamma(y)$ in the abstract program, then in the transformation to a concrete program the realization of the union operation would depend upon both the representation of T and the representation of $\Gamma(y)$. Thus the choice of these representations would have to be made jointly to ensure that the union could be performed efficiently. But in transforming **for** $z \in \Gamma(y)$ **do** $T := T \cup \{z\}$, one can deal separately with the transformation of $T := T \cup \{z\}$, which only involves the representation of T, and the transformation of the iterative control mechanism **for** $z \in \Gamma(y)$ **do** ... , which only involves the representation of $\Gamma(y)$.

This decoupling is particularly advantageous since Γ is an input and T is an output of our program. Although we will not consider the matter explicitly when we choose representations, in the "real world" the representation of Γ has to be suitable for some program segment that computes Γ, and the representation of T has to be suitable for some other program segment that uses T. In this situation, anything which couples the choice of these representations could complicate the programming task disastrously.

On the other hand, by replacing $T := T \cup \Gamma(y)$ by a **for** statement, we are excluding certain ways of implementing the union operation. Although it will turn out that these implementations are not desirable, this is not evident from the abstract algorithm. Our arguments for the replacement are merely heuristic, and do not guarantee that it is a step in the right direction. More generally, while data representation structuring is a systematic way of constructing programs, it is not a magic tool that insures optimal design choices.

At this point we must admit that, although the initial version of our abstract algorithm is conditionally correct, it is possible that it may never terminate. The difficulty is that $y :=$ a member of T may repeatedly set y to the same member of T. But once **for** $z \in \Gamma(y)$ **do** $T := T \cup \{z\}$ has been performed for a particular y, it is a waste of time to repeat this operation for the same y. Indeed if y is chosen to be the same node ad infinitum, the program will never terminate.

To overcome this difficulty we will partition T into a set P of *processed* nodes that have already been chosen as y, and a set U of *unprocessed* nodes that have not yet been chosen. Then, by always choosing y to be an unprocessed node, we can guarantee that each execution of the **while**-statement body will increase the number of processed nodes, so that termination must occur within N steps.

The first step is to modify the abstract program by introducing P and U as local set variables, along with appropriate statements for maintaining their values:

node {**exp**} x; **set procedure** Γ {**node exp**}; **set** {**var**} T;

$\vdots$

{**true**}
begin set P, U;
$T := \{x\}$; $P := \{\}$; $U := \{x\}$;
{**geninv** I: $T \subseteq \Gamma^*(x)$ **and** $x \in T$ **and** $P \cup U = T$ **and** $P \cap U = \{\}$}
{**whileinv**: $\Gamma(P) \subseteq T$}
while $\neg\ \Gamma(T) \subseteq T$ **do**
    begin node y;
    $y :=$ a member of T;
    begin$_I$ $P := P \cup \{y\}$; $U := U - \{y\}$ **end**;
    {**geninv** II: $y \in \Gamma^*(x)$ **and** $y \in P$ **and** $\Gamma(P - \{y\}) \subseteq T$}
    for $z \in \Gamma(y)$ **do**
        if $z \notin T$ **then**
            begin$_I$ $T := T \cup \{z\}$; $U := U \cup \{z\}$ **end**
    {$\Gamma(y) \subseteq T$}
    end
end
{$T = \Gamma^*(x)$} .

Since only the new variables P and U are affected by this modification, the assertions in the original abstract program remain valid.

Initially x, which is the only member of T, is unprocessed. Each time a member of T is chosen as y, it becomes processed. Each time a new node z is added to T, it is unprocessed. (Note the necessity of the qualification "new", which is reflected in the test $z \notin T$ in the body of the **for** statement. If z already belongs to T, it may be a processed node.) It is easy to see that P and U will always form a partition of T, so that $P \cup U = T$ and $P \cap U = \{\}$ can be added to the general invariant I. However, this invariant is only continuously true if the two blocks subscripted with I are regarded as indivisible actions. As discussed in Section 4.2.5, we will subscript the beginning of a block with the name of a general invariant whenever that invariant may be temporarily falsified within the block.

Just prior to the **for** statement, y is placed in P, and neither y nor P are changed by the **for** statement body. Thus $y \in P$ can be added to the general invariant II.

Initially $\Gamma(P) \subseteq T$ holds since P is empty. Assume that this condition holds at the beginning of the **while**-statement body. Then $\Gamma(P-\{y\}) \subseteq T$ will hold after y is added to P, and will continue to hold throughout the **for** statement since y and P are never changed and T is only enlarged. Thus $\Gamma(P-\{y\}) \subseteq T$ can be added to II. Then since this condition still holds upon completion of the **for** statement, and the **for** statement achieves $\Gamma(y) \subseteq T$, the condition $\Gamma(P) \subseteq T$ will again hold upon completion of the **while**-statement body. Thus $\Gamma(P) \subseteq T$ is an invariant of the **while** statement (but not a general invariant).

If U is empty then the partition condition implies $P = T$, and the invariant $\Gamma(P) \subseteq T$ implies $\Gamma(T) \subseteq T$, which is a sufficient condition for terminating the **while** statement. Thus we may replace

$$\text{while } \neg\ \Gamma(T) \subseteq T \text{ do } ...$$

by

$$\text{while } \neg\ \text{empty}(U) \text{ do } ...\quad.$$

Of course, the old test $\neg\ \Gamma(T) \subseteq T$ may become false while U is still nonempty, but this only means that our program may continue to loop unnecessarily. Correctness is not affected, since we never used the assumption that $\neg\ \Gamma(T) \subseteq T$ held at the beginning of the **while**-statement body.

At this stage, it is clear that U will be a nonempty subset of T when a member of T is chosen as y. Thus we may replace

$$y := \text{a member of } T$$

by

$$y := \text{a member of } U\quad.$$

By restricting the choice of y to U, we insure that each execution of the **while**-statement body will add a new node to P. Thus the number of such executions cannot exceed the bound N on the number of nodes in the graph.

Each execution of the **for**-statement body iterates over the immediate successors of y or, equally well, over the edges that emanate from y. Thus, since the **for** statement is executed for distinct nodes y, the total number of executions of its body cannot exceed the bound E on the number of edges in the graph.

The body of the conditional statement within the **for** statement always adds a new node to T, which initially contains the single member x. Thus the total number of executions of this body cannot exceed $N - 1$.

These bounds on the number of executions of various parts of our program are as close as we can come to understanding efficiency on the abstract level, since time and space requirements, even to an order of magnitude, will depend upon the choice of representations and the realization of primitive operations. In fact, since they determine the relative frequency with which various primitive operations will be performed, the bounds on number of executions will be crucial for deciding which representations should be used to obtain an efficient concrete program.

The intermediate assertions have served their purpose in demonstrating the correctness of our abstract program, and can now be discarded. Actually there is a small but significant exception. Since $P \cup U = T$ and $z \notin T$ will hold just prior to $T := T \cup \{z\}$, the assertion $z \notin U$ will hold afterwards, so that the following statement $U := U \cup \{z\}$ will insert a *new* member into U. This fact will turn out to be significant for the choice of the representation of U.

At this stage the abstract program illustrates a concept that will reappear in later sections and play a central role in the development of data representation structuring. Consider a variable that is local to a program (or at least whose final value is not used outside of the program). Such a variable is said to be *auxiliary* if all of its occurrences lie within statements whose only effect is to assign to the variable. More generally, a set of variables is said to be *auxiliary* if all of their occurrences lie within statements whose only effect is to assign to members of the set.

The importance of this concept is that the value of an auxiliary variable cannot affect the flow of control or the values of any nonauxiliary variable. As a consequence, one can eliminate auxiliary variables, by deleting their declarations and the statements that assign to them, without affecting the behavior of the program.

(Auxiliary variables are defined in [Owicki 76]. However, the basic concept goes back at least as far as [Lucas 68].)

The set variable P is easily seen to be auxiliary in our abstract program, and can therefore be eliminated. Thus, stripped of the scaffolding used to construct it, the abstract program is

```
node {exp} x; set procedure Γ {node exp}; set {var} T;
    ⋮
{true}
begin set U;
T:={x};  U:={x};
while ⌐ empty(U) do
    begin node y;
    y:=a member of U;
    U:=U−{y};
    for z ∈ Γ(y) do if z ∉ T then
        begin
        T:=T ∪ {z};
        {z ∉ U}
        U:=U ∪ {z}
        end
    end
end
{T=Γ*(x)}   .
```

Exercises

1. The call-by-name variant of the set-iterating **for** statement

    for $K \in S$ **do** B

   can be defined as

    begin set S'; $S' := \{\}$;
    while $\lnot$ **empty**$(S - S')$ **do**
    　　begin node K;
    　　$K :=$ a member of $S - S'$;
    　　B;
    　　$S' := S' \cup \{K\}$
    　　end
    end

   where S' is an identifier that does not occur in the original **for** statement. Use this definition to derive the following inference rule of specification logic [Hoare 72b]:

   Suppose

    K and S' are distinct identifiers of phrase types
    　　node expression and **set expression**,
    S is a set expression,
    B is a statement,
    I is an assertion,
    Σ is a finite set of specifications,

   such that

    K does not occur free in Σ, S, or I,
    S' does not occur free in Σ, S, or B.

   Let $\{S_1 \ldots , S_m\} = \mathscr{F}_{\text{sta-like}}(B)$ and $S_{m+1}, \ldots , S_n$ be any other identifiers distinct from K and S'. Then

   $$\frac{\Sigma \ \& \ S_1 \# K \ \& \ \ldots \ \& \ S_n \# K \ \& \ S_1 \# S' \ \& \ \ldots \ \& \ S_n \# S' \Rightarrow}{\{I \text{ and } S' \subseteq S \text{ and } K \in S - S'\} \ B \ \{I \mid_{S' \to S' \cup \{K\}}\}}{\Sigma \ \& \ S_1 \# S \ \& \ \ldots \ \& \ S_m \# S \to \{I \mid_{S' \to \{\}}\} \ \textbf{for } K \in S \ \textbf{do } B \ \{I \mid_{S' \to S}\}} \quad .$$

2. Weaken the inference rule given above to describe the more indeterminate situation where B can be executed more than once (but at most a finite number or times) for the same member of S. Show informally that the abstract program given in the previous section remains correct with this more indeterminate kind of **for** statement.

3. Transform the fast division program described in Exercise 4 after Section 1.3.5 to make n an auxiliary variable that can be eliminated from the program.

4. Write an abstract program to solve the "single-source single-sink" reachability problem, i.e. write a program that accepts two nodes x and v and the function Γ, and sets a logical variable *reachable* to **true** if and only if $v \in \Gamma^*(x)$. The simplest approach is to modify the program developed in the previous section to terminate with an appropriate **goto** when and if v is added to T.

   A more complex but efficient approach is possible if the input also includes an "immediate predecessor function" $\Gamma^\dagger$ such that $y \in \Gamma^\dagger(x)$ if and only if $\langle y, x \rangle \in$ **edge**. Then one can alternate between generating the set of nodes that can be reached from x and generating the set of nodes that can be reached backwards from v. Termination occurs when these sets intersect or when either set is complete.

5.1.3 The Representation of Finite Sets

We have purposely chosen an algorithm involving finite sets since there is no universally "best" way of representing such sets. Inevitably, choosing a representation to make one primitive operation as efficient as possible will force other primitive operations to be less efficient than in some other representation. Thus a wise choice of a representation can only be made in light of the particular needs of the abstract program, i.e. which primitive operations are used and with what relative frequencies. Moreover, it is often advantageous to choose distinct representations for different set variables.

The following are four fairly obvious ways of representing a set S:

(1) One can enumerate S with an array. Thus S might be the image of the segment of an array W over the interval $\boxed{a \quad b}$:

$$S = \{W \uparrow \boxed{a \quad b}\} \quad .$$

This representation has the advantage that one can insert an element into S in constant time, i.e. in a time independent of the size of S, by simply appending the element to the array segment at one end or the other. One can also test whether S is empty in constant time by simply testing $a > b$.

However, unless there is some control over the number of times a set member may occur in the array segment, the size of the segment can grow far larger than the size of S. This is a sufficiently serious defect to make this representation unsuitable for our purposes.

(2) One can enumerate S by an array segment without duplicate elements:

$$S = \{W \uparrow \boxed{a \quad b}\} \text{ and } \mathbf{ord}_{\neq} W \uparrow \boxed{a \quad b} \quad .$$

Prohibiting duplication insures that $\# \boxed{a \quad b} = \# S$, so that any bound on the size of S provides a bound on storage requirements. Not only can the emptiness of S be tested in constant time, as in (1), but more generally the size of S can be determined in constant time. On the other hand, to test whether a particular element belongs to S one must perform a linear search, in time of order $\# S$.

The price of avoiding duplication is the time required to insert an element into S. In general, one must perform a linear search, in time of order $\# S$, to see if the element is already present. However, this search can be avoided if it is known that the element being inserted does not belong to S, so that a *new* element can be inserted in constant time. This is one of several cases where a fine distinction in the nature of a primitive operation can have a major effect on its efficiency.

Another case is deletion. To delete a *specified* element from S one must perform a linear search to locate the element, in time of order $\# S$. However, to delete an *unspecified member*, i.e. to choose an arbitrary member of S and delete it, one can simply remove an element from one end of the array segment, in constant time.

Finally, consider iterating over the set S, i.e. executing **for** $K \in S$ **do** B. Excluding the time required to execute B repeatedly $\# S$ times, the control of this iteration will require an array scan taking time of order $\# S$.

(3)   If an ordering relation can be defined for the type of elements in S, then one can enumerate S by a strictly ordered array segment:

$$S = \{ W \uparrow \boxed{a \quad b} \} \text{ and ord}_< W \uparrow \boxed{a \quad b} \ .$$

Now binary search can be used in place of linear search, so that an element can be tested for membership in time of order $\log \# S$. On the other hand, when an element is inserted or a specified element is deleted, it may be necessary to move a sizeable subsegment of the array to preserve the ordering. Thus the time required to insert an element, even when it is known to be new, is of order $\# S$ in the worst case. The order of magnitude times for the other operations discussed in (2) remain unchanged.

(4)   Suppose S is known always to be a subset of some fixed, finite universe $\mathscr{U}$ (which would be **node** in the case of a set of nodes). Then S can be represented by a logical array C with domain $\mathscr{U}$ such that $C(x)$ records whether x belongs to S:

$$(\forall x \in \mathscr{U}) \ C(x) = (x \in S) \ .$$

Of course, Algol W does not permit the domain of an array to be an arbitrary finite universe such as **node**, but conceptually this is a straightforward extension of the language.

The number of elements in C is $\# \mathscr{U}$, which may be much larger than the maximum size of S. In many cases, however, this is compensated by the fact that an individual logical array element is much smaller than an array element that must represent a member of S.

In general this kind of representation, called a *characteristic vector*, is complementary to enumeration by an array. Testing membership, or inserting or deleting a specified element can be done in constant time by testing or setting a single array element. However, testing emptiness or deleting an unspecified member requires searching C up to the first true element, which needs time of order $\# \mathscr{U} - \# S$ in the worst case and $\# \mathscr{U} / \# S$ on the average. (Note that the situation deteriorates as S becomes smaller.) Even worse, determining size or iterating over all members of S requires a scan of the entire array, using time of order $\# \mathcal{U}$, regardless of the size of S.

There are many other useful representations of sets, often involving tree or list structures. These include *heaps*, which will be introduced in Section 5.2.3, hash tables [Morris 68], and binary search trees [Nievergelt 73]. Good general references are [Aho 74] and [Knuth 73].

Exercises

1. To each of the representations we have discussed, one could add an integer variable recording the size of S. For each representation, how would this affect the time requirements for the various primitive operations?

2. Suppose that a primitive operation is needed that replaces a set by its union with another set, i.e. that achieves the effect of $S := S \cup T$. Assume that the same representation is used for S and T. For each of the representations discussed above, what would be an efficient method for realizing this operation, and what would be the order of magnitude time requirement? In which cases would it be seriously inefficient to expand $S := S \cup T$ into for $z \in T$ do $S := S \cup \{z\}$?

3. Suppose that a set is represented redundantly by giving both an enumerating array without duplicates and a characteristic vector. What are the order of magnitude time requirements for the primitive operations discussed in the above section?

5.1.4   Representation of the Set Variables T and U

Having discussed the general properties of several representations of sets, we return to the specific problem of determining reachability in a directed graph. We have established the correctness of the abstract program given at the end of Section 5.1.2. Now we must choose representations for the abstract variables in this program and use these representations to transform the program into concrete form.

Fortunately, this kind of problem is not monolithic. In many cases, the representations of different data types, or even of different variables of the same type, can be considered in isolation from one another. In this case, we will separately consider the representations of the set variables T and U, the set function Γ, and finally the representation of nodes themselves.

Consider T. In the abstract program it is subject to three operations: the initialization $T := \{x\}$, which is only performed once, the membership test $z \notin T$, which is performed at most E times, and the insertion $T := T \cup \{z\}$, which is performed at most $N-1$ times. It is obviously more important to optimize the membership test and insertion than the initialization. For this purpose, the best of the four representations discussed in the previous section is clearly the characteristic vector (4), which permits both a membership test and an insertion to be performed in constant time.

Actually, this conclusion is premature. Since T is an output variable, its representation must be suitable, not only to the program we are writing to produce its value, but also to some other program that will use this value. In a real application, this might cause us to choose a different representation for T, or to simultaneously compute T in more than one representation (see Exercise 1 below), or to convert T to another representation after it has been computed. But to keep our example tractable we will assume that a characteristic vector is suitable for the program that will use the value of T.

Now we must transform our program to replace the abstract variable T by a concrete variable representing its value. To do this, we will use the following general method:

(1) One or more concrete variables are introduced to store the representation of one or more abstract variables.

(2) A general invariant called the *representation invariant* is introduced, which describes the relationship between the abstract and concrete variables.

(3) Each assignment to an abstract variable (or more generally, each assignment that affects the representation invariant) is augmented with assignments to the concrete variables that reestablish the representation invariant (or achieve it, in the case of an initialization).

(4) Each expression that contains an abstract variable but occurs outside of an assignment to an abstract variable is replaced by an expression that does not contain abstract variables but is guaranteed by the representation invariant to have the same value.

The last step will render the abstract variables auxiliary, so that their declarations and assignments can be eliminated.

In the present case, the concrete variable will be a characteristic vector whose domain is **node:**

logical array {var} C **(node)**　.

This array must be specified globally since it represents the output of our program. The representation invariant is

$$CI: \ (\forall z \in \text{node}) \ C(z) = (z \in T) \ .$$

To achive CI the initialization $T := \{x\}$ can be augmented with

for $z \in$ **node do** $C(z) := (z = x)$　.

The only other assignment to T is $T := T \cup \{z\}$. To reestablish CI after this assignment, we add $C(z) := \textbf{true}$.

The only occurrence of T in an expression outside of an assignment to T is in the test $z \notin T$. According to CI this test is equivalent to, and can therefore be replaced by, $\neg \ C(z)$.

The result of this transformation is

node {exp} x; **set procedure** Γ {**node** exp};
set {var} T; **logical array** {var} C (**node**);
$\vdots$

{**true**}
begin set U;
$T:=\{x\}$; **for** $z \in$ **node do** $C(z):=(z=x)$;
{**geninv** CI: $(\forall z \in$ **node**$)$ $C(z)=(z \in T)$}
$U:=\{x\}$;
while $\neg$ **empty**(U) **do**
   begin node y;
   $y:=$ a member of U;
   $U:=U-\{y\}$;
   for $z \in \Gamma(y)$ **do if** $\neg$ $C(z)$ **then**
     begin
     begin$_{CI}$ $T:=T \cup \{z\}$; $C(z):=$**true end**;
     $\{z \notin U\}$
     $U:=U \cup \{z\}$
     end
   end
end
$\{T=\Gamma^*(x)$ **and** $(\forall z \in$ **node**$)$ $C(z)=(z \in \Gamma^*(x))\}$.

Again we have used a subscript to indicate that a general invariant may be temporarily falsified in the interior of a block. We have also extended the consequent of the program to express the result $\Gamma^*(x)$ in terms of the concrete variable C.

At this stage T is an auxiliary variable and can be eliminated from the program. The representation invariant CI can also be dropped, since it has served its purpose in demonstrating the correctness of the program transformation.

Next we consider the set variable U. Besides the initialization $U:=\{x\}$, it is subject to three operations, each of which will be performed no more than N times: the emptiness test $\neg$ **empty**(U), the choice and deletion of an unspecified member $y:=$ a member of U; $U:=U-\{y\}$, and the insertion $U:=U \cup \{z\}$, in which z is guaranteed to be a new member by the preceding assertion $z \notin U$.

Because of the emptiness test and the choice of an unspecified member, a characteristic vector would be an unsuitable representation for U. In fact, of the representation methods discussed in Section 5.1.3, only enumeration by an array without duplicate elements (2) permits all three of the frequent operations to be performed in constant time. (Since U is a local variable, we do not need to consider the requirements of an external program.)

To implement this representation we introduce, at the same block level as U, the concrete variables

node array $W(1::N)$; **integer** a, b

and the representation invariant

$$WI: \boxed{1 \quad | a \quad b|} \text{ and } U = \{W \uparrow \boxed{|a \quad b|}\} \text{ and } \textbf{ord}_{\neq} W \uparrow \boxed{|a \quad b|} \ .$$

(Here the partition diagram insures that 1 is a suitable lower bound for the domain of W. The fact that N is a suitable upper bound will be established later.) To achieve this invariant, the initialization $U := \{x\}$ is augmented with $a := 1;\ b := 1;\ W(1) := x$.

The transformation of the abstract operation of choosing and deleting an unspecified member of U is somewhat complicated, since it involves both replacing an expression containing U and augmenting an assignment to U, and since indeterminacy must be resolved. The representation invariant implies that the indeterminate expression "a member of U" can be replaced by $W(k)$ for any value of k in $\boxed{a \quad b}$ (which must be a nonempty interval since U is nonempty). Then after the next operation $U := U - \{y\}$, the representation invariant can be regained by deleting the kth element from the segment of W over $\boxed{a \quad b}$.

Clearly this deletion can be done more easily if $W(k)$ is located at one end or the other of the array segment. Thus we may either (1) replace "a member of U" by $W(a)$ and add $a := a+1$ after $U := U - \{y\}$, or (2) replace "a member of U" by $W(b)$ and add $b := b-1$ after $U := U - \{y\}$. Notice that the freedom to make these especially efficient choices is a consequence of leaving "a member of U" indeterminate at the abstract level.

The only other assignment to U is $U := U \cup \{z\}$. Here, since the precedent $z \notin U$ insures that duplication will be avoided, WI can be regained by appending z to the upper end of the array segment, i.e. by adding the statements $b := b+1;\ W(b) := z$. (Note that appending z to the lower end of the array segment might violate the partition diagram $\boxed{1 \quad |a \quad b|}$.)

Finally, WI implies that the test $\neg$ **empty** (U) can be replaced by $a \le b$. Thus we have

node {**exp**} x; **set procedure** Γ {**node exp**};
logical array {**var**} C (**node**);

$\vdots$

{**true**}
begin set U; **node array** $W(1::N)$; **integer** a, b;
for $z \in$ **node do** $C(z) := (z = x)$;
$U := \{x\}$; $a := 1$; $b := 1$; $W(1) := x$;
{**geninv** WI: $\boxed{1\ \ \boxed{a}\ \ \boxed{b}}$ **and** $U = \{W \uparrow \boxed{a}\ \boxed{b}\}$ **and** $\text{ord}_{\neq} W \uparrow \boxed{a}\ \boxed{b}\}$
while $a \leq b$ **do**
    begin node y;
$$y := \begin{bmatrix} W(a) & \text{①} \\ W(b) & \text{②} \end{bmatrix};$$
    $\textbf{begin}_{WI}\ U := U - \{y\}; \begin{bmatrix} a := a+1 & \text{①} \\ b := b-1 & \text{②} \end{bmatrix}$ **end**;
    for $z \in \Gamma(y)$ **do if** $\neg\ C(z)$ **then**
        begin
        $C(z) :=$ **true**;
        $\{z \notin U\}$
        $\textbf{begin}_{WI}\ U := U \cup \{z\}$; $b := b+1$; $W(b) := z$ **end**
        end
    end
end
$\{(\forall z \in \textbf{node})\ C(z) = (z \in \Gamma^*(x))\}$.

The variable b is initialized to one and is only increased by the statement $b := b+1$, which can be performed at most $N-1$ times. Thus $b \leq N$ will hold throughout the program. This implies $\boxed{1\ \ \boxed{b}} \subseteq \boxed{1\ \ N}$, which in conjunction with $\boxed{1\ \ \boxed{a}\ \ \boxed{b}}$ implies $\boxed{a}\ \boxed{b} \subseteq \boxed{1\ \ N}$, so that the declared bounds of W are adequate to avoid subscript errors.

The circled numbers represent the alternative ways of implementing the choose-and-delete operation. When option ① is used, nodes are added to one end of $W \uparrow \boxed{a}\ \boxed{b}$ and removed from the other. As a consequence, W behaves as a *queue*, i.e. its element values are removed in the same order as they are entered. When option ② is used, nodes are added and removed from the same end of $W \uparrow \boxed{a}\ \boxed{b}$. As a consequence, W behaves as a *stack*, i.e. when a node is removed it is always the most recently entered node remaining in the stack.

The difference between ① and ② has a profound effect upon the order in which the members of $\Gamma^*(x)$ are processed by our algorithm. When ① is used, the nodes in $\Gamma^*(x)$ enter T in a *breadth-first* order, i.e. in increasing order of the minimum number of steps from x. When ② is used, these nodes enter T in a *depth-first* order, i.e. after a node y has entered T, all nodes that can be reached from y (via a path which does not go through a member of T) will enter T before any other nodes.

In our further development of the reachability program, we will only consider option ①, which causes breadth-first search. We will return to the topic of depth-first search in Section 5.4.1.

At this stage, U is an auxiliary variable that can be eliminated, along with the intermediate assertions.

The transformation method illustrated in this section is similar in spirit to that of [Hoare 72c] and [Jones 80]. The relationship between abstract and concrete variables that we call a representation invariant is divided by these authors into two components: a function (called an abstraction function by Hoare and a retrieve function by Jones) mapping concrete into abstract values, and an invariant relationship that is limited to concrete values.

Exercises

1. Suppose that the abstract variable T is retained while the concrete variables W, a, and b are introduced, and option ① is used so that W behaves as a queue. Show that the representation invariant WI can be strengthened to

    $$\boxed{1 \;|\; a \quad b} \text{ and } U=\{W\uparrow \boxed{a \quad b}\} \text{ and } T=\{W\uparrow \boxed{1 \quad b}\}$$
    $$\text{and } \text{ord}_{\neq} W\uparrow \boxed{1 \quad b} \;.$$

    This indicates that W, a, and b provide a compound representation of U and T, where the representation of T is redundant since T is also represented by the characteristic vector C (as in Exercise 3 after Section 5.1.3). By making W and b nonlocal one can produce the redundant representation of $T=\Gamma^*(x)$ as output.

2. Since the abstract reachability program never looks at nodes or edges that cannot be reached from x, the bounds on the number of executions of various operations can be tightened from N and E to $\# \Gamma^*(x)$ and the number of edges that emanate from members of $\Gamma^*(x)$. If these numbers are much smaller than N, then the use of a characteristic vector to represent T becomes undesirable since the slowest part of the program will be the initialization **for** $z \in$ **node do** $C(z):=(z=x)$. In this situation it is better to dispense with the characteristic vector and to use W to enumerate both T and U, as discussed in the previous exercise.

    Transform the abstract program by using this representation.

    (*Hint*: You will need to implement the test $z \notin T$ by a linear search. This can be accomplished by introducing a logical variable *present* and inserting a statement, immediately before the conditional statement that tests $z \notin T$, to achieve the assertion $present = (z \in T)$.)

3. Transform the abstract programs discussed in Exercise 4 after Section 5.1.2 to introduce representations for the set variables. In the version that searches both forward from x and backwards from v, you should be able to fit two enumerating array segments within a single array with domain $\boxed{1 \quad N}$.

5.1.5   Representation of the Function Γ

Next we consider the representation of the input function Γ. In this case the abstract-to-concrete transformation will have a rather different flavor than in the previous section, since Γ is used but not changed by our program, and since its usage controls an iteration. Once we have decided upon a representation and introduced appropriate concrete variables and a representation invariant, there will be no assignments to be augmented, and our only task will be to use the representation invariant to eliminate the single occurrence of Γ in our program without changing its behavior.

This occurrence of Γ controls the iteration in

> **for** $z \in \Gamma(y)$ **do if** $\neg\ C(z)$ **then**
>   **begin** $C(z) := $ **true**; $b := b+1$; $W(b) := z$ **end**   .

To clarify the way in which this statement depends upon Γ, it is helpful to define

> **procedure** *itersucc*(**node** {**exp**} y; **procedure** p {**node exp**});
>   **for** $z \in \Gamma(y)$ **do** $p(z)$.

Then the above statement can be replaced by the call

> *itersucc*$(y,\ \lambda(\textbf{node } \{\textbf{exp}\}\ z).$
>   **if** $\neg\ C(z)$ **then**
>   **begin** $C(z) := $ **true**; $b := b+1$; $W(b) := z$ **end**$)$.

The advantage of this transformation is that the dependence of our program upon Γ is localized in the procedure *itersucc*, so that the effects of the representation of Γ can be considered without reference to the rest of the program. The unusual aspect of the transformation, which is typical of the encapsulation of iterative constructs, is that *itersucc* is a higher-order procedure. Indeed, the transformation of **for** $z \in \Gamma(y)$ **do** S into *itersucc*$(y,$ $\lambda(\textbf{node}\{\textbf{exp}\}\ z).\ S)$ is completely analogous to the transformation of **for** $K := L$ **until** U **do** S into *iterate*$(L, U, \lambda(\textbf{integer}\ \{\textbf{exp}\}\ K).\ S)$ which was discussed in Section 4.1.1.

Frequently in this chapter we will call parameters by name, as in *itersucc*, even when call by value would have the same effect. Although call by value would be more efficient in the final executable version of the program, it is even more efficient to eliminate the procedure from the final version by using the copy rule, and for this purpose call by name is simpler.

Since Γ is a function from nodes to sets of nodes, its representation must provide, for each node y, a representation of the set $\Gamma(y)$. Suppose we choose to represent each $\Gamma(y)$ by a characteristic vector, which is a logical array with domain **node**. Then Γ itself can be represented by an array of characteristic vectors with domain **node**, which is equivalent to a two-dimensional logical array with domain **node** × **node**. Thus we may represent Γ by a concrete variable

> **logical array** {exp} G(**node, node**)   ,

with the representation invariant

$$(\forall y, z \in \textbf{node})\ G(y, z) = (z \in \Gamma(y))\ \ .$$

With this representation, an obvious realization of *itersucc* is

> **procedure** *itersucc*(**node** {exp} y; **procedure** p {**node exp**});
>   **for** $z \in \textbf{node}$ **do if** $G(y, z)$ **then** $p(z)$.

This is a standard way of representing the edge structure of a graph; the array G is often called an adjacency matrix in graph theory. Unfortunately, it is seriously inefficient for the algorithm we are considering, as well as many other algorithms for determining properties of graphs. As we have already pointed out in Section 5.1.3, characteristic vectors can be an inefficient way of controlling iterations over sets. In this case, a call of *itersucc*(y, p) will execute p exactly # $\Gamma(y)$ times, but *itersucc* itself, since it must test $G(y, z)$ for each node z, will require a time of order N, which may be far larger than # $\Gamma(y)$.

As an alternative, suppose we represent each $\Gamma(y)$ by an enumerating array without duplication. Since the size of these arrays will vary for different y, it would be undesirable to collect them into an array of arrays. Instead we will concatenate the array segments for different y into a single array G, which will contain one element for each edge in the graph. Then we will introduce two auxiliary arrays GL and GU such that $GL(y)$ and $GU(y)$ delimit the segment of G that enumerates $\Gamma(y)$.

Thus we introduce the concrete variables

> **node array** {exp} $G(1::E)$; **integer array** {exp} GL, GU(**node**)

and the representation invariant

$$(\forall y \in \textbf{node})\ (\Gamma(y) = \{G \uparrow \boxed{GL(y)\ \ GU(y)}\}$$
$$\textbf{and ord}_{\neq} G \uparrow \boxed{GL(y)\ \ GU(y)})\ \ .$$

With this representation, *itersucc* can be realized by

> **procedure** *itersucc*(**node** {exp} y; **procedure** p {**node exp**});
>   **for** $i := GL(y)$ **until** $GU(y)$ **do** $p(G(i))$.

Now the time required by *itersucc*(y, p), exclusive of the time required for executing p, is of order # $\boxed{GL(y)\ \ GU(y)} = $ # $\Gamma(y)$. It is easy to see that this leads to an execution time for the entire reachability program of order $N + E$.

Exercises

1. Although the two transformations of *itersucc* given above have only been justified informally, a transformation similar to the second of these can be carried out formally in the style of Section 5.1.4. We begin by rewriting the abstract version of *itersucc*, using the definition of the set-iterating **for** statement given in Exercise 1 after Section 5.1.2, as

    > **procedure** *itersucc*(**node** {exp} y; **procedure** p {**node exp**});
    >   **begin set** S'; $S' := \{\}$;
    >   **while** $\neg$ **empty**$(\Gamma(y) - S')$ **do**
    >   **begin node** z; $z :=$ a member of $\Gamma(y) - S'$;
    > $p(z)$; $S' := S' \cup \{z\}$
    >   **end**
    >   **end** .

    Now suppose G, GL, and GU are introduced to represent Γ as a concatenated sequence of enumerating arrays, so that the representation invariant

    $$(\forall y \in \mathbf{node})\ \big(\Gamma(y) = \{G \uparrow \boxed{GL(y)\quad GU(y)}\}$$
    $$\text{and ord}_{\neq}\ G \uparrow \boxed{GL(y)\quad GU(y)}\big)$$

    holds throughout the body of *itersucc*. To represent S', introduce the concrete integer variable i as a local variable of the procedure body, with the representation invariant

    $$\boxed{GL(y)\quad i\quad GU(y)} \text{ and } S' = \{G \uparrow \boxed{GL(y)\quad i}\} \ .$$

    Then transform the body of *itersucc*, in the manner illustrated in Section 5.1.4, to eliminate Γ and make S' auxiliary.

2. What happens to the second realization of *itersucc* given in the above section if the prohibition of duplicate elements is removed from the representation invariant for Γ? How does this affect the reachability program?

5.1.6 Representing Nodes

At this stage, we have developed the following program:

> **node** {exp} x; **node array** {exp} $G(1::E)$;
> **integer array** {exp} GL, GU(**node**); **logical array** {var} C(**node**);
>
> $\vdots$
>
> $\{(\forall y \in \textbf{node})\ (\Gamma(y) = \{G \uparrow \boxed{GL(y) \quad GU(y)}\}$
>   **and** $\text{ord}_{\neq}\ G \uparrow \boxed{GL(y) \quad GU(y)}\)\ \}$
> **begin**
> **procedure** *itersucc*(**node** {exp} y; **procedure** p {**node exp**});
>   **for** $i := GL(y)$ **until** $GU(y)$ **do** $p(G(i))$;
> **node array** $W(1::N)$; **integer** a, b;
> **for** $z \in$ **node do** $C(z) := (z = x)$;
> $a := 1$; $b := 1$; $W(1) := x$;
> **while** $a \leq b$ **do**
>   **begin node** y;
> $y := W(a)$; $a := a + 1$;
>   *itersucc*$(y, \lambda(\textbf{node}\ \{\text{exp}\}\ z)$.
>   **if** $\neg\ C(z)$ **then**
>   **begin** $C(z) := \textbf{true}$; $b := b + 1$; $W(b) := z$ **end**)
>   **end**
> **end**
> $\{(\forall z \in \textbf{node})\ C(z) = (z \in \Gamma^*(x))\}$.

Notice that, since it is a requirement to be met by the external program that computes G, GL, and GU, the representation invariant for Γ occurs as the precedent of this program.

Our final task is to represent nodes themselves. All that happens to nodes in our program is that they are tested for equality and used to index arrays. This reflects the fact that, as far as a directed graph is concerned, nodes are anonymous objects with no structure or arithmetic.

In this situation an obvious and reasonable decision is to represent nodes by integers. Indeed since N is a bound on the number of nodes, we can represent nodes by integers in the interval $\boxed{1 \quad N}$.

We could carry out the kind of transformation used previously, in which each node variable, node-valued array, and node-subscripted array would be replaced by a corresponding concrete entity. But this would be formal overkill. Since **node** is in one-to-one correspondence with a subset of $\boxed{1 \quad N}$, the logic of our program will be unaffected if we simply assume that **node** *is* a subset of $\boxed{1 \quad N}$. Then **node** can be replaced by **integer** when it is used as the data type of a variable, expression, or array element, and by $\boxed{1 \quad N}$ when it is used as an array domain or as a set to be iterated over. (If **node** is smaller than $\boxed{1 \quad N}$ then C will contain extra elements and the initializing **for** statement will assign to these elements, but this will not affect the correctness of the program.)

Thus the final concrete version of our program for reachability is

> **integer** {**exp**} x; **integer array** {**exp**} $G(1::E)$;
> **integer array** {**exp**} GL, $GU(1::N)$; **logical array** {**var**} $C(1::N)$;
> $\vdots$
> {**node** $\subseteq \boxed{1 \quad N}$ **and** $(\forall y \in \textbf{node})\ (\Gamma(y) = \{G \uparrow \boxed{GL(y) \quad GU(y)}\}$
>   **and ord**$_{\neq} G \uparrow \boxed{GL(y) \quad GU(y)}$) }
> **begin**
> **procedure** *itersucc*(**integer** {**exp**} y; **procedure** p {**integer exp**});
>   **for** $i := GL(y)$ **until** $GU(y)$ **do** $p(G(i))$;
> **integer array** $W(1::N)$; **integer** a, b;
> **for** $z := 1$ **until** N **do** $C(z) := (z = x)$;
> $a := 1$; $b := 1$; $W(1) := x$;
> **while** $a \le b$ **do**
>   **begin integer** y;
> $y := W(a)$; $a := a + 1$;
>   *itersucc*$\big(y$, $\lambda(\textbf{integer}\ \{\textbf{exp}\}\ z)$.
>   **if** $\neg\ C(z)$ **then**
>   **begin** $C(z) := \textbf{true}$; $b := b + 1$; $W(b) := z$ **end**)
>   **end**
> **end**
> $\{(\forall z \in \textbf{node})\ C(z) = (z \in \Gamma^*(x))\}$.

Of course, to obtain a highly efficient version of this program one would eliminate the procedure call and lambda expression by applying the copy rule and beta reduction.

The reader may wonder why we did not take nodes to be integers at the beginning of our development. The reason is not that it would have made anything we needed to do more difficult, but rather the converse. The data type **integer** has primitive operations, such as addition or the ordering relation, that are meaningless for nodes. By keeping track of **node** as a distinct data type, we have made it obvious that these operations are not to be applied to the representation of nodes.

We leave it to the reader to check that the execution time of this program is of order $N + E$.

Exercise

1. Implicit in the above discussion is the assumption that the representation of nodes by integers in $\boxed{1 \quad N}$ is suitable for the external programs which produce Γ and use $\Gamma^*(x)$. Assuming that the needs of the external programs require it, how might one handle each of the following situations?

    (a) Nodes are represented by pairs of integers in the block $\boxed{1 \quad N_1} \times \boxed{1 \quad N_2}$.

    (b) Nodes are represented by pairs $\langle i, j \rangle$ of integers such that $i \in \boxed{1 \quad N_1}$ and $j \in \boxed{1 \quad i}$.

    (c) Nodes are represented by a small set of integers that is not a subset of any small interval.

5.1.7 The Computation of Paths

Although the program developed in the preceding sections determines the set of nodes that can be reached from a given node, it does not compute the paths by which these nodes can be reached. In this section we will extend this program to record such paths. First we will extend the abstract program by adding an abstract array of paths. Then we will transform the program to replace this array by a more concrete and efficient encoding.

As defined in Section 5.1.1, a finite nonempty sequence $\langle x_0, \ldots, x_n \rangle$ of nodes is a *path* from x_0 to x_n if x_i is an immediate successor of x_{i-1} for each i in $\boxed{1 \quad n}$. We wish to compute an array *Path* such that, for each node $w \in \Gamma^*(x)$, *Path*(w) is a path from x to w.

Thus we extend the abstract program developed in Section 5.1.2 by introducing the abstract nonlocal array

node sequence array $\{$**var**$\}$ *Path*(**node**)   ,

where **node sequence** is a new data type whose values are finite sequences of nodes. Each time a node is added to T, a path from x to that node will be recorded in *Path*. Thus the program will maintain the general invariant

PI: $(\forall w \in T)$ *Path*(w) is a path from x to w ,

which will imply the desired property of *Path* when $T = \Gamma^*(x)$ at the conclusion of the program.

Initially, since T is set to $\{x\}$, *PI* can be achieved by setting *Path*(x) to $\langle x \rangle$. Each time a new node is added to T, this node will be an immediate successor of y, and y will already belong to T. Thus *Path*(y) will be a path from x to y, and the concatenation *Path*$(y) \oplus_{\text{seq}} \langle z \rangle$ will be a path from x to z, so that the assignment *Path*$(z) := $ *Path*$(y) \oplus_{\text{seq}} \langle z \rangle$ will regain *PI*. Thus our extended abstract program is

node {**exp**} x; **set procedure** Γ {**node exp**}; **set** {**var**} T;
node sequence array {**var**} $Path(\textbf{node})$;

$\vdots$

{**true**}
begin set U; $T := \{x\}$; $Path(x) := \langle x \rangle$;
{**geninv** PI: $(\forall w \in T)$ $Path(w)$ is a path from x to w}
$U := \{x\}$;
while $\neg$ **empty**(U) **do**
    begin node y; $y :=$ a member of U; $U := U - \{y\}$;
    for $z \in \Gamma(y)$ **do if** $z \notin T$ **then**
        begin
        {$x \in T$ **and** $y \in T$ **and** $z \in \Gamma(y)$ **and** $z \notin T$}
        $Path(z) := Path(y) \oplus_{\mathrm{seq}} \langle z \rangle$; $T := T \cup \{z\}$;
        {$z \notin U$}
        $U := U \cup \{z\}$
        end
    end
end
{$T = \Gamma^*(x)$ **and** $(\forall w \in \Gamma^*(x))$ $Path(w)$ is a path from x to w} .

Here the assertion $x \in T$ **and** $y \in T$ **and** $z \in \Gamma(y)$ **and** $z \notin T$ is a consequence of the reasoning in Section 5.1.2 that will be needed to establish the correctness of the transformation of our path-recording extension into a more concrete form. To simplify the exposition of this transformation, we have chosen the order of the two assignment statements following this assertion so that the general invariant PI will hold continuously.

It would be straightforward to represent $Path$ by a two-dimensional array with a row for each path, but this would be grossly inefficient in both space and time. A much more compact representation can be obtained by taking advantage of the fact that each path stored in $Path$ consists of a previously stored path plus a single additional node. Thus $Path$ can be represented by an array of "back links",

    node array {**var**} $Link(\textbf{node})$,

such that each $Path(w)$, except the initial $Path(x) = \langle x \rangle$, consists of the previously stored $Path(Link(w))$ plus the single node w.

More precisely, we add to PI the representation invariant

$$Path(x) = \langle x \rangle \text{ and } (\forall w \in T - \{x\})$$
$$(Link(w) \in T \text{ and } Path(w) = Path(Link(w)) \oplus_{\mathrm{seq}} \langle w \rangle) .$$

To maintain this invariant it is sufficient to assign $Link(z) := y$ each time z is added to T. Thus

$$Path(z) := Path(y) \oplus_{\mathrm{seq}} \langle z \rangle; \quad T := T \cup \{z\}$$

becomes

$$Link(z) := y; \ Path(z) := Path(y) \oplus_{\text{seq}} \langle z \rangle; \ T := T \cup \{z\} \quad .$$

Actually, the reason why *PI* is preserved by these assignments is more subtle than it might appear at first glance. It depends critically upon the fact that, since z is a new node being added to T, the assignments to $Link(z)$ and $Path(z)$ do not overwrite previously stored information.

Assume that

$$PI \text{ and } x \in T \text{ and } y \in T \text{ and } z \in \Gamma(y) \text{ and } z \notin T$$

holds before executing $Link(z) := y$. Since $z \notin T$, the assignment $Link(z) := y$ will not affect $Link(w)$ for any $w \in T - \{x\}$, so that *PI* will remain true and $Link(z) := y$ will give

$$PI \text{ and } x \in T \text{ and } y \in T \text{ and } z \in \Gamma(y) \text{ and } z \notin T \text{ and } Link(z) = y \quad .$$

Then, since $z \notin T$ and $x \in T$ and $y \in T$, the assignment $Path(z) := Path(y) \oplus_{\text{seq}} \langle z \rangle$ will not affect $Path(x)$, or $Path(y)$, or $Path(w)$ for any $w \in T - \{x\}$, or $Path(Link(w))$ when $Link(w) \in T$. Thus *PI* will remain true and the assignment to $Path(z)$ will give

$$PI \text{ and } x \in T \text{ and } y \in T \text{ and } z \in \Gamma(y) \text{ and } z \notin T$$
$$\text{and } Link(z) = y \text{ and } Path(z) = Path(y) \oplus_{\text{seq}} \langle z \rangle \quad .$$

At this point $Path(z)$ will be a path from x through y to z, and $Link(z) \in T$ and $Path(z) = Path(Link(z)) \oplus_{\text{seq}} \langle z \rangle$ will hold. In conjunction with *PI*, this implies that *PI* will continue to hold after z is inserted into the set T.

The representation of *Path* by *Link* is unusual in being *incomplete*. There are arrays of paths such that no value of *Link* would make the representation invariant true. However, such arrays never occur as the value of *Path*, so that the incomplete representation is adequate for this particular program. Indeed, this incompleteness is the underlying reason why we can obtain such a compact representation.

At this stage *Path* is an auxiliary variable in our program and can be eliminated. The rest of the transformation into concrete form follows Sections 5.1.4 to 5.1.6.

Since *Link* is an output variable and the way in which it represents *Path* is rather implicit, it is useful to give a procedure which will make any particular path explicit. A convenient approach is to give a higher-order procedure *iterpath* such that, after our path-finding program has been executed to obtain *Link*, the call $iterpath(y, p)$ for any $y \in \Gamma^*(x)$ will cause the execution of $p(x_0), p(x_1), \ldots, p(x_n)$ for some path $\langle x_0, x_1, \ldots, x_n \rangle$ from x to y.

It is difficult to formulate *iterpath* iteratively since the back links in *Link* lead from y towards x rather than x towards y. Fortunately, the problem can be solved by a straightforward use of recursion:

procedure *iterpath*(**node value** y; **procedure** p {**node exp**});
  if $y = x$ **then** $p(x)$ **else**
        begin *iterpath*($Link(y), p$); $p(y)$ **end**   .

Exercises

1. Using the logic of Chapter 1 and the rule for array assignment given in Section 2.3.2, give a formal proof of

    $\{PI \text{ and } x \in T \text{ and } y \in T \text{ and } z \in \Gamma(y) \text{ and } z \notin T\}$
    $Link(z) := y; \ Path(z) := Path(y) \oplus_{\text{seq}} \langle z \rangle; \ T := T \cup \{z\}$
    $\{PI\}$.

2. Introduce the recording of paths into the single-source single-sink programs derived in Exercise 4 after Section 5.1.2. In the version that searches both forward from x and backward from v, you will obtain backward links from some intermediate node to x and forward links to v. This will lead to a more interesting version of *iterpath*.

5.2 FINDING SHORTEST PATHS

5.2.1 Directed Graphs with Edge Lengths

So far, we have been concerned with finding paths in directed graphs. We now turn to a more difficult but closely related problem: finding shortest paths in directed graphs whose edges have lengths.

In addition to the set **node** and the function Γ which have been used to describe a directed graph, we will assume that there is a function δ from edges to nonnegative real numbers. Specifically, if $y \in \Gamma(x)$, we say that $\delta(x, y) \geq 0$ is the *length* of the edge from x to y.

For example, Figure 5.2 illustrates the same graph as Figure 5.1, with the addition of edge lengths given by the function δ such that

x:	A	A	B	B	B	C	C	D	D
y:	B	D	B	C	E	A	F	E	G
$\delta(x,y)$:	3	4	1	2	3	7	3	1	2

For a path $\langle x_0, \ldots, x_n \rangle$, we define the *length* of the path to be the sum $\sum_{i=1}^{n} \delta(x_{i-1}, x_i)$ of the lengths of its edges. Then if y is reachable from x the minimum of the lengths of all paths from x to y is called the *minimum distance* from x to y and is written $\delta^*(x, y)$.

For example, in Figure 5.2 there are an endless number of paths from **A** to **E**: $\langle \mathbf{A}, \mathbf{D}, \mathbf{E} \rangle$ with length 5, $\langle \mathbf{A}, \mathbf{B}, \mathbf{E} \rangle$ with length 6, $\langle \mathbf{A}, \mathbf{B}, \mathbf{B}, \mathbf{E} \rangle$ with length 7, etc. The minimum distance $\delta^*(\mathbf{A}, \mathbf{E})$ is the length of the shortest of these paths, which is 5.

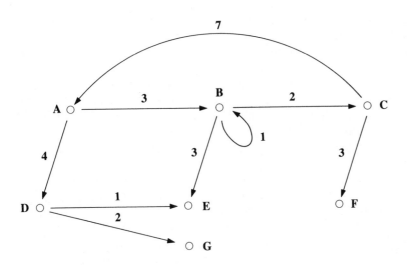

Figure 5.2   A Directed Graph whose Edges have Lengths.

Since edge lengths are nonnegative, path lengths and minimum distances are also nonnegative. However, the length of a path will be zero (which is obviously a minimum distance) if either the path contains zero steps or all of its edges have zero length.

5.2.2   An Abstract Program for Minimum Distances

We now consider the obvious extension of the problem posed in Section 5.1.2: Given a directed graph with edge lengths, to determine the minimum distance from a given node x to each node that can be reached from x. At the abstract level, the input to our program will be the node x, the function Γ from nodes to sets of nodes, and the function δ from pairs of nodes to reals. The output will be a set variable T whose final value, as before, will be $\Gamma^*(x)$, and a real array D with domain **node**, whose final value will be $D(z) = \delta^*(x, z)$ for all $z \in \Gamma^*(x)$.

The single-source abstract algorithm we are going to describe was originally given in [Dijkstra 59]. However, we will begin with an intuitive explanation that is based on a conversation many years ago with R. W. Floyd (who is also responsible for an efficient multiple-source algorithm [Floyd 62]).

Imagine the directed graph being traversed by racing amoebas. Initially there is a single amoeba at node x. The amoebas travel at a fixed speed (of one distance unit per time unit), and whenever an amoeba reaches a node it fissions into enough amoebas to traverse all of the outgoing edges. Intuitively, it is evident that the first amoeba to reach a node will have traversed the shortest path from x to that node in a time equal to the minimum distance.

For example, suppose the amoeba race occurs in the graph of Figure 5.2, starting at node **A**. Figure 5.3 shows the state of the race 3.5 time units after the start. At time zero, two amoebas left **A** moving towards **B** and **D**. The latter amoeba is still enroute, but the former has arrived at **B** and fissioned into three descendents which are now traversing the edges emanating from **B**.

Our abstract program will simulate such an amoeba race. The program will keep track of the instantaneous state of the race by executing a sequence of state changes reflecting the events that would change the state of an actual race. Most critically, these state changes will be executed in the same order as the corresponding events would occur in an actual race.

For our purposes, the state of the amoeba race can be characterized by four variables:

(1) The set P of nodes that have already been reached by amoebas.
(2) The set U (disjoint from P) of nodes that have not yet been reached, but have amoebas racing towards them.
(3) The set T, which is the union of P and U.
(4) A real array D with domain **node**, such that:
   (a) For all $y \in P$, $D(y)$ is the time node y was first reached by an amoeba.
   (b) For all $y \in U$, $D(y)$ is the future time at which node y will first be reached by an amoeba that is currently racing towards it on an incoming edge.

For example, the state of the race shown in Figure 5.3 is

$P = \{A, B\}$
$U = \{C, D, E\}$
$T = \{A, B, C, D, E\}$

y:	A	B	C	D	E	F	G
$D(y)$:	0	3	5	4	6	–	–

For the nodes in P, the array D records the first time of arrival, which is the minimum distance from x. However, this may not be the case for nodes in U. For example, in the above state $D(E) = 6$, reflecting the fact that the first currently existing amoeba will reach **E** at time 6. But as the race unfolds, a descendent of the amoeba currently racing towards **D** will reach **E** at time 5.

The state does not specify the status of losing amoebas, i.e. of amoebas that will not reach their target node until after some other currently

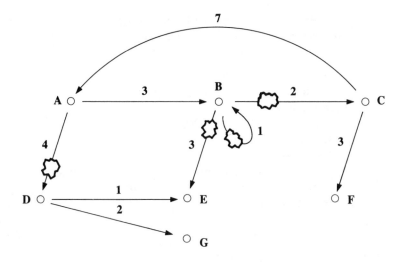

Figure 5.3   An Amoeba Race 3.5 Time Units after Starting at Node **A**.

existing amoeba. Ultimately we are only interested in the arrival times of winners, and a loser or its descendents can never catch up with a winner since all amoebas travel at the same speed.

If U is empty, then there is no amoeba racing towards a previously unreached node, so that the race is over except for the irrelevant behavior of losers. Otherwise, the next state-changing event will be the next arrival of an amoeba at a previously unreached node. This node y will be the member of U for which $D(y)$ has the smallest value, and it will be reached at time $D(y)$.

When the node y is reached, it leaves U and enters the set P. Then, for each $z \in \Gamma(y)$, a descendent amoeba is created which will reach z at time $D(y) + \delta(y, z)$. If z is not in T, then the new descendent is the first amoeba to move towards z, so that z must be added to T and to U, and $D(z)$ must be set to $D(y) + \delta(y, z)$. If z is already in U, then some other amoeba is already racing towards z and will arrive there at time $D(z)$, so that $D(z)$ should only be reset to $D(y) + \delta(y, z)$ if this new arrival time is less than the current value of $D(z)$. Finally, if z is in P then z has already been reached, and the new descendent is clearly a loser who will not affect the state.

To start the race, we can use the initial state $P=\{\}$, $U=\{x\}$, $T=\{x\}$, $D(x)=0$, in which a single amoeba is scheduled to arrive at node x at time zero.

This argument leads to the following abstract program:

328   DATA REPRESENTATION STRUCTURING

node {exp} x; **set procedure** Γ {node exp};
real procedure δ {node exp, node exp};
set {var} T; **real array** {var} D(node);

$\vdots$

$\{(\forall y \in \textbf{node})(\forall z \in \Gamma(y)) \, \delta(y, z) \ge 0\}$
begin set P, U;
$T := \{x\}$; $P := \{\}$; $U := \{x\}$; $D(x) := 0$;
while $\lnot$ **empty**(U) **do**
   begin node y;
   $y :=$ a member of U for which $D(y)$ is a minimum;
   begin $P := P \cup \{y\}$; $U := U - \{y\}$ **end**;
   for $z \in \Gamma(y)$ **do**
     if $z \notin T$ **then**
       begin $T := T \cup \{z\}$; $U := U \cup \{z\}$;
       $D(z) := D(y) + \delta(y, z)$
       end
     else if $z \in U$ **and** $\big(D(z) > D(y) + \delta(y, z)\big)$ **then**
       $D(z) := D(y) + \delta(y, z)$
   end
   end
$\{T = \Gamma^*(x) \text{ and } (\forall z \in \Gamma^*(x)) \, D(z) = \delta^*(x, z)\}$

A program of this kind, in which events within the computer mimic events in the "real" world, is called a *simulation* program. The development of such programs is an important and intensely studied subject which goes far beyond the scope of this book. Two good introductory texts are [Fishman 78] and [Pritsker 79].

In the present instance, however, our real goal is to find minimum distances rather than to simulate amoebas. Since the connection between these goals is only intuitive, it is desirable to buttress this intuition with assertions.

The minimum-distance program is closely related to the abstract reachability program given in Section 5.1.2 (before the removal of the auxiliary variable P). The only difference is that the minimum-distance program keeps track of the array D and uses this array to constrain the indeterminate choice of a member of U. Since constraining an indeterminacy cannot destroy the validity of assertions, all of the assertions in the reachability program are equally valid for the minimum-distance program. But now we must augment these assertions with appropriate properties of the array D:

node $\{$**exp**$\}$ x; **set procedure** Γ $\{$**node exp**$\}$;
real procedure δ $\{$**node exp, node exp**$\}$;
set $\{$**var**$\}$ T; **real array** $\{$**var**$\}$ $D($**node**$)$;

$\vdots$

$\{(\forall y \in$ **node**$)(\forall z \in \Gamma(y))\ \delta(y, z) \geq 0\}$
begin set P, U;
$T := \{x\}$; $P := \{\}$; $U := \{x\}$; $D(x) := 0$;
$\{$**geninv** I: $T \subseteq \Gamma^*(x)$ **and** $x \in T$ **and** $P \cup U = T$ **and** $P \cap U = \{\}$
  and $(\forall z \in T)\ D(z) \geq \delta^*(x, z)$ (1)
  and $D(x) = 0$ (2)
  and $(\forall v \in P)\ (\forall w \in U)\ D(v) \leq D(w)\ \}$ (3)
$\{$**whileinv**: $\Gamma(P) \subseteq T$
  and $(\forall v \in P)\ (\forall z \in \Gamma(v))\ D(z) \leq D(v) + \delta(v, z)\ \}$ (4)
while $\lnot$ **empty**(U) **do**
 begin node y;
 $y :=$ a member of U for which $D(y)$ is a minimum;
 begin$_I$ $P := P \cup \{y\}$; $U := U - \{y\}$ **end**;
 $\{$**geninv** II: $y \in \Gamma^*(x)$ **and** $y \in P$ **and** $\Gamma(P - \{y\}) \subseteq T$
  and $D(y) \geq \delta^*(x, y)$ (1)
  and $(\forall v \in P)\ D(v) \leq D(y)$ **and** $(\forall w \in U)\ D(y) \leq D(w)$ (3)
  and $(\forall v \in P - \{y\})\ (\forall z \in \Gamma(v))\ D(z) \leq D(v) + \delta(v, z)\ \}$ (4)
 for $z \in \Gamma(y)$ **do**
  if $z \notin T$ **then**
   begin$_{I,II}$ $T := T \cup \{z\}$; $U := U \cup \{z\}$;
   $D(z) := D(y) + \delta(y, z)$
  end
  else if $z \in U$ **and** $\big(D(z) > D(y) + \delta(y, z)\big)$ **then**
   $D(z) := D(y) + \delta(y, z)$
 $\{\Gamma(y) \subseteq T$
  and $\big(\forall z \in \Gamma(y)\big)\ D(z) \leq D(y) + \delta(y, z)\ \}$ (4)
 end
end
$\{T = \Gamma^*(x)$
 and $\big(\forall z \in \Gamma^*(x)\big)\ D(z) = \delta^*(x, z)\ \}$.   (5)

Here the lines containing new parts of assertions are numbered. These numbers refer to the following arguments:

(1) Upon initialization, $(\forall z \in T)\ D(z) \geq \delta^*(x, z)$ holds since $T = \{x\}$, $D(x) = 0$, and the minimum distance from x to itself is zero. Assume this

condition holds at the beginning of an iteration of the **while**-statement body. Then, since y is chosen from a subset of T, $D(y) \geq \delta^*(x, y)$ will hold when the **for** statement begins. Moreover, this condition will continue to hold throughout the execution of the **for** statement, since y will be a member of $P = T - U$, so that $D(y)$ will not be assigned to. Thus for each $z \in \Gamma(y)$, $D(y) + \delta(y, z)$ will be at least $\delta^*(x, y) + \delta(y, z)$, which is the length of a path from x through y to z, and therefore at least $\delta^*(x, z)$. Thus the assignments $D(z) := D(y) + \delta(y, z)$ will preserve $(\forall z \in T) \, D(z) \geq \delta^*(x, z)$, which will continue to hold throughout the iteration of the **while**-statement body.

(2)   Initially $D(x) = 0$. Since no element of D is ever increased or made negative, this condition is preserved throughout the program.

(3)   Initially, $(\forall v \in P) \, (\forall w \in U) \, D(v) \leq D(w)$ holds since P is empty. Assume this condition holds at the beginning of an iteration of the **while**-statement body. Then the choice of y to be a member of U for which $D(y)$ is a minimum gives $(\forall v \in P) \, D(v) \leq D(y)$ **and** $(\forall w \in U) \, D(y) \leq D(w)$, and since this condition is preserved by moving y from U into P, it will hold at the beginning of the **for** statement.

Within the **for** statement, since $y \in P$ and the **for** statement does not change P or $D(z)$ for any $z \in P$, the condition $(\forall v \in P) \, D(v) \leq D(y)$ will continue to hold. Moreover, since the **for** statement does not change $D(y)$ and never sets an element of D to a value less than $D(y)$, the condition $(\forall w \in U) \, D(y) \leq D(w)$ will also continue to hold. Finally, since these two conditions imply $(\forall v \in P) (\forall w \in U) \, D(v) \leq D(w)$, this condition will continue to hold throughout the iteration of the **while**-statement body.

This argument is illustrated in Figure 5.4.

(4)   Initially $(\forall v \in P) \, (\forall z \in \Gamma(v)) \, D(z) \leq D(v) + \delta(v, z)$ holds since P is empty. Assume that this condition holds at the beginning of an iteration of the **while**-statement body. Then at the beginning of the **for** statement, after y has been added to P, the condition $(\forall v \in P - \{y\}) \, (\forall z \in \Gamma(v)) \, D(z) \leq D(v) + \delta(v, z)$ holds. Moreover, this condition is preserved since the **for** statement does not change P or y or $D(v)$ for any $v \in P - \{y\}$, and never increases $D(z)$ for any z.

Each execution of the **for**-statement body achieves $D(z) \leq D(y) + \delta(y, z)$ in one of the following ways:

  (a) If $z \notin T$, then $D(z)$ will be set to $D(y) + \delta(y, z)$.
  (b) If $z \in U$, then $D(z)$ will be set to $D(y) + \delta(y, z)$ unless it already possesses a smaller value.
  (c) If $z \in P$, then $D(z) \leq D(y) + \delta(y, z)$ is assured by the condition $(\forall v \in P) \, D(v) \leq D(y)$ in II.

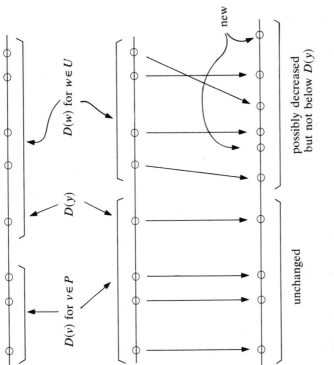

Figure 5.4 The Behavior of D.

$y :=$ a member of U for which $D(y)$ is a minimum;

$\mathbf{begin}_1\ P := P \cup \{y\};\ U := U - \{y\}\ \mathbf{end};$

$\mathbf{for}\ z \in \Gamma(y)\ \mathbf{do}\ \ldots$

Once $D(z) \leq D(y) + \delta(y, z)$ has been achieved for some z it will remain true since the **for** statement does not change $D(y)$ and never increases $D(z)$ for any z. Thus when the **for** statement terminates every $z \in \Gamma(y)$ will satisfy $D(z) \leq D(y) + \delta(y, z)$. In conjunction with $(\forall v \in P - \{y\})$ $(\forall z \in \Gamma(v))$ $D(z) \leq D(v) + \delta(v, z)$, this implies that $(\forall v \in P)$ $(\forall z \in \Gamma(v))$ $D(z) \leq D(v) + \delta(v, z)$ will again hold at the end of the **while**-statement body.

(5)   When the program terminates U will be empty, so that P will be equal to $T = \Gamma^*(x)$. Then the invariant of the **while**-statement implies

$$\left(\forall v \in \Gamma^*(x)\right) \left(\forall z \in \Gamma(v)\right) D(z) \leq D(v) + \delta(v, z) \quad .$$

Moreover, the general invariant I insures that $D(x) = 0$. It follows that $\left(\forall z \in \Gamma^*(x)\right) D(z) \leq \delta^*(x, z)$, i.e. that every path from x to a reachable z will have a length at least $D(z)$. The proof is by induction on the number of steps. The only path of zero steps goes from x to itself, and its length is given exactly by $D(x) = 0$. Any path of $n + 1$ steps from x to z can be divided into a path of n steps from x to v and an edge from v to z, for some v such that $v \in \Gamma^*(x)$ and $z \in \Gamma(v)$. The length of the n-step path is at least $D(v)$ by the induction hypothesis, and the length of the edge is $\delta(v, z)$. Thus the length of the $(n+1)$-step path is at least $D(v) + \delta(v, z)$, which is in turn at least $D(z)$.

In conjunction with the condition $(\forall z \in T) D(z) \geq \delta^*(x, z)$ in I and $T = \Gamma^*(x)$ in the consequent of the program, the above result implies $\left(\forall z \in \Gamma^*(x)\right) D(z) = \delta^*(x, z)$.

As with the reachability program, the body of the **while** statement can be performed no more than N times, since it adds new nodes to P, the body of the **for** statement can be performed no more than E times, since it processes distinct edges, and the statement following **if** $z \notin T$ **then** can be performed no more than $N - 1$ times, since it adds new nodes to T, which starts with one member. However, the second occurrence of $D(z) := D(y) + \delta(y, z)$ can be performed up to (almost) E times.

In addition to establishing the correctness of the abstract program, the assertions we have developed indicate a useful simplification. Consider the test $z \in U$ **and** $\left(D(z) > D(y) + \delta(y, z)\right)$. When this test is executed, the general invariant II insures that $(\forall v \in P) D(v) \leq D(y)$, the general invariant I insures $P \cup U = T$, and the prior test in the conditional statement insures $z \in T$. Thus $D(z) > D(y) + \delta(y, z)$ implies $z \notin P$, and therefore $z \in U$. It follows that the test $z \in U$ is unnecessary and can be eliminated.

Our intermediate assertions have served their purpose and can now be deleted, with the exception of two assertions about membership in U that will influence the transformation to concrete form. As in the reachability program, P is an auxiliary variable and may be eliminated. Thus the final form of the abstract program is

node {exp} x; **set procedure** Γ {**node exp**};
real procedure δ {**node exp, node exp**};
set {**var**} T; **real array** {**var**} D(node);
$\vdots$
$\{(\forall y \in \textbf{node})\ (\forall z \in \Gamma(y))\ \delta(y, z) \geq 0\}$
begin set U;
$T := \{x\};\ U := \{x\};\ D(x) := 0;$
while $\neg$ **empty**(U) **do**
    begin node y;
    $y :=$ a member of U for which $D(y)$ is a minimum;
    $U := U - \{y\}$;
    for $z \in \Gamma(y)$ **do**
        if $z \notin T$ **then**
            begin
            $T := T \cup \{z\}$;
            $\{z \notin U\}$
            $U := U \cup \{z\}$;
            $D(z) := D(y) + \delta(y, z)$
            end
        else if $D(z) > D(y) + \delta(y, z)$ **then**
            $\{z \in U\}$
            $D(z) := D(y) + \delta(y, z)$
    end
end
$\{T = \Gamma^*(x)\ \textbf{and}\ (\forall z \in \Gamma^*(x))\ D(z) = \delta^*(x, z)\}$.

Exercises

1. Where does the reasoning in the above section depend upon the precedent that edge lengths must be nonnegative?

2. Extend the abstract minimum-distance program to compute shortest paths from x to each member of $\Gamma^*(x)$ by adding an array *Path* satisfying the general invariant

    $(\forall w \in T)\ Path(w)$ is a path from x to w of length $D(w)$.

    Show that the resulting program can be transformed into a more concrete form by representing *Path* by an array of back links satisfying the representation invariant

    $Path(x) = \langle x \rangle\ \textbf{and}\ (\forall w \in T - \{x\})$
        $(Link(w) \in P\ \textbf{and}\ Path(w) = Path(Link(w)) \oplus_{\text{seq}} \langle w \rangle)$.

3. Write an abstract single-source single-sink minimum-distance program, i.e. one which determines whether a specific node v can be reached from x and, if so, computes the minimum distance $\delta^*(x, v)$. As in Exercise 4 after Section 5.1.2, one can either develop a straightforward modification of the program given above or, if an immediate predecessor function $\Gamma^\dagger$ is supplied as input, develop a more complex program that searches both forward from x and backwards from v. The latter version can be thought of as a simulation of a race with amoebas running forward from x and backwards from v, so that the shortest path from x to v will be traversed by a pair of amoebas that meet at an intermediate point. (Note, however, that this meeting point might not be a node.)

5.2.3 Representing U by a Heap

Since the usage of the set variable T in the abstract minimum-distance program is the same as in the reachability program, the representation of T by a characteristic vector, as discussed in Section 5.1.4, will permit all the primitive operations on T except its initialization to be executed in constant time. Similarly, the usage of Γ is the same as in the reachability program, so that the argument in Section 5.1.5 in favor of a representation by enumerating arrays remains valid.

However, the usage of U in the minimum-distance program is changed by the fact that y must be chosen to be the (usually) specific member of U for which $D(y)$ is a minimum, rather than an arbitrary member of U. If we were to represent U by an enumerating array without duplicates this choice and deletion operation would require a time of order N, and the entire program would require a time of order N^2. A similar problem would arise with the use of a characteristic vector.

On the other hand, the choice and deletion operation could be done in constant time if U were represented by an enumerating array that was ordered in accordance with the values of D. But the primitive operation of inserting a new element into U would require a time of order N and, even worse, each change in the value of an element of D would necessitate rearranging the enumerating array in time of order N. Thus the entire program would require time of order $E \cdot N$.

A way out of this dilemma is to represent U by an entity called a *heap*, which was invented by [Williams 64] and refined by [Floyd 64]. The basic idea is to arrange the nodes in U as an almost-balanced binary tree such that $D(y) \leq D(z)$ whenever z is a subnode of y in the tree. In this representation it is possible to delete the node with minimum D, to insert a new node, or to alter the value of D at a given node all in time of order $\log N$. Thus the entire program will require a time of order $(N + E) \cdot \log N$. This will be better than the alternatives discussed above as long as the graph is reasonably sparse. (However, when E comes close to its maximum possible value N^2, the use of an enumerating array without duplicates, with total time of order N^2, becomes superior.)

A heap is considerably more complex than the kinds of representations discussed previously. As a first step in its formulation we must define binary trees. Conventionally, such trees are defined to be directed graphs of a certain kind. For our purposes, however, it is simpler to regard all binary trees as subsets of a particular directed graph called the *completely infinite binary tree*, which is illustrated in Figure 5.5.

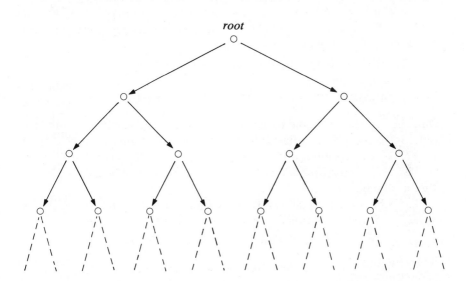

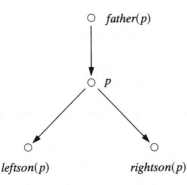

Figure 5.5   The Completely Infinite Binary Tree and its Primitive Operations.

To avoid confusion with the directed graph that is being examined by our program, we will call the nodes of the completely infinite binary tree *positions*, and we will introduce the data types **position** and **position set** to range over positions and sets of positions respectively. Each position p has exactly two immediate successors, called *leftson*(p) and *rightson*(p). A particular position called *root* has no immediate predecessors, while every other position p has exactly one immediate predecessor called *father*(p).

We write $p \sqsubseteq q$ if the position q is reachable from the position p (i.e. if $q \in \Gamma^*(p)$). The use of the symbol $\sqsubseteq$ emphasizes that this relation is a partial ordering, i.e. that it obeys the laws

(1) Transitivity: ($p \sqsubseteq q$ **and** $q \sqsubseteq r$) **implies** $p \sqsubseteq r$,
(2) Reflexivity: $p \sqsubseteq p$,
(3) Antisymmetry: ($p \sqsubseteq q$ **and** $q \sqsubseteq p$) **implies** $p = q$.

(Only the first two laws hold for arbitrary directed graphs, but antisymmetry holds for the completely infinite binary tree since it contains no cyclic paths.)

The special position *root* can be characterized in terms of reachability: It is the only position from which every position can be reached, i.e. such that ($\forall p \in$ **position**) $root \sqsubseteq p$.

Let S be a set of positions. If every finite path that ends in S belongs entirely to S, then S is called a *tree*. More formally, we define

$$Tree(S) = (\forall r \in S)\ (\forall q \in \textbf{position})\ q \sqsubseteq r \textbf{ implies } q \in S\ .$$

It is easy to see that a nonempty tree must contain *root*, and that if p is a tree member other than *root*, *father*(p) must also belong to the tree.

The idea of arranging the nodes in U to form a binary tree can be formalized by saying that there must be a one-to-one correspondence between U and a finite set S of positions that is a tree. Thus we will augment our program by introducing

> **position set** S

along with two arrays for keeping track of the correspondence between U and S:

> **node array** *nodeof*(**position**);
> **position array** *posof*(**node**)   .

The relationship between U and these concrete variables is asserted by the representation invariant

> *TI*: *Tree*(S)
> **and** $\{nodeof \restriction S\} = U$ **and** $\{posof \restriction U\} = S$
> **and** ($\forall p \in S$) $posof(nodeof(p)) = p$
> **and** ($\forall y \in U$) $nodeof(posof(y)) = y$.

Here the last three lines define the concept of a one-to-one correspondence. This concept can also be expressed in terms of the notions of inverse and bijection described in Section 2.3.4: The second line implies that there is a function *nodeof'* from S to U such that $(\forall p \in S)\ nodeof'(p) = nodeof(p)$, and a function *posof'* from U to S such that $(\forall y \in U)\ posof'(y) = posof(y)$. Then the last two lines imply that *nodeof'* and *posof'* are inverses of one another, and therefore bijections.

The main primitive operation to be performed upon this representation is the interchange of the nodes associated with two positions. This operation is accomplished by the following procedure, which exchanges the array elements *nodeof*(*p*) and *nodeof*(*q*) and then modifies *posof* to reestablish the one-to-one correspondence:

> **procedure** *swap*(**position** {**exp**} *p*, *q*);
> {**pa**: *nodeof # p & nodeof # q & posof # p & posof # q*}
> {*TI* **and** *p, q ∈ S*}
> **begin node** *m, n*;
> $m := nodeof(p);\ n := nodeof(q);$
> $nodeof(p) := n;\ nodeof(q) := m;$
> $posof(n) := p;\ posof(m) := q$
> **end**
> {*TI*}   .

We must now formalize the relation of the heap to the array D. As a first step, we note that the value of D that "occurs" at a tree position p is $D(nodeof(p))$. This composition of *nodeof* with D will be used so often that it is useful to declare it as a functional procedure:

> **real procedure** *V*(**position** {**exp**} *p*); $D(nodeof(p))$.

Henceforth, we will call $V(p) = D(nodeof(p))$ the *weight* of *p*.

Since *swap* exchanges *nodeof*(*p*) and *nodeof*(*q*) without changing D, it has the effect of interchanging the weights $V(p)$ and $V(q)$. In effect, we can think of *swap* as an exchange operation for the "abstract array" V that preserves the invariant *TI*. More precisely, if α is a ghost parameter of type **assertion procedure**(**real procedure**(**position exp**)), then *swap* satisfies

> **procedure** *swap*(**position** {**exp**} *p*, *q*);
> {**pa**: *nodeof # p & nodeof # q & nodeof # α*
>   *& posof # p & posof # q & posof # α* }
> {*TI* **and** *p, q ∈ S* **and** $\alpha([V \mid p: V(q) \mid q: V(p)])$}
> **begin node** *m, n*;
> $m := nodeof(p);\ n := nodeof(q);$
> $nodeof(p) := n;\ nodeof(q) := m;$
> $posof(n) := p;\ posof(m) := q$
> **end**
> {*TI* **and** $\alpha(V)$}   .

The relationship of the heap to D is that, whenever $q \sqsubseteq r$ holds between two positions in S, the weight of q is at most the weight of r. This *heap property* is expressed by the representation invariant

   HI: $Heap(S, V)$,

where *Heap* is defined by

>   **assertion procedure** *Heap*
>   **(position set {exp}** S**; real procedure** V **{position exp})**;
> $(\forall q, r \in S) (q \sqsubseteq r$ **implies** $V(q) \le V(r))$.

More succinctly, $Heap(S, V)$ asserts that $V \uparrow S$ is a monotone function, as defined in Section 2.3.4. (However, some of the consequences of monotonicity discussed in that section hold only for total, rather than partial orderings.)

Notice that $Heap(S, V)$ is meaningful even when S is not a tree. Also notice that although HI, in conjunction with TI, describes the representation of U by S, *nodeof*, and *posof*, it also involves the array D via the procedure V, so that D can be thought of as a "parameter" of the representation of U.

The invariant HI expresses the heap property by relating arbitrarily distant positions in S. An alternative is to focus on the relationship between a member of S and its immediate neighbors. Suppose we define

>   **logical procedure** *upgood*
>   **(position {exp}** p**; real procedure** V **{position exp})**;
>   **if** $father(p) \in S$ **then** $V(father(p)) \le V(p)$ **else true**;
>   **logical procedure** *downgood*
>   **(position {exp}** p**; real procedure** V **{position exp})**;
> $\big($**if** $leftson(p) \in S$ **then** $V(p) \le V(leftson(p))$ **else true**$\big)$
>   **and** $\big($**if** $rightson(p) \in S$ **then** $V(p) \le V(rightson(p))$
>   **else true**$\big)$;
>   **logical procedure** *goleft*
>   **(position {exp}** p**; real procedure** V **{position exp})**;
> $leftson(p) \in S$ **and** $\big(V(leftson(p)) \le V(p)\big)$ **and**
> $\big($**if** $rightson(p) \in S$ **then** $V(leftson(p)) \le V(rightson(p))$
>   **else true**$\big)$;
>   **logical procedure** *goright*
>   **(position {exp}** p**; real procedure** V **{position exp})**;
> $rightson(p) \in S$ **and** $\big(V(rightson(p)) \le V(p)\big)$ **and**
> $\big($**if** $leftson(p) \in S$ **then** $V(rightson(p)) \le V(leftson(p))$
>   **else true**$\big)$.

Then, as the reader may verify, the following properties hold:

$Heap(S, V)$ **and** $p \in S$ **implies**
$$upgood(p, V) \text{ and } downgood(p, V) \quad , \tag{1}$$
$Heap(S, V)$ **implies** $Heap(S-\{p\}, [V \mid p: w])$, $\qquad(2)$
$upgood(p, V)$ **and** $V(p) \le w$ **implies** $upgood(p, [V \mid p: w])$, (3)
$downgood(p, V)$ **and** $w \le V(p)$ **implies**
$$downgood(p, [V \mid p: w]) \quad , \tag{4}$$
$\neg\, downgood(p, V)$ **implies** $(goleft(p, V) \text{ **or** } goright(p, V))$, (5)
$upgood(root, V)$. $\qquad\qquad\qquad\qquad\qquad\qquad\qquad\qquad$ (6)

A much less trivial property is:

Theorem 1   If $Tree(S)$ and $Heap(S-\{p\}, V)$ and $upgood(p, V)$
   and $downgood(p, V)$, then $Heap(S, V)$.

Proof: We assume $p \in S$ since otherwise the theorem is obviously true.
Suppose $q \in S$ and $r \in S$ and $q \sqsubseteq r$. Then we must show $V(q) \le V(r)$.

(a) If neither q nor r is p, then $Heap(S-\{p\}, V)$ gives $V(q) \le V(r)$.

(b) If both q and r are p, then trivially $V(q) = V(p) = V(r)$.

(c) Suppose $q \ne p$ and $r = p$. Then there must be a path of at least one
    step from q to p, and this path must contain $father(p)$, so that
    $q \sqsubseteq father(p) \sqsubseteq p$. Moreover, since p belongs to S, which is a tree,
    $father(p)$ must belong to S. Since q and $father(p)$ belong to S,
    neither is p, and $q \sqsubseteq father(p)$, $Heap(S-\{p\}, V)$ implies
    $V(q) \le V(father(p))$. Since $father(p)$ belongs to S, $upgood(p, V)$
    implies $V(father(p)) \le V(p)$. Thus $V(q) \le V(father(p)) \le V(p)$
    $= V(r)$.

(d) Suppose $q = p$ and $r \ne p$. Then there must be a path of at least one
    step from p to r, and this path must contain either $leftson(p)$ or
    $rightson(p)$. We assume the first case (the argument for the second
    case is completely analogous), so that $p \sqsubseteq leftson(p) \sqsubseteq r$. Then since r
    belongs to S, which is a tree, $leftson(p)$ must belong to S. Since
    $leftson(p)$ and r belong to S, neither is p, and $leftson(p) \sqsubseteq r$,
    $Heap(S-\{p\}, V)$ implies $V(leftson(p)) \le V(r)$. Since $leftson(p)$
    belongs to S, $downgood(p, V)$ implies $V(p) \le V(leftson(p))$. Thus
    $V(q) = V(p) \le V(leftson(p)) \le V(r)$. $\qquad\qquad\qquad\qquad$ []

In this theorem, $Heap(S-\{p\}, V)$ can be thought of as asserting that S is a
heap with a "hole" at p, and the theorem as saying that such a hole will
vanish if it satisfies both $upgood(p, V)$ and $downgood(p, V)$.

The next theorem shows how a hole in a heap can be removed by
changing its weight to that of a neighboring position:

Theorem 2 Suppose *Tree(S)* and *Heap(S − {p}, V)*. Then:

(a) If ⌐ *upgood(p, V)* then *Heap(S, [V | p: V(father(p))])*
(b) If *goleft(p, V)* then *Heap(S, [V | p: V(leftson(p))])*
(c) If *goright(p, V)* then *Heap(S, [V | p: V(rightson(p))])*.

Proof: We assume $p \in S$, since otherwise the theorem is obviously true.

(a) Suppose ⌐ *upgood(p, V)*, and let $V' = [V | p: V(father(p))]$. From *Heap(S − {p}, V)* we have *Heap(S − {p}, V')*. Then by Theorem 1, to show *Heap(S, V')* we need only show *upgood(p, V')* and *downgood(p, V')*. To show *upgood(p, V')*, we note that $V'(father(p)) = V(father(p)) = V'(p)$. To show *downgood(p, V')*:

   (i) Suppose *leftson(p)* belongs to S. From ⌐ *upgood(p, V)* we know that *father(p)* also belongs to S. Moreover, since *father(p)* and *leftson(p)* are both distinct from p, these positions belong to S − {p}. Thus *Heap(S − {p}, V)* implies $V(father(p)) \le V(leftson(p))$, which implies $V'(p) \le V'(leftson(p))$.

   (ii) Suppose *rightson(p)* belongs to S. By an argument analogous to (i), we have $V'(p) \le V'(rightson(p))$.

(b) Suppose *goleft(p, V)* and let $V' = [V | p: V(leftson(p))]$. Again *Heap(S − {p}, V)* implies *Heap(S − {p}, V')*, so that by Theorem 1 we need only show *upgood(p, V')* and *downgood(p, V')*.
To show *upgood(p, V')*:
   Suppose *father(p)* belongs to S. From *goleft(p, V)* we know that *leftson(p)* also belongs to S. Moreover, since *father(p)* and *leftson(p)* are both distinct from p, these positions belong to S − {p}. Then *Heap(S − {p}, V)* implies $V(father(p)) \le V(leftson(p))$, which implies $V'(father(p)) \le V'(p)$.
To show *downgood(p, V')*:

   (i) $V'(p) = V(leftson(p)) = V'(leftson(p))$.

   (ii) Suppose *rightson(p)* belongs to S. From *goleft(p, V)* we have $V(leftson(p)) \le V(rightson(p))$. Then $V'(p) \le V'(rightson(p))$.

(c) The argument here is analogous to (b).   ⬚

From this theorem, we can go on to determine when a hole in a heap can be moved by exchanging its weight with that of an adjacent position:

Theorem 3 Suppose *Tree(S)* and *Heap(S−{p}, V)*. Then:

    (a) If $\neg$ *upgood(p, V)* then
                father(p) ∈ *S* and *Heap(S−{father(p)}, V″)*
                and *downgood(father(p), V″)*,
          where $V″=[V\,|\,p{:}\ V(father(p))\,|\,father(p){:}\ V(p)]$.
    (b) If *goleft(p, V)* then
                leftson(p) ∈ *S* and *Heap(S−{leftson(p)}, V″)*
                and *upgood(leftson(p), V″)*,
          where $V″=[V\,|\,p{:}\ V(leftson(p))\,|\,leftson(p){:}\ V(p)]$.
    (c) If *goright(p, V)* then
                rightson(p) ∈ *S* and *Heap(S−{rightson(p)}, V″)*
                and *upgood(rightson(p), V″)*,
          where $V″=[V\,|\,p{:}\ V(rightson(p))\,|\,rightson(p){:}\ V(p)]$.

Proof:

    (a) Since $\neg$ *upgood(p, V)*, we know *father(p)* ∈ *S* and $V(father(p))$
    $>V(p)$. From Theorem 2a, we have *Heap(S, [V | p: V(father(p))])*
    and, by property (1), *downgood(father(p), [V | p: V(father(p))])*.
    Then by property (2) we have *Heap(S−{father(p)},V″)* and by
    property (4) we have *downgood(father(p), V″)*.
Parts (b) and (c) are left to the reader.   ☐

Now suppose we have a heap with a hole that satisfies *downgood*. If
upgood is also satisfied, then Theorem 1 shows that the hole vanishes.
Otherwise, Theorem 3a permits us to move the hole upwards by exchanging
weights with its father and insures that the new hole will also satisfy
downgood. Thus we can repeatedly move the hole along an upward path
until it vanishes.

On the other hand, suppose we have a heap with a hole that satisfies
upgood. If *downgood* is also satisfied, then Theorem 1 shows that the hole
vanishes. Otherwise, property (5) insures that either *goleft* or *goright* is
satisfied, so that Theorem 3b or 3c permits us to move the hole downwards
by exchanging weights with one of its sons, and insures that the new hole will
also satisfy *upgood*. Thus we can repeatedly move the hole along a downward path until it vanishes.

This reasoning leads to the following pair of procedures for eliminating
holes from heaps:

```
procedure ascend(position {var} p);
    {pa: nodeof # p & posof # p}
    {TI and p ∈ S and Heap(S−{p}, V) and downgood(p, V)}
    {whileinv: TI and p ∈ S and Heap(S−{p}, V)
        and downgood(p, V) }
    while ⌐ upgood(p, V) do
        begin swap(p, father(p)); p:= father(p) end
    {TI and Heap(S, V)};
procedure descend(position {var} p);
    {pa: nodeof # p & posof # p}
    {TI and p ∈ S and Heap(S−{p}, V) and upgood(p, V)}
    {whileinv: TI and p ∈ S and Heap(S−{p}, V)
        and upgood(p, V) }
    while ⌐ downgood(p, V) do
        if goleft(p, V) then
            begin swap(p, leftson(p)); p:= leftson(p) end
        else {goright(p, V)}
            begin swap(p, rightson(p)); p:= rightson(p) end
    {TI and Heap(S, V)}   .
```

In each of these procedures the successive values of p trace out a path within the finite set S. Thus termination is insured by the fact that a finite set of positions cannot contain an infinite path.

The condition p ∈ S is needed in the precedents of *ascend* and *descend* to insure that p ∈ S will hold for the first call of *swap*.

At this point it is convenient to use the copy rule to eliminate the calls of *upgood*, *downgood*, and *goleft*. In the procedure *ascend*, the presence of p ∈ S and Tree(S) in the invariant implies that *father*(p) ∈ S can be replaced by p≠root:

```
procedure ascend(position {var} p);
    {pa: nodeof # p & posof # p}
    {TI and p ∈ S and Heap(S−{p}, V) and downgood(p, V)}
    while (p≠root) and (V(father(p))>V(p)) do
        begin swap(p, father(p)); p:= father(p) end
    {TI and Heap(S, V)}   .
```

A similar treatment of *descend* reveals redundant testing that can be eliminated by using **goto**'s and labels. The reader may verify that *descend* can be transformed into

```
        procedure descend(position {var} p);
            {pa: nodeof # p & posof # p}
            {TI and p ∈ S and Heap(S−{p}, V) and upgood(p, V)}
            begin
   loop:   if leftson(p) ∈ S then
                begin
                if rightson(p) ∈ S and (V(rightson(p))<V(leftson(p)))
                    then goto tryright else goto tryleft
                end
            else if rightson(p) ∈ S then goto tryright else goto quit;
 tryleft:   if V(leftson(p))<V(p) then goto left else goto quit;
tryright:   if V(rightson(p))<V(p) then goto right else goto quit;
    left:   {goleft(p, V)}
            swap(p, leftson(p)); p:=leftson(p); goto loop;
   right:   {goright(p, V)}
            swap(p, rightson(p)); p:=rightson(p); goto loop;
    quit:   {downgood(p, V)}
            end
            {TI and Heap(S, V)}   .
```

Having developed these procedures, we may now transform the abstract minimum-distance program of Section 5.2.2 by using a heap to represent U. We introduce the concrete variables

> **position set** S;
> **node array** $nodeof(\textbf{position})$; **position array** $posof(\textbf{node})$;

and the representation invariants

> TI: $Tree(S)$
> **and** $\{nodeof \upharpoonright S\}=U$ **and** $\{posof \upharpoonright U\}=S$
> **and** $(\forall p \in S)\ posof(nodeof(p))=p$
> **and** $(\forall y \in U)\ nodeof(posof(y))=y$

and

> HI: $Heap(S, V)$.

To achieve these invariants initially we augment the assignments

> $U:=\{x\}$; $D(x):=0$

with

> $S:=\{root\}$; $nodeof(root):=x$; $posof(x):=root$.

As a consequence of the one-to-one correspondence expressed by *TI*, the sets *U* and *S* have the same size. Thus the **while**-statement test $\neg$ **empty**(U) can be replaced by $\neg$ **empty**(S).

Next we consider the abstract deletion operation

$$y := \text{a member of } U \text{ for which } D(y) \text{ is a minimum};$$
$$U := U - \{y\} \quad .$$

Since *S* is a nonempty tree, it must contain the node *root*. Then the heap property *Heap*(*S*, *V*) implies $(\forall q \in S) \ V(root) \le V(q)$, the definition of *V* implies $(\forall q \in S) \ D(nodeof(root)) \le D(nodeof(q))$, and the fact that *nodeof* is a one-to-one correspondence from *S* to *U* implies $(\forall z \in U)$ $D(nodeof(root)) \le D(z)$. Thus we can take *y* to be *nodeof*(*root*). However, if we try to maintain the one-to-one correspondence by augmenting $U := U - \{y\}$ with $S := S - \{root\}$, then unless *root* is the only member of *S* its deletion will cause *S* to cease being a tree.

In this case we must proceed in a more roundabout manner. We begin by taking *p* to be a terminal member of *S*, i.e. a position whose deletion will preserve *Tree*(*S*). Next we perform *swap*(*p*, *root*) to make *p* the member of *S* with least weight. Then, after setting *y* to *nodeof*(*p*) and deleting *y* from *U* and *p* from *S*, both the one-to-one correspondence and *Tree*(*S*) will remain true.

However, the swap operation will leave holes in the heap at the positions *root* and *p*, and the hole at *root* will remain after *p* is deleted. Since property (6) insures *upgood*(*root*, *V*), this hole can be eliminated by using the procedure *descend*.

Thus the representation invariants will be preserved if we transform the abstract choice and deletion operation into

```
if S = {root} then
    begin_TI y := nodeof(root); U := U − {y}; S := {} end
else
    begin_HI position p;
    {Heap(S, V) and # S ≥ 2}
    p := a member of S such that Tree(S − {p});
    {Heap(S, V) and root ∈ S and p ∈ S and p ≠ root
        and Tree(S − {p}) }
    swap(p, root);
    {Heap(S − {root, p}, V) and V(p) ≤* {V ↑ S}
        and root ∈ S and p ∈ S and p ≠ root and Tree(S − {p}) }
    y := nodeof(p);
    begin_TI U := U − {y}; S := S − {p} end;
    {Heap(S − {root}, V) and root ∈ S and upgood(root, V)}
    p := root; descend(p)
    end    .
```

Next we consider the abstract operation

$$U := U \cup \{z\}; \; D(z) := D(y) + \delta(y, z) \quad ,$$

which inserts a new member into U and initializes the corresponding value of D. Let p be a nonmember of S such that $S \cup \{p\}$ is a tree. If we augment $U := U \cup \{z\}$ by inserting p into S and setting *nodeof* and *posof* to put z and p into correspondence, then the one-to-one correspondence between U and S will be preserved and S will remain a tree.

Moreover, before the insertion of p, $Tree(S)$ and $p \notin S$ will imply that *leftson*(p) and *rightson*(p) do not belong to S. Since these positions are distinct from p they will still not belong to S after the insertion of p, so that *downgood*(p, V) will hold. This insures that the hole in the heap at p can be eliminated by calling *ascend*(p). Thus the abstract insertion operation can be transformed into

> **begin**$_{HI}$ **position** p;
> $\{Heap(S, V)$ **and** $z \notin U\}$
> $p :=$ a nonmember of S such that $Tree(S \cup \{p\})$;
> $\{Heap(S, V)$ **and** $z \notin U$ **and** $p \notin S$ **and** $Tree(S \cup \{p\})$
>   **and** *leftson*(p), *rightson*$(p) \notin S \cup \{p\}$ $\}$
>   **begin**$_{TI}$ $U := U \cup \{z\}$; $S := S \cup \{p\}$;
>   *nodeof*$(p) := z$; *posof*$(z) := p$
>   **end**;
> $D(z) := D(y) + \delta(y, z)$;
> $\{Heap(S-\{p\}, V)$ **and** $p \in S$ **and** *downgood*$(p, V)\}$
> *ascend*(p)
> **end** .

Finally, we consider the second occurrence of

$$D(z) := D(y) + \delta(y, z) \quad ,$$

which decreases the value of D for a node in U. This operation creates a hole in the heap by decreasing the weight of the position $p = posof(z)$. However, property (4) insures that p will still satisfy *downgood*(p, V), so that the hole can be eliminated by calling *ascend*(p). Thus the above operation can be transformed into

> **begin**$_{HI}$ **position** p;
> $\{Heap(S, V)$ **and** $z \in U$ **and** $D(z) > D(y) + \delta(y, z)\}$
> $D(z) := D(y) + \delta(y, z)$;
> $p := posof(z)$;
> $\{Heap(S-\{p\}, V)$ **and** $p \in S$ **and** *downgood*$(p, V)\}$
> *ascend*(p)
> **end** .

At this stage, the representation invariants and other intermediate assertions have served their purpose, and U has become an auxiliary variable which can be eliminated. This leads to the following program:

```
node {exp} x; set procedure Γ {node exp};
real procedure δ {node exp, node exp};
set {var} T; real array {var} D(node);
⋮
{(∀y ∈ node) (∀z ∈ Γ(y)) δ(y, z) ≥ 0}
begin position set S;
node array nodeof(position); position array posof(node);
... Declarations of swap, V, ascend, and descend ...
T := {x}; D(x) := 0;
S := {root}; nodeof(root) := x; posof(x) := root;
while ⌐ empty(S) do
    begin node y;
    if S = {root} then
        begin y := nodeof(root); S := {} end
    else
        begin position p;
        p := a member of S such that Tree(S − {p});
        swap(p, root); y := nodeof(p); S := S − {p};
        p := root; descend(p)
        end;
    for z ∈ Γ(y) do
        if z ∉ T then
            begin T := T ∪ {z};
                begin position p;
                p := a nonmember of S such that Tree(S ∪ {p});
                S := S ∪ {p}; nodeof(p) := z; posof(z) := p;
                D(z) := D(y) + δ(y, z); ascend(p)
                end
            end
        else if D(z) > D(y) + δ(y, z) then
            begin position p;
            D(z) := D(y) + δ(y, z);
            p := posof(z); ascend(p)
            end
    end
end
{T = Γ*(x) and (∀z ∈ Γ*(x)) D(z) = δ*(x, z)}   .
```

Exercises

1. Use specification logic to derive the following procedure assumption for the
    procedure *swap*:

    $(\forall$ **position exp** $p)$ $(\forall$ **position exp** $q)$

    $(\forall$ **assertion procedure(real procedure(position exp))** $\alpha)$

    $(nodeof \# p$ & $nodeof \# q$ & $nodeof \# \alpha$
       & $posof \# p$ & $posof \# q$ & $posof \# \alpha \Rightarrow$
       $\{TI$ **and** $p, q \in S$ **and** $\alpha([V \,|\, p: V(q) \,|\, q: V(p)])\}$

          $swap(p, q)$ $\{TI$ **and** $\alpha(V)\}$ $)$
    & $(\forall$ **exp-like** $e)$ $(nodeof \# e$ & $posof \# e \Rightarrow swap \# e)$.

    In this derivation you will need to use global assumptions $(\Sigma'$ in rule (R26) for
    procedure declarations) including the static assertion $\{V = nodeof \cdot D\}$, which
    describes the meaning of the function procedure V, as well as various noninter-
    ference assumptions about global identifiers.

2. Show that $Heap(S-\{p\}, V)$ implies $(upgood(p, V)$ **or** $downgood(p, V))$. Then
    use this result to write a procedure satisfying

    procedure *eliminatehole*(**position** $\{$**var**$\}$ $p)$;

       $\{$**pa**: $nodeof \# p$ & $posof \# p\}$
       $\{TI$ **and** $p \in S$ **and** $Heap(S-\{p\}, V)\}$

       $\vdots$

       $\{TI$ **and** $Heap(S, V)\}$.

    Although the need for this procedure does not arise in the minimum-distance
    problem, it can occur in other simulation problems where the time of a future
    event such as arrival at a graph node may be changed arbitrarily rather than just
    decreased.

5.2.4 Representing Trees by Intervals

Since the positions of the completely infinite binary tree form a countably
infinite set, we can represent them by positive integers, i.e. we can take
position to be the set of integers that are larger than zero. One particular
choice for this representation is to number the positions in the order
obtained by scanning successive levels from left to right, as shown in Figure
5.6. The advantage of this choice is that the primitive operations on positions
can be computed easily:

      integer procedure *root*; 1;
      integer procedure *leftson*(**integer** $\{$**exp**$\}$ $p)$; $p \times 2$;
      integer procedure *rightson*(**integer** $\{$**exp**$\}$ $p)$; $p \times 2 + 1$;
      integer procedure *father*(**integer** $\{$**exp**$\}$ $p)$; p **div** 2   .

Notice that $father(root) = 0 \notin$ **position**.

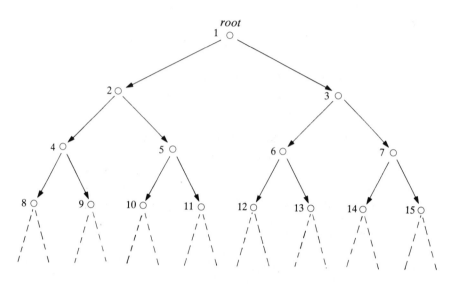

Figure 5.6   Representing Positions by Integers.

Beyond the definition of these procedures, the only effect of introducing this representation into our program is to replace the data type **position** by **integer** and the data type **position set** by **integer set**. (The domain of the array *nodeof* must be an interval containing every integer that can ever belong to *S*. The size of this interval will become apparent later.)

We are left with the problem of representing the integer set *S*. Here we will find that it is not necessary to provide a representation for arbitrary finite sets of integers. In fact, by resolving the indeterminacy in our program appropriately, we will be able to constrain *S* so that its value is always an interval beginning with 1.

Thus to represent *S* we introduce the concrete variable

> **integer** *slim*;

and the representation invariant

$$SI: S = \boxed{1 \quad slim} \quad .$$

As illustrated in Figure 5.7, the interval $\boxed{1 \quad slim}$ will always be an almost-balanced tree. Of course, there are trees (even almost-balanced ones) that are not intervals, but this only means that our representation is *incomplete*, i.e. that some members of the range of the abstract variable are unrepresentable. If we can transform our program in a way that preserves the invariant *SI*, we will have insured that such unrepresentable values are never assigned to *S*. As an added benefit this will imply that *S* is always almost-balanced, so that *ascend* and *descend* can be executed in time of order log *N*.

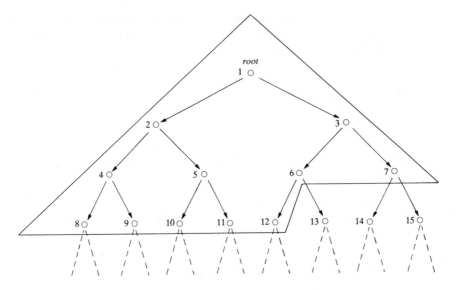

Figure 5.7   Representing Trees by Intervals.

The transformation to concrete form involves the following steps:

(1) In the procedure *descend*, since *leftson(p)* and *rightson(p)* are never less than one, the tests *leftson(p)* ∈ *S* and *rightson(p)* ∈ *S* can be replaced by *leftson(p)* ≤ *slim* and *rightson(p)* ≤ *slim* respectively. Moreover, since *leftson(p)* < *rightson(p)*, *rightson(p)* ∈ *S* implies *leftson(p)* ∈ *S*. In other words, the invariant *SI* limits *S* to trees in which every position with a rightson also has a leftson. Thus the conditional expression

> **if** *leftson(p)* ∈ *S* **then** ...
> **else if** *rightson(p)* ∈ *S* **then goto** *tryright* **else goto** *quit*

can be simplified to

> **if** *leftson(p)* ∈ *S* **then** ... **else goto** *quit*   .

(2) In the main program, the assignment *S*:={*root*} must be augmented with *slim*:=*root*.

(3) The test ⌐ **empty**(*S*) can be replaced by *slim* > 0.

(4) The test *S*={*root*} can be replaced by *slim*=*root*.

(5) The assignment *S*:={} must be augmented with *slim*:=0.

(6) The indeterminate assignment *p*:= a member of *S* such that *Tree(S−{p})* can be replaced by *p*:=*slim*. When the indeterminacy is resolved in this way, *SI* can be preserved by augmenting *S*:=*S*−{*p*} with *slim*:=*slim*−1.

(7) The indeterminate assignment $p := $ a nonmember of S such that $Tree(S \cup \{p\})$ can be replaced by $p := slim + 1$. When the indeterminacy is resolved in this way, SI can be preserved by augmenting $S := S \cup \{p\}$ with $slim := slim + 1$.

Since $S = \boxed{1 \quad slim}$ has the same size as U, it is always a subinterval of $\boxed{1 \quad N}$. Thus, since the elements of $nodeof(p)$ are only accessed when $p \in S$, the domain of $nodeof$ can be taken to be $\boxed{1 \quad N}$.

At this stage the invariant SI has served its purpose, and S has been transformed into an auxiliary variable which can be eliminated. Our program has the form:

```
node {exp} x; set procedure Γ {node exp};
real procedure δ {node exp, node exp};
set {var} T; real array {var} D(node);
    ⋮
{(∀y ∈ node) (∀z ∈ Γ(y)) δ(y, z) ≥ 0}
begin integer slim;
node array nodeof(1::N); integer array posof(node);
integer procedure root; 1;
integer procedure leftson(integer {exp} p); p × 2;
integer procedure rightson(integer {exp} p); p × 2 + 1;
integer procedure father(integer {exp} p); p div 2;
procedure swap(integer {exp} p, q);
    begin node m, n;
    m := nodeof(p); n := nodeof(q);
    nodeof(p) := n; nodeof(q) := m;
    posof(n) := p; posof(m) := q
    end;
real procedure V(integer {exp} p); D(nodeof(p));
procedure ascend(integer {var} p);
    while (p ≠ root) and (V(father(p)) > V(p)) do
        begin swap(p, father(p)); p := father(p) end;
procedure descend(integer {var} p);
    begin
loop: if leftson(p) ≤ slim then
        begin
        if (rightson(p) ≤ slim) and (V(rightson(p)) < V(leftson(p)))
            then goto tryright else goto tryleft
        end
    else goto quit;
tryleft: if V(leftson(p)) < V(p) then goto left else goto quit;
```

```
tryright:  if V(rightson(p)) < V(p) then goto right else goto quit;
    left:  swap(p, leftson(p)); p := leftson(p); goto loop;
   right:  swap(p, rightson(p)); p := rightson(p); goto loop;
    quit:  end;
        T := {x}; D(x) := 0;
        slim := root; nodeof(root) := x; posof(x) := root;
        while slim > 0 do
            begin node y;
            if slim = root then
                begin y := nodeof(root); slim := 0 end
            else
                begin integer p;
                p := slim; swap(p, root); y := nodeof(p); slim := slim − 1;
                p := root; descend(p)
                end;
            for z ∈ Γ(y) do
                if z ∉ T then
                    begin T := T ∪ {z};
                        begin integer p;
                        p := slim + 1; slim := slim + 1;
                        nodeof(p) := z; posof(z) := p;
                        D(z) := D(y) + δ(y, z);
                        ascend(p)
                        end
                    end
                else if D(z) > D(y) + δ(y, z) then
                    begin integer p;
                    D(z) := D(y) + δ(y, z);
                    p := posof(z); ascend(p)
                    end
            end
        end
        {T = Γ*(x) and (∀z ∈ Γ*(x)) D(z) = δ*(x, z)}
```

To produce a fully concrete program, representations must be introduced for the variable T, the procedure Γ, and the data type **node**. The appropriate transformations are the same as those discussed in Sections 5.1.4 to 5.1.6.

*5.3 USING A HEAP TO SORT

In this section we digress from the topic of directed graphs to show how a heap can be used to sort an array segment. Historically, this was the first use of the concept of a heap [Williams 64, Floyd 64].

The basic idea is to construct a heap by inserting each array element, and then to construct an ordered array by repeatedly removing the smallest member of the heap. Since both insertion of an arbitrary element and deletion of the smallest member can be performed in time of order log n, the entire sort requires time of order $n \cdot \log n$.

*5.3.1 An Abstract Program

As in Section 5.2.3, the heap will be a set of positions of the completely infinite binary tree:

> **position set** S .

Now, however, there is no analogue of the one-to-one correspondence between S and a set of graph nodes. Instead, the weights of the positions in S are specified directly by an array:

> **real array** V(**position**) .

(We assume that the elements of the array to be sorted have data type **real**.) Since there is no one-to-one correspondence, the invariant TI is simply

> TI: $Tree(S)$.

The procedure $swap$ is now simply a procedure for exchanging two elements of the array V. However, except for the simpler form of TI and the change of V from a procedure to an array, this new version of $swap$ has the same abstract behavior as in Section 5.2.3:

> **procedure** $swap$(**position** {**exp**} p, q);
> {**pa**: $V \# p$ & $V \# q$ & $V \# \alpha$}
> {TI **and** $p, q \in S$ **and** $\alpha([V \mid p: V(q) \mid q: V(p)])$}
> **begin real** t; $t := V(p)$; $V(p) := V(q)$; $V(q) := t$ **end**
> {TI **and** $\alpha(V)$} ,

where α is a ghost parameter of type **assertion procedure**(**real array** {**exp**} (**position**)).

As before, the invariant HI is

> HI: $Heap(S, V)$.

Aside from the change in the type of V, the definitions of $Heap$, $upgood$, $downgood$, $goleft$, and $goright$ are the same as before, and the theorems about these procedures remain valid. Thus, since $swap$ has the same abstract behavior, the definitions and specifications of $ascend$ and $descend$ remain the same.

The sorting program performs two iterations over the array segment to be sorted. The order of the first iteration has no effect on the abstract algorithm, but we will eventually find that descending order will lead to a more efficient concrete program. In each step of the first iteration a new position p is added to S, in a way which preserves $Tree(S)$, and $V(p)$ is set to the current element of X. Then, since p is a hole in the heap that satisfies $downgood(p, V)$ (because $leftson(p)$ and $rightson(p)$ do not belong to S), $ascend(p)$ is called to eliminate the hole.

The second iteration scans X in ascending order. Each step removes the member p of S for which V has the minimum value and assigns this minimum value to the current element of X. Thus the processed segment of X will be in increasing order and the values in this segment will all be smaller or equal to the values remaining in the heap. As in Section 5.2.3, $Heap(S, V)$ insures that the minimum of V occurs at $root$ but, unless it is the only member of S, $root$ cannot be removed from S without falsifying $Tree(S)$. Again the solution is to take p to be a position whose removal will preserve $Tree(S)$ and to swap the values $V(p)$ and $V(root)$ before removing p. Then after p has been removed, the heap will have a hole at $root$ that satisfies $upgood(root, V)$ (because $root$ has no father), so that $descend$ can be called to eliminate the hole.

This argument leads to the following abstract program:

$\{\boxed{a\quad b} \subseteq \textbf{dom } X \textbf{ and } X = X_0\}$
begin position set S; **real array** V(position); **integer** k;
... Declarations of *swap*, *ascend*, and *descend* ...
$S := \{\}$;
$\{\textbf{geninv } TI\text{: } Tree(S)\}$
$\{\textbf{geninv } HI\text{: } Heap(S, V)\}$
$k := b + 1$;
$\{\textbf{geninv } I1\text{: } \boxed{a\quad k\quad b} \textbf{ and } X\uparrow \boxed{a\quad k} \oplus V\uparrow S \sim X_0 \uparrow \boxed{a\quad b}\}$
while $a < k$ **do**
    begin$_{HI}$ **position** p;
    $p := $ some nonmember of S such that $Tree(S \cup \{p\})$;
    begin$_{I1}$ $k := k - 1$; $S := S \cup \{p\}$; $V(p) := X(k)$ **end**;
    $\{Heap(S - \{p\}, V) \textbf{ and } downgood(p, V) \textbf{ and } p \in S\}$
    $ascend(p)$
    end;
$\{\boxed{a\quad k} = \{\}\}$
$\{\textbf{geninv } I2\text{: } \textbf{ord}_\leq X\uparrow \boxed{a\quad k} \textbf{ and } \{X\uparrow \boxed{a\quad k}\} \leq^* \{V\uparrow S\}\}$
while $k \leq b$ **do**
    if $S = \{root\}$ **then**
        begin$_{I1,I2}$ $X(k) := V(root)$; $S := \{\}$; $k := k + 1$ **end**
    else

$\mathbf{begin}_{HI}$ **position** p;
$p :=$ some member of S such that $Tree(S-\{p\})$;
$swap(p, root)$;
$\{Heap(S-\{root, p\}, V)$ **and** $V(p) \leq^* \{V \uparrow S\}$
    and $root \in S$ **and** $p \in S$ **and** $p \neq root$
      and $Tree(S-\{p\})\}$
$\mathbf{begin}_{I1,I2}$ $X(k) := V(p)$; $S := S-\{p\}$; $k := k+1$ **end**;
$\{Heap(S-\{root\}, V)$ **and** $root \in S$ **and** $upgood(root, V)\}$
$p := root$; $descend(p)$
end

end
$$\{X \uparrow \boxed{a \quad b} \sim X_0 \uparrow \boxed{a \quad b} \text{ and } \mathbf{ord}_{\leq} X \uparrow \boxed{a \quad b}\} \quad .$$

Here we have used the general invariants $I1$ and $I2$ to convey information that would otherwise have to be repeated in invariants of the **while** statements and intermediate assertions. Notice that, within the rearrangement condition

$$X \uparrow \boxed{a \quad} k \oplus V \uparrow S \sim X_0 \uparrow \boxed{a \quad b} \quad ,$$

the general concatenation operator $\oplus$, defined in Section 2.3.7, is applied to a function $V \uparrow S$ whose domain is not a set of integers.

Before transforming the abstract program into concrete form, we note two properties of the program that will be relevant to this transformation. The first is that whenever $swap(p, q)$ is called, the positions p and q will be distinct members of S. The second is that the dependency upon X of the invariants $I1, I2$, and TI, which must be preserved by calls of $swap$, is limited to the segment of X over the interval $\boxed{a \quad} k$.

*5.3.2 A Concrete Program

The transformation of the abstract sorting program into concrete form is similar to that described in Section 5.2.4. Again, we represent positions by integers as in Figure 5.6, so that *root, leftson, rightson*, and *father* have the definitions given in Section 5.2.4. Then we represent the set S by the integer variable *slim*, with the representation invariant

$$SI: S = \boxed{1 \quad slim} \quad .$$

Again, the indeterminacy in the two assignments to p can be resolved in a way that preserves this invariant. We replace $p :=$ some nonmember of S

such that $Tree(S \cup \{p\})$ by $p := slim + 1$, and we replace $p :=$ some member of S such that $Tree(S - \{p\})$ by $p := slim$.

The following program is the result of these transformations. In it we have applied the copy rule to eliminate the procedures *ascend* and *descend*. The domain of V is taken to be $\boxed{1 \quad b-a+1}$ since $\# \boxed{1 \quad slim} = \# S \le \# \boxed{a \quad b} = \# \boxed{1 \quad b-a+1}$, so that $\boxed{1 \quad slim} \subseteq \boxed{1 \quad b-a+1}$.

$\{\boxed{a \quad b} \subseteq \mathbf{dom}\ X \text{ and } X = X_0\}$
begin real array $V(1::b - a + 1)$; **integer** k, $slim$;
... Declarations of *root*, *leftson*, *rightson*, and *father* ...
procedure $swap(\mathbf{integer}\ \{\mathbf{exp}\}\ p,\ q)$;
$\quad \{p \in \boxed{1 \quad slim} \text{ and } q \in \boxed{1 \quad slim} \text{ and } p \ne q\}$
$\quad$ **begin real** t; $t := V(p)$; $V(p) := V(q)$; $V(q) := t$ **end**;
$slim := 0$; $k := b + 1$;
while $a < k$ **do**
$\quad$ **begin integer** p;
$\quad\quad p := slim + 1$; $k := k - 1$; $slim := slim + 1$; $V(p) := X(k)$;
$\quad\quad$ **while** $(p \ne root)$ **and** $(V(father(p)) > V(p))$ **do**
$\quad\quad\quad$ **begin** $swap(p, father(p))$; $p := father(p)$ **end**
$\quad$ **end**;
while $k \le b$ **do**
$\quad$ **if** $slim = root$ **then**
$\quad\quad$ **begin** $X(k) := V(root)$; $slim := 0$; $k := k + 1$ **end**
$\quad$ **else**
$\quad\quad$ **begin integer** p;
$\quad\quad p := slim$; $swap(p, root)$;
$\quad\quad X(k) := V(p)$; $slim := slim - 1$; $k := k + 1$; $p := root$;
$loop$: **if** $leftson(p) \le slim$ **then**
$\quad\quad\quad$ **begin**
$\quad\quad\quad$ **if** $(rightson(p) \le slim)$
$\quad\quad\quad\quad$ **and** $(V(rightson(p)) < V(leftson(p)))$
$\quad\quad\quad$ **then goto** $tryright$ **else goto** $tryleft$
$\quad\quad\quad$ **end**
$\quad\quad\quad$ **else goto** $quit$;
$tryleft$: **if** $V(leftson(p)) < V(p)$ **then goto** $left$ **else goto** $quit$;
$tryright$: **if** $V(rightson(p)) < V(p)$ **then goto** $right$ **else goto** $quit$;
$left$: $swap(p, leftson(p))$; $p := leftson(p)$; **goto** $loop$;
$right$: $swap(p, rightson(p))$; $p := rightson(p)$; **goto** $loop$;
$quit$: **end**
end
$\{X \upharpoonright \boxed{a \quad b} \sim X_0 \upharpoonright \boxed{a \quad b} \text{ and } ord_\le X \upharpoonright \boxed{a \quad b}\}$.

*5.3.3 Further Transformations to Improve Efficiency

The program given in the previous section is fully concrete, in the sense that all of its data types and primitive operations are provided by Algol W. Nevertheless, further transformations can be used to improve its efficiency.

Consider the sequence of calls of *swap* that occur during a single iteration of either outer **while** statement. The last assignment in each call of *swap* (except the final call) will set an element of *V* that will be immediately reset during the next call of *swap*. This is an obvious inefficiency that can be eliminated by transformation.

To represent the array *V* we introduce two concrete variables:

real array $V1(1::b-a+1)$

in the main program and

real z

in each of the blocks in which the integer variable p is declared. Of course, these variables are really no more concrete than *V* itself; we are only calling them "concrete" to emphasize the parallel with the transformations discussed previously. In fact, $V1$ and V will have the same values except that within the blocks in which p and z are declared the value of $V(p)$ will be given by z rather than by $V1(p)$.

More precisely, the general invariant

$$VI: \quad V \uparrow \boxed{1 \quad slim} = V1 \uparrow \boxed{1 \quad slim}$$

will hold during the main program. During the bodies of the blocks where p and z are declared, however, this invariant will be in abeyance and, after initialization, the general invariant

$$VII: \quad V \uparrow \boxed{1 \quad slim} = [V1 \mid p: z] \uparrow \boxed{1 \quad slim}$$

will hold instead.

The invariant *VII* will hold at the beginning of each call of $swap(p, q)$. If the body of *swap* is augmented with the assignment $V1(p) := V1(q)$, then it is straightforward to see that

$$V \uparrow \boxed{1 \quad slim} = [V1 \mid q: z] \uparrow \boxed{1 \quad slim}$$

will hold when the body of *swap* is completed. It follows that each of the following blocks will preserve *VII*:

$$\textbf{begin}_{VII} \; swap(p, father(p)); \; p := father(p) \; \textbf{end};$$
$$\textbf{begin}_{VII} \; swap(p, root);$$
$$\quad X(k) := V(p); \; slim := slim - 1; \; k := k+1; \; p := root \; \textbf{end};$$
$$\textbf{begin}_{VII} \; swap(p, leftson(p)); \; p := leftson(p) \; \textbf{end};$$
$$\textbf{begin}_{VII} \; swap(p, rightson(p)); \; p := rightson(p) \; \textbf{end} \quad .$$

In the main program, the initialization will achieve *VI* by making $\boxed{1 \quad slim}$ empty. Then in the first block where p and z are declared, *VII* will be achieved if we augment $V(p) := X(k)$ with $z := X(k)$; $V1(p) := X(k)$. (Actually $V1(p) := X(k)$ is not needed to achieve *VII*, but it will serve to simplify later developments.) At the end of this block, *VI* can be regained by the assignment $V1(p) := z$.

In the second block where p and z are declared, *VII* will be achieved if $p := slim$ is augmented with $z := V1(slim)$. Again, at the end of the block *VI* can be regained by the assignment $V1(p) := z$.

At this stage we have

$\{\boxed{a \quad b} \subseteq \textbf{dom } X \textbf{ and } X = X_0\}$
begin real array V, $V1(1 :: b - a + 1)$; **integer** k, $slim$;
... Declarations of *root*, *leftson*, *rightson*, and *father* ...
procedure *swap*(**integer** {**exp**} p, q);
$\quad \{p \in \boxed{1 \quad slim} \textbf{ and } q \in \boxed{1 \quad slim} \textbf{ and } p \neq q \textbf{ and } VII\}$
$\quad$ **begin real** t;
$\quad t := V(p)$; $V(p) := V(q)$; $V(q) := t$;
$\quad V1(p) := V1(q)$
$\quad$ **end**;
$\quad \{V \uparrow \boxed{1 \quad slim} = [V1 \mid q: z] \uparrow \boxed{1 \quad slim}\}$
$slim := 0$; $k := b + 1$;
$\{\textbf{geninv } VI: V \uparrow \boxed{1 \quad slim} = V1 \uparrow \boxed{1 \quad slim}\}$
while $a < k$ **do**
$\quad$ **begin**$_{VI}$ **integer** p; **real** z;
$\quad p := slim + 1$; $k := k - 1$; $slim := slim + 1$; $V(p) := V(k)$;
$\quad z := X(k)$; $V1(p) := X(k)$;
$\quad \{\textbf{geninv } VII: V \uparrow \boxed{1 \quad slim} = [V1 \mid p: z] \uparrow \boxed{1 \quad slim}\}$
$\quad$ **while** $(p \neq root)$ **and** $(V(father(p)) > V(p))$ **do**
$\quad\quad$ **begin**$_{VII}$ *swap*$(p, father(p))$; $p := father(p)$ **end**;
$\quad V1(p) := z$
$\quad$ **end**;
while $k \leq b$ **do**
$\quad$ **if** $slim = root$ **then**
$\quad\quad$ **begin** $X(k) := V(root)$; $slim := 0$; $k := k + 1$ **end**
$\quad$ **else**
$\quad\quad$ **begin**$_{VI}$ **integer** p; **real** z;
$\quad\quad p := slim$; $z := V1(slim)$;

$\{$**geninv** *VII*: $V \uparrow \boxed{1 \quad slim} = [V1 \mid p: z] \uparrow \boxed{1 \quad slim}\}$

    begin$_{VII}$

    swap$(p, root)$;

    $\{V \uparrow \boxed{1 \quad slim} = [V1 \mid root: z] \uparrow \boxed{1 \quad slim}$

    and $p \neq root \}$

    $X(k) := V(p)$; $slim := slim - 1$; $k := k + 1$; $p := root$

    end;

  loop: **if** $leftson(p) \leq slim$ **then**

      begin

      if $\big(rightson(p) \leq slim\big)$

             and $\big(V(rightson(p)) < V(leftson(p))\big)$

        then goto *tryright* **else goto** *tryleft*

      end

    else goto *quit*;

  tryleft: **if** $V\big(leftson(p)\big) < V(p)$ **then goto** *left* **else goto** *quit*;

  tryright: **if** $V\big(rightson(p)\big) < V(p)$ **then goto** *right* **else goto** *quit*;

    left: **begin**$_{VII}$ *swap*$\big(p, leftson(p)\big)$; $p := leftson(p)$ **end**;

        goto *loop*;

    right: **begin**$_{VII}$ *swap*$\big(p, rightson(p)\big)$; $p := rightson(p)$ **end**;

        goto *loop*;

    quit: $V1(p) := z$

    end

end

$\{X \uparrow \boxed{a \quad b} \sim X_0 \uparrow \boxed{a \quad b}$ **and** $\text{ord}_{\leq} X \uparrow \boxed{a \quad b}\}$.

To make V auxiliary we must replace all expressions containing V that occur outside of assignments to V by equivalent expressions that do not contain V. In the cases where *VII* holds, we may replace $V(p)$ by z and, since $leftson(p)$, $rightson(p)$, and $father(p)$ are all distinct from p, we may replace V by $V1$ in $V(leftson(p))$, $V(rightson(p))$, and $V(father(p))$.

There are two other cases. For the assignment $X(k) := V(root)$, the invariant *VI* shows that $V(root)$ can be replaced by $V1(root)$. For the assignment $X(k) := V(p)$, the preceding assertion shows that $V(p)$ can be replaced by $V1(p)$.

Once V has been made auxiliary, its declaration and assignments may be eliminated. In particular, the body of *swap* reduces to

    begin real t; $t := z$; $V1(p) := V1(q)$ **end** .

Here t has also become auxiliary, so that the body of *swap* can be reduced further to $V1(p) := V1(q)$.

The elimination of V and t leads to the following program:

```
{ a  b  ⊆ dom X and X=X₀}
begin real array V1(1::b−a+1); integer k, slim;
... Declarations of root, leftson, rightson, and father ...
procedure swap(integer {exp} p, q);
    {p ∈ 1  slim  and q ∈ 1  slim  and p≠q}
    V1(p):=V1(q);
slim:= 0; k:=b+1;
while a<k do
    begin integer p; real z;
    p:=slim+1; k:=k−1; slim:=slim+1;
    z:=X(k); V1(p):=X(k);
    while (p≠root) and (V1(father(p))>z) do
        begin swap(p, father(p)); p:=father(p) end;
    V1(p):=z
    end;
while k≤b do
    if slim=root then
        begin X(k):=V1(root); slim:=0; k:=k+1 end
    else
        begin integer p; real z;
        p:=slim; z:=V1(slim); swap(p, root);
        X(k):=V1(p); slim:=slim−1; k:=k+1; p:=root;
loop:   if leftson(p)≤slim then
            begin
            if (rightson(p)≤slim)
                    and (V1(rightson(p))<V1(leftson(p)))
                then goto tryright else goto tryleft
            end
        else goto quit;
tryleft:  if V1(leftson(p))<z then goto left else goto quit;
tryright: if V1(rightson(p))<z then goto right else goto quit;
left:  swap(p, leftson(p)); p:=leftson(p); goto loop;
right: swap(p, rightson(p)); p:=rightson(p); goto loop;
quit:  V1(p):=z
        end
end
{X ↑ a  b  ∼ X₀ ↑ a  b  and ord≤ X ↑ a  b }  .
```

A final transformation can be used to reduce the storage requirements of this program. In the first part of the program the active portion of $V1$, which is the segment over $\boxed{1 \quad slim}$, grows at the same rate as the inactive portion of X, which is the segment over $\boxed{k \quad b}$. Similarly, in the second part of the program the active portion of $V1$ shrinks at the same rate as the inactive portion of X. Thus it should be possible to use the inactive portion of X to represent the active portion of $V1$, so that the program will only use a constant amount of local storage.

Since the inactive portion of X varies at its left end while the active portion of $V1$ varies at its right end, it is necessary for the elements of $V1$ to occur in X in reverse order. The situation is described by the representation invariant

$$XI: \ k = b + 1 - slim \ \textbf{and} \ (\forall q \in \boxed{1 \quad slim}) \ V1(q) = X(b + 1 - q) \quad .$$

If we regard the statement pairs

$$slim := 0; \ k := b + 1$$
$$k := k - 1; \ slim := slim + 1$$
$$\{slim = root\} \ slim := 0; \ k := k + 1$$
$$slim := slim - 1; \ k := k + 1$$

as indivisible, then the first part of XI is already maintained by our program. To maintain the second part we add assignments to X as follows:

(1) In the body of $swap$, $V1(p) := V1(q)$ is augmented with $X(b + 1 - p) := V1(q)$.

(2) The assignment $V1(p) := X(k)$ is augmented with $X(b + 1 - p) := X(k)$.

(3) Both of the assignments $V1(p) := z$ are augmented with $X(b + 1 - p) := z$.

Here we are adding assignments to the array X, which is already used by our program. However, it is easily seen that each of the added assignments only affects $X \uparrow \boxed{k \quad b}$, while the rest of the program only depends upon $X \uparrow \boxed{a \quad k}$.

Now $V1$ can be made auxiliary by replacing $V1(q)$ by $X(b + 1 - q)$ outside of assignments to $V1$. Similarly k can be made auxiliary by replacing k by $b + 1 - slim$.

Some further simplifications occur. The assignments $X(b + 1 - p)$ $:= X(b + 1 - slim)$ and $X(b + 1 - slim) := X(b + 1 - p)$ can be eliminated since they both occur in contexts where $p = slim$. The assignment $X(b + 1 - slim) := X(b + 1 - root)$ can be eliminated since it occurs in a context where $slim = root$.

After the auxiliary variables and the above assignments have been eliminated, the second outer **while** statement has the form

$$\textbf{while} \ b + 1 - slim \leq b \ \textbf{do}$$
$$\quad \textbf{if} \ slim = root \ \textbf{then begin} \ slim := 0 \ \textbf{end}$$
$$\quad \textbf{else} \ \ldots \quad .$$

Since $root=1$, this is equivalent to

> **while** $slim \geq 1$ **do if** $slim=1$ **then** $slim:=0$ **else** $\ldots$,

which can clearly be replaced by

> **while** $slim>1$ **do** $\ldots$.

Our final program is

$$\{\boxed{a \quad b} \subseteq \textbf{dom } X \textbf{ and } X=X_0\}$$

```
begin integer slim;
    ... Declarations of root, leftson, rightson, and father ...
    procedure swap(integer {exp} p, q); X(b+1−p):=X(b+1−q);
    slim:=0;
    while a<b+1−slim do
        begin integer p; real z;
        p:=slim+1; slim:=slim+1; z:=X(b+1−slim);
        while (p≠root) and (X(b+1−father(p))>z) do
            begin swap(p, father(p)); p:=father(p) end;
        X(b+1−p):=z
        end;
    while slim>1 do
        begin integer p; real z;
        p:=slim; z:=X(b+1−slim); swap(p, root);
        slim:=slim−1; p:=root;
loop:   if leftson(p)≤slim then
            begin
            if (rightson(p)≤slim)
                and (X(b+1−rightson(p))<X(b+1−leftson(p)))
                then goto tryright else goto tryleft
            end
        else goto quit;
tryleft:   if X(b+1−leftson(p))<z then goto left else goto quit;
tryright:  if X(b+1−rightson(p))<z then goto right else goto quit;
left:   swap(p, leftson(p)); p:=leftson(p); goto loop;
right:  swap(p, rightson(p)); p:=rightson(p); goto loop;
quit:   X(b+1−p):=z
        end
    end
```

$$\{X \uparrow \boxed{a \quad b} \sim X_0 \uparrow \boxed{a \quad b} \textbf{ and ord}_\leq X \uparrow \boxed{a \quad b}\}   .$$

Like *mergesort* in Section 3.2.2 and *quicksort* in Section 3.2.3, this program will sort an array segment of n elements in time of order $n \cdot \log n$. Its advantage over *mergesort* is that it requires only a constant amount of storage. Its advantage over *quicksort* is that the time bound of $n \cdot \log n$ extends to the worst case.

Exercises

1.　The program for sorting by repeated insertions, described in Exercise 4 after Section 2.3.3, involves successive exchanges of array elements similar to the calls of *swap* whose efficiency was improved by the transformation discussed in the above section. Improve the efficiency of the insertion-sorting program by a similar transformation. The basic idea is to "represent" the nonlocal array X by another nonlocal array $X1$ that satisfies the general invariants $X = X1$ in the outer block of the program and $X = [X1 \mid c: y]$ in the inner block, where c and y are appropriate local variables of the inner block. The result of the transformation will be a program that sorts $X1$ instead of X.

2.　The inefficiency caused by successive calls of *swap* also occurs in the program for finding minimum distances in a directed graph. Show that this inefficiency can be eliminated by a transformation similar to that described in the above section. One begins by using the copy rule to expand the calls of *ascend* and *descend* in the version of the program developed in Section 5.2.3. In the main block of this program, one declares the concrete variables

$\quad$ **node array** *nodeof*1(**position**); **position array** *posof*1(**node**);

and the procedure

$\quad$ **real procedure** $V1$(**position** $\{\textbf{exp}\}$ p); $D(nodeof1(p))$.

Then in each subsidiary block in which the position p is declared, one declares the concrete variable

$\quad$ **node** t;

In the main program, the general invariant

$\quad$ *NI*: $nodeof \uparrow S = nodeof1 \uparrow S$
$\quad\quad$ **and** $posof \uparrow U = posof1 \uparrow U$
$\quad\quad$ **and** $V \uparrow S = V1 \uparrow S$

is imposed. In the subsidiary blocks where p and t are declared, *NI* is held in abeyance, and

$\quad$ *NII*: $nodeof \uparrow S = [nodeof1 \mid p: t] \uparrow S$
$\quad\quad$ **and** $posof \uparrow U = [posof1 \mid t: p] \uparrow U$
$\quad\quad$ **and** $V \uparrow S = [V1 \mid p: D(t)] \uparrow S$

is imposed. The procedure *swap* is augmented to satisfy

$\quad$ $\{NII$ **and** $p \in S$ **and** $q \in S$ **and** $p \neq q\}$
$\quad$ $swap(p, q)$
$\quad$ $\{nodeof \uparrow S = [nodeof1 \mid q: t] \uparrow S$
$\quad\quad$ **and** $posof \uparrow U = [posof1 \mid t: q] \uparrow U$
$\quad\quad$ **and** $V \uparrow S = [V1 \mid q: D(t)] \uparrow S \}$.

Then these invariants can be used to make *nodeof* and *posof* auxiliary, and also to replace calls of V by $V1$.

5.4　FINDING STRONGLY CONNECTED COMPONENTS

As a final example, we apply the methodology of data representation structuring to an unusually difficult and ingenious algorithm [Tarjan 72] for finding the strongly connected components of a finite directed graph. Our development was inspired by an unpublished presentation of this algorithm by D. E. Knuth.

Two nodes x and y in a directed graph are said to be *strongly connected* if and only if $y \in \Gamma^*(x)$ **and** $x \in \Gamma^*(y)$, i.e. if each node is reachable from the other. The set of nodes that are strongly connected to x is called the *strongly connected component generated by x*.

In the graph shown in Figure 5.1, for example, each of the nodes **A**, **B**, and **C** generates the strongly connected component {**A**, **B**, **C**}. Each of the remaining nodes generates the strongly connected component that is the singleton set containing that node.

It is easy to see that $y \in \Gamma^*(x)$ **and** $x \in \Gamma^*(y)$ is an equivalence relation. As a consequence, the strongly connected components generated by two nodes are either the same or disjoint, and the union of the strongly connected components generated by all nodes is the set of all nodes. In other words, the strongly connected components form a partition of the set of all nodes in the graph. A further consequence is that a strongly connected component is generated by each of its members.

Our development will progress through three stages. We will begin with an abstract recursive program for performing depth-first search. Then by introducing additional abstract variables and operations upon these variables, we will obtain an abstract program for finding strongly connected components. Finally, we will introduce representations for the abstract variables and transform the program into concrete form.

Although this presentation will show why Tarjan's algorithm works, it will hardly make it obvious. Data representation structuring, indeed programming methodology in general, cannot provide the ingenuity that is needed to invent this kind of algorithm. But it can provide a clear retrospective explanation.

5.4.1　Recursive Depth-First Search

In Section 5.1 we developed a program that, when the set of unprocessed nodes was represented by a stack, would sequence through the nodes that were reachable from a given node in depth-first order. We now want to accomplish the same task with a recursive procedure.

The set $\Gamma^*(x)$ of nodes that are reachable from x is the union of {x} with the sets of nodes that are reachable from each of the immediate successors of x. Thus one might expect that, if initially T is the empty set, then the procedure

> **procedure** *search*(**node** {**exp**} *x*);
>   **begin** $T := T \cup \{x\}$; **for** $y \in \Gamma(x)$ **do** *search*(*y*) **end**

would reset T to $\Gamma^*(x)$. But in fact this procedure will never terminate if it encounters a cyclic path in the graph. To avoid this problem, it is sufficient to make the procedure ignore nodes that are already present in T:

> **procedure** *search*(**node** {**exp**} *x*);
>   **if** $x \notin T$ **then**
>   **begin** $T := T \cup \{x\}$; **for** $y \in \Gamma(x)$ **do** *search*(*y*) **end**   .

However, to prove the correctness of this procedure we must describe its behavior when T is not initially empty, and to do so we must formalize the idea of one node being reachable from another via a path that avoids some part of the graph.

Let T be a set of nodes, and consider a path $\langle x_0, \ldots, x_n \rangle$ such that none of the nodes $x_0, \ldots, x_{n-1}$ belongs to T. We call such a path *T-free* (despite the fact that the final node may belong to T). It is easy to see that a path of zero steps is T-free for any T, and that an edge is a T-free path if and only if its initial node does not belong to T. More interestingly, if a path is viewed as a composition of subpaths, then it is T-free if and only if all of the subpaths are T-free.

We write $\Gamma^*(x, T)$ for the set of nodes that can be reached from x via T-free paths. We also write $\Gamma^*(S, T)$ for the set of nodes that can be reached from some member of S via T-free paths. These definitions are a straightforward generalization of the Γ^*-notation introduced in Section 5.1.1, in which $\Gamma^*(x)$ reappears as the special case $\Gamma^*(x, \{\})$.

Our argument about the procedure *search* will depend upon two rather subtle properties of T-free paths. First consider the set

$$\Gamma^*(S_1, T) \cup \Gamma^*(S_2, T \cup \Gamma^*(S_1, T))   .$$

Since a $T \cup \Gamma^*(S_1, T)$-free path is also a T-free path, every member of this set must belong to $\Gamma^*(S_1 \cup S_2, T)$. More surprisingly, the converse also holds. For suppose there is a T-free path from some member u of $S_1 \cup S_2$ to a node x. If any member y of $\Gamma^*(S_1, T)$ occurs on this path, then there is a T-free path from some $s \in S_1$ to y and a T-free path from y to x:

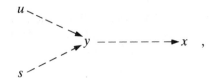

so that the composition of these paths shows that $x \in \Gamma^*(S_1, T)$. On the other hand, if no member of $\Gamma^*(S_1, T)$ occurs on the path from u to x, then this path is $T \cup \Gamma^*(S_1, T)$-free and begins with a member of S_2, so that $x \in \Gamma^*(S_2, T \cup \Gamma^*(S_1, T))$. Thus

$$\Gamma^*(S_1, T) \cup \Gamma^*(S_2, T \cup \Gamma^*(S_1, T)) = \Gamma^*(S_1 \cup S_2, T) \quad . \qquad (1)$$

Secondly, suppose $x \notin T$, and consider the set

$$\{x\} \cup \Gamma^*(\Gamma(x), T \cup \{x\}) \quad .$$

If $z \in \{x\}$ then the zero-step path from x to z, which is T-free, establishes $z \in \Gamma^*(x, T)$. If $z \in \Gamma^*(\Gamma(x), T \cup \{x\})$ then there is an edge from x to some y, which is T-free since $x \notin T$, and a T-free path from y to z. Thus the composite path

$$x \longrightarrow y - - - \rightarrow z$$

is T-free. so that $z \in \Gamma^*(x, T)$.

Conversely, suppose $z \in \Gamma^*(x, T)$, so that there is a T-free path from x to z. If $z = x$ then $z \in \{x\}$. Otherwise, the last occurrence of x on the path must occur before z, so that the path can be decomposed into a path from x to the last occurrence of x, an edge from x to some distinct node y, and a $T \cup \{x\}$-free path from y to z:

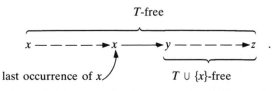

$$T\text{-free}$$

Then.the edge from x to y gives $y \in \Gamma(x)$ and the path from y to z gives $z \in \Gamma^*(y, T \cup \{x\})$, so that $z \in \Gamma^*(\Gamma(x), T \cup \{x\})$. Thus

$$\text{If } x \notin T \text{ then } \{x\} \cup \Gamma^*(\Gamma(x), T \cup \{x\}) = \Gamma^*(x, T) \quad . \qquad (2)$$

We can now show that the procedure call $search(x)$ will increase T by adding the nodes that can be reached from x via T-free paths. More precisely, $search$ will satisfy

$$\{T = T_0\} \; search(x) \; \{T = T_0 \cup \Gamma^*(x, T_0)\} \quad ,$$

where T_0 is a ghost parameter of type **set expression** and it is assumed that T does not interfere with x or T_0.

As is typical with recursive procedures, we assume this specification about calls of $search$ in proving a similar specification of the body of the declaration of $search$. The first step is to show that, for any node sets T_1 and S,

$$\{T = T_1\} \; \textbf{for } y \in S \textbf{ do } search(y) \; \{T = T_1 \cup \Gamma^*(S, T_1)\} \quad .$$

This is most easily shown by induction on the size of S. It is trivial when S is empty. Otherwise, there will be a smaller set S' and a node y_{final} such that $S = S' \cup \{y_{final}\}$ and **for** $y \in S$ **do** $search(y)$ is equivalent to **for** $y \in S'$ **do** $search(y)$; $search(y_{final})$. Then if $T = T_1$ beforehand, the induction hypothesis shows that **for** $y \in S'$ **do** $search(y)$ will achieve $T = T_1 \cup \Gamma^*(S', T_1)$, and the assumption about recursive calls, with x replaced by y_{final} and T_0 by $T_1 \cup \Gamma^*(S', T_1)$, shows that $search(y_{final})$ will achieve

$$T = T_1 \cup \Gamma^*(S', T_1) \cup \Gamma^*(y_{final}, T_1 \cup \Gamma^*(S', T_1)) \quad .$$

By property (1), this implies

$$T = T_1 \cup \Gamma^*(S' \cup \{y_{final}\}, T_1) = T_1 \cup \Gamma^*(S, T_1) \quad .$$

Now suppose that the body of the declaration of *search* is executed with T_0 as the initial value of T. If $x \in T_0$ then $\Gamma^*(x, T_0) = \{x\}$, since the only T_0-free path beginning with $x \in T_0$ is the zero-step path. Thus $T = T_0 \cup \Gamma^*(x, T_0)$ will hold without any assignment to T. On the other hand, suppose $x \notin T_0$. Then $T := T \cup \{x\}$ will achieve $T = T_0 \cup \{x\}$, and the specification we have shown about the **for** statement, with T_1 replaced by $T_0 \cup \{x\}$ and S replaced by $\Gamma(x)$, implies that **for** $y \in \Gamma(x)$ **do** $search(y)$ will achieve

$$T = T_0 \cup \{x\} \cup \Gamma^*(\Gamma(x), T_0 \cup \{x\}) \quad .$$

By property (2), this implies $T = T_0 \cup \Gamma^*(x, T_0)$.

Thus we have

```
procedure search(node {exp} x);
    {T = T₀}
    if x ∉ T then
        begin T := T ∪ {x}; for y ∈ Γ(x) do search(y) end
    {T = T₀ ∪ Γ*(x, T₀)}   .
```

Strictly speaking, the annotation of this procedure declaration should include the parameter assumptions $T \# x$ & $T \# T_0$. For simplicity, however, we will omit the obvious and often lengthy parameter assumptions of the procedures developed in this and later sections.

If $search(x)$ is called with $T = T_0$, then the set of nodes to which *search* will be applied, either directly or recursively, will be $\Gamma^*(x, T_0)$. For later developments, we will need to have this set available just after execution of the **for** statement in the body of *search*. It cannot be obtained from the current value of T, which combines $\Gamma^*(x, T_0)$ with T_0. Thus we will introduce a second global set variable M and extend *search* so that $M = \Gamma^*(x, T_0)$ holds just after the **for** statement.

The overall effect of the call $search(x)$ upon M will be to increase M by $\Gamma^*(x, T_0)$. Upon entrance, if $x \in T$ then x will be inserted into M. Otherwise the initial value of M will be saved as a local variable and M will be reset to $\{x\}$, so that the **for** statement will achieve $M = \{x\} \cup \Gamma^*(\Gamma(x), T_0 \cup \{x\}) = \Gamma^*(x, T_0)$. Then M will be reset to the union of its current value and its initial value:

```
procedure search(node {exp} x);
  {T = T₀ and M = M₀}
  if x ∈ T then M := M ∪ {x} else
    begin set Msave; Msave := M;
    T := T ∪ {x}; M := {x};
    for y ∈ Γ(x) do search(y);
    {T = T₀ ∪ Γ*(x, T₀) and M = Γ*(x, T₀) and Msave = M₀}
    M := Msave ∪ M
    end
  {T = T₀ ∪ Γ*(x, T₀) and M = M₀ ∪ Γ*(x, T₀)}   .
```

The justification of the assertions that appear here is basically the same as before. Beginning with the assumption that recursive calls satisfy

$$\{T = T_0 \text{ and } M = M_0\} \ search(x)$$
$$\{T = T_0 \cup \Gamma^*(x, T_0) \text{ and } M = M_0 \cup \Gamma^*(x, T_0)\} \quad ,$$

one can use property (1) to show

$$\{T = T_1 \text{ and } M = M_1\} \ \text{for } y \in S \ \text{do } search(y)$$
$$\{T = T_1 \cup \Gamma^*(S, T_1) \text{ and } M = M_1 \cup \Gamma^*(S, T_1)\} \quad .$$

Then property (2) can be used to show that the body of the declaration of *search* satisfies the same specification as was assumed for the recursive calls. The details are left to the reader.

Our main program will initialize T and M to be the empty set and then apply *search* to each node of the graph. The overall effect will be to set T (and M) to $\Gamma^*(\text{node}, \{\}) = \Gamma^*(\text{node}) = \text{node}$:

```
{true}
begin set T, M; T := {}; M := {};
  begin
  ... Declaration of search ...
  for y ∈ node do search(y)
  end
{T = node}
end   .
```

(The reason for enclosing the declaration of *search* in a subsidiary block will become apparent later.)

It should be emphasized that the purpose of this program is not just to achieve the trivial final assertion, but to produce a sequence of states satisfying the intermediate assertion within the body of *search*. In particular, in the next section we will add more statements to the program whose correctness will depend upon the validity of the assertion $T = T_0 \cup \Gamma^*(x, T_0)$ and $M = \Gamma^*(x, T_0)$ that occurs after the **for** statement in the body of *search*.

However, further developments will not change the calling tree of our program. Thus at this stage we can express the total execution time of the program in terms of the execution time of individual calls. Suppose we refer to a call $search(x)$ as *terminal* if $x \in T$ and *nonterminal* if $x \notin T$. Since a nonterminal call adds the new node x to T, and T grows from the empty set to the entire set of nodes, there will be exactly one nonterminal call $search(x)$ for each node x, and the number of nonterminal calls will be #**node**.

Terminal calls will not perform subcalls, and each nonterminal call $search(x)$ will perform #$\Gamma(x)$ immediate subcalls. Thus the total number of calls from within the body of *search* will be $\sum_{x \in \textbf{node}} \#\Gamma(x) = \#\textbf{edge}$. In addition, there will be #**node** calls from the main program, so that the total number of calls will be #**node** + #**edge**, and the number of terminal calls will be #**edge**.

Now suppose there are constants α, β, and δ such that the time required by a call $search(x)$, exclusive of the time for subcalls, is bounded by α if the call is terminal and by $\beta + \delta \cdot \#\Gamma(x)$ if the call is nonterminal. Then the total time for the program will be bounded by

$$
\begin{aligned}
&\alpha \cdot \#\textbf{edge} + \sum_{x \in \textbf{node}} \left(\beta + \delta \cdot \#\Gamma(x)\right) \\
&= \alpha \cdot \#\textbf{edge} + \beta \cdot \#\textbf{node} + \delta \cdot \left(\sum_{x \in \textbf{node}} \#\Gamma(x)\right) \\
&= \beta \cdot \#\textbf{node} + (\alpha + \delta) \cdot \#\textbf{edge} \\
&\leq \beta \cdot N + (\alpha + \delta) \cdot E \quad,
\end{aligned}
$$

which is of order $N + E$.

Of course, this result depends upon our ability to produce a concrete program in which a terminal call can be performed in constant time and a nonterminal call $search(x)$ can be performed in time of order $\#\Gamma(x)$. We will eventually achieve this goal by introducing an unusual data representation.

Exercise

1. Use specification logic to formalize the correctness argument for the program developed in the above section. In your proof you will need to use rule (R26) for proper procedure declarations with

$$
\Sigma_{\text{proc}} = (\forall \textbf{node exp } x) (\forall \textbf{set exp } T_0) (\forall \textbf{set exp } M_0)
$$
$$
(T \# x \,\&\, T \# T_0 \,\&\, T \# M_0 \,\&\, M \# x \,\&\, M \# T_0 \,\&\, M \# M_0 \Rightarrow
$$
$$
\{T = T_0 \text{ and } M = M_0\}
$$
$$
search(x)
$$
$$
\{T = T_0 \cup \Gamma^*(x, T_0) \text{ and } M = M_0 \cup \Gamma^*(x, T_0)\})
$$
$$
\,\&\, (\forall \textbf{exp-like } e) (T \# e \,\&\, M \# e \Rightarrow search \# e)
$$

and

$$
\Sigma' = \textbf{gv}(T) \,\&\, \textbf{gv}(M) \,\&\, M \# T \,\&\, T \# \Gamma \,\&\, M \# \Gamma \quad.
$$

You will also need to use the rule for the abstract **for** statement given in Exercise 1 after Section 5.1.2.

5.4.2 An Abstract Program for Strongly Connected Components

We now want to extend the program developed in the previous section to compute the set of strongly connected components. We introduce an output variable SCC, of type **set of sets** (of nodes), which is initialized to the empty set. Within the procedure $search(x)$, immediately after execution of the **for** statement, we will be able to determine whether a certain subset of T is the strongly connected component generated by x and, if so, we will insert this component into SCC.

 We will also introduce a set variable U to keep track of the members of T which have not yet been placed in SCC. Since the strongly connected components are disjoint and we do not wish to output the same component more than once, each time a component is inserted into SCC it will be a subset of U which will then be deleted from U. In fact, the component will consist of the members of U that were not present in U when the current call of *search* began execution.

 Thus we have

```
set procedure Γ {node exp};
set of sets {var} SCC;
⋮
{true}
begin set T, U, M; SCC:={}; T:={}; U:={}; M:={};
{geninv UI: SCC is a set of strongly connected components
        and T−U = U SCC and U⊆T }
    begin
    procedure search(node {exp} x);
        if x∈T then M:= M ∪ {x} else
            begin set Usave, Msave;
            Usave:= U; Msave:= M;
            begin_UI T:= T ∪ {x}; U:= U ∪ {x} end;
            M:={x};
            for y∈Γ(x) do search(y);
            {T=T_0 ∪ Γ*(x, T_0) and M=Γ*(x, T_0)}
            if U−Usave is the strongly connected component
                    generated by x then
                begin_UI
                SCC:= SCC ∪ {U−Usave}; U:= U−(U−Usave)
                end;
            M:= Msave ∪ M
            end;
        for y∈node do search(y)
        end
    {T=node}
    end  .
```

Whenever a new member is added to T it is also added to U. The only other operation affecting U is the removal and output of a subset that is a strongly connected component. Thus as indicated by the general invariant UI, U will always be a subset of T such that $T-U$ is the union $\bigcup SCC$ of the strongly connected components that have been placed in SCC. By placing this general invariant before the block in which *search* is declared, we indicate that it is a *global* invariant, i.e. that it holds throughout the execution of *search* at all recursive levels.

Of course, the test "$U-Usave$ is the strongly connected component generated by x" begs the question of how one finds strongly connected components. However, we will eventually be able to replace it with a more constructive test.

Next, we want to show that a call *search*(x) will increase both of the sets U and $T-U$, i.e. that

$$\{T=T_0 \text{ and } U=U_0\} \ search(x) \ \{U_0 \subseteq U \text{ and } T_0-U_0 \subseteq T-U\} \quad .$$

As usual we will assume this specification about recursive calls while proving that it is met by the body of the declaration of *search*.

Consider an execution of the procedure body beginning with a state in which $T=T_0$ and $U=U_0$. If $x \in T$ then the procedure body will not change T or U and will obviously meet the above specification. On the other hand, if $x \notin T$ then the assignment $Usave := U$ will achieve the general invariant

$$UII: \ Usave = U_0 \subseteq U \text{ and } T_0 - U_0 \subseteq T - U \quad .$$

Assignments to M will obviously preserve UII. Since x is not a member of T or its subset U, the assignments $T := T \cup \{x\}$; $U := U \cup \{x\}$ will preserve UII and also achieve $x \in U - U_0$. Since each recursive call is assumed to increase U and $T-U$, the sequence of such calls performed by **for** $y \in \Gamma(x)$ **do** *search*(y) will also preserve UII and $x \in U - U_0$. Finally $Usave \subseteq U$ implies that $U := U - (U - Usave)$ is equivalent to (and can be replaced by) the simpler statement $U := Usave$, which obviously preserves UII.

Thus we have

```
set procedure Γ {node exp};
set of sets {var} SCC;
  ⋮
{true}
begin set T, U, M; SCC:={}; T:={}; U:={}; M:={};
{geninv UI: SCC is a set of strongly connected components
        and T−U = ∪ SCC and U⊆ T }
    begin
    procedure search(node {exp} x);
        {T = T₀ and U = U₀}
        if x∈ T then M:= M ∪ {x} else
            begin set Usave, Msave; Usave:= U;
            {geninv UII: Usave= U₀ ⊆ U and T₀− U₀ ⊆ T− U}
            Msave:= M;
            begin_UI T:= T ∪ {x}; U:= U ∪ {x} end;
            M:= {x};
            {x∈ U− U₀}
            for y∈ Γ(x) do search(y);
            {T= T₀ ∪ Γ*(x, T₀) and M= Γ*(x, T₀) and x∈ U− U₀}
            if  U− Usave  is the  strongly  connected  component
                    generated by x then
                begin_UI SCC:= SCC ∪ {U− Usave}; U:= Usave
                end;
            M:= Msave ∪ M
            end;
        {U₀ ⊆ U and T₀− U₀ ⊆ T− U}
    for y∈ node do search(y)
    end
{T= node}
end  .
```

Notice that *UII* is a *local* invariant of the procedure *search*, since it contains
the local variable *Usave* and the ghost parameters T_0 and U_0. Thus it
describes a particular level of recursion, in contrast to the global assertion *UI*
which holds for all levels of recursion.

Finally we come to the crux of the behavior of the abstract program. We
will show that, if x is reachable from every member of U before a call of
search(x), then there will be a path from every member of U after the call to
some member of U before the call. In other words, we will show that the
specification of *search* can be strengthened to

$$\{T= T_0 \text{ and } U= U_0 \text{ and } (\forall u\in U)\, x\in \Gamma^*(u)\}$$
$$search(x)$$
$$\{U_0\subseteq U \text{ and } T_0- U_0\subseteq T- U \text{ and } (\forall u\in U)(\exists v\in U_0)\, v\in \Gamma^*(u)\} .$$

In proving this specification, we will also be able to find a constructive equivalent of the test that $U - Usave$ is the strongly connected component generated by x.

Suppose $T = T_0$ **and** $U = U_0$ **and** $(\forall\ u \in U)\, x \in \Gamma^*(u)$ holds before execution of the procedure body. If $x \in T$, then U will not be changed, so that $(\forall\ u \in U)\, (\exists\ v \in U_0)\, v \in \Gamma^*(u)$ will hold since there is a path from every member of U to itself.

On the other hand, suppose $x \notin T$. Then we can show that $(\forall u \in U)$ $x \in \Gamma^*(u)$ holds throughout the execution of the procedure body and can therefore be added to the local invariant UII. This condition is preserved by adding x to U since x is reachable from itself, and it is obviously preserved if U is replaced by its subset $Usave$. The critical point is to show that it is preserved by the recursive calls of $search(y)$ within the **for** statement.

Let U_{before} and U_{after} be the values of U before and after such a call, and suppose x is reachable from every member of U_{before}. Then its immediate successor $y \in \Gamma(x)$ will also be reachable from these members, so that the assumption about recursive calls implies that from every $u \in U_{after}$ one can reach some $v \in U_{before}$. By path composition it follows that x can be reached from every member of U_{after}:

$$u - - - - \to v - - - - - \to x \longrightarrow y \ .$$

$$\in U_{after} \qquad \in U_{before} \qquad\qquad\qquad \in \Gamma(x)$$

Now consider the situation immediately after execution of the **for** statement. From UI, UII, the assertion following the **for** statement, and the argument given above, we know that the following conditions will hold:

> SCC is a set of strongly connected components
> **and** $T - U = \cup\ SCC$ **and** $U \subseteq T$
> **and** $Usave = U_0 \subseteq U$ **and** $T_0 - U_0 \subseteq T - U$
> **and** $T = T_0 \cup \Gamma^*(x, T_0)$ **and** $M = \Gamma^*(x, T_0)$ **and** $x \in U - U_0$
> **and** $(\forall u \in U)\, x \in \Gamma^*(u)$.

Let z be any member of $U - U_0$. Since z belongs to U, it does not belong to $T - U$, nor to its subset $T_0 - U_0$. Then since z does not belong to U_0, it does not belong to T_0. Thus T_0 is disjoint from $U - U_0$. Moreover, since $z \in U \subseteq T = T_0 \cup \Gamma^*(x, T_0) = T_0 \cup M$, we have $z \in M$. Thus $U - U_0$ is a subset of M.

Since $M = \Gamma^*(x, T_0)$, every node in M is reachable from x. On the other hand, since $(\forall u \in U)\, x \in \Gamma^*(u)$, x is reachable from every node in U. Thus every node in $M \cap U$ is strongly connected to x, so that $M \cap U$ is a subset of the strongly connected component generated by x.

Since $U_0 \subseteq U$, $M \cap U$ is the union of the disjoint subsets $M \cap (U - U_0)$ and $M \cap U_0$. Moreover, since $U - U_0 \subseteq M$, the first of these subsets is $U - U_0$.

Thus every node in $U - U_0$ is strongly connected to x, and if $U - U_0$ is the entire strongly connected component generated by x then $M \cap U_0$ is empty.

On the other hand, if $U - U_0$ is not the entire strongly connected component generated by x, then there must be a cyclic path from $x \in U - U_0$ back to x which passes outside of $U - U_0$. Let v be the first node on this path which lies outside of $U - U_0$. Then there is a path from x to v in which every nonfinal node lies in $U - U_0$ and, since T_0 is disjoint from $U - U_0$, this path is T_0-free. Thus v belongs to $\Gamma^*(x, T_0) = M$, and since $\Gamma^*(x, T_0) \subseteq T$, v also belongs to T. But v cannot belong to $T - U$, since this would violate the fact that $T - U$ is the union of a set of strongly connected components by establishing a strong connection between a member of $T - U$ and x, which lies in $U - U_0$ and therefore outside of $T - U$. Moreover, v does not belong to $U - U_0$. Thus v belongs to $T - (T - U) - (U - U_0) = U_0$ and also to M, so that $M \cap U_0$ is nonempty.

Thus the test of whether $U - Usave = U - U_0$ is the strongly connected component generated by x is equivalent to, and can be replaced by, a test of whether $M \cap U_0 = M \cap Usave$ is empty. Moreover, if these tests are false then there is a path from x to a node v in U_0 that in conjunction with the existence of a path from any node in U to x, implies the desired consequent of $search(x)$:

$$(\forall u \in U)\, (\exists\, v \in U_0)\ v \in \Gamma^*(u)\ .$$

On the other hand, if the tests are true then the consequent will obviously be achieved by the assignment $U := Usave$.

As a special case of the specification we have proved for $search$, if U is empty before executing $search(x)$ then the precedent will be satisfied and the consequent will imply that U will again be empty after execution. Thus each execution of $search$ in the main program will satisfy the specification for this procedure and will leave U empty. At the conclusion of the program we will have $U = \{\}$ and $T = \textbf{node}$, so that the set $T - U$, which is the union of the strongly connected components which have been placed in SCC, will be the entire set of nodes in the graph.

Thus our abstract program is

set procedure Γ {node exp};
set of sets {var} SCC;

$\vdots$

{true}
begin set T, U, M; $SCC := \{\}$; $T := \{\}$; $U := \{\}$; $M := \{\}$;
{**geninv** UI: SCC is a set of strongly connected components
    and $T - U = \bigcup SCC$ and $U \subseteq T$ }
  begin
  procedure *search*(**node** {exp} x);
    $\{T = T_0$ and $U = U_0$ and $(\forall u \in U)\, x \in \Gamma^*(u)\}$
    if $x \in T$ **then** $M := M \cup \{x\}$ **else**
      begin set $Usave$, $Msave$; $Usave := U$;
      {**geninv** UII: $Usave = U_0 \subseteq U$ and $T_0 - U_0 \subseteq T - U$
        and $(\forall u \in U)\, x \in \Gamma^*(u)$ }
      $Msave := M$;
      begin$_{UI}$ $T := T \cup \{x\}$; $U := U \cup \{x\}$ **end**;
      $M := \{x\}$;
      $\{x \in U - U_0\}$
      for $y \in \Gamma(x)$ **do** *search*(y);
      $\{T = T_0 \cup \Gamma^*(x, T_0)$ and $M = \Gamma^*(x, T_0)$ and $x \in U - U_0\}$
      if empty($M \cap Usave$) **then**
        $\{U - Usave$ is the strongly connected component
          generated by x }
        begin$_{UI}$ $SCC := SCC \cup \{U - Usave\}$; $U := Usave$
        end;
      $M := Msave \cup M$
      end;
    $\{U_0 \subseteq U$ and $T_0 - U_0 \subseteq T - U$
      and $(\forall u \in U)\, (\exists v \in U_0)\, v \in \Gamma^*(u)$ }
  for $y \in$ **node do** *search*(y)
  end
end
$\{SCC$ is a set of strongly connected components
  and $\bigcup SCC =$ **node** } .

5.4.3 Transformation to a Concrete Program

In preparation for the transformation of our abstract program into concrete
form, we omit the intermediate assertions, which have served their purpose,
except for the occurrence of $U \subseteq T$ in the global general invariant UI. We
also move the assignment $M := Msave \cup M$ backward into both branches of
the preceding conditional statement:

```
set procedure Γ {node exp};
set of sets {var} SCC:
   ⋮
{true}
begin set T, U, M; SCC:={}; T:={}; U:={}; M:={};
{geninv UI: U ⊆ T}
      begin
      procedure search(node {exp} x);
         if x ∈ T then M := M ∪ {x} else
            begin set Usave, Msave; Usave := U;
            Msave := M; T:= T ∪ {x}; U:= U ∪ {x}; M:={x};
            for y ∈ Γ(x) do search(y);
            if empty(M ∩ Usave) then
                begin SCC:= SCC ∪ {U − Usave};
                U:= Usave; M:= Msave ∪ M
                end
            else M:= Msave ∪ M
            end;
         for y ∈ node do search(y)
         end
      end
{SCC is a set of strongly connected components
   and ∪ SCC=node }    .
```

To represent U we introduce the concrete variables

node array $A(1::N)$; **integer** p .

The segment of A over $\boxed{1 \quad p}$ will enumerate the members of U without duplication. This leads to the global representation invariant

$$AI: \boxed{1 \quad p \quad \#T} \text{ and } U=\{A \upharpoonright \boxed{1 \quad p}\} \text{ and } \text{ord}_{\neq} A \upharpoonright \boxed{1 \quad p}$$

(where the partition diagram precludes subscript errors, since $\#T \leq N$).

To achieve this invariant initially, when U is empty, we set p to zero. To maintain the invariant we augment the assignment $U:= U \cup \{x\}$, which inserts a new member into U, with $p:= p + 1; A(p):= x$. We also augment the assignment $U:= Usave$ with $p:= psave$, where $psave$ is a local variable of $search$ used to save the value possessed by p when $search$ began execution.

The argument that the latter augmentation preserves the representation invariant is more subtle than it might seem at first glance. It depends upon the fact that the recursive calls of $search$ performed by the **for** statement will not decrease the interval $\boxed{1 \quad p}$ nor alter the segment of A over the initial value of this interval. To demonstrate this, we must show that $search$ satisfies the specification

$$\{A = A_0 \text{ and } p = p_0\}$$
$$search(x)$$
$$\{\,\boxed{1 \;\; p_0 \;\; p}\;\text{ and } A \uparrow \boxed{1 \;\; p_0} = A_0 \uparrow \boxed{1 \;\; p_0}\,\}\quad.$$

As usual, we will assume this specification about recursive calls in proving that it is met by the body of *search*.

Suppose $A = A_0$ and $p = p_0$ holds before execution of the body of *search*. If $x \in T$ this condition will obviously be preserved, since there will be no assignments to A or p, and it will imply the consequent of the above specification. Otherwise, the assignments $Usave := U$; $psave := p$ will achieve the local general invariant

$$AII:\; \boxed{1 \;\; p_0 \;\; p}\;\text{ and } A \uparrow \boxed{1 \;\; p_0} = A_0 \uparrow \boxed{1 \;\; p_0}$$
$$\text{and } Usave = \{A \uparrow \boxed{1 \;\; p_0}\}\text{ and } psave = p_0\quad.$$

It is easy to see that this invariant is preserved by the only assignments within its scope which interfere with it:

$$p := p + 1;\; A(p) := x$$

and

$$p := psave\quad.$$

Less trivially, it is also preserved by the recursive calls of *search* in the **for** statement. To see this, let $A_{before}, p_{before}, A_{after},$ and p_{after} be the values of A and p before and after such a call. If AII holds beforehand, then

$$\boxed{1 \;\; p_0 \;\; p_{before}}\;\text{ and } A_{before} \uparrow \boxed{1 \;\; p_0} = A_0 \uparrow \boxed{1 \;\; p_0}$$
$$\text{and } Usave = \{A_{before} \uparrow \boxed{1 \;\; p_0}\}\text{ and } psave = p_0\quad.$$

The specification of recursive calls gives

$$\boxed{1 \;\; p_{before} \;\; p_{after}}\;\text{ and }$$
$$A_{after} \uparrow \boxed{1 \;\; p_{before}} = A_{before} \uparrow \boxed{1 \;\; p_{before}}\quad.$$

From these conditions, we may infer

$$\boxed{1 \;\; p_0 \;\; p_{after}}\;\text{ and } A_{after} \uparrow \boxed{1 \;\; p_0} = A_0 \uparrow \boxed{1 \;\; p_0}$$
$$\text{and } Usave = \{A_{after} \uparrow \boxed{1 \;\; p_0}\}\text{ and } psave = p_0\quad,$$

which shows that AII will hold after the call of *search*.

The local invariant AII implies the desired consequent of the body of *search*:

$$\boxed{1 \;\; p_0 \;\; p}\;\text{ and } A \uparrow \boxed{1 \;\; p_0} = A_0 \uparrow \boxed{1 \;\; p_0}\quad.$$

It also implies that the global invariant AI will be preserved by the assignments $U := Usave$; $p := psave$.

Next, we introduce the concrete variable

integer array $Q(\textbf{node})$.

This array will provide two items of information. In the first place, if $u \in U$ then $Q(u)$ will give the position of u in the array A, i.e. $Q(u) \in \boxed{1 \quad p}$ and $A(Q(u)) = u$. In the second place, for any node u, $Q(u)$ will indicate whether u belongs to $T - U$, U, or neither set. For this purpose, if $u \notin T$ then $Q(u)$ will be zero, and if $u \in T - U$ then $Q(u)$ will be some integer that is so large that it cannot occur in $\boxed{1 \quad p}$. In practice, a sufficiently large integer is $N + 1$, but to show the logic of our program more clearly, we will write ∞ for this integer.

Thus we introduce the global representation invariant

> QI: ($\forall u \in$ **node**) **if** $u \notin T$ **then** $Q(u) = 0$
> **else if** $u \in U$ **then** $Q(u) \in \boxed{1 \quad p}$ **and** $A(Q(u)) = u$
> **else** $Q(u) = \infty$.

Since T is empty initially, QI can be achieved by setting all elements of Q to zero. To preserve QI when a new node is added to T and U, we must augment $U := U \cup \{x\}$; $p := p + 1$; $A(p) := x$ with $Q(x) := p$. To preserve QI when U is reset to its subset *Usave*, we must reset $Q(u)$ to ∞ for each u in the set $U - Usave$, which is equal to the set $\{A \uparrow psave\boxed{\quad p}\}$ as a consequence of AI and AII.

At this stage, we have

> **set procedure** Γ {**node** exp};
> **set of sets** {**var**} SCC;
>
> $\vdots$
>
> {**true**}
> **begin set** T, U, M;
> **node array** $A(1::N)$; **integer array** $Q(\textbf{node})$; **integer** p;
> $SCC := \{\}$; $T := \{\}$; $U := \{\}$; $M := \{\}$;
> {**geninv** UI: $U \subseteq T$}
> $p := 0$;
> {**geninv** AI: $\boxed{1 \quad p \quad \#T}$
>   **and** $U = \{A \uparrow \boxed{1 \quad p}\}$ **and** $\text{ord}_{\neq} A \uparrow \boxed{1 \quad p}$ }
> **for** $y \in$ **node do** $Q(y) := 0$;
> {**geninv** QI: ($\forall u \in$ **node**) **if** $u \notin T$ **then** $Q(u) = 0$
>   **else if** $u \in U$ **then** $Q(u) \in \boxed{1 \quad p}$ **and** $A(Q(u)) = u$
>   **else** $Q(u) = \infty$ }

```
begin
procedure search(node {exp} x);
    {A = A_0 and p = p_0}
    if x ∈ T then M := M ∪ {x} else
        begin set Usave, Msave; integer psave;
        Usave := U; psave := p;
        {geninv AII: │1  p_0│  p│ and A ↑ │1  p_0│ = A_0 ↑ │1  p_0│
            and Usave = {A ↑ │1  p_0│} and psave = p_0 }
        Msave := M;
            begin_{AI,QI} T := T ∪ {x};
            U := U ∪ {x}; p := p + 1; A(p) := x; Q(x) := p;
            M := {x}
            end;
        for y ∈ Γ(x) do search(y);
        if empty(M ∩ Usave) then
            begin_{AI,QI} SCC := SCC ∪ {U − Usave};
            U := Usave;
            for k := psave + 1 until p do Q(A(k)) := ∞;
            p := psave; M := Msave ∪ M
            end
        else M := Msave ∪ M
        end;
    {│1  p_0│  p│ and A ↑ │1  p_0│ = A_0 ↑ │1  p_0│}
    for y ∈ node do search(y)
    end
end
{SCC is a set of strongly connected components
    and ∪ SCC = node}   .
```

Finally we must deal with the set M. To represent M we introduce the concrete variable

integer mp ,

whose value will be the smallest integer in $\boxed{1 \quad p}$ such that $A(p) \in M$, or ∞ if no such integer exists. (Again, ∞ can be taken to be any integer, such as $N + 1$, that is too large to ever belong to $\boxed{1 \quad p}$.) Thus we introduce the global representation invariant

MI: $mp = \text{Min } \mathcal{P}(M, A \uparrow \boxed{1 \quad p})$.

Here Min S denotes the smallest integer in the set S if S is nonempty, or ∞ if S is empty. As defined in Section 2.3.8, $\mathcal{P}(M, X)$ denotes the preimage of M under X, i.e. the set of members of **dom** X that are mapped by X into members of M.

Notice that the variable mp gives an *ambiguous* representation of M, i.e. we cannot express M in terms of mp and the other concrete variables. Nevertheless, we will see that mp provides just the information about M that is actually needed by the algorithm.

Since M is empty initially, we can achieve MI by setting mp to ∞. Within *search*, when $x \in T$, QI implies

$$\text{Min } \mathcal{P}(\{x\}, A \uparrow \boxed{1 \quad p}) = Q(x)$$

(even when $x \in T - U$), which with MI implies that

$$\text{Min } \mathcal{P}(M \cup \{x\}, A \uparrow \boxed{1 \quad p})$$

is the minimum of mp and $Q(x)$. Thus MI will be preserved if $M := M \cup \{x\}$ is augmented with **if** $Q(x) < mp$ **then** $mp := Q(x)$.

On the other hand, if $x \notin T$ then augmenting $Msave := M$ with $mpsave := mp$, where $mpsave$ is a local integer variable, will achieve the local invariant

$$MII: \ mpsave = \text{Min } \mathcal{P}(Msave, A \uparrow \boxed{1 \quad p_0}) \quad ,$$

which will be maintained by the rest of the body of *search* since, by AII, the segment of A over $\boxed{1 \quad p_0}$ will not be changed.

The global invariant MI may be falsified by $p := p + 1$; $A(p) := x$, but it will be regained if we augment $M := \{x\}$ with $mp := p$.

Now consider the test whether $M \cap Usave$ is empty. Since $Usave = \{A \uparrow \boxed{1 \quad p_0}\}$, law (4) in Section 2.3.8 shows that $M \cap Usave$ will be empty if and only if $\mathcal{P}(M, A \uparrow \boxed{1 \quad p_0})$ is empty. But MI and $\boxed{1 \quad p_0 \mid p}$ imply that this set will be empty if and only if $mp > p_0$.

Thus if $M \cap Usave$ is empty then Min $\mathcal{P}(Msave \cup M, A \uparrow \boxed{1 \quad p_0})$ will be Min $\mathcal{P}(Msave, A \uparrow \boxed{1 \quad p_0})$, which is $mpsave$ according to MII. Since $p_0 = psave$, it follows that MI will be preserved if $p := psave$; $M := Msave \cup M$ is augmented with $mp := mpsave$.

On the other hand, suppose $M \cap Usave$ is nonempty, so that $mp \leq p_0$. The integer Min $\mathcal{P}(Msave \cup M, A \uparrow \boxed{1 \quad p})$ is the minimum of the three quantities

$$\text{Min } \mathcal{P}(Msave, A \uparrow \boxed{1 \quad p_0}) = mpsave \ ,$$
$$\text{Min } \mathcal{P}(Msave, A \uparrow p_0 \boxed{\quad p}) \ ,$$
$$\text{Min } \mathcal{P}(M, A \uparrow \boxed{1 \quad p}) = mp \ .$$

However, since $mp \leq p_0$, the second of these quantities must be larger than the third. Thus MI will be preserved if $M := Msave \cup M$ is augmented with the assignment to mp of the minimum of $mpsave$ and mp.

Thus we have

> **set procedure** Γ {**node** exp};
> **set of sets** {**var**} SCC;
> $\vdots$
> {**true**}
> **begin set** T, U, M;
> **node array** $A(1::N)$; **integer array** Q(node); **integer** p, mp;
> $SCC := \{\}$; $T := \{\}$; $U := \{\}$; $M := \{\}$;
> {**geninv** UI: $U \subseteq T$}
> $p := 0$;
> {**geninv** AI: $\boxed{1 \quad p \quad \#T}$
>   **and** $U = \{A \uparrow \boxed{1 \quad p}\}$ **and** $\mathrm{ord}_{\neq} A \uparrow \boxed{1 \quad p}$ }
> **for** $y \in$ **node do** $Q(y) := 0$;
> {**geninv** QI: $(\forall u \in$ **node**$)$ **if** $u \notin T$ **then** $Q(u) = 0$
>   **else if** $u \in U$ **then** $Q(u) \in \boxed{1 \quad p}$ **and** $A(Q(u)) = u$
>   **else** $Q(u) = \infty$ }
> $mp := \infty$;
> {**geninv** MI: $mp = \mathrm{Min}\ \mathcal{P}(M, A \uparrow \boxed{1 \quad p})$}
>   **begin**
>   **procedure** $search$(**node** {exp} x);
> $\{A = A_0$ **and** $p = p_0\}$
>   **if** $x \in T$ **then**
>   **begin**$_{MI}$ $M := M \cup \{x\}$;
>   **if** $Q(x) < mp$ **then** $mp := Q(x)$
>   **end**
>   **else**
>   **begin set** $Usave$, $Msave$; **integer** $psave$, $mpsave$;
> $Usave := U$; $psave := p$;
>   {**geninv** AII: $\boxed{1 \quad p_0 \quad p}$ **and** $A \uparrow \boxed{1 \quad p_0} = A_0 \uparrow \boxed{1 \quad p_0}$
>   **and** $Usave = \{A \uparrow \boxed{1 \quad p_0}\}$ **and** $psave = p_0$ }
> $Msave := M$; $mpsave := mp$;
>   {**geninv** MII: $mpsave = \mathrm{Min}\ \mathcal{P}(Msave, A \uparrow \boxed{1 \quad p_0})$}

$\mathbf{begin}_{AI,QI,MI}\ T:=T\ \cup\ \{x\};$
$U:=U\ \cup\ \{x\};\ p:=p+1;\ A(p):=x;\ Q(x):=p;$
$M:=\{x\};\ mp:=p$
end;
for $y\in\Gamma(x)$ **do** $search(y);$
if $\mathbf{empty}(M\ \cap\ Usave)$ **then**
$\quad\mathbf{begin}_{AI,QI,MI}\ SCC:=SCC\ \cup\ \{U-Usave\};$
$\quad U:=Usave;$
$\quad$**for** $k:=psave+1$ **until** p **do** $Q(A(k)):=\infty;$
$\quad p:=psave;\ M:=Msave\ \cup\ M;\ mp:=mpsave$
$\quad$**end**
else
$\quad\mathbf{begin}_{MI}\ M:=Msave\ \cup\ M;$
$\quad$**if** $mpsave<mp$ **then** $mp:=mpsave$
$\quad$**end**
end;
$\{\boxed{1\ \ p_0}\ \ p\ \text{ and }\ A\uparrow\boxed{1\ \ p_0}=A_0\uparrow\boxed{1\ \ p_0}\}$
for $y\in$ **node do** $search(y)$
end
end
$\{SCC$ is a set of strongly connected components
and $\cup\ SCC=$**node** $\}$.

Now we can replace the expressions involving abstract variables that occur outside of assignments to these variables by equivalent expressions involving concrete variables. By QI, the test $x\in T$ can be replaced by $Q(x)\neq0$. By AII and MI, as we have already seen, the test $\mathbf{empty}(M\ \cap\ Usave)$ can be replaced by $mp>psave$. Finally, by AI and AII, the set expression $U-Usave$ in the assignment to SCC can be replaced by $\{A\uparrow\boxed{psave\ \ p}\}$.

These replacements render the abstract variables T, U, M, $Usave$, and $Msave$ auxiliary. After their elimination, we have

set procedure Γ {**node exp**};
set of sets {**var**} $SCC;$
$\vdots$
{**true**}
begin node array $A(1::N);$ **integer array** $Q($**node**$);$ **integer** $p,\ mp;$
$SCC:=\{\};\ p:=0;$ **for** $y\in$ **node do** $Q(y):=0;\ mp:=\infty;$
$\quad$**begin**

```
procedure search(node {exp} x);
    if Q(x) ≠ 0 then
        begin if Q(x) < mp then mp := Q(x) end
    else
        begin integer psave, mpsave;
        psave := p; mpsave := mp;
        p := p + 1; A(p) := x; Q(x) := p; mp := p;
        for y ∈ Γ(x) do search(y);
        if mp > psave then
            begin SCC := SCC ∪ {{A 1 psave    p }};
            for k := psave + 1 until p do Q(A(k)) := ∞;
            p := psave; mp := mpsave
            end
        else if mpsave < mp then mp := mpsave
        end;
    for y ∈ node do search(y)
    end
end
{SCC is a set of strongly connected components
    and ∪ SCC = node}    .
```

Representations for the function Γ and for nodes can be provided as in
Sections 5.1.5 and 5.1.6. (Note, however, that if **node** is a proper subset of
$\boxed{1 \quad N}$ then the iteration **for** $y \in$ **node do** $search(y)$ must exclude integers in
$\boxed{1 \quad N}$ that do not represent nodes.) A possible representation of the output
SCC is left to the reader as an exercise.

If we assume that the output of a strongly connected component via
SCC requires a time proportional to its size then, since each node belongs to
exactly one component, the total time required for output statements will be
of order N. A similar argument applies to the **for** statement that sets $Q(A(k))$
to ∞ for each k in the outputted component. The rest of the program obeys
the timing restrictions discussed in Section 5.4.1, and therefore requires a
time of order $N + E$.

Exercise

1. Transform the above program to represent the output variable SCC by an array
   out, with domain **node**, using the representation invariant

   $$S \in SCC \text{ if and only if } (\exists \ x \in \cup SCC) \ S = \mathscr{P}(\{out(x)\}, out) \quad .$$

   This is a standard method for representing a partition of a finite set.

APPENDIX A
NOTATION FOR SYNTACTIC DEFINITION

A.1 BACKUS-NAUR FORM

One of the most significant aspects of the development of Algol 60 [Naur 60, 63] was the use of a precise and formal notation, called Backus normal form, Backus-Naur form, or simply BNF, to specify syntax. Although the concept underlying BNF was already known in mathematical linguistics [Chomsky 56], it was independently discovered by J. Backus, who first suggested its application to the definition of programming languages [Backus 59]. Since then, with occasional extensions or modifications, BNF has become the standard tool for describing the syntax of programming languages. In this appendix we give an explanation of this notation, including several extensions that will be used in Appendix B.

The underlying idea is best seen through simple examples (which are not meant to describe the actual syntax of Algol W). Consider the fragment of a programming language used in Section 1.1. Its syntax might be described in English as follows:

(1)   A statement can be:

        (a)   An action,

or   (b)   **if** L **then** S, where L is a logical expression and S is a statement,

or   (c)   **if** L **then** S_1 **else** S_2, where L is a logical expression and S_1 and S_2 are statements,

or   (d)   **while** L **do** S, where L is a logical expression and S is a statement,

or   (e)   **begin** Q **end**, where Q is a statement sequence.

383

(2)   A statement sequence can be:

   (a)   A statement,

or   (b) $S; Q$, where S is a statement and Q is a statement sequence.

In BNF, the above description becomes

⟨statement⟩ ::= ⟨action⟩
⟨statement⟩ ::= **if** ⟨logical expression⟩ **then** ⟨statement⟩
⟨statement⟩ ::= **if** ⟨logical expression⟩ **then** ⟨statement⟩
   else ⟨statement⟩
⟨statement⟩ ::= **while** ⟨logical expression⟩ **do** ⟨statement⟩
⟨statement⟩ ::= **begin** ⟨statement sequence⟩ **end**
⟨statement sequence⟩ ::= ⟨statement⟩
⟨statement sequence⟩ ::= ⟨statement⟩ ; ⟨statement sequence⟩

The names in angular brackets, such as ⟨statement⟩ and ⟨logical expression⟩, are called *nonterminal symbols* or *phrase class names*, and denote sets of language phrases that have the same syntactic behavior. On the other hand, symbols such as **if** and **then** and the semicolon, which actually belong to the language being described, are called *terminal symbols*. A syntax description is given by a set of formulas, called *productions*, with the form $N ::= S$, where N is a nonterminal symbol and S is a string that can contain both nonterminal and terminal symbols. Roughly speaking, a production of the form $N ::= S$ means that S is a possible form for a phrase in the set denoted by N.

   More precisely, every syntactically correct phrase p in the set denoted by the nonterminal symbol N can be *derived* by the following process:

   (1)   Let p be N.
   (2)   As long as p contains one or more nonterminal symbols, replace some nonterminal N in p by the right side of some production whose left side is N.

For example, a derivation of a phrase in the set denoted by ⟨statement⟩ might consist of the following steps:

⟨statement⟩
if ⟨logical expression⟩ **then** ⟨statement⟩ **else** ⟨statement⟩
if ⟨logical expression⟩ **then begin** ⟨statement sequence⟩ **end**
   else ⟨statement⟩
if ⟨logical expression⟩ **then begin** ⟨statement⟩ ;
   ⟨statement sequence⟩ **end else** ⟨statement⟩
if ⟨logical expression⟩ **then begin** ⟨statement⟩ ;
   ⟨statement⟩ **end else** ⟨statement⟩
if ⟨logical expression⟩ **then begin** ⟨action⟩ ;
   ⟨statement⟩ **end else** ⟨statement⟩
if ⟨logical expression⟩ **then begin** ⟨action⟩ ;
   ⟨action⟩ **end else** ⟨statement⟩

if ⟨logical expression⟩ **then begin** ⟨action⟩ ;
  ⟨action⟩ **end else while** ⟨logical expression⟩ **do** ⟨statement⟩
if ⟨logical expression⟩ **then begin** ⟨action⟩ ;
  ⟨action⟩ **end else while** ⟨logical expression⟩ **do** ⟨action⟩

Of course, to complete this derivation we would have to replace the remaining nonterminals, using productions for ⟨logical expression⟩ and ⟨action⟩ that would be available if we had a description of a complete language instead of just a fragment. Ultimately, we would obtain a string of terminal symbols that, by definition, would be a syntactically correct statement.

The derivation of a phrase can be displayed more perspicuously by a *derivation tree*, in which nonterminal symbols occur as nonterminal nodes, terminal symbols appear as terminal nodes, and the subnodes of each nonterminal node describe the replacement of that node. The tree for the above derivation is given in Figure A.1. (Of course, to complete the derivation tree we would have to add subtrees below the five remaining nonterminal nodes.)

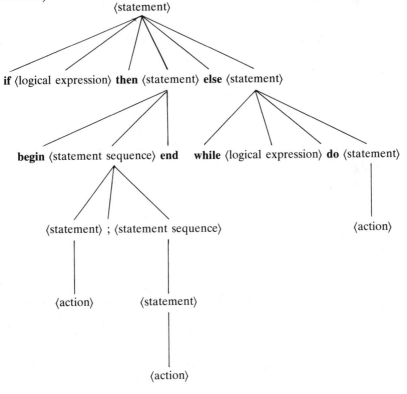

Figure A.1   Derivation Tree for **if** ⟨logical expression⟩ **then begin** ⟨action⟩ ;
  ⟨action⟩ **end else while** ⟨logical expression⟩ **do** ⟨action⟩ .

A derivation tree provides a proof that the string obtained by reading its terminal nodes from left to right is a syntactically correct phrase. Beyond this however, it displays the way in which a phrase is divided into its immediate subphrases, which obviously affects its meaning (at least, if we make the plausible assumption that the meaning of a phrase is a function of the meanings of its subphrases). For example, the tree in Figure A.1 shows the following decomposition into subphrases:

if ⟨logical expression⟩ **then begin** ⟨action⟩ ; ⟨action⟩ **end**
else while ⟨logical expression⟩ **do** ⟨action⟩

At this point, the problem of *ambiguity* arises. Consider the statement:

if ⟨logical expression⟩ **then if** ⟨logical expression⟩
then ⟨action⟩ **else** ⟨action⟩

For this phrase, there are two distinct derivation trees, shown in Figure A.2, which describe two different decompositions into subphrases:

if ⟨logical expression⟩ **then**
   if ⟨logical expression⟩ **then** ⟨action⟩ **else** ⟨action⟩

and

if ⟨logical expression⟩ **then**
   if ⟨logical expression⟩ **then** ⟨action⟩
else ⟨action⟩

which in turn imply different meanings. The existence of more than one derivation tree for the same phrase (from the same nonterminal) is called *ambiguity*, and is normally a defect in a language design.

In this particular case, one way of removing the ambiguity is to limit the forms of statements that can occur between **then** and **else** to a phrase class called ⟨simple statement⟩. The following productions give an unambiguous syntax:

⟨statement⟩ ::= ⟨simple statement⟩
⟨statement⟩ ::= **if** ⟨logical expression⟩ **then** ⟨statement⟩
⟨statement⟩ ::= **if** ⟨logical expression⟩ **then** ⟨simple statement⟩
   else ⟨statement⟩
⟨statement⟩ ::= **while** ⟨logical expression⟩ **do** ⟨statement⟩
⟨simple statement⟩ ::= ⟨action⟩
⟨simple statement⟩ ::= **begin** ⟨statement sequence⟩ **end**
⟨statement sequence⟩ ::= ⟨statement⟩
⟨statement sequence⟩ ::= ⟨statement⟩ ; ⟨statement sequence⟩

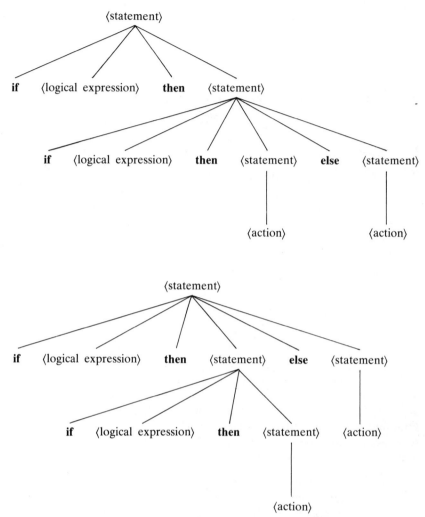

Figure A.2   Two Derivation Trees for **if** ⟨logical expression⟩ **then**
⟨logical expression⟩ **then** ⟨action⟩ **else** ⟨action⟩

In this syntax, the only permissible subphrase decomposition is

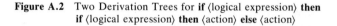

       if ⟨logical expression⟩ **then**
           if ⟨logical expression⟩ **then** ⟨action⟩ **else** ⟨action⟩

which is described by the derivation tree in Figure A.3.

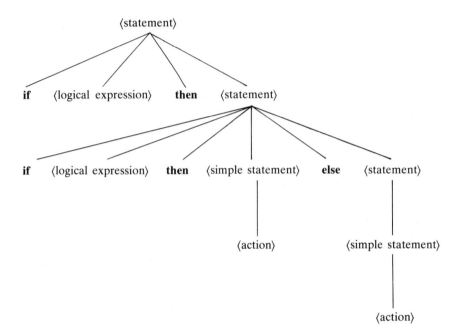

Figure A.3   Derivation Tree for **if** ⟨logical expression⟩ **then**
⟨logical expression⟩ **then** ⟨action⟩ **else** ⟨action⟩
with an Unambiguous Set of Productions.

To explore further the relation between syntax, subphrase decomposition, and meaning, consider a simple language in which expressions are sequences of identifiers separated by + or −. Both of the following production sets describe the correct set of phrases:

⟨expression⟩ ::= ⟨identifier⟩
⟨expression⟩ ::= ⟨expression⟩ + ⟨identifier⟩
⟨expression⟩ ::= ⟨expression⟩ − ⟨identifier⟩

or

⟨expression⟩ ::= ⟨identifier⟩
⟨expression⟩ ::= ⟨identifier⟩ + ⟨expression⟩
⟨expression⟩ ::= ⟨identifier⟩ − ⟨expression⟩

But there is a difference in subphrase decomposition, as can be seen for the expression $x - y + z$. Under the two production sets, this phrase is given the distinct derivation trees shown in Figure A.4. According to the first set of productions, the operators + and − associate to the left, e.g. $x - y + z = (x - y) + z$, while according to the second set of productions, these operators associate to the right, e.g. $x - y + z = x - (y + z)$. Since + and − are left-associative in conventional mathematical

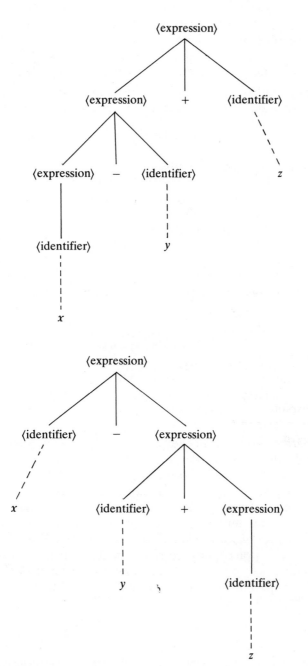

Figure A.4   Derivation Trees for $x - y + z$ with Two Different Production Sets.

notation (and in Algol W), only the first set of productions describes sub-phrase decomposition correctly.

Now suppose that we wish to add a multiplication operator. To reflect conventional notation we want decompositions such as $x \times y + z$ and $x + y \times z$, i.e. we want multiplication to "bind more tightly" than addition or subtraction. The solution is to say that an expression is a sequence of terms separated by $+$ or $-$, where a term is a sequence of identifiers separated by $\times$:

> ⟨expression⟩ ::= ⟨term⟩
> ⟨expression⟩ ::= ⟨expression⟩ + ⟨term⟩
> ⟨expression⟩ ::= ⟨expression⟩ − ⟨term⟩
> ⟨term⟩ ::= ⟨identifier⟩
> ⟨term⟩ ::= ⟨term⟩ × ⟨identifier⟩

Next, to add the use of parentheses, we want to say that a parenthesized expression can occur anywhere that an identifier can. If we introduce ⟨primary⟩ to denote "anywhere an identifier can occur", we get:

> ⟨expression⟩ ::= ⟨term⟩
> ⟨expression⟩ ::= ⟨expression⟩ + ⟨term⟩
> ⟨expression⟩ ::= ⟨expression⟩ − ⟨term⟩
> ⟨term⟩ ::= ⟨primary⟩
> ⟨term⟩ ::= ⟨term⟩ × ⟨primary⟩
> ⟨primary⟩ ::= ⟨identifier⟩
> ⟨primary⟩ ::= (⟨expression⟩)

Nonterminal symbols like ⟨expression⟩, ⟨term⟩, and ⟨primary⟩, that are used to show the subphrase decomposition of various operations, are often called *levels of precedence*. In the description of Algol W in Appendix B, six such nonterminals are needed to describe the syntax of expressions.

This general method of describing syntax has been studied extensively in theoretical computer science, where finite sets of productions of the form $N ::= S$ are called *context-free grammars* [Hopcroft 69]. The subject is also of considerable practical importance, since a major component of any compiler is a procedure, called a *parser*, that converts the input program into its (hopefully unique) derivation tree [Aho 72, Gries 71, Backhouse 79].

Exercise

1. The following set of productions describes an unorthodox language of expressions which is quite different from either Algol W or conventional mathematical notation, despite the fact that the same symbols are used:

$\langle \text{expression} \rangle ::= \langle \text{term} \rangle$
$\langle \text{expression} \rangle ::= - \langle \text{expression} \rangle$
$\langle \text{term} \rangle ::= \langle \text{factor} \rangle$
$\langle \text{term} \rangle ::= \langle \text{factor} \rangle + \langle \text{term} \rangle$
$\langle \text{term} \rangle ::= \langle \text{factor} \rangle \times \langle \text{term} \rangle$
$\langle \text{factor} \rangle ::= \langle \text{primary} \rangle$
$\langle \text{factor} \rangle ::= / \langle \text{primary} \rangle$
$\langle \text{primary} \rangle ::= a$
$\langle \text{primary} \rangle ::= b$
$\langle \text{primary} \rangle ::= c$
$\langle \text{primary} \rangle ::= (\langle \text{expression} \rangle)$

Determine which of the following strings are syntactically correct according to this set of productions, i.e. which strings can be derived from the nonterminal symbol $\langle \text{expression} \rangle$. Give derivation trees for the correct strings.

$-a+b+c$
$a+b-c$
$a \times b + /c$
$--/c$
$-//c$
$(a+b) / c$

A.2 EXTENSIONS OF BACKUS-NAUR FORM

Although Backus-Naur productions can be used to describe a real programming language such as Algol W, an extremely large number of productions is required. Indeed, to describe precisely the rules for parameter and subscript matching it is necessary to use an infinite number of productions. Thus we introduce several extensions of our notation to permit a single production to stand for a set of productions.

To condense a group of productions with the same left side, we write

$$N ::= S_1 \mid ... \mid S_n$$

as an abbreviation for

$$N ::= S_1$$
$$\vdots$$
$$N ::= S_n$$

For example, the productions used in the previous section to describe a simple language of expressions can be written as

$\langle \text{expression} \rangle ::= \langle \text{term} \rangle \mid \langle \text{expression} \rangle + \langle \text{term} \rangle$
    $\mid \langle \text{expression} \rangle - \langle \text{term} \rangle$
$\langle \text{term} \rangle ::= \langle \text{primary} \rangle \mid \langle \text{term} \rangle \times \langle \text{primary} \rangle$
$\langle \text{primary} \rangle ::= \langle \text{identifier} \rangle \mid (\langle \text{expression} \rangle)$

More generally, to indicate several alternatives within part of the right side of a production, we write

$$N ::= S_0 \, [\![S_1 \mid \ldots \mid S_n]\!] \, S_{n+1}$$

(where some of the strings S_i may be empty) as an abbreviation for

$$N ::= S_0 S_1 S_{n+1}$$
$$\vdots$$
$$N ::= S_0 S_n S_{n+1}$$

For example,

⟨scale factor⟩ ::= $'$ $[\![\mid + \mid -]\!]$ ⟨integer number⟩

abbreviates

⟨scale factor⟩ ::= $'$ ⟨integer number⟩
⟨scale factor⟩ ::= $'$ +⟨integer number⟩
⟨scale factor⟩ ::= $'$ −⟨integer number⟩

It is also useful to introduce a notation for repetition. We write $[\![S]\!]^k$, where k is a nonnegative integer, to stand for the string $SS \ldots S$ containing k occurrences of S. For example,

⟨identifier⟩ ::= ⟨letter⟩ $[\![⟨\text{letter or digit}⟩]\!]^3$

is an abbreviation for

⟨identifier⟩ ::=
    ⟨letter⟩ ⟨letter or digit⟩ ⟨letter or digit⟩ ⟨letter or digit⟩

A slight extension of this notation is particularly useful for describing languages, such as Algol W, in which lists of items separated by commas play a major role. For $k \geq 1$, we write $[\![S]\!]^k_\odot$ to stand for the string $S,S, \ldots ,S$ consisting of k occurrences of S separated by commas. For example,

⟨real variable⟩ ::= ⟨real array variable $([\![*]\!]^3_\odot)$⟩ $([\![⟨\text{subscript}⟩]\!]^3_\odot)$

is an abbreviation for

⟨real variable⟩ ::= ⟨real array variable $(*, *, *)$⟩
    (⟨subscript⟩, ⟨subscript⟩, ⟨subscript⟩)

(Here ⟨real array variable $(*, *, *)$⟩ is the name of a class of phrases that denote three-dimensional real arrays.) Note that repetition can occur either inside or outside of the angular brackets that enclose nonterminal symbols.

Finally, we introduce the concept of *production schemas*. A production schema looks like a production except that it contains occurrences of one or more special symbols called *metavariables*. The schema also gives a description of the ranges of these metavariables. It stands for the set of those productions that can be obtained by replacing all occurrences of each metavariable by some member of its range.

Numeric metavariables will be used to indicate varying numbers of repetitions. For example, the schema

$$\langle \text{identifier} \rangle ::= \langle \text{letter} \rangle \; [\![\langle \text{letter or digit} \rangle]\!]^i$$
$$\text{where } 0 \le i \le 255$$

stands for the 256 productions

$$\langle \text{identifier} \rangle ::= \langle \text{letter} \rangle$$
$$\langle \text{identifier} \rangle ::= \langle \text{letter} \rangle \; \langle \text{letter or digit} \rangle$$
$$\langle \text{identifier} \rangle ::= \langle \text{letter} \rangle \; \langle \text{letter or digit} \rangle \; \langle \text{letter or digit} \rangle$$
$$\vdots$$

Similarly,

$$\langle \text{real variable} \rangle ::= \langle \text{real array variable } ([\![*]\!]^n_\odot) \rangle \; ([\![\langle \text{subscript} \rangle]\!]^n_\odot)$$
$$\text{where } n \ge 1$$

stands for the infinite sequence of productions

$$\langle \text{real variable} \rangle ::= \langle \text{real array variable } (*) \rangle \; (\langle \text{subscript} \rangle)$$
$$\langle \text{real variable} \rangle ::= \langle \text{real array variable } (*, *) \rangle$$
$$(\langle \text{subscript} \rangle, \langle \text{subscript} \rangle)$$
$$\langle \text{real variable} \rangle ::= \langle \text{real array variable } (*, *, *) \rangle$$
$$(\langle \text{subscript} \rangle, \langle \text{subscript} \rangle, \langle \text{subscript} \rangle)$$
$$\vdots$$

We will also use symbolic metavariables, denoted by Greek letters, which range over sets of symbol strings. For example, the schema

$$\langle \tau \text{ term} \rangle ::= \langle \tau \text{ factor} \rangle$$
$$\text{where } \tau \in \{\textbf{integer, real, long real, logical}\}$$

stands for the four productions

$$\langle \text{integer term} \rangle ::= \langle \text{integer factor} \rangle$$
$$\langle \text{real term} \rangle ::= \langle \text{real factor} \rangle$$
$$\langle \text{long real term} \rangle ::= \langle \text{long real factor} \rangle$$
$$\langle \text{logical term} \rangle ::= \langle \text{logical factor} \rangle$$

It is important to notice that, when forming an instance of a production schema containing several metavariables, occurrences of distinct metavariables may be replaced by different integers or symbol strings, but occurrences of the same metavariable must be replaced by the same integer or symbol string.

A few metavariable ranges will be used in many schemas. For this reason, we introduce the following *standard* metavariables, whose ranges will be fixed throughout the description in Appendix B:

m: ranges over integers at least one.

n: ranges over integers at least one.

τ: ranges over the data types, i.e. **integer**, **real**, **long real**, and **logical**.

τ_{num}: ranges over the numeric data types, i.e. **integer**, **real**, and **long real**.

α: ranges over dimension lists, i.e. lists of one or more asterisks, separated by commas.

θ: ranges over phrase types (defined in Section B.3.1).

π: ranges over lists of one or more phrase types, separated by commas.

Exercise

1. The following productions and production schemas appear in Appendix B. In each case describe the set of productions being abbreviated.

⟨real number⟩ ::= ⟨unscaled real⟩
   | [[⟨unscaled real⟩ | ⟨integer number⟩ |]] ⟨scale factor⟩
⟨unscaled real⟩ ::= [[⟨digit⟩]]^i . [[⟨digit⟩]]^j
   where $i \geq 0$, $j \geq 0$, and $i + j \geq 1$
⟨simple variable declaration⟩ ::= τ [[⟨τ variable binder⟩]]$_{\odot}^{n}$
⟨elementary τ_{num} expression⟩ ::= [[+ | −]] ⟨τ_{num} term⟩
⟨τ_0 term⟩ ::= ⟨τ_1 term⟩ / ⟨τ_2 factor⟩
   where τ_0, τ_1, and τ_2 are given by column 6 of Table B.1
⟨array declaration⟩ ::=
   τ **array** [[⟨τ array variable ([[*]]$_{\odot}^{n}$) binder⟩]]$_{\odot}^{m}$
   ([[⟨lower bound⟩ :: ⟨upper bound⟩]]$_{\odot}^{n}$)

APPENDIX B
THE SYNTAX OF A SUBSET OF ALGOL W

This appendix describes the syntax of the portion of Algol W used in this book. It also includes a few additional facilities for input-output and real arithmetic that are likely to be needed in simple programs. As much as possible, we have used the notation discussed in Appendix A, but a few constraints on the syntax are stated in informal English. The order in which language features are presented follows the division of the book into chapters.

In order to emphasize programming methodology rather than a particular programming language, we have purposely avoided many interesting and useful aspects of Algol W. These include complex numbers, character and bit strings, references and records, subarray designators, expression blocks, certain forms of the **for** statement, **case** statements, **assert** statements, character-oriented input-output, exception handling, and a miscellany of implicitly declared procedures and variables. Those aspects of interest to a language designer are discussed in [Wirth 66]. However, this reference is a preliminary description differing in many details from the actually implemented language, which is thoroughly described in [Sites 72].

Our productions frequently deviate from those given in either [Wirth 66] or [Sites 72]. We have tried to choose nonterminal names that match the terminology used in the main text, to unify the description of several constructs, to make the behavior of types and binders as explicit as possible, and to formalize the parameter and subscript matching rules. For the last purpose, we have used the extended parameter specifiers which were introduced in Section 3.1.2.

Our description assumes that a complete program is a single string of characters, although in reality this string is broken up by a division into individual punched cards. However, the breaks between cards are ignored by the compiler, except that the last eight columns of each card are skipped. (For large or important programs, it is convenient to place sequential card numbers or identifying symbols in these columns as a protection against missing or out-of-order cards.) Thus the first column of each card immediately follows the 72nd column of the preceding card.

It is unwise to try to pack a program onto a minimal number of cards; line breaks and indentation should be used to reveal the structure of the program as clearly as possible to human readers. However, one must remember that these visual cues, which do not influence the Algol W compiler, can mask syntactic errors. The omission of a semicolon or comma is especially hard to perceive at the end of a line. Even harder is a missing blank at the end of a line that runs all the way to column 72 and is followed by a line beginning in column one.

We continue to show reserved words in lower-case boldface and implicitly declared identifiers in lower-case italics, although these words are actually punched in upper case. Aside from this convention, and the use of extended parameter specifiers, the symbols in the productions are those used for the IBM 360/370 implementation of the language (with an 029 keypunch). However, in many cases one or more alternative symbols, not used in the actual implementation, are shown *below* the correct symbol. For example,

$$\langle\text{logical factor}\rangle ::= \neg \ \langle\text{logical primary}\rangle$$
$$\textbf{not}$$

Some of these alternative symbols, such as lower case letters, $\neq, \leq, \geq, \times, \{$, and $\}$ are used in this book, the others occur frequently in the computing literature or in other Algol-like languages. Hopefully this will provide—without confusion—a limited ability to read Algol-like languages in general.

It should be emphasized that the symbols $\langle, \rangle, ::=, |, [\![$, and $]\!]$, Greek letters (symbolic metavariables), and superscripts (numeric metavariables) are part of the syntactic notation and do not occur in Algol W programs. (Actually the symbol $|$ is used as an operator in a part of Algol W not used in this book.)

B.1   SYNTAX FOR CHAPTER 1

B.1.1   Basic Symbols

⟨letter⟩ ::= A | B | C | D | E | F | G | H | I | J | K | L
a b c d e f g h i j k l
| M | N | O | P | Q | R | S | T | U | V | W | X | Y | Z
m n o p q r s t u v w x y z

⟨digit⟩ ::=   0 | 1 | 2 | 3 | 4 | 5 | 6 | 7 | 8 | 9

⟨letter or digit⟩ ::= ⟨letter⟩ | ⟨digit⟩

⟨reserved word⟩ ::= **true** | **false** | **integer** | **real** | **logical**
| **long** | **array** | **procedure** | **begin** | **end** | **if** | **then**
| **else** | **div** | **rem** | **abs** | **short** | **and** | **or** | **go** | **to**
| **goto** | **for** | **until** | **do** | **while** | **comment** | **value**
| **result** | **step** | ⟨extra reserved word⟩

⟨extra reserved word⟩ ::= **null** | **complex** | **bits** | **string**
| **reference** | **record** | **case** | **of** | **shr** | **shl** | **is**
| **assert** | **algol** | **fortran**

⟨identifier⟩ ::= ⟨letter⟩ $[\![$⟨letter or digit⟩$]\!]^i$
where $0 \le i \le 255$

⟨integer number⟩ ::= $[\![$⟨digit⟩$]\!]^i$
where $i \ge 1$

⟨unscaled real⟩ ::= $[\![$⟨digit⟩$]\!]^i$. $[\![$⟨digit⟩$]\!]^j$
where $i \ge 0$, $j \ge 0$, and $i+j \ge 1$

⟨scale factor⟩ ::= $'_{10}$ $[\![$ | + | − $]\!]$ ⟨integer number⟩

⟨real number⟩ ::= ⟨unscaled real⟩
| $[\![$⟨unscaled real⟩ | ⟨integer number⟩ | $]\!]$ ⟨scale factor⟩

⟨long real number⟩ ::= ⟨real number⟩ L | ⟨integer number⟩ L

⟨string character⟩ ::= ⟨normal string character⟩ | $""$

⟨string⟩ ::= $"$ $[\![$⟨string character⟩$]\!]^i$ $"$
where $1 \le i \le 256$

⟨comment⟩ ::= **comment** ⟨comment body⟩ ;
                         {   }

⟨comment body⟩ ::= $[\![$⟨comment character⟩$]\!]^i$
where $i \ge 0$

An identifier must not be the same as any reserved word, including the extra reserved words, which are used in full Algol W but not in the sublanguage used in this book.

Strings denote sequences of characters. Although we will not discuss the string-manipulation facilities of Algol W (in which strings are an additional data type), we will use strings as constant parameters in output statements. (See Section C.2.)

A ⟨normal string character⟩ is any keypunch character except the quotation mark ". A ⟨comment character⟩ is any keypunch character except the semicolon.

Blanks (unpunched card columns) can be interspersed freely in an Algol W program, without changing its syntactic structure or meaning, except for the following restrictions:

(1) Blanks must not occur within reserved words, identifiers, or numbers.

(2) Blanks occurring within strings are meaningful components of the strings.

(3) When a reserved word, identifier, or number is immediately followed by a reserved word, identifier, number, or comment body, they must be separated by at least one blank.

Comments may be interspersed freely in a program, without affecting its syntactic structure or meaning, except in the middle of a reserved word, identifier, number, string, or comment.

B.1.2   Simple Variable Declarations

$$\langle \text{declaration} \rangle ::= \langle \text{simple variable declaration} \rangle$$
$$\langle \text{simple variable declaration} \rangle ::= \tau \; [\![\langle \tau \text{ variable binder} \rangle]\!]_{\odot}^{n}$$
$$\langle \tau \text{ variable binder} \rangle ::= \langle \tau \text{ variable identifier} \rangle$$
$$\langle \tau \text{ variable identifier} \rangle ::= \langle \text{identifier} \rangle$$

The last three productions are schemas in which τ is a standard symbolic metavariable ranging over the four data types **integer**, **real**, **long real**, and **logical**. (However, note that reserved words such as **integer** are not written in boldface when they occur within the names of nonterminal symbols.) In the second production, n is a standard numeric metavariable ranging over the integers 1, 2, 3, ...

The scope of a declaration and its binders is the immediately enclosing block (excluding lower and upper bounds of array declarations that are immediately enclosed by this block). Two binders with the same scope must be distinct identifiers. Except for implicitly declared identifiers, every identifier occurrence in a complete program must be bound.

Each binder establishes the (phrase) type of the identifier occurrences that it binds. For example, any occurrence of x that is bound by the declaration **real** x must appear in a derivation tree as

$$\vdots$$
⟨real variable identifier⟩
|
⟨identifier⟩
|
⟨letter⟩
|
x

B.1.3 Variables and Expressions

⟨τ variable⟩ ::= ⟨τ variable identifier⟩
⟨τ expression⟩ ::= ⟨simple τ expression⟩
   | ⟨conditional τ expression⟩
⟨conditional τ_0 expression⟩ ::= **if** ⟨logical expression⟩
then ⟨τ_1 expression⟩ **else** ⟨τ_2 expression⟩
  where τ_0, τ_1, and τ_2 are given by column 1 of Table B.1
⟨simple τ expression⟩ ::= ⟨elementary τ expression⟩
⟨simple τ_0 expression⟩ ::= ⟨elementary τ_1 expression⟩
  $[\![$ = | ¬= $]\!]$ ⟨elementary τ_2 expression⟩
      ≠
  where τ_0, τ_1, and τ_2 are given by column 2 of Table B.1
⟨simple τ_0 expression⟩ ::= ⟨elementary τ_1 expression⟩
  $[\![$ < | <= | > | >= $]\!]$ ⟨elementary τ_2 expression⟩
      ≤   ≥
  where τ_0, τ_1, and τ_2 are given by column 3 of Table B.1
⟨elementary τ expression⟩ ::= ⟨τ term⟩
⟨elementary τ_{num} expression⟩ ::= $[\![$ + | − $]\!]$ ⟨τ_{num} term⟩
⟨elementary τ_0 expression⟩ ::=
  ⟨elementary τ_1 expression⟩ $[\![$ + | − $]\!]$ ⟨τ_2 term⟩
  where τ_0, τ_1, and τ_2 are given by column 4 of Table B.1
⟨elementary logical expression⟩ ::=
  ⟨elementary logical expression⟩ **or** ⟨logical term⟩
                       ∨
⟨τ term⟩ ::= ⟨τ factor⟩
⟨τ_0 term⟩ ::= ⟨τ_1 term⟩ * ⟨τ_2 factor⟩
                   ×
  where τ_0, τ_1, and τ_2 are given by column 5 of Table B.1
⟨τ_0 term⟩ ::= ⟨τ_1 term⟩ / ⟨τ_2 factor⟩
  where τ_0, τ_1, and τ_2 are given by column 6 of Table B.1
⟨integer term⟩ ::= ⟨integer term⟩ $[\![$ **div** | **rem** $]\!]$ ⟨integer factor⟩
                      ÷
⟨logical term⟩ ::= ⟨logical term⟩ **and** ⟨logical factor⟩
                  ∧
⟨τ factor⟩ ::= ⟨τ primary⟩

τ_1	τ_2	τ_0						
		1	2	3	4	5	6	7
integer	integer	integer	logical	logical	integer	integer	long real	permitted
integer	real	real	logical	logical	real	long real	real	—
integer	long real	long real	logical	logical	long real	long real	long real	—
real	integer	real	logical	logical	real	long real	real	permitted
real	real	real	logical	logical	real	long real	real	permitted
real	long real	real	logical	logical	real	long real	real	permitted
long real	integer	long real	logical	logical	long real	long real	long real	permitted
long real	real	real	logical	logical	real	long real	real	permitted
long real	long real	long real	logical	logical	long real	long real	long real	permitted
logical	logical	logical	logical	—	—	—	—	permitted

Operators:

1	2	3	4	5	6	7
if- **then-** **else**	= ¬=	∨ ⩽ ∧ ⩾	+ −	*	/	:=

Table B.1   Operation Types as a Function of their Argument Types.

$\langle$long real factor$\rangle$ ::= $\langle \tau_{\text{num}}$ factor$\rangle$ ** $\langle$integer primary$\rangle$

$\qquad\qquad\qquad\qquad\qquad\uparrow$

$\langle$logical factor$\rangle$ ::= $\neg$ $\langle$logical primary$\rangle$

$\qquad\qquad\qquad$**not**

$\langle \tau$ primary$\rangle$ ::= $\langle \tau$ constant$\rangle$ $|$ $\langle \tau$ variable$\rangle$ $|$ $(\langle \tau$ expression$\rangle)$

$\langle \tau_{\text{num}}$ primary$\rangle$ ::= **abs** $\langle \tau_{\text{num}}$ primary$\rangle$

$\langle$real primary$\rangle$ ::= **short** $\langle \tau_{\text{num}}$ primary$\rangle$

$\langle$long real primary$\rangle$ ::= **long** $\langle \tau_{\text{num}}$ primary$\rangle$

$\langle \tau_{\text{num}}$ constant$\rangle$ ::= $\langle \tau_{\text{num}}$ number$\rangle$

$\langle$logical constant$\rangle$ ::= **true** $|$ **false**

The standard metavariable τ_{num} ranges over the three numeric data types **integer**, **real**, and **long real**. When a production schema contains the metavariables τ_0, τ_1, and τ_2, it stands for the set of productions that can be obtained by replacing these metavariables in accordance with the appropriate column of Table B.1, which expresses τ_0 as a function of τ_1 and τ_2. An occurrence of "—" in Table B.1 indicates that the corresponding values of τ_1 and τ_2 are not permitted.

The syntax of logical expressions in Algol W is somewhat different than conventional mathematical notation. There are no multiple relations, and relations must be parenthesized when joined by **and** or **or**. For example, $x < y < z$ must be written as $(x < y)$ **and** $(y < z)$. In this book we have not followed this syntax in the logical expressions that occur within assertions.

The operators **short** and **long** can be used to convert any type of number to a single or double precision floating-point representation.

B.1.4 Statements

$\langle$complete program$\rangle$ ::= $\langle$statement$\rangle$

$\langle$statement$\rangle$ ::= $\langle$simple statement$\rangle$ $|$ $\langle$conditional statement$\rangle$

$\qquad$ $|$ $\langle$while statement$\rangle$

$\langle$simple statement$\rangle$ ::= $\langle$empty statement$\rangle$ $|$ $\langle$block$\rangle$

$\qquad$ $|$ $\langle$assignment statement$\rangle$

$\langle$empty statement$\rangle$ ::=

$\langle$block$\rangle$ ::= **begin** $[\![\langle$declaration$\rangle$;$]\!]^i$ $\langle$statement sequence$\rangle$ **end**

$\qquad$ where $i \geq 0$

$\langle$statement sequence$\rangle$ ::= $[\![\langle$statement$\rangle$;$]\!]^i$ $\langle$statement$\rangle$

$\qquad$ where $i \geq 0$

$\langle$assignment statement$\rangle$ ::= $\langle \tau_1$ variable$\rangle$:= $\langle \tau_2$ expression$\rangle$

$\qquad$ where τ_1 and τ_2 are given by column 7 of Table B.1

$\langle$conditional statement$\rangle$ ::=

$\qquad$ **if** $\langle$logical expression$\rangle$ **then** $\langle$statement$\rangle$

$\qquad$ $|$ **if** $\langle$logical expression$\rangle$ **then** $\langle$simple statement$\rangle$

$\qquad\qquad$ **else** $\langle$statement$\rangle$

$\langle$while statement$\rangle$ ::= **while** $\langle$logical expression$\rangle$ **do** $\langle$statement$\rangle$

As discussed in Section A.1, the distinction between statements and simple statements is made to avoid ambiguities involving conditional statements. The only context that requires a statement to be simple is the part of the two-way conditional statement between **then** and **else**.

The empty statement is simply an empty string of characters. Its execution leaves the state of the computation unchanged.

A block (excluding lower and upper bounds in immediately enclosed array declarations) is the scope of the binders in the declarations and label definitions that it immediately encloses. Since these binders have the same scope, they must be distinct identifiers.

In the schema describing assignment statements, the permissible values of the metavariables are described by column 7 of Table B.1. When τ_1 and τ_2 are permitted in this schema, τ_2 is said to be *assignment compatible* with τ_1.

It is important to distinguish the three symbols $=$, $:=$, and $::=$. The first is the relational operator of equality, the second is the assignment operator, and the third is a symbol of the syntax-defining notation, which never occurs in Algol W programs.

Probably the most common trivial syntactic error in Algol W is a misplaced semicolon. Aside from its use within procedure declaration headings, the semicolon plays two distinct roles: it marks the end of comments and it separates adjacent declarations and statements in a block. In the latter role, it behaves more like a comma in English than a period.

To check that the usage of semicolons in a program is correct, first eliminate all comments, including the semicolons that terminate the comments. Then there should be a semicolon after every declaration, and after every statement that is followed by another statement (or a label definition), but not after those statements that are followed by **end**, **else**, a comma, or a right parenthesis.

B.1.5 Implicitly Declared Procedures

⟨simple statement⟩ ::=
  ⟦ *read* | *readon* ⟧ (⟦⟨read parameter⟩⟧$_\odot^n$)
  | ⟦ *write* | *writeon* ⟧ (⟦⟨write parameter⟩⟧$_\odot^n$)
  | *iocontrol* (⟨integer expression⟩)
⟨read parameter⟩ ::= ⟨τ variable⟩
⟨write parameter⟩ ::= ⟨τ expression⟩ | ⟨string⟩
⟨integer primary⟩ ::=
  ⟦ *entier* | *truncate* | *round* ⟧ (⟨τ_{num} expression⟩)
⟨real primary⟩ ::=
  ⟦ *sqrt* | *exp* | *ln* | *log* | *sin* | *cos* | *arctan* ⟧
  (⟨τ_{num} expression⟩)

⟨long real primary⟩ ::=
  〚 *longsqrt* | *longexp* | *longln* | *longlog* | *longsin*
    | *longcos* | *longarctan* 〛 (⟨τ_{num} expression⟩)
⟨logical primary⟩ ::= *odd* (⟨integer expression⟩)

The identifiers *read, readon, write, writeon,* and *iocontrol* are implicitly declared procedure identifiers denoting built-in procedures for input and output (whose meaning is described in Appendix C). Thus the first production above is actually a special case of the general syntax for procedure statements, which will be given in Section B.3.5. Similarly, the remaining identifiers above are implicitly declared function-procedure identifiers, and the last four productions are special cases of the general syntax for function designators.

The functions *entier, truncate,* and *round* provide three methods for converting real numbers to integers. *entier(x)* gives the unique integer i such that $i \leq x < i+1$. Then

$$truncate(x) = \textbf{if } x \geq 0 \textbf{ then } entier(x) \textbf{ else } -entier(-x)$$
$$round(x) = \textbf{if } x \geq 0 \textbf{ then } truncate(x + 0.5) \textbf{ else } truncate(x - 0.5).$$

Most of the remaining functions are single-precision and double-precision versions of common elementary functions from mathematics. *ln* and *longln* produce logarithms to the base e, while *log* and *longlog* produce logarithms to the base 10.

Exercise

1. In each of the following cases, we give a nonterminal symbol of Algol W along with a phrase that is supposed to be derivable from the nonterminal symbol, but that in fact contains one or more syntactic errors. In each case, correct the syntactic errors without changing the intuitive meaning, and without changing the form of the phrase more than necessary. In the first two cases, give a derivation tree for the corrected phrase from the designated nonterminal. Assume that nonlocal identifiers behave as though declared by **integer** k, n; **real** x, y. (Note that Greek letters, superscripts, and the symbols 〚, 〛, and | are all part of notation for abbreviating sets of productions, and should not appear in derivation trees.)

⟨logical expression⟩ $0 < k \leq n$
⟨statement⟩ **begin real** z; $z := x/-y$; **end**
⟨real expression⟩ $-3 \times' - 3 \times -3$
⟨statement⟩ $n := n \ast\ast\ n$
⟨statement⟩ **if** $n > 0$ **then**
    while $n \neq 0$ **do** $n := n-1$;
  else $n := 1$
⟨statement⟩ **begin integer** i, **real** z;
    begin $i := 0$; $z := 1$ **end**
    begin $i := i+1$; $z := z$ **div** 2 **end**
  end

B.2 SYNTAX FOR CHAPTER 2

B.2.1 Array Declarations

$\langle$declaration$\rangle ::= \langle$array declaration$\rangle$

$\langle$array declaration$\rangle ::=$

$\quad \tau$ **array** $[\![\langle \tau$ array variable $([\![*]\!]_\odot^n)$ binder$\rangle]\!]_\odot^m$

$\quad ([\![\langle$lower bound$\rangle :: \langle$upper bound$\rangle]\!]_\odot^n)$

$\qquad \vdots$

$\langle$lower bound$\rangle ::= \langle$integer expression$\rangle$

$\langle$upper bound$\rangle ::= \langle$integer expression$\rangle$

$\langle \tau$ array variable (α) binder$\rangle ::= \langle \tau$ array variable (α) identifier$\rangle$

$\langle \tau$ array variable (α) identifier$\rangle ::= \langle$identifier$\rangle$

It is a syntactic error to use an n-dimensional array in an array designator with the wrong number of subscripts. To make this explicit in our syntax, we must include dimensionality as part of the type of an array identifier. For this purpose we will use a *dimension list*, which is a list of $n \geq 1$ asterisks separated by commas. (This rather unusual notation is chosen because of its similarity to specifiers for array parameters.) The standard symbolic metavariable α ranges over dimension lists.

B.2.2 Variables and Expressions Involving Arrays

$\langle \tau$ variable$\rangle ::= \langle \tau$ array variable $([\![*]\!]_\odot^n)\rangle ([\![\langle$subscript$\rangle]\!]_\odot^n)$

$\langle$subscript$\rangle ::= \langle$integer expression$\rangle$

$\langle \tau$ array variable $(\alpha)\rangle ::= \langle \tau$ array variable (α) identifier$\rangle$

$\langle \tau$ primary$\rangle ::= \langle \tau$ array expression $([\![*]\!]_\odot^n)\rangle ([\![\langle$subscript$\rangle]\!]_\odot^n)$

$\langle \tau$ array expression $(\alpha)\rangle ::= \langle \tau$ array variable $(\alpha)\rangle$

These productions introduce an intentional ambiguity. For example, Figure B.2 shows two derivation trees for a $\langle$real primary$\rangle$ of the form $\langle$real array variable $(*)\rangle (\langle$subscript$\rangle)$. The first tree reflects the view that the value of the primary is the value of a variable that is obtained by applying the array to a subscript. The second tree reflects the view that the value of the primary is obtained by applying to a subscript the function that is the value of the entire array.

This ambiguity is permissible since both derivation trees give rise to the same meaning. It must be included to permit the full variety of parameters discussed in Section B.3.

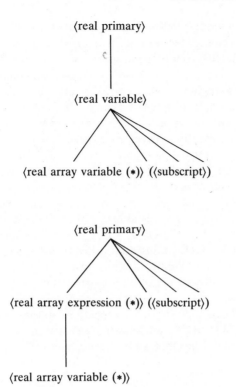

⟨real primary⟩

⟨real variable⟩   (1)

⟨real array variable (*)⟩ (⟨subscript⟩)

⟨real primary⟩

⟨real array expression (*)⟩ (⟨subscript⟩)   (2)

⟨real array variable (*)⟩

Figure B.2 Two Derivation Trees for a ⟨real primary⟩ of the
Form ⟨real array variable (*)⟩ (⟨subscript⟩).

B.3 SYNTAX FOR CHAPTER 3

In Section 3.1.2, we claimed that the use of extended specifiers insures that
the copy rule will preserve syntactic correctness. In this section, we give a
syntactic description that is sufficiently formal to permit this claim to be
demonstrated. In this description we use production schemas containing
metavariables whose ranges are in turn described by productions. This kind
of two-level grammar was invented by A. van Wijngaarden and first used
extensively in the definition of Algol 68 [van Wijngaarden 69].

To orient the reader to the details that follow, we begin with an explanation of why the copy rule preserves syntactic correctness. In this explanation
we will ignore call by value and result.

The set of phrase types, which is the range of the metavariable θ, is
defined by the productions in Section B.3.1. For each phrase type θ, there is

a nonterminal $\langle\theta$ binder$\rangle$ describing binders that establish θ, a nonterminal $\langle\theta$ identifier$\rangle$ describing identifier occurrences that are bound by a $\langle\theta$ binder$\rangle$, and a nonterminal $\langle\theta\rangle$ describing phrases of type θ. In Section B.3.5, we show that syntactic correctness is preserved by a *type-correct* substitution, which is a substitution that replaces free occurrences of $\langle\theta$ identifier$\rangle$, after appropriate parenthesization, by phrases that can be derived from $\langle\theta\rangle$. Thus we must show that the substitution prescribed by the copy rule is type-correct.

Consider a declaration **procedure** $P(FL); S$, where the formal parameter list FL binds the formal parameters $F_1 , \dots , F_n$. By the syntax of formal parameter lists, the type information in FL determines unique $\theta_1, \dots , \theta_n$ such that the occurrence of each F_i in FL is a $\langle\theta_i$ binder$\rangle$, so that the binding structure insures that each free occurrence of F_i in S is a $\langle\theta_i$ identifier$\rangle$. At the same time, this syntax also establishes that (excepting the anomalous behavior of call by value) FL is a $\langle\theta_1 , \dots , \theta_n$ formal parameter list$\rangle$. Then the syntax of procedure declarations establishes that P is a $\langle$procedure$(\theta_1 , \dots , \theta_n)$ binder$\rangle$, so that the binding structure insures that each occurrence of P bound by the procedure declaration is a $\langle$procedure$(\theta_1 , \dots , \theta_n)$ identifier$\rangle$.

Now suppose $P(A_1 , \dots , A_n)$ is a procedure statement containing such an occurrence. Then the syntax for procedure statements establishes that $A_1 , \dots , A_n$ is a $\langle\theta_1 , \dots , \theta_n$ actual parameter list$\rangle$, and the syntax of actual parameter lists establishes that each A_i must be a $\langle\theta_i\rangle$. Thus the substitution

$$S\Big|_{F_1, \dots, F_n \rightarrow A_1, \dots, A_n}$$

prescribed by the copy rule is type-correct.

B.3.1   Phrase Types

$$\langle\text{phrase type}\rangle ::= \tau \text{ \textbf{variable}} \mid \tau \text{ \textbf{expression}}$$
$$\text{var} \qquad\qquad \text{exp}$$
$$\mid \tau \text{ \textbf{array variable}} (\langle\text{dimension list}\rangle)$$
$$\text{var}$$
$$\mid \tau \text{ \textbf{array expression}} (\langle\text{dimension list}\rangle)$$
$$\text{exp}$$
$$\mid \text{\textbf{statement}} \mid \text{\textbf{procedure}} (\langle\text{phrase type list}\rangle)$$
$$\mid \tau \text{ \textbf{procedure}} (\langle\text{phrase type list}\rangle)$$
$$\langle\text{phrase type list}\rangle ::= [\![\langle\text{phrase type}\rangle]\!]_\odot^n$$
$$\langle\text{dimension list}\rangle ::= [\![*]\!]_\odot^n$$

The standard metavariables θ, π, and α respectively range over the sets of phrase types, phrase type lists, and dimension lists which are described by these productions. The phrase type **statement** includes parameterless proper procedures, since the two notions are equivalent in Algol W. Similarly, the phrase type τ **expression** includes parameterless τ function procedures.

B.3.2 Formal Parameter Lists

$\langle [\![\theta]\!]_\odot^n$ formal parameter list$\rangle ::= \langle [\![\theta]\!]_\odot^n$ specifier$\rangle$

$\langle \pi, [\![\theta]\!]_\odot^n$ formal parameter list$\rangle ::=$
$\quad \langle \pi$ formal parameter list$\rangle$; $\langle [\![\theta]\!]_\odot^n$ specifier$\rangle$

$\langle [\![\tau$ variable $]\!]_\odot^n$ specifier$\rangle ::=$
$\quad \tau [\![\{\mathbf{var}\} \mid \mathbf{result} \mid \mathbf{value\ result}]\!] [\![\langle \tau$ variable binder$\rangle]\!]_\odot^n$

$\langle [\![\tau$ expression $]\!]_\odot^n$ specifier$\rangle ::=$
$\quad \tau [\![\{\mathbf{exp}\} \mid \mathbf{procedure}]\!] [\![\langle \tau$ expression binder$\rangle]\!]_\odot^n$

$\langle [\![\tau$ expression $]\!]_\odot^n$ specifier$\rangle ::=$
$\quad \tau\ \mathbf{value}\ [\![\langle \tau$ variable binder$\rangle]\!]_\odot^n$

$\langle [\![\tau$ array variable $(\alpha)]\!]_\odot^n$ specifier$\rangle ::=$
$\quad \tau\ \mathbf{array}\ \{\mathbf{var}\}\ [\![\langle \tau$ array variable (α) binder$\rangle]\!]_\odot^n (\alpha)$

$\langle [\![\tau$ array expression $(\alpha)]\!]_\odot^n$ specifier$\rangle ::=$
$\quad \tau\ \mathbf{array}\ \{\mathbf{exp}\}\ [\![\langle \tau$ array expression (α) binder$\rangle]\!]_\odot^n (\alpha)$

$\langle [\![$ statement $]\!]_\odot^n$ specifier$\rangle ::=$
$\quad \mathbf{procedure}\ [\![\langle$ statement binder$\rangle]\!]_\odot^n$

$\langle [\![$ procedure $(\pi)]\!]_\odot^n$ specifier$\rangle ::=$
$\quad \mathbf{procedure}\ [\![\langle$ procedure (π) binder$\rangle]\!]_\odot^n \{\pi\}$

$\langle [\![\tau$ procedure $(\pi)]\!]_\odot^n$ specifier$\rangle ::=$
$\quad \tau\ \mathbf{procedure}\ [\![\langle \tau$ procedure (π) binder$\rangle]\!]_\odot^n \{\pi\}$

The schemas given above are complicated by the need to describe compound specifiers. The reader who has difficulty should first try to understand the productions that are obtained by taking $n=1$; these productions describe a sublanguage in which each specifier contains a single formal parameter.

When n is restricted to one, the first two schemas imply that a $\langle \theta_1, \ldots, \theta_n$ formal parameter list$\rangle$ has the form $\langle \theta_1$ specifier$\rangle$; $\ldots$; $\langle \theta_n$ specifier$\rangle$, and the remaining schemas imply that each $\langle \theta_i$ specifier$\rangle$ contains a $\langle \theta_i$ binder$\rangle$, along with appropriate information determining θ_i. The only exception is $\tau\ \mathbf{value}\ F$, which is a $\langle \tau$ expression specifier$\rangle$ containing a $\langle \tau$ variable binder$\rangle$. This reflects the fact that a formal parameter called by value can be used as a variable, e.g. on the left of an assignment statement, while the corresponding actual parameter can be an expression, e.g. a constant or compound expression.

As an illustration of the description of compound specifiers, consider deriving the formal parameter list $\mathbf{integer}\ \{\mathbf{exp}\}\ i, j;\ \mathbf{real}\ \{\mathbf{var}\}\ x, y$ from the nonterminal symbol $\langle$integer expression, integer expression, real variable, real variable formal parameter list$\rangle$. The necessary productions are obtained from the following substitutions:

$$\left.\begin{array}{l}\pi \ \rightarrow \textbf{integer expression, integer expression}\\ \theta \ \rightarrow \textbf{real variable}\\ n \ \rightarrow 2\end{array}\right\} \begin{array}{l}\text{in the second}\\ \text{schema}\end{array}$$

$$\left.\begin{array}{l}\theta \ \rightarrow \textbf{integer expression}\\ n \ \rightarrow 2\end{array}\right\} \text{ in the first schema}$$

$$\left.\begin{array}{l}\tau \ \rightarrow \textbf{integer}\\ n \ \rightarrow 2\end{array}\right\} \text{ in the fourth schema}$$

$$\left.\begin{array}{l}\tau \ \rightarrow \textbf{real}\\ n \ \rightarrow 2\end{array}\right\} \text{ in the third schema}$$

The scope of the binders in a formal parameter list consists of the formal parameter list itself and the immediately following procedure body. Since binders with the same scope must be distinct identifiers, the same identifier must not occur more than once in the same formal parameter list.

Although the parts of specifiers in curly brackets are used throughout this book, they are not actually part of Algol W and must be replaced by comments in real programs. Because of their omission from Algol W, certain syntactic errors are only detected during program execution.

B.3.3   Procedure Declarations

⟨declaration⟩ ::= ⟨procedure declaration⟩
⟨procedure declaration⟩ ::=
  procedure ⟨statement binder⟩ ; ⟨statement⟩
  | **procedure** ⟨procedure (π) binder⟩
    (⟨π formal parameter list⟩) ; ⟨statement⟩
  | τ **procedure** ⟨τ expression binder⟩ ; ⟨τ expression⟩
  | τ **procedure** ⟨τ procedure (π) binder⟩
    (⟨π formal parameter list⟩) ; ⟨τ expression⟩

In general, a proper procedure declaration establishes the phrase type **procedure**(π) for the identifier that it binds, and a τ function procedure declaration establishes the phrase type τ **procedure** (π), where in each case π is determined by the formal parameter list. However, a parameterless proper procedure declaration establishes the phrase type **statement**, and a parameterless τ function procedure declaration establishes the phrase type τ **expression**.

B.3.4   Binders and Identifiers

⟨θ binder⟩ ::= ⟨θ identifier⟩
⟨θ identifier⟩ ::= ⟨identifier⟩

These production schemas show that identifiers and their binders are classified by phrase type. Several particular instances of these schema have occurred in previous sections.

Without additional restrictions, the second schema would lead to ambiguity. This ambiguity is resolved by the proviso that the phrase type of an identifier occurrence is determined by the type of the binder which binds it. More precisely, for each phrase type θ, the production $\langle \theta$ identifier$\rangle ::= \langle$identifier$\rangle$ can only be used to described identifier occurrences that are bound by binders which are described by the production $\langle \theta$ binder$\rangle ::= \langle \theta$ identifier$\rangle$.

In a complete program, all free identifier occurrences must be implicitly declared identifiers. The type of such occurrences is given in Table B.3. The types of *read*, *readon*, *write*, and *writeon* are special cases, since these identifiers stand for "generic" procedures that can accept a variety of number and types of actual parameters. In the context of calls of *write* and *writeon*, **string** is an additional data type, so that strings can be used as constant write parameters, i.e.

$$\langle \text{string expression} \rangle ::= \langle \text{string} \rangle$$

Implicitly declared identifiers cannot be used as actual parameters.

Identifier	*Phrase Type*
entier *truncate* *round*	**integer procedure(real expression)**
sqrt *exp* *ln* *log* *sin* *cos* *arctan*	**real procedure(real expression)**
longsqrt *longexp* *longln* *longlog* *longsin* *longcos* *longarctan*	**long real procedure(long real expression)**
odd	**logical procedure(integer expression)**
read *readon*	**procedure(τ_1 variable, ... , τ_n variable)** where $n \geq 1$ and $\tau_1, ... , \tau_n \in$ {**integer, real, long real, logical**}
write *writeon*	**procedure(τ_1 expression, ... , τ_n expression)** where $n \geq 1$ and $\tau_1, ... , \tau_n \in$ {**integer, real, long real, logical, string**}
iocontrol	**procedure(integer expression)**
intfieldsize	**integer variable** (See Section C.2)

Table B.3   Phrase Types of Implicitly Declared Identifiers.

B.3.5 Procedure Statements and Function Designators

⟨simple statement⟩ ::= ⟨statement identifier⟩
⟨τ primary⟩ ::= ⟨τ expression identifier⟩
⟨τ array expression (α)⟩ ::= ⟨τ array expression (α) identifier⟩
⟨simple statement⟩ ::= ⟨procedure statement⟩
⟨procedure statement⟩ ::=
    ⟨procedure (π)⟩ (⟨π actual parameter list⟩)
⟨procedure (π)⟩ ::= ⟨procedure (π) identifier⟩
⟨τ primary⟩ ::= ⟨τ function designator⟩
⟨τ function designator⟩ ::=
    ⟨τ procedure (π)⟩ (⟨π actual parameter list⟩)
⟨τ procedure (π)⟩ ::= ⟨τ procedure (π) identifier⟩
⟨θ actual parameter list⟩ ::= ⟨θ⟩
⟨π, θ actual parameter list⟩ ::=
    ⟨π actual parameter list⟩, ⟨θ⟩

The first two productions show the contexts in which statement and τ expression identifiers can occur; such occurrences can be viewed as calls of parameterless procedures. The third production shows that array expression identifiers can occur as array expressions in much the same way that simple expression identifiers can occur as primaries. (The analogy would be better if we could view these occurrences as calls of parameterless "array" procedures, but Algol W does not permit procedures that return array values. In fact, array expression identifiers are the only kind of identifiers that can be bound by specifiers but not by declarations.)

The remaining productions describe procedure calls that contain actual parameters.

We can now show that type-correct substitutions preserve syntactic correctness:

(1) Let θ be any phrase type other than τ **expression** or **statement**, and consider any occurrence of a θ identifier that is not a binder. Among all the productions we have given, the only production that can describe such an occurrence has the form

⟨θ⟩ ::= ⟨θ identifier⟩

Thus syntactic correctness will be preserved if the occurrence is replaced by any phrase that can be derived from the nonterminal ⟨θ⟩.

(2) Consider an occurrence of a τ expression identifier that is not a binder. The only production that can describe such an occurrence has the form

⟨τ primary⟩ ::= ⟨τ expression identifier⟩

Thus the production

⟨τ primary⟩ ::= (⟨τ expression⟩)

shows that syntactic correctness will be preserved if the occurrence is replaced by (E), where E is any phrase that can be derived from $\langle \tau$ expression$\rangle$.

(3) Consider an occurrence of a statement identifier that is not a binder. The only production that can describe such an occurrence is

$\langle$simple statement$\rangle$ $::=$ $\langle$statement identifier$\rangle$

Thus the productions

$\langle$simple statement$\rangle$ $::=$ $\langle$block$\rangle$
$\langle$block$\rangle$ $::=$ **begin** $\langle$statement sequence$\rangle$ **end**
$\langle$statement sequence$\rangle$ $::=$ $\langle$statement$\rangle$

show that syntactic correctness will be preserved if the occurrence is replaced by **begin** S **end**, where S is any phrase that can be derived from $\langle$statement$\rangle$.

In summary, any nonbinding occurrence of $\langle \theta$ identifier$\rangle$ can be replaced by any phrase derived from $\langle \theta \rangle$, providing that the phrase is parenthesized if θ is τ **expression**, enclosed in **begin** ... **end** if θ is **statement**, and left unchanged otherwise.

In real Algol W, the parameter matching rules for call by value and result are slightly more relaxed than is indicated by this syntactic description. Consider a procedure statement or function designator beginning with an identifier that is bound by a procedure declaration containing the specifier τ_1 **value**. Then the corresponding actual parameter may be a phrase of type τ_2 **expression**, where τ_2 is assignment compatible with τ_1 (i.e. where τ_1 and τ_2 are permitted by column 7 of Table B.1). Similarly, for the specifier τ_1 **result** the corresponding actual parameter may be a phrase of type τ_2 **variable** where τ_1 is assignment compatible with τ_2, and for the specifier τ_1 **value result** the corresponding actual parameter may be a phrase of type τ_2 **variable**, where τ_1 and τ_2 are each assignment compatible with the other. The general intent is that τ_1 and τ_2 must insure the syntactic correctness of the initial and final assignment statements in the expansion of the procedure body caused by call by value or result.

In our formal syntactic description, we have ignored this relaxation of the parameter matching rules, since its formulation would introduce excessive complications.

Exercise

1. Give a derivation tree for the following block:

> **begin real array** $X(1::10)$;
> **procedure** $P(\text{**real array**} \{\text{**exp**}\} \ Y(*); \text{**real**} \{\text{**var**}\} \ Z); \ Z := Y(1);$
> $P(X, X(2))$
> **end**

B.4   SYNTAX FOR CHAPTER 4

B.4.1   The for Statement

⟨statement⟩ ::= ⟨for statement⟩
⟨for statement⟩ ::= **for** ⟨integer expression binder⟩ :=
⟦⟨lower bound⟩ **until** ⟨upper bound⟩
    | ⟨upper bound⟩ **step** −1 **until** ⟨lower bound⟩⟧
do ⟨statement⟩

The scope of the binder in a **for** statement is the **for** statement itself, excluding lower and upper bounds. Note that, since the identifier occurrences bound by this binder have type **integer expression**, they cannot be assigned to within the body of the **for** statement.

B.4.2   Labels and goto Statements

⟨statement sequence⟩ ::= ⟨statement⟩
    | ⟨statement⟩ ; ⟨statement sequence⟩
    | ⟨label definition⟩ ⟨statement sequence⟩
⟨label definition⟩ ::= ⟨label binder⟩ :
⟨label binder⟩ ::= ⟨label identifier⟩
⟨label identifier⟩ ::= ⟨identifier⟩
⟨simple statement⟩ ::= ⟨goto statement⟩
⟨goto statement⟩ ::= ⟦ **goto** | **go to** ⟧ ⟨label⟩
⟨label⟩ ::= ⟨label identifier⟩

The first production replaces the production for ⟨statement sequence⟩ given in Section B.1.4.

The scope of a label binder is the immediately enclosing block, with the usual exclusion of array bounds.

The syntax permits a label to be attached to the end of a block, so that jumping to the label from within the block causes an exit from the block, e.g.

begin ... *finish*: **end**

Strictly speaking, *finish* labels an empty statement that is the last statement in the block.

Although it is consistent to regard **label** as an additional phrase type, Algol W is anomalous in this regard. Although labels are represented by identifiers, they cannot be used as formal or actual parameters. In practice, this limitation does not cause difficulties since, in any situation where a label parameter would be useful, one can use a **goto** statement as a statement parameter instead.

APPENDIX C
INPUT AND OUTPUT IN ALGOL W

In this appendix we describe enough of the input and output facilities of Algol W to permit the writing of complete programs for testing and using simple algorithms. Input-output is the main aspect of Algol W that, although adequate for teaching purposes, is insufficient to support many practical programming applications. Except for the possibility of combining Algol W programs with FORTRAN or machine-language subroutines, the only input which can be read by an Algol W program is a sequence of punched cards, and the only output which can be written is a sequence of printed pages. (Of course, the program really reads images of cards and writes images of pages which are stored on magnetic disks or tapes, but this fact is irrelevant to the programmer.)

There are two fundamentally different facilities for reading cards. One method treats the input as a sequence of *data items*, each of which denotes a numerical or logical value. The other method, not described here, treats the input as a sequence of individual characters. There is a similar dichotomy of output facilities; in this case we will say enough about character-oriented output to permit the printing of titles and headings.

413

C.1 INPUT

The input to be read by an Algol W program must be contained on a deck of punched cards that is separate from the program itself. In contrast to the program, all 80 card columns are used. For most purposes, the separation between cards is ignored; for example, a data item can start on one card and finish on the next.

Except for string-oriented input, the input data is a sequence of items denoting numerical or logical values. The format for each data item is exactly the same as for numerical or logical constants in a program, except that numerical items can be prefixed with an optional $+$ or $-$ sign:

$$\langle \text{data item} \rangle ::= [\![\; | \; + \; | \; - \;]\!] \; \langle \tau_{num} \text{ constant} \rangle \; | \; \langle \text{logical constant} \rangle$$

Adjacent data items must be separated by one or more blanks, while individual data items must not contain blanks.

The data items in the input sequence are read, in order, by a succession of read operations. Within the program, the statement

$$readon \; ([\![\langle \text{read parameter} \rangle]\!]_{\odot}^{n})$$

where

$$\langle \text{read parameter} \rangle ::= \langle \tau \text{ variable} \rangle$$

performs one read operation for each parameter, from left to right. Each operation reads one data item from the input and makes it the current value of the corresponding parameter. Corresponding data items and parameters must be assignment compatible, i.e. their types must satisfy the following relationship:

read parameter	data item
integer	integer
real	integer, real, or long real
long real	integer, real, or long real
logical	logical .

The implicitly declared identifier *read* may be used instead of *readon*. The only difference is that, before the first data item is read, the input medium will be advanced to the first column of the next card, unless it is already positioned at the first column of a card. This facility has a potential for inadvertently skipping data items, which makes its use inadvisable.

If a program attempts to read beyond the end of the input data card deck, it is terminated with an error message. Regrettably, there is no way in a program to test whether the input has been exhausted.

C.2 OUTPUT

A statement of the form

$$[\![\; write \mid writeon \;]\!] \; ([\![\langle\text{write parameter}\rangle]\!]_{\odot}^{n})$$

where

$$\langle\text{write parameter}\rangle ::= \langle\tau \text{ expression}\rangle \mid \langle\text{string}\rangle$$

causes the value of each parameter, from left to right, to be printed as a data item.

Suppose that the printed representation of a data item uses n characters. Then, according to the type of the corresponding write parameter, this printed representation will be preceded and followed by blanks:

type	number of blanks on left	number of blanks on right
integer	$intfieldsize - n$	2
real	$14 - n$	2
long real	$22 - n$	2
logical	$6 - n$	2
string	0	0 .

Here *intfieldsize* is an implicitly declared integer variable that can be set by the program to determine the width of printed integer data items; if it is not reset its value will be 14. Note that, aside from the possibility of resetting *intfieldsize*, the total width of the character sequence printed by a nonstring write parameter is determined by the parameter itself, independently of the data being printed. An attempt to print an integer data item such that $n > intfieldsize$ will cause an asterisk to be printed.

Scale factors are only used in the printing of real and long real numbers with very large or very small magnitudes. Strings are printed exactly as written, except that the enclosing quotation marks are removed, and the pairs $''''$ are replace by single quotation marks $''$.

For example, the statement

$$write('''''TEST''''=''', 25, -25.0, 25'9, \textbf{true})$$

would print the following sequence of characters:

$$''TEST''=\quad ⑫\quad 25\quad ⑦\quad -25.00000\quad ④\quad 2.500000'+10\quad ④\quad TRUE\quad ②$$

where the circled integers indicate numbers of blank spaces.

In printing, characters are divided into lines of up to 132 characters, and lines are grouped into pages of up to 60 lines. The following rules determine when a data item (including its preceding blanks) will begin a new line or page:

(1) A data item will begin a new line if the item (including the blank spaces placed on its right) will not fit into the remaining space of the current line.

(2)   A new line will begin a new page if it will not fit into the remaining space of the current page.

(3)   The first data item printed by each execution of a *write* statement (as opposed to *writeon*) will begin a new line.

(4)   An execution of the statement *iocontrol*(2) will cause the next data item to be printed to begin a new line.

(5)   An execution of the statement *iocontrol*(3) will cause the next data item to be printed to begin a new page.

The use of *iocontrol*(2) is illustrated by the following complete program for printing the squares of the integers 1 to 100:

```
begin integer n;
write("THE FIRST HUNDRED SQUARES");
iocontrol(2);
n := 0;
while n ≠ 100 do begin n := n+1; writeon(n×n) end
end   .
```

Performing *iocontrol*(2) forces the first execution of *writeon*$(n \times n)$ to begin a new line. Thereafter, the lines are filled out with integers.

C.3   AN EXAMPLE OF A COMPLETE PROGRAM

Consider writing a complete program for testing a statement that computes factorials. More specifically, the program is to execute some number of "cases", where each case consists of reading an integer, computing its factorial, and printing the integer and its factorial. Even though this is a rather vague specification, it is useful to construct the program in a top-down fashion.

The first step is to determine the number of cases and iterate over them. The simplest approach is to require the first input item to be a count of the number of cases. Then we have

```
begin integer cases;
readon(cases);
"Write heading";
{whileinv: cases is the number of cases yet to be done}
while cases > 0 do
   begin
   cases := cases - 1;
   "Process one case"
   end
end   .
```

We have included a step that prints a heading for the output, but we postpone the details until we see what the output for each case will be like. Note that the concept of an invariant assertion is still valid, even though the assertion has been written in English.

At first sight, one might expect the following form for "Process one case":

> "Read input";
> "Compute Factorial";
> "Write output" .

But this neglects the possibility that the factorial may be undefined for the input value. A better plan for "Process one case" is:

> **begin integer** n;
> *readon*(n);
> **if** $n < 0$ **then** "Process invalid input"
> **else** "Process valid input"
> **end** .

Then "Process valid input" expands easily into

> **begin long real** f;
> "Set f to n!";
> *write*(n, **short** f)
> **end** .

Here we have chosen to make f a long real variable, since the factorial function can easily exceed the range of an integer variable. To insure adequate accuracy, we compute f in double precision, but print it in single precision. Then "Set f to n!" is simply the program given in Section 1.3.1, except that f is a long real variable rather than an integer variable. (Of course, we are lucky that we do not have to modify this program to accomplish the change in arithmetic.)

Next we fill in "Process invalid input":

> *write*(n, "   ⑤   UNDEFINED") .

The circled integer indicates the number of blanks; it is chosen to make UNDEFINED line up (on the right) with the values of f printed for valid cases. Finally "Write heading" can be filled in with

> *write*("   ⑬   N   ⑨   FACT(N)");
> *write*(" ") .

The blanks in the first statement are chosen to line up N and FACT(N) with the values of n and f printed for valid cases. The second statement inserts a blank line between the heading and the lines for each case.

The complete program is

```
comment Test Program for Factorial Computation;
begin integer cases;
readon(cases);
comment write heading;
    write("          ⑬          N     ⑨      FACT(N)");
    write(" ");
{whileinv: cases is the number of cases yet to be done}
while cases > 0 do
    begin
    cases := cases − 1;
        begin integer n;
        readon(n);
        if n < 0 then
            comment process invalid input;
            write(n, "    ⑤   UNDEFINED")
        else comment process valid input;
            begin long real f;
            {n ≥ 0}
                begin integer k;
                k := 0; f := 1;
                {whileinv: f=k! and 0 ≤ k ≤ n}
                while k ≠ n do
                    begin k := k + 1; f := k × f end
                end;
            {f=n!}
            write(n, short f)
            end
        end
    end
end   .
```

Exercises

1. Write a complete program to read the number of cases to be performed and then, for each case, read a real number x and an integer n, and output

    (a) The values of x and n.
    (b) x^n, computed by evaluating the expression $x**n$.
    (c) x^n, computed by one of the slow algorithms in Exercise 1 after Section 1.3.3.
    (d) x^n, computed by one of the fast algorithms in Section 1.3.5.
    (e) A count of the number of multiplications performed by the fast algorithm.

    Provision should be made for giving an error message if $n < 0$.

2. Write a procedure for producing a readable table of a real function of two arguments. The procedure should have the form

    > **procedure** *printtable*(**integer value** *nx, ny*;
    > **real value** *minx, miny, stepx, stepy*;
    > **real procedure** f {**real exp, real exp**}); ... .

    The procedure should tabulate $f(x, y)$ for

    $$x = minx + i \times stepx \text{ where } i \in \boxed{0 \quad nx-1}$$
    and
    $$y = miny + j \times stepy \text{ where } j \in \boxed{0 \quad ny-1} \quad .$$

    The table should be organized into rows and columns so that each value of x corresponds to a row, and appears at the left of the row, and each value of y corresponds to a column, and appears at the head of the column.

    This problem becomes harder if ny is so large that the table is wider than the paper on which it is printed. In this case, one can print out the table as a sequence of vertical strips which can be pasted together.

REFERENCES

Aho 72
Aho, A. V. and Ullman, J. D., *The Theory of Parsing, Translation, and Compiling, Vol. I: Parsing,* Prentice-Hall, Englewood Cliffs, N.J. (1972).

Aho 74
Aho, A. V., Hopcroft, J. E., and Ullman, J. D., *The Design and Analysis of Computer Algorithms,* Addison-Wesley, Reading, Mass. (1974).

Backhouse 79
Backhouse, R. C., *Syntax of Programming Languages: Theory and Practice,* Prentice-Hall International, London (1979).

Backus 59
Backus, J. W., "The syntax and semantics of the proposed international algebraic language of the Zurich ACM–GAMM Conference", *Proceedings of the International Conference on Information Processing,* June 1959, 125–132, UNESCO, Paris (1960).

Barron 63
Barron, D. W., Buxton, J. N., Hartley, D. F., Nixon, E., and Strachey, C., "The main features of CPL", *Computer Journal* **6** (2), 134–143 (July 1963).

Chomsky 56
Chomsky, N., "Three models for the description of language", *IRE Transactions on Information Theory* **IT–2** (3), 113–124 (September 1956).

Clint 72
Clint, M. and Hoare, C. A. R., "Program proving: Jumps and functions", *Acta Informatica* **1** (3), 214–224 (1972).

Crandall 78
Crandall, R. E., "On the '3x+1' problem", *Mathematics of Computation* **32**, 1281–1292 (October 1978).

Dahl 68
Dahl, O.-J., Myhrhaug, B., and Nygaard, K., *Simula 67 Common Base Language,* Norwegian Computing Centre, Oslo (1968).

Dahl 72
Dahl, O.-J. and Hoare, C. A. R., "Hierarchical program structures", in Dahl, O.-J., Dijkstra, E. W., and Hoare, C. A. R., *Structured Programming,* Academic Press, London, 175–220 (1972).

Dijkstra 59
Dijkstra, E. W., "A note on two problems in connexion with graphs", *Numerische Mathematik* **1**, 269–271 (1959).

Dijkstra 60
Dijkstra, E. W., "Recursive programming", *Numerische Mathematik* **2**, 312–318 (1960), reprinted in *Programming Systems and Languages,* ed. S. Rosen, McGraw-Hill, New York, 221–227 (1967).

Dijkstra 68
Dijkstra, E. W., "Go to statement considered harmful", *Comm. ACM* **11** (3), 147–148 (March 1968).

Dijkstra 71
Dijkstra, E. W., *A Short Introduction to the Art of Programming,* EWD 316, Technische Hogeschool Eindhoven (August 1971).

Dijkstra 72
Dijkstra, E. W., "Notes on structured programming", in Dahl, O.-J., Dijkstra, E. W., and Hoare, C. A. R., *Structured Programming,* Academic Press, London, 1–82 (1972).

Dijkstra 75
Dijkstra, E. W., "Guarded commands, nondeterminacy and formal derivation of programs", *Comm. ACM* **18** (8), 453–457 (August 1975).

Dijkstra 76
Dijkstra, E. W., *A Discipline of Programming,* Prentice-Hall, Englewood Cliffs, N.J. (1976).

Dorn 72
Dorn, W. S. and McCracken, D. D., *Numerical Methods with Fortran IV Case Studies,* Wiley, New York (1972).

van Emden 79
van Emden, M. H., "Programming with verification conditions", *IEEE Transactions on Software Engineering* **SE-5** (2), 148–159 (March 1979).

Fishman 78
Fishman, G. S., *Principles of Discrete Event Simulation,* Wiley, New York (1978).

Floyd 62
Floyd, R. W., "Algorithm 97: Shortest path", *Comm. ACM* **5** (6), 345 (June 1962).

Floyd 64
Floyd, R. W., "Algorithm 245: Treesort 3", *Comm. ACM* **7** (12), 701 (December 1964).

Floyd 67a
Floyd, R. W., "Assigning meanings to programs", in Mathematical Aspects of Computer Science, ed. J. T. Schwartz, *Proceedings of Symposia in Applied Mathematics* **19**, American Mathematical Society, Providence, 19–32 (1967).

Floyd 67b
Floyd, R. W., "Nondeterministic algorithms", *Journal ACM* **14** (4), 636–644 (October 1967).

Foley 71
Foley, M. and Hoare, C. A. R., "Proof of a recursive program: Quicksort", *Computer Journal* **14** (4), 391–395 (November 1971).

Gentzen 35
Gentzen, G., "Untersuchungen über das logisiche Schliessen", *Mathematische Zeitschrift* **39**, 176–210, 405–431 (1935).
Translation: "Investigations into logical deduction", in *The Collected Papers of Gerhard Gentzen,* ed. M. E. Szabo, North-Holland, Amsterdam, 68–131 (1969).

Graham 75
Graham, S. L. and Rhodes, S. P., "Practical syntactic error recovery", *Comm. ACM* **18** (11), 639–650 (November 1975).

Gries 71
Gries, D., *Compiler Construction for Digital Computers,* Wiley (1971).

Gries 80
Gries, D. and Levin, G., "Assignment and procedure call proof rules", *ACM Transactions on Programming Languages and Systems* **2** (4), 564–579 (October 1980).

Guttag 77
Guttag, J. V., "Abstract data types and the development of data structures", *Comm. ACM* **20** (6), 396–404 (June 1977).

Hamming 71
Hamming, R. W., *Introduction to Applied Numerical Analysis,* McGraw-Hill, New York (1971).

Hoare 62
Hoare, C. A. R., "Quicksort", *Computer Journal* **5** (1), 10–15 (April 1962).

Hoare 69
Hoare, C. A. R., "An axiomatic basis for computer programming", *Comm. ACM* **12** (10), 576–580 and 583 (October 1969).

Hoare 71a
Hoare, C. A. R., "Proof of a program: FIND", *Comm. ACM* **14** (1), 39–45 (January 1971).

Hoare 71b
Hoare, C. A. R., "Procedures and parameters: An axiomatic approach", in *Symposium on Semantics of Algorithmic Languages,* ed. E. Engeler, Lecture Notes in Mathematics No. 188, Springer-Verlag, Berlin, 102–116 (1971).

Hoare 72a
Hoare, C. A. R., "Notes on data structuring", in Dahl, O.-J., Dijkstra, E. W., and Hoare, C. A. R., *Structured Programming,* Academic Press, London, 83–174 (1972).

Hoare 72b
Hoare, C. A. R., "A note on the for statement", *BIT* **12** (3), 334–341 (1972).

Hoare 72c
Hoare, C. A. R., "Proof of correctness of data representations", *Acta Informatica* **1** (4), 271–281 (1972).

Hoare 73
Hoare, C. A. R. and Wirth, N., "An axiomatic definition of the programming language PASCAL", *Acta Informatica* **2** (4), 335–355 (1973).

Hopcroft 69
Hopcroft, J. E. and Ullman, J. D., *Formal Languages and their Relation to Automata,* Addison-Wesley, Reading (1969).

Jones 80
Jones, C. B., *Software Development: A Rigorous Approach,* Prentice-Hall International, London (1980).

Knuth 73
Knuth, D. E., *The Art of Computer Programming, Vol. 3: Sorting and Searching,* Addison-Wesley, Reading (1973).

Knuth 74
Knuth, D. E., "Structured programming with **go to** statements", *Computing Surveys* **6** (4), 261–301 (December 1974).

Landin 65
Landin, P. J., "A correspondence between Algol 60 and Church's lambda-notation", *Comm. ACM* **8** (2,3), 89–101 and 158–165 (February–March 1965).

Landin 66a
Landin, P. J., "A λ-calculus approach", in *Advances in Programming and Non-Numerical Computation,* ed. L. Fox, Pergamon Press, 97–141 (1966).

Landin 66b
Landin, P. J., "The next 700 programming languages", *Comm. ACM* **9** (3), 157–166 (March 1966).

Liskov 75
Liskov, B., "An introduction to CLU", in *New Directions in Algorithmic Languages 1975,* ed. S. A. Schuman, IRIA, Rocquencourt, 139–156 (1975).

London 78
London, R. L., Guttag, J. V., Horning, J. J., Lampson, B. W., Mitchell, J. G., and Popek, G. J., "Proof rules for the programming language Euclid", *Acta Informatica* **10** (1), 1–26 (1978).

Lucas 68
Lucas, P., "Two constructive realizations of the block concept and their equivalence", IBM Laboratory Vienna, Technical Report TR 25.085 (28 June 1968).

McCarthy 60
McCarthy, J., "Recursive functions of symbolic expressions and their computation by machine, Part I", *Comm. ACM* **3** (4), 184–195 (April 1960).

McCarthy 63
McCarthy, J., "A basis for a mathematical theory of computation", in *Computer Programming and Formal Systems,* ed. P. Braffort and D. Hirshberg, North-Holland, Amsterdam, 33–70 (1963).

McCarthy 67
McCarthy, J. and Painter, J., "Correctness of a compiler for arithmetic expressions", in Mathematical Aspects of Computer Science, ed. J. T. Schwartz, *Proceedings of Symposia in Applied Mathematics* **19,** American Mathematical Society, Providence, 33–41 (1967).

Morgan 70
Morgan, H. L., "Spelling correction in systems programs", *Comm. ACM* **13** (2), 90–94 (February 1970).

Morris 68
Morris, R., "Scatter storage techniques", *Comm. ACM* **11** (1), 38–44 (January 1968).

Naur 60
Naur, P. et al., "Report on the algorithmic language ALGOL 60", *Comm. ACM* **3** (5), 299–314 (May 1960).

Naur 63
Naur, P. et al., "Revised report on the algorithmic language ALGOL 60", *Comm. ACM* **6** (1), 1–17 (January 1963).

Naur 66
Naur, P., "Proof of algorithms by general snapshots", *BIT* **6** (4), 310–316 (1966).

Nievergelt 73
Nievergelt, J. and Reingold, E. M., "Binary search trees of bounded balance", *SIAM Journal Computing* **2** (1), 33–43 (March 1973).

Owicki 76
Owicki, S. and Gries, D., "An axiomatic proof technique for parallel programs", *Acta Informatica* **6,** 319–340 (1976).

Pritsker 79
Pritsker, A. A. B. and Pegden, C. D., *Introduction to Simulation and SLAM,* Halstead Press (1979).

Randell 64
Randell, B. and Russell, L. J., *Algol 60 Implementation; The Translation and Use of Algol 60 Programs on a Computer,* Academic Press, New York 1964.

Reynolds 72
Reynolds, J. C., "Definitional interpreters for higher-order programming languages", *Proceedings 25th National ACM Conference,* Boston, August 1972, Association for Computing Machinery, New York, 717–740.

Reynolds 78a
Reynolds, J. C., "Syntactic control of interference", *Conference Record of the Fifth Annual Symposium on Principles of Programming Languages,* Tucson, January 1978, Association for Computing Machinery, New York, 39–46.

Reynolds 78b
Reynolds, J. C., 'Programming with transition diagrams", in *Programming Methodology, A Collection of Papers by Members of IFIP WG 2.3*, ed. D. Gries, Springer-Verlag, Berlin, 153–165 (1978).

Reynolds 79
Reynolds, J. C., "Reasoning about arrays", *Comm. ACM* **22** (5), 290–299 (May 1979).

Reynolds 81
Reynolds, J. C., "Idealized Algol and its specification logic", Computer and Information Science, Syracuse University, Report 1–81 (July 1981).

Sedgewick 77
Sedgewick, R., "The analysis of Quicksort programs", *Acta Informatica* **7** (4), 327–355 (1977).

Sedgewick 78
Sedgewick, R., "Implementing Quicksort programs", *Comm. ACM* **21** (10), 847–857 (October 1978).

Sites 72
Sites, R. L., *Algol W Reference Manual*, STAN-CS-71-230, Stanford University Computer Science Department (February 1972).

Slagle 69
Slagle, J. R. and Dixon, J. K., "Experiments with some programs that search game trees", *Journal ACM* **16** (2), 189–207 (April 1969).

Stoy 77
Stoy, J. E., *Denotational Semantics: The Scott-Strachey Approach to Programming Language Theory*, MIT Press, Cambridge, Mass. (1977).

Tarjan 72
Tarjan, R., "Depth-first search and linear graph algorithms", *SIAM Journal Computing* **1** (2), 146–160 (June 1972).

Tennent 76
Tennent, R. D., "The denotational semantics of programming languages", *Comm. ACM* **19** (8), 437–453 (August 1976).

Tennent 81
Tennent, R. D., *Principles of Programming Languages*, Prentice-Hall International, London (1981).

Terras 76
Terras, R., "A stopping time problem on the positive integers", *Acta Arithmetica* **30**, 241–252 (1976).

Warshall 62
Warshall, S., "A theorem on Boolean matrices", *Journal ACM* **9** (1), 11–12 (January 1962).

van Wijngaarden 69
van Wijngaarden, A. (ed.), Mailloux, B. J., Peck, J. E. L., and Koster, C. H. A., "Report on the algorithmic language ALGOL 68", MR 101, Mathematisch Centrum, Amsterdam (February 1969), also *Numerische Mathematik* **14**, 79–218 (1969).

Williams 64
Williams, J. W. J., "Algorithm 232: Heapsort", *Comm. ACM* **7** (6), 347–348 (June 1964).

Wirth 66
Wirth, N. and Hoare, C. A. R., "A contribution to the development of ALGOL", *Comm. ACM* **9** (6), 413–432 (June 1966).

Wirth 71a
Wirth, N., "The programming language PASCAL", *Acta Informatica* **1** (1), 35–63 (1971).

Wirth 71b
Wirth, N., "Program development by stepwise refinement", *Comm. ACM* **14** (4), 221–227 (April 1971).

Wulf 76
Wulf, W. A., London, R. L., and Shaw, M., "An introduction to the construction and verification of Alphard programs", *IEEE Transactions on Software Engineering* **SE-2** (4), 253–265 (December 1976).

INDEX

abs, 14, 401.
Absolute error, **61,** 62, 66–68.
Abstract program, 60, 289,
    298, 301–8, 321–22,
    325–34, 352–54,
    363–74.
Abstract specification logic,
    203, 247–51, 251–52,
    257.
Abstraction function, 315.
Actual parameter, **158–59,**
    160–62, 166–68, 170,
    182, 217, 252–55,
    406–10, 412.
Adding assumptions, inference
    rule, **218.**
Addition, 14, 68, 399–401.
Adjacency matrix, 317.
Algebra, 121, 134.
Algol 60, xii, 56, 157, 383.
Algol 68, xii, 161, 245, 405.
Algol W, 33, 114, 160, 298,
    395–416,
    advantages, xii, 56, 75, 88,
    130, 157, 171, 260,
    limitations, 10–11, 161, 243,
    278, 298, 413.
Allocation, 54, 75.
Almost balanced tree, **192,** 198,
    334, 348.
Alpha-beta heuristic, 155.
Alpha conversion, 55–58, **57,**
    89–90, 92, 159, 164–65,
    211, 261.
Alpha variant, **57.**
Alphabetic ordering, 108, 132,
    136.
Alternative sign, **391–92,** 394,
    396.
Alternative symbols, 396.
Ambiguity, 11, 15–16, 298,
    379, **386–88,** 404–5,
    409.
Amoeba race, 325–28, 334.
Ampersand, 167, 213–14,
    218.
Analysis of algorithms, 61.
and, 5, **15,** 129–30, 214,
    399–401.
Antisymmetry, 100, 108, 336.
APL, 56, 114.
Application, **95, 221.**
Approximation, 61–69, 71.
Arc, **286,** 299.

Array, **73–76,** 73–155, **148–49,**
    172–77, 182, 183, 194,
    209, 251–56, 308–10,
    404.
Array assignment, inference
    rule, **112,** 112–14, **150,**
    251, 256, 324.
Array declaration, inference
    rule, **256.**
Array designator, **74,** 96, 162,
    209, 216–17, 251–55,
    395, 404–5.
Array element
    noninterference,
    inference rule, **253.**
Array parameter, 172–77,
    182–83, 407.
Array segment noninter-
    ference, inference rule,
    253, 253–55.
ascend (procedure), 342.
Assertion, **19,** 19–27, 38–42, 51,
    78, 89, 96, 149–50, 167,
    181, 201, 205, 211–12,
    273–75,
    relevant, 283, 292, 295,
    static, **213,** 219–20, 241–43,
    253, 257.
Assertion procedure, **212,** 216,
    217, 338.
Assignment:
    array, 112, 114, 173,
    inference rule, **112,** 113,
    114, **150, 251,** 256, 324,
    compatible, **402,** 411, 414,
    simple, inference rule, **44,**
    47–48, 91, 111–12, **223,**
    226, **248,**
    statement, **12,** 16, 70, 205,
    226, 401–2.
Associativity, 119, 120, 134,
    135, 388.
Assumption, **214,** 218–19, 221,
    226–27.
Asterisk, 98, 172, 300, 404,
    415.
Auxiliary variable, **306,** 307,
    311.
Axiom, **220–21,** 223–24, 248,
    249, 251–53, 256–57.

Back link, 322–24, 333.
Backus, J. W., 383,
Backus-Naur form, 383–94.

Balance, *see* Almost balanced
    tree.
Based on (termination), **22.**
begin, 4, 401.
Behavior pattern, 1–7.
Beta reduction, **244,** 244–47,
    320.
Bijection, 119, **120,** 120–22,
    133–34, 139–40,
    336–37.
Binary search, program, 102–9,
    181, 309.
Binary tree, 195, 334–43,
    335–36, 347–49.
Binder, **56,** 406, 408–9.
Binding, 55–58, 75–76, 89–92,
    159, 162–65, 182–83,
    203, 207, 211, 244,
    260–61, 272–73,
    398–99, 406, 408–9,
    412.
Binding occurrence, **56.**
Blank, 396, 398, 414, 415.
Block, **4,** 10, 53, 56, 75–76,
    226–28, 272, 284, 285,
    287, 401–2, *see also*
    Compound statement,
    Parenthesization,
    expression, 180–81, 395.
Block (set of integer
    sequences), **150.**
Block structure, 203, 226.
BNF, 383–94.
Body, 18, 158, 226, 261.
Boldface, 12, 396.
Bottom-up programming, 7.
Bound, lower and upper, **74,**
    75–76, 149, 260–61,
    404, 412.
Bound occurrence, **56,** 159.
Bracket, curly, 20, 24, 98,
    100, 161, 167, 182,
    396, 408.
Breadth-first, **314,** 347–48.
Built-in procedure, 16, 395,
    402–3, 409, 414–16.

Call, **158.**
Call by address, 171–72, 203.
Call by name, **169,** 170–73, 203,
    240–43, 262, 266–69,
    316.
Call by reference, 171–72,
    203.

Call by value or result, **169–70**, 171–73, 177, 181–83, 203, 237–40, 244, 262, 266–69, 316, 407, 411.
Calling tree, **189**, 189–94, 198, 200, 368.
Cartesian product, **131, 149**, 149–50.
Category, 121, 136.
Characteristic vector, **309–10**, 310–12, 315–17, 334.
Chomsky, N., 383.
Choose and delete, *see* Deletion.
Clint, M., 275.
Closed subroutine, 160.
cod, 95, 96, 98, 112.
Codomain, **95**, 96, 98, 112.
Collision, 91–92, 159, 163–65.
Column, **149**, 150, 396, 414.
Combining assumptions, inference rule, **218**.
Comma, 162, 392, 396.
Comment, **5**, 23–26, 167, 182, 397–98, 402.
Commutivity, 134.
Compiler, 10, 61, 160–61, 201.
Complete program, **55**, 401, 409, 416–19.
Component interval, **81**.
Composition, **119**, 119–21, 123, 124, 133, 138.
Compound specifier, **162**, 173, 182, 407–8.
Compound statement, 206, *see also* Block,
inference rule, **44, 220**.
Concatenation, 130–36, **131**, 139–42, 146, 354, *see also* Sequence concatenation.
Conclusion, **43, 217**.
Concrete program, **298**, *see also* Transformation.
Concurrent computation, 168, 289–90.
Conditional correctness, **22**, 40, 43, 51.
Conditional expression, **16**, 80, 100, 128–30, 399–401.
Conditional statement, **3–4**, 10, 287, 386–88, 401–2,
inference rules, **49, 220**.
Congruence, 134.
Conjunction of assumptions, 213–14, 218.
Conjunction of specifications, inference rule, **52, 221**.
Consequent, **20**.
Constancy, inference rule, **223**, 234.
Constant, **14–15, 69–70**, 397–98, 401.

Context-free grammar, 390.
Continuation semantics, 210, 275.
Control structure, 1, 7, 259, 272, 281, 286.
Coproduct, 136.
Copy rule, 158–60, **159**, 163–65, 172, 180, 182–85, 202, 208–9, 247, 316, 320, 342, 355, 405–6.
Counting zeroes in array, program, 78.
Current value, 12, 96.
Cyclic path, 336, 364, 373.

Dahl, O.-J., 298.
Data representation structuring, 60, 289, **297–98**, 297–382.
Date type, **15**, 16, 69–71, 144, **162**, 204, 213, 297–98, 320, 394, 398, 409.
Declaration, 53–55, 162, 182–83, 226, 401,
array, 74, 149, 194, 404.
inference rule, **256**.
binding by 56, 75–76, 159, 162, 182–83, 398–99, 406, 408,
function procedure, 157, 180, 181, 408,
inference rule, **257**, 258,
general inference rule, **55**, 58,
proper procedure, 157–60, 181, 207–10, 406, 408,
inference rule, 228–43, **231–32**, 246–50, **249**, 347, 368,
simple variable, 53–54, 69, 398,
inference rule, **226–27**, 251.
Decreasing order, **103**, 144.
Deletion, 308–9, 313–14, 334, 344.
Depth, **189–90**.
Depth-first search, **315**, recursive program, 363–68.
Derivation, **384**, *see also* Inference rule.
Derivation tree, 222, **385**, 385–91, 398–99, 403, 404–5, 411.
descend (procedure), 342–43, 349.
Describes, **205**.
Diagram, 78–85, 286–90.
Difference, *see* Subtraction.
Differentiation, 68–69.
Dijkstra, E. W., 1, 7, 22, 32, 185, 271, 272, 289, 325.

Dimension list, **172**, 182–83, 404, 406.
Direct semantics, 210.
Direct substitution, **84**.
Directed graph, **299–301**, **324–25**, 335–36.
Discharging assumptions, **227**.
Disjoint, **81**.
Disjoint union, **131**, 131–34, 136, 139.
Disjunction of specifications, inference rule, **52, 221**.
Distance, *see* Minimum distance.
div, 14, 59, 70, 107, 399.
Dividing line, **83**.
Division, **14**, 59, 70, 107, 399–401.
programs, 13–14, 27–30, 35, 307.
do, 5, 259, 401, 412.
dom, 79, 95, *see also* Domain.
Domain:
of array, **74**, 75, 79, 149, 256, 309,
of function, **95**, 96–98, 112.
Domain constancy, inference rule, **256**.
Double precision, **63–65**, 69–71, 401, 417.
downgood (procedure), 338.
Duplicate values, 103, 308, 318,
program for removing, 118.
Dynamic array allocation, 75–76.
Dynamic scope, 54.

Edge, **299**, 324–25.
Efficiency, *see* Execution time, Storage.
Element, of array, **74**.
Elementary function, 402–3, 409.
eliminatehole (procedure), 347.
else, 3, 16, 399, 401.
van Emden, M. H., 281.
Empty array, 75, 97.
Empty function, **97**, 98, 134, 141–42.
Empty set, 80, 82, 90, 97–98, 150, 218.
Empty statement, **51**, 272–73, 401–2, 412,
inference rule, **51, 221**.
end, 4, 401.
End line, **83**.
entier (procedure), 402–3, 409.
Enumeration, **308–9**, 310, 312–15, 317–18, 334, 375.

Environment, 203–10, **204,**
    221, 275.
Equality, 15–16, 74, **95,**
    399–401, 402.
Equivalence, **41, 100,** 122, 363.
Erasure, **83.**
Error, 61,
    input, 65–68, 414, 417–19,
    numerical, 61–69, 71,
    parameter matching,
        160–61, 167,
    propagation, 65–69,
    subscript, 61, **74–75,** 77,
        87–88, 112, 128, 171,
        251, 375,
    syntactic, 10–11, 396, 403,
        408.
Evaluation, avoided or
    repeated, 129–30,
    170–71, 181, 240–43.
Exchange, 114, 115–17, 119,
    122–23, 125–26, 146,
    174, 362, *see also swap.*
Execution time, 32–34, 107,
    114, 160, 170, 172, 173,
    177, 187, 189–95,
    197–99, 200–1, 286,
    291, 294, 305, 308–10,
    313, 316–17, 332, 334,
    348, 356, 361–62, 368,
    382.
Existential quantifier, *see*
    Quantifier.
exp, 161–63, 173, 180, 182–83,
    406–7.
Exponential function, 402–3,
    409,
    program, 71.
Exponentiation, 70, 401,
    program, 26–27, 166–67,
    265, 419.
        fast, 30–35, 201, 281–86,
        288–90, 294, 419,
    proof, 226, 228, 239.
Expression, 12, 14–16, **15,**
    70–71, 161–63, 180, 182,
    205, 214, 388–91,
    399–401, 404–5, 406,
    410, *see also*
        Conditional expression,
        Function designator,
        Lambda expression,
        Relation,
    array, 114, 173, 183, 216,
        404–6, 410,
    block, 180–81, 395,
    logical, **3, 15,** 20, 24, 212,
        401.
Expression-like, **215,** 215–16,
    222.
Extended specifier, **161,** 173,
    177–78, 180, 182, 202,
    396, 405, 408.

Factorial, programs, 17–22, 89,
    109–10, 201, 264–65,
    416–18,
    procedures, 163–67, 168–69,
        172, 184–85,
    proof, 113, 224–25, 227,
        232–39, 253–56.
Factors, program for finding,
    118.
false, 8, 15, 41, 219–20, 401.
father (procedure), **336,**
    347.
Fibonacci numbers, programs,
    36–37, 111, 187,
    proof, 47, 48, 49–51.
Final state, **205.**
Fixed point representation,
    61–62.
Fixed-point theory, 210,
    250.
Floating point
    representation,
    62–65, 69.
Flowchart, 7–10, 38–42, 286.
Floyd, R. W., 38, 43, 155, 290,
    325, 334, 351.
for statement, **259–62,** 259–71,
    280, 412,
    binding by, 182, 260–61, 412,
    bound-altering, 266–67,
    descending, **270–71,**
    inference rules, 262–71, **263,**
        267, 270,
    invariant, 262–66, **264,** 271,
    set-iterating, **303,** 316,
        365–66,
        inference rule, 307, 368,
    variants, **262,** 266–69.
forinv, 262–66, **264,** 271.
Formal definition, 172,
    204–10, 213–17.
Formal parameter, **158–59,**
    160–70, 181–83, 207,
    278, 406, 407–8, 412,
    binding by, 159, 182–83, 244,
        406, 408.
FORTRAN, 148, 171, 260,
    413.
Free occurrence, **56,** 159, 213,
    222, 302, 409.
Free substitution, inference
    rule, 211, **219,** 221.
Function, **95,** 95–98, 102–3,
    108, 112–14, 119–24,
    130–34, 136, 137–42,
    150, 204,
    as array value, 95–96,
    112–14, 149, 404.
Function designator, **180,** 182,
    402–3, 410.
Function procedure, 157,
    180–83, 201, 216,
    402–3, 406–10,

inference rule, **257,** 258.

Gadbow, W. J., 137, 195.
General invariant, **283, 284,**
    285, 302, 304, 311,
    354.
Generic procedure, 409.
geninv, 284, *see also* General
    invariant.
Gentzen, G., 214.
Ghost identifier, *see* Identifier.
Ghost parameter, **230,** 232,
    237–38, 241–43, 337,
    352, 365.
Global invariant, 370.
Global occurrence, **159,**
    164–67, **182,** 215–16,
    232, 239, 245.
goleft (procedure), 338.
Good array designators,
    inference rule, **252,**
    252–55.
Good variable, **216–17,** 223,
    226, 233, 251,
    inference rule, **248,** 252.
goright (procedure), 338.
goto 210, **272,** 272–95, 307,
    342, 412,
    inference rule, 276–81,
        277–78.
Grammar, 390.
Graph, **95,** *see also* Directed
    graph.
Greatest common divisor,
    program, 38.
Greek letter, 393, 396.
Gries, D., 29, 203, 294, 306.
Group, 121
gv, 216–17, *see also* Good
    variable.

Heap, 310, **334,** 334–54.
Heap (assertion procedure),
    338.
Higher-order procedure,
    177–81, **179,** 183, 187,
    203–4, 240–43, 316–18,
    323–24.
Hoare, C. A. R., 20, 43, 60,
    112, 195, 198, 203,
    240, 262, 275, 298,
    307, 315, 395.
Hole, 110, 124, 339–42,
    344–45, 353.

IBM 360/370, 59, 63–65, 396.
Idealized computer, 60–61.
Identifier, **14,** 163, 204–5, 213,
    222, 397–99, 406,
    408–9,
    collision, 91–92, 159,
        163–65,
    control, 261,

ghost, **29,** 110, 123, 230, 232, 237, 241,
implicitly declared, **55,** 395, 396, 398, 402–3, 409,
primed, 164.
Identity function, **119,** 119–20, 121, 138.
if, 3, 16, 399, 401.
Image, **97,** 97–100, 114, 120, 123, 133, 138, 141–42.
Immediate successor, **300,** 316–18.
Implication, **41,** 52, 103, 210, **213–14,** 218–19, 223–24.
Implicit declaration, *see* Identifier.
implies, 103, 171, 180, 214, 219–20.
Inclusion, of relations, 99, **100,** 104.
Increasing order, **102–3,** 212.
Increasing zero, program, 108–9.
Independence, of assertions, 283, 292.
Indeterminacy, **289,** 289–90, 292–94, 298, 302, 303, 307, 313–14, 328, 348, 354,
of specifications, 95, 145–46.
Indivisible action, 283, 285, 304.
Induction, on tree depth, 191–93.
Infer, **43.**
Inference rule, 42–52, 55, 58, 112, 150,
in specification logic, 217–24, 226–27, 231–32, 246, 248–49, 251–53, 256, 257, 263, 267, 270, 277–78, 307,
derivation, 219, 223–24, 248–52, 256, 258, 267–69, 307.
Infinity, 377.
Injective, 108, **120,** 121.
Input, 402–3, 409, 413–14, 416–19.
Input-preserving program, **29,** 110, 155.
Insertion, 308–9, 313, 334, 345.
Instance, **43, 217.**
Integer, 14–16, 54, 58–60, 394, 397–98, 414–15.
integer set (data type), 213, 253, 263, 348.
Integration, notation, 91.
Interchange, *see* Exchange.
Interference, **166,** 166–73, 176–77, 188, 203–6, 210–11, *see also*

Specification of noninterference.
Intermediate line, 82, **83.**
Intersection, 66, 131, 138, 141,
of array with interval, program, 142–43,
of arrays, program, 137, 143,
of function with set, **140,** 140–43, 146.
Interval, **78,** 124, 259–60, 262,
diagram, 78–80, **79,** 81–82, 85–88, 213, 253, 262–63.
Invariant, 281.
of **for** statement, 262–66, **264,** 271,
general, **283, 284,** 285, 302, 304, 311, 354,
global and local, 370–71,
representation, **311,** 315,
of **while** statement, **18,** 20–21, 23, 25, 31, 48–49, 51, 417.
Inverse, **120,** 120–22, 337.
Irregular, **80,** 87, 262, 264.
iterate (procedure), 178–79, 243–45, 262.
Iteration, **5,** 199–200, 259–60, 271, *see also* Set.

Jensen's device, 171, 241–43, 246–47.
Jones, C. B., 298, 315.

Key, ordering by, 144–48, 201.
Knuth, D. E., 200, 363.

L-value, 204.
Label, 210, **272,** 272–95, 342, 412,
binding, 272, 412,
inference rule, 276–81, **277–78.**
Lambda calculus, 56, 244.
Lambda expression, 243–47, **244,** 316, 320.
Landin, P. J., 202, 204.
Left shift, program, 110, 114, 124, 136.
leftson (procedure), **336,** 347.
Length, **130, 324.**
Less than, **108.**
Levin, G., 29, 203.
Lexicographic ordering, 132, 136.
Linear search, program, 100–2, 273–75, 278–81, 308.
LISP, 56, 130, 201, 245.
Local invariant, 371.
Local variable, 52–55, **53,** 168, 172, 194.
Logarithm, 34, 402–3, 409.

logical, 15, 54, 394.
Logical word, 59.
London, R. L., 203
long, 401.
long real, 69–71, 394.
Longest run, program, 109.
Lower-case letter, 12, 396.
Lucas, P., 306.

McCarthy, J., 112, 155, 201.
Macro, 157, 160.
Map, **95.**
Mathematical facts, 45–46, 219–20,
inference rule for introducing, **219.**
Maximum finding, program, 93–95, 99–100, 102, 115–17, 174–75, 265–66.
Meaning, 162, 203–10, 213–17, 275, 386–88.
Membership, 308–9.
Memory, 58, *see also* Storage.
Merging, programs, 127–30, 176–77, 187–89, 291–94,
with keys, 145,
with overwriting, 137, 195,
proofs, 135, 146–48,
strict, 137.
Metavariable, **43, 217, 392–94,** 396, 405.
Min, **379.**
Minimax of an array, program, 150–55.
Minimum and maximum finding, program, 95.
Minimum distance, **324,** program, 325–51, 362.
Modus ponens, inference rule, **218,** 221.
Monoid, 121, 134.
Monotone, 108, **121,** 121–22, 338.
Monotonicity argument, 107, 108, 189, 197.
Morris, F. L., 82, 95.
Multidimensional array, **148–49,** 148–50.
Multiple-source, 301, 325.
Multiplication, 14, 68, 70–71, 399–401,
programs, 27, 35.
Myhrhaug, B., 298.

Naur, P., 38, 157, 383.
Negation, logical, **15,** 90, 214, 401.
Node, **299, 301,** 319–21.
Noninterference decomposition, inference rules, **222.**

Nonterminal symbol, **384,** 392, 396.
Normalization, **63.**
Numeric metavariable, **393–94,** 396.
Numerical analysis, 69.
Nygaard, K., 298.

odd (procedure), **15–16,** 213, 403, 409.
One-dimensional array, **74.**
One-to-one correspondence, *see* Bijection.
Open subroutine, 160.
Operator, 14–15, 399–401.
or, 15, 129–30, 214, 399–401.
ord, 103, *see also* Ordered function.
Order of magnitude, **33–34,** 107, 160, 198.
Ordered array, *see* Ordered function.
Ordered function, 102–4, **103,** 108, 120, 123–24, 133, 144, 212, 309.
Ordering relation, 15, 82, 98, 100, 102–4, 108, 132, 136, 144, 336, 396, 399–401.
Output, 402–3, 409, 413, 415–16, 416–19.
Overflow, 34, **59,** 60–61, **65,** 261, 280.
Owicki, S., 306.

pa, 167, *see also* Parameter assumption.
Painter, J., 112.
Pair, 131.
Parallel computation, 168, 289–90.
Parameter, **158–59,** 158–83, 278, 405–10.
Parameter assumption, **166–67,** 176, 226, 229, 233, 240, 366.
Parameter matching, 160–63, 180, 202, 391, 396, 405–6, 411.
Parameterless procedure, 178, 180, 182–83, 406, 408, 410.
Pardee, O. O'M., 144.
Parenthesization, 4–5, 21, 92, 410–11.
Parser, 201–2, 390.
Partial order, **100,** 336.
Partition, **81,** 82–83, 303–4, 363, 382,
    diagram, 79–88, **80–81,** 103–4, 134, 262,
    program, 125–26, 148, 175, 196–97, 200, 271, 295.

Pascal, xii, 148, 157, 178.
Path, **300,** 321, 324–25,
    cyclic, 336, 364, 373,
    T-free, **364,** 364–65.
Path finding, programs, 321–24, 333.
Permissible, **275, 288.**
Permutation, 121.
Phrase class name, **384.**
Phrase type **162–63,** 182–83, 204–5, 211–13, 217, 278, 302, 405–6.
Physical word, 59.
PL/I, 16, 56, 114, 171.
Pointwise extension, **98,** 98–100, 103–4.
Position, **336,** 347–48.
Precedence, 390.
Precedent, **20.**
Predecessor, immediate, **307–8,** 334.
Predicate calculus, 89.
Preimage, **137,** 137–43, 146, 379.
Premiss, **43, 217.**
Preorder, **100.**
Primitive operation, 297, 308–10, 320.
Problem-oriented type, 144, 213, **297–98,** 301, 320, 321, 336, 369.
Procedure, 157–202, **158–60, 181–83,** 203–4, 207–10, 212, 215–16, 243–45, 405–11.
    built-in, 16, 395, 402–3, 409, 414–16,
    implementation, 160, 172,
    inference rules, 228–43, **231–32,** 246–50, **249, 257,** 258.
Procedure assumption, 228–32.
Procedure parameter, 177–79, 180, 182–83, 243, 407, 409.
Procedure statement, 157, **158–60,** 182, 207–10, 233–34, 402–3, 406, 410.
Product, 131, 149–50, 171,
    of interval, program, 89.
Production, **384,** 396.
Production schema, **392–94,** 405.
Program proving, xii, 42, 51, 172, 181, 201, 203–4.
Propagation of errors, 65–69.
Proper procedure, 157–60, 181–83, 207–10, 215–16, 402–3, 405–10,

inference rule, 228–43, **231–32,** 246–50, **249,** 347, 368.
Punched card, 396, 413–14.

Quantifier, 78, **89,** 89–93, 162–63,
    binding by, 89, 162–63,
    introduction and removal, inference rule, **219,**
    of specification, **214, 216,** 219, 223–24.
Queue, 314–15.
quicksort (procedure), 195–200.
Quotation mark, 398, 415.
Quotient, **14,** 134.

Radix, **58.**
Range information, 20, 26, 40, 264.
Reachability, **300,** 336, 363, **364,** 364–65,
    program, 301–8, 310–24, 328.
real, 69–71, 394.
Real number, 61–71, 397–98, 414–15.
Real-time programming, 60, 198.
Realignment, 119, **122,** 122–24, 130, 132, 133–36, 139, 141–42.
Rearrangement, 119, **122,** 122–23, 131, 133–35, 139–42,
    stable, **146,** 146–48, 195, 198.
Record, 144, 201, 298, 395.
Recursion, 160, **184,** 184–202, 209–10, 231–32, 235–36, 239, 250, 258, 280–81, 323–24, 363–82,
    mutual, 195, 232.
Recursive function, 201.
Redex, beta, **244,** 246.
Reductio ad absurdum, inference rule, **219.**
Redundant testing, 34, 130, 282, 292, 294.
Reflexivity, 100, **104,** 108, 122, 336.
Regular, **80,** 82, 262, 269.
Relation, **15,** 98–100, 102–4, 396, 399–401.
Relative error, **62,** 66–68.
rem, 14, 59, 70, 399.
Remainder, **14,** *see also* Division.
Removing duplicate values, program, 118.
Removing squares, program, 144.

Renaming, *see* Alpha
   conversion.
repeat (procedure), 178,
   240–41.
Repetition, in productions,
   392, 394, 396.
Replication, **83.**
Representation, 298, 319–21,
   322–24, 347–49, 382,
   ambiguous, **298,** 379,
   compound, **298,** 315, 377,
   decoupling, 303, 310,
   incomplete, **298,** 323, 348,
   invariant, **311,** 315,
   of numbers, 58–65,
   redundant, 310, 315, 377,
   of sets, 308–18, 334, 375–82.
Reserved word, 12, 396,
   397–98.
Restriction, **96,** 96–100, 103–4,
   114, 120, 131–34,
   138–42.
Result, of function, **95.**
result, (specifier), 169–70, 407.
Retrieve function, 315.
Reynolds, J. C., 78, 203, 250,
   281.
rightson (procedure), **336,** 347.
Rimkus, C. J., 108–9.
rnd, **61.**
root, **336,** 347.
round (procedure), 402–3, 409.
Roundoff, 61–62.
Row, **149,** 150.
Rule of inference, *see* Inference
   rule.
Run, program for finding
   longest, 109.

S-expression, parser, 201–2.
Satisfies, **205.**
Scale factor, **70,** 397, 415.
Scaling, 62.
Schema, **392–94,** 405.
Scope, 53–54, **56,** 75–76, *see
   also* Binding.
Search, *see* Binary search,
   Depth-first search,
   Linear search.
Segment, 76, **80,** 96, **150.**
Self-implication, inference
   rule, **218.**
Semantics, 172, 204–10,
   213–17.
Semicolon, 162, 396, 398, 402.
Separating assumptions,
   inference rule, **218.**
Sequence, **130,** 148, 205–6.
Sequence concatenation, **130,**
   131–33, 136.
Set:
   iteration over, 303, 308–10,
   316–18,

representation, 308–18, 334,
   375–82.
set (data type), **301.**
set of sets (data type), 369.
Shift, 124, *see also* Left shift.
short, 401.
Side effect, 181.
Simple assignment, inference
   rule, **44,** 47–48, 91,
   111–12, **223,** 226, **248.**
Simple parameter, **162,** 170,
   182, 407.
Simple statement, 386–88,
   401–2.
Simple variable declaration,
   53–54, 69, 398,
   inference rule, **226–27,** 251.
SIMULA 67, 298.
Simulation, 326–28, **328,** 347.
Single-argument function
   variation, **112–14,** 120,
   122–23, 150.
Single precision, **63–65,** 69–71,
   401, 417.
Single-source, 301, 325.
Single-source single-sink,
   307–8, 315, 324, 334.
Singleton set, 79, **98–99,** 103,
   122.
Sites, R. L., 180, 261, 395.
Size, **79–80,** 82–83, 98, 103,
   131, 140, 150, 308–10,
   of problem, 185, 186, 187,
   195, 200.
Smallest factors, program,
   118.
SNOBOL, 56.
Sorting, programs:
   using a heap, 351–62,
   by insertion, 118, 123, 148,
   362,
   by maximum finding,
   115–18, 119, 123, 124,
   148, 174–75, 271,
   by merging, 187–95,
   by partitioning, 195–200,
   by range partitioning, 200–1.
Specification, 19–23, 24,
   39–40, 203–4, 206,
   210–17, *see also*
   Inference rule,
   of good variable, **216–17,**
   223, 226, 233, 248, 251,
   252,
   implication, 210, **213–14,**
   218, 223–24,
   indeterminate, 95, 145–46,
   limitations of, 22, 87–88,
   251,
   of noninterference, 166–67,
   176, 206–7, 210, **214–16,**
   221–23, 226, 230–31,
   234, 251, 252–53,

quantified, **214, 216,** 219,
   223–24,
   of statement, **20,** 24, 39, 206,
   213, 275–76,
   of static assertion, **213,** 219–20,
   241–43, 253, 257,
   universal, 203, **210,** 210–11,
   217, 220.
Specification logic, 203–4,
   210–58, 263–64,
   266–71, 275–81, 307,
   347, 368.
Specifier, **160,** 160–63, 167, 169,
   172–73, 177–78,
   180–83, 207, 226,
   407–8,
   binding by, 159, 182–83, 244,
   406, 408.
Square, program for finding
   largest, 155.
Square removal, program, 144.
Square root, 402–3, 409,
   programs, 30, 35.
Stability, **146,** 146–48, 195, 198.
Stack, 314.
Standard form, 79, 81.
Standard metavariable, **394,**
   406.
Standard ordering, **98,** 108,
   132, 136.
State, **12–14,** 24–25, **204,**
   204–10, 275.
Statement, **3,** 3–6, 12, 20, 51,
   158, 178, 183, 205–6,
   214, 259, 272, 383–88,
   401–2, 406, 410, 412.
Statement compounding,
   inference rule, **44, 220.**
Statement-like, **215,** 215–16,
   222, 234.
Statement parameter, 178, 183,
   203, 240, 407.
Static assertion, **213,** 219, 241,
   253, 257.
Static implication, inference
   rule, **219.**
Static scope, 54.
step, 270, 412.
Step (of path), **300.**
Stepwise refinement, **7,** 19, 20,
   416.
Stopper, **198,** 295.
Storage, 54, 55, 58, 60–61, 75,
   114, 157, 160, 173, 177,
   194–95, 199–200, 305,
   308–9, 322–23, 359–60,
   361–62.
Store, 204.
Strachey, C., 204.
Strengthening precedent, in-
   ference rule, **45, 220.**
Strict order, **103,** 108, 121.
Strictly monotone, **108,** 121.

String, 202, 395, 397–98, 409, 415.
Stronger (relating assertions), **40–41.**
Strongly connected component, **363,** program for finding, 369–82.
Structured program, **7,** 157, 272, 286, 298.
Subphrase, 92, 385–90.
Subroutine, 157, 160.
Subscript:
 of array, **74,** 114, 149, 216–17, 404,
 of block, **285,** 304,
 error, 61, **74–75,** 77, 87–88, 112, 128, 171, 251, 375,
 of identifier, 29.
Subset, **79,** 90, 98, 131, 138, 150.
Substitution, 43–44, 90–93, **92,** 159, 163–64, 207, 211, 219, 244,
 of partition diagrams, **84,**
 type-correct, **182,** 406, 410–11.
Substitution law, **207,** 207–9, 211.
Subtraction, 14, 399–401,
 of arrays, program, 143,
 of set from function, **142,** 142–44,
 of sets, **114,** 131, 138, 142.
Successor, immediate, **300,** 316–18.
sum (procedure), 171, 241–43, 246–47.
Summation, **76, 85,** 91.
 of array, programs, 76–78, 85–88, 179, 243–45, 247, 260, 262–63, 272, proofs, 87–88, 264.
Surjective, **120.**
swap (in heap), 337, 347, 352, 358.
swap (values of variables), 240, 256.
Symbolic metavariable, **393–94,** 396, 405.
Symmetry, 100, 122, 294.
Syntax, 10–12, 163, 167, 201–2, 383–412.

T-free, **364,** 364–65.
Table of two-argument function, program, 419.

Tableau, **46,** 46–48, 50–51, **225.**
Tarjan, R., 363.
Temporary variable, 37, 53.
Terminal node, **189,** 344.
Terminal symbol, **384.**
Termination, 6, 18–19, 22, 40, 42, 51, 87–88, 184, 200, 201, 205–6, 261, 285, 294, 303, 342.
then, 3, 16, 399, 401.
Top-down programming, **7,** 19, 20, 416.
Total correctness, 22.
Total interval, **81.**
Total order, **100.**
Totality, 100, 108.
Towers of Hanoi, program, 185–87.
Transformation:
 into concrete program, 60, 289, 298, 310–21, **311,** 322–24, 343–51, 354–55, 374–82,
 to improve efficiency, 356–62.
Transition diagram, **286,** 286–90, 292–94, 301.
Transitivity, **99,** 100, 108, 122, 136, 336.
Transposition, program, 155.
Tree, 189–95, 310, 334–43, 347–49, 385–91.
Tree (assertion procedure), **336.**
Trigonometric functions, 402–3, 409.
true, 8, 15, 41, 401.
truncate (procedure), 402–3, 409.
Type, 162–63, 297–98, *see also* Data type, Phrase type, Problem-orientated type.

Underflow, **65.**
Union, **90,** 98, 131, 138, 150, 218, 303, 310, *see also* Disjoint union, of set of sets, 370.
Universal quantifier, *see* Quantifier.
until, 259, 412.
upgood (procedure), 338.
User-defined type, *see* Problem-orientated type.

V (procedure), 337, 352.
Vacuously true, **90,** 99.
Valid tableau, **46, 225.**
Value, 12, 15, 204–5, 414, array, 95–96, **96,** 112–14, 149, 404–5.
value (specifier), 169–70, 407.
var, 161–63, 173, 175, 182, 406–7.
Variable, 12, 14–16, 52–55, 69, 73–74, 149, 161–63, 182, 204–5, 209, 214–15, 216–17, 226–28, 398–401, 404–6,
 abstract and concrete, 310–11, 356,
 array, 95, 173, 175, 182, 215, 404–6,
 auxiliary, **306,** 307, 311,
 good **216–17,** 223, 226, 233, 251,
 inference rule, **248,** 252,
 local, 52–55, **53,** 168, 169, 172, 194,
 logical, 15, 29,
 temporary, 37, 53.
Variation, **112–14,** 120, 122–23, 150.
Vector product, program, 171, 246–47.
Verification condition, **38–40.**

Weakening consequent, inference rule, **45,** 220.
Weaker (relating assertions), **40–41.**
Weight, **337.**
while statement, **5,** 5–7, 10, 20–21, 23, 25, 78, 187, 243, 259, 262, 287, 401, inference rule, **49,** 211–12, **220,** invariant, **18,** 20–21, 23, 25, 51, 417.
whiledo (procedure), 187, 243.
whileinv, 25, *see also* **while** statement.
van Wijngaarden, A., 161, 405.
Williams, J. W. J., 334, 351.
Winograd, S., 108.
Wirth, N., 7, 112, 148, 203, 395.
Word length, **58–59.**
Working backwards, 47–48, 51.
Worst-case, 198, 199, 309, 362.

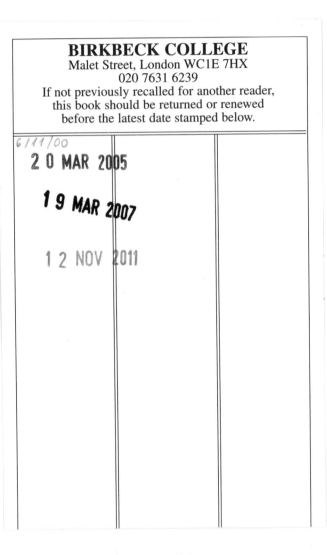